Illustrated Series™

Microsoft® 365 Office 2021

Introductory

Cengage

Australia • Brazil • Canada • Mexico • Singapore • United Kingdom • United States

Cengage

Illustrated Series® Collection Microsoft® Office 365® & Office 2021 Introductory
David W. Beskeen, Carol Cram, Jennifer Duffy, Lisa Friedrichsen, Lynn Wermers

SVP, Product: Erin Joyner
VP, Product: Thais Alencar
Product Director: Mark Santee
Senior Product Manager: Amy Savino
Product Assistant: Ciara Horne
Learning Designer: Zenya Molnar
Content Manager: Grant Davis
Digital Delivery Quality Partner: Jim Vaughey
Developmental Editors: Julie Boyles, Barbara Clemens, Mary-Terese Cozzola, Karen Porter
VP, Product Marketing: Jason Sakos
Director, Product Marketing: Danaë April
Executive Product Marketing Manager: Jill Staut
IP Analyst: Ann Hoffman
IP Project Manager: Ilakkiya Jayagopi
Production Service: Lumina Datamatics, Inc.
Designer: Erin Griffin
Cover Image Source: Getty Images

Mac Users: If you're working through this product using a Mac, some of the steps may vary. Additional information for Mac users is included with the Data files for this product.

Disclaimer: This text is intended for instructional purposes only; data is fictional and does not belong to any real persons or companies.

Disclaimer: The material in this text was written using Microsoft Windows 10 and Office 365 Professional Plus and was Quality Assurance tested before the publication date. As Microsoft continually updates the Windows 10 operating system and Office 365, your software experience may vary slightly from what is presented in the printed text.

For product information and technology assistance, contact us at **Cengage Customer & Sales Support, 1-800-354-9706 or support.cengage.com.**

For permission to use material from this text or product, submit all requests online at **www.copyright.com.**

Library of Congress Control Number: 2022903946

Student Edition ISBN: 978-0-357-67492-5
K12 ISBN: 978-0-357-67494-9
Looseleaf ISBN: 978-0-357-67493-2*
*Looseleaf available as part of a digital bundle

Cengage
200 Pier 4 Boulevard
Boston, MA 02210
USA

Cengage is a leading provider of customized learning solutions with employees residing in nearly 40 different countries and sales in more than 125 countries around the world. Find your local representative at **www.cengage.com.**

To learn more about Cengage platforms and services, register or access your online learning solution, or purchase materials for your course, visit **www.cengage.com.**

Notice to the Reader

Printed in the United States of America
Print Number: 01 Print Year: 2022

Brief Contents

Contents

Integration

Access 2021

Integration

Illustrated Series™

Microsoft® 365 Office 2021

Introductory

Getting to Know Microsoft Office Versions

Cengage is proud to bring you the next edition of Microsoft Office. This edition was designed to provide a robust learning experience that is not dependent upon a specific version of Office.

Microsoft supports several versions of Office:

- **Office 365:** A cloud-based subscription service that delivers Microsoft's most up-to-date, feature-rich, modern productivity tools direct to your device. There are variations of Office 365 for business, educational, and personal use. Office 365 offers extra online storage and cloud-connected features, as well as updates with the latest features, fixes, and security updates.
- **Office 2021:** Microsoft's "on-premises" version of the Office apps, available for both PCs and Macs, offered as a static, one-time purchase and outside of the subscription model.
- **Office Online:** A free, simplified version of Office web applications (Word, Excel, PowerPoint, and OneNote) that facilitates creating and editing files collaboratively.

Office 365 (the subscription model) and Office 2021 (the one-time purchase model) had only slight differences between them at the time this content was developed. Over time, Office 365's cloud interface will continuously update, offering new application features and functions, while Office 2021 will remain static. Therefore, your onscreen experience may differ from what you see in this product. For example, the more advanced features and functionalities covered in this product may not be available in Office Online or may have updated from what you see in Office 2021.

For more information on the differences between Office 365, Office 2021, and Office Online, please visit the Microsoft Support site.

Cengage is committed to providing high-quality learning solutions for you to gain the knowledge and skills that will empower you throughout your educational and professional careers.

Thank you for using our product, and we look forward to exploring the future of Microsoft Office with you!

Using SAM Projects and Textbook Projects

SAM Projects allow you to actively apply the skills you learned live in Microsoft Word, Excel, PowerPoint, or Access. Become a more productive student and use these skills throughout your career.

To complete SAM Textbook Projects, please follow these steps:

SAM Textbook Projects allow you to complete a project as you follow along with the steps in the textbook. As you read the module, look for icons that indicate when you should download **sam↓** your SAM Start file(s) and when to upload **sam↑** the final project file to SAM for grading.

Everything you need to complete this project is provided within SAM. You can launch the eBook directly from SAM, which will allow you to take notes, highlight, and create a custom study guide, or you can use a print textbook or your mobile app. Download IOS or Download Android.

To get started, launch your SAM Project assignment from SAM, MindTap, or a link within your LMS.

Step 1: Download Files

- Click the "Download All" button or the individual links to download your **Start File** and **Support File(s)** (when available). You must use the SAM Start file.
- Click the Instructions link to launch the eBook (or use the print textbook or mobile app).
- Disregard any steps in the textbook that ask you to create a new file or to use a file from a location outside of SAM.
- Look for the SAM Download icon **sam↓** to begin working with your start file.
- Follow the module's step-by-step instructions until you reach the SAM Upload icon **sam↑**.
- Save and close the file.

Step 2: Save Work to SAM

- Ensure you rename your project file to match the Expected File Name.
- Upload your in-progress or completed file to SAM. You can download the file to continue working or submit it for grading in the next step.

Step 3: Submit for Grading

- Upload the completed file to SAM for immediate feedback and to view the available Reports.
    - The **Graded Summary Report** provides a detailed list of project steps, your score, and feedback to aid you in revising and resubmitting the project.
    - The **Study Guide Report** provides your score for each project step and links to the associated training and textbook pages.
- If additional attempts are allowed, use your reports to assist with revising and resubmitting your project.
- To re-submit the project, download the file saved in step 2.
- Edit, save, and close the file, then re-upload and submit it again.

For all other SAM Projects, please follow these steps:

To get started, launch your SAM Project assignment from SAM, MindTap, or a link within your LMS.

Step 1: Download Files

- Click the "Download All" button or the individual links to download your **Instruction File**, **Start File**, and **Support File(s)** (when available). You must use the SAM Start file.
- Open the Instruction file and follow the step-by-step instructions. Ensure you rename your project file to match the Expected File Name (change _1 to _2 at the end of the file name).

Step 2: Save Work to SAM

- Upload your in-progress or completed file to SAM. You can download the file to continue working or submit it for grading in the next step.

Step 3: Submit for Grading

- Upload the completed file to SAM for immediate feedback and to view available Reports.
    - The **Graded Summary Report** provides a detailed list of project steps, your score, and feedback to aid you in revising and resubmitting the project.
    - The **Study Guide Report** provides your score for each project step and links to the associated training and textbook pages.
- If additional attempts are allowed, use your reports to assist with revising and resubmitting your project.
- To re-submit the project, download the file saved in step 2.
- Edit, save, and close the file, then re-upload and submit it again.

For additional tips to successfully complete your SAM Projects, please view our Common Student Errors Infographic.

Creating Documents with Word

CASE You have been hired to work at JCL Talent, Inc., a business support services company that provides employment and recruitment services for employers and job seekers. Shortly after reporting to your new office, Dawn Lapointe, Director of JCL Talent – Technical Careers division, asks you to use Word to create a memo to staff and a tip sheet for job seekers.

Module Objectives

After completing this module, you will be able to:

- Understand word processing software
- Explore the Word window
- Start a document
- Save a document
- Select text
- Format text using the Mini toolbar and the Ribbon
- View and navigate a document
- Cut and paste text
- Copy and paste text
- Format with fonts
- Set document margins
- Add bullets and numbering
- Insert a graphic
- Apply a theme

Files You Will Need

IL_WD_1-1.docx
Support_WD_1-2.jpg
IL_WD_1-3.docx
Support_WD_1-4.jpg
IL_WD_1-5.docx
Support_WD_1-6.jpg

Understand Word Processing Software

Learning Outcomes
- Identify the features of Word
- State the benefits of using a word processing program

A **word processing program** is a software program that includes tools for entering, editing, and formatting text and graphics. Microsoft Word is a powerful word processing program that allows you to create and enhance a wide range of documents quickly and easily. **FIGURE 1-1** shows the first page of a report created using Word and illustrates some of the Word features you can use to enhance your documents. The electronic files you create using Word are called **documents**. One of the benefits of using Word is that document files can be stored on a hard disk, flash drive, or other physical storage device, or to OneDrive or another Cloud storage place, making them easy to transport, share, and revise. **CASE** *Before beginning your memo, you explore the editing and formatting features available in Word.*

DETAILS

You can use Word to accomplish the following tasks:

- **Type and edit text**
  The Word editing tools make it simple to insert and delete text in a document. You can add text to the middle of an existing paragraph; replace text with other text; undo an editing change; and correct typing, spelling, and grammatical errors with ease.

- **Copy and move text from one location to another**
  Using the more advanced editing features of Word, you can copy or move text from one location and insert it in a different location in a document. You also can copy and move text between documents. This means you don't have to retype text that is already entered in a document.

- **Format text and paragraphs with fonts, colors, and other elements**
  The sophisticated formatting tools in Word allow you to make the text in your documents come alive. You can change the size, style, and color of text; add lines and shading to paragraphs; and enhance lists with bullets and numbers. Creatively formatting text helps to highlight important ideas in your documents.

- **Format and design pages**
  The page-formatting features in Word give you power to design attractive newsletters, create powerful résumés, and produce documents such as research papers, business cards, brochures, and reports. You can change paper size, organize text in columns, and control the layout of text and graphics on each page of a document. For quick results, Word includes preformatted cover pages, pull quotes, and headers and footers, as well as galleries of coordinated text, table, and graphic styles. If you are writing a research paper, Word makes it easy to manage reference sources and create footnotes, endnotes, and bibliographies.

- **Enhance documents with tables, charts, graphics, screenshots, and videos**
  Using the powerful graphics tools in Word, you can spice up your documents with pictures, videos, photographs, screenshots, lines, preset quick shapes, and diagrams. You also can illustrate your documents with tables and charts to help convey your message in a visually interesting way.

- **Use Mail Merge to create form letters and mailing labels**
  The Word Mail Merge feature allows you to send personalized form letters to many different people. You can also use Mail Merge to create mailing labels, directories, email messages, and other types of documents.

- **Share documents securely**
  The security features in Word make it quick and easy to remove comments, tracked changes, and unwanted personal information from your files before you share them with others. You can also add a password or a digital signature to a document and convert a file to a format suitable for publishing on the web.

FIGURE 1-1: A report created using Word

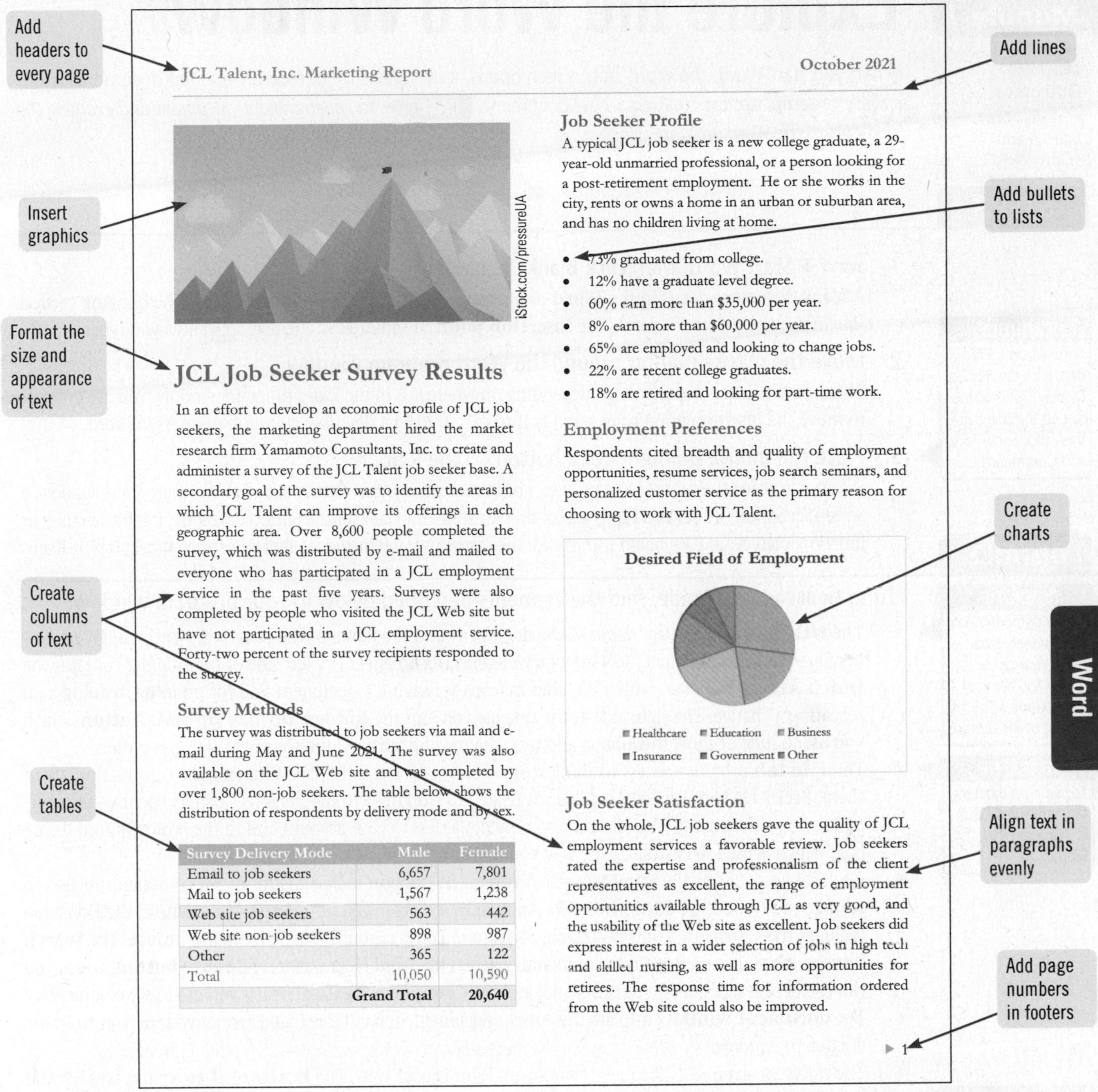

JCL Talent, Inc. Marketing Report October 2021

JCL Job Seeker Survey Results

In an effort to develop an economic profile of JCL job seekers, the marketing department hired the market research firm Yamamoto Consultants, Inc. to create and administer a survey of the JCL Talent job seeker base. A secondary goal of the survey was to identify the areas in which JCL Talent can improve its offerings in each geographic area. Over 8,600 people completed the survey, which was distributed by e-mail and mailed to everyone who has participated in a JCL employment service in the past five years. Surveys were also completed by people who visited the JCL Web site but have not participated in a JCL employment service. Forty-two percent of the survey recipients responded to the survey.

Survey Methods

The survey was distributed to job seekers via mail and e-mail during May and June 2021. The survey was also available on the JCL Web site and was completed by over 1,800 non-job seekers. The table below shows the distribution of respondents by delivery mode and by sex.

Survey Delivery Mode	Male	Female
Email to job seekers	6,657	7,801
Mail to job seekers	1,567	1,238
Web site job seekers	563	442
Web site non-job seekers	898	987
Other	365	122
Total	10,050	10,590
	Grand Total	20,640

Job Seeker Profile

A typical JCL job seeker is a new college graduate, a 29-year-old unmarried professional, or a person looking for a post-retirement employment. He or she works in the city, rents or owns a home in an urban or suburban area, and has no children living at home.

- 73% graduated from college.
- 12% have a graduate level degree.
- 60% earn more than $35,000 per year.
- 8% earn more than $60,000 per year.
- 65% are employed and looking to change jobs.
- 22% are recent college graduates.
- 18% are retired and looking for part-time work.

Employment Preferences

Respondents cited breadth and quality of employment opportunities, resume services, job search seminars, and personalized customer service as the primary reason for choosing to work with JCL Talent.

Job Seeker Satisfaction

On the whole, JCL job seekers gave the quality of JCL employment services a favorable review. Job seekers rated the expertise and professionalism of the client representatives as excellent, the range of employment opportunities available through JCL as very good, and the usability of the Web site as excellent. Job seekers did express interest in a wider selection of jobs in high tech and skilled nursing, as well as more opportunities for retirees. The response time for information ordered from the Web site could also be improved.

1

Planning a document

Before you create a new document, it's a good idea to spend time planning it. Identify the message you want to convey, the audience for your document, and the elements, such as tables or charts, you want to include. You should also think about the tone and look of your document—are you writing a business letter, which should be written in a pleasant, but serious, tone and have a formal appearance, or are you creating a flyer that must be colorful, eye-catching, and fun to read? The purpose and audience for your document determine the appropriate design. Planning the layout and design of a document involves deciding how to organize the text, selecting the fonts to use, identifying the graphics to include, and selecting the formatting elements that will enhance the message and appeal of the document. For longer documents, such as newsletters, it can be useful to sketch the layout and design of each page before you begin.

Explore the Word Window

Learning Outcomes
- Create a blank document
- Open Word

When you start Word, the Word start screen opens. It includes a list of recently opened documents and a gallery of templates for creating a new document. **CASE** *You open a blank document and examine the elements of the Word program window.*

STEPS

TROUBLE
If the Ribbon is hidden, click the Ribbon Display Options button on the title bar, then click Show Tabs and Commands.

1. **sam Start Word, then click Blank document**
   A blank document opens in the **Word program window**, as shown in **FIGURE 1-2**. The blinking vertical line in the document window is the **insertion point**. It indicates where text appears as you type.
2. **Move the mouse pointer around the Word program window**
   The mouse pointer changes shape depending on where it is in the Word program window. You use pointers to move the insertion point or to select text to edit. **TABLE 1-1** describes common pointers in Word.
3. **Place the mouse pointer over a button on the Ribbon**
   When you place the mouse pointer over a button or some other elements of the Word program window, a ScreenTip appears. A **ScreenTip** is a label that identifies the name of the button or feature, briefly describes its function, conveys any keyboard shortcut for the command, and includes a link to associated help topics, if any.

DETAILS

QUICK TIP
If your computer has touchscreen capability, your Quick Access toolbar may also include a Touch/Mouse Mode button.

QUICK TIP
To display a different tab, you simply click its name on the Ribbon.

TROUBLE
Click the View tab, then click the Ruler check box in the Show group to display the rulers if they are not already displayed.

Using FIGURE 1-2 as a guide, find the elements described below in your program window:

- The **title bar** displays the name of the document and the name of the program. Until you give a new document a different name, its temporary name is Document1. The left side of the title bar contains the **Quick Access toolbar**, which includes buttons for saving a document and for undoing, redoing, and repeating a change. The right side of the title bar contains the **Ribbon Display Options button**, which you use to hide or show the Ribbon and tabs, the resizing buttons, and the program Close button.
- The **File tab** provides access to **Backstage view** where you manage files and the information about them. Backstage view includes commands related to working with documents, such as opening, printing, and saving a document. The File tab also provides access to your account and to the Word Options dialog box, which is used to customize the way you use Word.
- The Ribbon contains the Word tabs. Each **tab** on the Ribbon includes buttons for commands related to editing and formatting documents. The commands are organized in **groups**. For example, the Home tab includes the Clipboard, Font, Paragraph, Styles, and Editing groups. The Ribbon also includes the **Search box**, which you can use to find a command or access the Word Help system, the **Share button**, which you can use to save a document to the Cloud, and the **Comments button**, which you use to see comments.
- The **document window** displays the current document. You enter text and format your document in the document window.
- The rulers appear in the document window in Print Layout view. The **horizontal ruler** displays left and right document margins as well as the tab settings and paragraph indents, if any, for the paragraph in which the insertion point is located. The **vertical ruler** displays the top and bottom document margins.
- The vertical and **horizontal scroll bars** are used to display different parts of the document in the document window. The scroll bars include **scroll boxes** and **scroll arrows**, which you use to scroll.
- The **status bar** displays the page number of the current page, the total number of pages and words in the document, and the status of spelling and grammar checking. It also includes the view buttons, the Zoom slider, and the Zoom level button. You can customize the status bar to display other information.
- The **view buttons** on the status bar allow you to display the document in Focus Mode, Read Mode, Print Layout, or Web Layout view. The **Zoom slider** and the **Zoom level button** provide quick ways to enlarge and decrease the size of the document in the document window, making it easy to zoom in on a detail of a document or to view the layout of the document as a whole.

FIGURE 1-2: Elements of the Word program window

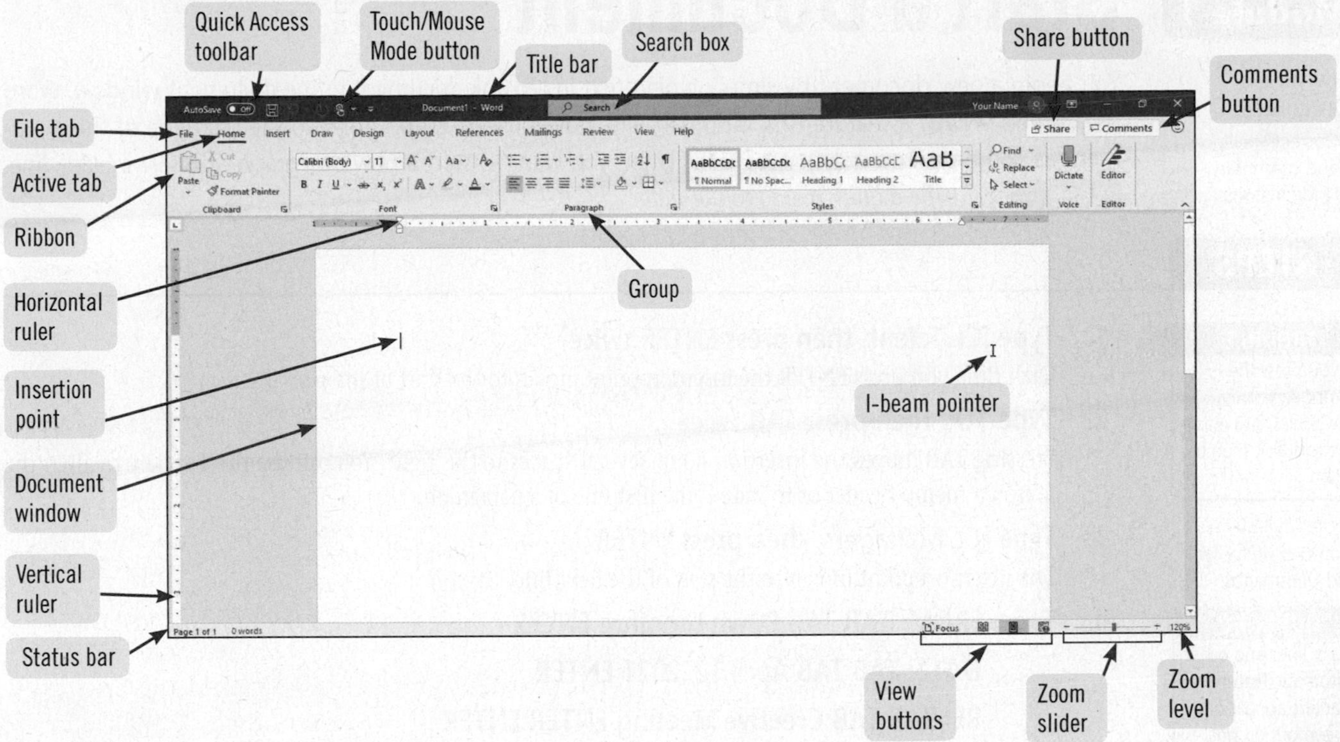

TABLE 1-1: Common mouse pointers in Word

name	pointer	use to
I-beam pointer		Move the insertion point in a document or to select text
Click and Type pointers, including left-align and center-align		Move the insertion point to a blank area of a document in Print Layout or Web Layout view; double-clicking with a Click and Type pointer automatically applies the Paragraph formatting (alignment and indentation) required to position text or a graphic at that location in the document
Selection pointer		Click a button or other element of the Word program window; appears when you point to elements of the Word program window
Right-pointing arrow pointer		Select a line or lines of text; appears when you point to the left edge of a line of text in the document window
Hand pointer		Open a hyperlink; appears when you point to a hyperlink in a task pane or when you press CTRL and point to a hyperlink in a document
Hide white space pointer		Hide the white space in the top and bottom margins of a document in Print Layout view
Show white space pointer		Show the white space in the top and bottom margins of a document in Print Layout view

Word
Module 1

Start a Document

Learning Outcomes
- Correct spelling and grammar
- Undo actions

You begin a new document by simply typing text in a blank document in the document window. Word uses **word wrap**, a feature that automatically moves the insertion point to the next line of the document as you type. You only press ENTER when you want to start a new paragraph or insert a blank line.

CASE *You type a quick memo to the staff.*

STEPS

TROUBLE
If you press the wrong key, press BACKSPACE to erase the mistake, then try again.

1. **Type JCL Talent, then press ENTER twice**
   Each time you press ENTER the insertion point moves to the start of the next line.
2. **Type TO:, then press TAB twice**
   Pressing TAB moves the insertion point several spaces to the right. You can use the TAB key to align the text in a memo header or to indent the first line of a paragraph.
3. **Type JCL Managers, then press ENTER**
   The insertion point moves to the start of the next line.

QUICK TIP
Wavy lines and other automatic feature markers appear on screen but do not print.

4. **Type: FROM: TAB TAB Dawn Lapointe ENTER**
   DATE: TAB TAB April 12, 2021 ENTER
   RE: TAB TAB Creative Meeting ENTER ENTER
   Red wavy or blue double lines may appear under the words you typed, indicating a possible spelling or grammar error. Spelling and grammar checking is one of the many automatic features you will encounter as you type. **TABLE 1-2** describes several automatic features. You can correct any typing errors you make later.

TROUBLE
To reverse an AutoCorrect adjustment, immediately click the Undo button on the Quick Access toolbar.

5. **Type The next creative staff meeting will be held on the 18th of April at 3 p.m. in the conference room on the ground floor., then press SPACEBAR**
   As you type, notice that the insertion point moves automatically to the next line of the document. You also might notice that Word automatically changed "18th" to "18th" in the memo. This feature is called **AutoCorrect**. AutoCorrect automatically makes typographical adjustments and detects and adjusts typing errors, certain misspelled words (such as "taht" for "that"), and incorrect capitalization as you type.

QUICK TIP
If you want uniform spacing between lines and paragraphs, apply the No Spacing style to the document by clicking the No Spacing button in the Styles group on the Home tab before you begin to type. Alternatively, select the text and then click the No Spacing button.

6. **Type Heading the agenda will be the accessibility design of our new Recruitment Tips webpage. The page is scheduled for September.**
   When you type the first few characters of "September," the Word AutoComplete feature displays the complete word in a ScreenTip. **AutoComplete** suggests text to insert quickly into your documents. You can ignore AutoComplete for now. Your memo should resemble **FIGURE 1-3**.
7. **Press ENTER, then type Anna Jocharz has been hired to draft content. A preliminary content outline is attached. Prior to the meeting, please review the web content accessibility guidelines recommended by the World Wide Web Consortium.**
   When you press ENTER and type the new paragraph, notice that Word adds more space between the paragraphs than it does between the lines in each paragraph. This is part of the default style for paragraphs in Word, called the **Normal style**.
8. **Position the I pointer after for (but before the space) in the last sentence of the first paragraph, then click to move the insertion point after for**
9. **Press BACKSPACE three times, then type to launch in**
   Pressing BACKSPACE removes the character before the insertion point.
10. **Move the insertion point before staff in the first sentence, then press DELETE six times to remove the word "staff" and the space after it**
    Pressing DELETE removes the character after the insertion point. **FIGURE 1-4** shows the revised memo.

FIGURE 1-3: Memo text in the document window

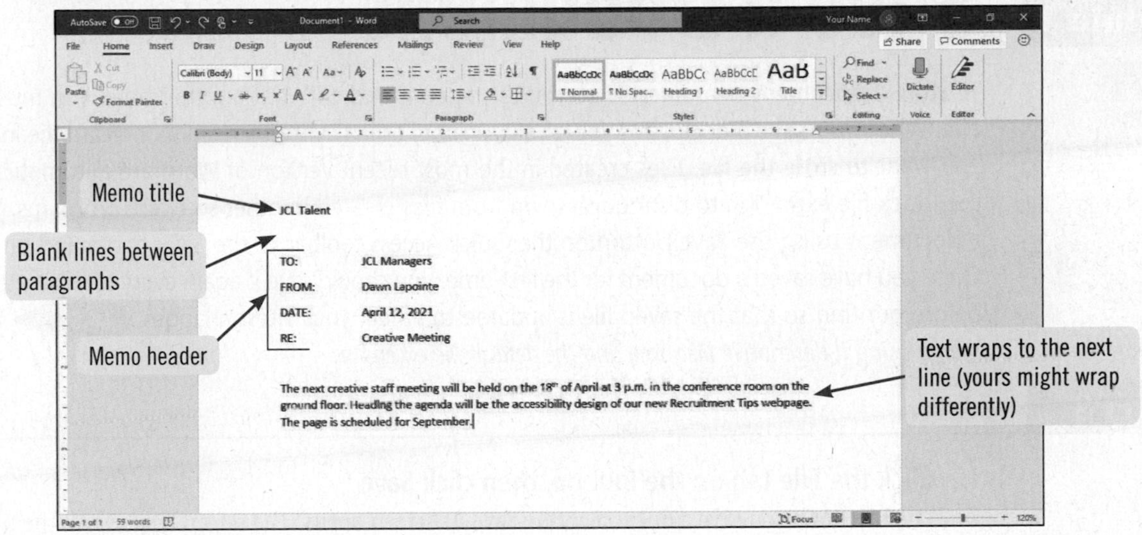

FIGURE 1-4: Edited memo text

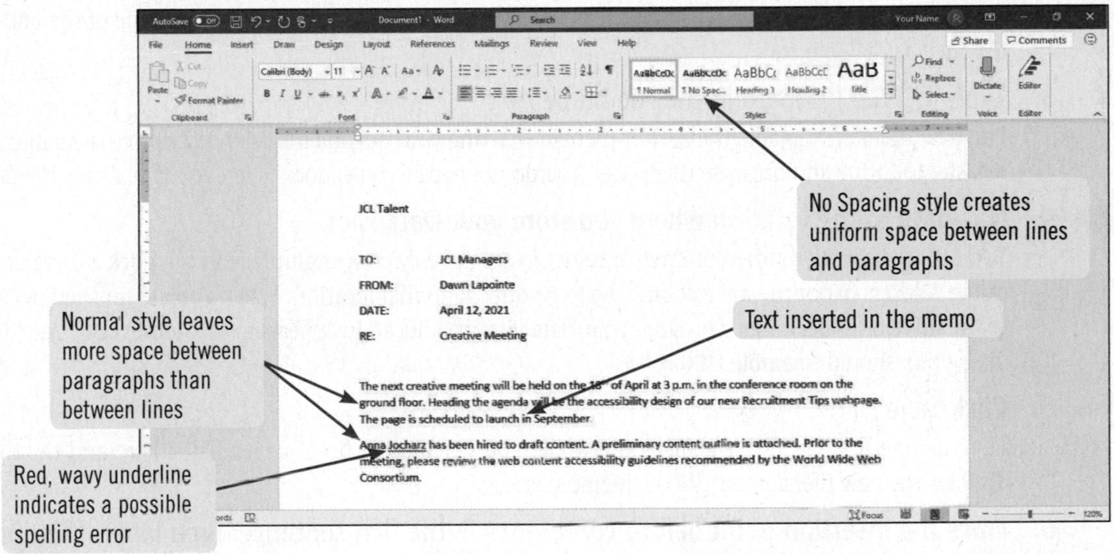

TABLE 1-2: Automatic features that appear as you type in Word

feature	what appears	to use
AutoComplete	A ScreenTip suggesting text to insert appears as you type	Press ENTER to insert the text suggested by the ScreenTip; continue typing to reject the suggestion
AutoCorrect	A small blue box appears when you place the pointer over text corrected by AutoCorrect; an AutoCorrect Options button appears when you point to the blue box	Word automatically corrects typos, minor spelling errors, and capitalization, and adds typographical symbols (such as © and ™) as you type; to reverse an AutoCorrect adjustment, click the AutoCorrect Options arrow, then click the option that will undo the action
Spelling and Grammar	A red wavy line under a word indicates a possible misspelling or a repeated word; a blue double line under text indicates a possible grammar error	Right-click red- or blue-underlined text to display a shortcut menu of correction options; click a correction option to accept it and remove the colored underline, or click Ignore to leave the text as is

Save a Document

Learning Outcome
- Save a document

To store a document permanently so you can open it and edit it at another time, you must save it as a **file**. When you **save** a document you give it a name, called a **filename**, and indicate the location where you want to store the file. Files created in the most recent version of Word are automatically assigned the .docx file extension to distinguish them from files created in other software programs. You can save a document using the Save button on the Quick Access toolbar or the Save command on the File tab. Once you have saved a document for the first time, you should save it again every few minutes and always before printing so that the saved file is updated to reflect your latest changes. **CASE** *You save your memo using a descriptive filename and the default file extension.*

STEPS

1. **Click the File tab on the Ribbon, then click Save**
   The first time you save a document, the Save As screen opens. The screen displays all the places you can save a file to, including OneDrive, your PC (identified as This PC), or a different location.

2. **Click Browse in the Save As screen**
   The Save As dialog box opens, similar to **FIGURE 1-5**. The default filename, JCL Talent, appears in the File name box. The default filename is based on the first few words of the document. The default file type, Word Document, appears in the Save as type list box. **TABLE 1-3** describes the functions of some of the buttons in the Save As dialog box.

> **TROUBLE**
> If you don't see the extension .docx as part of the filename, the setting in Windows to display file extensions is not active.

3. **Type IL_WD_1_Memo in the File name box**
   The new filename replaces the default filename. Giving your documents brief descriptive filenames makes it easier to locate and organize them later. You do not need to type .docx when you type a new filename.

4. **Navigate to the location where you store your Data Files**
   You can navigate to a different drive or folder in several ways. For example, you can click a drive or folder in the Address bar or the navigation pane to go directly to that location. When you are finished navigating to the drive or folder where you store your Data Files, that location appears in the Address bar. Your Save As dialog box should resemble **FIGURE 1-6**.

> **QUICK TIP**
> You can also double-click a drive or folder in the folder window to change the active location.

5. **Click Save**
   The document is saved to the drive and folder you specified in the Save As dialog box, and the title bar displays the new filename, IL_WD_1_Memo.docx.

6. **Place the insertion point before conference in the first sentence, type large, then press SPACEBAR**
   You can continue to work on a document after you have saved it with a new filename.

7. **Click the Save button on the Quick Access toolbar**
   Your change to the memo is saved. After you save a document for the first time, you must continue to save the changes you make to the document.

> **QUICK TIP**
> You also can press CTRL+S to save a document.

Using keyboard shortcuts

A **shortcut key** is a function key, such as F1, or a combination of keys, such as CTRL+S, that you press to perform a command. For example, instead of using the Cut, Copy, and Paste commands on the Ribbon or the Mini toolbar, you can use the **keyboard shortcuts** CTRL+X to cut text, CTRL+C to copy text, and CTRL+V to paste text. You can also press CTRL+S to save changes to a document instead of clicking the Save button on the Quick Access toolbar or clicking Save on the File tab. Becoming skilled at using keyboard shortcuts can help you quickly accomplish many of the tasks you perform in Word. If a keyboard shortcut is available for a command, then it is listed in the ScreenTip for that command.

FIGURE 1-5: Save As dialog box

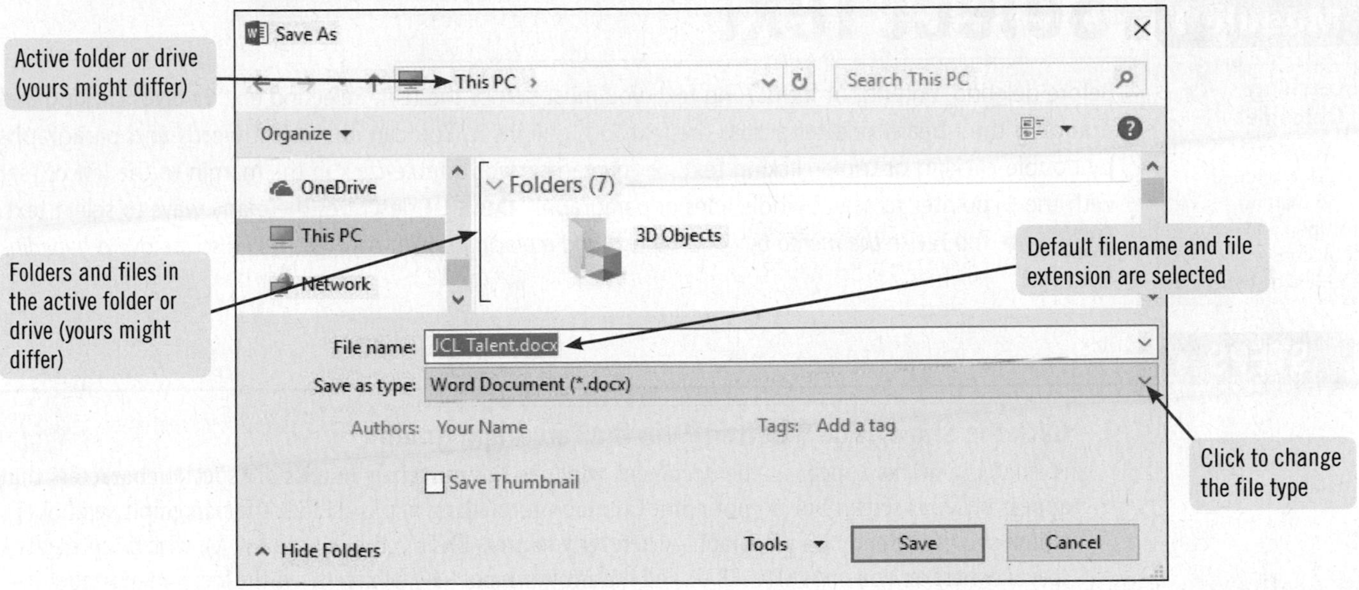

FIGURE 1-6: File to be saved to the Module 1 folder

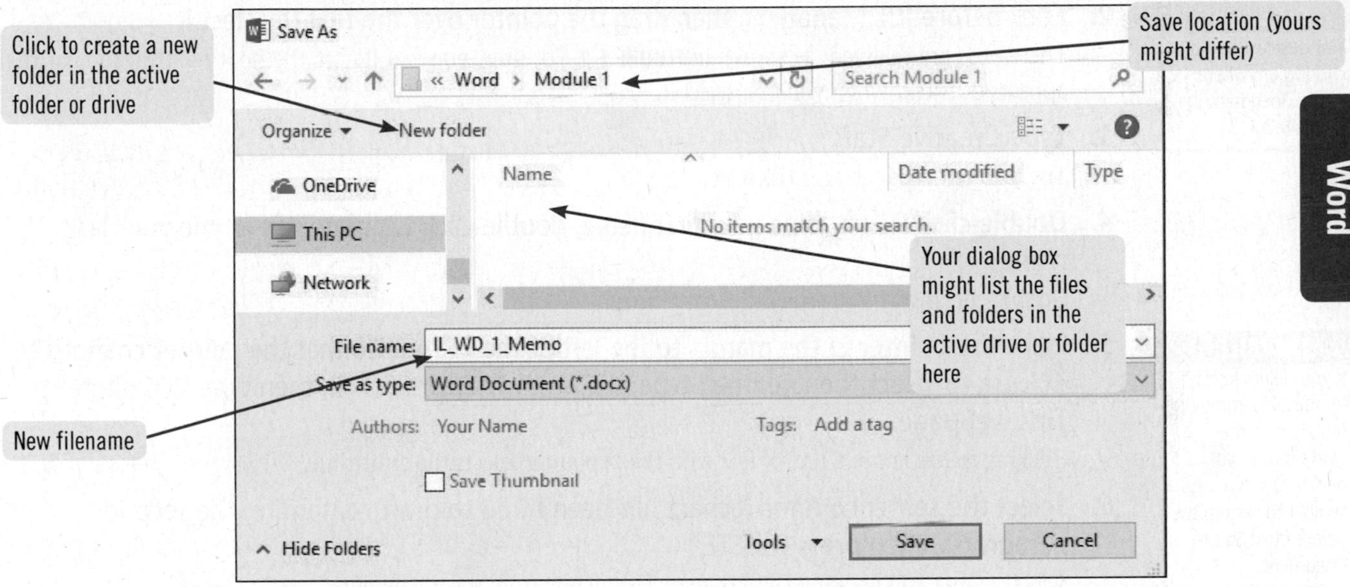

TABLE 1-3: Save As dialog box buttons

button	use to
Back	Navigate back to the last location shown in the Address bar
Forward	Navigate to the location that was previously shown in the Address bar
Up to	Navigate to the location above the current location in the folder hierarchy
Organize	Open a menu of commands related to organizing the selected file or folder, including Cut, Copy, Delete, Rename, and Properties
New folder	Create a new folder in the current folder or drive
Change your view	Change the way folder and file information is shown in the folder window in the Save As dialog box; click the Change your view button to toggle between views, or click the arrow to open a menu of view options

Select Text

Learning Outcomes
- Select text
- Show and hide formatting
- Undo and redo actions
- Manage hyperlinks

Before deleting, editing, or formatting text, you must **select** the text. Selecting text involves clicking and dragging the I-beam pointer across the text to highlight it. You can also select words and paragraphs by double-clicking or triple-clicking text, or you can click or double-click in the margin to the left of text with the pointer to select whole lines or paragraphs. **TABLE 1-4** describes the many ways to select text.
CASE *You revise the memo by selecting text and replacing it with new text. You also remove a hyperlink from text.*

STEPS

1. **Click the Show/Hide ¶ button ¶ in the Paragraph group**
   Formatting marks appear in the document window. **Formatting marks** are special characters that appear on your screen but do not print. Common formatting marks include the paragraph symbol (¶), which shows the end of a paragraph—wherever you press ENTER; the dot symbol (.), which represents a space—wherever you press SPACEBAR; and the arrow symbol (→), which shows the location of a tab stop—wherever you press TAB. Working with formatting marks turned on can help you to select, edit, and format text with precision.

QUICK TIP
You deselect text by clicking anywhere in the document window.

2. **Click before JCL Managers, then drag the pointer over the text to select it**
   The words are selected, as shown in **FIGURE 1-7**. For now, you can ignore the floating Mini toolbar that appears over text when you first select it.
3. **Type Creative Staff**
   The text you type replaces the selected text.
4. **Double-click Dawn, type your first name, double-click Lapointe, then type your last name**
   Double-clicking a word selects the entire word.

TROUBLE
If you delete text by mistake, immediately click the Undo button on the Quick Access toolbar to restore the deleted text to the document.

5. **Place the pointer in the margin to the left of the RE: line so that the pointer changes to , click to select the line, then type RE:, press TAB, press TAB, then type Recruitment Tips webpage**
   Clicking to the left of a line of text with the pointer selects the entire line.
6. **Select the sentence Anna Jocharz has been hired to draft content. in the second paragraph, then press DELETE**
   Selecting text and pressing DELETE removes the text from the document.
7. **Click after the period at the end of the second paragraph, press SPACEBAR, then type See www.w3.org for more information.**
   When you press SPACEBAR after typing the web address, Word automatically formats the web address as a hyperlink. A **hyperlink** is text that when clicked opens a webpage in a browser window. Text that is formatted as a hyperlink appears as colored, underlined text. You want to remove the hyperlink formatting.
8. **Right-click www.w3.org, then click Remove Hyperlink**
   Removing a hyperlink removes the link, but the text remains.

QUICK TIP
Always save before and after editing text.

9. **Click ¶, then click the Save button on the Quick Access toolbar**
   Formatting marks are turned off, and your changes to the memo are saved. The Show/Hide ¶ button is a **toggle button**, which means you can use it to turn formatting marks on and off. The edited memo is shown in **FIGURE 1-8**.

FIGURE 1-7: Text selected in the memo

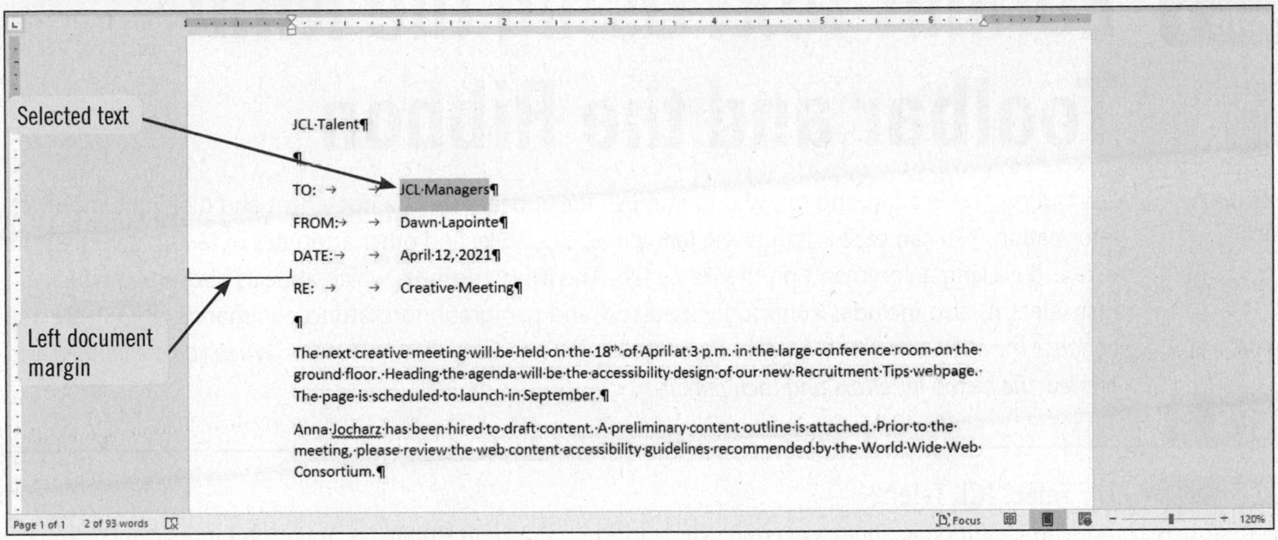

FIGURE 1-8: Edited memo with replacement text

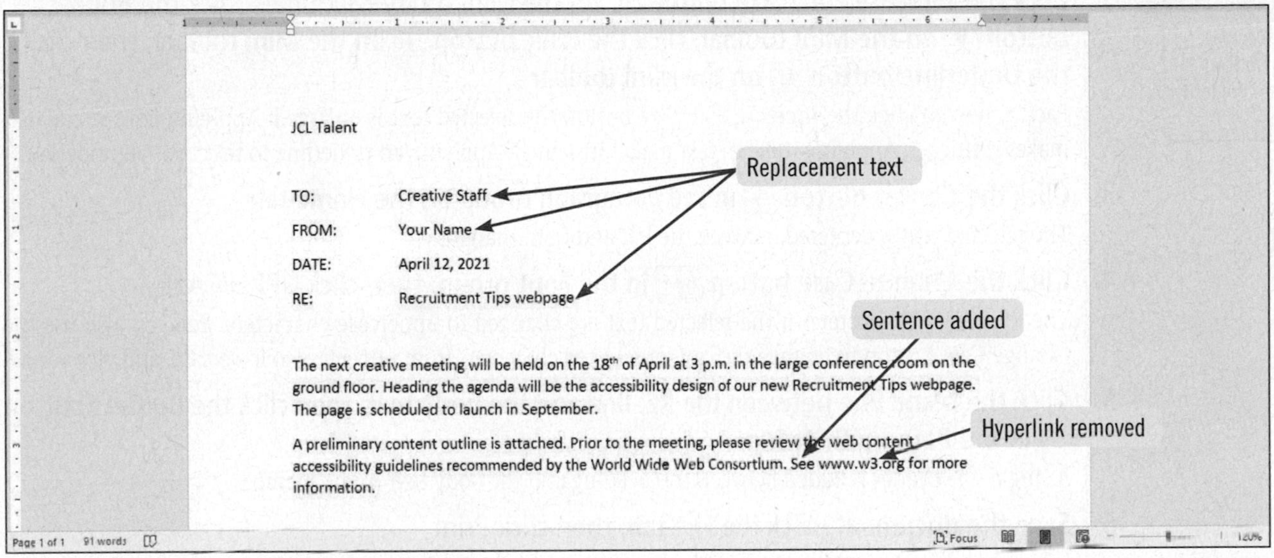

TABLE 1-4: Methods for selecting text

to select	use the pointer to
Any amount of text	Drag over the text
A word	Double-click the word
A line of text	Move the pointer to the left of the line, then click
A sentence	Press and hold CTRL, then click the sentence
A paragraph	Triple-click the paragraph or double-click with the pointer to the left of the paragraph
A large block of text	Click at the beginning of the selection, press and hold SHIFT, then click at the end of the selection
Multiple nonconsecutive selections	Select the first selection, then press and hold CTRL as you select each additional selection
An entire document	Triple-click with the pointer to the left of any text; press CTRL+A; or click the Select button in the Editing group on the Home tab, and then click Select All

Word
Module 1

Format Text Using the Mini Toolbar and the Ribbon

Learning Outcomes
- Modify text formatting
- Print a document
- Modify print settings
- Close a document

Formatting text is a fast and fun way to improve the appearance of a document and highlight important information. You can easily change the font, color, size, style, and other attributes of text by selecting the text and clicking a command on the Home tab. The **Mini toolbar**, which appears above text when you first select it, also includes commonly used text and paragraph formatting commands. **CASE** *You enhance the appearance of the memo by formatting the text using the Mini toolbar. When you are finished, you preview the memo for errors and then print it.*

STEPS

TROUBLE
If the Mini toolbar disappears, right-click the selection to display it again.

QUICK TIP
Click the Decrease Font Size button to decrease the font size.

1. **Select JCL Talent**
   The Mini toolbar appears over the selected text, as shown in **FIGURE 1-9**. You click a formatting option on the Mini toolbar to apply it to the selected text. **TABLE 1-5** describes the function of the buttons on the Mini toolbar. The buttons on the Mini toolbar are also available on the Ribbon.
2. **Click the Increase Font Size button on the Mini toolbar six times, click the Bold button on the Mini toolbar, click the Italic button on the Mini toolbar, then click the Underline button on the Mini toolbar**
   Each time you click the Increase Font Size button the selected text is enlarged. Applying bold to the text makes it thicker. Applying italic to text makes it slanted. Applying an underline to text adds an underline.
3. **Click the Center button in the Paragraph group on the Home tab**
   The selected text is centered between the left and right margins.
4. **Click the Change Case button in the Font group, then click UPPERCASE**
   The lowercase characters in the selected text are changed to uppercase characters. You can also use the Change Case button to change the case of selected characters from uppercase to lowercase, and vice versa.
5. **Click the blank line between the RE: line and the body text, then click the Borders button in the Paragraph group**
   A single line border is added between the heading and the body text in the memo.
6. **Save the document, click the File tab, then click Print**
   Information related to printing the document appears on the Print screen in Backstage view. Options for printing the document appear on the left side of the Print screen and a preview of the document as it will look when printed appears on the right side, as shown in **FIGURE 1-10**. Before you print a document, it's a good habit to examine it closely so you can identify and correct any problems.
7. **Click the Zoom In button on the status bar five times, then proofread your document carefully for errors**
   The document is enlarged in print preview. If you notice errors in your document, you need to correct them before you print. To do this, press ESC or click the Back button in Backstage view, correct any mistakes, save your changes, click the File tab, and then click the Print command again to be ready to print the document.
8. **Click the Print button on the Print screen**
   A copy of the memo prints using the default print settings. To change the current printer, change the number of copies to print, select which pages of a document to print, or modify another print setting, you simply change the appropriate setting on the Print screen before clicking the Print button.
9. **sam Click the File tab, then click Close**
   The document closes, but the Word program window remains open.

FIGURE 1-9: Mini toolbar

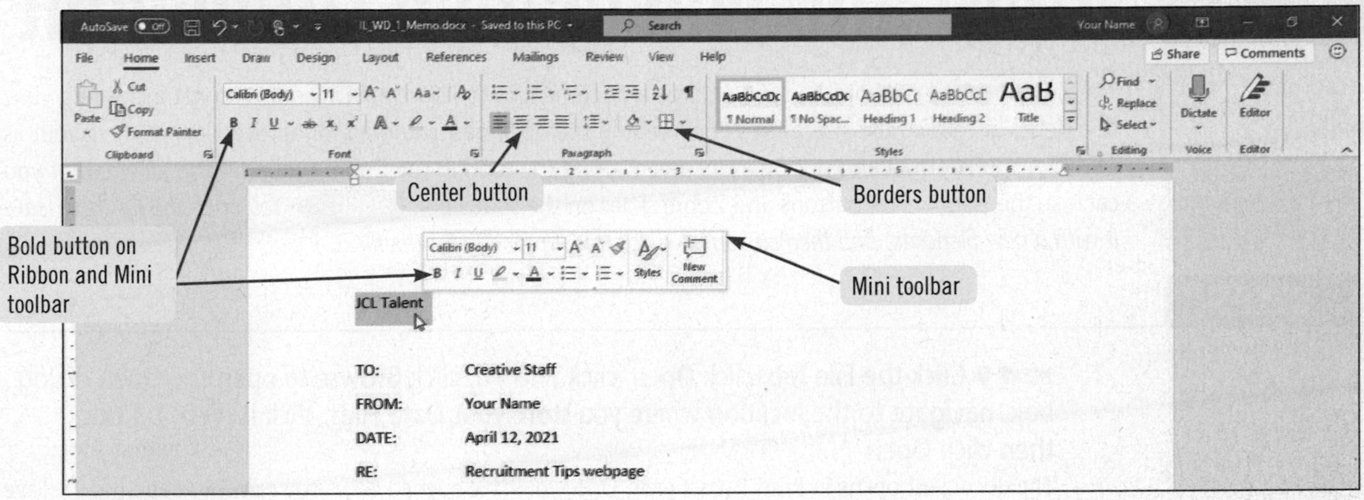

FIGURE 1-10: Preview of the completed memo

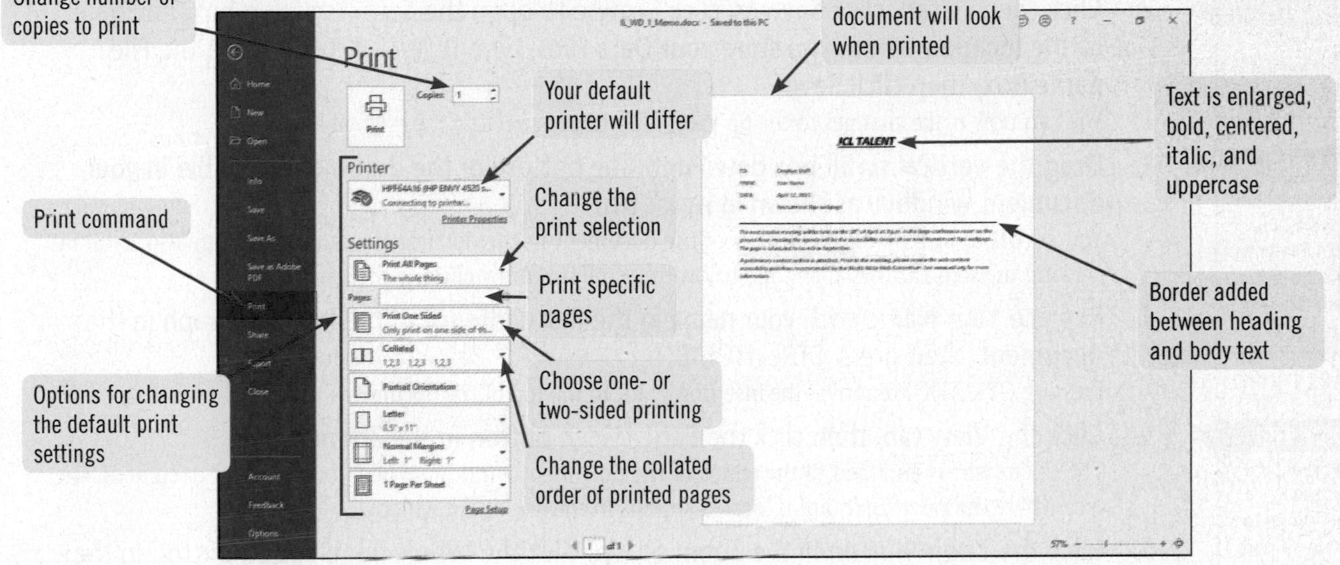

TABLE 1-5: Buttons on the Mini toolbar

button	use to	button	use to
Calibri (Body)	Change the font of text	B	Apply bold to text
11	Change the font size of text	I	Apply italic to text
A^	Make text larger	U	Apply an underline to text
A˅	Make text smaller	(highlight)	Apply colored highlighting to text
(format painter)	Copy the formats applied to selected text to other text	A	Change the color of text
(styles)	Apply a style to text	(bullets)	Apply bullets to paragraphs
(new comment)	Insert a new comment	(numbering)	Apply numbering to paragraphs

Word

Word
Module 1

View and Navigate a Document

Learning Outcomes
- Open documents
- Zoom in and out
- Manage document properties

The Zoom feature in Word lets you enlarge a document in the document window to get a close-up view of a detail or reduce the size of the document in the document window for an overview of the layout as a whole. You zoom in and out on a document using the tools in the Zoom group on the View tab or you can use the Zoom level buttons and Zoom slider on the status bar. **CASE** *You open the tip sheet, save it with a new filename, and then customize a document property for the file.*

STEPS

1. **sam Click the File tab, click Open, click This PC, click Browse to open the Open dialog box, navigate to the location where you store your Data Files, click IL_WD_1-1.docx, then click Open**
   The document opens in Print Layout view. Once you have opened a file, you can edit it and use the Save or the Save As command to save your changes. You use the **Save** command when you want to save the changes you make to a file, overwriting the stored file. You use the **Save As** command when you want to leave the original file intact and create a duplicate file with a different filename, file extension, or location.

TROUBLE
Click the Enable Editing button if necessary.

2. **Click the File tab, click Save As, click Browse to open the Save As dialog box, navigate to the location where you store your Data Files, type IL_WD_1_TipSheet in the File name box, then click Save**
   You can now make changes to the tip sheet file without affecting the original file.

TROUBLE
If you do not see the vertical scroll box, move the pointer to the right side of the document window to display it.

3. **Drag the vertical scroll box down until the bottom of the document is visible in your document window, as shown in FIGURE 1-11**
   You **scroll** to display different parts of the document in the document window. You can also scroll by clicking the scroll arrows above and below the scroll bar, or by clicking the scroll bar.
4. **Replace Your Name with your name in the first sentence of the last paragraph in the document, then press CTRL+HOME**
   Pressing CTRL+HOME moves the insertion point to the top of the document.

QUICK TIP
Click the Multiple Pages button in the Zoom group to display two or more pages of a multi-page document in the document window.

5. **Click the View tab, then click the Page Width button in the Zoom group**
   The document is enlarged to the width of the document window. When you enlarge a document, the area where the insertion point is located appears in the document window.
6. **Click the Zoom button in the Zoom group, click the Whole page option button in the Zoom dialog box, then click OK to view the entire document**
   You use the Zoom dialog box to select a zoom level for displaying the document in the document window.
7. **Move the Zoom slider on the status bar to the right until the Zoom percentage is approximately 200%, then click the Zoom Out button [–] until the zoom level is 120%**
   Dragging the Zoom slider enlarges or reduces a document in the document window. You can also click the Zoom Out and Zoom In buttons to change the zoom level.
8. **Click the File tab, then click Info**
   The right side of the Info screen in Backstage view shows the document properties for the file. **Document properties** are user-defined details about a file that describe its contents and origin, including the name of the author, the title of the document, and keywords that you can assign to help organize and search your files.
9. **Click the Add a title box in the Properties section of the Info screen, type Tips, then click outside the box**
   The new Title property for the document appears in Backstage view as shown in as shown in FIGURE 1-12
10. **Click Back button to return to the Home tab, then save your changes**
    The document appears at 120% zoom in Print Layout view.

FIGURE 1-11: Zoom slider

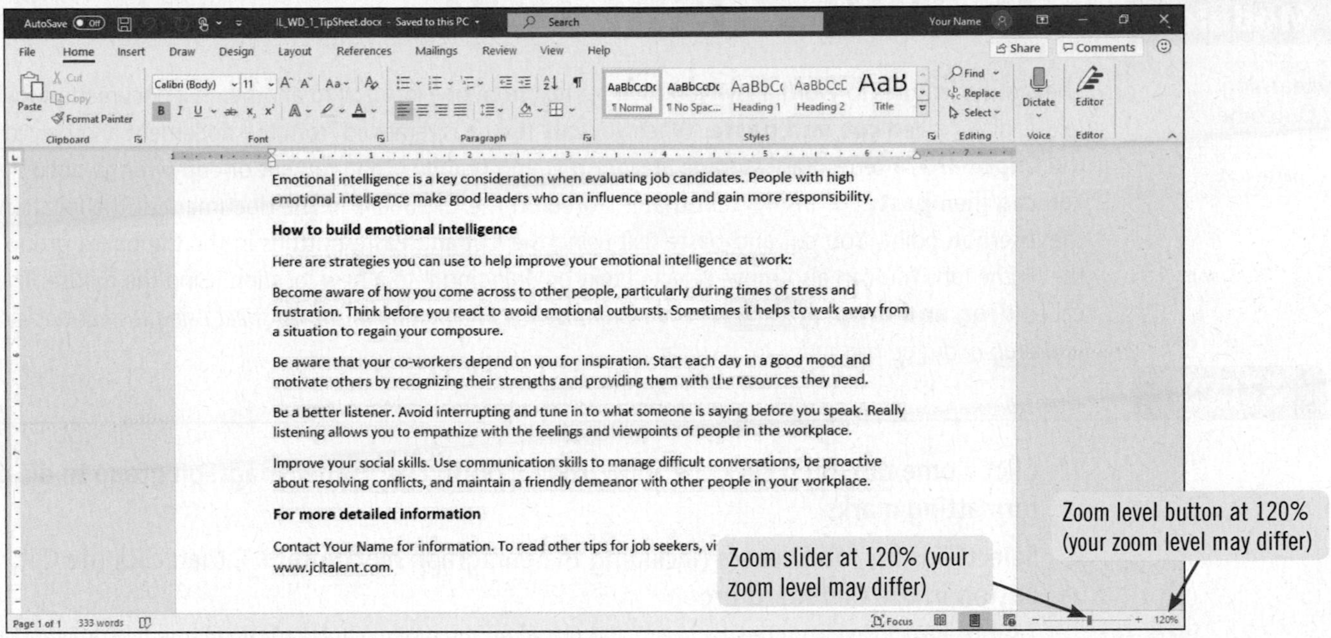

FIGURE 1-12: Document properties in Backstage view

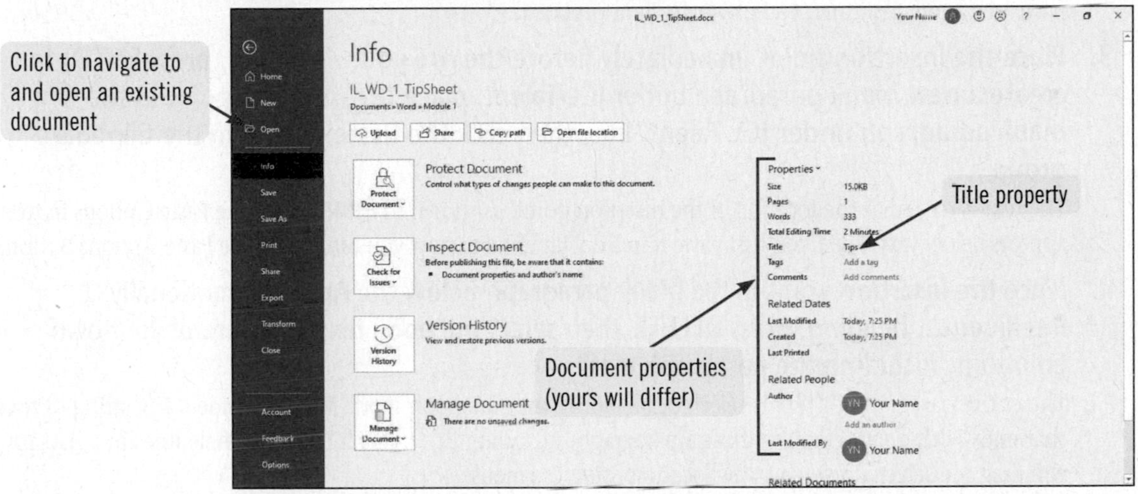

Word

Using Word document views

Document views are different ways of displaying a document in the document window. Each Word view provides features that are useful for working on different types of documents. The default view, **Print Layout view,** displays a document as it will look on a printed page. Print Layout view is helpful for formatting text and pages, including adjusting document margins, creating columns of text, inserting graphics, and formatting headers and footers. Also useful is **Read Mode view,** which displays document text so that it is easy to read on screen. Other Word views are helpful for performing specialized tasks. **Web Layout view** allows you to format webpages or documents that will be viewed on a computer screen. In Web Layout view, a document appears just as it will when viewed with a web browser. Outline view is useful for editing and formatting longer documents that include multiple headings. **Outline view** allows you to reorganize text by moving the headings. Finally, **Draft view**, shows a simplified layout of a document, without margins, headers and footers, or graphics. When you want to quickly type and edit text, it's often easiest to work in Draft view. You switch between views by clicking the view buttons on the status bar or by using the commands on the View tab. Changing views does not affect how the printed document will appear. It simply changes the way you view the document in the document window.

Word
Module 1

Cut and Paste Text

Learning Outcome
- Cut, copy, and paste text

The editing features in Word allow you to move text from one location to another in a document. Moving text is often called **cut and paste**. When you **cut** text, it is removed from the document and placed on the **Clipboard**, a temporary storage area for text and graphics that you cut or copy from a document. You can then **paste**, or insert, text that is stored on the Clipboard in the document at the location of the insertion point. You cut and paste text using the Cut and Paste buttons in the Clipboard group on the Home tab. You can also move selected text by dragging it to a new location using the mouse. This is called **drag and drop**. CASE *You reorganize the information in the tip sheet using the cut-and-paste and drag-and-drop methods.*

STEPS

1. **Click Home tab, then click the Show/Hide ¶ button ¶ in the Paragraph group to display formatting marks**
2. **Select Tips for Job Seekers (including the paragraph mark after it), then click the Cut button in the Clipboard group**
   The text is removed from the document and placed on the system clipboard. Word uses two different clipboards: the system **clipboard**, which holds just one item and is not visible, and the **Office Clipboard** (the Clipboard), which holds up to 24 items and can be displayed. When you cut-and-paste or copy-and-paste items one at a time, you use the system clipboard.
3. **Place the insertion point immediately before the Are you... heading, press ENTER to create a new blank paragraph under JCL Talent, place the insertion point in the new blank paragraph under JCL Talent, Inc., then click the Paste button in the Clipboard group**
   The text is pasted at the location of the insertion point, as shown in **FIGURE 1-13**. The Paste Options button appears below text when you first paste it in a document. For now you can ignore the Paste Options button.
4. **Place the insertion point in the blank paragraph below the Are you emotionally intelligent... heading, press DELETE, then select the body text Be aware of your own emotions, including the paragraph mark**
   The entire paragraph of text is selected, including the paragraph mark. Word considers any string of text that ends with a paragraph mark as a paragraph, including titles, headings, and single lines in a list. You will drag the selected text to a new location using the mouse.
5. **Press and hold the mouse button over the selected text, then drag the pointer's vertical line to the beginning of the Control how you express... paragraph, as shown in FIGURE 1-14**
   You drag the insertion point to where you want the text to be inserted when you release the mouse button.
6. **Release the mouse button, click to deselect the text, then save your changes**
   The selected text is moved to the location of the insertion point. Text is not placed on the Clipboard when you drag and drop it.

QUICK TIP
As you drag, the pointer changes to , and a black vertical line, which is the insertion point, moves with the pointer.

QUICK TIP
If you make a mistake, click the Undo button on the Quick Access toolbar, then try again.

Highlighting text in a document

The Highlight tool allows you to mark and find important text in a document. **Highlighting** is transparent color that is applied to text using the Highlight pointer. To highlight text, click the Text Highlight Color arrow in the Font group on the Home tab, select a color, then use the I-beam part of the pointer to select the text you want to highlight. Click to turn off the Highlight pointer. To remove highlighting, select the highlighted text, click then click No Color. Highlighting prints, but it is used most effectively when a document is viewed on screen.

FIGURE 1-13: Moved text with Paste Options button

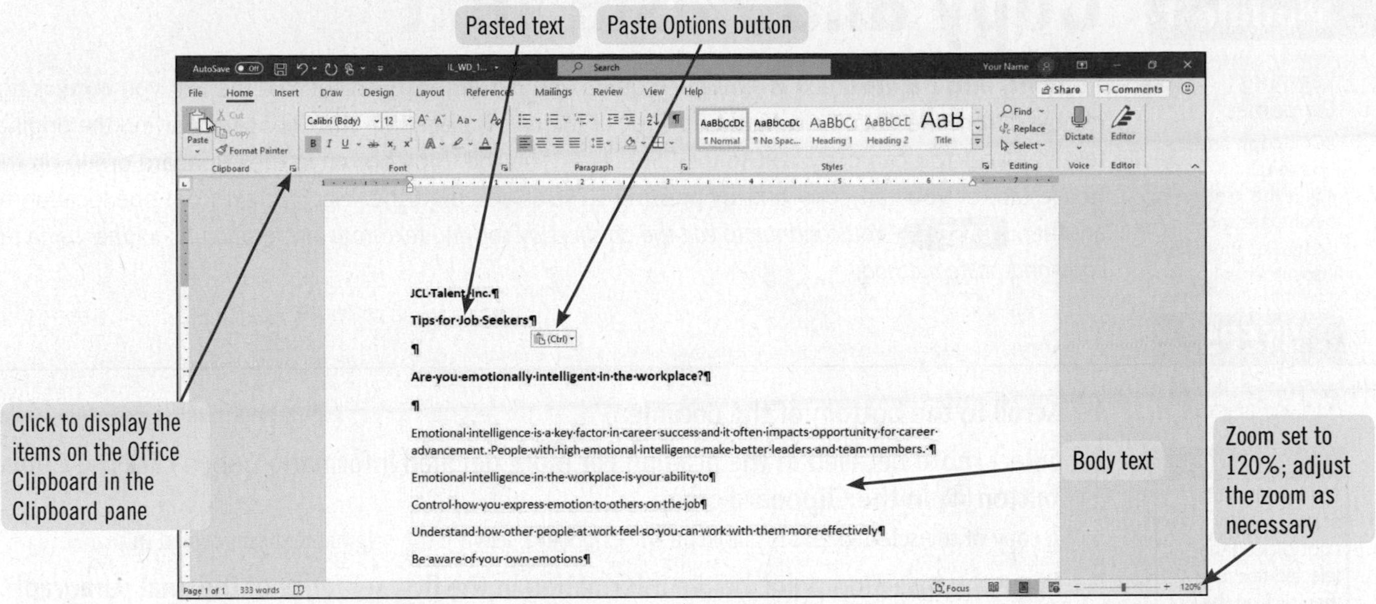
Pasted text
Paste Options button
Click to display the items on the Office Clipboard in the Clipboard pane
Body text
Zoom set to 120%; adjust the zoom as necessary
JCL·Talent,·Inc.¶
Tips·for·Job·Seekers¶
Are·you·emotionally·intelligent·in·the·workplace?¶
Emotional·intelligence·is·a·key·factor·in·career·success·and·it·often·impacts·opportunity·for·career·advancement.·People·with·high·emotional·intelligence·make·better·leaders·and·team·members.·¶
Emotional·intelligence·in·the·workplace·is·your·ability·to¶
Control·how·you·express·emotion·to·others·on·the·job¶
Understand·how·other·people·at·work·feel·so·you·can·work·with·them·more·effectively¶
Be·aware·of·your·own·emotions¶

FIGURE 1-14: Dragging and dropping text in a new location

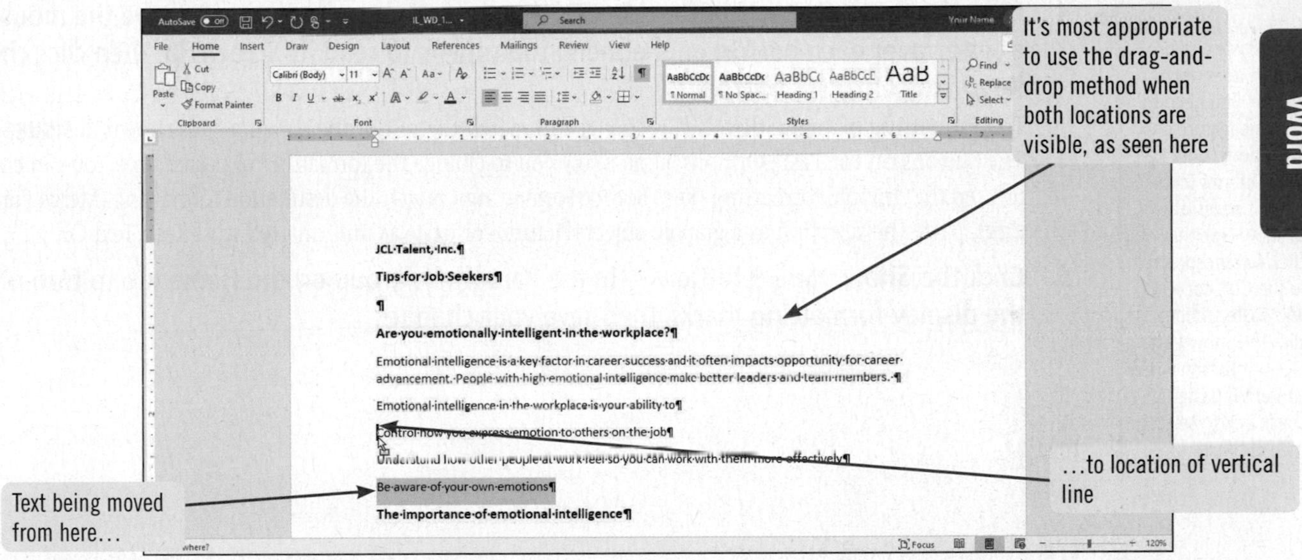
It's most appropriate to use the drag-and-drop method when both locations are visible, as seen here
...to location of vertical line
Text being moved from here...
JCL·Talent,·Inc.¶
Tips·for·Job·Seekers¶
Are·you·emotionally·intelligent·in·the·workplace?¶
Be·aware·of·your·own·emotions¶
The·importance·of·emotional·intelligence¶

Using the Undo, Redo, and Repeat commands

Word remembers the editing and formatting changes you make so that you can easily reverse or repeat them. You can reverse the last action you took by clicking the Undo button on the Quick Access toolbar, or you can undo a series of actions by clicking the Undo arrow and selecting the action you want to reverse. When you undo an action using the Undo arrow, you also undo all the actions above it in the list—that is, all actions that were performed after the action you selected. Similarly, you can keep the change you just reversed by using the Redo button on the Quick Access toolbar. The Redo button appears only immediately after clicking the Undo button to undo a change.

If you want to repeat an action you just completed, you can use the Repeat button on the Quick Access toolbar. For example, if you just typed "thank you," clicking inserts "thank you" at the location of the insertion point. If you just applied bold, clicking applies bold to the currently selected text. You also can repeat the last action you took by pressing F4.

Word

Word Module 1

Copy and Paste Text

Learning Outcomes
- Cut, copy, and paste text
- Split the window
- Compare and combine multiple documents

Copying and pasting text is similar to cutting and pasting text, except that the text you **copy** is not removed from the document. Rather, a copy of the text is placed on the Clipboard, leaving the original text in place. You can copy text to the Clipboard using the Copy button in the Clipboard group on the Home tab, or you can copy text by pressing CTRL as you drag the selected text from one location to another. **CASE** *You continue to edit the tip sheet by copying text from one location to another using the copy-and-paste method.*

STEPS

QUICK TIP
You can also cut or copy text by right-clicking the selected text, and then clicking the Cut or Copy command on the menu that opens.

TROUBLE
If the Paste Options button does not appear, you need to turn the feature on in Options. Click File, click Options (click More if necessary to show Options), click Advanced, scroll to the Cut, copy, and paste section, click the Show Paste Options button when content is pasted check box to select it, then click OK.

1. **Scroll to the bottom of the document**
2. **Select more detailed in the heading For more detailed information, then click the Copy button in the Clipboard group**

   A copy of the selected text is placed on the Clipboard, leaving the original text you copied in place.
3. **Place the insertion point before information in the first sentence of the final paragraph, then click the Paste button**

   The text "more detailed" is inserted in the final paragraph, as shown in **FIGURE 1-15**. Notice that the pasted text is formatted differently than the paragraph in which it was inserted.
4. **Click the Paste Options button (Ctrl) that appears next to the text, move the mouse pointer over each button on the menu that opens to read its ScreenTip, then click the Keep Text Only (T) button**

   The formatting of "more detailed" is changed to match the rest of the paragraph, as shown in **FIGURE 1-16**. The buttons on the Paste Options menu allow you to change the formatting of pasted text. You can choose to keep the original formatting (Keep Source Formatting), match the destination formatting (Merge Formatting), paste the selection as a graphic object (Picture), or paste as unformatted text (Keep Text Only).
5. **Click the Show/Hide ¶ button ¶ in the Paragraph group on the Home tab to turn off the display formatting marks, then save your changes**

Splitting the document window to copy and move items in a long document

If you want to copy or move items between parts of a long document, it can be useful to split the document window into two panes. This allows you to display the item you want to copy or move in one pane and the destination for the item in the other pane. To split a window, click the Split button in the Window group on the View tab, and then drag the horizontal split bar that appears to the location where you want to split the window. Once the document window is split into two panes, you can use the scroll bars in each pane to display different parts of the document. To copy or move an item from one pane to another, you can use the Cut, Copy, and Paste commands, or you can drag the item between the panes. When you are finished editing the document, double-click the split bar to restore the window to a single pane, or click the Remove Split button in the Window group on the View tab.

FIGURE 1-15: Text pasted in document

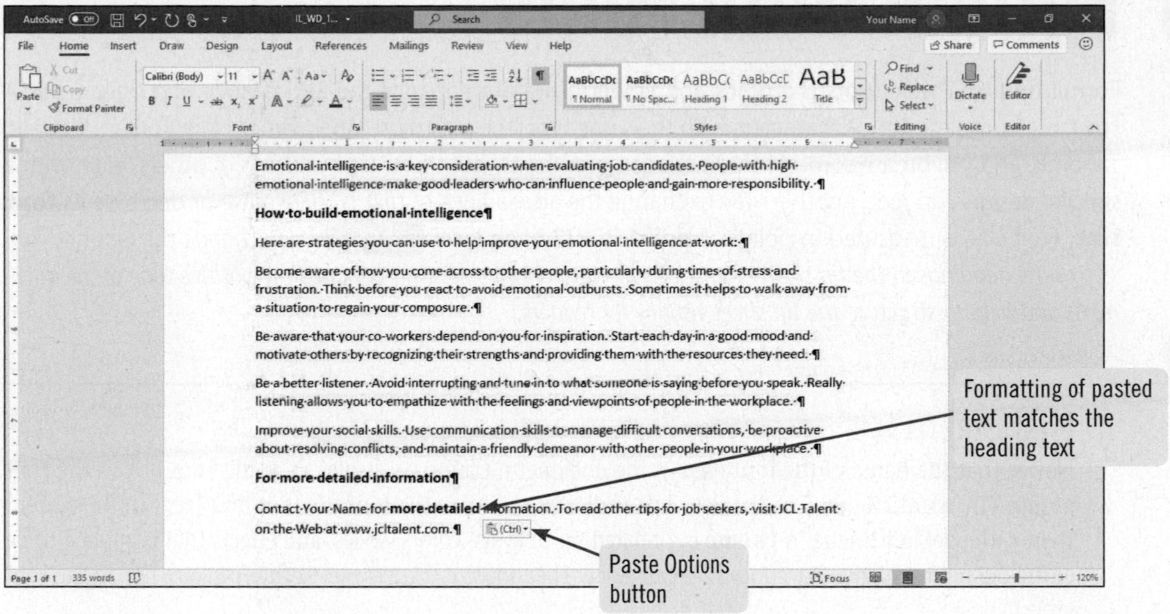

FIGURE 1-16: Copied text in document

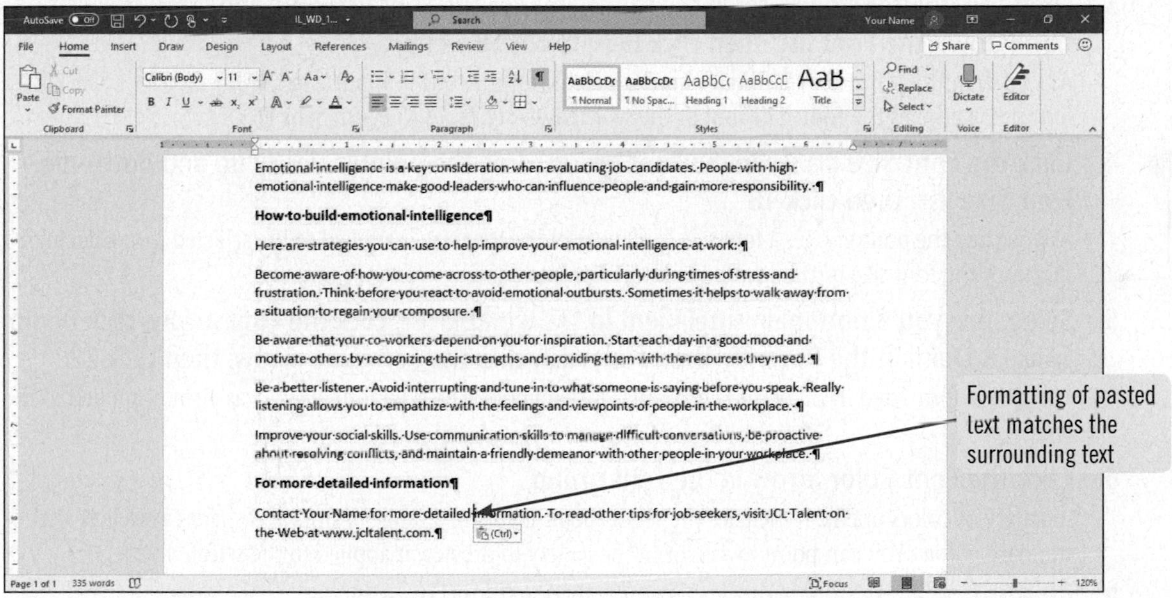

Word

Copying and moving items between documents

You can also use the Clipboard to copy and move items between documents. To do this, open both documents and the Clipboard pane. With multiple documents open, copy or cut an item from one document and then switch to the other document and paste the item. To switch between open documents, point to the Word icon on the taskbar, and then click the document you want to appear in the document window. You can also display more than one document at the same time by clicking the Arrange All button or the View Side by Side button in the Window group on the View tab.

Word Module 1

Format with Fonts

Learning Outcome
- Modify text formatting

Formatting text with fonts is a quick and powerful way to enhance the appearance of a document. A **font** is a complete set of characters with the same typeface or design. Arial, Times New Roman, Courier, Tahoma, and Calibri are some of the more common fonts, but there are hundreds of others, each with a specific design and feel. Another way to change the appearance of text is to increase or decrease its **font size**. Font size is measured in points. A **point** is 1/72 of an inch. **CASE** *You change the font and font size of the headings in the tip sheet. You select a font and font sizes that enhance the positive tone of the document and help to structure the tip sheet visually for readers.*

STEPS

1. **Press CTRL+HOME**
   Notice that the name of the font used in the document, Calibri, is displayed in the Font box in the Font group. The word "(Body)" in the Font box indicates Calibri is the font used for body text in the current theme, the default theme. A **theme** is a related set of fonts, colors, styles, and effects that is applied to an entire document to give it a cohesive appearance. The font size, 11, appears in the Font Size box in the Font group.

> **QUICK TIP**
> There are two types of fonts: **serif fonts** have a small stroke, called a serif, at the ends of characters; **sans serif fonts** do not have a serif.

2. **Select Tips for Job Seekers, then click the Font arrow in the Font group**
   The Font list, which shows the fonts available on your computer, opens as shown in **FIGURE 1-17**. The font names are formatted in the font. Font names can appear in more than one location on the Font list.

3. **Drag the pointer slowly down the font names in the Font list, drag the scroll box to scroll down the Font list, then click Berlin Sans FB Demi**
   As you drag the pointer over a font name, a preview of the font is applied to the selected text. Clicking a font name applies the font. The font of the selected text changes to Berlin Sans FB Demi.

> **QUICK TIP**
> You can also type a font size in the Font Size box.

4. **Click the Font Size arrow in the Font group, drag the pointer slowly up and down the Font Size list, then click 18**
   As you drag the pointer over a font size, a preview of the font size is applied to the selected text. Clicking 18 increases the font size of the selected text to 18 points.

5. **Select Are you emotionally intelligent in the workplace?, click the Font arrow, click Berlin Sans FB Demi in the Recently Used Fonts list, click the Font Size arrow, then click 22**
   The title is formatted in 22-point Berlin Sans FB Demi bold. The bold formatting was already applied to the text.

6. **Click the Font Color arrow in the Font group**
   A gallery of colors opens. It includes the set of theme colors in a range of tints and shades as well as a set of standard colors. You can point to a color in the gallery to preview it applied to the selected text.

7. **Click the Blue, Accent 1 color as shown in FIGURE 1-18, then deselect the text**
   The color of the title text changes to blue. The active color on the Font Color button also changes to blue.

> **TROUBLE**
> If the Mini toolbar closes, select the text again.

8. **Scroll down, select the heading The importance of emotional intelligence, then, using the Mini toolbar, click the Font arrow, click Berlin Sans FB Demi, click the Font Size arrow, click 14, click [A], then deselect the text**
   The heading is formatted in 14-point Berlin Sans FB Demi bold with a blue color.

9. **Repeat Step 8 to apply 14-point Berlin Sans FB Demi blue to the How to build emotional intelligence and For more detailed information headings, press CTRL+HOME, then save your changes**
   Compare your document to **FIGURE 1-19**.

FIGURE 1-17: Font list

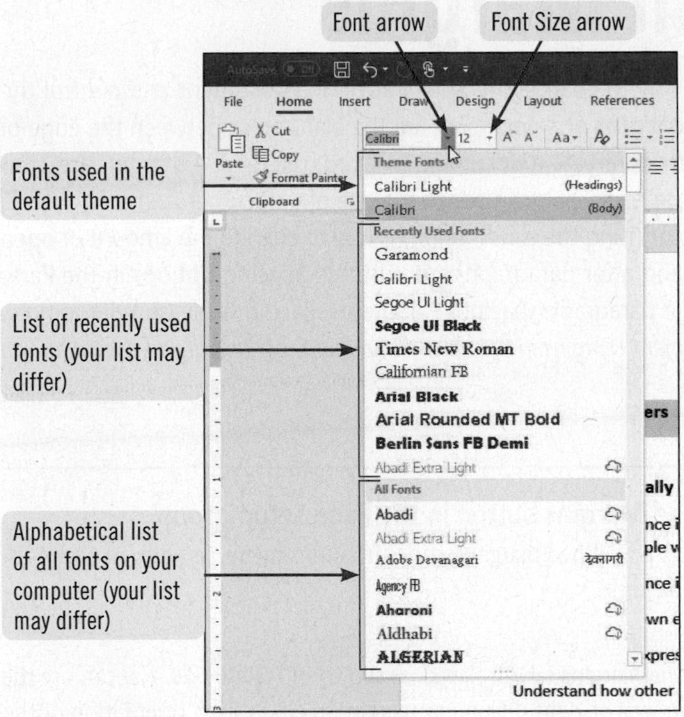

FIGURE 1-18: Font Color Palette

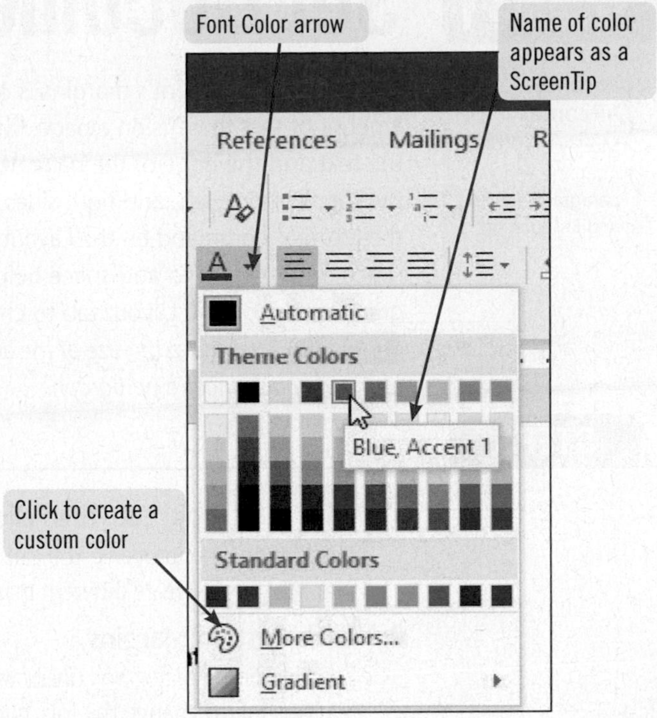

FIGURE 1-19: Document formatted with fonts

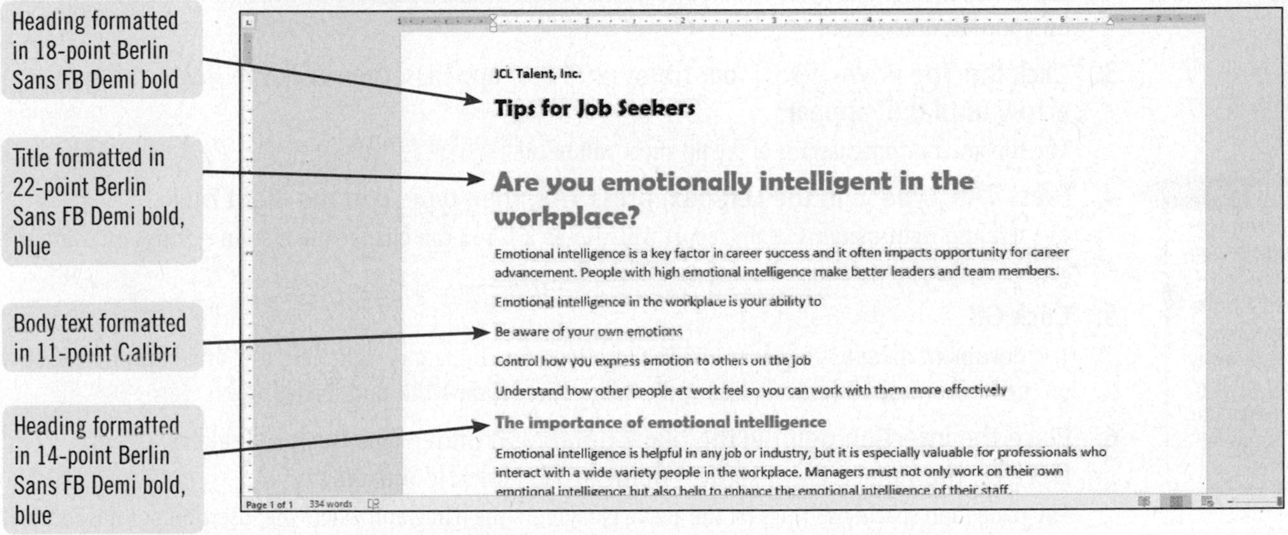

Applying shadows and other text effects to text

The Word Text Effects and Typography feature allows you to add visual appeal to your documents by adding special text effects to text, including outlines, shadows, reflections, and glows. The feature also includes a gallery of preformatted combined text effect styles, called **WordArt**, that you can apply to your text to format it quickly and easily. To apply a WordArt style to text, simply select the text, click the Text Effects and Typography button in the Font group on the Home tab, and select a WordArt style from the gallery. To apply an individual text effect style, such as a shadow, outline, reflection, or glow, select the text, click the Text Effects and Typography button, point to the type of text effect you want to apply, and then select a style from the gallery that opens. Experiment with combining text effect styles to give your text a striking appearance.

If you are unhappy with the way text is formatted, you can use the Clear All Formatting command to return the text to the default format settings—11-point Calibri. Select the text, then click the Clear All Formatting button in the Font group on the Home tab.

Word
Module 1

Set Document Margins

Learning Outcomes
- Modify page setup
- Alter line and paragraph spacing and indentation

Changing a document's margins is one way to change the appearance of a document and control the amount of text that fits on a page. The **margins** of a document are the blank areas between the edge of the text and the edge of the page. When you create a document in Word, the default margins are 1" at the top, bottom, left, and right sides of the page. You can adjust the size of a document's margins using the Margins command on the Layout tab or using the rulers. Another way to change the amount of open space on a page is to add space before and after paragraphs. You use the Spacing options in the Paragraph group on the Layout tab to change paragraph spacing. Paragraph spacing is measured in points. **CASE** *You reduce the size of the document margins in the tip sheet so that more text fits on the page. You also add space under a paragraph.*

STEPS

1. **Click the Layout tab, then click the Margins button in the Page Setup group**
   The Margins menu opens. You can select predefined margin settings from this menu, or you can click Custom Margins to create different margin settings.

2. **Click Custom Margins**
   The Page Setup dialog box opens with the Margins tab displayed, as shown in **FIGURE 1-20**. You can use the Margins tab to change the top, bottom, left, or right document margin; to change the orientation of the pages from portrait to landscape; and to alter other page layout settings. **Portrait orientation** means a page is taller than it is wide; **landscape orientation** means a page is wider than it is tall. This tip sheet uses portrait orientation.

3. **Click the Top down arrow four times until 0.6" appears, then click the Bottom down arrow until 0.6" appears**
   The top and bottom margins of the tip sheet will be .6".

4. **Press TAB, type .6 in the Left box, press TAB, then type .6 in the Right box**
   The left and right margins of the report will also be .6". You can change the margin settings by using the arrows or by typing a value in the appropriate box.

> **QUICK TIP**
> The minimum allowable margin settings depend on your printer and the size of the paper you are using. Word displays a warning message if you set margins that are too narrow for your printer.

5. **Click OK**
   The document margins change to .6". The location of each margin (right, left, top, and bottom) is shown on the horizontal and vertical rulers at the intersection of the white and shaded areas.

6. **Place the insertion point in the blank paragraph under Tips for Job Seekers, press DELETE, then place the insertion point in Tips for Job Seekers**
   The paragraph spacing settings for the active paragraph (the paragraph where the insertion point is located) are shown in the Before and After text boxes in the Paragraph group on the Layout tab.

7. **Click the Before up arrow in the Spacing section in the Paragraph group once until 6 pt appears, then click the After up arrow in the Spacing section in the Paragraph group four times until 30 pt appears**
   Six points of space are added before the Tips for Job Seekers paragraph, and 30 points of space are added after, as shown in **FIGURE 1-21**.

FIGURE 1-20: Margins tab in Page Setup dialog box

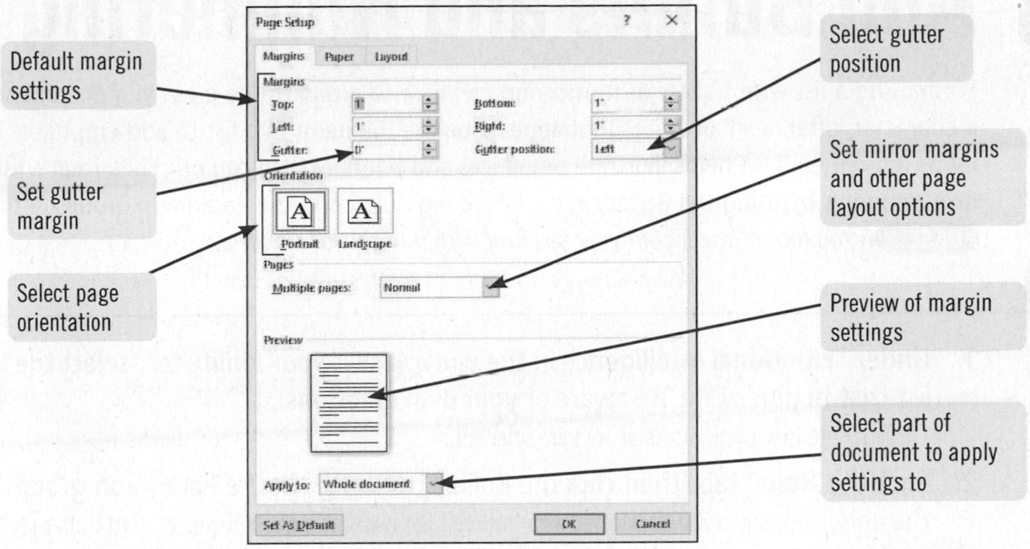

FIGURE 1-21: Info sheet with smaller margins and space after a paragraph

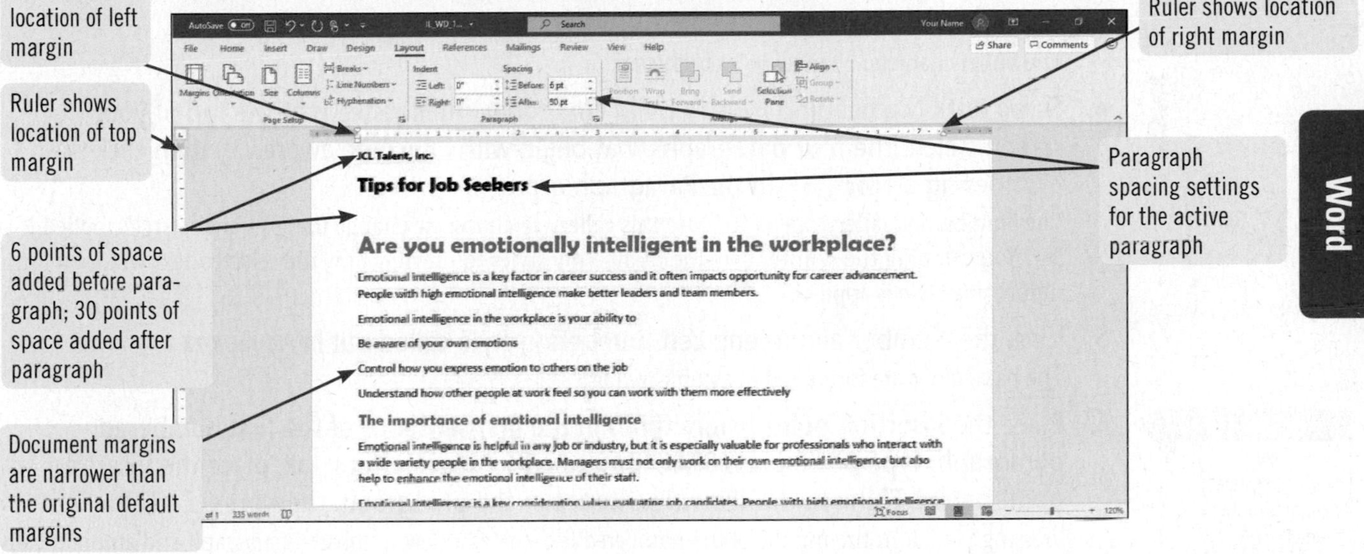

Changing orientation, margin settings, and paper size

By default, the documents you create in Word use an 8 ½" × 11" paper size in portrait orientation with the default margin settings. You can change the orientation, margin settings, and paper size to common settings using the Orientation, Margins, and Size buttons in the Page Setup group on the Layout tab. You can also adjust these settings and others in the Page Setup dialog box. For example, to change the layout of multiple pages, use the Multiple pages arrow on the Margins tab to create pages that use mirror margins, that include two pages per sheet of paper, or that are formatted using a book fold. **Mirror margins** are used in a document with facing pages, such as a magazine, where the margins on the left page of the document are a mirror image of the margins on the right page. Documents with mirror margins have inside and outside margins, rather than right and left margins. Another type of margin is a gutter margin, which is used in documents that are bound, such as books. A gutter adds extra space to the left, top, or inside margin to allow for the binding. Add a gutter to a document by adjusting the setting in the Gutter position box on the Margins tab. To change the size of the paper used, use the Paper size arrow on the Paper tab to select a standard paper size, or enter custom measurements in the Width and Height boxes.

Add Bullets and Numbering

Learning Outcome
- Create numbered and bulleted lists

Formatting a list with bullets or numbering can help to organize the ideas in a document. A **bullet** is a character, often a small circle, that appears before the items in a list to add emphasis. Formatting a list as a numbered list helps illustrate sequences and priorities. You can quickly format a list with bullets or numbering by using the Bullets and Numbering buttons in the Paragraph group on the Home tab.

CASE *You format the lists in your tip sheet with numbers and bullets.*

STEPS

1. **Under "Emotional intelligence in the workplace is your ability to", select the three-line list that begins with "Be aware of your own emotions..."**
   Three single-line paragraphs of text are selected.
2. **Click the Home tab, then click the Bullets button in the Paragraph group**
   The three paragraphs are formatted as a bulleted list using the most recently used bullet style as shown in FIGURE 1-22.
3. **Click a bullet in the list to select all the bullets, click the Bullets arrow in the Paragraph group, click the check mark bullet style, then click the document to deselect the text**
   The bullet character changes to a check mark.
4. **Scroll until the heading How to build emotional intelligence is at the top of your screen, select the four paragraphs that begin with "Become aware...", then click the Numbering arrow in the Paragraph group**
   The Numbering gallery opens. You use this gallery to choose or change the numbering style applied to a list. You can drag the pointer over the numbering styles to preview how the selected text will look if the numbering style is applied.
5. **Click the Number alignment: Left numbering style called out in FIGURE 1-23**
   The paragraphs are formatted as a numbered list.
6. **Place the insertion point before times in the first sentence of the first numbered paragraph, type peak, press SPACEBAR to add a space after peak, place the insertion point before Think in the second sentence of the paragraph, then press ENTER**
   Pressing ENTER in the middle of the numbered list creates a new numbered paragraph and automatically renumbers the remainder of the list. Similarly, if you delete a paragraph from a numbered list, Word automatically renumbers the remaining paragraphs.
7. **Click 1 in the list**
   Clicking a number in a list selects all the numbers, as shown in FIGURE 1-24.
8. **Click the Bold button in the Font group, then save your changes**
   The numbers are all formatted in bold. Notice that the formatting of the items in the list does not change when you change the formatting of the numbers. You can also use this technique to change the formatting of bullets in a bulleted list.

QUICK TIP
To remove a bullet or number, select the paragraph(s), then click the Bullets button or the Numbering button.

FIGURE 1-22: Bullets applied to list

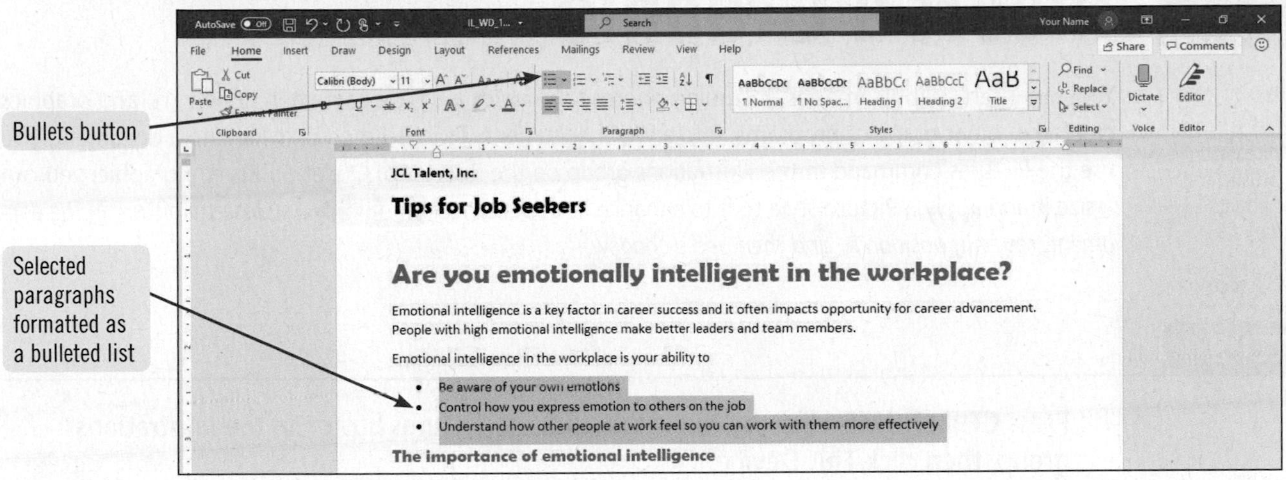

FIGURE 1-23: Numbering gallery

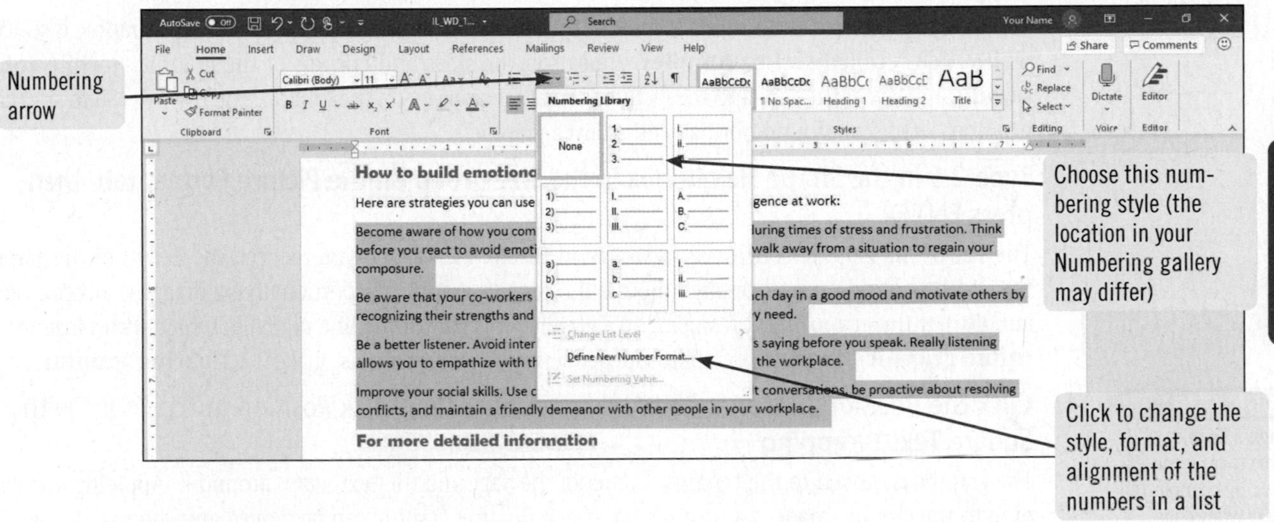

FIGURE 1-24: Numbered list

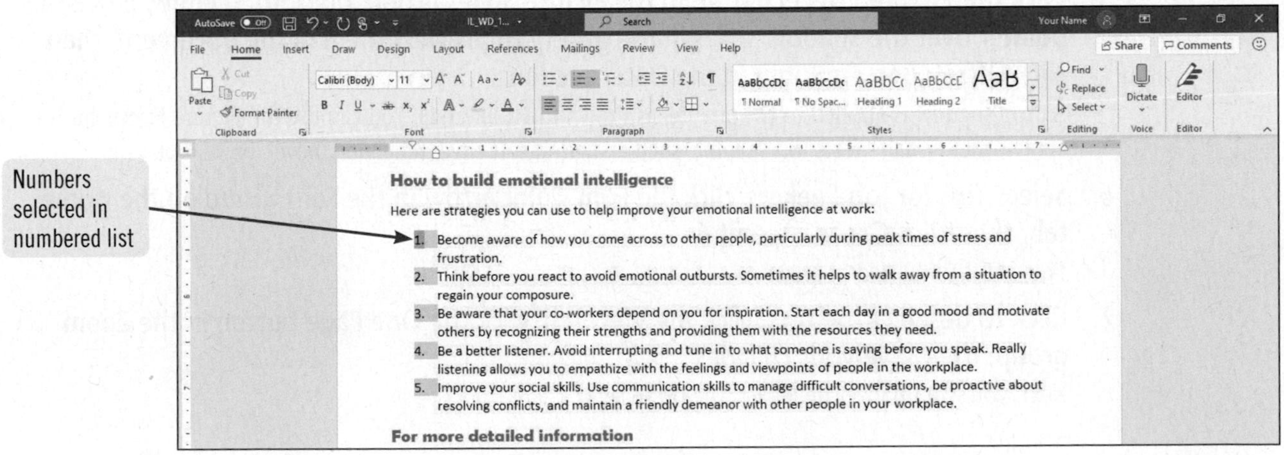

Word
Module 1

Insert a Graphic

Learning Outcomes
- Insert pictures
- Apply artistic and picture effects
- Apply styles to objects
- Format objects

You can insert graphic images, including photos taken with a digital camera, scanned art, and graphics created in other graphics programs, into a Word document. To insert a graphic file into a document, you use the Pictures command in the Illustrations group on the Insert tab. Once you insert a graphic, you can resize it and apply a Picture style to it to enhance its appearance. **CASE** *You insert a picture in the document, resize it, position it, and then add a shadow.*

STEPS

1. **Press CTRL+HOME, click the Insert tab, click the Pictures button in the Illustrations group, then click This Device**
   The Insert Picture dialog box opens. You use this dialog box to locate and insert graphic files. Most graphic files are **bitmap graphics**, which are often saved with a .bmp, .png, .jpg, .tif, or .gif file extension.
2. **Navigate to the location where you store your Data Files, click the file Support_WD_1-2.jpg, then click Insert**
   The picture is inserted as an inline graphic at the location of the insertion point. When a graphic is selected, white circles, called **sizing handles**, appear on the sides and corners of the graphic, a white **rotate handle** appears at the top, and the Picture Format tab appears on the Ribbon. You use this tab to size, crop, position, wrap text around, format, and adjust a graphic.
3. **Type 2.5 in the Shape Height box in the Size group on the Picture Format tab, then press ENTER**
   The size of the graphic is reduced, as shown in FIGURE 1-25. When you reduced the height of the graphic, the width reduced proportionally. You can also resize a graphic proportionally by dragging a corner sizing handle. Until you apply text wrapping to a graphic, it is part of the line of text in which it was inserted (an **inline graphic**). To move a graphic independently of text, you must make it a **floating graphic**.
4. **Click the Position button in the Arrange group, then click Position in Top Right with Square Text Wrapping**
   The graphic is moved to the top-right corner of the page and the text wraps around it. Applying text wrapping to the graphic made it a floating graphic. A floating graphic can be moved anywhere on a page. You can also move a floating graphic to a new location by dragging it using the mouse.
5. **Click the Picture Effects button in the Picture Styles group, point to Shadow, move the pointer over the shadow styles in the gallery to preview them in the document, then click Offset: Bottom Right in the Outer section**
   A drop shadow is applied to the picture, as shown in FIGURE 1-26. You can use the Picture Effects button to apply other visual effects to a graphic, such as a glow, soft edge, reflection, bevel, or 3-D rotation.
6. **Select Tips for Job Seekers, click the Font Color arrow in the Font group on the Home tab, then click Green, Accent 6**
   The text is formatted in green.
7. **Click to deselect the text, click the View tab, click the One Page button in the Zoom group, then save your changes**
   Next, you will finalize the look of the tip sheet.

QUICK TIP
Change a floating graphic to an inline graphic by changing the text-wrapping style to In Line with Text.

FIGURE 1-25: Inline graphic in document

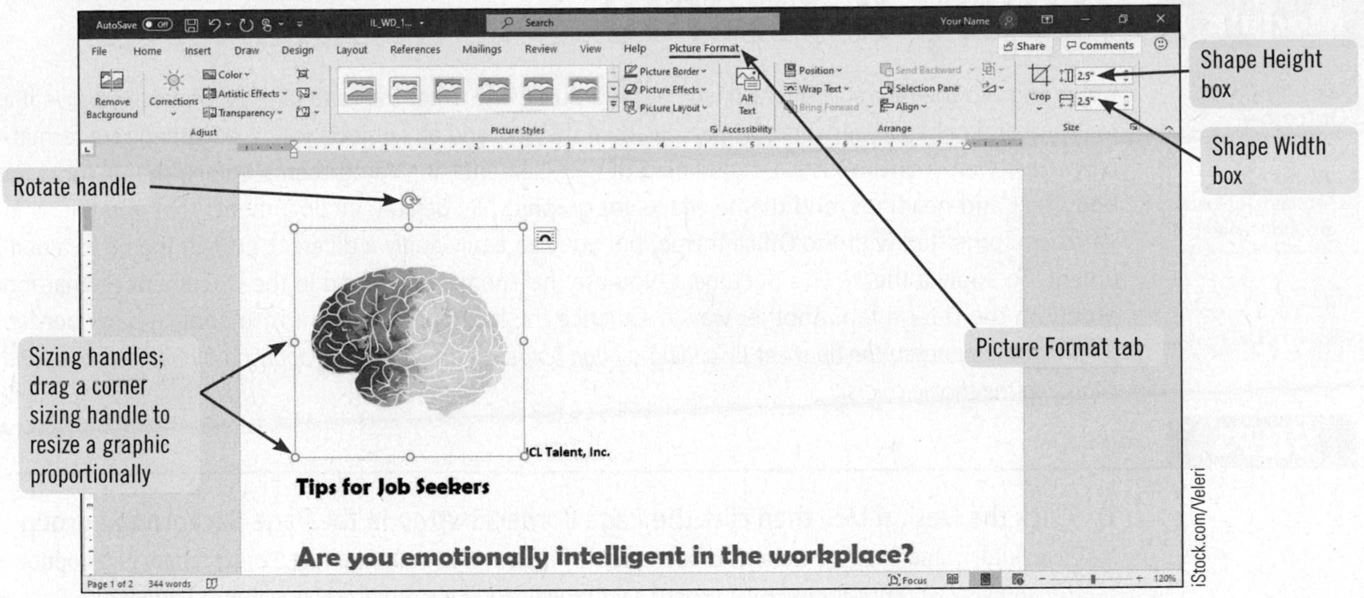
Shape Height box
Shape Width box
Rotate handle
Sizing handles; drag a corner sizing handle to resize a graphic proportionally
Picture Format tab
JCL Talent, Inc.
Tips for Job Seekers
Are you emotionally intelligent in the workplace?
iStock.com/Veleri

FIGURE 1-26: Floating graphic with shadow effect applied

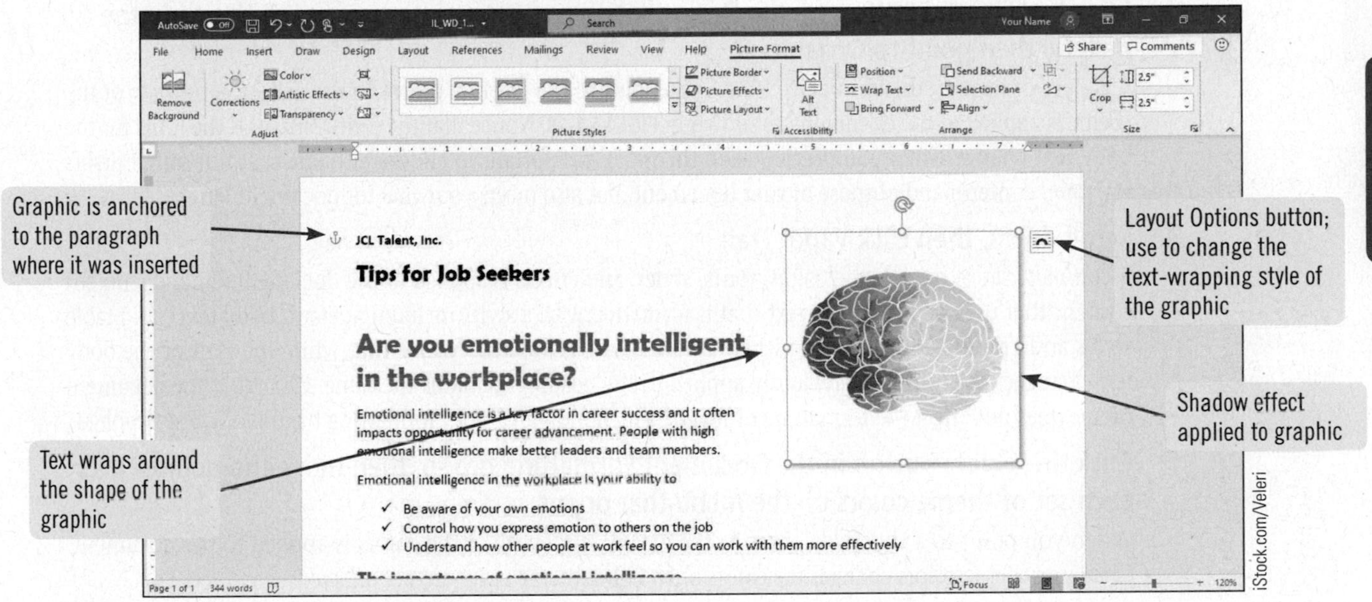
Graphic is anchored to the paragraph where it was inserted
Layout Options button; use to change the text-wrapping style of the graphic
Shadow effect applied to graphic
Text wraps around the shape of the graphic
JCL Talent, Inc.
Tips for Job Seekers
Are you emotionally intelligent in the workplace?
Emotional intelligence is a key factor in career success and it often impacts opportunity for career advancement. People with high emotional intelligence make better leaders and team members.
Emotional intelligence in the workplace is your ability to
Be aware of your own emotions
Control how you express emotion to others on the job
Understand how other people at work feel so you can work with them more effectively
iStock.com/Veleri

Word

Enhancing pictures with styles and effects

A fun way to give a document personality and flair is to apply a style or an effect to a picture. To apply a style, select the picture and then choose from the style options in the Styles group on the Picture Format tab. Styles include a preset mixture of effects, such as shading, borders, shadows, and other settings. The Effects command in the Styles group on the Picture Format tab gives you the power to apply a customized variety of effects to an object, including a shadow, bevel, glow, reflection, soft edge, or 3-D rotation. To apply an effect, select the object, click the Picture Effects arrow, point to the type of effect you want to apply, and then select from the options in the gallery that opens. To further customize an effect, click the Options command for that type of effect at the bottom of the gallery to open the Format Picture pane. The best way to learn about styles and effects is to experiment by applying them to a picture and seeing what works. To return a picture to its original settings, click the Reset Picture button in the Adjust group on the Picture Format tab.

Apply a Theme

Learning Outcomes
- Change document themes
- Format page background elements

Changing the theme applied to a document is a quick way to set the tone of a document and give it a polished and cohesive appearance, particularly if the text and any objects in the document are formatted with styles. A **theme** is a set of unified design elements, including theme colors, theme fonts for body text and headings, and theme effects for graphics. By default, all documents that you create in Word are formatted with the Office theme, but you can easily apply a different built-in theme to a document. To apply a theme to a document, you use the Themes command in the Document Formatting group on the Design tab. Another way to enhance the look of a document is to apply a page border.

CASE *You polish the tip sheet by adding a page border to the document, applying a built-in theme, and changing the theme colors.*

STEPS

1. **Click the Design tab, then click the Page Borders button in the Page Background group**
   The Borders and Shading dialog box opens, as shown in **FIGURE 1-27**. The Page Border tab includes options for applying a border around each page of a document, and for customizing the look of borders.
2. **Click the Box button on the Page Border tab, then click OK**
   A single line page border is added to the document.
3. **Click the Themes button on the Design tab, move the pointer over each theme in the gallery, then point to Organic**
   A gallery of built-in themes opens. When you point to the Organic theme in the gallery, a preview of the theme is applied to the document, as shown in **FIGURE 1-28**. Notice that the font colors and the fonts for the body text change when you preview each theme. It's important to choose a theme that not only mirrors the tone, content, and purpose of your document, but also meets your goal for document length.
4. **Scroll down, then click Vapor Trail**
   A complete set of new theme colors, fonts, styles, and effects is applied to the document. Only document content that uses theme colors, text that is formatted with a style (including default body text), and table styles and graphic effects change when a new theme is applied. Notice that while the font of the body text changed, the font you previously applied to the headings remains the same. Changing the document theme does not affect the formatting of text to which individual font formatting has already been applied.
5. **Click the Colors button in the Document Formatting group, then move the pointer over each set of theme colors on the menu that opens**
   When you point to a theme color set in the gallery, a preview of the colors is applied to the document. Changing theme colors changes the colors only. Other theme styles are not affected.
6. **Click Blue**
   The Blue theme colors are applied to the document, as shown in **FIGURE 1-29**.
7. **sam Save the document, submit the document to your instructor, close the file, then exit Word**

FIGURE 1-27: Page Border tab in Borders and Shading dialog box

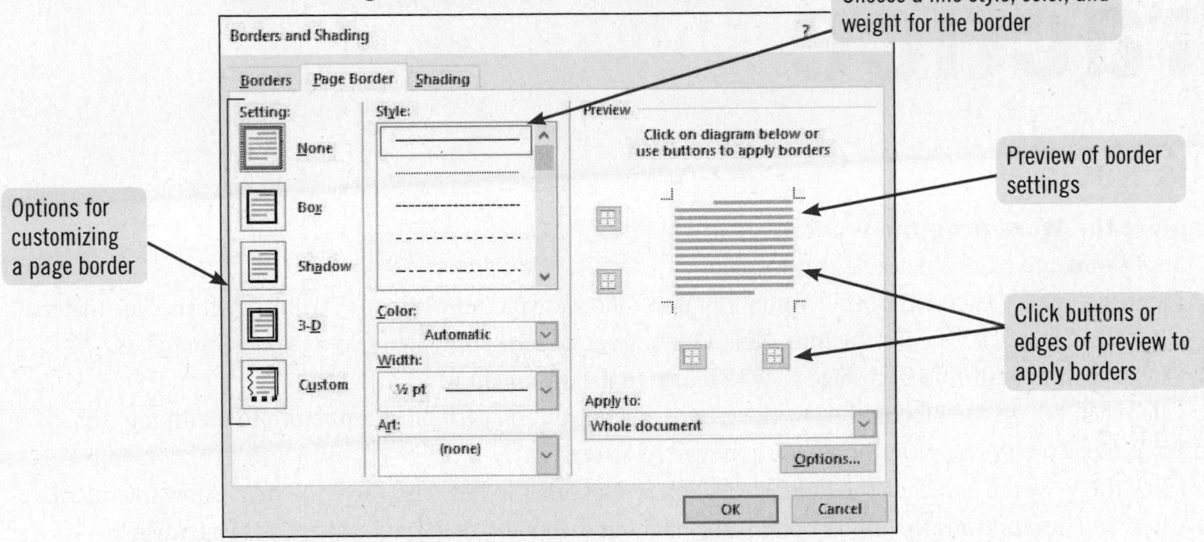

FIGURE 1-28: Organic theme previewed in document

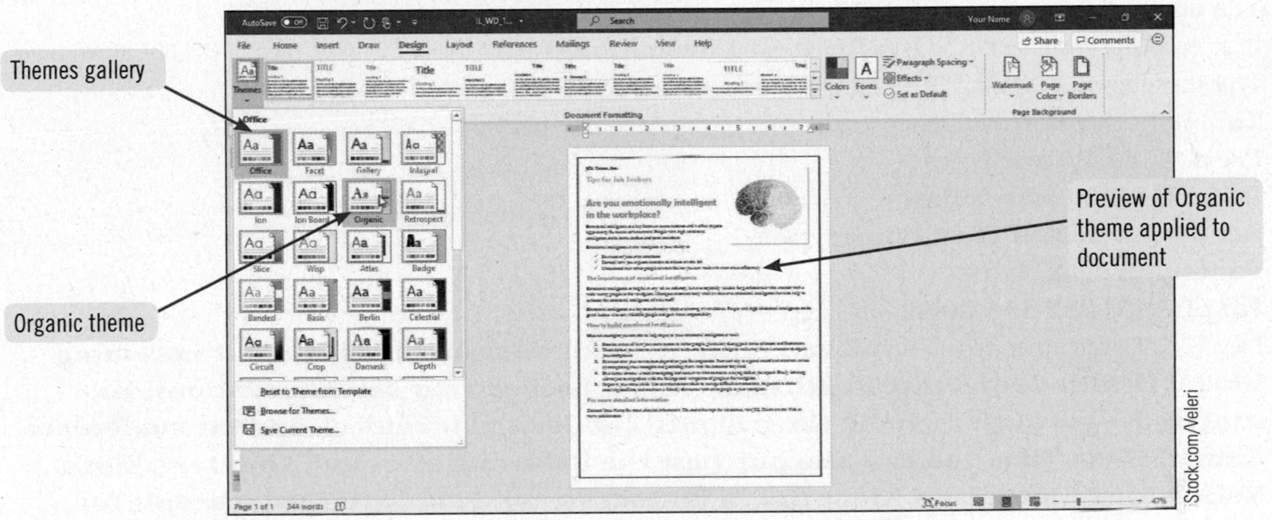

FIGURE 1-29: Vapor Trail theme and Blue theme colors applied to document

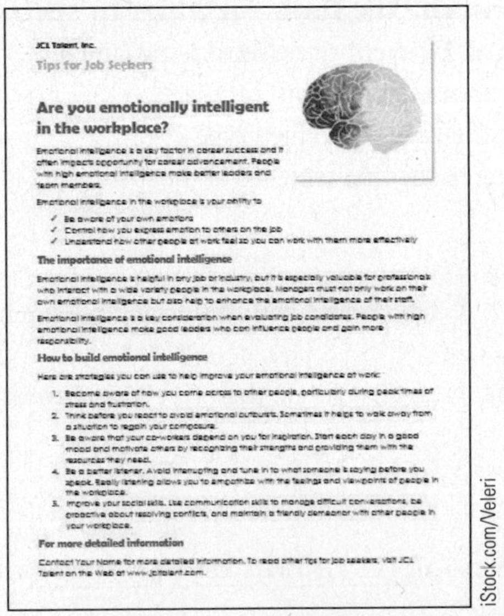

Word

Practice

Skills Review

1. **Explore the Word program window.**
   - **a.** Start Word and open a new, blank document.
   - **b.** Identify as many elements of the Word program window as you can without referring to the module material.
   - **c.** Click the File tab, then click the Info, New, Open, Save, Save As, Print, Share, and Export commands.
   - **d.** Click the Back button in Backstage view to return to the document window.
   - **e.** Click each tab on the Ribbon, review the groups and buttons on each tab, then return to the Home tab.
   - **f.** Point to each button on the Home tab and read its ScreenTip.
   - **g.** Click the View tab and click the Ruler check box several times to hide and show the ruler. Show the ruler.
   - **h.** Click the View buttons to view the blank document in each view, then return to Print Layout view.
   - **i.** Use the Zoom slider to zoom all the way in and all the way out on the document, then return to 120%.
2. **Start a document.**
   - **a.** In a new blank document, type **Health West International** at the top of the page, then press ENTER two times.
   - **b.** Type the following, pressing TAB as indicated and pressing ENTER at the end of each line:
     To: TAB TAB **Matthew Chao**
     From: TAB TAB **Your Name**
     Date: TAB TAB **Today's date**
     Re: TAB TAB **Health West Conference**
     Pages: TAB TAB **1**
     Fax: TAB TAB **212-555-0043**
   - **c.** Press ENTER again, then type **Thank you for confirming your attendance at our upcoming Global Health Conference in February. I have booked your accommodations. Your conference package includes three nights, continental breakfast, and the conference dinner. If you like, you can also purchase the following add-ons: Exhibitor's Kiosk, Networking Lunch, and Night Out in Boston. Please see the attached schedule for conference dates and details.**
   - **d.** Press ENTER, then type **To make a payment, please call me at 617-555-0156 or visit our website at www.healthwest5.com. Payment must be received in full by the 3rd of October to hold your room. We look forward to seeing you!**
   - **e.** Insert **Fireside Chat Social Hour,** before Networking Lunch.
   - **f.** Insert **Insurance** before Conference in the first sentence.
   - **g.** Use BACKSPACE to delete 1 in the Pages: line, then type **2**.
   - **h.** Use DELETE to delete upcoming in the first sentence of the first paragraph.
3. **Save a document.**
   - **a.** Click the File tab, then click Save.
   - **b.** Save the document as **IL_WD_1_ChaoFax** with the default file extension to the location where you store your Data Files.
   - **c.** After your name, type a comma, press SPACEBAR, then type **Conference Manager**.
   - **d.** Save the document.
4. **Select text.**
   - **a.** Turn on formatting marks.
   - **b.** Select the Re: line, then type **Re:** TAB TAB **Global Health Insurance Conference**

Skills Review (continued)

c. Select three in the third sentence, then type **two**.
d. Select 3rd of October in the second sentence of the last paragraph, type **15th of November**, select room, then type **reservation**.
e. Delete the sentence We look forward to seeing you!
f. Turn off the display of formatting marks, then save the document.

5. Format text using the Mini toolbar.

a. Select Health West International, click the Increase Font Size button on the Mini toolbar eight times, apply bold, then click the Decrease Font Size button on the Mini toolbar twice.
b. Center Health West International on the page.
c. Change the case of Health West International to uppercase.
d. Apply a bottom border under Health West International.
e. Apply bold to the following words in the fax heading: To:, From:, Date:, Re:, Pages:, and Fax:.
f. Apply yellow highlighting to 15th of November.
g. Use the Undo, Redo, and Repeat buttons to undo the highlighting, redo the highlighting, undo, repeat, then undo the highlighting again.
h. Remove the hyperlink from the website address, then underline 15th of November.
i. Italicize the last sentence of the first paragraph.
j. Read the document using the Read Mode view.
k. Return to Print Layout view, zoom in on the document, then proofread the fax.
l. Correct any typing errors in your document, then save the document. Compare your document to **FIGURE 1-30**.
m. Preview the document in Print Preview, identify each printing option available to you on the Print screen in Backstage view, then print the document only if required to do so by your instructor.
n. Return to Print Layout view, save, submit the fax per your instructor's directions, then close the document.

FIGURE 1-30

HEALTH WEST INTERNATIONAL

To: Matthew Chao
From: Your Name, Conference Manager
Date: September 5, 2021
Re: Global Health Insurance Conference
Pages: 2
Fax: 212-555-0043

Thank you for confirming your attendance at our Global Health Insurance Conference in February. I have booked your accommodations. Your conference package includes two nights, continental breakfast, and the conference dinner. If you like, you can also purchase the following add-ons: Exhibitor's Kiosk, Fireside Chat Social Hour, Networking Lunch, and Night Out in Boston. *Please see the attached schedule for conference dates and details.*

To make a payment, please call me at 617-555-0156 or visit our website at www.healthwest5.com. Payment must be received in full by the 15th of November to hold your reservation.

6. View and navigate a document.

a. Open the file IL_WD_1-3.docx from the location where you store your Data Files, then save it as **IL_WD_1_HealthWest** in the File name box.
b. Switch to Page Width view, then scroll through the document to get a feel for its contents.
c. Use the Zoom dialog box to view the Whole Page.
d. Use the Zoom slider to set the Zoom percentage at approximately 100%.
e. Read the document using the Read Mode view. (*Hint*: Press ESC to leave Read Mode view.)

Skills Review (continued)

- **f.** Return to Print Layout view, zoom in, scroll to the bottom of the document, then replace Your Name with your name in the final sentence.
- **g.** Add the Title property **Global** to the document properties in the file, return to Print Layout view, change the zoom level to 120%, then save your changes.

7. Cut and paste text.

- **a.** Turn on the display of formatting marks.
- **b.** Select the first body paragraph that begins We aim… (including the paragraph mark after it), cut it to the clipboard, then paste the paragraph before the heading Experience and expertise across the globe.
- **c.** Delete the heading The Health West International Difference.
- **d.** In the list of locations, move the Middle East paragraph after the Europe paragraph.
- **e.** Move the United States paragraph after the Greater China paragraph.
- **f.** Move the Southeast Asia paragraph before the United States paragraph.
- **g.** Move the Greater China paragraph after the Europe paragraph, then save your changes.

8. Copy and paste text.

- **a.** Scroll to the bottom of the document, then remove the hyperlink in the final paragraph.
- **b.** Select the sentence Get an online quote at www.healthwest5.com., then copy the sentence to the clipboard.
- **c.** Scroll to the top of the page, add a blank paragraph under the Health West International heading, then paste the sentence at the location of the blank paragraph.
- **d.** Use the Paste Options button to Keep Source formatting.
- **e.** Format the pasted sentence in italic, turn off formatting marks, then save your changes.

9. Format with fonts.

- **a.** Format the heading Health West International in 20-point Calibri Light with a Blue, Accent 1 font color.
- **b.** Format the heading The industry leader in global health benefits in 12-point Calibri Light with a Gold, Accent 4 font color.
- **c.** Format Experience and expertise across the globe, Global member support, and Clinical expertise in 12-point Calibri Light with a Gold, Accent 4 font color.
- **d.** Apply bold formatting to the last paragraph in the document, then change the font color to Blue, Accent 1.
- **e.** Scroll up, select Health West International, click the Text Effects and Typography arrow, preview several WordArt styles applied to the text, then apply one of the styles.
- **f.** Click the Undo button, add an Offset: Bottom Right shadow to the title, then save your changes.

10. Set document margins.

- **a.** Change the left and right margins to 2".
- **b.** View the document in Multiple Pages view.
- **c.** Change the left and right margins to 1.5".
- **d.** Change all four document margins to .7".
- **e.** Change the zoom level to 120%, then add 24 points of space before the heading The industry leader in global health benefits.
- **f.** Save your changes.

11. Add bullets and numbering.

- **a.** Select the five-line list of locations that begins with Europe and ends with United States, then format it as a bulleted list using the circle bullet symbol.
- **b.** Change the font color of the bullets to Blue, Accent 1.
- **c.** Press and hold CTRL to select the headings Experience and expertise across the globe, Global member support, and Clinical expertise, then apply numbering.
- **d.** Click 1 in the list, then change the font color of the numbers to Blue, Accent 1.
- **e.** Save your changes.

Skills Review (continued)

12. Insert a graphic.

a. Click in the first body paragraph to move the insertion point to the top of the document, then open the Insert Picture dialog box.

b. Navigate to the location where you store Data Files, then insert the file **Support_ WD_1-4.jpg**.

c. Change the height of the graphic to 1.2 using the Shape Height box in the Size group on the Picture Format tab.

d. Use the Position command to wrap text around the graphic and position it in the Top Left with Square Text Wrapping.

e. Apply the Double Frame, Black picture style to the graphic.

f. Click the Reset Picture arrow in the Adjust Group on the Picture Format tab, reset the picture, then apply the Simple Frame, White picture style.

g. Change the font size of Health West International to 28 point.

h. Click before The industry leader in global health benefits heading, press ENTER, change the font size of the heading to 18 point, then save your changes.

13. Apply a theme.

a. Change the view to One Page, click the Design tab, click the Page Borders button, then apply a single line box border to the page.

b. Use the Themes feature, preview several different themes applied to the document. Apply a theme, zoom in and out on the document to evaluate its suitability, then apply another theme, zoom in and out, and so forth.

c. Apply the View theme.

d. Change all four document margins to .6" to better fit the text on the page.

e. Zoom in on the bottom of the document, then add 24 points of space above the last paragraph.

f. Change the theme colors to Red.

g. Zoom in on the top of the document, then change the font color of the Get an online quote… paragraph to Brown, Accent 5.

h. Change the font color of the four light brown headings to Orange, Accent 3. Compare your document to **FIGURE 1-31**.

i. Save your changes, preview the document, submit it per your instructor's directions, then close the document and exit Word.

FIGURE 1-31

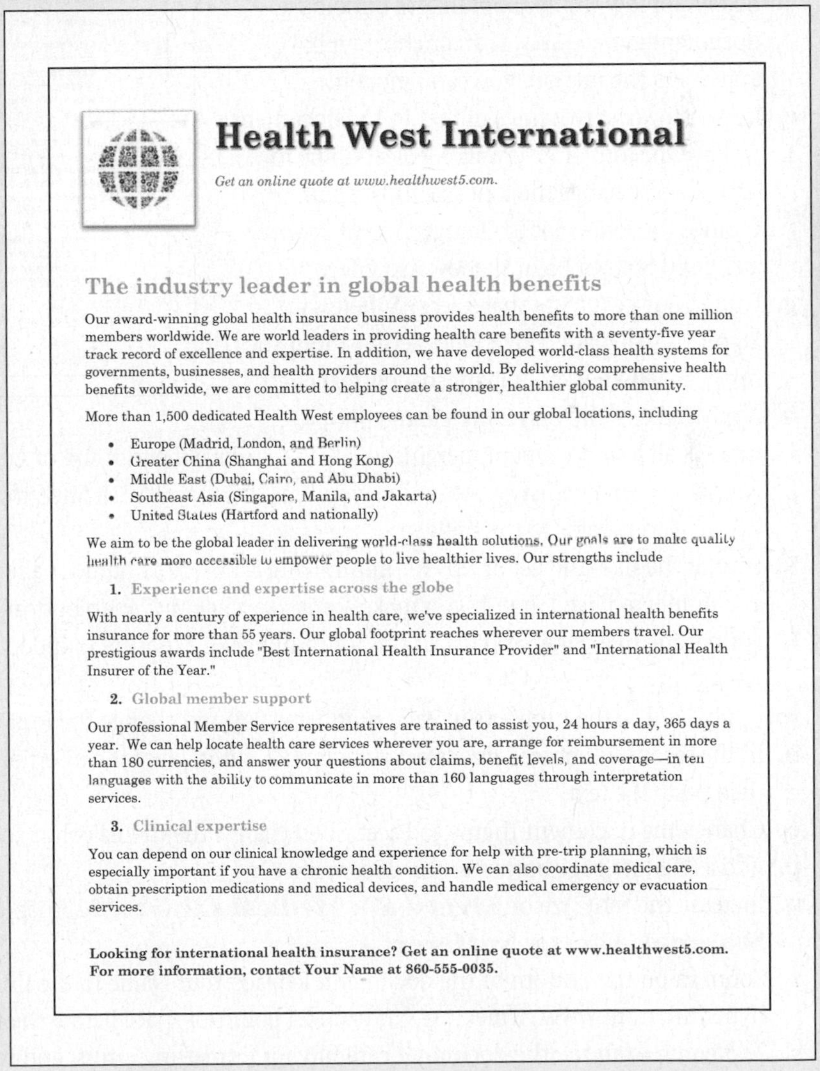

Health West International

Get an online quote at www.healthwest5.com.

The industry leader in global health benefits

Our award-winning global health insurance business provides health benefits to more than one million members worldwide. We are world leaders in providing health care benefits with a seventy-five year track record of excellence and expertise. In addition, we have developed world-class health systems for governments, businesses, and health providers around the world. By delivering comprehensive health benefits worldwide, we are committed to helping create a stronger, healthier global community.

More than 1,500 dedicated Health West employees can be found in our global locations, including

- Europe (Madrid, London, and Berlin)
- Greater China (Shanghai and Hong Kong)
- Middle East (Dubai, Cairo, and Abu Dhabi)
- Southeast Asia (Singapore, Manila, and Jakarta)
- United States (Hartford and nationally)

We aim to be the global leader in delivering world-class health solutions. Our goals are to make quality health care more accessible to empower people to live healthier lives. Our strengths include

1. Experience and expertise across the globe

With nearly a century of experience in health care, we've specialized in international health benefits insurance for more than 55 years. Our global footprint reaches wherever our members travel. Our prestigious awards include "Best International Health Insurance Provider" and "International Health Insurer of the Year."

2. Global member support

Our professional Member Service representatives are trained to assist you, 24 hours a day, 365 days a year. We can help locate health care services wherever you are, arrange for reimbursement in more than 180 currencies, and answer your questions about claims, benefit levels, and coverage—in ten languages with the ability to communicate in more than 160 languages through interpretation services.

3. Clinical expertise

You can depend on our clinical knowledge and experience for help with pre-trip planning, which is especially important if you have a chronic health condition. We can also coordinate medical care, obtain prescription medications and medical devices, and handle medical emergency or evacuation services.

Looking for international health insurance? Get an online quote at www.healthwest5.com. For more information, contact Your Name at 860-555-0035.

iStock.com/bubaone

Word

Independent Challenge 1

You work at the Riverwalk Medical Clinic, a large outpatient medical facility staffed by family physicians, specialists, nurses, and other allied health professionals. Your boss has drafted an information sheet to help seasonal allergy sufferers and asks you to edit and format it so that it is eye catching and attractive.

FIGURE 1-32

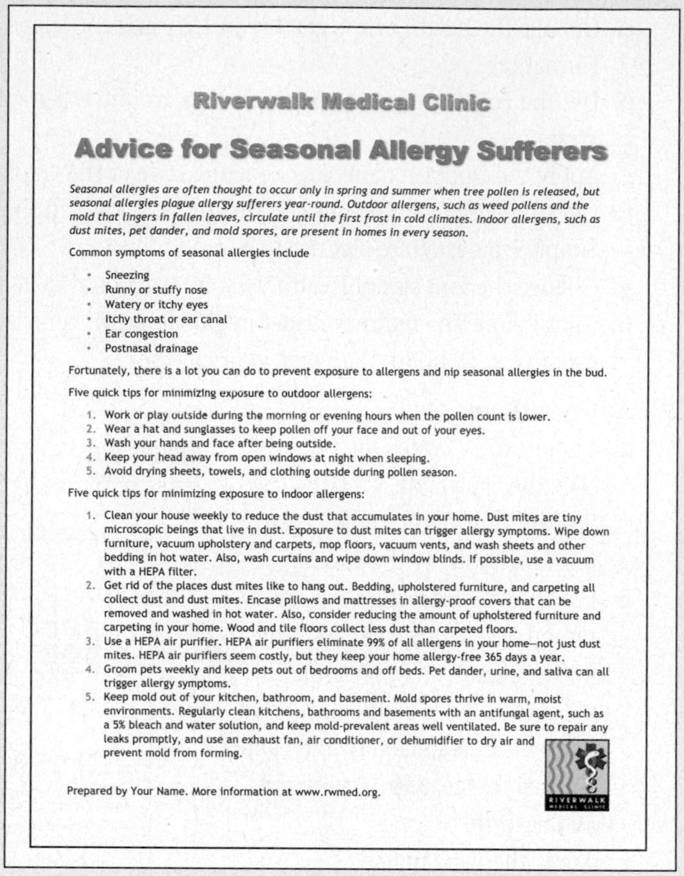

Riverwalk Medical Clinic

Advice for Seasonal Allergy Sufferers

Seasonal allergies are often thought to occur only in spring and summer when tree pollen is released, but seasonal allergies plague allergy sufferers year-round. Outdoor allergens, such as weed pollens and the mold that lingers in fallen leaves, circulate until the first frost in cold climates. Indoor allergens, such as dust mites, pet dander, and mold spores, are present in homes in every season.

Common symptoms of seasonal allergies include

- Sneezing
- Runny or stuffy nose
- Watery or itchy eyes
- Itchy throat or ear canal
- Ear congestion
- Postnasal drainage

Fortunately, there is a lot you can do to prevent exposure to allergens and nip seasonal allergies in the bud.

Five quick tips for minimizing exposure to outdoor allergens:

1. Work or play outside during the morning or evening hours when the pollen count is lower.
2. Wear a hat and sunglasses to keep pollen off your face and out of your eyes.
3. Wash your hands and face after being outside.
4. Keep your head away from open windows at night when sleeping.
5. Avoid drying sheets, towels, and clothing outside during pollen season.

Five quick tips for minimizing exposure to indoor allergens:

1. Clean your house weekly to reduce the dust that accumulates in your home. Dust mites are tiny microscopic beings that live in dust. Exposure to dust mites can trigger allergy symptoms. Wipe down furniture, vacuum upholstery and carpets, mop floors, vacuum vents, and wash sheets and other bedding in hot water. Also, wash curtains and wipe down window blinds. If possible, use a vacuum with a HEPA filter.
2. Get rid of the places dust mites like to hang out. Bedding, upholstered furniture, and carpeting all collect dust and dust mites. Encase pillows and mattresses in allergy-proof covers that can be removed and washed in hot water. Also, consider reducing the amount of upholstered furniture and carpeting in your home. Wood and tile floors collect less dust than carpeted floors.
3. Use a HEPA air purifier. HEPA air purifiers eliminate 99% of all allergens in your home—not just dust mites. HEPA air purifiers seem costly, but they keep your home allergy-free 365 days a year.
4. Groom pets weekly and keep pets out of bedrooms and off beds. Pet dander, urine, and saliva can all trigger allergy symptoms.
5. Keep mold out of your kitchen, bathroom, and basement. Mold spores thrive in warm, moist environments. Regularly clean kitchens, bathrooms and basements with an antifungal agent, such as a 5% bleach and water solution, and keep mold-prevalent areas well ventilated. Be sure to repair any leaks promptly, and use an exhaust fan, air conditioner, or dehumidifier to dry air and prevent mold from forming.

Prepared by Your Name. More information at www.rwmed.org.

a. Open the file IL_WD_1-5.docx from the drive and folder where you store your Data Files, save it as **IL_WD_1_AllergyInfo**, then read the document to get a feel for the content. **FIGURE 1-32** shows how you will format the info sheet.

b. Show the rulers in your document window if they are not already visible.

c. Accept or ignore all suggested spelling and grammar changes in the document.

d. Insert the Riverwalk Medical Clinic logo file Support_WD_1-6.jpg at the top of the document. Change the height of the logo to 1", then position the logo in the bottom right with square text wrapping. (*Hint*: Zoom in and out on the document as necessary. If an anchor symbol appears in the margin, you can ignore it.)

e. Center the first two lines of text in the document.

f. Change the font of Riverwalk Medical Clinic to Arial Black. Change the font size to 18 point. Change the font color to Orange, Accent 2. Apply an Offset: Bottom Right shadow text effect.

g. Format Advice for Seasonal Allergy Sufferers in 28-point Arial Black with a Blue, Accent 1 font color. Apply an Offset: Bottom Right shadow text effect.

h. Apply italic to the first body paragraph.

i. Change all four document margins to .5", then reduce the font size of Advice for Seasonal Allergy Sufferers by 2 points.

j. Format the six-line list of common symptoms (beginning with Sneezing) as a bulleted list, then apply the Blue, Accent 1 font color to the bullets.

k. Format the five-line list of tips for minimizing exposure to outdoor allergens (beginning with Work or play outside) as a numbered list. (*Hint*: If you make a mistake, click the Undo button and try again.)

l. Format the five-paragraph list of tips for minimizing exposure to indoor allergens, beginning with Clean your house weekly, as a numbered list.

m. Apply bold to the numbers in each numbered list, and change the font color of the numbers to Blue, Accent 1.

n. In the second numbered list, select paragraph 2, cut it, place the insertion point before Groom in the new paragraph 3, then paste the text.

o. Change the document theme to Facet, then change the theme colors to Blue Green.

p. Add a Shadow page border to the document.

q. Increase the font size of **Riverwalk Medical Clinic** to 22, then add 12 points of space after **Advice for Seasonal Allergy Sufferers**.

r. Zoom in on the bottom of the document. Replace Your Name in the final line with your name, remove the hyperlink from www.rwmed.org, and add 24 points of space before the final line paragraph.

s. Zoom out, examine the document carefully for formatting errors, and make any necessary adjustments so that all the text fits on one page.

t. Save the document, submit it per your instructor's directions, then close the file and exit Word.

Independent Challenge 2

Yesterday you interviewed for a job as the administrative assistant in the Business Department at Jericho College. You spoke with several people at the college, including Sonia Alvarado, director of human resources, whose business card is shown in **FIGURE 1-33**. You need to write a follow-up letter to Ms. Alvarado, thanking her for the interview and expressing your interest in the college and the position. She also asked you to send her some samples of your work as evidence of your Word skills.

a. Start Word and save a new blank document as **IL_WD_1_AlvaradoLetter** to the location where you store your Data Files.

b. Begin the letter by clicking the No Spacing button in the Styles group. You use this button to apply the No Spacing style to the document so that your document does not include extra space between paragraphs.

c. Type a personal letterhead for the letter that includes your name, address, telephone number, email address, and webpage or LinkedIn address, if you have one. Remove any hyperlinks. Accept or undo any automatic corrections. (*Note: Format the letterhead after you finish typing the letter.*)

d. Four lines below the bottom of the letterhead, type today's date.

e. Four lines below the date, type the inside address, referring to **FIGURE 1-33** for the information. Include the recipient's title, college name, and full mailing address.

FIGURE 1-33

f. Two lines below the inside address, type **Dear Ms. Alvarado:** for the salutation.

g. Two lines below the salutation, type the body of the letter, leaving a blank space between each paragraph, according to the following guidelines:
- In the first paragraph, thank her for the interview. Then restate your interest in the position and express your desire to work for the college. Add any specific details you think will enhance the power of your letter.
- In the second paragraph, note that you are enclosing three samples of your work, and explain something about the samples you are enclosing.
- Type a short final paragraph.

h. Two lines below the last body paragraph, type a closing, then four lines below the closing, type the signature block. Be sure to include your name in the signature block.

i. Two lines below the signature block, type an enclosure notation. (*Hint*: An enclosure notation usually includes the word "Enclosures" or the abbreviation "Enc." followed by the number of enclosures in parentheses.)

j. Edit your letter for clarity and precision. Move sentences if necessary, replace words with more precise words, and correct any spelling or grammar errors.

k. Change the font of the letter to a serif font, such as Times New Roman, Garamond, or something similar. Adjust the font size so the letter can be read easily.

l. Format the letterhead using fonts, font colors, text effects, borders, themes, paragraph spacing, paragraph alignment, change case, and other formatting features. Be sure the design of your letterhead reflects your personality and is suitable for a professional document.

m. Change the Title document property to **Letter**.

n. Save your changes, preview the letter, submit it per your instructor's directions, then close the document and exit Word.

Visual Workshop

Create the letter shown in **FIGURE 1-34**. Before beginning to type, click the No Spacing button in the Styles group on the Home tab. Type the letter before formatting the letterhead and applying the theme. To format the letterhead, change the font size of the first line of text to 40 point and apply the Gradient Fill: Blue, Accent color 5, Reflection WordArt style. Change the font color of the address line to Blue, Accent 5. Add the bottom border to the letterhead. When the letterhead is formatted, change the font size of the body text to 12 point, apply the Organic theme, then change the font color of the letterhead text to Green, Accent 1. Save the document as **IL_WD_1_SakuraDoksa** to the location where you store your Data Files, submit the letter to your instructor, then close the document and exit Word.

FIGURE 1-34

Sakura-Doksa Tech Services

Mission Office Park, 7800 Sakura-Doksa Way, Detroit, MI 48213, www.sakuradoksa.com

November 12, 2021

Mr. Orlando Howley
34 Oak Street
Lansing, MI 48910

Dear Mr. Howley:

We are writing to let you know that beginning in January you will be able to attend a no-cost technology services evaluation at the Sakura-Doksa Tech Services facility in your neighborhood. During this two-hour class, you will learn from our certified instructors:

- How tech services can help streamline your business functions.
- What hardware and software solutions might meet your business needs.
- How to reduce risk and maintain effective security for your business systems.

For more information on this and other Sakura-Doksa Tech Services products and services, visit Sakura-Doksa Tech Services on the web at www.sakuradoksa.com.

Sincerely,

Your Name
Customer Services Coordinator

Editing and Formatting Documents

CASE You have been asked to edit and format a research report on job growth in the tech sector. After editing the report and applying styles to format the text, you plan to add page numbers, a header, footnotes, and a bibliography to the report. Finally, before distributing the report file electronically, you will strip the file of private information.

Module Objectives

After completing this module, you will be able to:

- Insert comments
- Find and replace text
- Check spelling and grammar
- Research information
- Change line spacing and indents
- Apply styles to text
- Insert page numbers and page breaks
- Add headers and footers
- Add footnotes and endnotes
- Insert citations
- Create a bibliography
- Inspect a document

Files You Will Need

IL_WD_2-1.docx
IL_WD_2-2.docx
IL_WD_2-3.docx
IL_WD_2-4.docx

Insert Comments

Learning Outcome
- Add comments

You can collaborate on documents with colleagues in different ways. One way is to insert comments into a document when you want to ask questions or provide information to other reviewers. A **comment** is text that appears to the right of your document in Print Layout view. Shading appears in the document at the point where you inserted the comment. A comment icon may appear to the right of the commented text. Each reviewer is assigned a unique color automatically, which is applied to the background of the reviewer's initials. **CASE** *Your colleague, Dawn Lapointe, read the draft of the report and inserted comments. You open the report to review and respond to Dawn's comments. You add and edit comments.*

STEPS

1. **sam Start Word, open the file IL_WD_2-1.docx from the location where you store your Data Files, save it as IL_WD_2_TechJobs, change the zoom level to 100%, then click the Review tab**
   Simple Markup is the default option in the Display for Review box in the Tracking group on the Review tab. A different markup option may be selected if another user was working on the computer before you. With this option, comments appear along the right side of the page. If you see comment icons and no comment wording, then click a comment icon to read the comment. If you want to see all comments, click the Show Comments button in the Comments group.

QUICK TIP
When you click the reviewer's initials, a person card for the reviewer appears; use this to communicate quickly with reviewers.

2. **Click the Display for Review arrow in the Tracking group, then click All Markup**
   In the second body paragraph, the text "job" is shaded in a color, indicating the text is associated with the comment.
3. **Select the word Sector in the title (the first line), then click the New Comment button in the Comments group**
   The word "Sector" is shaded, and space for a comment appears to the right of the document. Your name or the name assigned to your computer appears. To navigate between comments in a long document, use the Next and Previous buttons in the Comments group.

TROUBLE
If you don't see the Reply box, click the Reply button, type your reply, then click anywhere in the document text.

4. **Type This title is approved by the web team., then click the Post comment button or, if a Post comment button does not appear in your comment, click anywhere in the document text**
   Your comment appears as shown in **FIGURE 2-1**.
5. **Click Dawn's first comment (starts with "This is…"), click the Reply box in the comment, type I am compiling a list., then click the Post reply button**
   Your response appears indented under the original comment.

FIGURE 2-1: New comment in document

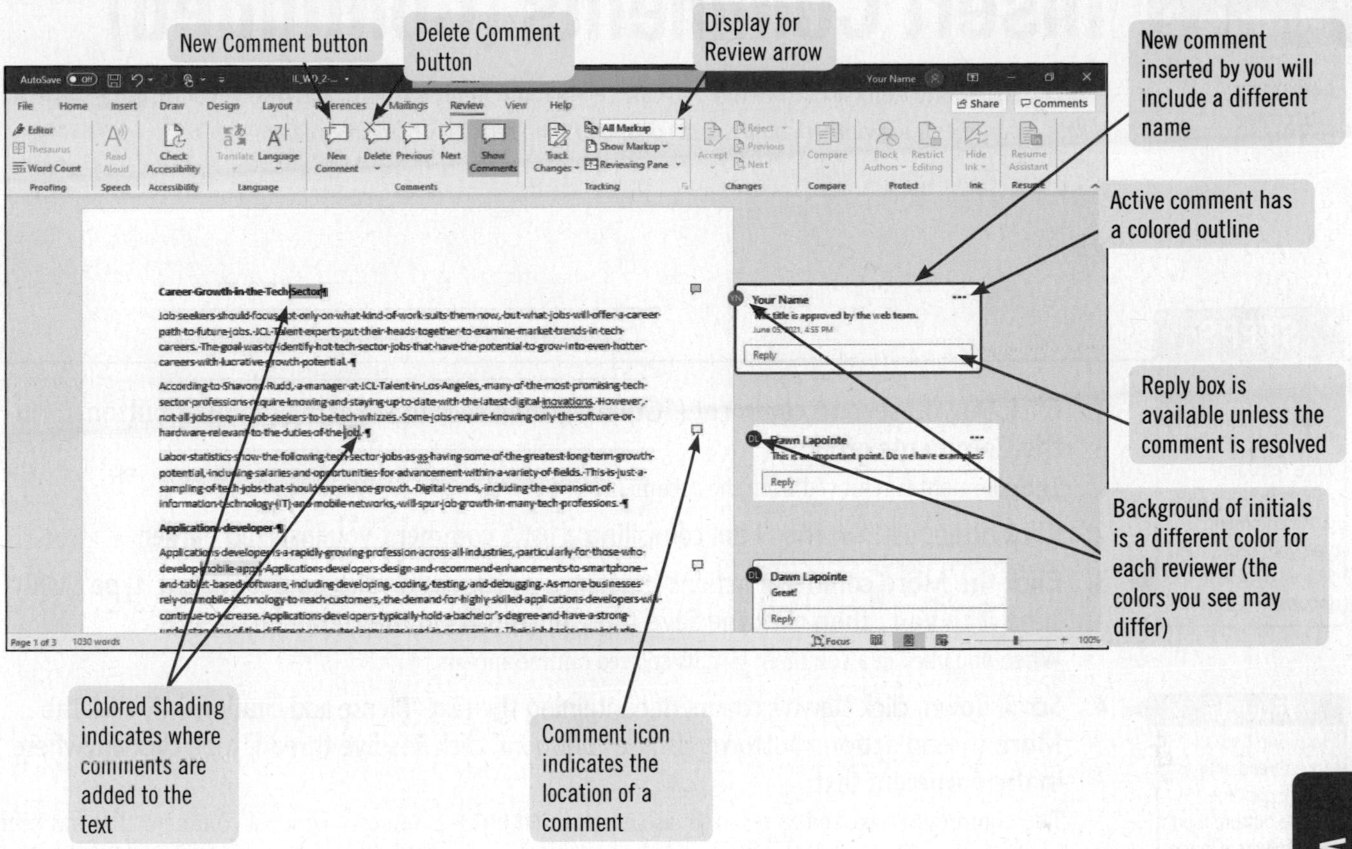
New Comment button
Delete Comment button
Display for Review arrow
New comment inserted by you will include a different name
Active comment has a colored outline
Reply box is available unless the comment is resolved
Background of initials is a different color for each reviewer (the colors you see may differ)
Colored shading indicates where comments are added to the text
Comment icon indicates the location of a comment

Word

Insert Comments (Continued)

Learning Outcome
- Manage comments

After inserting and editing comments, you can delete them, reply to them, and resolve them. **CASE** *You delete a comment, view other comment actions, and then reply to and resolve comments.*

STEPS

TROUBLE
If you don't see the More comment actions button, click in the comment, type your reply, then click anywhere in the document text.

TROUBLE
If you don't see the More thread actions button, click the Resolve button, then click anywhere in the document text.

QUICK TIP
To delete all comments in a document, click the Delete Comment arrow, then click Delete All Comments in Document.

1. **Click Dawn's second comment ("Great!"), then click the Delete Comment button in the Comments group**
   The comment is removed from the document.
2. **Click after "list." in the "I am compiling a list." comment you inserted earlier**
3. **Click the More comment actions button in the reply, click Edit comment, type I will send it to you., then click the Save reply button in the comment**
   When you click in a comment box, its colored outline appears.
4. **Scroll down, click Dawn's comment containing the text "Please add citations…", click the More thread actions button in the comment, click Resolve thread, then click anywhere in the document text**
   The comment is marked as resolved, as shown in **FIGURE 2-2**. You can reopen a comment that has been marked as resolved by clicking the comment icon or the comment itself and then clicking the Reopen button in the comment.
5. **Click All Markup in the Tracking group, click No Markup, then save your changes**
   Selecting No Markup hides the comments. Hiding the comments does not remove them from the document. It simply hides them from view on the screen. You will keep the comments hidden while you format the document.

FIGURE 2-2: Resolved comment in document

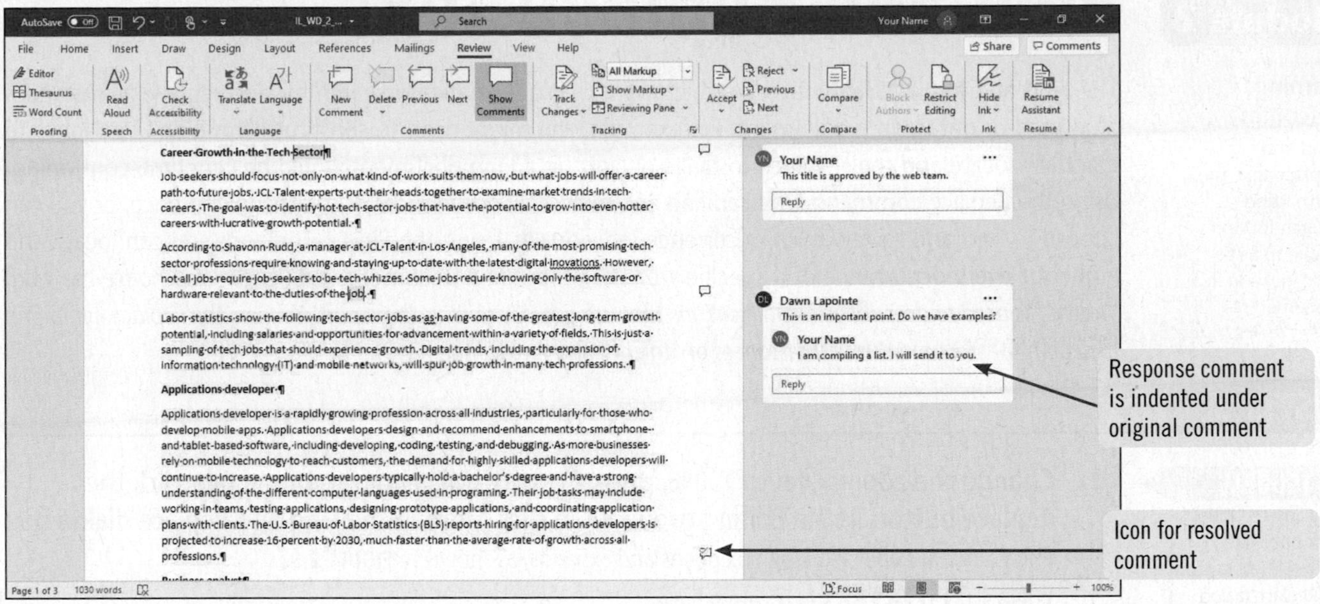

Inking comments in Word

If you are working in Touch mode on a touch-enabled device, you can draw or write comments using your finger, a digital pen, or a mouse. The type of inking features available to you will depend on your device. To begin, click the Draw tab on the Ribbon, click a pen in the Drawing Tools group to create an ink comment, and then use your finger, stylus, or mouse to draw or write in the document. On some devices, you can change the color and type of pen stroke to use for inking by using the Pen button in the Drawing Tools group. You can hide inked comments using the Hide Ink button in the Ink group on the Review tab. When you are finished inking a comment, click anywhere in the document. If you are on a touch-enabled device and want to switch your device to Touch mode and use the full range of inking features available in Word, you can add the Touch/Mouse Mode button to the Quick Access toolbar by clicking the Customize Quick Access Toolbar button on the Quick Access toolbar, and then clicking Touch/Mouse Mode. To use Touch mode, click the Touch/Mouse Mode button, and then click Touch.

Find and Replace Text

Learning Outcomes
- Find and replace text and formatting
- Search for text
- Move to a specific location in a document

The Find and Replace feature in Word allows you to automatically search for and replace all instances of a word or phrase in a document. For example, you might need to substitute "position" for "job". To manually locate and replace each instance of "job" in a long document would be very time-consuming. Using the Replace command, you can find and replace all occurrences of specific text at once, or you can choose to find and review each occurrence individually. Using the Find command, you can locate and highlight every occurrence of a specific word or phrase in a document. **CASE** *You notice the word "talent" is used to describe job qualifications that are actually skills in the report. You use the Replace command to search the document for all instances of "talent" and replace them with "skill".*

STEPS

TROUBLE
If any Search Options check boxes are selected in your Find and Replace dialog box, deselect them. If Format appears under the Find what or Replace with box, click in the box, then click the No Formatting button.

QUICK TIP
To find, review, and replace each occurrence individually, click Find Next.

1. **Change the zoom level to 120%, press CTRL+HOME, click the Home tab, click the Replace button in the Editing group, then click More in the Find and Replace dialog box**
   The Find and Replace dialog box opens and expands, as shown in **FIGURE 2-3**.
2. **Type talent in the Find what box**
   The text "talent" is the text that will be replaced.
3. **Press TAB, then type skill in the Replace with box**
   The text "skill" will replace the text "talent".
4. **Click the Match case check box in the Search Options section to select it**
   Selecting the Match case check box tells Word to find only exact matches for the uppercase and lowercase characters you entered in the Find what text box. You want to replace all instances of "talent" in the body text of the report. You do not want to replace "Talent" in the proper name "JCL Talent".
5. **Click Replace All**
   Clicking Replace All changes all occurrences of "talent" to "skill" in the press release. A message box reports eight replacements were made.
6. **Click OK to close the message box, then click Close in the Find and Replace dialog box**
   Word replaced "talent" with "skill" in eight locations but did not replace "Talent" in the company name. To find or replace text that is formatted a certain way, click the Find arrow in the Editing group, click Advanced Find, click Format in the Find and Replace dialog box, and then select the appropriate format options. To find or replace special characters such as em dashes and paragraph marks, click Special in the Find and Replace dialog box.
7. **Click the Find button in the Editing group**
   Clicking the Find button opens the Navigation pane, which is used to browse a longer document by headings, by pages, or by specific text. The Find command allows you to quickly locate all instances of text in a document. You use it to verify that Word did not replace "Talent" in JCL Talent.
8. **Type Talent in the search box in the Navigation pane**
   The word "Talent" is highlighted and selected in the document, as shown in **FIGURE 2-4**.
9. **Click the Close button in the Navigation pane**
   The highlighting is removed from the text when you close the Navigation pane.
10. **Press CTRL+HOME, then save the document**

FIGURE 2-3: Find and Replace dialog box

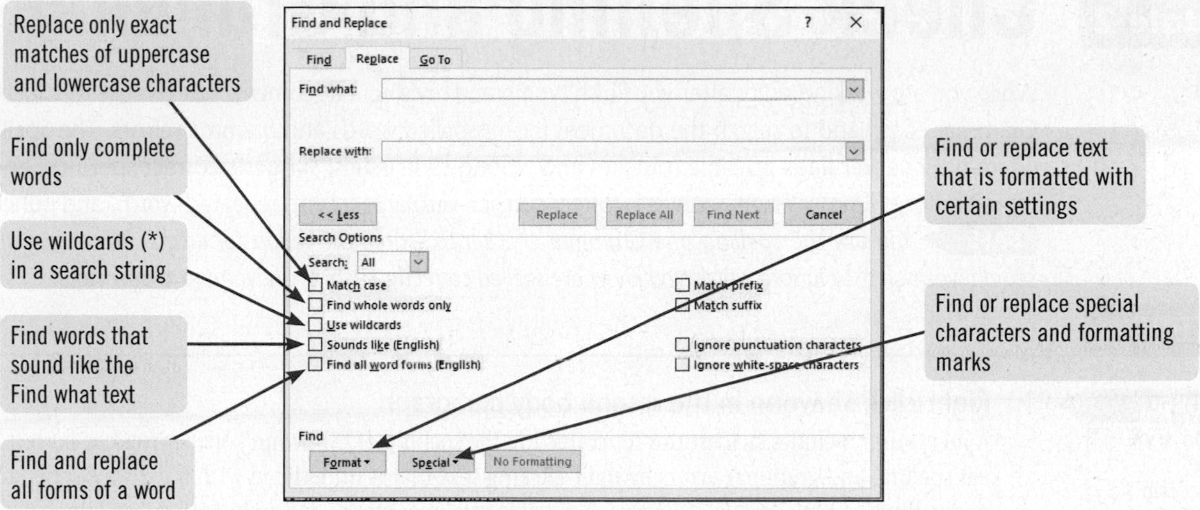

FIGURE 2-4: Found text highlighted in document

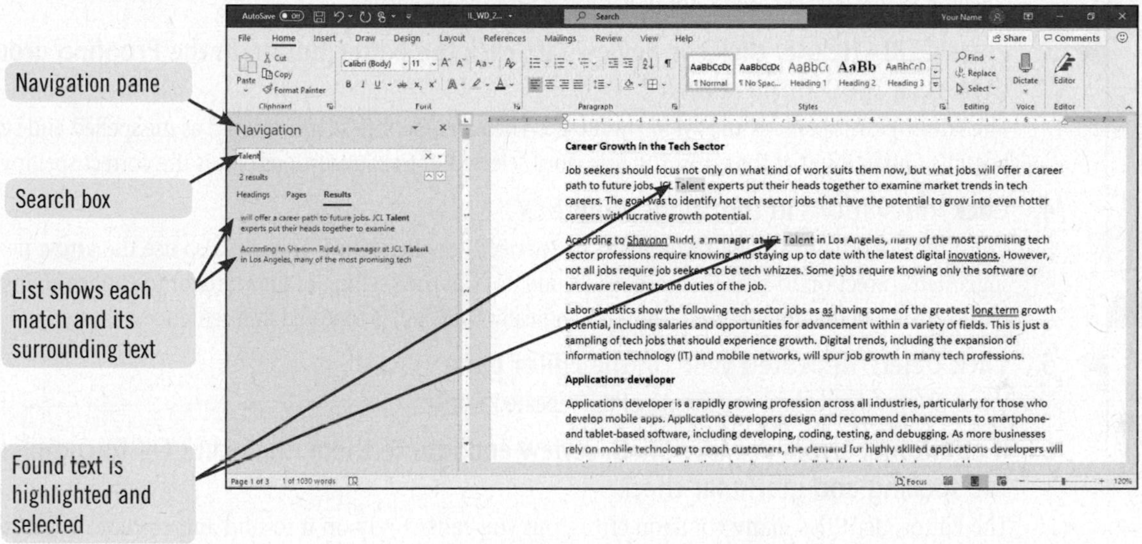

Navigating a document using the Navigation pane and the Go to command

Rather than scrolling to move to a different place in a longer document, you can use the Navigation pane to quickly move the insertion point to a specific page, a specific heading, or specific text. One way to open the Navigation pane is by clicking the Page number button on the status bar, then clicking the link in the Navigation pane for the type of item, headings or pages, you want to use to navigate the document.

To move to a specific page, section, line, table, graphic, or other item in a document, you use the Go To tab in the Find and Replace dialog box. On the Go To tab in the Find and Replace dialog box, select the type of item you want to find in the Go to what list, enter the relevant information about that item, and then click Next to move the insertion point to the item.

Word
Module 2

Check Spelling and Grammar

Learning Outcome
- Check spelling and grammar

While you are working on or after you finish typing and revising a document, you can use the Spelling and Grammar command to search the document for misspelled words and grammar errors. The Spelling and Grammar checker flags possible mistakes and writing style issues, suggests correct spellings, and offers remedies for grammar errors such as incorrect subject–verb agreement, repeated words, and punctuation.

CASE *You use the Spelling and Grammar checker to search the report for errors. Before beginning the search, you select to ignore words you know are spelled correctly, such as Shavonn, a proper noun.*

STEPS

TROUBLE
If Shavonn is not flagged as misspelled, skip to Step 3.

QUICK TIP
To change the language used by the Word proofing tools, click the Language button in the Language group on the Review tab, click Set Proofing Language, select the language you prefer in the dialog box that opens, then click OK.

QUICK TIP
To add a word to the Dictionary so it is not flagged as misspelled, click Add to Dictionary.

1. **Right-click Shavonn in the second body paragraph**
   A menu that includes suggestions for correcting the spelling of "Shavonn" opens. You can correct individual spelling and grammar errors by right-clicking text that is underlined with a red wavy line (a possible misspelling), a blue double underline (a possible grammar error), or purple dotted line (a possible writing style issue), and then selecting a correction. Although "Shavonn" is not in the Word dictionary, it is a proper name that is spelled correctly in the document.
2. **Click Ignore All**
   Clicking Ignore All tells Word not to flag "Shavonn" as misspelled.
3. **Press CTRL+HOME, click the Review tab, click the Editor button in the Proofing group, then click Total Suggestions**
   The Editor pane opens, as shown in **FIGURE 2-5**. The pane identifies "inovations" as misspelled and suggests possible corrections for the error. The first word selected in the Suggestions box is the correct spelling.
4. **Click innovations in the Suggestions box**
   Word replaces the misspelled word with the correctly spelled word. You can also use the arrow next to a suggested correction to hear the word read aloud, to hear the spelling of the word, or to change all instances of the error in a document. Next, the pane indicates that "as" is repeated in a sentence.
5. **Click Delete Repeated Word in the Editor pane**
   Word deletes the second occurrence of the repeated word.
6. **If additional errors are identified, review and ignore them, then click OK to complete the spelling and grammar check**
   The Editor identifies many common errors, but you cannot rely on it to find and correct all spelling and grammar errors in your documents, or to always suggest a valid correction. Always proofread your documents carefully.
7. **Click the Close button in the Editor pane, press CTRL+HOME, then save the document**

Searching for information

The Search feature on the References tab gives you quick access to information about document text, including definitions, images, and other material from online sources. For example, you might use Search to see the definition of a word used in a document or to hear the word pronounced. To use Search, select the text you want to look up in your document, right-click it, then click Search. You can also select text, then click the Search button in the Research group on the References tab. The Search pane opens and displays images and web links related to the selected text. Click the More button to display only pictures, web information, or help articles.

FIGURE 2-5: Editor pane

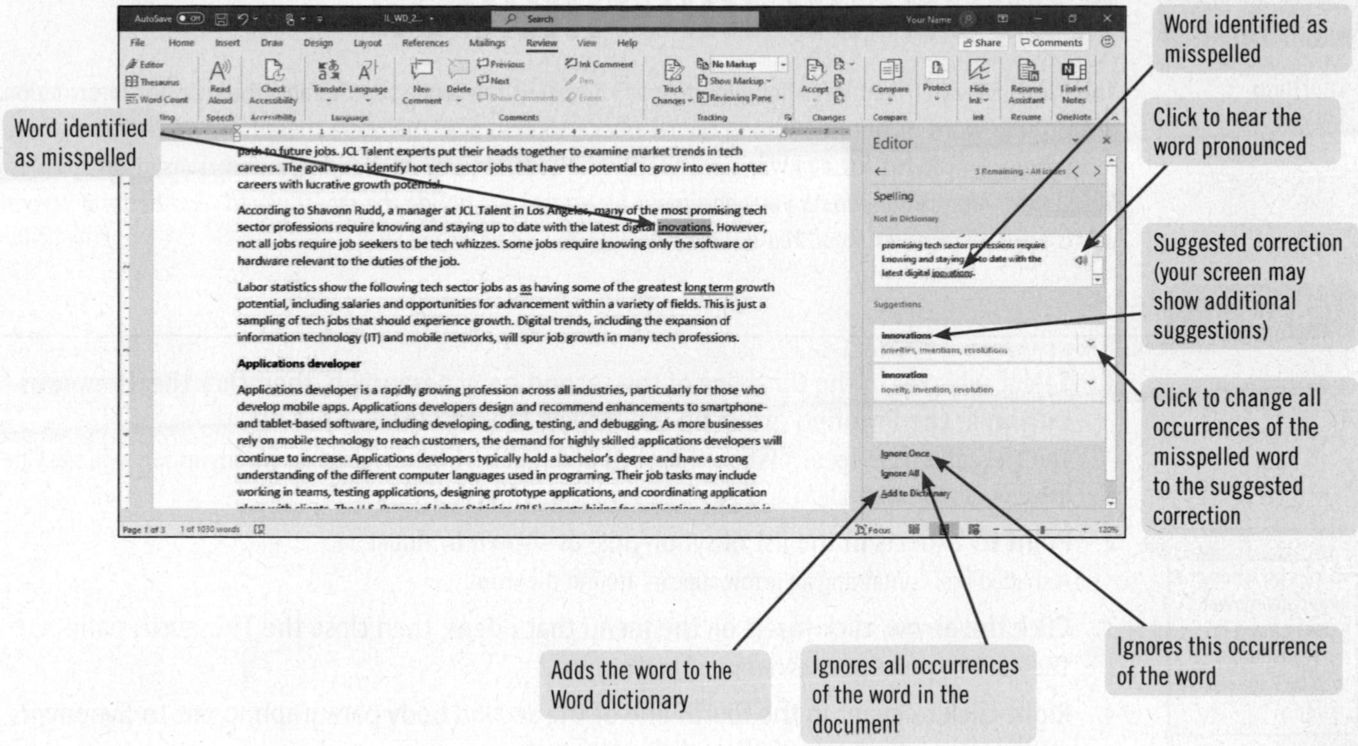

Inserting text with AutoCorrect

As you type, AutoCorrect automatically corrects many commonly misspelled words. By creating your own AutoCorrect entries, you can set Word to insert text that you type often, such as your name or contact information, or to correct words you misspell frequently. For example, you could create an AutoCorrect entry so that the name "Mary T. Watson" is automatically inserted whenever you type "mtw" followed by a space. You create Auto-Correct entries and customize other AutoCorrect and AutoFormat options using the AutoCorrect dialog box. To open the AutoCorrect dialog box, click the File tab, click Options, click Proofing in the Word Options dialog box that opens, and then click AutoCorrect Options. On the AutoCorrect tab in the AutoCorrect dialog box, type the text you want to be corrected automatically in the Replace box (such as "mtw"), type the text you want to be inserted in its place automatically in the With box (such as "Mary T. Watson"), and then click Add. The AutoCorrect entry is added to the list. Click OK to close the AutoCorrect dialog box, and then click OK to close the Word Options dialog box. Word inserts an AutoCorrect entry in a document when you press SPACEBAR or a punctuation mark after typing the text you want Word to correct. For example, Word inserts "Mary T. Watson" when you type "mtw" followed by a space. If you want to remove an AutoCorrect entry you created, simply open the AutoCorrect dialog box, select the AutoCorrect entry you want to remove in the list, click Delete, click OK, and then click OK to close the Word Options dialog box.

Research Information

Learning Outcomes
- Find synonyms
- Check the word count

The Word Research features allow you to quickly search reference sources and the web for information related to a word or phrase. Among the reference sources available are a thesaurus, which you can use to look up synonyms for awkward or repetitive words, as well as dictionary and translation sources.

CASE *After proofreading your document for errors, you decide the report would read better if several words were more professional. You use the thesaurus to find synonyms.*

STEPS

1. **Select whizzes in the third line of the second body paragraph, then click the Thesaurus button in the Proofing group on the Review tab**

   The Thesaurus pane opens. "Whizzes" appears in the search box, and possible synonyms for "whizzes" are listed under the search box.

> **QUICK TIP**
> To look up synonyms for a different word, type the word in the search box, then click the search button.

2. **Point to experts in the list of synonyms, as shown in FIGURE 2-6**

   A shaded box containing an arrow appears around the word.

3. **Click the arrow, click Insert on the menu that opens, then close the Thesaurus pane**

   The word "experts" replaces "whizzes" in the report.

4. **Right-click relevant in the fourth line of the second body paragraph, point to Synonyms on the menu that opens, then click pertinent**

   The word "pertinent" replaces "relevant" in the report.

5. **Select the three paragraphs of body text under the "Career Growth..." title, then click the Word Count button in the Proofing group**

   The Word Count dialog box opens, as shown in **FIGURE 2-7**. The dialog box lists the number of pages, words, characters, paragraphs, and lines included in the selected text. Notice that the status bar also displays the number of words included in the selected text and the total number of words in the entire document. If you want to view the page, character, paragraph, and line count for the entire document, make sure nothing is selected in your document, and then click Word Count in the Proofing group.

6. **Click Close, then save the document**

Reading a document aloud using Word

The Word Read Aloud feature reads a document aloud for you. Reading a document aloud can help you hear grammar errors, discover missing words, or notice other writing issues you might not notice when proofreading a document on screen. As Word reads the document aloud, each word is highlighted on the screen as it is pronounced. To read a document aloud using Word, move the insertion point to the beginning of the document, then click the Read Aloud button in the Speech group on the Review tab. A toolbar of playback controls opens at the top of the document window and Word begins to read aloud. You can use the Settings button on the playback controls to change the reading speed or the reading voice. The Previous, Next, Pause, and Play buttons allow you to pause and resume the reading, or to navigate through the document paragraph by paragraph. When you are finished reading the document aloud using Word, click the Stop button on the playback controls.

FIGURE 2-6: Thesaurus pane

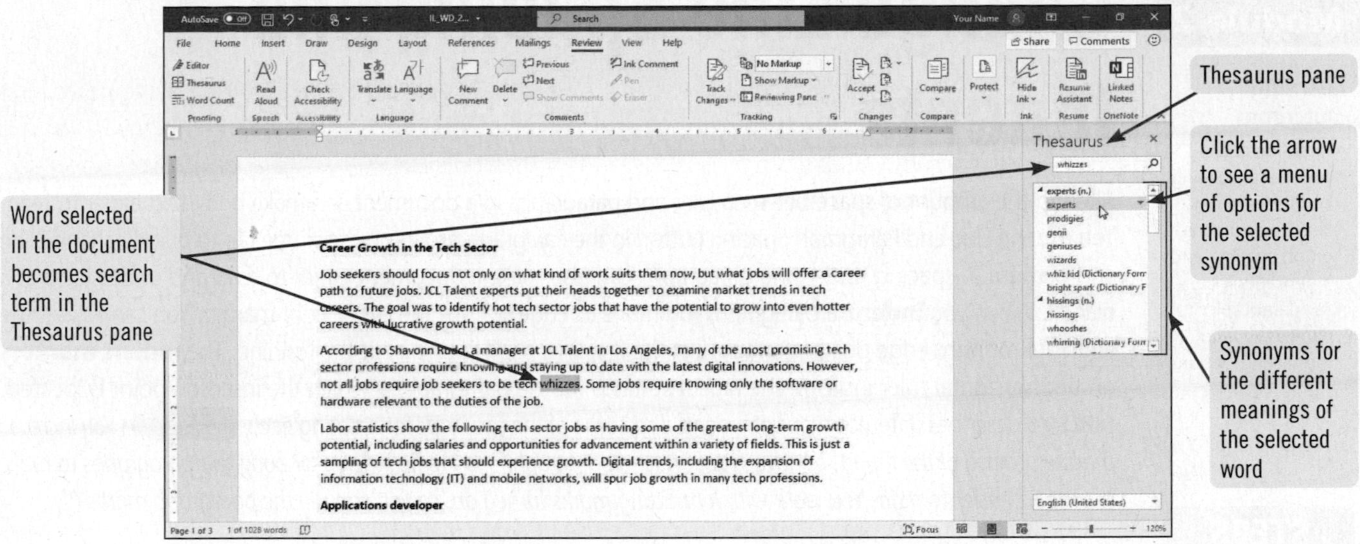

FIGURE 2-7: Word Count dialog box

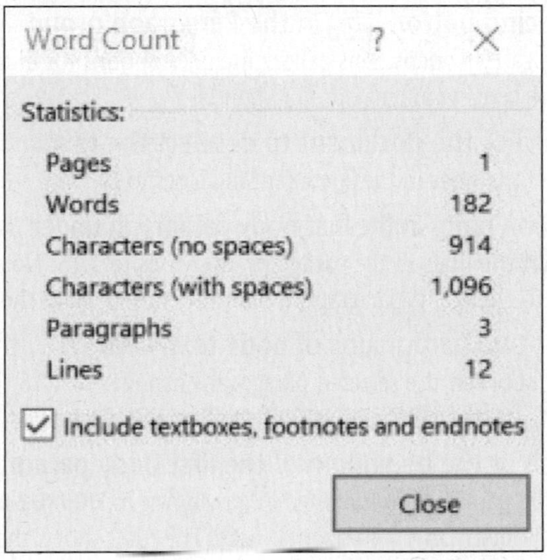

Using a add-ins for Word

Add-ins are small programs embedded in Word that allow you to access information on the web without having to leave Word. For example, you can look up something on Wikipedia, insert an online map in one of your documents, or access dictionaries and other reference sources, all from within Word using an add-in. To find and install an add-in, click the Get Add-ins button in the Add-ins group on the Insert tab to open the Office Add-ins gallery. The Store tab in the Office Add-ins gallery includes a searchable list of the add-ins available to you, which you can also browse by category. Some add-ins are free, and some require purchase.

To install an add-in, click the Add button next to it on the Store tab. To use an add-in after you have installed it, click the My Add-ins button on the Insert tab to open the Office Add-ins gallery with the My Add-ins tab displayed. Select the Add-in you want to use on this tab, and then click Add. A new button for the add-in may be added to your ribbon. When you no longer need an add-in you have installed, you can remove it by right-clicking the add-in on the My Add-in tab in the Office Add-ins gallery, and then clicking Remove.

Change Line Spacing and Indents

Learning Outcomes
- Alter line and paragraph spacing and indentation
- Set line and paragraph spacing and indentation
- Set paragraph pagination and formatting options

Altering the amount of space between lines and paragraphs in a document can make body text easier to read. You use the Line and Paragraph Spacing button in the Paragraph group on the Home tab to quickly change line and paragraph spacing. Indenting paragraphs can also make a document easier to read and understand at a glance. When you **indent** a paragraph, you move its edge in from the left or right margin. You can indent the entire left or right edge of a paragraph, just the first line, or all lines except the first line. The **indent markers** on the horizontal ruler indicate the indent settings for the paragraph in which the insertion point is located. **TABLE 2-1** describes different types of indents and some of the methods for creating each. **CASE** *You increase the line spacing of the report, remove space under a paragraph, and create indents for body text paragraphs to make the report easier to read. You work with formatting marks turned on, so you can see the paragraph marks (¶).*

STEPS

1. **Press CTRL+HOME, click the Home tab, click the Show/Hide ¶ button [¶] in the Paragraph group, press CTRL+A to select the entire document, then click the Line and Paragraph Spacing button [icon] in the Paragraph group**
   The Line Spacing gallery opens. This gallery includes options for increasing the space between lines. Both line and paragraph spacing are measured in points.
2. **Click 2.0, then click the document to deselect the text**
   The space between the lines in the document increases to 2.
3. **Place the insertion point in the first body paragraph under the title, click [icon] then click 1.15**
   The space between the lines in the paragraph decreases to 1.15. Notice that you do not need to select an entire paragraph to change its paragraph formatting; simply place the insertion point in the paragraph.
4. **Select the next two paragraphs of body text, click [icon], then click 1.15**
   The line spacing between the selected paragraphs changes to 1.15. To change the paragraph-formatting features of more than one paragraph, you must select the paragraphs.
5. **Click before Job at the beginning of the first body paragraph, then press TAB**
   The first line of the paragraph is indented ½", as shown in **FIGURE 2-8**. Notice the First Line Indent marker is located at the ½" mark on the horizontal ruler. The ruler shows the indent settings for the paragraph in which the insertion point is located. Pressing TAB is a quick way to indent the first line of a paragraph ½".
6. **Place the insertion point in the second body paragraph, then drag the First Line Indent marker [icon] right to the ½" mark on the horizontal ruler**
   FIGURE 2-9 shows the First Line Indent marker being dragged. The first line of the second body paragraph is indented 1/2". Dragging the First Line Indent marker indents only the first line of a paragraph.
7. **Place the insertion point in the third body paragraph, then drag the Hanging Indent marker [icon] right to the ½" mark on the ruler**
   Take care to drag the Hanging Indent marker and not the Left Indent marker. **FIGURE 2-10** shows the Hanging Indent marker being dragged. The lines under the first line of the third body paragraph are indented ½". Dragging the Hanging Indent marker indents the subsequent lines of a paragraph more than the first line.
8. **Place the insertion point in the first body paragraph, click [icon], click Remove Space After Paragraph, then save your changes**
   The space between the first and second body paragraphs is eliminated. Using the Line and Paragraph Spacing button is a quick way to add or remove space between paragraphs. You can also change the paragraph spacing settings for the active paragraph using the Spacing Before and After boxes in the Paragraph group on the Layout tab.

QUICK TIP
Word recognizes any string of text that ends with a paragraph mark as a paragraph, including titles, headings, and single lines in a list.

QUICK TIP
If the rulers are not displayed, click the View tab, then click the Ruler check box.

TROUBLE
Take care to drag only the First Line Indent marker. If you make a mistake, click the Undo button [icon], then try again.

FIGURE 2-8: First line indent

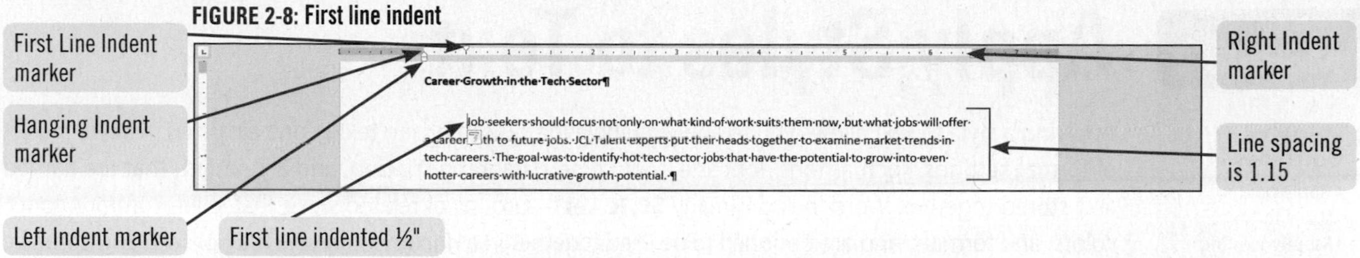

FIGURE 2-9: Dragging the First Line Indent marker

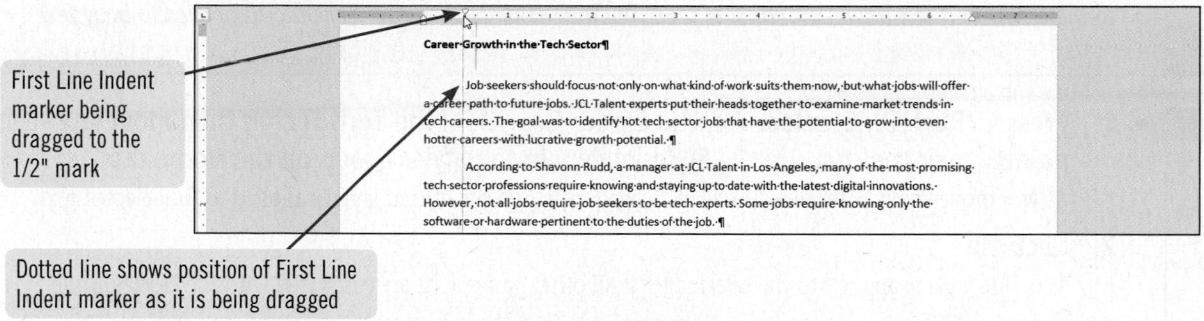

FIGURE 2-10: Dragging the Hanging Indent marker

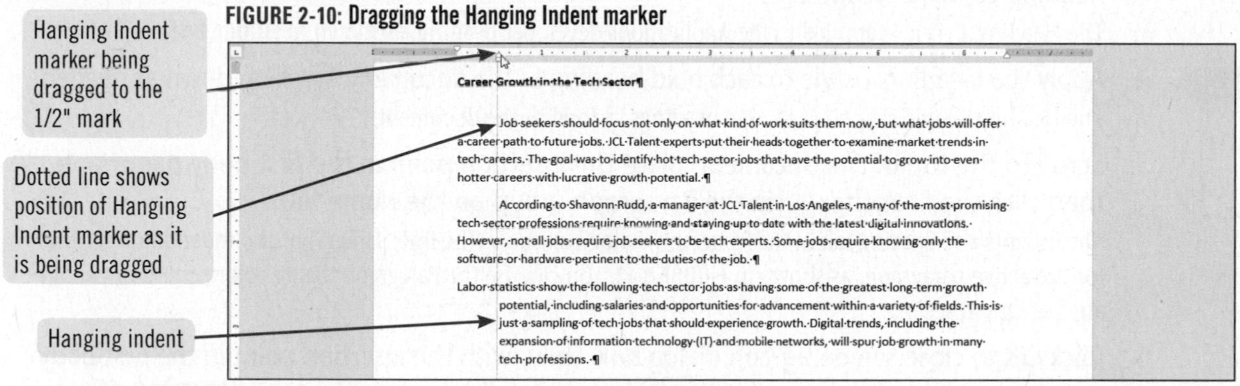

TABLE 2-1: Types of indents

indent type: description	to create
Left indent: left edge of a paragraph is moved in from the left margin	Drag the Left Indent marker on the ruler to the right to the position where you want the left edge of the paragraph to align; when you drag the left indent marker, all the indent markers move as one
Right indent: right edge of a paragraph is moved in from the right margin	Drag the Right Indent marker on the ruler to the left to the position where you want the right edge of the paragraph to align
First line indent: first line of a paragraph is indented more than the subsequent lines	Drag the First Line Indent marker on the ruler to the right to the position where you want the first line of the paragraph to begin; or activate the First Line Indent marker in the tab indicator, and then click the ruler at the position where you want the first line of the paragraph to begin
Hanging indent: subsequent lines of a paragraph are indented more than the first line	Drag the Hanging Indent marker on the ruler to the right to the position where you want the hanging indent to begin; or activate the Hanging Indent marker in the tab indicator, and then click the ruler at the position where you want the second and remaining lines of the paragraph to begin; when you drag the hanging indent marker, the left indent marker moves with it
Negative indent (or Outdent): left edge of a paragraph is moved to the left of the left margin	Drag the Left Indent marker on the ruler left to the position where you want the negative indent to begin; when you drag the left indent marker, all markers move as one

Word
Module 2

Apply Styles to Text

Learning Outcomes
- Apply built-in styles to text
- Modify existing styles

Applying a style to text allows you to apply multiple format settings to text in one easy step. A **style** is a set of format settings, such as font, font size, font color, paragraph spacing, and alignment, that are named and stored together. Word includes many **Style sets**—groups of related styles that share common fonts, colors, and formats, and are designed to be used together in a document to give it a polished and cohesive look. Each Style set includes styles for a title, subtitle, several heading levels, body text, and other text elements. By default, all text is formatted using the Normal style. CASE *You apply title and heading styles to the report to make the report easier to read. You also modify the Normal style that is applied to body text.*

STEPS

QUICK TIP
To change the active Style set, click the Design tab, click the More button in the Document Formatting group, then select a different style set.

1. **Press CTRL+HOME, select the title Career Growth in the Tech Sector, then move the pointer over the styles in the Styles gallery in the Styles group on the Home tab**
   As you move the pointer over a style in the gallery, a preview of that style is applied to the selected text.
2. **Click Title**
   The Title style is applied to the selected text. All other paragraphs are formatted with the Normal style.
3. **Select Applications developer, click Heading 1 in the Styles group, then click the heading to deselect the text**
   The Heading 1 style is applied to the Applications developer heading, as shown in FIGURE 2-11.

QUICK TIP
The body text paragraphs are formatted with the Normal style.

4. **Apply the Heading 1 style to each bold heading in the document, scrolling down as needed**
   The Heading 1 style is applied to nine headings in total in the document.
5. **Scroll to the top of the document, place the insertion point in the first body paragraph, then click the Launcher in the Paragraph group on the Home tab**
   The Indents and Spacing tab in the Paragraph dialog box shows the line, paragraph, and indentation settings for the active paragraph, as shown in FIGURE 2-12. You can use the Paragraph dialog box to check or change any paragraph setting.
6. **Click OK to close the paragraph dialog box, then, with the insertion point in the first body paragraph, right-click Normal in the Styles group, click Update Normal to Match Selection**
   The format of each paragraph formatted with the Normal style in the document is changed to match the first body paragraph. The title and headings are indented now, too because the Heading 1 and Title styles are based on the Normal style. When the Normal style changed, the styles based on the Normal style changed, too.

TROUBLE
If you apply the wrong style, click the Undo button on the Quick Access toolbar, then right-click the style name in the Styles group again.

7. **Right-click Heading 1 in the Styles group, click Modify, click the Style based on arrow in the Modify Style dialog box, click (no style), then click OK**
   The Heading 1 style is now based on no style and the indent is removed from the headings in the document. You can use the Modify Style dialog box to change any format setting in a style.
8. **Right-click Title in the Styles group, click Modify, click the Style based on arrow in the Modify Style dialog box, click (no style), then click OK**
   The Title style is now based on no style and the indent is removed from the title in the document.
9. **Select the Career Growth... title, click the Increase Font Size button in the Font group, click the Font Color arrow, click Blue, Accent 1, Darker 25%, click the Line and Paragraph Spacing button in the Paragraph group, click Add Space After Paragraph, deselect the title, then save your changes**
   The font size of the title is increased, the font color changes to dark blue, and extra space is added after the title paragraph, as shown in FIGURE 2-13. You can modify the format of text to which a style has been applied without changing the style itself.

FIGURE 2-11: Styles applied to the report

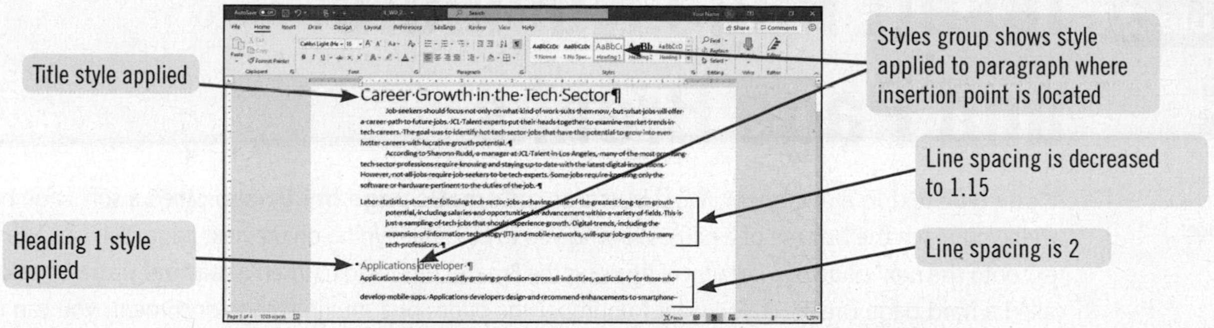

FIGURE 2-12: Indents and Spacing tab in Paragraph dialog box

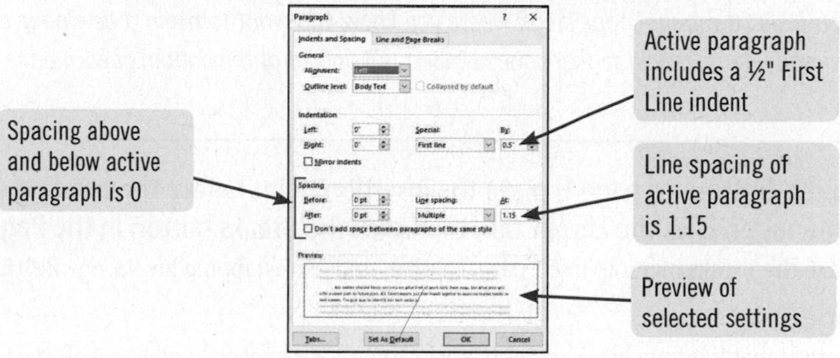

FIGURE 2-13: Modified styles applied to the document

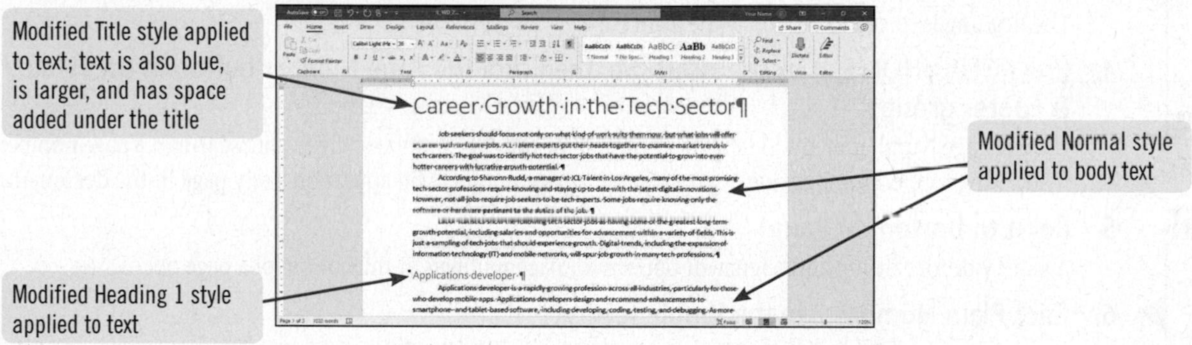

Changing the Style set

Changing the Style set applied to a document is a quick way to give a document a different look and design. Style sets include font and paragraph settings for headings and body text. When you change the Style set, a complete set of new fonts and colors is applied to the entire document. All the body text and all the headings that have been formatted with a style change to the format settings for the active Style set. To change the Style set, you click one of the Style sets available in the Document Formatting group on the Design tab. You can also change the color scheme or font used in the active Style set by clicking the Colors or Fonts buttons in the Document Formatting group and then selecting from the available color schemes or font options.

You can also save a group of font and paragraph settings as a new Style set. To do this, click the More button in the Document Formatting group, and then click Save as a New Style Set. If you want to return a document to its original Style set, click the More button, and then click Reset to the Default Style Set.

Insert Page Numbers and Page Breaks

Learning Outcomes
- Insert page, section, and column breaks
- Insert page numbers

As you type text in a document, Word inserts an **automatic page break** (also called a soft page break) when you reach the bottom of a page, allowing you to continue typing on the next page. You can also force text onto the next page of a document by using the Breaks command to insert a **manual page break** (also called a hard page break). If you want to number the pages of a multiple-page document, you can insert a page number field to add a page number to each page. A **field** is a code that serves as a placeholder for data that changes in a document, such as a page number or the current date. When you use the Page Number button on the Insert tab to add page numbers to a document, you insert the page number field at the top, bottom, or side of any page, and Word automatically numbers all the pages in the document for you. **CASE** *You insert a manual page break where you know you want to begin a new page of the report, and then you add a page number field so that page numbers will appear at the bottom of each page in the document.*

STEPS

> **QUICK TIP**
> Pressing CTRL+ENTER is a fast way to insert a manual page break.

1. **Scroll to the bottom of page 1, place the insertion point before the heading Customer service manager, click the Layout tab, then click the Breaks button in the Page Setup group**
   You also use the Breaks menu to insert page, column, and text-wrapping breaks. See **TABLE 2-2**.
2. **Click Page**
   Word inserts a manual page break before "Customer service manager" and moves all the text following the page break to the beginning of the next page, as shown in **FIGURE 2-14**.

> **QUICK TIP**
> To delete a page break, select it and then press DELETE. Page breaks are only visible when formatting marks are turned on.

3. **Scroll down, place the insertion point before the heading Intelligence analyst on page 2, press and hold CTRL, then press ENTER**
   The heading is forced to the top of the third page.
4. **Press CTRL+HOME, click the Insert tab, then click the Page Number button in the Header & Footer group**
   Use the Page Number menu to select the position for the page numbers. If you choose to add a page number field to the top, bottom, or side of a document, a page number will appear on every page in the document.

> **QUICK TIP**
> To change the location or formatting of page numbers, click the Page Number button, point to a page number location, then select a format from the gallery.

5. **Point to Bottom of Page**
   A gallery of formatting and alignment options for page numbers at the bottom of a page opens.
6. **Click Plain Number 2 in the Simple section**
   A page number field containing the number 1 is centered in the Footer area at the bottom of page 1 of the document, as shown in **FIGURE 2-15**. The document text is gray, or dimmed, because the Footer area is open. Text that is inserted in a Footer area appears at the bottom of every page in a document.
7. **Double-click the document text**
   The page number is now dimmed because it is located in the Footer area, which is no longer the active area. When the document is printed, the page numbers appear as normal text.

> **QUICK TIP**
> To remove page numbers from a document, click the Page Number button, then click Remove Page Numbers.

8. **Press CTRL+HOME, click the View tab, click the Multiple Pages button in the Zoom group, then save the document**
   Word numbered each page of the report automatically, and each page number is centered at the bottom of the page, as shown in **FIGURE 2-16**.

FIGURE 2-14: Manual page break in document

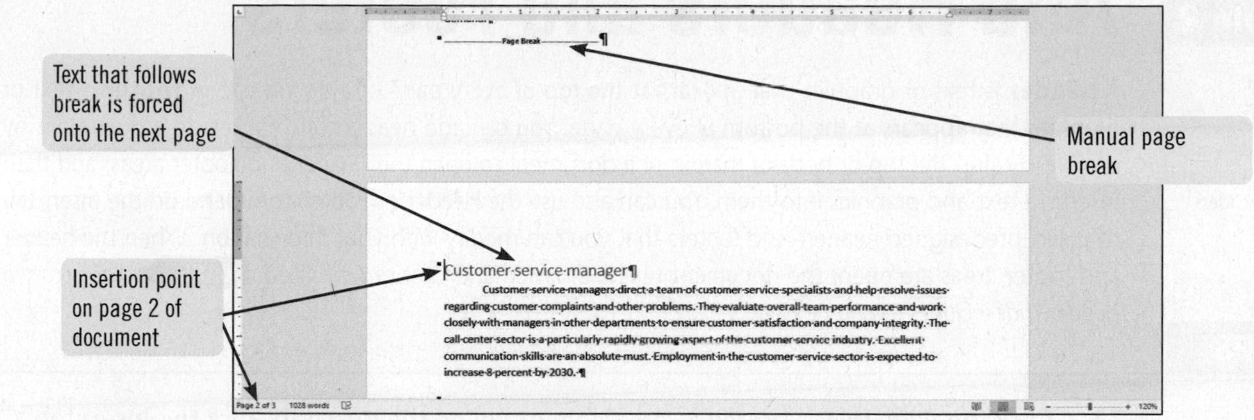
Text that follows break is forced onto the next page
Manual page break
Insertion point on page 2 of document
Page Break
Customer·service·manager¶
Customer·service·managers·direct·a·team·of·customer·service·specialists·and·help·resolve·issues·regarding·customer·complaints·and·other·problems.·They·evaluate·overall·team·performance·and·work·closely·with·managers·in·other·departments·to·ensure·customer·satisfaction·and·company·integrity.·The·call·center·sector·is·a·particularly·rapidly·growing·aspect·of·the·customer·service·industry.·Excellent·communication·skills·are·an·absolute·must.·Employment·in·the·customer·service·sector·is·expected·to·increase·8·percent·by·2030.·¶

FIGURE 2-15: Page number in document

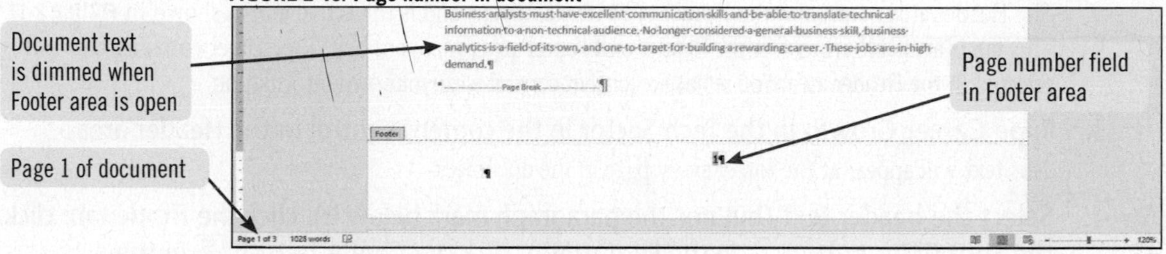

FIGURE 2-16: Pages 1, 2, and 3

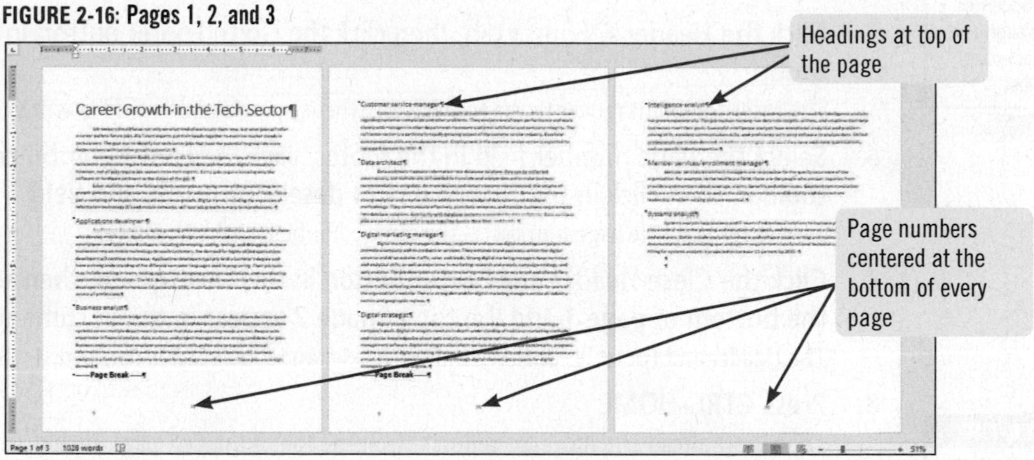

TABLE 2-2: Types of breaks

break	function
Page	Forces the text following the break to begin at the top of the next page
Column	Forces the text following the break to begin at the top of the next column
Text Wrapping	Forces the text following the break to begin at the beginning of the next line

Word
Module 2

Add Headers and Footers

Learning Outcomes
- Insert headers and footers
- Manage headers and footers

A **header** is text or graphics that appears at the top of every page of a document. A **footer** is text or graphics that appears at the bottom of every page. You can add headers and footers to a document by double-clicking the top or bottom margin of a document to open the Header and Footer areas, and then inserting text and graphics into them. You can also use the Header or Footer command on the Insert tab to insert predesigned headers and footers that you can modify with your information. When the header and footer areas are open, the document text is dimmed and cannot be edited. CASE *You create a header that includes the name of the report.*

STEPS

1. **Click the Page Width button in the Zoom group on the View tab, click the Insert tab, then click the Header button in the Header & Footer group**
   A gallery of built-in header designs opens.
2. **Scroll down the gallery to view the header designs, scroll up the gallery, then click Blank**
   The Header area opens and the Header & Footer tab opens and is the active tab, as shown in **FIGURE 2-17**. This tab is available whenever the Header and Footer areas are open. The [Type Here] **content control** is selected in the Header area. You replace a content control with your own information.
3. **Type Career Growth in the Tech Sector in the content control in the Header area**
   This text will appear at the top of every page in the document.
4. **Select the header text (but not the paragraph mark below it), click the Home tab, click the Font Color button in the Font group, click the Center button in the Paragraph group, click the Borders button, then click in the Header area to deselect the text**
   The text is the same blue used in the document and is centered in the Header area with a bottom border.
5. **Click the Header & Footer tab, then click the Go to Footer button in the Navigation group**
   The insertion point moves to the Footer area, where a page number field is centered in the Footer area.
6. **Select the page number field in the footer, click the Font Color button on the Mini toolbar, then click in the Footer area to deselect the text and field**
   The footer text (the page number) is the same color blue as the headings.
7. **Click the Close Header and Footer button in the Close group, then scroll down until the bottom of page 1 and the top of page 2 appear in the document window**
   The Header and Footer areas close, and the header and footer text is dimmed, as shown in **FIGURE 2-18**.
8. **Press CTRL+HOME**
   The report already includes the report title at the top of the first page, making the header information redundant.
9. **Position the pointer over the header text at the top of page 1, double-click the header to open the Header area, click the Different First Page check box in the Options group on the Header and Footer tab, then click the Close Header and Footer button**
   The header and footer text is removed from the Header and Footer areas on the first page.
10. **Click Show/Hide ¶ button in the Paragraph group on the Home tab, click the View tab, click the Multiple Pages button in the Zoom group, then save your changes**
    The headers and footers and all the pages in the document are shown in **FIGURE 2-19**.

QUICK TIP
You can also use the Insert Alignment Tab button in the Position group on the Header & Footer tab to left-, center-, and right-align text in the Header and Footer areas.

QUICK TIP
To remove headers or footers from a document, click the Header or Footer button, and then click Remove Header or Remove Footer.

FIGURE 2-17: Header area

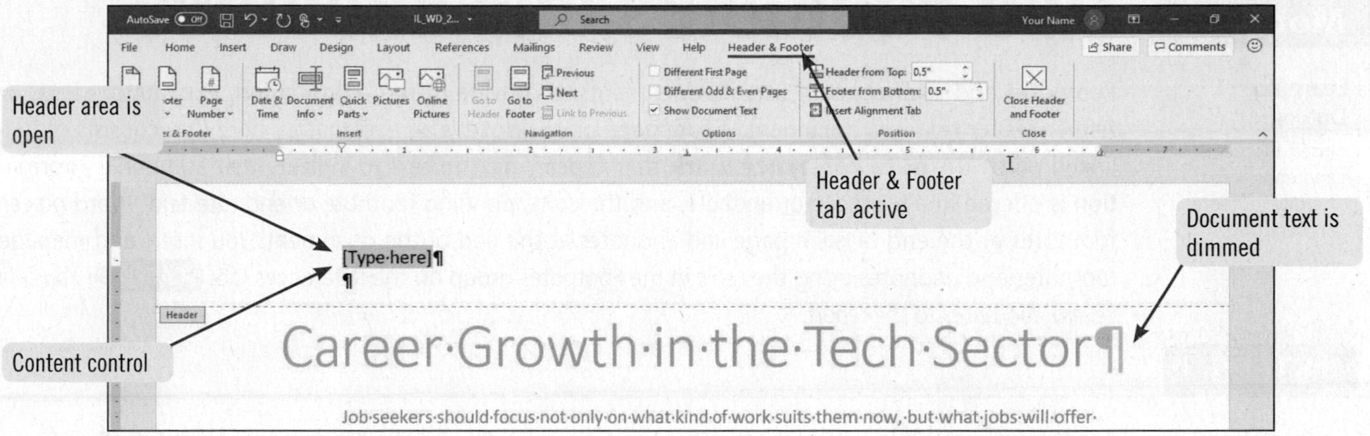

FIGURE 2-18: Header and footer in document

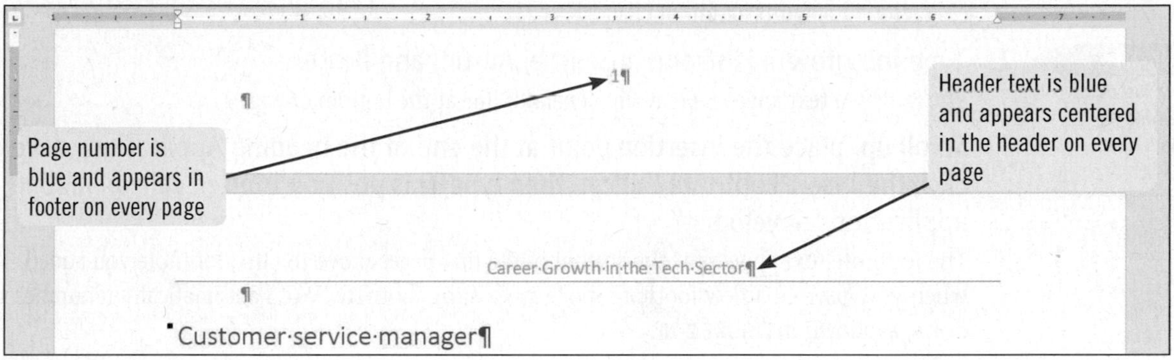

FIGURE 2-19: Header and footer on pages 2 and 3

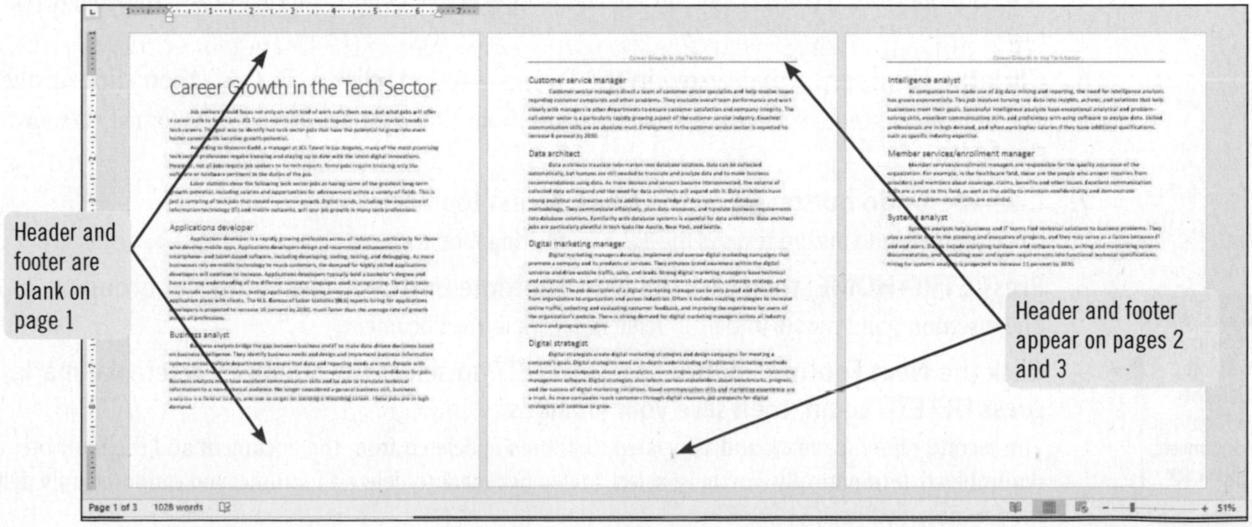

Word

Add Footnotes and Endnotes

Learning Outcomes
- Insert footnotes and endnotes
- Modify footnote and endnote properties

Footnotes and endnotes are used in documents to provide further information, explanatory text, or references for text in a document. A **footnote** or **endnote** is an explanatory note that consists of two linked parts: the **note reference mark** that appears next to text to indicate that additional information is offered in a footnote or endnote, and the corresponding footnote or endnote text. Word places footnotes at the end of each page and endnotes at the end of the document. You insert and manage footnotes and endnotes using the tools in the Footnotes group on the References tab. **CASE** *You add several footnotes to the report.*

STEPS

1. **Click the 100% button in the Zoom group, scroll until the Business analyst heading is at the top of your screen, place the insertion point at the end of the last body paragraph (after "demand."), click the References tab, then click the Insert Footnote button in the Footnotes group**

   A note reference mark, in this case a superscript 1, appears after "demand.", and the insertion point moves below a separator line at the bottom of the page. A note reference mark can be a number, a symbol, a character, or a combination of characters.

QUICK TIP
To delete a footnote, select the note reference mark, then press DELETE.

2. **Type Job growth is strong in Seattle, Austin, and Boston.**

   The footnote text appears below the separator line at the bottom of page 1.

3. **Scroll up, place the insertion point at the end of the heading Applications developer, click the Insert Footnote button, then type This position is often called "mobile applications developer."**

   The footnote text appears at the bottom of the first page, above the first footnote you added. Notice that when you inserted a new footnote above an existing footnote, Word automatically renumbered the footnotes, as shown in **FIGURE 2-20**.

4. **Place the insertion point at the end of the paragraph under the Applications developer heading, click the Insert Footnote button, then type Many hold a master's degree.**

   The footnote text appears between the text for footnotes 1 and 3 at the bottom of the page.

5. **Click the Launcher in the Footnotes group**

   The Footnote and Endnote dialog box opens. You can use this dialog box to change the location of footnote and endnote text, to convert footnotes to endnotes, and to change the formatting of the note reference marks.

6. **Click the Number format arrow in the Format section, click A, B, C,..., then click Apply**

   The note reference marks in the document change from 1, 2, 3 format to an A, B, C format, as shown in **FIGURE 2-21**.

7. **Click the Undo button on the Quick Access toolbar**

   Clicking the Undo button restores the 1,2,3 numbering format.

8. **Press CTRL+HOME, then click the Next Footnote button in the Footnotes group**

   The insertion point moves to the "1" reference mark in the document.

QUICK TIP
To convert all footnotes to endnotes, click the Launcher in the Footnotes group, click Convert, click OK, then click Close.

9. **Click the Next Footnote button, press DELETE to select the number 2 reference mark, press DELETE again, then save your changes**

   The second reference mark and associated footnote are deleted from the document and the footnotes are renumbered automatically. You must select a reference mark to delete a footnote; you cannot simply delete the footnote text itself.

FIGURE 2-20: Renumbered footnotes in the document

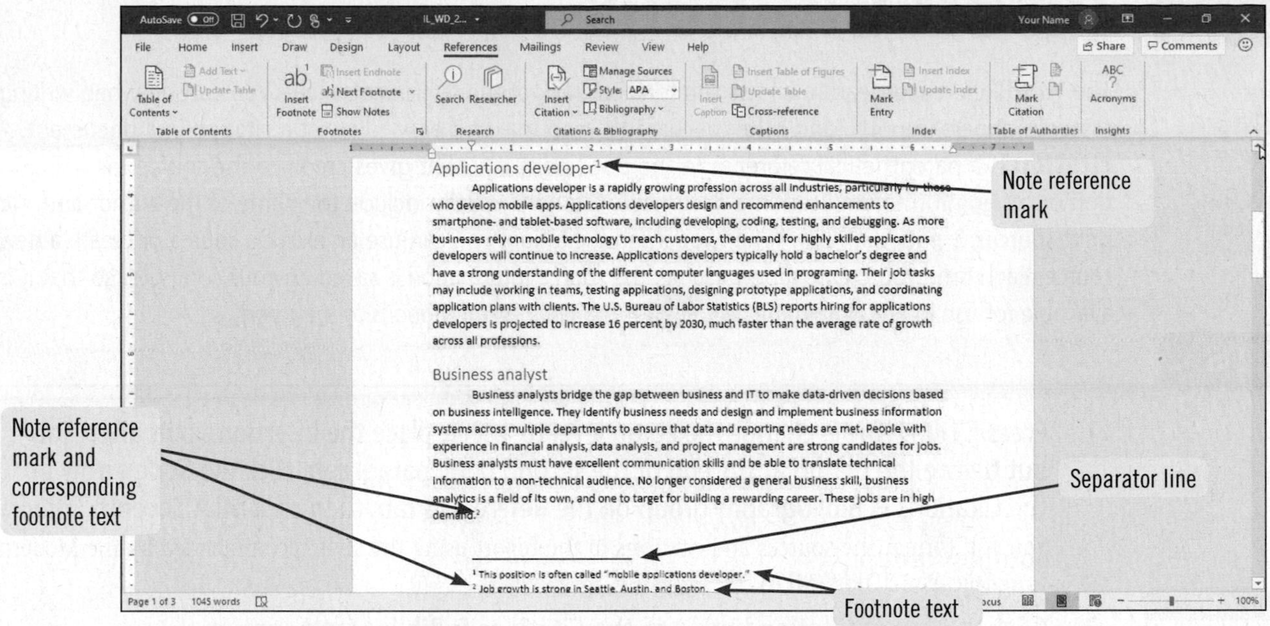

FIGURE 2-21: Note reference marks in new format

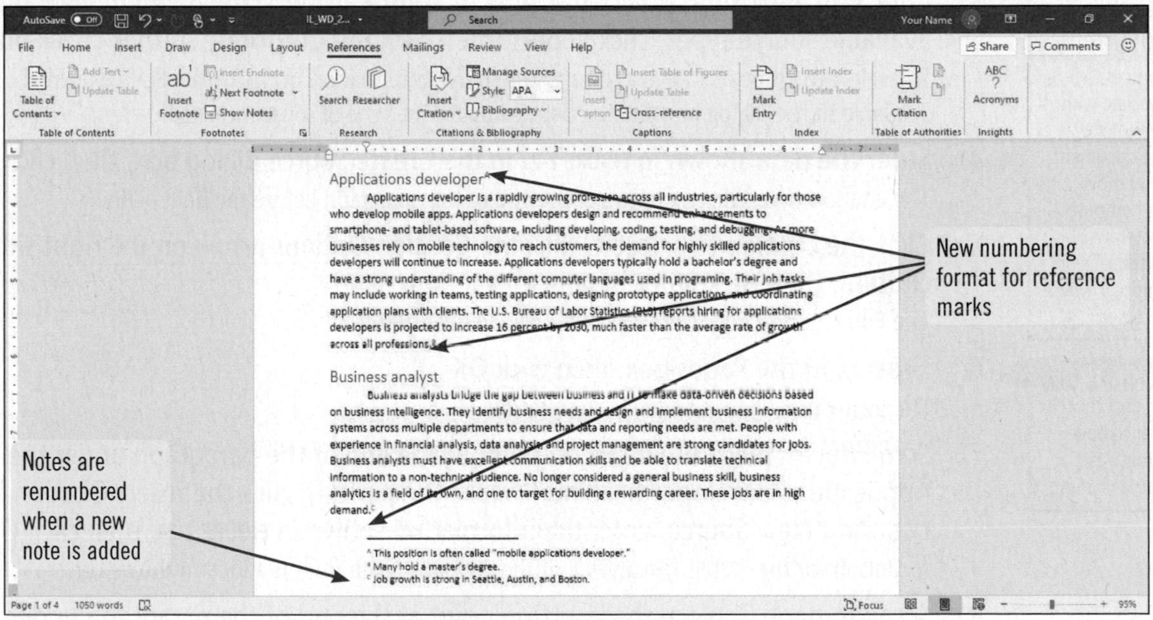

Word

Insert Citations

Learning Outcomes
- Add a source to a document
- Insert a citation
- Edit a citation

The Word References feature allows you to keep track of the reference sources you consult when writing research papers, reports, and other documents, and makes it easy to insert a citation in a document. A **citation** is a parenthetical reference in the document text that gives credit to the source for a quotation or other information used in a document. Citations usually include the name of the author and, for print sources, a page number. When you insert a citation, you can use an existing source or create a new source. Each time you create a new source, the source information is saved on your computer so that it is available for use in any document. CASE *You add several citations to the report.*

STEPS

QUICK TIP
When you create a new source for a document, it appears automatically in the bibliography when you generate it.

QUICK TIP
Only sources that you associate with a document stay with the document when you move it to another computer. The master list of sources remains on the computer where it was created.

QUICK TIP
You can also choose to add or remove the author, year, or title from a citation.

1. **Press CTRL+HOME, change the zoom level to 120%, place the insertion point after "job" but before the period at the end of the second body paragraph, click the Style arrow in the Citations & Bibliography group on the References tab, then click MLA Seventh Edition**
   You will format the sources and citations in the report using the style recommended by the Modern Language Association (MLA).
2. **Click the Insert Citation button in the Citations & Bibliography group**
   A list of the sources (one) already used in the file opens. You can choose to cite this source, create a new source, or add a placeholder for a source. When you add a new citation to a document, the source is added to the list of master sources stored on the computer. The new source is also associated with the document.
3. **Click Add New Source, click the Type of Source arrow, scroll down to view the available source types, click Report, then click the Corporate Author check box**
   You select the type of source and enter the source information in the Create Source dialog box. The fields available in the dialog box change, depending on the type of source selected.
4. **Enter the data shown in FIGURE 2-22 in the Create Source dialog box, then click OK**
   The citation (JCL Talent) appears at the end of the paragraph before the final period.
5. **Click the citation to select it, click the Citation Options arrow on the right side of the citation, then click Edit Citation**
   The Edit Citation dialog box opens, as shown in **FIGURE 2-23**.
6. **Type 15 in the Pages box, then click OK**
   The page number 15 is added to the citation.
7. **Scroll down, place the insertion point at the end of the paragraph under the Applications developer heading (before the period), click the Insert Citation button, click Add New Source, enter the information shown in FIGURE 2-24, then click OK**
   A citation for the Web publication that the data was taken from is added to the report.
8. **Scroll to page 2, place the insertion point at the end of the paragraph under the Customer service manager heading (before the period) click the Insert Citation button, then click U.S. Bureau of Labor Statistics in the list of sources**
   The citation (U.S. Bureau of Labor Statistics) appears at the end of the paragraph.
9. **Press CTRL+END, then repeat Step 8 to insert a U.S. Bureau of Labor Statistics citation at the end of the last paragraph in the document**
10. **Scroll up to page 2, place the insertion point at the end of the paragraph under the Data architect heading (before the period) click the Insert Citation button, click Add New Placeholder, type NYT, click OK, then save your changes**
    You added a citation placeholder for a source that you still need to add to the document.

FIGURE 2-22: Creating a report source

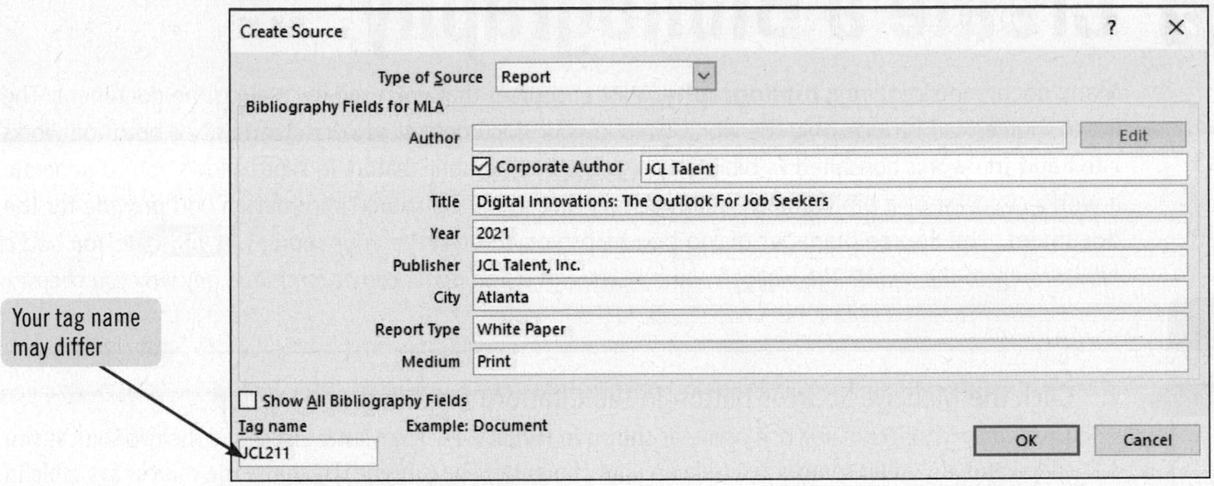

FIGURE 2-23: Edit Citation dialog box

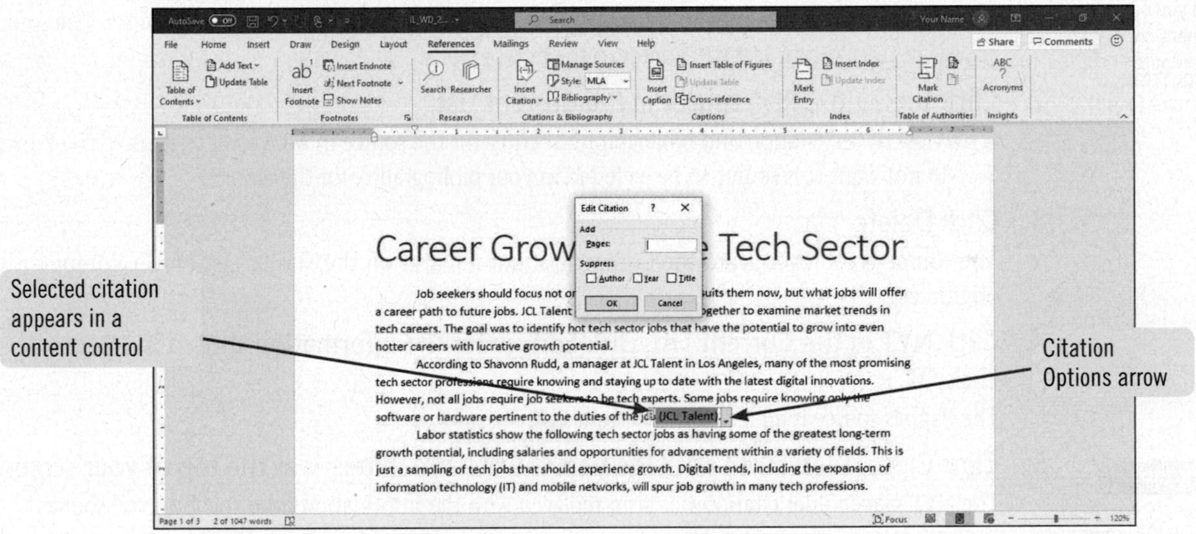

FIGURE 2-24: Adding a Web publication source

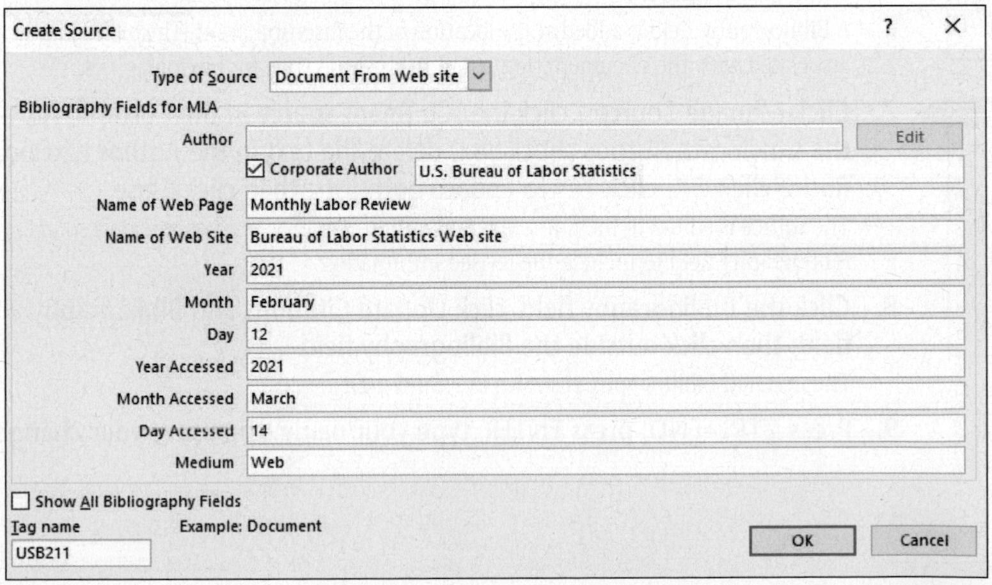

Word

Word
Module 2

Create a Bibliography

Learning Outcomes
- Add and delete sources
- Edit a source
- Insert a bibliography field

Many documents require a **bibliography**, a list of sources that you used in creating the document. The list of sources can include only the works cited in your document (a **works cited** list) or both the works cited and the works consulted (a bibliography). The Bibliography feature in Word allows you to generate a works cited list or a bibliography automatically, based on the source information you provide for the document. The Source Manager dialog box helps you to organize your sources. CASE *You add a bibliography to the report. The bibliography is inserted as a field and it can be formatted any way you choose.*

STEPS

QUICK TIP
You must copy sources from the Master List to the Current List for the sources to be available when you open the document on another computer.

1. **Click the Manage Sources button in the Citations & Bibliography group**
   The Source Manager dialog box opens, as shown in **FIGURE 2-25**. The Master List shows the two sources you added and any other sources available on your computer. The Current List shows the sources available in the current document, as well as the NYT placeholder you added. A check mark next to a source indicates the source is cited in the document. You use the tools in the Source Manager dialog box to add, edit, and delete sources from the lists, and to copy sources between the Master and Current Lists. The sources that appear in the Current List will appear in the bibliography.
2. **Click the Singh, Riya source in the Current List**
   A preview of the citation and bibliographical entry for the source in MLA style appears in the Preview box. You do not want this source to be included in your bibliography for the report.
3. **Click Delete**
   The source is removed from the Current List but remains on the Master List on the computer where it originated.
4. **Click NYT in the Current List, click Edit, enter the information shown in FIGURE 2-26, then click OK**
   The Pappas source is added to the Current List.
5. **Click Close, then scroll until the heading Data Architect is at the top of your screen**
   The NYT placeholder citation has been replaced with the information from the "Pappas" source.
6. **Press CTRL+END to move the insertion point to the end of the document, click the Bibliography button in the Citations & Bibliography group, then click Bibliography in the Built-in gallery**
   A Bibliography field is added at the location of the insertion point. The bibliography includes all the sources associated with the document, formatted in the MLA style for bibliographies.
7. **Click Manage Sources, click the JCL Talent source in the Current List, click Edit, deselect the Corporate Author check box, delete the text in the Author text box, type Shavonn Rudd, click OK, click Yes to update both lists, then click Close**
   The source is edited to include a different author name. When you update a source, you need to update the Bibliography field to include the revised information.
8. **Click the Bibliography field, click Update Citations and Bibliography at the top of the field, then click outside the Bibliography field**
   The updated Bibliography is shown in **FIGURE 2-27**.
9. **Press CTRL+END, press ENTER, type your name, then save your changes**

QUICK TIP
Click References in the Built-in gallery to insert a References list. Click Works Cited in the Built-in gallery to insert a Works Cited list.

QUICK TIP
To change the style used for citations and the bibliography, click the Style arrow in the Citations & Bibliography group, then select a different style.

FIGURE 2-25: Source Manager dialog box

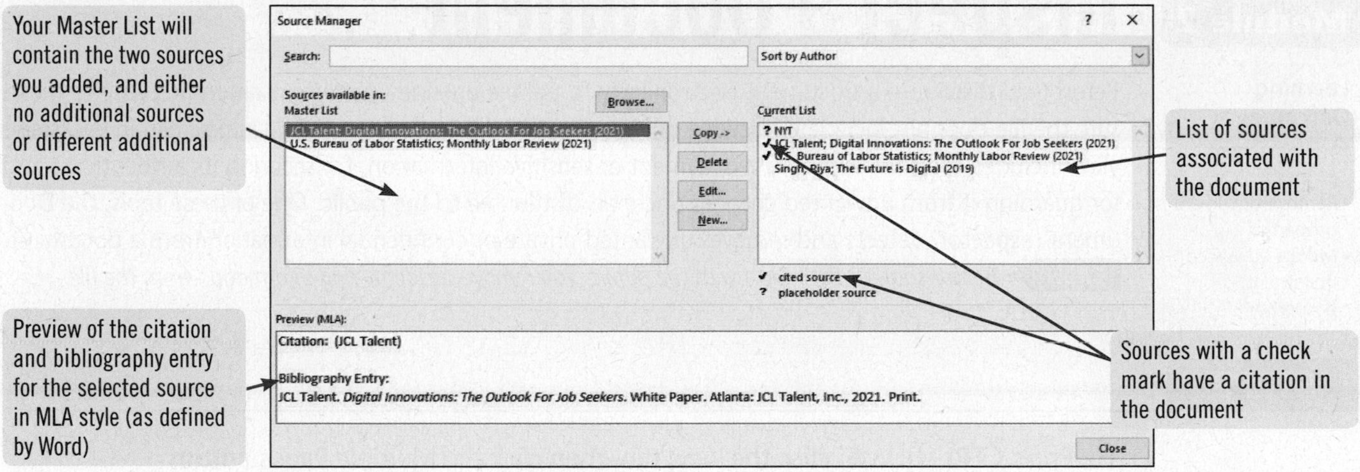

FIGURE 2-26: Adding a periodical source

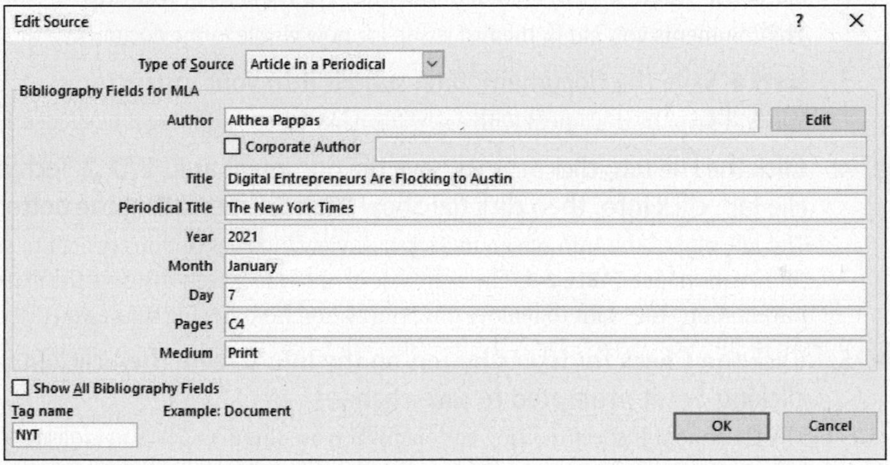

FIGURE 2-27: Bibliography field in document

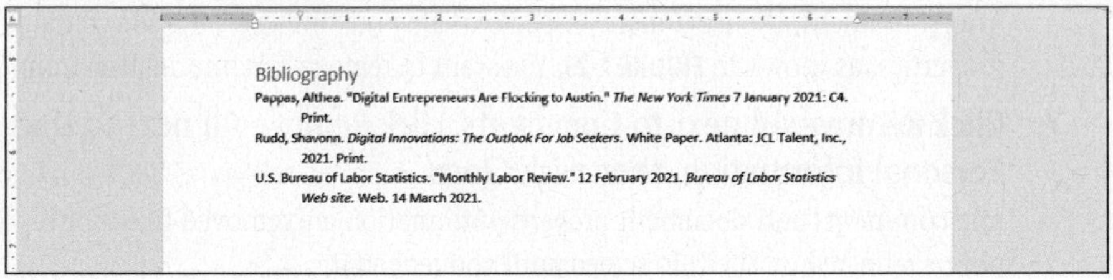

Finding and citing sources with the Word Researcher

The Word Researcher tool helps you find citable sources, quotations, images, and other material for a research paper. Using Researcher, you can search for journal articles and websites that relate to a topic, add information from those sources into a document, automatically create a citation for the source, and automatically create and update a bibliography—all without having to manually enter the source information. To begin, click the Researcher button in the Research group on the References tab to open the Researcher pane. Type a keyword for your topic in the search box, press ENTER, and then explore the list of sources related to your topic. When you find a source that is useful to you, you can select text (or an image) from it and add the selection to your document, choosing to add text only or to add the text and a citation. When you add a citation, Word automatically creates a bibliography that is updated each time you add additional material to the document. To avoid plagiarism, be sure to paraphrase text that is not a quote, and always include citations giving credit for any content that is not your original work. Also, always verify that the bibliographies you create using Word are formatted in the most up-to-date MLA, APA, Chicago, or other style.

Word

Inspect a Document

Learning Outcomes
- Edit document properties
- Remove document properties
- Modify advanced document properties

Before you distribute a document electronically to people outside your organization, it's wise to make sure the file does not include embedded private or confidential information. The Info screen in Backstage view includes tools for stripping a document of sensitive information, for securing its authenticity, and for guarding it from unwanted changes once it is distributed to the public. One of these tools, the Document Inspector, detects and removes unwanted private or confidential information from a document.

CASE *Before sharing the report with the public, you remove all identifying information from the file.*

STEPS

1. **Press CTRL+HOME, click the View tab, then click the Multiple Pages button**
   The completed document is shown in **FIGURE 2-28**.
2. **Click the Review tab, click No Markup, then click All Markup**
   The comments you hid in the first lesson are now visible in the document.
3. **sam Save the document, then submit it to your instructor**
   You will save the document with a new file name before stripping it of all identifying information.
4. **Click the File tab, click Save As, save the document as IL_WD_2_TechJobs_Inspected, click the File tab, click Info, then click the Show All Properties link at the bottom of the Info screen**
   The left side of the Info screen in Backstage view includes options related to stripping the file of private information. See **TABLE 2-3**. The right side of the Info screen displays the expanded document property information. You want to remove this information from the file before you distribute it electronically.
5. **Click the Check for Issues button on the Info screen, then click Inspect Document, clicking Yes if prompted to save changes**
   The Document Inspector dialog box opens. You use this dialog box to indicate which private or identifying information you want to search for and remove from the document.
6. **Make sure all the check boxes are selected, then click Inspect**
   After a moment, the Document Inspector dialog box indicates the file contains comments and document properties, as shown in **FIGURE 2-29**. You want to remove this information from the file.
7. **Click Remove All next to Comments, click Remove All next to Document Properties and Personal Information, then click Close**
   The comments and document property information are removed from the report file, but the change will not be reflected on the Info screen until you reopen it.
8. **Click the Back button on the Info screen, save your changes to the document, click the File tab, then click Info**
   The comments have been removed from the file. The Info screen shows the document properties have been removed from the file.
9. **Submit the document to your instructor, close the file, then exit Word**

QUICK TIP
To recover unsaved changes to a file, click Manage Document on the Info screen, then click Recover Unsaved Documents.

QUICK TIP
A document property, such as author name, might appear automatically in a content control in a document. Stripping a file of document properties does not remove information from a content control.

FIGURE 2-28: Formatted document

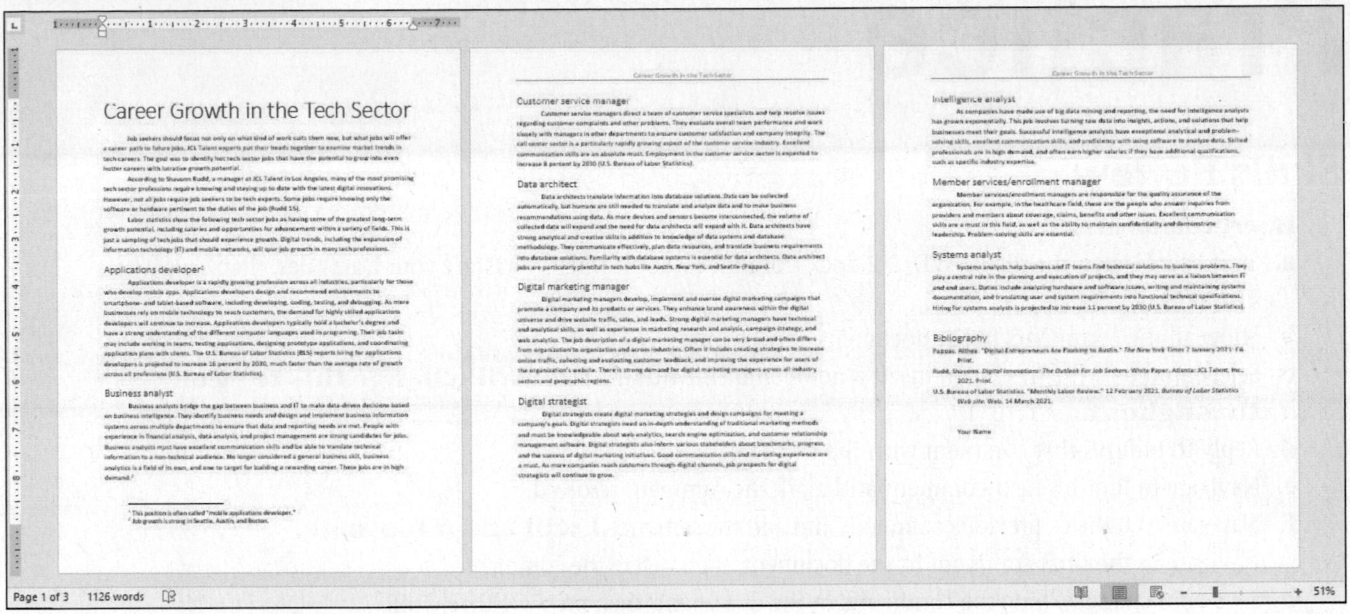

FIGURE 2-29: Results after inspecting document

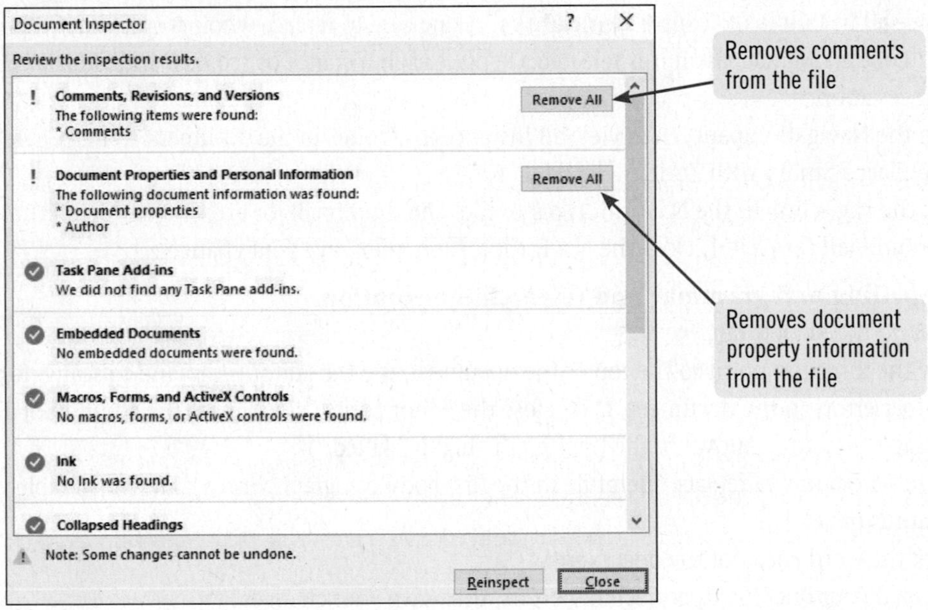

TABLE 2-3: Options on the Info screen

option	use to
Protect Document	Mark a document as final so that it is read-only and cannot be edited; encrypt a document so that a password is required to open it; restrict what kinds of changes can be made to a document and by whom; restrict access to editing, copying, and printing a document and add a digital signature to a document to verify its integrity
Check for Issues	Detect and remove unwanted information from a document, including document properties and comments; check for content that people with disabilities might find difficult to read; and check the document for features that are not supported by previous versions of Microsoft Word
Manage Document	Browse and recover draft versions of unsaved files

Practice

Skills Review

1. **Insert comments.**
   a. Start Word, open the file IL_WD_2-2.docx from the location where you store your Data Files, then save it as **IL_WD_2_Zone**.
   b. Show all the comments in the document, if necessary.
   c. Select Studio in the title, then insert a new comment with the text **I will change this to "Zone" throughout.**
   d. Reply to Judith's first comment with the text **OK.**
   e. Navigate to Judith's next comment and mark the comment resolved.
   f. Navigate to Judith's previous comment and add the sentence **I will add a footnote.**
   g. Navigate to the final comment in the document, then delete the comment.
   h. Save your changes, hide the comments in the document, then press CTRL+HOME.
2. **Find and replace text.**
   a. Using the Replace command, replace all instances of "2017" with **2019**.
   b. Replace all instances of "Studio" with **Zone**, taking care to match the case when you perform the replace.
   c. Replace all instances of "course" with **class,** taking care to replace whole words only when you perform the replace. (*Hint*: Deselect Match case if it is selected.) Replace each instance of "course" individually rather than replacing all instances at once.
   d. Open the Navigation pane, then view all instances of "zone" in the document to make sure no errors occurred when you replaced Studio with Zone.
   e. Click the Pages link in the Navigation pane, click the thumbnail for each page to scroll through the document, click the thumbnail for page 1, close the Navigation pane, then save your changes.
3. **Check spelling and grammar and research information.**
   a. Switch to the Review tab.
   b. Move the insertion point to the top of the document, use the Editor command to search for and correct spelling and grammar errors in the document, then close the Editor pane. (*Hint*: Ignore the addition of a question mark following "massage" and the removal of the hyphen in "highly-skilled.")
   c. Use the Thesaurus to replace "helpful" in the first body paragraph with a different suitable word, then close the Thesaurus pane.
   d. Check the word count of the document.
   e. Proofread your document, correct any errors, then save your changes.
4. **Change line spacing and indents.**
   a. Change the line spacing of the entire document to 1.5.
   b. Change the line spacing of the first body paragraph to 1.15.
   c. Indent the first line of the first body paragraph .3". (*Hint*: Use the Paragraph dialog box.)
   d. Remove the paragraph space under the first body paragraph, then save your changes.
5. **Apply styles to text.**
   a. Apply the Title style to the title "The Global Fitness Zone".
   b. Apply the Subtitle style to the subtitle "A Health, Fitness, and Rehabilitation Facility".
   c. Apply the Heading 1 style to each red heading in the document.
   d. Apply the Heading 2 style to each green heading in the document.
   e. With the insertion point in the first body paragraph, update the Normal style to match the first body paragraph.

Skills Review (continued)

- **f.** Modify the Title style to be based on no style.
- **g.** Modify the Subtitle, Heading 1, and Heading 2 styles to be based on no style.
- **h.** Change the theme of the document to Gallery. (*Hint*: Use the Design tab.)
- **i.** Select the title, change the font size to 36, change the font color to Red, Accent 1, Darker 25%, then apply bold.
- **j.** Select the subtitle, change the font size to 14, then add 24 points of space after the paragraph.
- **k.** Select the heading "Welcome…", add 6 points of space after the paragraph, then update the Heading 1 style to match the selection
- **l.** Select the heading "Benefits of Exercise", add 6 points of space before the paragraph, and 3 points of space after the paragraph, then update the Heading 2 style to match the selection.
- **m.** Scroll to the bottom of page 1, click the first item in the bulleted list, add 6 points of space before the paragraph, then save your changes.

6. Insert page numbers and page breaks.

- **a.** Scroll to the bottom of page 2, then insert a manual page break before the heading "Facilities and Services".
- **b.** Insert page numbers in the document at the bottom of the page. Select the Accent Bar 1 page number style from the gallery.
- **c.** Close the Footer area, scroll through the document to view the page number on each page.
- **d.** Turn on formatting marks, delete the manual page break at the bottom of page 2, then save your changes to the document.

7. Add headers and footers.

- **a.** Double-click the Footer area, then use the Go to Header button to move the insertion point to the Header area.
- **b.** Click the Header button, scroll down the gallery of built-in header designs, then select the Filigree header.
- **c.** Click the Document title content control in the header, then type **The Global Fitness Zone**.
- **d.** Replace the text in the Author content control with your name, press END to move the insertion point out of the content control, then press SPACEBAR. (*Note*: If your name does not appear in the header, right-click the Author content control, click Remove Content Control, then type your name in the header.)
- **e.** Close headers and footers, then scroll to view the header and footer on each page.
- **f.** Open headers and footers, select the text in the Header area, including the paragraph mark after your name, change the alignment of the selected text to left, then remove the first line indent. (*Hint*: You can drag the indent marker on the ruler or use the Paragraph dialog box to remove the first line indent.)
- **g.** Remove the header and footer from the first page of the document, close headers and footers, then save your changes.

8. Add footnotes and endnotes.

- **a.** Press CTRL+HOME, scroll down, place the insertion point at the end of the first body paragraph, insert a footnote, then type **Active people live longer and feel better!**
- **b.** Place the insertion point at the end of the first paragraph under the Getting Started heading, insert a footnote, then type **Each day is 1,440 minutes. We help you set aside 30 of them for physical activity.**
- **c.** Place the insertion point at the end of the Getting Started heading, insert a footnote, type **Always consult a physician before beginning an exercise program.**
- **d.** Change the number format of the footnotes to *, †, ‡, then save your changes.

9. Insert citations.

- **a.** Place the insertion point at the end of the second paragraph under the Benefits of Exercise heading (after "down from 52% in 2019" but before the period), then be sure the style for citations and bibliography is set to MLA Seventh Edition.
- **b.** Insert a citation, add a new source, enter the source information shown in the Create Source dialog box in **FIGURE 2-30**, then click OK.

Word

Skills Review (continued)

c. Place the insertion point at the end of the second paragraph under the Getting Started heading, insert a citation, then select Shree, Maxine from the list of sources.

d. Edit the citation to include the page number **22**.

e. Scroll to page 2, place the insertion point at the end of the "Be a morning exerciser" paragraph in the bulleted list, but before the ending period, insert a citation for WebMD, then save your changes.

FIGURE 2-30

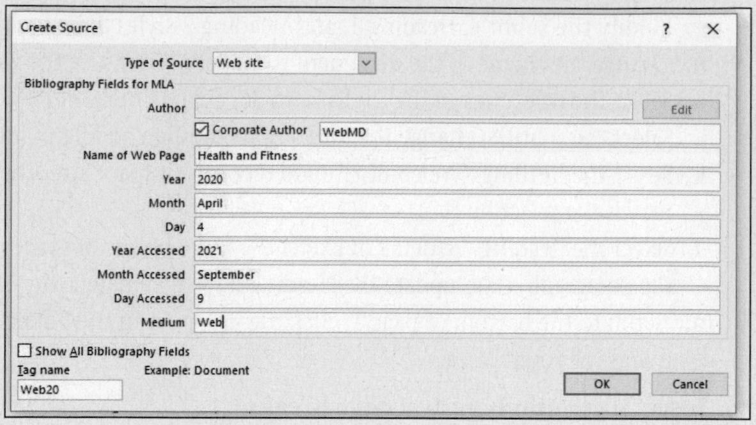

10. Create a bibliography.

a. Press CTRL+END, then insert a bibliography labeled **Works Cited**.

b. Open the Source Manager dialog box.

c. Delete the National Heart/Lung Health Institute source from the Current list.

d. Select the source Health, National Institute of: ... in the Current List, click Edit, click the Corporate Author check box, edit the entry so it reads **National Institute of Health**, click OK, then click Close.

e. Update the bibliography field.

f. With the bibliography field selected, click the Bibliographies button above the Bibliography field, then select References.

g. Click the Bibliographies button again, select Bibliography, then save your changes. Pages 1 and 3 of the formatted document are shown in **FIGURE 2-31**.

h. Save your changes to the document, then submit it to your instructor without closing the document.

FIGURE 2-31

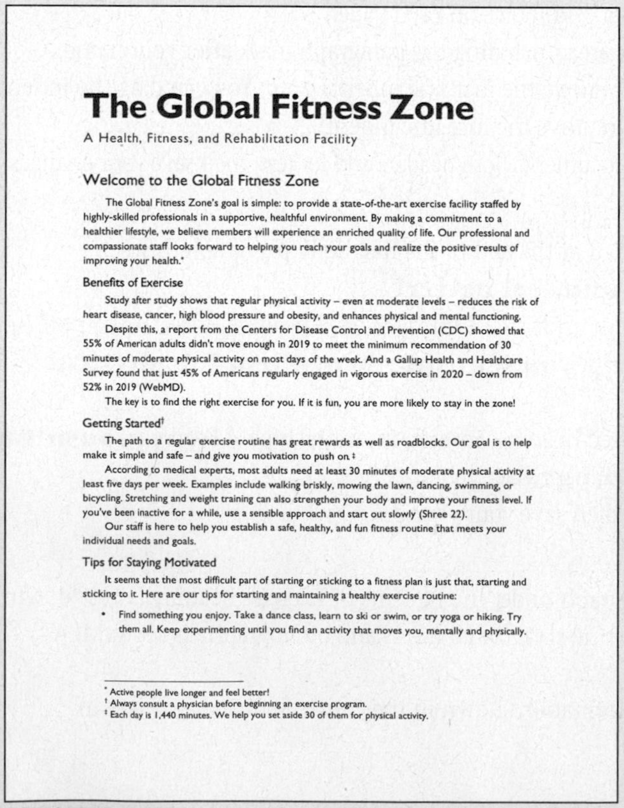

The Global Fitness Zone

A Health, Fitness, and Rehabilitation Facility

Welcome to the Global Fitness Zone

The Global Fitness Zone's goal is simple: to provide a state-of-the-art exercise facility staffed by highly-skilled professionals in a supportive, healthful environment. By making a commitment to a healthier lifestyle, we believe members will experience an enriched quality of life. Our professional and compassionate staff looks forward to helping you reach your goals and realize the positive results of improving your health.[*]

Benefits of Exercise

Study after study shows that regular physical activity – even at moderate levels – reduces the risk of heart disease, cancer, high blood pressure and obesity, and enhances physical and mental functioning.

Despite this, a report from the Centers for Disease Control and Prevention (CDC) showed that 55% of American adults didn't move enough in 2019 to meet the minimum recommendation of 30 minutes of moderate physical activity on most days of the week. And a Gallup Health and Healthcare Survey found that just 45% of Americans regularly engaged in vigorous exercise in 2020 – down from 52% in 2019 (WebMD).

The key is to find the right exercise for you. If it is fun, you are more likely to stay in the zone!

Getting Started[†]

The path to a regular exercise routine has great rewards as well as roadblocks. Our goal is to help make it simple and safe – and give you motivation to push on.[‡]

According to medical experts, most adults need at least 30 minutes of moderate physical activity at least five days per week. Examples include walking briskly, mowing the lawn, dancing, swimming, or bicycling. Stretching and weight training can also strengthen your body and improve your fitness level. If you've been inactive for a while, use a sensible approach and start out slowly (Shree 22).

Our staff is here to help you establish a safe, healthy, and fun fitness routine that meets your individual needs and goals.

Tips for Staying Motivated

It seems that the most difficult part of starting or sticking to a fitness plan is just that, starting and sticking to it. Here are our tips for starting and maintaining a healthy exercise routine:

- Find something you enjoy. Take a dance class, learn to ski or swim, or try yoga or hiking. Try them all. Keep experimenting until you find an activity that moves you, mentally and physically.

[*] Active people live longer and feel better!
[†] Always consult a physician before beginning an exercise program.
[‡] Each day is 1,440 minutes. We help you set aside 30 of them for physical activity.

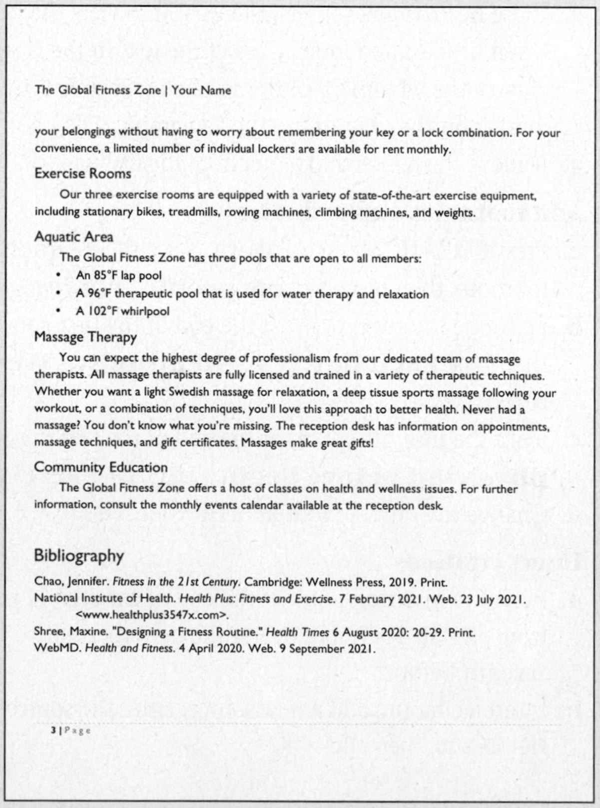

The Global Fitness Zone | Your Name

your belongings without having to worry about remembering your key or a lock combination. For your convenience, a limited number of individual lockers are available for rent monthly.

Exercise Rooms

Our three exercise rooms are equipped with a variety of state-of-the-art exercise equipment, including stationary bikes, treadmills, rowing machines, climbing machines, and weights.

Aquatic Area

The Global Fitness Zone has three pools that are open to all members:

- An 85°F lap pool
- A 96°F therapeutic pool that is used for water therapy and relaxation
- A 102°F whirlpool

Massage Therapy

You can expect the highest degree of professionalism from our dedicated team of massage therapists. All massage therapists are fully licensed and trained in a variety of therapeutic techniques. Whether you want a light Swedish massage for relaxation, a deep tissue sports massage following your workout, or a combination of techniques, you'll love this approach to better health. Never had a massage? You don't know what you're missing. The reception desk has information on appointments, massage techniques, and gift certificates. Massages make great gifts!

Community Education

The Global Fitness Zone offers a host of classes on health and wellness issues. For further information, consult the monthly events calendar available at the reception desk.

Bibliography

Chao, Jennifer. *Fitness in the 21st Century*. Cambridge: Wellness Press, 2019. Print.
National Institute of Health. *Health Plus: Fitness and Exercise*. 7 February 2021. Web. 23 July 2021. <www.healthplus3547x.com>.
Shree, Maxine. "Designing a Fitness Routine." *Health Times* 6 August 2020: 20-29. Print.
WebMD. *Health and Fitness*. 4 April 2020. Web. 9 September 2021.

3 | Page

Skills Review (continued)

11. Inspect a document.

a. Save a copy of the document as **IL_WD_2_Zone_Inspected** to the drive and folder where you store your Data Files.
b. Open the Navigation pane, click the Headings link, click the headings listed in the Navigation pane to scroll through the document, then close the Navigation pane.
c. Use the Go To command to move the insertion point to the top of page 1.
d. Use the Find and Replace dialog box to find all em dashes in the document, but do not replace the em dashes. (*Hint*: Scroll through the document using the Find Next button.)
e. Use the Find and Replace dialog box to find text formatted with the Heading 2 style, but do not replace the text.
f. Select a word in the document, look it up using the Search button on the References tab, then close the Search pane.
g. Show the comments in the document, then, using the Review tab, delete all the comments in the document.
h. Use the Check for Issues command to run the Document Inspector.
i. Remove all document property and personal information data from the document, then save your changes.
j. Submit a copy of the document to your instructor, close the document, then exit Word.

Independent Challenge 1

The Riverwalk Medical Clinic publishes a variety of newsletters and information reports related to health and wellness for patients. Your colleague has drafted a newsletter about staying healthy while traveling and forwarded the file to you. The file includes comments with instructions for finalizing the document. You need to add citations and footnotes and format the newsletter for distribution to patients.

Word

a. Start Word, open the file IL_WD_2-3.docx from the drive and folder where you store your Data Files, save it as **IL_WD_2_Newsletter**, then read the document to get a feel for its contents.
b. Show the comments in the document, scroll through the comments, reply to or resolve each comment, add a comment, then delete all comments from the document.
c. Format the newsletter using styles. Apply the Title style to the orange text, the Heading 1 style to the blue text, and the Heading 2 style to the green text. (You will format the masthead after formatting the body of the document.)
d. Apply a theme to the document. Choose a theme that suits the purpose and audience for the document. You can change the theme colors or style set if you wish.
e. Change the font size of the title so that the title fits on one line.
f. Modify the Heading 1 and Heading 2 styles so that the font, font size, font color, and paragraph spacing of the headings gives the newsletter an attractive and cohesive look.
g. Using styles, format the first three lines of the document as a masthead for the newsletter. The masthead for this document should be attractive, but should not compete with the title of the document for attention. After applying styles, apply other formats, such as font size, font color, text effects, paragraph alignment, and borders to customize the look of the masthead.
h. Add a header to the document using the Filigree header style. Type **Riverwalk Medical Clinic** in the Document title content control, then type your name in the Author content control. (*Hint*: If the Author content control shows different text, replace that text with your name.)
i. Add a page number to the bottom of each page using the page number style of your choice.
j. Remove headers and footers from the first page of the document.
k. Use the Find command or the Navigation pane to find the text specified in the table below, then add a footnote at each location, using the footnote text specified in the table.

Independent Challenge 1 (continued)

Find text	Footnote text
behavior and health of the traveler	**Behavior is a critical factor. For example, going outdoors in a malaria-endemic area could result in becoming infected.**
public health	**It is best to consult a travel medicine specialist.**
tweezers	**Pack these items in checked luggage.**
Sunscreen	**SPF 15 or greater.**

l. Change the Citations and Bibliography style to MLA Seventh Edition. Use the Find command or the Navigation pane to find the text specified in the table below, then add a citation at each location, using the source specified in the table. Some citations include a page number. Remember to insert the citation before the period at the end of a sentence.

Find text	Citation source	Citation page number
people travel	World Tourism Organization	15
consequences	World Health Organization	
Source:	Johnson, Margaret	50
prevalent in sub-Saharan Africa	Centers for Disease Control and Prevention	
pregnancy	Clinton, Edmund	92

m. Press CTRL+END, then add a bibliography to the newsletter.

n. Check the document for spelling and grammar errors, then use the thesaurus to replace a word with a synonym.

o. View the document in Multiple pages view, then make any formatting adjustments necessary so that the document flows smoothly between pages and is easy to read. **FIGURE 2-32** shows a sample first page of the newsletter.

p. Save the document, submit a copy to your instructor, close the document, then exit Word.

FIGURE 2-32

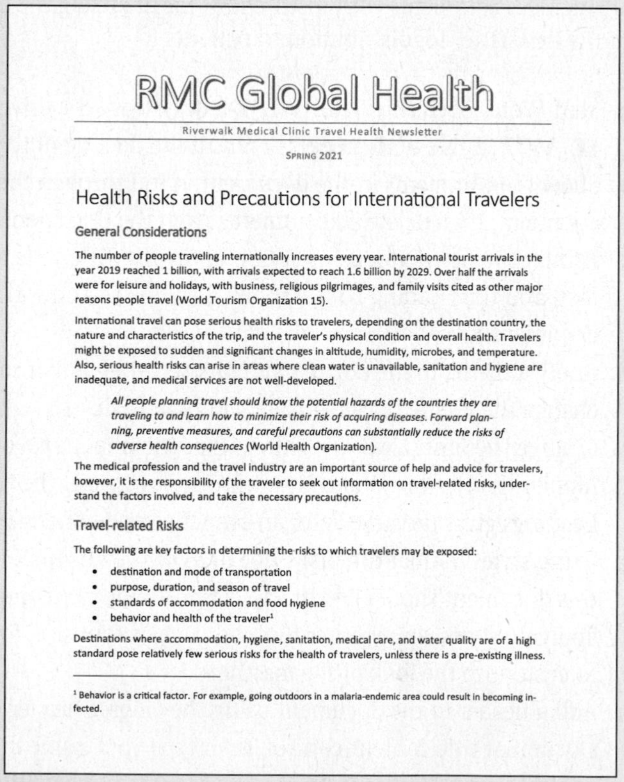

RMC Global Health

Riverwalk Medical Clinic Travel Health Newsletter

SPRING 2021

Health Risks and Precautions for International Travelers

General Considerations

The number of people traveling internationally increases every year. International tourist arrivals in the year 2019 reached 1 billion, with arrivals expected to reach 1.6 billion by 2029. Over half the arrivals were for leisure and holidays, with business, religious pilgrimages, and family visits cited as other major reasons people travel (World Tourism Organization 15).

International travel can pose serious health risks to travelers, depending on the destination country, the nature and characteristics of the trip, and the traveler's physical condition and overall health. Travelers might be exposed to sudden and significant changes in altitude, humidity, microbes, and temperature. Also, serious health risks can arise in areas where clean water is unavailable, sanitation and hygiene are inadequate, and medical services are not well-developed.

All people planning travel should know the potential hazards of the countries they are traveling to and learn how to minimize their risk of acquiring diseases. Forward planning, preventive measures, and careful precautions can substantially reduce the risks of adverse health consequences (World Health Organization).

The medical profession and the travel industry are an important source of help and advice for travelers, however, it is the responsibility of the traveler to seek out information on travel-related risks, understand the factors involved, and take the necessary precautions.

Travel-related Risks

The following are key factors in determining the risks to which travelers may be exposed:

- destination and mode of transportation
- purpose, duration, and season of travel
- standards of accommodation and food hygiene
- behavior and health of the traveler[1]

Destinations where accommodation, hygiene, sanitation, medical care, and water quality are of a high standard pose relatively few serious risks for the health of travelers, unless there is a pre-existing illness.

[1] Behavior is a critical factor. For example, going outdoors in a malaria-endemic area could result in becoming infected.

Independent Challenge 2

As an administrative assistant at a community college, you frequently format the research papers written by the members of your department. The format recommended by the *MLA Handbook for Writers of Research Papers*, a style guide that includes information on preparing, writing, and formatting research papers, is the standard format used by many schools, colleges, and universities. In this independent challenge, you will research the MLA guidelines for formatting a research paper and use the guidelines you find to format the pages of a research report.

FIGURE 2-33

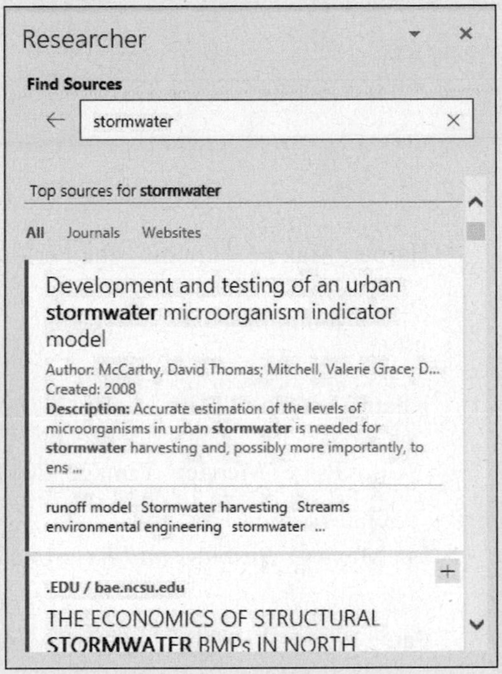

a. Use your favorite search engine to search the web for information on the MLA guidelines for formatting a research report. Use the keywords **MLA Style** and **research paper format** to conduct your search.

b. Look for information on the proper formatting for the following aspects of a research paper: paper size, margins, title page or first page of the report, line spacing, paragraph indentation, and page numbers. Also find information on proper formatting for citations and a works cited page. Print the information you find.

c. Start Word, open the file IL_WD_2-4.docx from the drive and folder where you store your Data Files, then save it as **IL_WD_2_Research**. Using the information you learned, format this document as a research report.

d. Correct spelling and grammar errors in the document. If possible, add "stormwater" to the Word dictionary.

e. Adjust the margins, set the line spacing, and add page numbers to the document in the format recommended by the MLA. Use **Stormwater Management: A Case Study** as the title for your sample report, use your name as the author name, and use the name of the course you are enrolled in currently as well as the instructor's name for that course. Make sure to format the title page exactly as the MLA style dictates.

f. Format the remaining text as the body of the research report. Indent the first line of each paragraph rather than use quadruple spacing between paragraphs.

g. Create five sources and insert five citations in the document—including at least one journal article and one website. If possible, use the Researcher tool to add sources and citations. **FIGURE 2-33** shows the Researcher pane with sample sources. You can also make up sources. (*Note*: For this practice document, you are allowed to make up sources. Never make up sources for real research papers.)

h. Add two citation placeholders to the document.

i. Create a works cited page, following MLA style. If necessary, edit the format of the citations and works cited page to conform to MLA format.

j. Save the document, submit a copy to your instructor, close the document, then exit Word.

Visual Workshop

Use a blank document to create the Works Cited page shown in **FIGURE 2-34**, then save the document as **IL_WD_2_WorksCited**. Use 12-point Times New Roman for the text, double-space the lines in the document, and apply a hanging indent to the paragraphs in the list. Format "Works Cited" with the Heading 1 style and center the heading at the top of the document. Add your name and a page number to the header, then format the header text in 12-point Times New Roman. Correct spelling and grammar errors, remove the document property information from the file, then submit a copy to your instructor.

FIGURE 2-34

Works Cited

Harper, Maxine. "Landing the Perfect Job." *eHow,* www.ehow.com/landing-32980-the-perfect-job.html.

Khatri, Jamaica. "Data Analyst." *The Vintage Book of Contemporary Professions,* edited by Roger Mendez, Vintage, 2019, pp. 204-07.

Lu, Maya C. *Business and Environmentalism.* Reed Publishers, 2020.

Patel, Simon. "10 Tips for Job Seekers." *Working: Business Careers for the Digital World,* 20 Aug. 2020, example.com/article/working. Accessed 14 June 2021.

Formatting Text and Graphics

CASE You have been asked to finalize a report on the activities of the Technology department that will be distributed to other departments at JCL Talent. After formatting the headings in the report, you use tabs and create tables to organize the information so that it is easy to understand. Finally, you illustrate the report with images, shapes, and SmartArt.

Module Objectives

After completing this module, you will be able to:

- Use the Format Painter
- Work with tabs
- Add borders and shading
- Insert a table
- Insert and delete rows and columns
- Apply a table style
- Insert online pictures
- Size and scale a graphic
- Draw and format shapes
- Arrange graphic objects
- Create SmartArt graphics

Files You Will Need

IL_WD_3-1.docx
IL_WD_3-2.docx
IL_WD_3-3.docx
IL_WD_3-4.docx
IL_WD_3-5.docx

Use the Format Painter

Learning Outcomes
- Apply formatting using the Format Painter
- Clear formatting
- Insert special characters

You can dramatically change the appearance of text by applying different font styles, font effects, and character-spacing effects. When you are satisfied with the formatting of specific text, you can quickly apply the same formats to other text in the document using the Format Painter. The **Format Painter** is a powerful Word feature that allows you to copy all the format settings applied to selected text to other text that you want to format the same way. **CASE** *You enhance the appearance of the text in the report on the activities of the Technology department by applying different font styles and text effects. You also insert the date and a copyright symbol in the document.*

STEPS

1. **sam Start Word, open the file IL_WD_3-1.docx from the location where you store your Data Files, save it as IL_WD_3_Update, then drag the Zoom slider to 100**
2. **Select the title Update: JCL Technical Careers Division, click the Text Effects and Typography button in the Font group on the Home tab, click the Fill: Blue; Accent color 1; Shadow style (the second WordArt style in the first row), click the Font Size arrow, click 24, click the Font Color arrow, then click Green, Accent 6, Darker 25%**
   The title is formatted in 24-point WordArt style, green.
3. **Select the heading Career Connections Webinar Series to display the Mini toolbar, click the Font Size arrow, click 14, click the Bold button B, click the Italic button I, click the Font Color arrow, click the Blue, Accent 1, Darker 25% color in the theme colors, then deselect the text**
   The heading is formatted in 14-point bold, italic, and blue.
4. **Select Career Connections Webinar Series, then click the Format Painter button in the Clipboard group on the Home tab**
   The pointer changes to .
5. **Scroll down, drag to select the heading Social Media Advertising Campaign, then deselect the text**
   The heading is formatted in 14-point bold, italic, and blue, as shown in **FIGURE 3-1**.
6. **Select Social Media Advertising Campaign again, then double-click the Format Painter button**
   Double-clicking the Format Painter button allows the Format Painter to remain active until you turn it off. By keeping the Format Painter active, you can apply formatting to multiple items.
7. **Scroll down, select the headings Upcoming Conferences and Technical Careers Division Personnel, then click the Format Painter button to turn off the Format Painter**
   The headings are formatted in 14-point bold, italic, and blue.
8. **Press CTRL+END, type Prepared by, press SPACEBAR and type your name followed by a comma, press SPACEBAR, click the Insert tab, then click the Insert Date and Time button in the Text group**
   The Date and Time dialog box opens with available formats for inserting the date and time.
9. **Select the third format in the list, click OK to insert the current date at the insertion point, press ENTER, then click the Symbol button in the Symbols group**
   A gallery of commonly used symbols opens similar to the one in **FIGURE 3-2**. You may see a different selection of symbols depending on which symbols you insert most frequently. You can insert a symbol from this gallery or click More Symbols to open a larger gallery of symbols.
10. **Click the copyright symbol © in the gallery, press SPACEBAR, type JCL Talent, click the Home tab, press CTRL+HOME, then save your changes**
    The copyright symbol is inserted before JCL Talent.

QUICK TIP
To change the WordArt style currently applied to text, select the text, click the Text Effects and Typography button, then select a different WordArt style from the gallery.

TROUBLE
Move the pointer over the document text to see .

QUICK TIP
You can also press ESC to turn off the Format Painter.

QUICK TIP
You can also click in the left margin to select the heading text.

QUICK TIP
To insert the date as a field that is updated automatically, select the Update automatically check box.

TROUBLE
If you do not see the copyright symbol, click More Symbols, select the code in the Character code box, type 00A9, click Insert, then click Close.

FIGURE 3-1: Formats copied and applied using the Format Painter

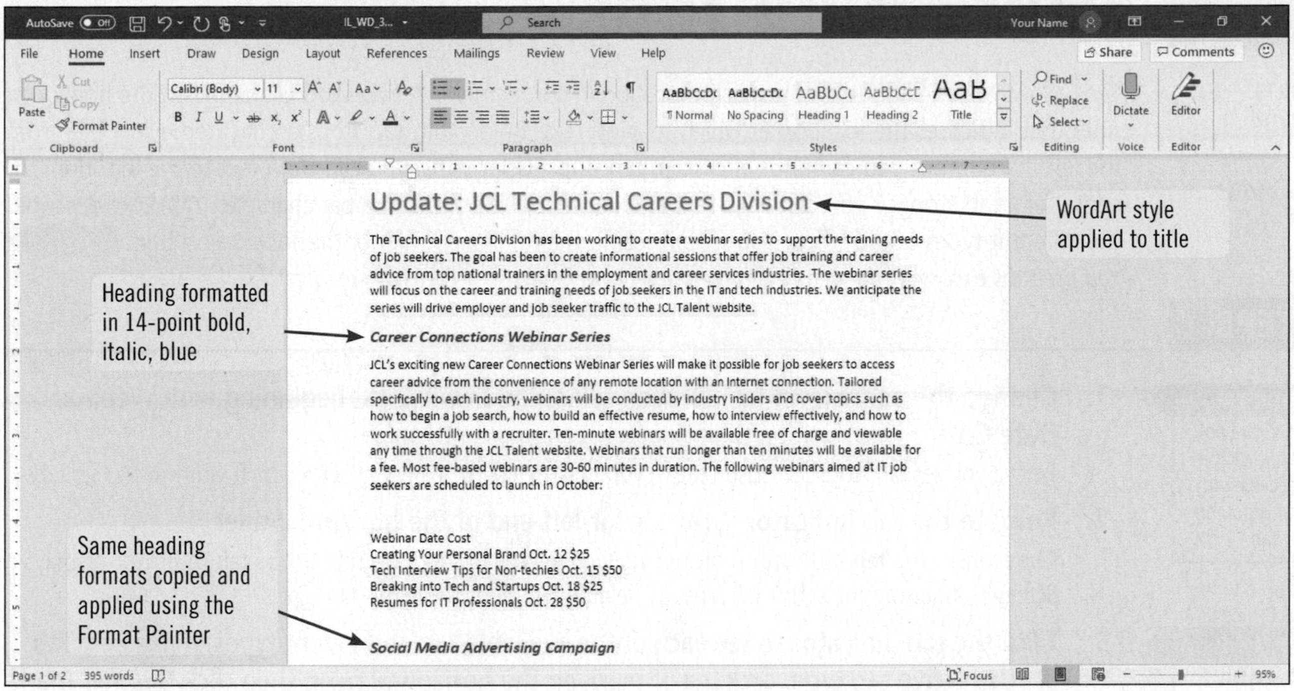

FIGURE 3-2: Symbol gallery

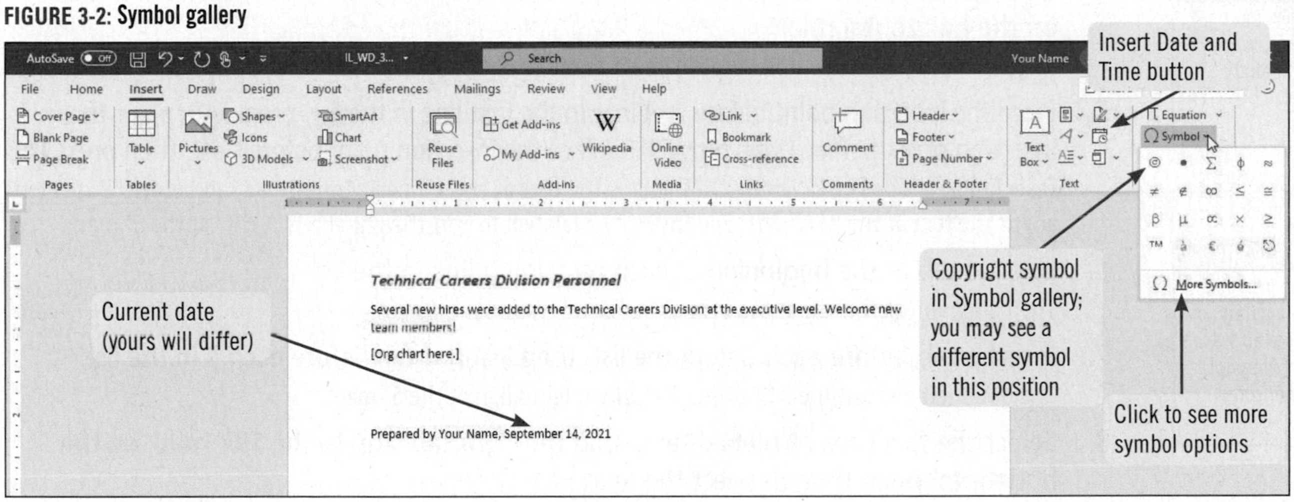

Clearing formatting from text

If you are unhappy with the way text is formatted, you can use the Clear All Formatting command to return the text to the default format settings. The default format includes font and paragraph formatting: text is formatted in 11-point Calibri, and paragraphs are left-aligned with 1.08 point line spacing, 8 points of space after, and no indents. To clear formatting from text and return it to the default format, select the text you want to clear, and then click the Clear All Formatting button in the Font group on the Home tab. If you prefer to return the text to the default font and remove all paragraph formatting, making the text 11-point Calibri, left-aligned, single spaced, with no paragraph spacing or indents, select the text and then click the No Spacing button in the Styles group on the Home tab.

Word
Module 3

Work with Tabs

Learning Outcome
- Set and use tab stops

Tabs allow you to align text at a specific location in a document. A **tab stop** is a point on the horizontal ruler that indicates the location at which to align text. By default, tab stops are located every 1/2" from the left margin, but you can also set custom tab stops. Using tabs, you can align text to the left, right, or center of a tab stop, or you can align text at a decimal point or insert a bar character. **TABLE 3-1** describes the different types of tab stops. You set tabs using the horizontal ruler or the Tabs dialog box. **CASE** *You use tabs to format the detailed information on webinars so it is easy to read.*

STEPS

QUICK TIP
If the rulers are not displayed, click the Ruler check box in the Show group on the View tab.

1. **Change the zoom level to 120, then select the five-line list beginning with Webinar Date Cost**
   Before you set tab stops for existing text, you must select the paragraphs for which you want to set tabs.

2. **Point to the tab indicator at the far-left end of the horizontal ruler**
   The icon in the tab indicator indicates the active type of tab; pointing to the tab indicator displays a ScreenTip naming the active tab type. By default, left tab is the active tab type.

QUICK TIP
To remove a tab stop, drag it off the ruler.

3. **Click the tab indicator to see each of the available tab and indent types, make Left Tab the active tab type, click the 1" mark on the horizontal ruler, then click the 3¾" mark on the horizontal ruler**
   Clicking the horizontal ruler inserts a tab stop of the active type for the selected paragraph or paragraphs. A left tab stop is inserted at the 1" mark and the 3¾" mark.

TROUBLE
If you click more than twice, keep clicking until the Right Tab icon again appears.

4. **Click the tab indicator twice so the Right Tab icon is active, then click the 5" mark on the horizontal ruler**
   A right tab stop is inserted at the 5" mark on the horizontal ruler, as shown in **FIGURE 3-3**.

5. **Place the insertion point before Webinar in the first line in the list, press TAB, place the insertion point before Date, press TAB, place the insertion point before Cost, then press TAB**
   Inserting a tab before "Webinar" left-aligns the text at the 1" mark, inserting a tab before "Date" left-aligns the text at the 3¾" mark, and inserting a tab before "Cost" right-aligns "Cost" at the 5" mark.

QUICK TIP
Place the insertion point in a paragraph to see the tab stops for that paragraph on the horizontal ruler.

6. **Insert a tab at the beginning of each remaining line in the list**
   The paragraphs left-align at the 1" mark.

7. **Insert a tab before each Oct. in the list, then insert a tab before each $ in the list**
   The dates left-align at the 3¾" mark. The prices right-align at the 5" mark.

8. **Select the five lines of tabbed text, drag the right tab stop to the 5½" mark on the horizontal ruler, then deselect the text**
   Dragging the tab stop moves it to a new location. The prices right-align at the 5½" mark.

QUICK TIP
Double-click a tab stop on the ruler to open the Tabs dialog box.

9. **Select the last four lines of tabbed text, click the Launcher in the Paragraph group, then click Tabs at the bottom of the Paragraph dialog box**
   The Tabs dialog box opens, as shown in **FIGURE 3-4**. You can use the Tabs dialog box to set tab stops, change the position or alignment of existing tab stops, clear tab stops, and apply tab leaders to tabs. **Tab leaders** are lines that appear in front of tabbed text.

10. **Click 3.75" in the Tab stop position list box, click the 2 option button in the Leader section, click Set, click 5.5" in the Tab stop position list box, click the 2 option button in the Leader section, click Set, click OK, deselect the text, then save your changes**
    A dotted tab leader is added before each 3.75" and 5.5" tab stop in the last four lines of tabbed text, as shown in **FIGURE 3-5**.

FIGURE 3-3: Left and right tab stops on the horizontal ruler

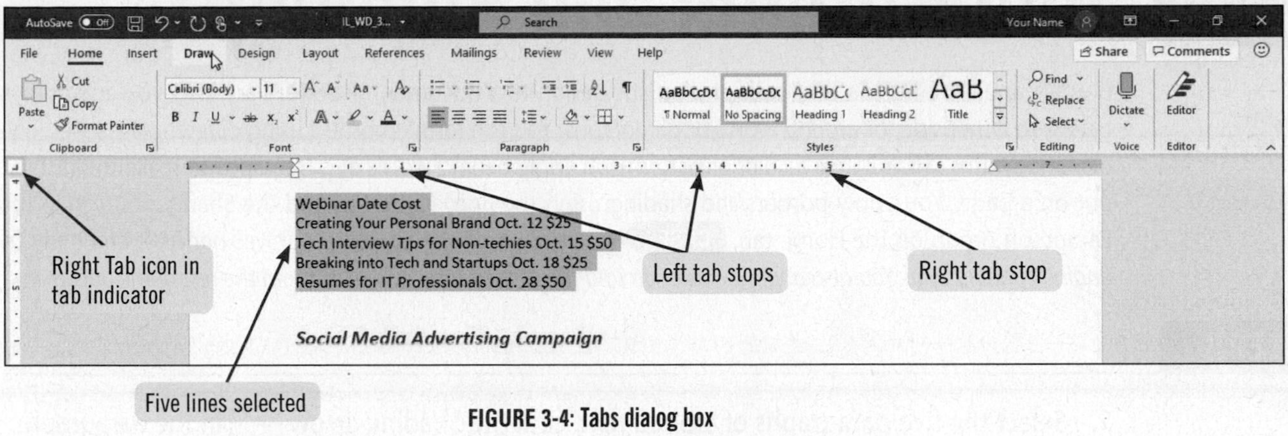

FIGURE 3-4: Tabs dialog box

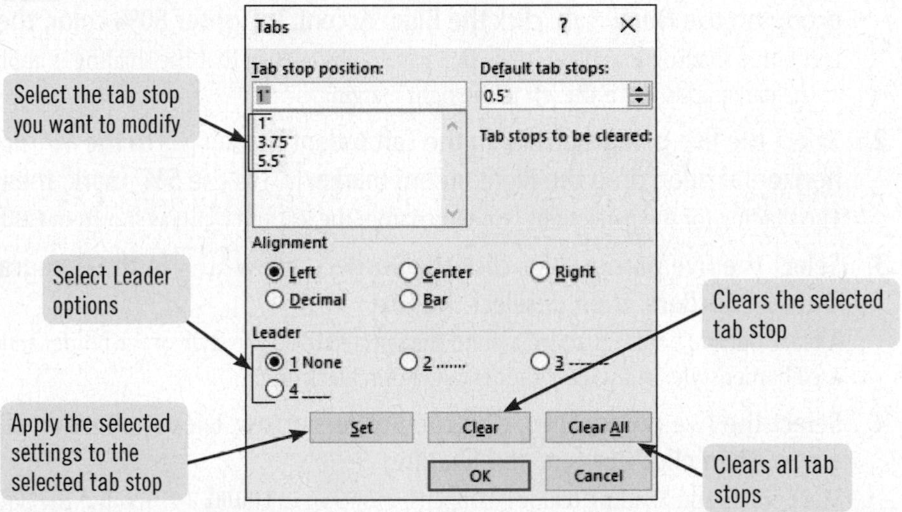

FIGURE 3-5: Tab leaders

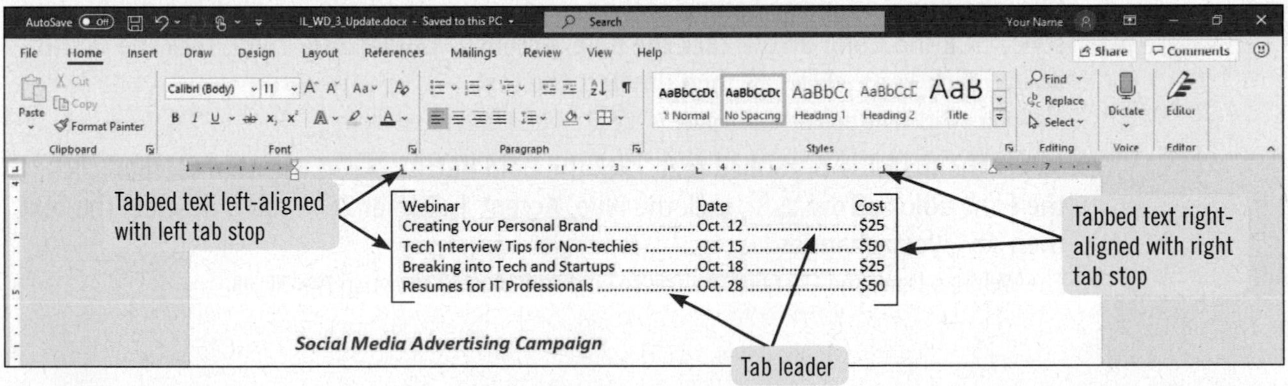

TABLE 3-1: Types of tabs

tab	use to
Left tab	Set the start position of text so that text runs to the right of the tab stop as you type
Center tab	Set the center align position of text so that text stays centered on the tab stop as you type
Right tab	Set the right or end position of text so that text moves to the left of the tab stop as you type
Decimal tab	Set the position of the decimal point so that numbers align around the decimal point as you type
Bar tab	Insert a vertical bar at the tab position

Add Borders and Shading

Learning Outcomes
- Apply shading to text
- Apply borders to text

Borders and shading can add color and artistic design to a document. **Borders** are lines you add above, below, to either side, or around words or paragraphs. You can format borders using different line styles, colors, and widths. **Shading** is a color or pattern you apply behind words or paragraphs to make them stand out on a page. You apply borders and shading using the Borders button and the Shading button in the Paragraph group on the Home tab. **CASE** *You enhance the tabbed text for webinar costs and dates by adding shading to it. You also apply a border around the tabbed text to set it off from the rest of the document.*

STEPS

1. **Select the five paragraphs of tabbed text, click the Shading arrow in the Paragraph group on the Home tab, click the Blue, Accent 1, Lighter 80% color, then deselect the text**
   Light blue shading is applied to the five paragraphs. Notice that the shading is applied to the entire width of the paragraphs, from the left to the right margin.
2. **Select the five paragraphs, drag the Left Indent marker to the ¾" mark on the horizontal ruler, drag the Right Indent marker to the 5¾" mark, then deselect the text**
   The shading for the paragraphs is indented from the left and right, as shown in **FIGURE 3-6**.
3. **Select the five paragraphs, click the Borders arrow in the Paragraph group, click Outside Borders, then deselect the text**
   A black outside border is added around the selected text. The style of the border added is the most recently used border style, in this case the default, a thin black line.
4. **Select the five paragraphs, click the Borders arrow, click No Border, click the Borders arrow, then click Borders and Shading**
   The Borders and Shading dialog box opens, as shown in **FIGURE 3-7**. You use the Borders tab to change the border style, color, and width, and to add boxes and lines to words or paragraphs.
5. **Click the Box icon in the Setting section, scroll down the Style list, click the double-line style, click the Color arrow, click the Blue, Accent 1, Darker 25% color, click the Width arrow, click ¾ pt, click OK, then deselect the text**
   A ¾-point dark blue double-line border is added around the tabbed text.
6. **Select the first line of tabbed text, click the Bold button B on the Mini toolbar, click the Font Color arrow, click the Blue, Accent 1, Darker 25% color, deselect the text, then save your changes**
   The Webinar, Date, and Cost text changes to bold dark blue, as shown in **FIGURE 3-8**.

Underlining text

Another way to call attention to text and to enhance the appearance of a document is to apply an underline style to words you want to highlight. The Underline arrow in the Font group displays straight, dotted, wavy, dashed, and mixed underline styles, along with a gallery of colors to choose from. To apply an underline to text, select it, click the Underline arrow, and then select an underline style from the list. For a wider variety of underline styles, click More Underlines in the list, and then select an underline style in the Font dialog box. You can change the color of an underline at any time by selecting the underlined text, clicking the Underline arrow, pointing to Underline Color, and then choosing from the options in the color gallery. If you want to remove an underline from text, select the underlined text, and then click the Underline button.

FIGURE 3-6: Shading applied to the tabbed text

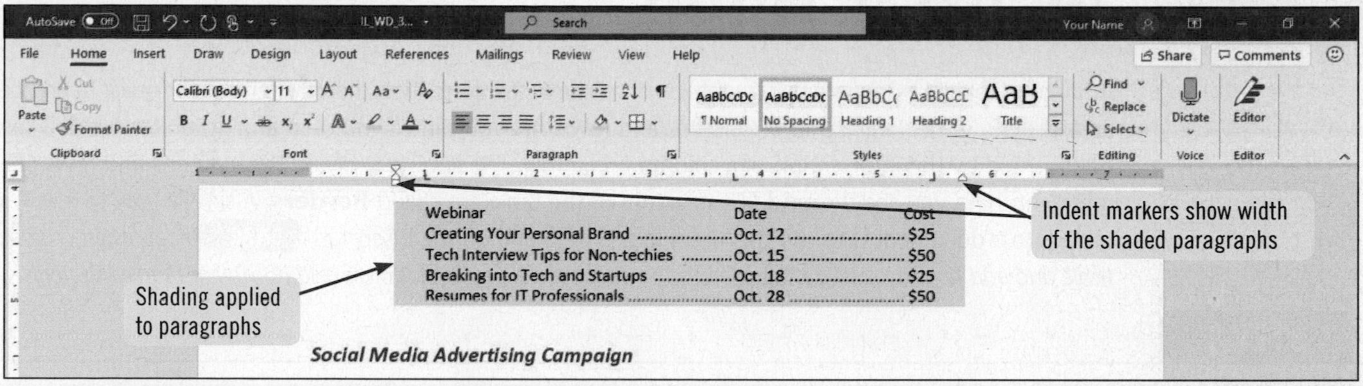

FIGURE 3-7: Borders tab in Borders and Shading dialog box

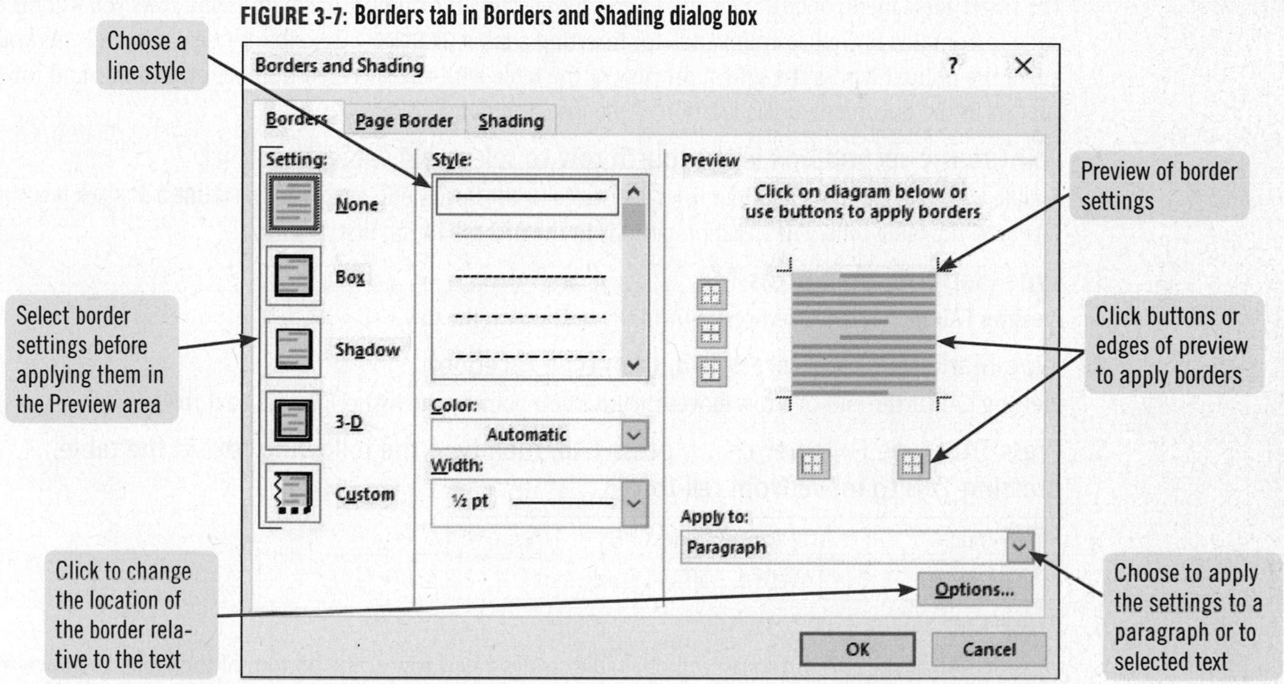

FIGURE 3-8: Borders and shading applied to the document

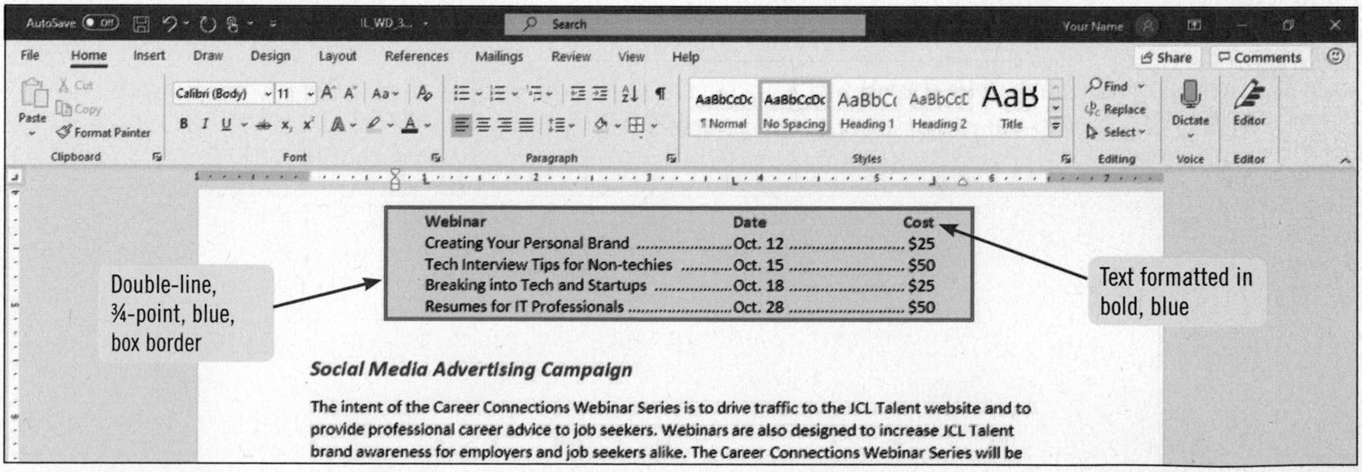

Word

Word
Module 3

Insert a Table

Learning Outcomes
- Insert a table
- Select and enter table data

Adding a table to a document is a useful way to illustrate information that is intended for quick reference and analysis. A **table** is a grid of columns and rows that you can fill with text and graphics. A **cell** is the box formed by the intersection of a column and a row. The lines that divide the columns and rows of a table and help you see the grid-like structure of the table are called **borders**. A simple way to insert a table into a document is to use the Insert Table command on the Insert tab. **CASE** *You insert a blank table and add text to organize the information about social media platforms and JCL Talent marketing goals.*

STEPS

1. **Scroll down, place the insertion point in the blank paragraph above the Upcoming Conferences heading, click the Insert tab, then click the Table button in the Tables group**
   The Insert Table menu opens. It includes a grid for selecting the number of columns and rows you want the table to contain, as well as commands for inserting a table. **TABLE 3-2** describes these commands. As you move the pointer across the grid, a preview of the table with the specified number of columns and rows appears in the document at the location of the insertion point.
2. **Point to the second box in the fourth row to select 2x4 Table, then click**
   A table with two columns and four rows is inserted in the document, as shown in **FIGURE 3-9**. Black borders surround the table cells. The insertion point is in the first cell in the first row.
3. **Type Platform, then press TAB**
   Pressing TAB moves the insertion point to the next cell in the row.
4. **Type Marketing Goal, press TAB, then type Facebook**
   Pressing TAB at the end of a row moves the insertion point to the first cell in the next row.
5. **Press TAB, type Follower count, press TAB, then type the following text in the table, pressing TAB to move from cell to cell**

Instagram	Brand awareness
LinkedIn	Website traffic/Conversions

6. **Press TAB**
   Pressing TAB at the end of the last cell of a table creates a new row at the bottom of the table, as shown in **FIGURE 3-10**. The insertion point is located in the first cell in the new row.

TROUBLE
If you pressed TAB after the last row, click the Undo button on the Quick Access toolbar to remove the new blank row.

7. **Type the following, pressing TAB to move from cell to cell and to create a new row**

WhatsApp	Website traffic
Twitter	Promoted tweets

8. **Save your changes**
   The completed table is shown in **FIGURE 3-11**.

FIGURE 3-9: Blank table

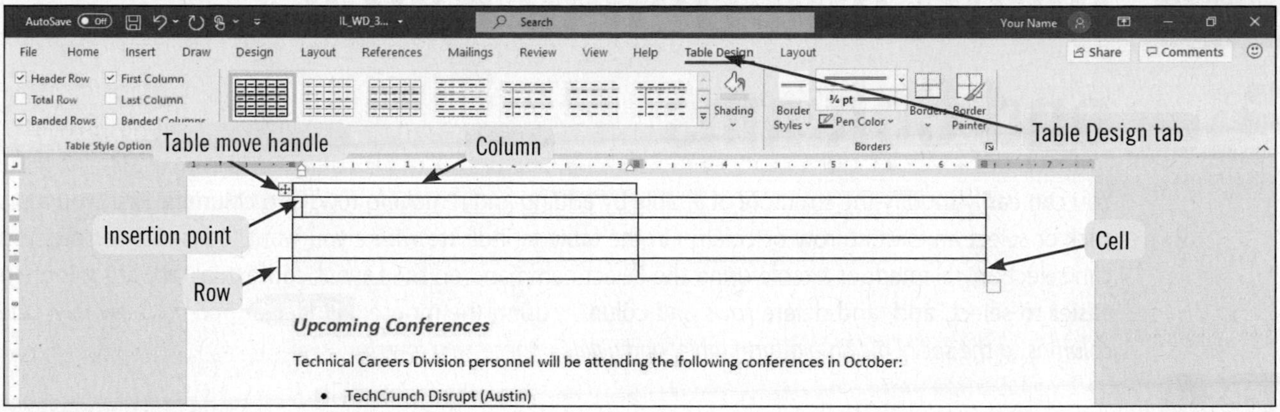

FIGURE 3-10: New row in table

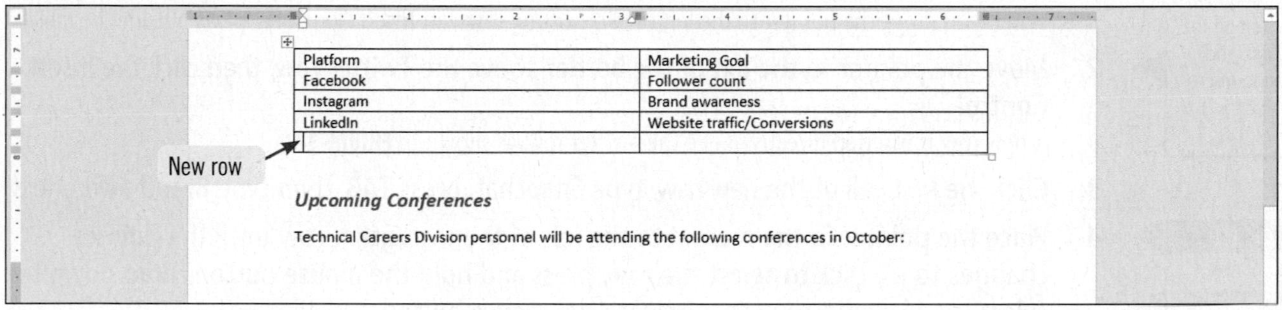

FIGURE 3-11: Text in the table

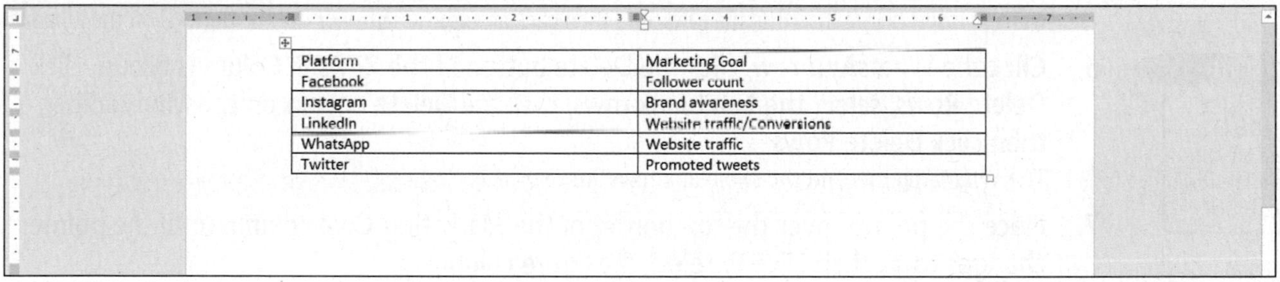

TABLE 3-2: Table menu commands

command	use to
Insert Table	Create a table with any number of columns and rows and select an AutoFit behavior
Draw Table	Create a complex table by drawing the table columns and rows
Convert Text to Table	Convert text that is separated by tabs, commas, or another separator character into a table
Excel Spreadsheet	Insert a blank Excel worksheet into the document as an embedded object
Quick Tables	Insert a preformatted table template and replace the placeholder data with your own data

Word

Word
Module 3

Learning Outcome
- Insert and delete rows and columns

Insert and Delete Rows and Columns

You can easily modify the structure of a table by adding and removing rows and columns. First, you must click or select an existing row or column in the table to indicate where you want to insert or delete. You can select any element of a table using the Select command on the Layout contextual tab, but it is often easier to select, add, and delete rows and columns using the mouse. **CASE** *You add new rows and columns to the social media platform table, and delete unnecessary rows.*

STEPS

QUICK TIP
You can also insert a row by right-clicking a row, clicking the Insert button on the Mini toolbar, and then clicking Insert Above or Insert Below.

QUICK TIP
If the end of row mark is not selected, you have selected only the text in the row, not the row itself.

QUICK TIP
If you select a row and press DELETE, you delete only the contents of the row, not the row itself.

QUICK TIP
To select a cell, place the pointer near the left border of the cell, then click.

QUICK TIP
You can use the arrow keys or press TAB to move the insertion point from cell to cell.

1. **Click the Home tab, click the Show/Hide ¶ button ¶ in the Paragraph group to display formatting marks, then move the pointer up and down the left edge of the table**
   An end of cell mark appears at the end of each cell, and an end of row mark appears at the end of each row. When you move the pointer to the left of two existing rows, an Insert Control appears outside the table.
2. **Move the pointer to the left of the border above the Twitter row, then click the Insert Control**
   A new row is inserted directly above the Twitter row, as shown in **FIGURE 3-12**.
3. **Click the first cell of the new row, type Snapchat, press TAB, then type Brand awareness**
4. **Place the pointer in the margin to the left of the Instagram row until the pointer changes to ↗, click to select the row, press and hold the mouse button, drag down to select the LinkedIn row, then release the mouse button**
   The Instagram and LinkedIn rows are selected, including the end of row marks.
5. **Click the Layout contextual tab, then click the Insert Below button in the Rows & Columns group**
   Two new rows are added below the selected rows. To insert multiple rows, you select the number of rows you want to insert before inserting the rows, and then click an Insert Control or use the buttons on the Ribbon.
6. **Click the WhatsApp row, click the Delete button in the Rows & Columns group, click Delete Rows, select the two blank rows, click the Delete button on the Mini toolbar, then click Delete Rows**
   The WhatsApp row and the two blank rows are deleted.
7. **Place the pointer over the top border of the Marketing Goal column until the pointer changes to ↓, then click to select the entire column**
8. **Click the Insert Right button in the Rows & Columns group, then type Cost Basis**
   A new column is inserted to the right of the Marketing Goal column, as shown in **FIGURE 3-13**.
9. **Place the pointer over the border between the Marketing Goal and Cost Basis columns at the top of the table, click the Insert Control, then type Budget in the first cell of the new column**
   A new column for Budget is added between the Marketing Goal and Cost Basis columns.
10. **Press DOWN ARROW to move the insertion point to the next cell in the Budget column, click the Home tab, click ¶ to turn off the display of formatting marks, enter the text shown in FIGURE 3-14 in each cell in the Budget and Cost Basis columns, then save your changes**
    Compare your table to **FIGURE 3-14**.

FIGURE 3-12: Inserted row

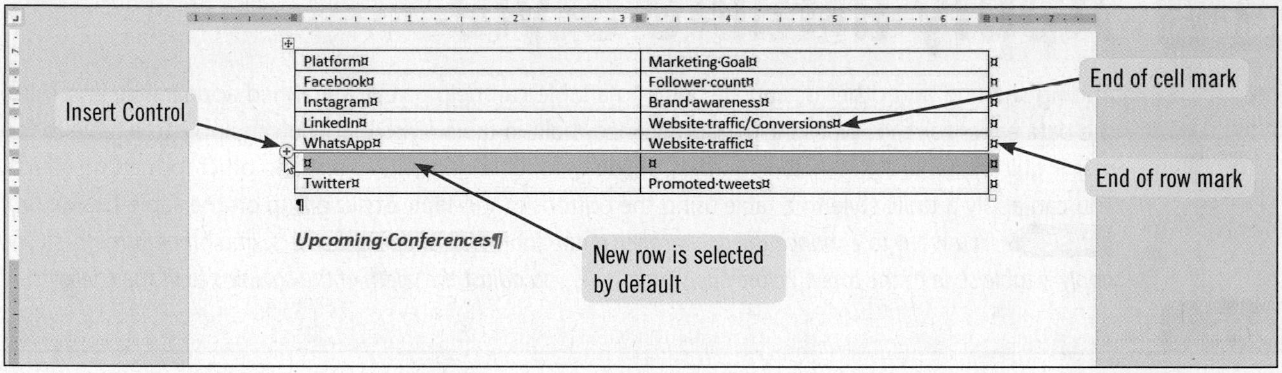
Platform¤ Marketing·Goal¤
Facebook¤ Follower·count¤
Instagram¤ Brand·awareness¤
LinkedIn¤ Website·traffic/Conversions¤
WhatsApp¤ Website·traffic¤
Twitter¤ Promoted·tweets¤
Upcoming·Conferences¶
Insert Control
End of cell mark
End of row mark
New row is selected by default

FIGURE 3-13: Inserted column

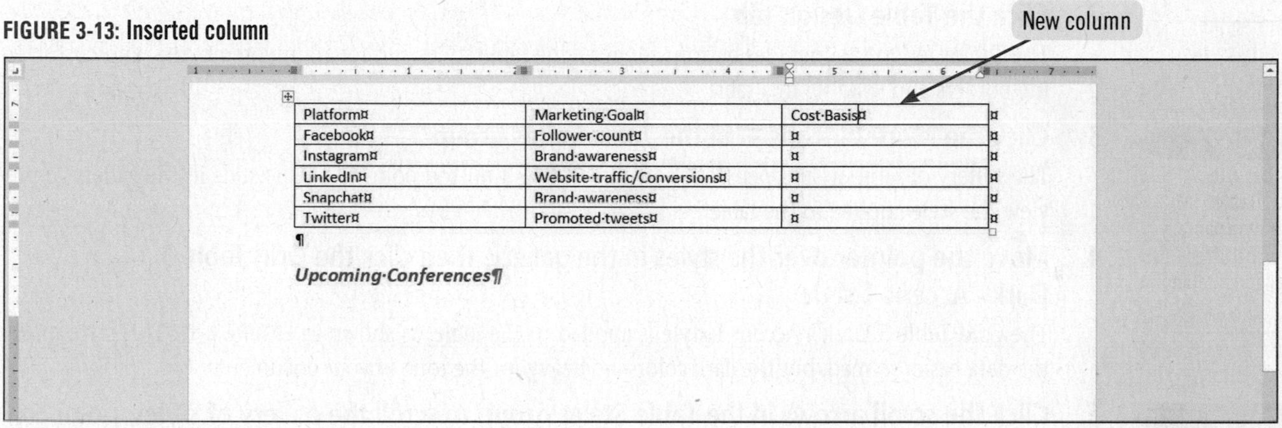

FIGURE 3-14: Text in Budget and Cost Basis columns

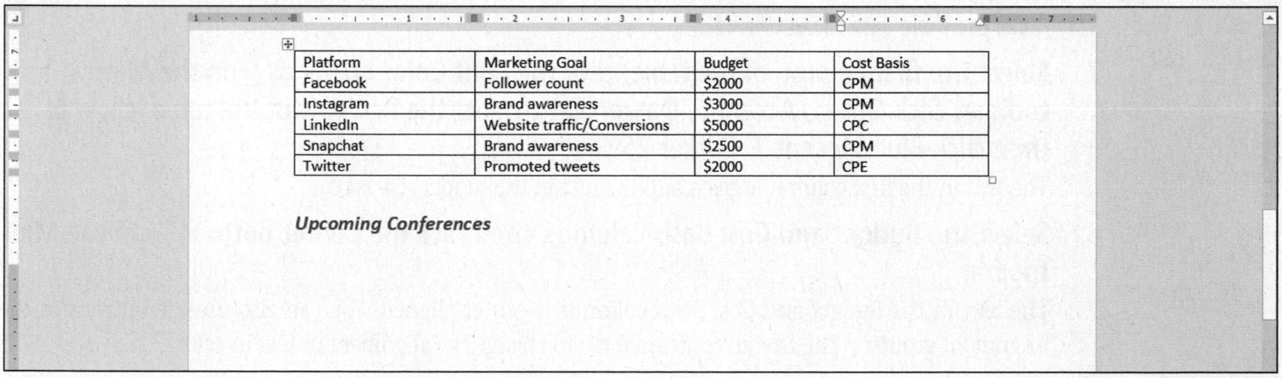

Word

Word
Module 3

Apply a Table Style

Learning Outcome
- Apply a table style

Adding shading and other design elements to a table can help give it a polished appearance and make the data easier to read. Word includes predefined, built-in table styles that you can apply to a table to format it quickly. Table styles include borders, shading, fonts, alignment, colors, and other formatting effects. You can apply a table style to a table using the buttons in the Table Styles group on the Table Design tab. **CASE** *You want to enhance the appearance of the table with shading, borders, and other formats, so you apply a table style to the table. Before applying a style, you adjust the width of the columns to fit the contents.*

STEPS

QUICK TIP
The insertion point must be in the table for the table contextual tabs to be active.

QUICK TIP
The number after the word "Table" in the Table style name is the row identifier in the gallery of table styles.

QUICK TIP
Click Clear in the gallery of table styles to remove all borders, shading, and other style elements from a table.

QUICK TIP
You can also use the Select button in the Table group on the Layout contextual tab to select a table, row, column, or cell.

1. **Click the Layout contextual tab, click the AutoFit button in the Cell Size group, then click AutoFit Contents**
   The width of the table columns is adjusted to fit the text. The Layout contextual tab includes buttons for modifying the structure and size of a table.
2. **Click the Table Design tab**
   The Table Design tab includes buttons for applying table styles and for adding, removing, and customizing borders and shading in a table.
3. **Click the More button in the Table Styles group**
   The gallery of table styles opens, as shown in **FIGURE 3-15**. You point to a table style in the gallery to preview the style applied to the table.
4. **Move the pointer over the styles in the gallery, then click the Grid Table 5 Dark - Accent 1 style**
   The Grid Table 5 Dark - Accent 1 style is applied to the table, as shown in **FIGURE 3-16**. This style makes the data easier to read, but the dark colors are heavy for the tone of your document.
5. **Click the scroll arrows in the Table Styles group to scroll the gallery of styles, point to several styles to see each style applied to the table, click the More button in the Table Styles group, then click the Grid Table 2 - Accent 3 style**
   The Grid Table 2 - Accent 3 style is applied to the table. This style makes the table data easier to read.
6. **In the Table Style Options group, click the Banded Rows check box to clear it**
   The shading is removed from alternating rows in the table. When the banded columns or banded rows setting is active, the odd columns or rows are formatted differently from the even columns or rows to make the table data easier to read.
7. **Select the first column of the table, click the Font Color arrow on the Mini toolbar, click Green, Accent 6, Darker 25%, select the first row of the table, click , then click Blue, Accent 1, Darker 25%**
   The text in the first column is green and the text in the header row is blue.
8. **Select the Budget and Cost Basis columns, then click the Center button on the Mini toolbar**
   The text in the Budget and Cost Basis columns is center-aligned. You can also use the buttons in the Alignment group on the Layout contextual tab to change the alignment of text in cells.
9. **Click the table move handle, click the Home tab, click the Center button in the Paragraph group on the Ribbon, then deselect the table**
   Clicking the table move handle selects the entire table. Clicking the Center button with the entire table selected centered the table between the margins, as shown in **FIGURE 3-17**.
10. **Press CTRL+HOME, then save your changes**

FIGURE 3-15: Gallery of table styles

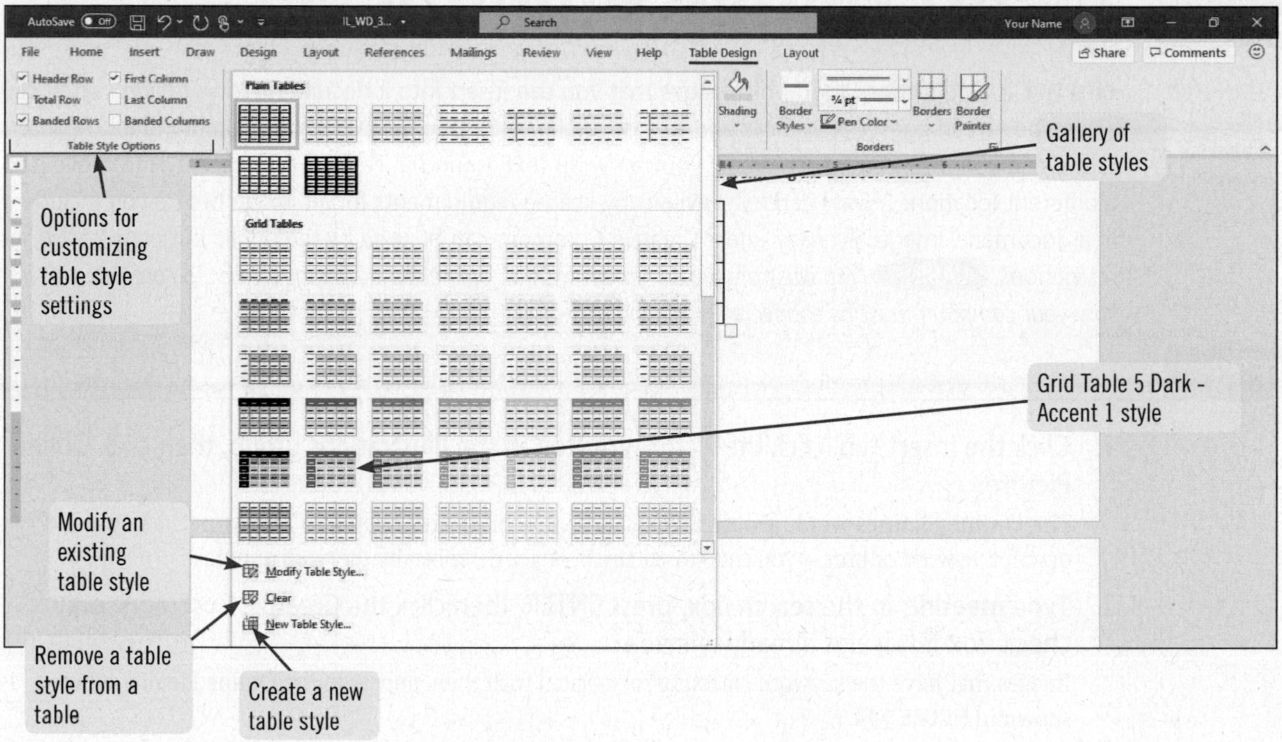

FIGURE 3-16: Grid Table 5 Dark - Accent 1 style applied to table

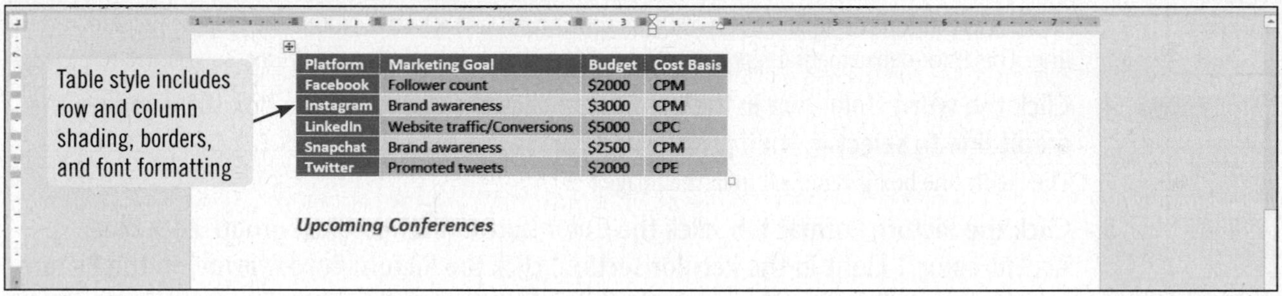

FIGURE 3-17: Completed table

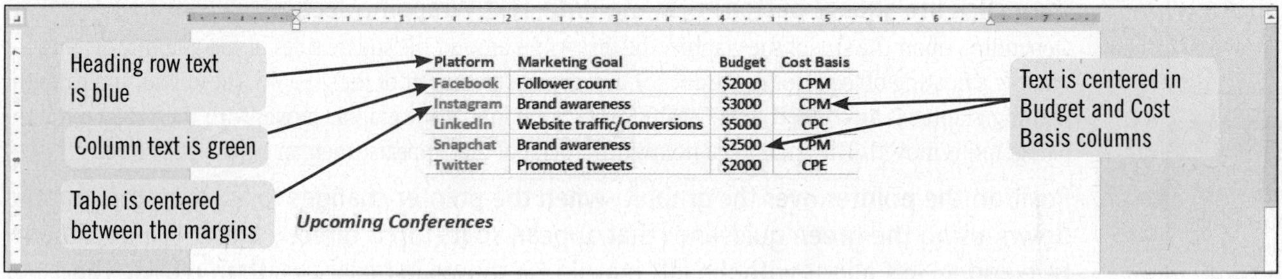

Insert Online Pictures

Learning Outcomes
- Insert pictures
- Wrap text around objects

Clip art is a collection of graphic images that you can insert into a document. Bing image search clip art images are images that you can add to a document using the Online Pictures command on the Insert tab. Once you insert a clip art image, you can wrap text around it, resize it, enhance it, and move it to a different location. Always carefully review any license requirements for an image before you include it in a document. Images licensed under Creative Commons can be used by the public but carry copyright restrictions. CASE *You illustrate the document with an online clip art image. Note: To complete this lesson, your computer must be connected to the Internet.*

STEPS

1. **Click the Insert tab, click the Pictures button in the Illustrations group, then click Online Pictures**

   The Online Pictures window opens. You can search for images related to a keyword. A **keyword** is a descriptive word or phrase you enter to obtain an image described by the word or phrase.

2. **Type meeting in the search box, press ENTER, then click the Creative Commons only check box if it is not already selected**

   Images that have the keyword "meeting" associated with them appear in the Online Pictures window, as shown in FIGURE 3-18.

3. **Click the Filter button, click Clipart, click the clip called out in FIGURE 3-18, then click Insert**

   The clip is inserted as an inline graphic at the location of the insertion point, as shown in FIGURE 3-19. Until you apply text wrapping to an inline graphic, it is part of the line of text in which it was inserted. Sizing handles appear on the square edges of the graphic when it is selected. Notice the graphic includes a credit line. This inter-departmental report does not require that you retain the credit line, so you will remove it.

   TROUBLE
   Select a different clip that has square dimensions if the clip shown in **FIGURE 3-18** is not available to you.

4. **Click the word Unknown in the credit line, click the border of the box surrounding the credit line to select it, then press DELETE**

   The credit line box is removed from the image.

   TROUBLE
   If your clip does not include a credit line, skip Step 4.

5. **Click the Picture Format tab, click the Color button in the Adjust group, click Blue, Accent color 1 Light in the Recolor section, click the Picture Border arrow in the Picture Styles group, click Blue, Accent 1, then deselect the graphic**

   The color of the image changes from black to blue, and a blue picture border is added. To move a graphic independently of the line of text in which it was inserted, you must make it a floating graphic.

6. **Click the image to select it, click the Layout Options button on the side of the image, then click the Square button in the With Text Wrapping section**

   Depending upon the size of the graphic, the text wraps around the square sides of the graphic, making the graphic a floating object. Notice the anchor that appears to the left of the graphic. The anchor indicates the floating graphic is **anchored** to the nearest paragraph, so that the graphic moves with the paragraph if the paragraph is moved. The anchor is a nonprinting symbol that appears when an object is selected.

   QUICK TIP
   To position a graphic anywhere on a page, you must apply text wrapping to it even if there is no text on the page.

7. **Position the pointer over the graphic, when the pointer changes to ✥, drag the graphic down, using the green guidelines that appear, so its top is directly under the document title and its left aligns with the left margin, as shown in FIGURE 3-20, then release the mouse button**

   The graphic is positioned below the title on the left side of the page.

   QUICK TIP
   To position a graphic using precise measurements, click the Position button, click More Layout Options, then adjust the settings on the Position tab in the Layout dialog box.

8. **Deselect the graphic, then save your changes.**

FIGURE 3-18: Online Pictures window

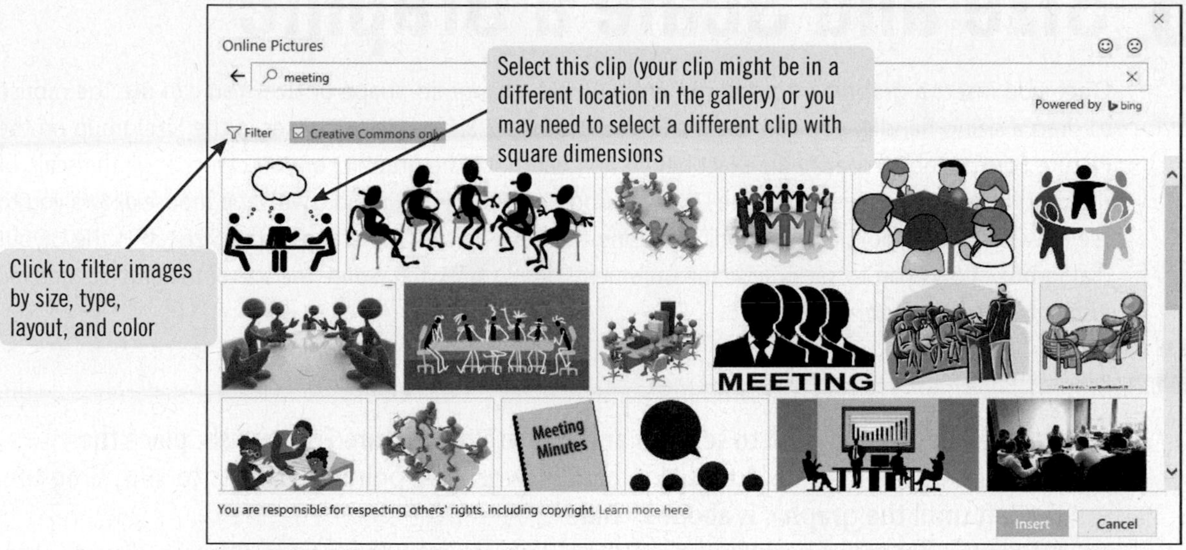

FIGURE 3-19: Inline graphic

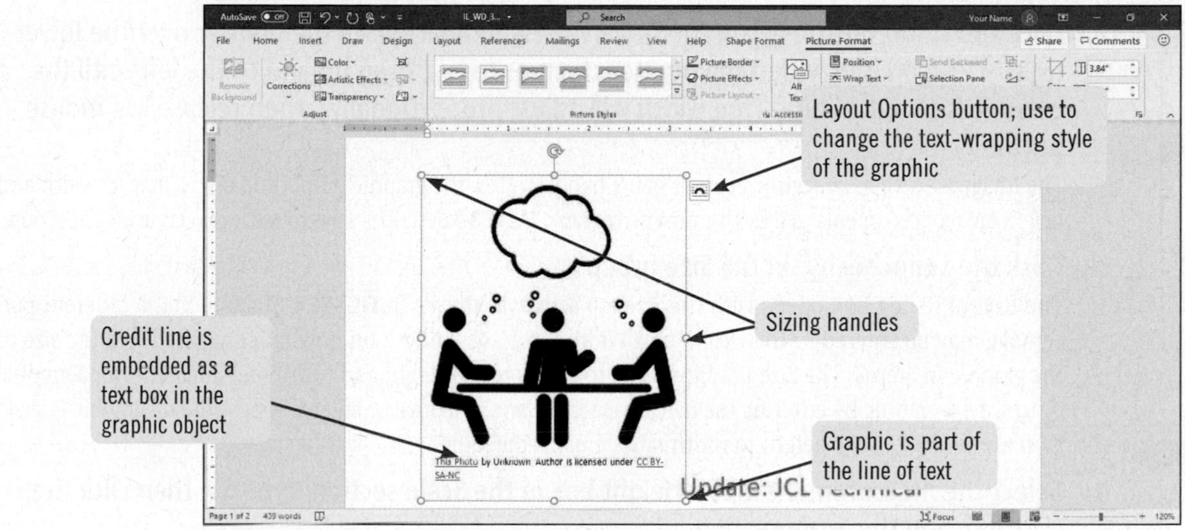

FIGURE 3-20: Graphic being moved to a new location

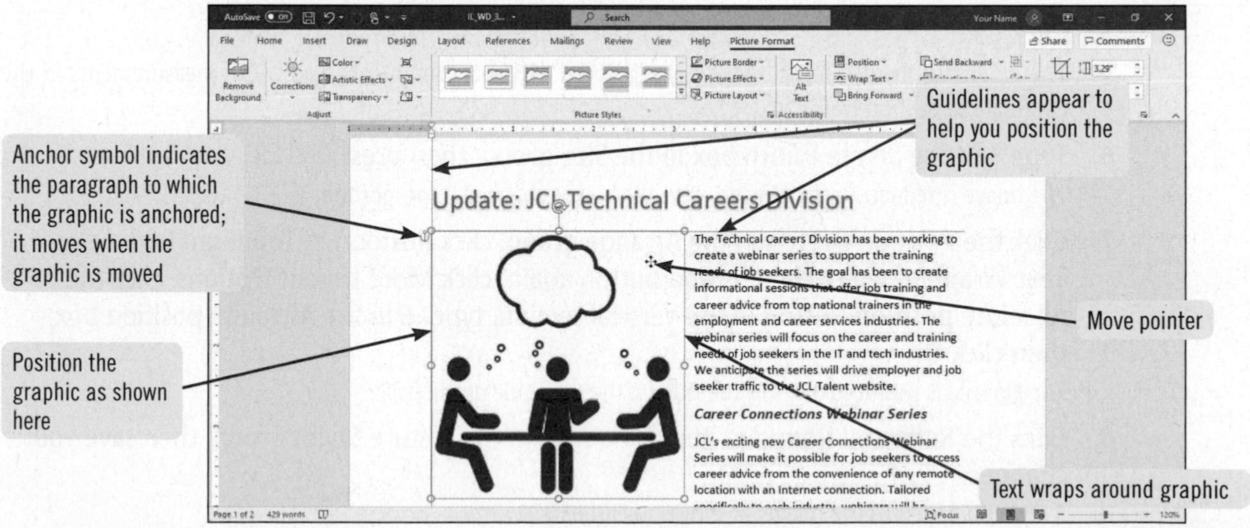

Size and Scale a Graphic

Learning Outcomes
- Format objects
- Scale a graphic

Once you insert a graphic into a document, you can change its shape or size. You can use the mouse to drag a sizing handle, you can use the Shape Width and Shape Height boxes in the Size group on the Picture Format tab to specify an exact height and width for the graphic, or you can change the scale of the graphic using the Size tab in the Layout dialog box. Resizing a graphic with the mouse allows you to see how the image looks as you modify it. Using the boxes in the Size group or the Size tab in the Layout dialog box allows you to set precise measurements. **CASE** *You reduce the size of the graphic that you inserted in the JCL document.*

STEPS

1. **Double-click the graphic to select it and activate the Picture Format tab, place the pointer over the middle-right sizing handle, when the pointer changes to ⇔, drag to the left until the graphic is about 2" wide**

   Refer to the ruler as you drag. When you release the mouse button, the image is taller than it is wide. Dragging a side, top, or bottom sizing handle changes only the width or height of a graphic.

> **QUICK TIP**
> As you drag the corner handle, refer to the measurements in the Size group on the Ribbon to best approximate the size of the image.

2. **Click the Undo button on the Quick Access toolbar, place the pointer over the lower-right sizing handle, when the pointer changes to ⤡, drag up and to the left until the graphic is about 2" high (the width will adjust proportionally), then release the mouse button**

   The image is smaller. Dragging a corner sizing handle resizes the graphic proportionally so that its width and height are reduced or enlarged by the same percentage. **TABLE 3-3** describes ways to resize objects using the mouse.

3. **Click the Launcher in the Size group**

   The Layout dialog box opens with the Size tab active, as shown in **FIGURE 3-21**. Note that a different percentage may be entered in the Height and Width boxes, depending on how much you reduced the size of the graphic in Step 2. The Size tab allows you to enter precise height and width measurements for a graphic or to scale a graphic by entering the percentage you want to reduce or enlarge it by. When a graphic is sized to **scale** (or scaled), its height to width ratio remains the same.

> **QUICK TIP**
> Deselect the Lock aspect ratio check box if you want to change a graphic's proportions.

4. **Select the measurement in the Height box in the Scale section, type 50, then click the Width box in the Scale section**

   The scale of the width changes to 50% and the Absolute measurements in the Height and Width sections decrease proportionally.

5. **Click OK**

   The height and width measurements are reduced to 50% of the height and width measurements in the Original size section of the dialog box.

6. **Type 1 in the Shape Width box in the Size group, then press ENTER**

   The image is reduced to be 1" wide, with the height changed in proportion.

7. **Click the Position button in the Arrange group, click Position in Top Right with Square Text Wrapping, click the Position button again, click More Layout Options, click the Absolute position button in the Vertical section, type .6 in the Absolute position box, then click OK**

   The graphic is positioned below the title on the right side of the page.

8. **Click the Reflected Rounded Rectangle style in the Picture Styles group, then save your changes**

   A style is applied to the image, as shown in **FIGURE 3-22**.

FIGURE 3-21: Size tab in the Layout dialog box

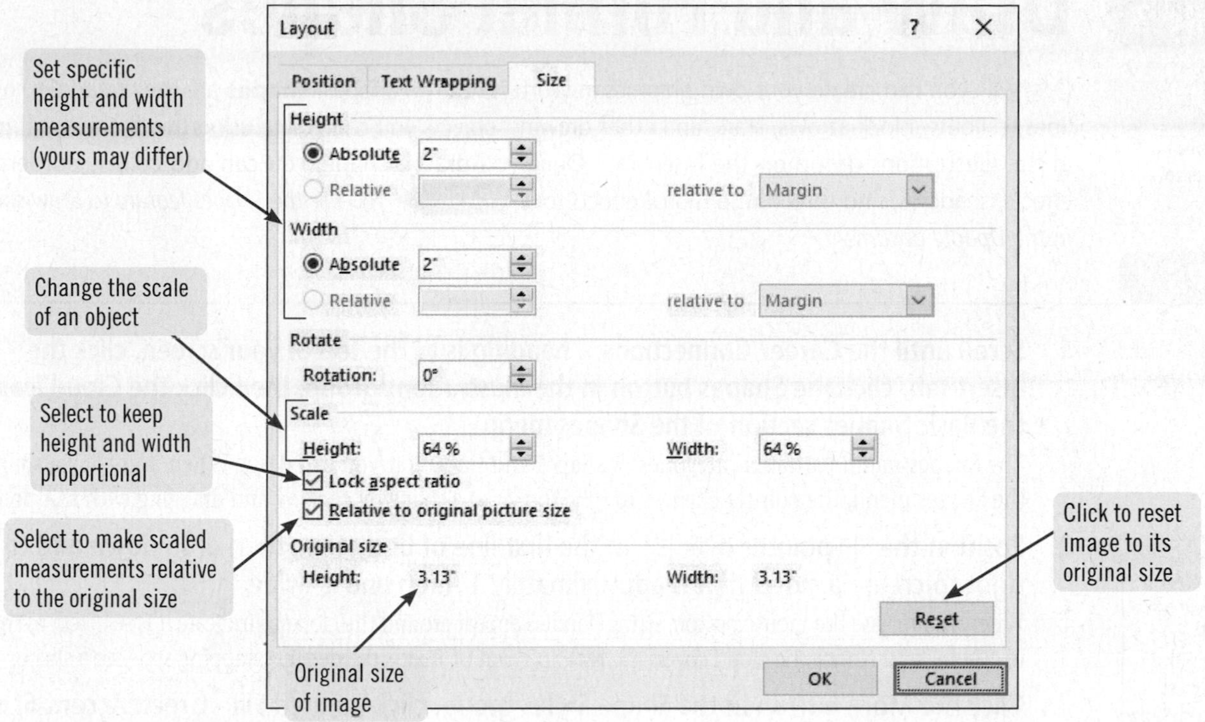

FIGURE 3-22: Style applied to resized image

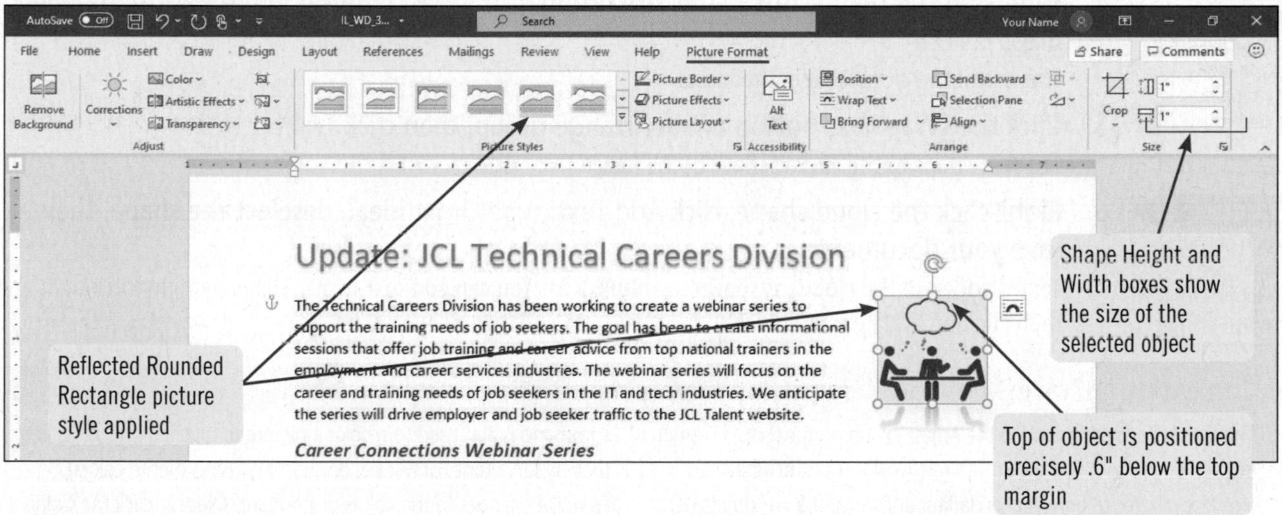

TABLE 3-3: Methods for resizing an object using the mouse

do this	to
Drag a corner sizing handle	Resize a clip art or bitmap graphic and maintain its proportions
Press SHIFT and drag a corner sizing handle	Resize any graphic object and maintain its proportions
Press CTRL and drag a side, top, or bottom sizing handle	Resize any graphic object vertically or horizontally while keeping the center position fixed
Press CTRL and drag a corner sizing handle	Resize any graphic object diagonally while keeping the center position fixed
Press SHIFT+CTRL and drag a corner sizing handle	Resize any graphic object while keeping the center position fixed and maintaining its proportions

Draw and Format Shapes

Learning Outcomes
- Insert shapes
- Apply styles to objects

One way you can create your own graphics in Word is to draw shapes. **Shapes** are the rectangles, ovals, lines, callouts, block arrows, stars, and other drawing objects you can create using the Shapes command in the Illustrations group on the Insert tab. Once you draw a shape, you can add colors, borders, fill effects, shadows, and three-dimensional effects to it. CASE *You use the Shapes feature to draw shapes in the Update document.*

STEPS

1. **Scroll until the Career Connections... heading is at the top of your screen, click the Insert tab, click the Shapes button in the Illustrations group, then click the Cloud icon in the Basic Shapes section of the Shapes menu**
   The Shapes menu contains categories of shapes and lines that you can draw. When you click a shape in the Shapes menu, the pointer changes to +. You draw a shape by clicking and dragging with this pointer.

2. **Position the + pointer over JCL in the first line of body text, then drag down and to the right to create a cloud that is approximately 1" high and 2" wide**
   When you release the mouse button, sizing handles appear around the cloud to indicate it is selected, as shown in **FIGURE 3-23**. Notice the cloud covers the text. In Front of Text is the default wrapping style for a shape.

3. **Click the More button in the Shape Styles group, click Colored Fill - Green Accent 6, click the Shape Effects button, point to Preset, then click Preset 5**
   The color of the cloud changes to green and the image is formatted with a bevel and shadow style.

4. **Type .8 in the Height box in the Size group, press TAB, type 1.2 in the Width box, then press ENTER**
   The size of the cloud shape is reduced.

5. **Click the Wrap Text button in the Arrange group, then click Tight**
   The text wraps to the curved shape of the image.

6. **Right-click the cloud shape, click Add Text, type Great idea!, deselect the shape, then save your document**
   Text is added to the cloud, as shown in **FIGURE 3-24**. You can add text to any shape by right-clicking it and then clicking Add Text or Edit Text.

QUICK TIP
To draw a perfect square or circle, click the Rectangle or Oval shape on the menu, then press SHIFT while you drag with the pointer.

QUICK TIP
You can also use the Layout Options button to change the text wrapping style applied to an object.

TROUBLE
The position of your cloud shape does not need to match the figure exactly.

Correcting pictures, changing colors, and applying artistic effects

The Corrections command in the Adjust group on the Picture Format tab allows you to adjust a picture's relative lightness **(brightness)**, alter the difference between its darkest and lightest areas **(contrast)**, and change the sharpness of an image. To make these adjustments, select the image and then click the Corrections button to open a gallery of preset percentages applied to the selected picture. Point to an option in the gallery to preview it in the document; click an option in the gallery to apply it. You can also fine-tune brightness, contrast, or sharpness by clicking Picture Corrections Options in the Corrections gallery, and then using the sliders in the Picture Corrections section of the Format Picture pane to adjust the percentage.

The Color command in the Adjust group is used to change the vividness and intensity of color in an image **(color saturation)**, and to change the "temperature" of a photo by bringing out the cooler blue tones or the warmer orange tones **(color tone)**. The Color command is also used to recolor a picture to give it a stylized effect, such as sepia tone, grayscale, or duotone (using theme colors). To make changes to the colors in a picture, select it, click the Color button, and then select one of the color modes or variations in the gallery that opens, or click Picture Color Options to fine-tune color settings using the Format Picture pane.

The Artistic Effects command in the Adjust group allows you to make a photo look like a drawing, a painting, a photocopy, a sketch, or some other artistic medium. To experiment with applying an artistic effect, select a photo, click the Artistic Effects button, and then point to each effect to preview it applied to the photo.

After you adjust a picture, you can undo any changes by clicking the Reset Picture arrow in the Adjust group. This command discards all formatting changes made to a picture, including size, cropping, borders, and effects.

FIGURE 3-23: Shape in document

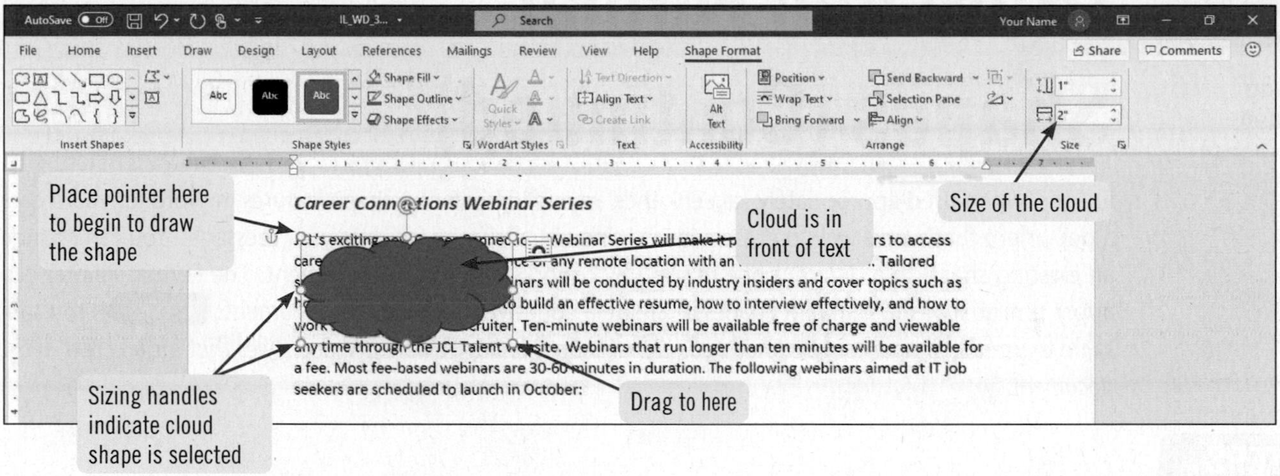

FIGURE 3-24: Text added to shape

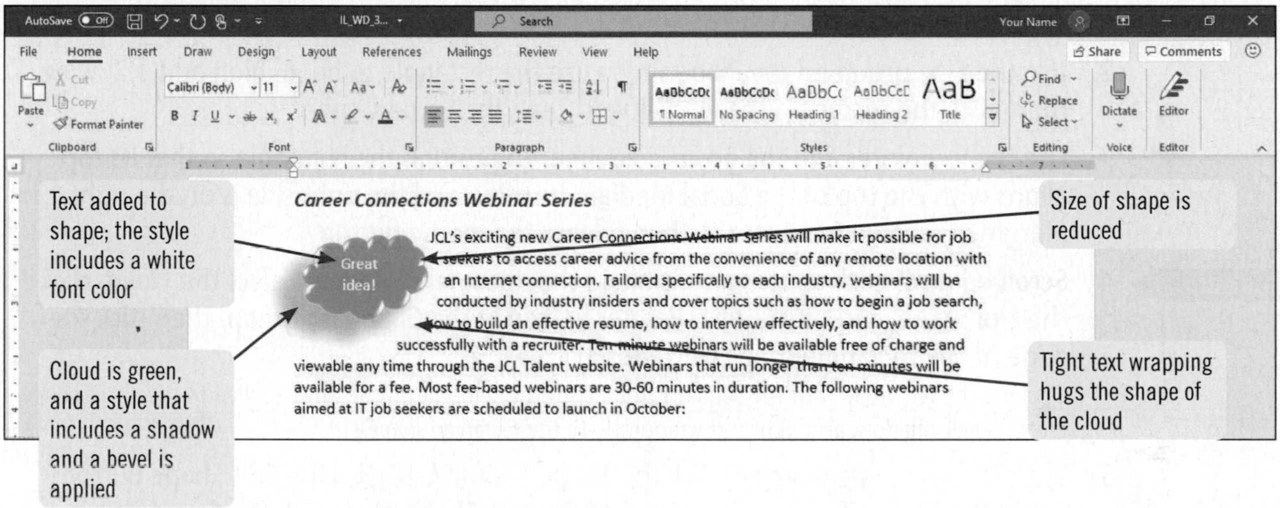

Adding alt text and checking documents for accessibility issues

It's important to design documents so that they are accessible to people of all abilities. The Alt Text command allows you to add a text description of a graphic image to a document so that people who are visually impaired and using a screen reader can access the content of the image. The alt text associated with an image should serve the same purpose and convey the same essential information as the image so that no information or functionality is lost for readers who are visually impaired. To add alt text to an image, select the image, click the Alt Text command in the Accessibility group on the Picture Format tab, and then type the alternative text description in the box on the Alt Text pane. When you are finished, close the Alt Text pane. You can edit alt text at any time by right-clicking an image and then clicking Edit Alt Text.

The Accessibility Checker locates elements of a document that might be a potential problem for readers with disabilities, and it offers suggestions on how to resolve each issue. For example, the Accessibility Checker might flag a graphic that does not include alt text, or it might issue a warning about formatting that makes text hard to read. To check a document for accessibility issues, click the Check Accessibility button in the Accessibility group on the Review tab. The results of the inspection appear in the Accessibility pane.

(Continued)

Word
Module 3

Draw and Format Shapes (Continued)

Learning Outcomes
- Use the Format Painter
- Change and modify shapes

Shapes, when used appropriately, can enhance any document. The shape features in Word let you create a document that works well to present ideas using visual cues to facilitate your message. You can change an existing shape to a different one to see which works best for the document. The Format Painter can apply similar styles to different shapes to create a cohesive design in the document. **CASE** *You continue to use the Shapes feature to add additional shapes and try different shape styles that include text in the document.*

STEPS

1. **Scroll down until the Social Media... heading is at the top of your screen, click the Insert tab, click the Shapes button in the Illustrations group, click the Rectangle icon in the Rectangles section, then use the + pointer to draw a rectangle below the Social Media... heading**
2. **Use the Size group on the Ribbon to resize the rectangle to be .6" high and 1.2" wide, right-click the rectangle shape, click Add Text, then type Genius!**
3. **Use the pointer and the green guidelines to position the rectangle so that its top aligns with the top of the Social Media... heading and the right side is on the right margin, as shown in FIGURE 3-25, then release the mouse button**
4. **Scroll up until both shapes are visible in the document window, select the cloud, click the Home tab, click the Format Painter button in the Clipboard group, then click the edge of the rectangle shape with the pointer**

   Clicking the rectangle with the Format Painter copied the formatting settings applied to the cloud shape—green, bevel, shadow, and tight text wrapping—to the rectangle shape.

> **TROUBLE**
> Press Undo and try again if the formatting is not applied.

5. **With the rectangle selected, click the Shape Format tab, click the Edit Shape button in the Insert Shapes group, point to Change Shape, then click the Cloud icon in the Basic Shapes section**

   The rectangle changes to a cloud. Notice that changing the object shape does not change the text or the format settings applied to the object.
6. **Select the Great idea! cloud, click the Edit Shape button, point to Change Shape, then click the Thought Bubble: Cloud icon in the Callouts section**

   The cloud changes to a thought bubble cloud.
7. **Position the pointer over the yellow adjustment handle on the thought bubble cloud, drag the handle down and left, similar in FIGURE 3-26, then release the mouse button**

   Dragging the adjustment handle modifies the shape of the thought bubble cloud.

> **TROUBLE**
> Do not be concerned if your cloud shape does not match the figure exactly.

8. **Save your changes**

FIGURE 3-25: Positioning the rectangle

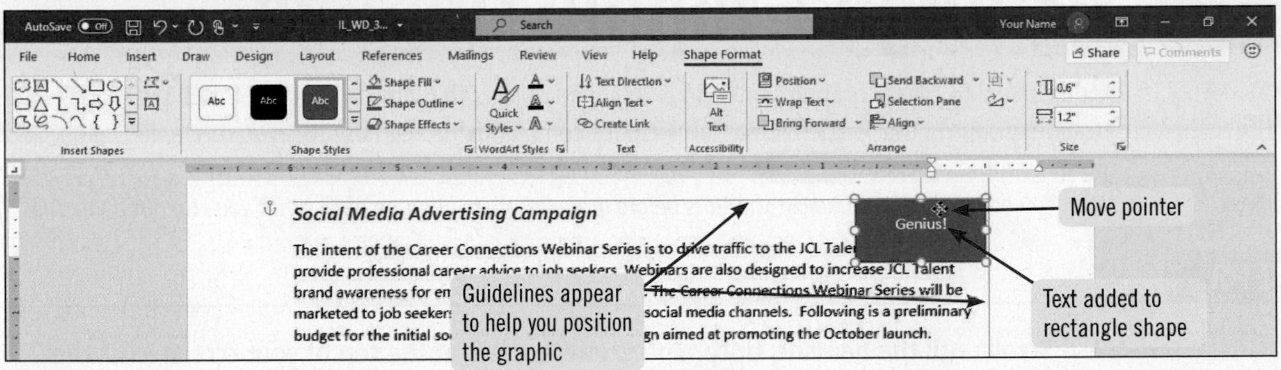

FIGURE 3-26: Cloud shapes in document

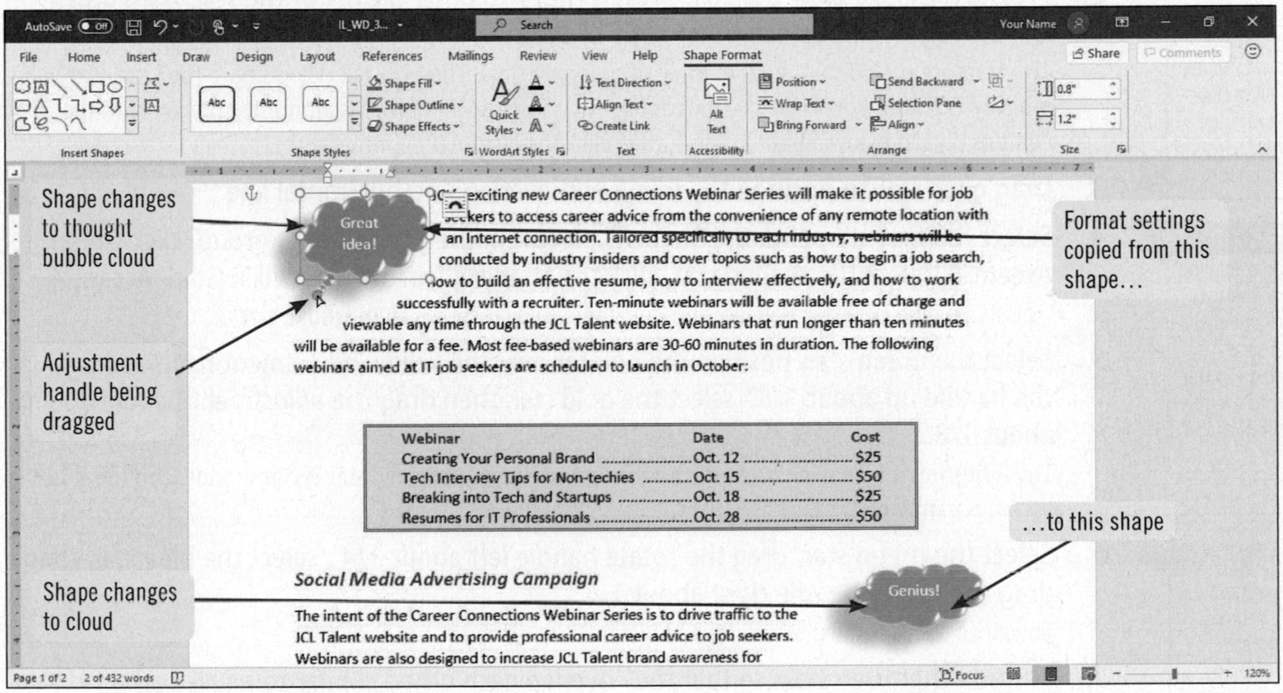

Enhancing graphic objects with styles and effects

Another way to make a document fun and visually appealing for the reader is to apply a style or an effect to a graphic object. To apply a style, select the object and then choose from the style options in the Styles group on the active Format tab for that type of object. Styles include a preset mixture of effects, such as shading, borders, shadows, and other settings. The Effects command in the Styles group on the active Format tab gives you the power to apply a customized variety of effects to an object, including a shadow, bevel, glow, reflection, soft edge, or 3-D rotation. To apply an effect, select the object, click the Effects command for that type of object, point to the type of effect you want to apply, and then select from the options in the gallery that opens. To further customize an effect, click the Options command for that type of effect at the bottom of the gallery to open the Format Shape pane. The best way to learn about styles and effects is to experiment by applying them to an object and seeing what works.

Word

Word Module 3

Arrange Graphic Objects

Learning Outcomes
- Format objects
- Arrange objects
- Paste objects

Another way to create graphics in Word is to create objects that are composed of multiple shapes. The Arrange group on the Shape Format tab includes commands you can use to layer, rotate, flip, align, and group graphic objects. **CASE** *You decide to illustrate page 2 of the document with a cluster of small stars. You edit, rotate, and adjust the stars before grouping them into one object that you can position easily.*

STEPS

1. **Scroll until the heading Upcoming Conferences is at the top of your screen, click the Insert tab, click the Shapes button in the Illustrations group, click the Star: 5 Points icon in the Stars and Banners section of the Shapes menu, then click a blank area of page 2**
   A 1" square star shape is inserted in the document.

> **QUICK TIP**
> To align shapes with each other, select two or more shapes, click the Align button in the Arrange group, then select an alignment option.

2. **Press CTRL+C to copy the star, press CTRL+V to paste a copy of the star, then press CTRL+V again to paste another copy of the star**
   Two stars are pasted for a total of three overlapping stars. These pasted objects have the same text wrapping style as the source object—In Front of Text. To paste an object as an inline graphic, click the Paste Options button below a pasted object, then click the Picture (P) option.
3. **Drag each star to position them in a non-overlapping horizontal line**

> **QUICK TIP**
> To change color, line weight, or line style of a shape outline, click the Shape Outline arrow in the Shape Styles group, then select from the options.

4. **Select the first star, click the Shape Fill arrow in the Shape Styles group, click Green, Accent 6, select the second star, click the Shape Fill arrow, then click Gold, Accent 4**
   One star is blue, one star is green, and one star is gold, as shown in in **FIGURE 3-27**.
5. **Select the green star, position the pointer over the yellow adjustment handle, drag the handle up about 1/8", select the gold star, then drag the adjustment handle down about 1/8"**
   The Adjustment handle changed the internal proportions. The green star becomes wider and the gold star becomes narrower.

> **QUICK TIP**
> To rotate a graphic object 90 degrees, click the Rotate Objects button in the Arrange group, then click Rotate Right or Rotate Left.

6. **Select the green star, drag the rotate handle left about 1/4", select the blue star, then drag the rotate handle right about 1/4"**
   The green star is rotated left and the blue star is rotated right.
7. **Position the three stars so that they overlap each other, similar to FIGURE 3-28**
   The stars are stacked in layers. Don't be concerned if the layering of your stars is different.
8. **Select the gold star, click the Bring Forward arrow in the Arrange group, then click Bring to Front**
   The gold star becomes the front layer of the stack of objects. You use the Bring Forward and Send Backward arrows to shift the order of the layers in a stack of graphic objects.

> **QUICK TIP**
> To flip a graphic object, click the Rotate Objects button, then click Flip Vertical or Flip Horizontal.

9. **Press and hold CTRL, click the blue star, click the green star so that all three stars are selected, click the Group Objects button in the Arrange group, then click Group**
   The three star objects become a single object with sizing handles around a surrounding border. Any formatting applied will affect all the objects within the grouped object.
10. **Type 1 in the Shape Height box in the Size group, type 1.2 in the Shape Width box, press ENTER, click the Position button in the Arrange group, click Position in Top Right with Square Text Wrapping, deselect the object, then save your changes**
    The size of the grouped object is reduced to 1" high and 1.2" wide, and the object is positioned in the top-right corner of the page, as shown in **FIGURE 3-29**.

FIGURE 3-27: Stars with fill color applied

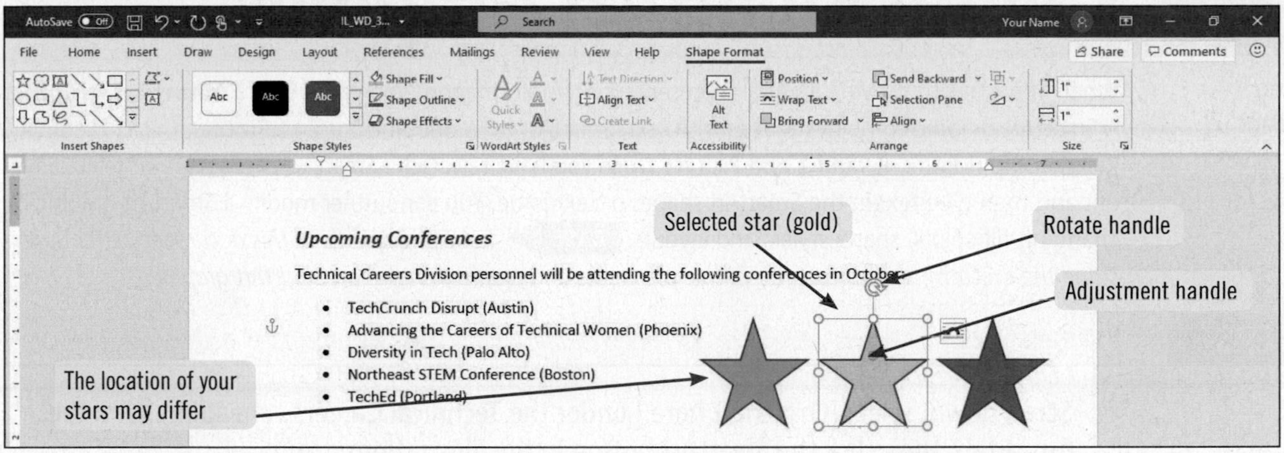

FIGURE 3-28: Stars layered in document

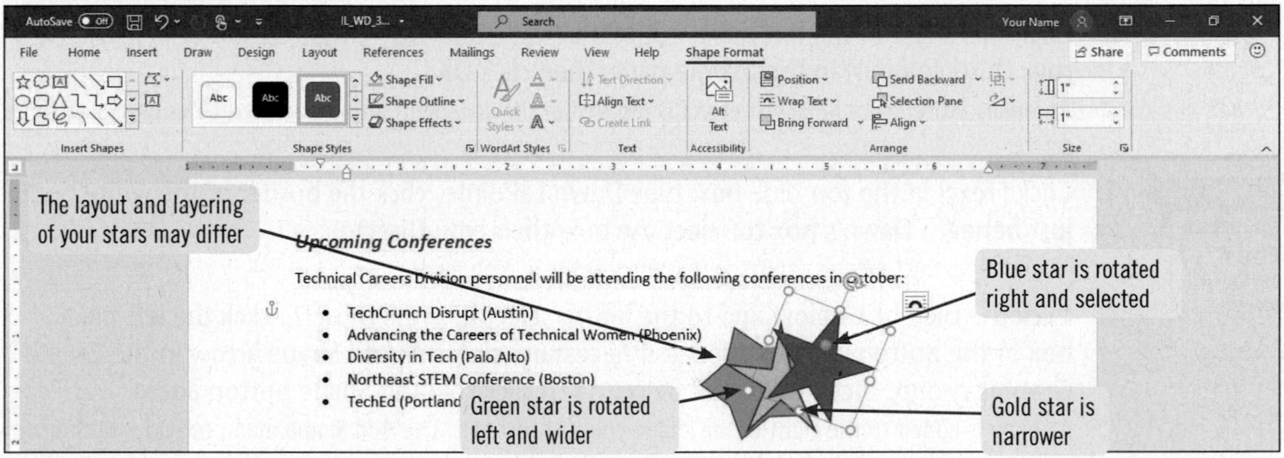

FIGURE 3-29: Grouped and resized object positioned in top corner

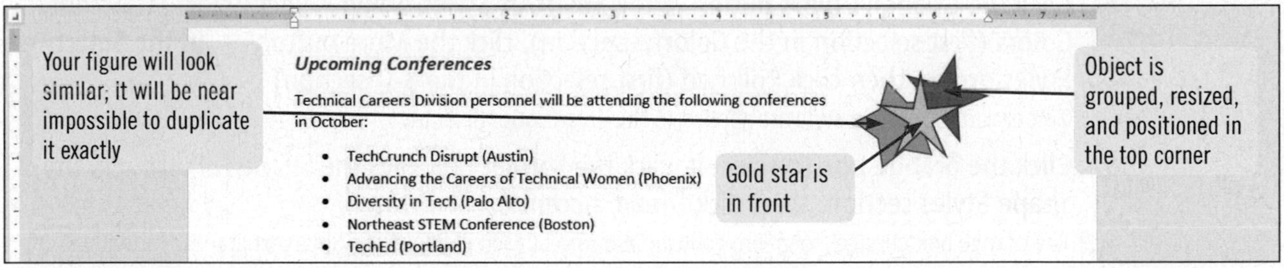

Creating an illustration in a drawing canvas

A **drawing canvas** is a workspace for creating your own graphics. It provides a frame-like boundary between an illustration and the rest of the document so that the illustration can be sized, formatted, and positioned like a single graphic object. If you are creating an illustration that includes multiple shapes, such as a flow chart, it is helpful to create the illustration in a drawing canvas. To draw shapes or lines in a drawing canvas, click the Shapes button in the Illustrations group on the Insert tab, click New Drawing Canvas to open a drawing canvas in the document, and then create and format your illustration in the drawing canvas. When you are finished, right-click the border of the drawing canvas and then click Fit to resize the drawing canvas to fit the illustration. You can then resize the illustration by dragging a border of the drawing canvas. Once you have resized a drawing canvas, you can wrap text around it and position it. By default, a drawing canvas has no border or background so that it is transparent in a document, but you can add fill and borders to it if you wish.

Create SmartArt Graphics

Learning Outcomes
- Insert SmartArt
- Customize SmartArt

When you want to provide a visual representation of information, you can create a **SmartArt graphic**. A SmartArt graphic combines shapes with text. SmartArt categories include List, Process, Cycle, Hierarchy, Relationship, Matrix, Pyramid, and Picture. Once you have selected a SmartArt category, you select a layout and then type text in the SmartArt shapes or text pane. You can further modify a SmartArt graphic by changing fill colors, shape styles, and layouts. **CASE** *To help recipients of this document better understand the executive structure at JCL Talent, you create an organizational chart SmartArt graphic.*

STEPS

1. **Scroll down, select [Org chart here.] under the Technical Careers... heading, click the Insert tab, then click the SmartArt button in the Illustrations group**
   The Choose a SmartArt Graphic dialog box opens. You use it to select the category of diagram you want to create and the layout and design for the diagram. The right pane shows a preview of the selected diagram layout.
2. **Click Hierarchy in the left pane, select the Name and Title Organization Chart style (first row, third column) in the middle pane, then click OK**
   An organization chart SmartArt object is inserted in the document and the SmartArt Design tab becomes active.
3. **Click [Text] in the top blue box, type Dawn LaPointe, click the border of the white box just beneath Dawn's box to select the box, then type Director**
   As you type, the font size adjusts so that the text fits in each text box.

QUICK TIP
You can type directly in the shapes, or you can use the text pane to enter the text.

4. **Click the blue box below and to the left to select it, press DELETE, click the left blue box in the bottom row to select it if necessary, click the Add Shape arrow in the Create Graphic group, click Add Shape Below, then click the Add Shape button again**
   A shape is added to the right of the shape you just inserted. The Add Shape menu provides options for adding more shapes below, above, before, and after to your SmartArt graphic. You can also add an Assistant shape. New shapes will be added depending upon which box is currently selected in the SmartArt graphic.
5. **Click the Change Colors button in the SmartArt Styles group, select Colorful - Accent Colors (first selection in the Colorful section), click the More button in the SmartArt Styles group, then click Polished (first selection in the 3-D section)**
   Colors and a SmartArt style are applied to the organizational chart.
6. **Click the orange box to select it, click the Format tab, click the Shape Fill arrow in the Shape Styles section, then click Green, Accent 6**
   The orange box changes to green. You can also format each element of a SmartArt graphic individually.
7. **Type the text shown in FIGURE 3-30 in each box the SmartArt graphic, click outside the object to deselect it, then save your changes**
8. **Click the View tab, then click Multiple Pages in the Zoom group**
   The completed document is shown in **FIGURE 3-31**.
9. **sam Submit the document to your instructor, close the file, then exit Word**

FIGURE 3-30: Organizational chart

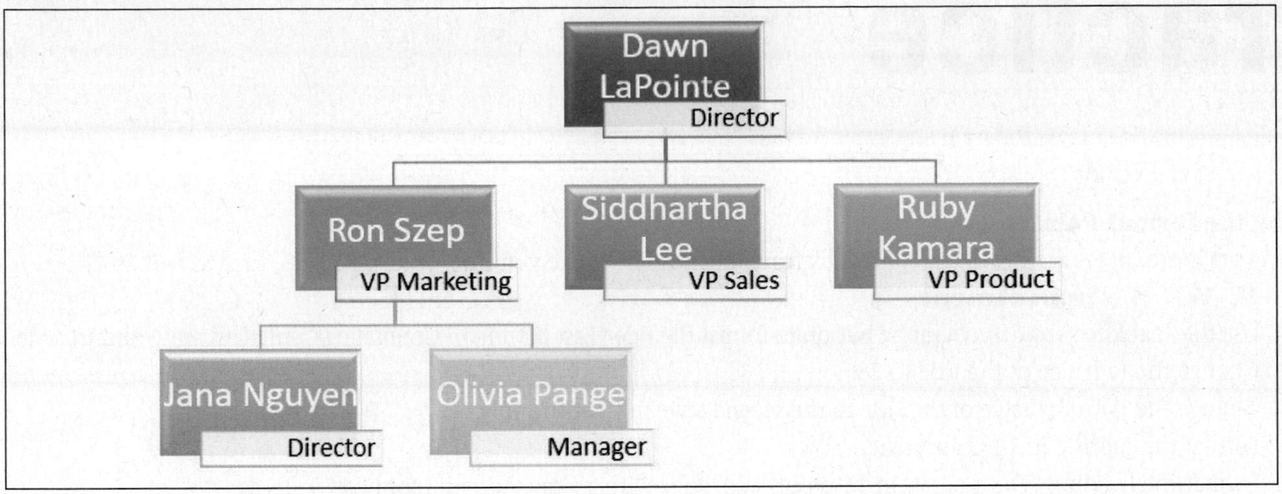

FIGURE 3-31: Completed document

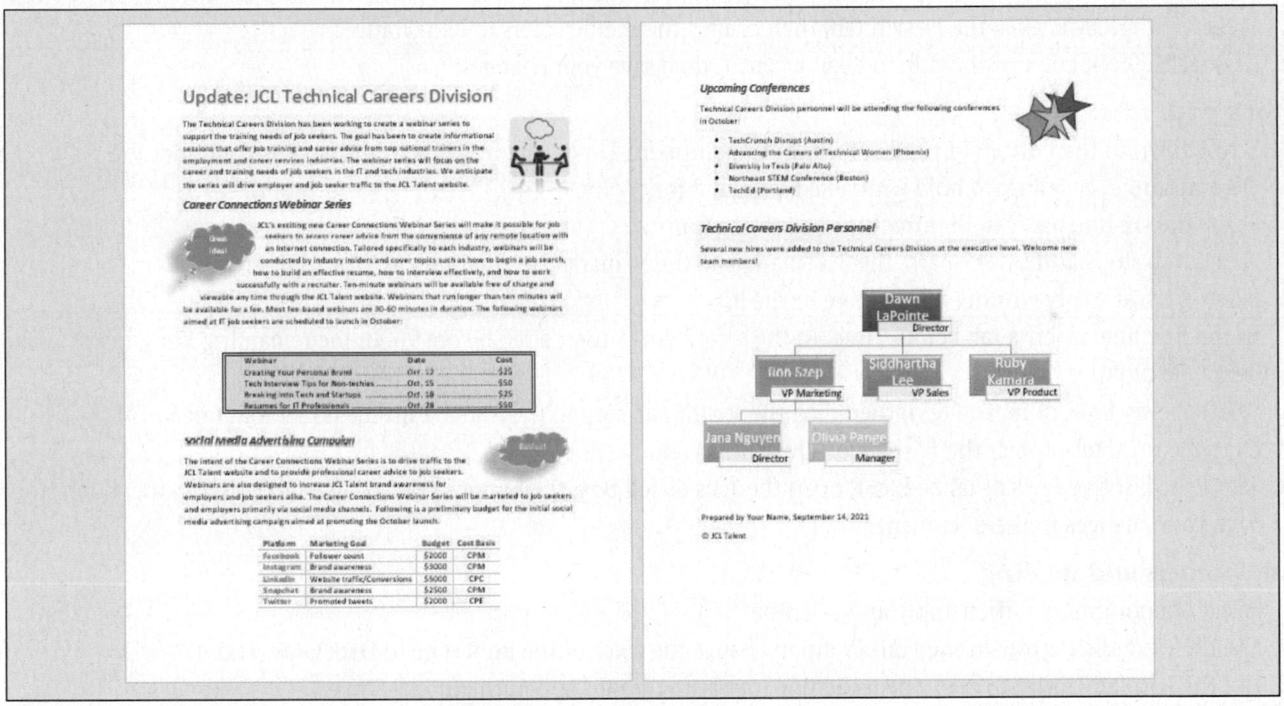

Update: JCL Technical Careers Division

The Technical Careers Division has been working to create a webinar series to support the training needs of job seekers. The goal has been to create informational sessions that offer job training and career advice from top national trainers in the employment and career services industries. The webinar series will focus on the career and training needs of job seekers in the IT and tech industries. We anticipate the series will drive employer and job seeker traffic to the JCL Talent website.

Career Connections Webinar Series

JCL's exciting new Career Connections Webinar Series will make it possible for job seekers to access career advice from the convenience of any remote location with an Internet connection. Tailored specifically to each industry, webinars will be conducted by industry insiders and cover topics such as how to begin a job search, how to build an effective resume, how to interview effectively, and how to work successfully with a recruiter. Ten-minute webinars will be available free of charge and viewable any time through the JCL Talent website. Webinars that run longer than ten minutes will be available for a fee. Most fee-based webinars are 30-60 minutes in duration. The following webinars aimed at IT job seekers are scheduled to launch in October:

Webinar	Date	Cost
Creating Your Personal Brand	Oct. 12	$25
Tech Interview Tips for Non-techies	Oct. 15	$50
Breaking into Tech and Startups	Oct. 18	$25
Resumes for IT Professionals	Oct. 28	$50

Social Media Advertising Campaign

The intent of the Career Connections Webinar Series is to drive traffic to the JCL Talent website and to provide professional career advice to job seekers. Webinars are also designed to increase JCL Talent brand awareness for employers and job seekers alike. The Career Connections Webinar Series will be marketed to job seekers and employers primarily via social media channels. Following is a preliminary budget for the initial social media advertising campaign aimed at promoting the October launch.

Platform	Marketing Goal	Budget	Cost Basis
Facebook	Follower count	$2000	CPM
Instagram	Brand awareness	$3000	CPM
LinkedIn	Website traffic/Conversions	$5000	CPC
Snapchat	Brand awareness	$2500	CPM
Twitter	Promoted tweets	$2000	CPE

Upcoming Conferences

Technical Careers Division personnel will be attending the following conferences in October:

- TechCrunch Disrupt (Austin)
- Advancing the Careers of Technical Women (Phoenix)
- Diversity in Tech (Palo Alto)
- Northeast STEM Conference (Boston)
- TechEd (Portland)

Technical Careers Division Personnel

Several new hires were added to the Technical Careers Division at the executive level. Welcome new team members!

Dawn LaPointe – Director
Ron Szep – VP Marketing
Siddhartha Lee – VP Sales
Ruby Kamara – VP Product
Jana Nguyen – Director
Olivia Pange – Manager

Prepared by Your Name, September 14, 2021

© JCL Talent

Practice

Skills Review

1. **Use the Format Painter.**
   a. Start Word, open the file IL_WD_3-2.docx from the location where you store your Data Files, then save it as **IL_WD_3_Appointments**.
   b. Use the Text Effects and Typography button to format the title "East Mountain Counseling Center" in any WordArt style.
   c. Change the font size of the title to 28.
   d. Change the WordArt style of the title to the second style in the third row.
   e. Format the subtitle in 14-point italic.
   f. Format the heading "Our policy" in 14-point bold, italic with a Gray, Accent 3 font color.
   g. Use the Format Painter to copy the format of the Our policy heading to the following headings: Five-step approach to scheduling appointments, Determining the time required for an appointment, and Processing new clients.
   h. Press CTRL+END to go to the end of the document, type **Last revised**, insert the current date using a format that includes the year as four digits, type **by**, then type your name followed by a period and a space.
   i. Type **East Mountain Counseling is an affiliate of PRG Health.**, then insert a trademark symbol (™) after Health. (*Hint*: The Trademark symbol is character code 2122.)
   j. Press CTRL+HOME, click the Design tab, then change the theme colors to Red Orange.
   k. Change the font color of the title to Red, Accent 3, then save your changes.
2. **Work with tabs.**
   a. Scroll down to the bottom of page 1, format "Appointment Time," the first line in the six-line list under the Determining... heading, in bold with a Red, Accent 3 font color.
   b. Select the six-line list of appointment time information.
   c. Set left tab stops at the 1½" mark, the 3¾" mark, and the 5" mark.
   d. Insert a tab at the beginning of each line in the list.
   e. In the first line, insert a tab before Time. In the second line, insert a tab before 90. In the remaining lines, insert a tab before 60 or 90.
   f. Select the six lines of tabbed text, then drag the second tab stop to the 4" mark on the horizontal ruler.
   g. Drag the third tab stop at the 5" mark off the ruler to remove it.
   h. Select the last five lines of tabbed text, open the Tabs dialog box, then apply a dotted line tab leader to the 4" tab stop.
   i. Save your changes to the document.
3. **Add borders and shading.**
   a. Select "Appointment," then apply an underline.
   b. Use the Underline arrow in the Font group to change the color of the underline to Dark Gray, Text 2.
   c. Use the Format Painter to copy the underline formatting from "Appointment" to "Time."
   d. Click the heading Determining..., add 6 points of space after the paragraph, then open the Borders and Shading dialog box.
   e. Use the Borders tab to apply a ½-point width, Dark Gray, Text 2 colored border below the heading.
   f. Use the Format Painter to apply the same paragraph and border settings to the other headings in the report: Our policy, Five-step approach..., and Processing new clients.
   g. Scroll to the end of the document, click in the Last revised... paragraph, then center the paragraph.
   h. Apply Dark Gray, Text 2, Lighter 80% shading to the paragraph.
   i. Add a ½ -point, dotted line, Dark Gray, Text 2 box border around the paragraph.
   j. Save your changes.

Skills Review (continued)

4. Insert a table.

a. Turn on formatting marks, click in the middle blank paragraph above the Processing new clients heading, then insert a table that contains two columns and three rows.

b. Type the text shown below, pressing TAB to add rows as necessary.

S. Beran	10-2
M. Kurosawa	1-5
C. Foth	2-7
M. Smith	2-4
P. Eriksen	12-6
F. Janda	10-3

c. Save your changes.

5. Insert and delete rows and columns.

a. Insert a row above the S. Beran row, type **Counselor** in the first cell, then type **Availability** in the second cell.

b. Delete the M. Smith row.

c. Insert a column to the left of the Counselor column, then type **Day** in the first cell.

d. Type the days of the work week, begin with Monday and end with Friday, in each empty cell in the new column.

e. Save your changes.

6. Apply a table style.

a. Select the table, then use the AutoFit command to fit the table to the contents.

b. Click the Table Design tab, preview table styles applied to the table, and then apply an appropriate style.

c. Apply the List Table 4 - Accent 3 style to the table, then remove the Banded Rows and First Column table style options.

d. Center the text in the Availability column.

e. Center the table between the margins, then save your changes.

7. Insert online pictures. (*Note:* To complete these steps, your computer must be connected to the Internet.)

a. Press CTRL+HOME, then open the Online Pictures window.

b. Search using Bing Image Search to find images related to the keyword **mountain**. Click the Filter link in the Online Pictures window, select Clipart on the Filter menu to filter the search results, then verify the Creative Commons only check box is selected.

c. Insert the mountain with orange sky image shown in **FIGURE 3-32**. (*Note:* Select a different image if this one is not available to you. It is best to select an image that is similar in shape to the image shown in **FIGURE 3-32**.)

d. Scroll down, click Unknown in the credit line, select the box that surrounds the credit line, then delete the credit line box, if necessary.

e. Use the Shape Width box in the Size group on the Picture Format tab to change the width of the image to 3".

f. Use the Position command to position the image in the top right with square text wrapping.

g. Apply a 1-point Black, Text 1 color picture border, then change the color of the image to Gold, Accent color 5 Light.

h. Use the Reset Picture arrow to reset the picture (but not the size).

i. Use the Artistic Effects button to apply the Glow Diffused artistic effect to the image (second row, fourth column).

j. Use the Color button to change the color tone to Temperature: 11200 K.

k. Use the Corrections button to adjust the brightness and contrast to Brightness: 0% (Normal) Contrast: −20%, then save your changes.

FIGURE 3-32

Word

Skills Review (continued)

8. **Size and scale a graphic.**
   - a. Resize the image proportionally so that it is about **1**" high and **1.5**" wide.
   - b. Drag the image so its top is aligned with the first line of body text and its left side is aligned with the left margin.
   - c. Resize the image so that it is precisely **1.18**" high and **1.78**" wide. Deselect the Lock aspect ratio check box, if necessary.
   - d. Position the image so its Horizontal absolute position is 0" to the right of the margin and its Vertical absolute position is 1" below the margin.
   - e. Add ¼-point Black, Text 1 picture border around the image, then save your changes.

9. **Draw and format shapes.**
   - a. Scroll until the Five-step approach… heading is at the top of your screen.
   - b. Click the Shapes button, click the Star: 7 Points shape, then click in the numbered list below the Five-step… heading.
   - c. Resize the shape to be **1**" high and **1.5**" wide.
   - d. Right-click the shape, click Add Text, type **New!**, select the text, then apply bold.
   - e. Fill the shape with Intense Effect – Gold, Accent 2, then apply the Preset 1 shape effect.
   - f. Change the shape of the object to Explosion: 8 Points (Stars and Banners section).
   - g. Apply square text wrapping, then position the shape so it aligns with the right margin and the first line of body text under the Five-step… heading. (*Hint*: Make sure the shape is under the border.)
   - h. Draw a rectangle shape over the numbered list, then resize it to **.5**" high and **.8**" wide.
   - i. Select the explosion shape, then use the Format Painter to copy the format of the explosion shape to the rectangle shape.
   - j. Change the shape of the rectangle to Star: 4 Points.
   - k. Position the Star: 4 Points shape to the left of the tabbed text at the bottom of page 1, so that it aligns with the left margin, then save your changes.

10. **Arrange graphic objects.**
    - a. Select the Star: 4 Points shape, copy it, then paste two copies.
    - b. Drag the two pasted copies of the star shape to a blank area of the page.
    - c. Change the fill color of one star to be Red, Accent 3.
    - d. Position the two stars so that they overlap each other slightly, then use the Bring Forward arrow to bring the gold star to the front.
    - e. Select the two stars, then use the Group arrow to group them into a single object.
    - f. Position the grouped object in the bottom right of the page with square text wrapping.
    - g. Select the single gold star on the left side of the page, rotate the shape 90 degrees to the left, then save your changes.

11. **Create SmartArt graphics.**
    - a. Scroll to the end of the document, click in the middle blank paragraph above the Last revised… shaded paragraph, then click the SmartArt button.
    - b. Select Process in the list of SmartArt types, select the Accent Process style, then click OK.
    - c. Change the colors of the SmartArt object to the Colorful Range - Accent Colors 5 to 6 style.
    - d. Enter text in the SmartArt object so that the process diagram appears as shown in **FIGURE 3-33**.
    - e. Resize the SmartArt object to be **3.2**" high, then save your changes.
    - f. Adjust the size or position of objects as needed to so that your document resembles the document shown in the figure. View your document in two-page view and compare it to the document shown in **FIGURE 3-34**.
    - g. Save your changes to the document, submit it to your instructor, close the file, and then exit Word.

FIGURE 3-33

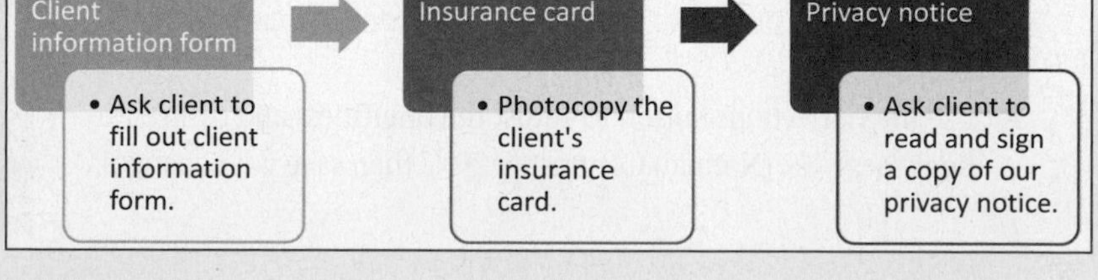
Client information form
• Ask client to fill out client information form.
Insurance card
• Photocopy the client's insurance card.
Privacy notice
• Ask client to read and sign a copy of our privacy notice.

FIGURE 3-34

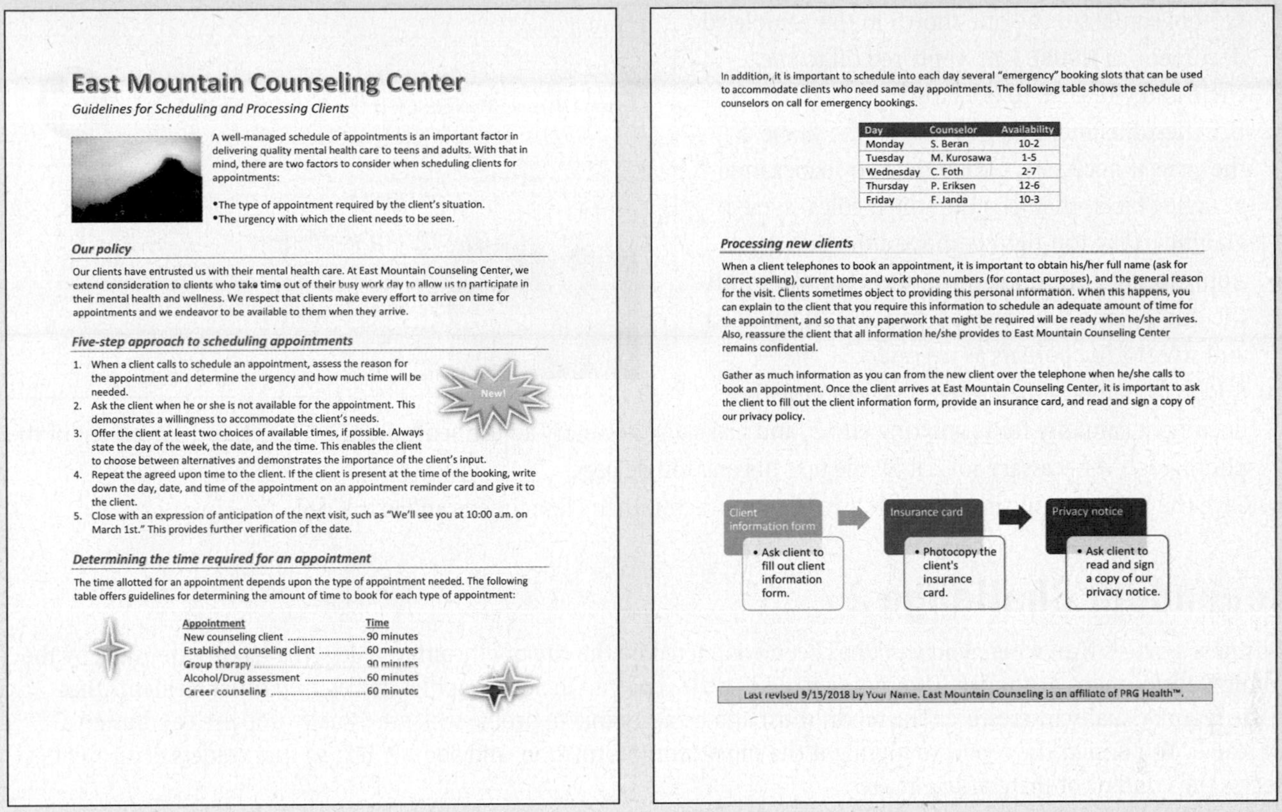

East Mountain Counseling Center

Guidelines for Scheduling and Processing Clients

A well-managed schedule of appointments is an important factor in delivering quality mental health care to teens and adults. With that in mind, there are two factors to consider when scheduling clients for appointments:

- The type of appointment required by the client's situation.
- The urgency with which the client needs to be seen.

Our policy

Our clients have entrusted us with their mental health care. At East Mountain Counseling Center, we extend consideration to clients who take time out of their busy work day to allow us to participate in their mental health and wellness. We respect that clients make every effort to arrive on time for appointments and we endeavor to be available to them when they arrive.

Five-step approach to scheduling appointments

1. When a client calls to schedule an appointment, assess the reason for the appointment and determine the urgency and how much time will be needed.
2. Ask the client when he or she is not available for the appointment. This demonstrates a willingness to accommodate the client's needs.
3. Offer the client at least two choices of available times, if possible. Always state the day of the week, the date, and the time. This enables the client to choose between alternatives and demonstrates the importance of the client's input.
4. Repeat the agreed upon time to the client. If the client is present at the time of the booking, write down the day, date, and time of the appointment on an appointment reminder card and give it to the client.
5. Close with an expression of anticipation of the next visit, such as "We'll see you at 10:00 a.m. on March 1st." This provides further verification of the date.

New!

Determining the time required for an appointment

The time allotted for an appointment depends upon the type of appointment needed. The following table offers guidelines for determining the amount of time to book for each type of appointment:

Appointment	Time
New counseling client	90 minutes
Established counseling client	60 minutes
Group therapy	90 minutes
Alcohol/Drug assessment	60 minutes
Career counseling	60 minutes

In addition, it is important to schedule into each day several "emergency" booking slots that can be used to accommodate clients who need same day appointments. The following table shows the schedule of counselors on call for emergency bookings.

Day	Counselor	Availability
Monday	S. Beran	10-2
Tuesday	M. Kurosawa	1-5
Wednesday	C. Foth	2-7
Thursday	P. Eriksen	12-6
Friday	F. Janda	10-3

Processing new clients

When a client telephones to book an appointment, it is important to obtain his/her full name (ask for correct spelling), current home and work phone numbers (for contact purposes), and the general reason for the visit. Clients sometimes object to providing this personal information. When this happens, you can explain to the client that you require this information to schedule an adequate amount of time for the appointment, and so that any paperwork that might be required will be ready when he/she arrives. Also, reassure the client that all information he/she provides to East Mountain Counseling Center remains confidential.

Gather as much information as you can from the new client over the telephone when he/she calls to book an appointment. Once the client arrives at East Mountain Counseling Center, it is important to ask the client to fill out the client information form, provide an insurance card, and read and sign a copy of our privacy policy.

Client information form
• Ask client to fill out client information form.
Insurance card
• Photocopy the client's insurance card.
Privacy notice
• Ask client to read and sign a copy of our privacy notice.

Last revised 9/15/2018 by Your Name. East Mountain Counseling is an affiliate of PRG Health™.

Independent Challenge 1

The Riverwalk Medical Clinic publishes a variety of helpful tips and information sheets related to health issues. Your colleague has assembled a "Fast Facts" sheet on Lyme disease and has asked you to format it so it highlights the important information regarding the disease. Design and formatting elements will make the document attractive to readers.

a. Start Word, open the file IL_WD_3-3.docx from the drive and folder where you store your Data Files, save it as **IL_WD_3_FastFacts**, then read the document to get a basic understanding of its contents.

b. Select the entire document, then change the font to 11-point Garamond.

c. Change all four document margins to Narrow .5.

d. Change the theme colors to Orange Red. (*Hint*: Use the Theme Colors button on the Design tab.)

e. Change the font size of the first line, "Riverwalk Medical Clinic—Fast Facts", to 14, and apply italic.

f. Change the font size of the second line, the title "Lyme Disease…", to 20.

g. Change the font size of the heading "How ticks spread the disease" to 14, apply bold, then add a single bottom border with the Gray, Text 2 color, and a width of 1/2 pt.

h. Use the Format Painter to copy the format of the "How ticks spread the disease" heading to the following headings in the tip sheet: Tick habitat and distribution, Symptoms and signs, Treatment and prognosis, and Protection from tick bites.

i. Insert an online picture that is a photograph. Select a photograph that is appropriate to the content. (*Hint*: Use the Filter link in the Online Pictures window to filter for photographs.)

j. Remove the credit line box from the image, if necessary.

k. Resize the image proportionally so that it is 2.5" wide, wrap text around the image, then position the photograph to the left of the "How ticks spread the disease" heading. **FIGURE 3-35** shows a sample layout.

l. Enhance the photograph with corrections, colors, artistic effects, borders, or styles.

Independent Challenge 1 (continued)

m. Using circle and cross shapes, create a medical symbol similar to the one shown in the completed document in **FIGURE 3-35**. Apply red fill to the circle and white fill to the cross.

n. Use the adjustment handle to alter the shape of the cross if necessary. Group the two shapes in to a single object, then position the medical symbol graphic in the top-right corner on the first page.

o. Apply font colors to the document that work with the photograph you selected, then adjust the color and style of the borders as necessary.

p. Add your name to the footer, then examine the document carefully for formatting errors, and make any necessary adjustments. Adjust the size and placement of the photograph if necessary so that all the text fits on a single page.

q. Save the information sheet, submit it to your instructor, then close the file and exit Word.

FIGURE 3-35

Riverwalk Medical Clinic—Fast Facts

Lyme Disease: Prevention is the Best Protection

Lyme disease, an inflammatory disease transmitted by the bite of a deer tick, has become a serious public health risk in certain areas of the United States and Canada. Campers, hikers, fishermen, outdoor enthusiasts, and other travelers or residents in endemic areas who have frequent or prolonged exposure to tick habitats during the spring and summer months are at increased risk for Lyme disease.

How ticks spread the disease

The bacterium that causes Lyme disease is spread by the bite of infected Ixodes ticks, commonly known as deer ticks. Ticks can attach to any part of the human body but are most often found in hairy areas such as the scalp, groin, and armpit. In most cases the tick must be attached for at least 48 hours before the bacteria can be transmitted. During the spring and summer months, when people spend more time outdoors, the young (nymphal) ticks are most often responsible for spreading the disease. These ticks are tiny (about the size of the head of a pin) and rarely noticed, making it difficult for people to find and remove an infected tick.

Independent Challenge 2

The business services firm where you work has been contracted by the city of Lincoln to redesign a report published by the Economic Development Authority. The client would like the report to include graphics, tables, and other elements that make the report visually interesting. The report must also be accessible to people who are visually impaired and using a screen reader. You design the report to highlight the important information, and add Alt Text so that readers of all abilities can access the content of the graphic images.

a. Start Word, open the file IL_WD_3-4.docx from the drive and folder where you store your Data Files, then save it as **IL_WD_3_Lincoln**.

b. Read the document to get a basic understanding of the contents, use CTRL+A to select all the text in the document, then clear all formatting from the text.

c. Determine the font and font sizes you will use for the body text, title, subtitle, and headings.

d. Select all the text again, change the style to No Spacing, then apply the font you intend to use for the body text to all the text in the report.

e. Format the title and subtitle using a font, font size, and font color of your choice.

f. Format the heading Mission using a font, font size, and font color of your choice, then, use the Format Painter to copy the formatting of the Mission heading to the Lincoln Advantage and Issues headings.

g. Format the subheading Services using a font, font size, and font color of your choice, then use the Format Painter to copy the formatting of the Services heading to the following headings: Project Finance, Real Estate Development, Business Loans, Technology/Innovation, Arts/Creativity, Geography, and Expected Population Growth.

h. Scroll to the bottom of the document. Above the final paragraph, insert a table with two columns and three rows, then enter the following text.

Years	Population Growth
2020–2040	18%
2040–2060	32% (projected)

i. Autofit the table to the content, apply an appropriate table style to the table, adjust the formatting, then center the table between the margins.

Independent Challenge 2 (continued)

j. Scroll to the top of the document. Using shapes, create a graphic to illustrate the document. The graphic should be composed of two or more shapes. For example, you might draw city buildings, an abstract design, or something else you think will represent the content.

k. Format the shapes with fills, outlines, and effects. Use the adjustment and rotate handles to alter the shapes as necessary.

l. Position the shapes so that they overlap, use the Bring Forward and Send Backward buttons to adjust the layers, then group the shapes into a single object.

m. Resize the grouped object, wrap text around it, and position it in the document.

n. Create a SmartArt graphic similar to **FIGURE 3-36**. Use the Alternating Hexagons SmartArt style (List group), then format the SmartArt graphic using colors, styles, and effects.

o. Resize the SmartArt graphic and position it in the document.

p. Use the Multiple Pages button to view both pages of the document, then adjust the size and position of the graphics.

q. Select the shapes graphic you created in steps j–m, use the Alt Text button to open the Alt Text pane, then mark the shapes graphic as decorative.

r. Select the SmartArt graphic, then type a description of the SmartArt graphic in the Alt Text pane.

s. Use the Check Accessibility button on the Review tab to check the document for accessibility issues.

t. Add your name to the footer, save your changes to the document, submit it to your instructor, close the file, and then exit Word.

FIGURE 3-36

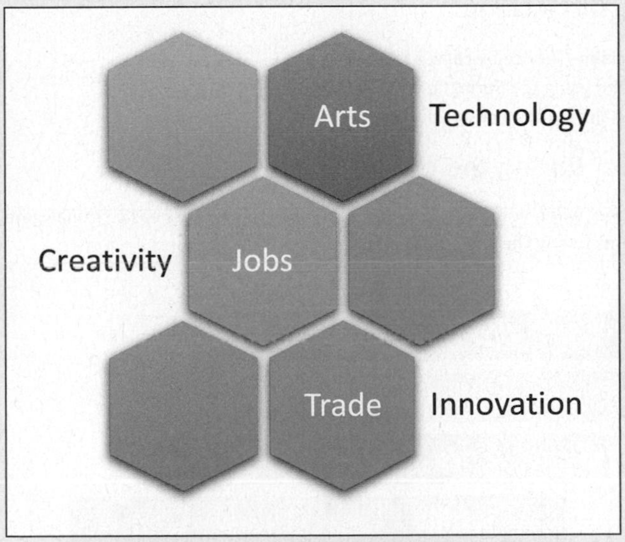

Visual Workshop

Open the file IL_WD_3-5.docx from the location where you store your Data Files, then save the document as **IL_WD_3_ClaimFlyer**. Create the one-page flyer shown in **FIGURE 3-37**. Use 12-point Calibri for the body text, 36-point Calibri for the title, 16-point Calibri for the subtitle, and 18-point Calibri for the headings. To create the SmartArt graphic object, use the Staggered Process style from the Process group. Add a registered trademark symbol ® after "Springfield" in each instance of "Springfield Mobile app". Add your name to the footer, then submit a copy of the flyer to your instructor.

FIGURE 3-37

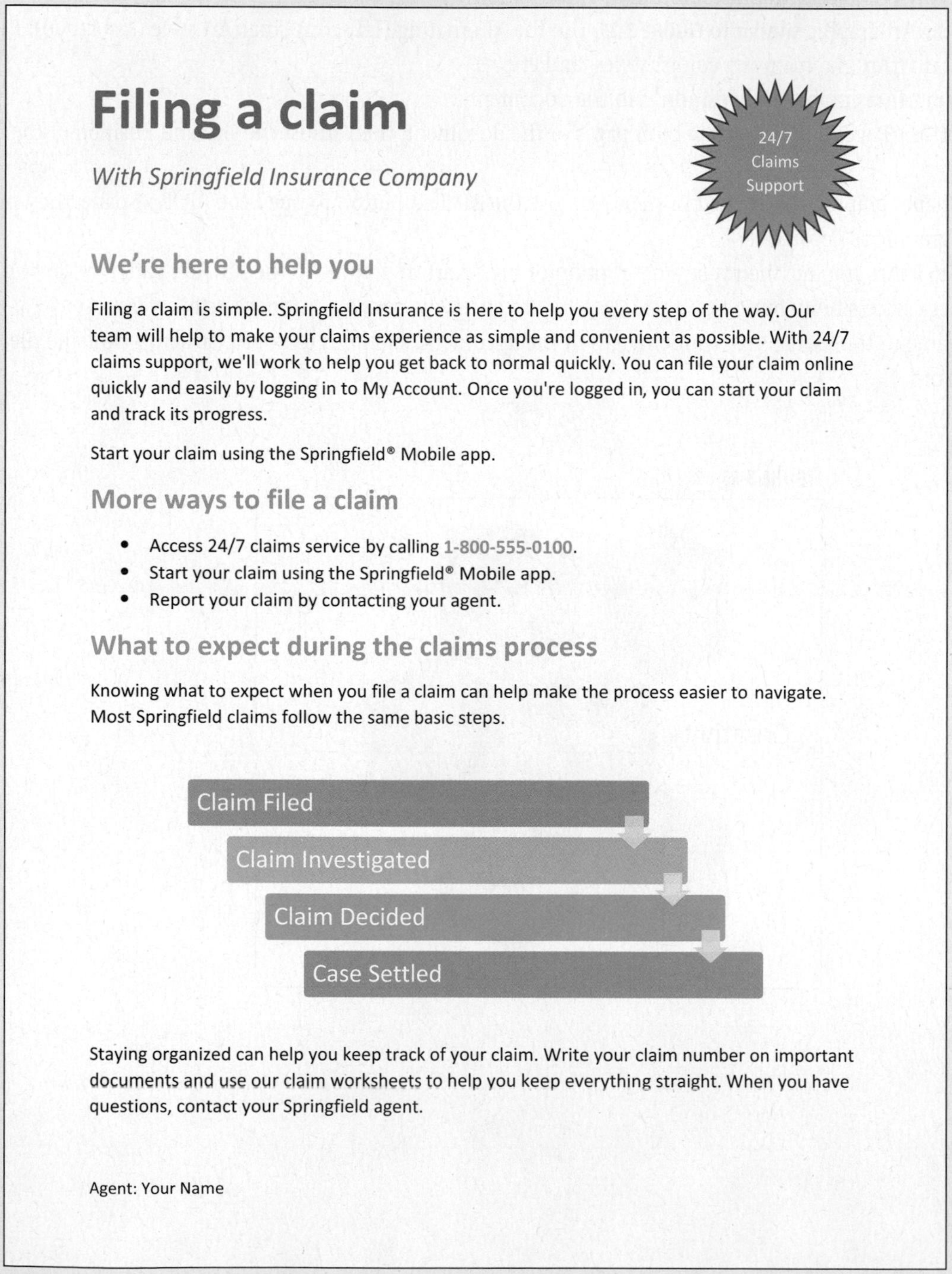

Filing a claim

With Springfield Insurance Company

24/7
Claims
Support

We're here to help you

Filing a claim is simple. Springfield Insurance is here to help you every step of the way. Our team will help to make your claims experience as simple and convenient as possible. With 24/7 claims support, we'll work to help you get back to normal quickly. You can file your claim online quickly and easily by logging in to My Account. Once you're logged in, you can start your claim and track its progress.

Start your claim using the Springfield® Mobile app.

More ways to file a claim

- Access 24/7 claims service by calling 1-800-555-0100.
- Start your claim using the Springfield® Mobile app.
- Report your claim by contacting your agent.

What to expect during the claims process

Knowing what to expect when you file a claim can help make the process easier to navigate. Most Springfield claims follow the same basic steps.

Claim Filed
Claim Investigated
Claim Decided
Case Settled

Staying organized can help you keep track of your claim. Write your claim number on important documents and use our claim worksheets to help you keep everything straight. When you have questions, contact your Springfield agent.

Agent: Your Name

Getting Started with Excel

CASE You have been hired as an assistant at JCL Talent, a company that provides recruitment services for employers and job seekers. You report to Dawn LaPointe, the director of technical careers. As Dawn's assistant, you create worksheets to analyze data from various company offices to help her make sound decisions on company expansion, investments, and new recruiting opportunities.

Module Objectives

After completing this module, you will be able to:

- Explore Excel
- Enter data
- Edit data
- Copy and move cell data
- Enter formulas and use AutoSum
- Copy formulas with relative cell references
- Copy formulas with absolute cell references
- Enter a formula with multiple operators
- Insert a function
- Switch worksheet views
- Choose print options

Files You Will Need

IL_EX_1-1.xlsx
IL_EX_1-2.xlsx
IL_EX_1-3.xlsx
IL_EX_1-4.xlsx
IL_EX_1-5.xlsx

Excel
Module 1

Explore Excel

Learning Outcomes
- Define key spreadsheet terms
- Open and save an Excel file
- Identify Excel window elements

Microsoft Excel is an **electronic spreadsheet program**, a computer program used to perform calculations and analyze and present numeric data. An Excel file, a **workbook**, is a collection of related worksheets contained within a single file with the file extension xlsx. A workbook is made up of one or more worksheets. A **worksheet** contains a grid of columns and rows where you can enter and manipulate data, perform calculations with data, and analyze data. **CASE** *You decide to review the distribution of technical postings in JCL's North American offices, to learn more about where and when these types of jobs have been posted.*

STEPS

TROUBLE
If you don't see the extension .xlsx on the filenames in the Save As dialog box, don't worry; Windows can be set up to display or not to display the file extensions.

QUICK TIP
You can open a blank workbook by clicking Blank workbook rather than Open.

1. **sam Click the Start button on the Windows taskbar, type Excel, click Excel, click Open, navigate to the location where you store your Data Files, click IL_EX_1-1.xlsx, then click Open**
2. **Click the File tab, click Save As on the navigation bar, click Browse, navigate to the location where you store your Data Files if necessary, type IL_EX_1_Postings in the File name box, then click Save**

   Using **FIGURE 1-1** as a guide, identify the following items:
   - The **Name box** is the box to the left of the formula bar that shows the cell reference or name of the active cell. "A1" appears in the Name box.
   - The **formula bar** is the area above the worksheet grid where you enter or edit data in the active cell.
   - The **worksheet window** is an area of the program window that displays part of the current worksheet, which can contain a total of 1,048,576 rows and 16,384 columns. The columns and rows intersect to form cells, where you can enter and manipulate text, numbers, formulas, or a combination of all three. Every cell has its own unique location or **cell address**, a cell's location, expressed by its column letter and row number such as A1.
   - The **cell pointer** is a dark rectangle that outlines the active cell in a worksheet. In the figure, the cell pointer outlines cell A1, so A1 is the active cell.
   - By default, a workbook file contains one worksheet named Sheet1—but you can have as many sheets as your computer's memory allows in a workbook. The New sheet button to the right of Sheet1 allows you to add worksheets to a workbook. **Sheet tab scrolling buttons** are triangles that let you navigate to additional sheet tabs when available; they're located to the left of the sheet tabs.
   - You can use the scroll bars to move around in a worksheet that is too large to fit on the screen at once.
   - The status bar provides a brief description of the active command or task in progress. The **mode indicator** on the left end of the status bar indicates the program's status, such as the Edit mode in Excel. You are in Edit mode any time you are entering or changing the contents of a cell. You can use the Zoom In and Zoom Out buttons in the status bar to increase or decrease the scale of the displayed worksheet.
   - You can use the **Search box** on the title bar to find a command or access the Excel Help system.
   - The AutoSave button on the Quick Access Toolbar is on if you are working on a file saved on OneDrive. When AutoSave is on, your file will be automatically saved as you make changes.
3. **Click cell B4**

   Cell B4 becomes the active cell. To activate a different cell, you can click the cell or press the arrow keys on your keyboard to move to it.

QUICK TIP
The button that opens in the lower-right corner of a range is the Quick Analysis tool.

4. **Click cell B4, drag to cell B11, then release the mouse button**

   You selected a group of cells and they are highlighted, as shown in **FIGURE 1-2**. A series of two or more adjacent cells in a column, row, or rectangular group of cells, notated using the cell address of its upper-left and lower-right corners, such as B4:B11, is called a **range**; you select a range when you want to perform an action on a group of cells at once, such as moving them or formatting them.

FIGURE 1-1: Open workbook

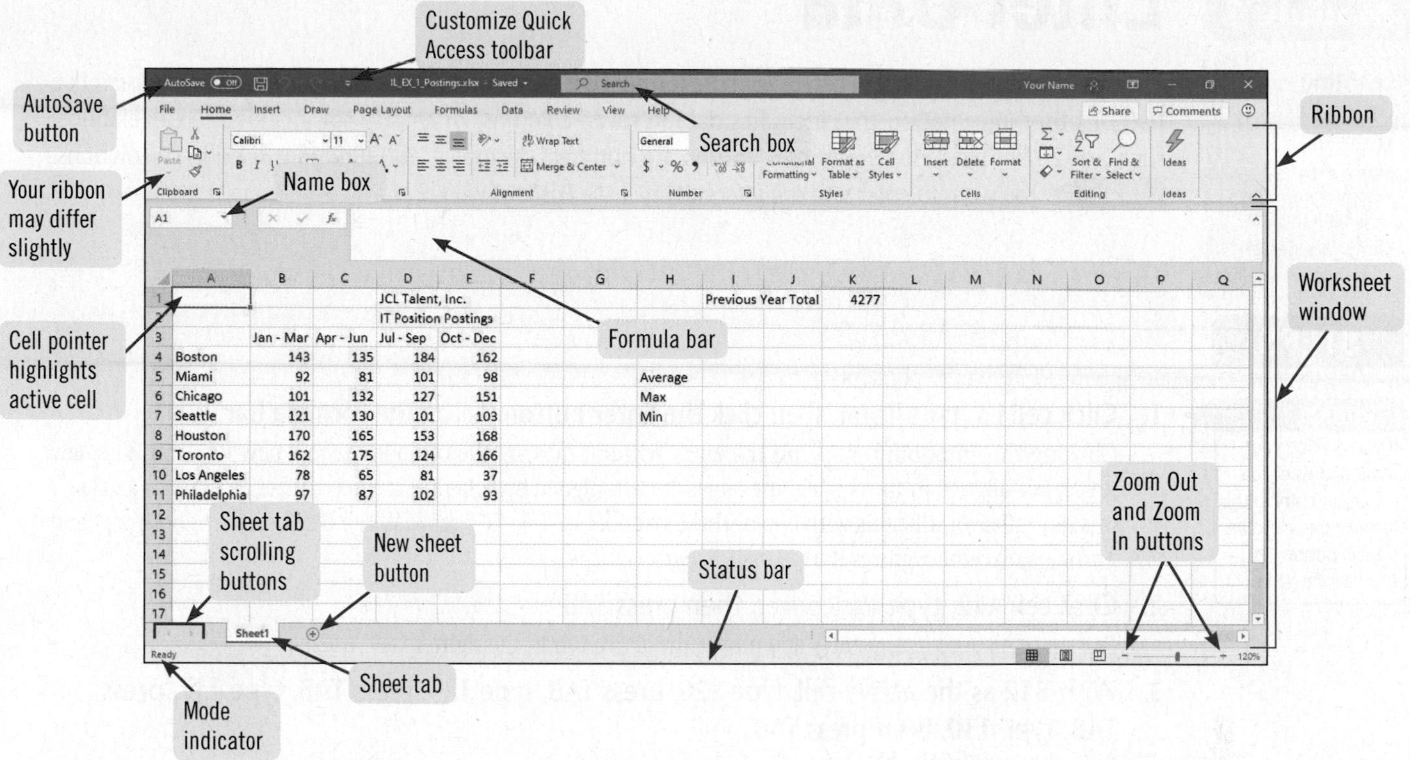

FIGURE 1-2: Selected range

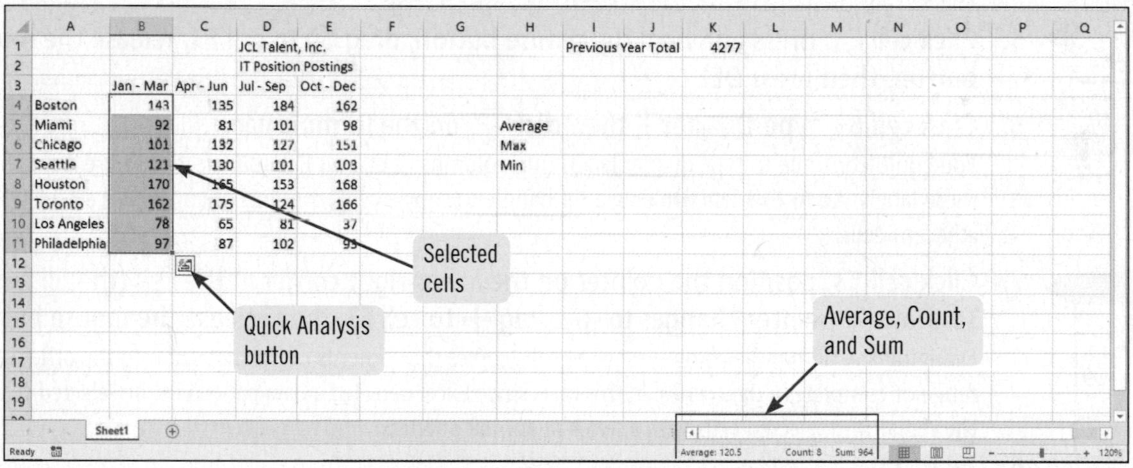

Navigating a worksheet

With over a million cells available in a worksheet, it is important to know how to move around in, or navigate, a worksheet. You can use the arrow keys on the keyboard ↑, ↓, →, or ← to move one cell at a time, or press PAGE UP or PAGE DOWN to move one screen at a time. To move one screen to the left, press ALT+PAGE UP; to move one screen to the right, press ALT+PAGE DOWN.

You can also use the pointer to click the desired cell. If the desired cell is not visible in the worksheet window, use the scroll bars or use the Go To command by clicking the Find & Select button in the Editing group on the Home tab on the ribbon. To quickly jump to the first cell in a worksheet, press CTRL+HOME; to jump to the last cell, press CTRL+END.

Excel
Module 1

Enter Data

Learning Outcomes
- Enter labels
- Enter values
- Copy data using the fill handle
- Enter a series of data with Auto Fill

To enter content in a cell, you can type in the formula bar or directly in the cell itself. **Labels** are descriptive text or other information that identifies data in rows, columns, or charts, not included in calculations, such as "2021 Sales" or "Expenses". **Values** are numbers, formulas, and functions used in calculations.

CASE *You want to enter and edit information in the Postings workbook.*

STEPS

QUICK TIP If you change your mind and want to cancel an entry in the formula bar, click the Cancel button on the formula bar.

1. **Click cell F3, type Total, then click the Enter button on the formula bar**
   Clicking the Enter button accepts the entry without moving the cell pointer to a new location. The new text is left-aligned in the cell because labels are left-aligned by default. Excel recognizes an entry as a value if it is a number or it begins with one of these symbols: +, –, =, @, #, or $. When a cell contains both text and numbers, Excel recognizes it as a label.
2. **Click cell A12, type Vancouver, then press TAB**
   Pressing TAB accepts the entry and moves the active cell to the right, to cell B12.
3. **With B12 as the active cell, type 120, press TAB, type 130, press TAB, type 117, press TAB, type 130, then press TAB**
   The quarterly data is displayed for the Vancouver office, as shown in **FIGURE 1-3**. The numbers are right-aligned because values are right-aligned by default. You want to replace the monthly labels in row 3 with quarter labels.

QUICK TIP If you want to clear a cell's content, including its formatting, click the Clear button in the Editing group, then click Clear All.

4. **Click cell B3, then press DEL**
   You can delete each cell entry individually or delete a range of cells.
5. **Click cell C3, press and hold the mouse button, drag to cell E3, release the mouse button, then press DEL**
6. **Click cell B3, type Quarter 1, then click on the formula bar**
   You could continue to type quarter labels into columns C, D, and E, but it is easier to use Auto Fill to enter these labels. **Auto Fill** lets you drag a fill handle to copy a cell's contents or continue a selected series into adjacent cells.

QUICK TIP You can insert a worksheet into a workbook by clicking the New sheet button.

7. **Click cell B3, position the pointer on the lower-right corner of the cell (the fill handle) so that the pointer changes to +, drag + to cell E3, then release the mouse button**
   Dragging the fill handle across a range of cells copies the contents of the first cell into the other cells in the range or completes a data series. In this case, since Excel detected a data pattern in the selected cells, it filled the remaining selected cells with a series of annual quarters.
8. **Click the Auto Fill Options button**
   Options for filling the selected range include Fill Series, which is selected, as shown in **FIGURE 1-4**. The other available options allow you to change to copying cells, fill the cells with formatting only, or fill the cells without formatting.
9. **Save your work**

FIGURE 1-3: Vancouver data entered

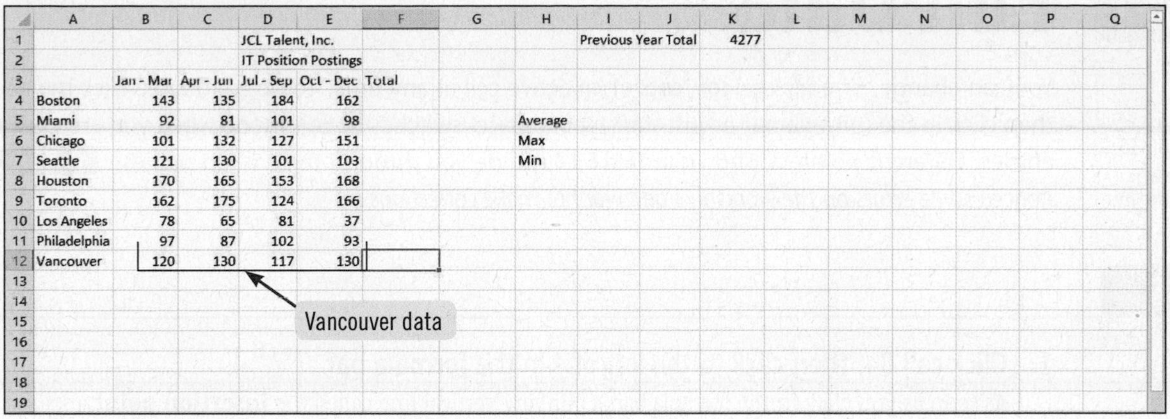

	A	B	C	D	E	F	H	I	K
1				JCL Talent, Inc.				Previous Year Total	4277
2				IT Position Postings					
3		Jan - Mar	Apr - Jun	Jul - Sep	Oct - Dec	Total			
4	Boston	143	135	184	162				
5	Miami	92	81	101	98		Average		
6	Chicago	101	132	127	151		Max		
7	Seattle	121	130	101	103		Min		
8	Houston	170	165	153	168				
9	Toronto	162	175	124	166				
10	Los Angeles	78	65	81	37				
11	Philadelphia	97	87	102	93				
12	Vancouver	120	130	117	130				

FIGURE 1-4: Auto Fill options

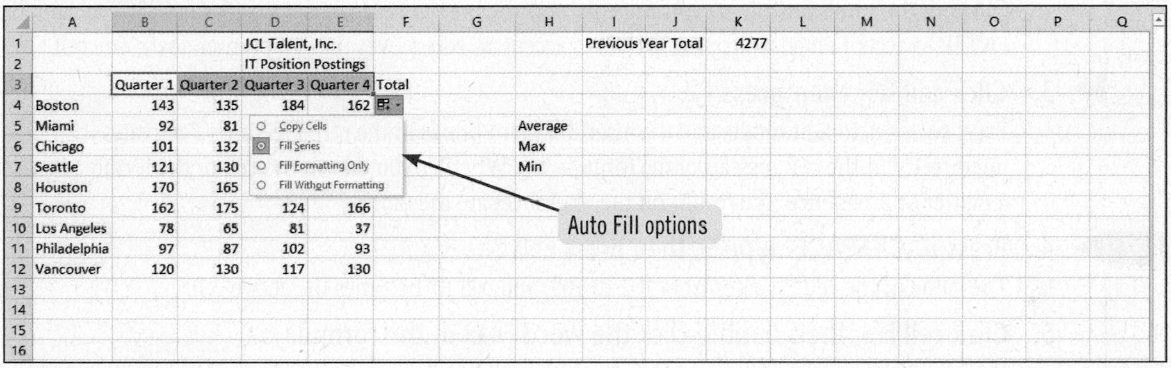

	A	B	C	D	E	F	H	I	K
1				JCL Talent, Inc.				Previous Year Total	4277
2				IT Position Postings					
3		Quarter 1	Quarter 2	Quarter 3	Quarter 4	Total			
4	Boston	143	135	184	162				
5	Miami	92	81				Average		
6	Chicago	101	132				Max		
7	Seattle	121	130				Min		
8	Houston	170	165						
9	Toronto	162	175	124	166				
10	Los Angeles	78	65	81	37				
11	Philadelphia	97	87	102	93				
12	Vancouver	120	130	117	130				

Inserting and deleting selected cells

As you add formulas to your workbook, you may need to insert or delete cells. To insert cells, click the Insert arrow in the Cells group on the Home tab, then click Insert Cells. The Insert dialog box opens, asking if you want to insert a cell and move the current active cell down or to the right of the new one. To delete one or more selected cells, click the Delete arrow in the Cells group, click Delete Cells, and in the Delete dialog box, indicate which way you want to move the adjacent cells. When using this option, be careful not to disturb row or column alignment that may be necessary to maintain the accuracy of cell references on the worksheet. You can also click the Insert button or Delete button in the Cells group to insert or delete a single cell. Excel automatically adjusts cell references within the formulas of any moved cells to reflect their new locations.

Using Auto Fill and Flash Fill

Auto Fill is an Excel feature that lets you drag a fill handle to copy a cell's contents or continue a series into adjacent cells. This can be used to enter the months of the year, days of the week, and custom lists of a series. Flash Fill, although similar to Auto Fill, isn't used to fill in a series of data. It is an Excel feature that looks for patterns in the data you enter and automatically fills or formats data in remaining cells based on those patterns. The filled data must be adjacent to the example data. Flash Fill often detects the pattern as you enter data and shows the new data in a light font. Pressing ENTER accepts the suggestion and enters the data. If Excel doesn't detect a pattern automatically, you can click the Flash Fill button in the Data Tools group on the Data tab to fill in the data.

Excel
Module 1

Edit Data

Learning Outcomes
- Edit cell entries in the formula bar
- Edit cell entries in the cell

You can change, or edit, the contents of an active cell at any time. To do so, double-click the cell, and then click in the formula bar or just start typing. Excel switches to Edit mode when you are making cell entries. Different pointers, shown in **TABLE 1-1**, guide you through the editing process. **CASE** *You noticed some errors on the worksheet and want to make corrections.*

STEPS

1. **Click cell B4, then click to the left of 4 in the formula bar**
   As soon as you click in the formula bar, a blinking vertical line called the **insertion point** appears on the formula bar at the location where new text will be inserted. See **FIGURE 1-5**.

QUICK TIP
On some keyboards, you might need to press F-LOCK to enable the function keys.

2. **Press DEL, type 3, then click the Enter button ✓ on the formula bar**
   Clicking the Enter button accepts the edit, and the Boston first quarter posting is 133. You can also press ENTER to accept an edit. Pressing ENTER to accept an edit moves the cell pointer down one cell.

3. **Click cell B6, then press F2**
   Excel switches to Edit mode, and the insertion point blinks in the cell. Pressing F2 activates the cell for editing directly in the cell instead of the formula bar. Whether you edit in the cell or the formula bar is simply a matter of preference; the results on the worksheet are the same.

QUICK TIP
If you notice a mistake *after* confirming a cell entry, click the Undo button on the Quick Access toolbar. The Undo button allows you to reverse up to 100 previous actions, one at a time. If you mistakenly undo an action, you can click the Redo button on the Quick Access toolbar.

4. **Press BACKSPACE, type 9, then press ENTER**
   The value in the cell changes from 101 to 109, and cell B7 becomes the active cell.

5. **Click cell H6, then double-click the word Max in the formula bar**
   Double-clicking a word in a cell selects it. When you selected the word, the Mini toolbar automatically opened.

6. **Type Maximum, then press ENTER**
   When text is selected, typing deletes it and replaces it with the new text.

7. **Double-click cell H7, click to the right of n, type imum, then click ✓**
   Double-clicking a cell activates it for editing directly in the cell. Compare your screen to **FIGURE 1-6**.

8. **Save your work**

Recovering unsaved changes to a workbook file

You can use Excel's AutoRecover feature to automatically save (Autosave) your work as often as you want. This means that if you suddenly lose power or if Excel closes unexpectedly while you're working, you can recover all or some of the changes you made since you saved it last. (Of course, this is no substitute for regularly saving your work; it's just added insurance.) To customize the AutoRecover settings, click the File tab, click Options, then click Save. AutoRecover lets you decide how often and in which location it should AutoSave files. When you restart Excel after losing power, you will see a new section, Recovered files, above the listing of recent files. You can click Show Recovered Files to access the saved and AutoSaved versions of files that were open when Excel closed.

FIGURE 1-5: Worksheet in Edit mode

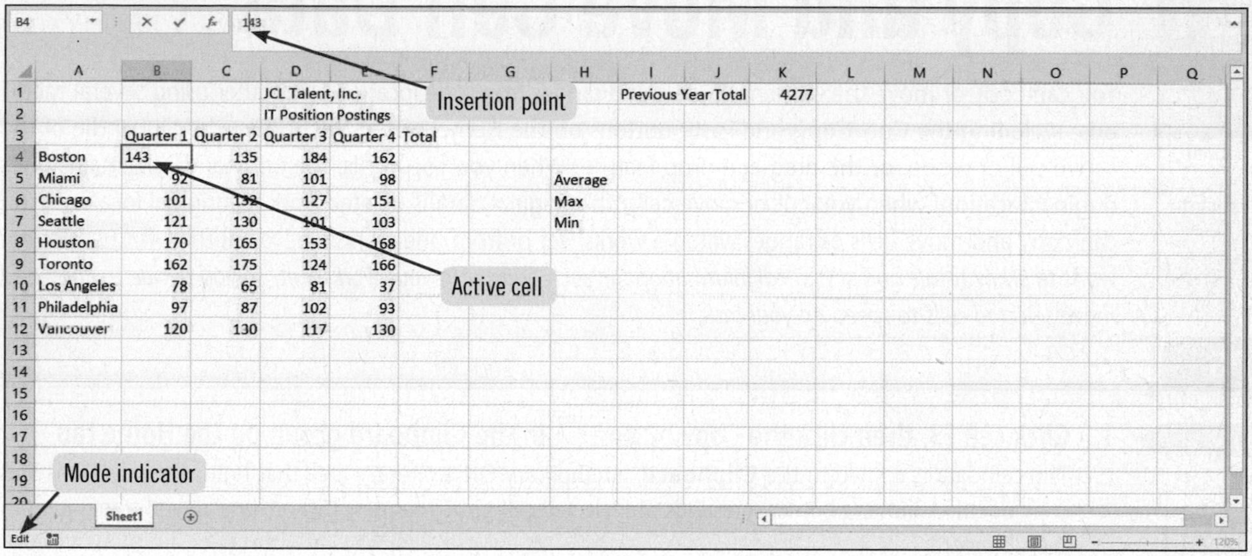

FIGURE 1-6: Edited worksheet

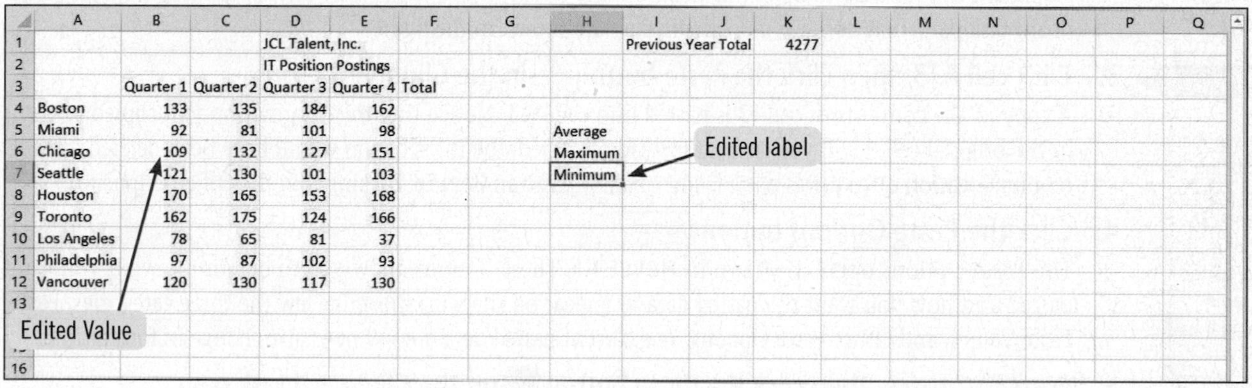

TABLE 1-1: Common pointers in Excel

name	pointer	use to	visible over the
Normal		Select a cell or range; indicates Ready mode	Active worksheet
Fill handle	+	Copy cell contents or series to adjacent cells	Lower-right corner of the active cell or range
I-beam		Edit cell contents in active cell or formula bar	Active cell in Edit mode or over the formula bar
Move		Change the location of the selected cell(s)	Perimeter of the active cell(s)
Copy		Create a duplicate of the selected cell(s)	Perimeter of the active cell(s) when CTRL is pressed
Column resize		Change the width of a column	Border between column heading indicators

Copy and Move Cell Data

Learning Outcomes
- Copy cell data to the Clipboard
- Paste a Clipboard entry
- Move a range

You can copy or move the contents in cells and ranges from one location to another using several methods, including the Cut, Copy, and Paste buttons on the Home tab on the ribbon, the fill handle of the active cell or range, or the drag-and-drop feature. When you copy cells, the original data remains in its original location; when you cut or move cells, the original data is deleted from its original location. You can copy and move cells or ranges within a worksheet or from one worksheet to another. **CASE** *You want to show totals and statistical information for each quarter in your worksheet, so you decide to copy and move selected cells to speed up your task.*

STEPS

QUICK TIP
To cut or copy selected cell contents, activate the cell, then select the characters within the cell that you want to cut or copy.

1. **Click cell F3, then click the Copy button in the Clipboard group on the Home tab**
   The cell data is copied to the **Clipboard**, a temporary Office storage area that holds the selections you copy or cut. A moving border surrounds the selected cell until you press ESC or copy an additional item to the Clipboard.
2. **Click the dialog box launcher in the Clipboard group**
   The Office Clipboard opens in the Clipboard task pane, as shown in **FIGURE 1-7**. When you copy or cut an item, it is cut or copied both to the Clipboard provided by Windows and to the Office Clipboard. The Office Clipboard can hold up to 24 of the most recently cut or copied items from any Office program. Your Clipboard task pane may contain more items than are shown in the figure.

QUICK TIP
You can have multiple items in the Clipboard resulting from multiple copy operations. You can paste these items individually or all the items at the same time by clicking the Paste All button.

3. **Click cell A13, then click the Paste button in the Clipboard group**
   A copy of the contents of cell F3 is pasted into cell A13. Notice that the information you copied remains in the original cell, F3; if you had cut instead of copied, the information would have been deleted from its original location once it was pasted. You can also paste an item by clicking it in the Office Clipboard.
4. **Click the Paste Options button (Ctrl)**
   The Paste Options open, as shown in **FIGURE 1-8**. These options allow you to determine what you want pasted and how you want the pasted data to appear on the worksheet. Review the three categories, Paste, Paste Values, and Other Paste Options. The current pasted data doesn't need any change in formatting.
5. **Press ESC twice, then click the Close button on the Clipboard task pane**
6. **Select the range H5:H7, point to any edge of the selected range until the pointer changes to , drag the range to cell A15, then release the mouse button**
   The move pointer displays an outline of the range you are dragging. When you release the mouse button, you "drop" the selection to the range A15:A17. When pasting an item from the Clipboard, you only need to specify the upper-left cell of the range where you want to paste the selection. If you press and hold CTRL while dragging and dropping, the information is copied instead of moved.

FIGURE 1-7: Copied data in Office Clipboard

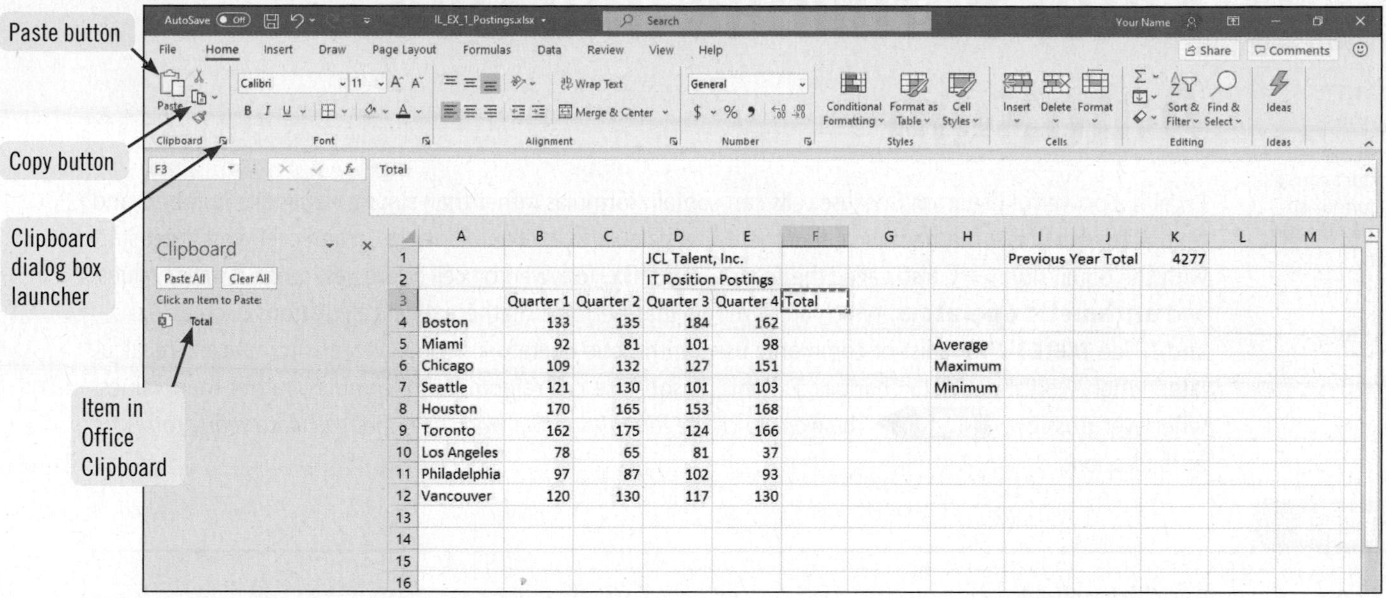

FIGURE 1-8: Paste options

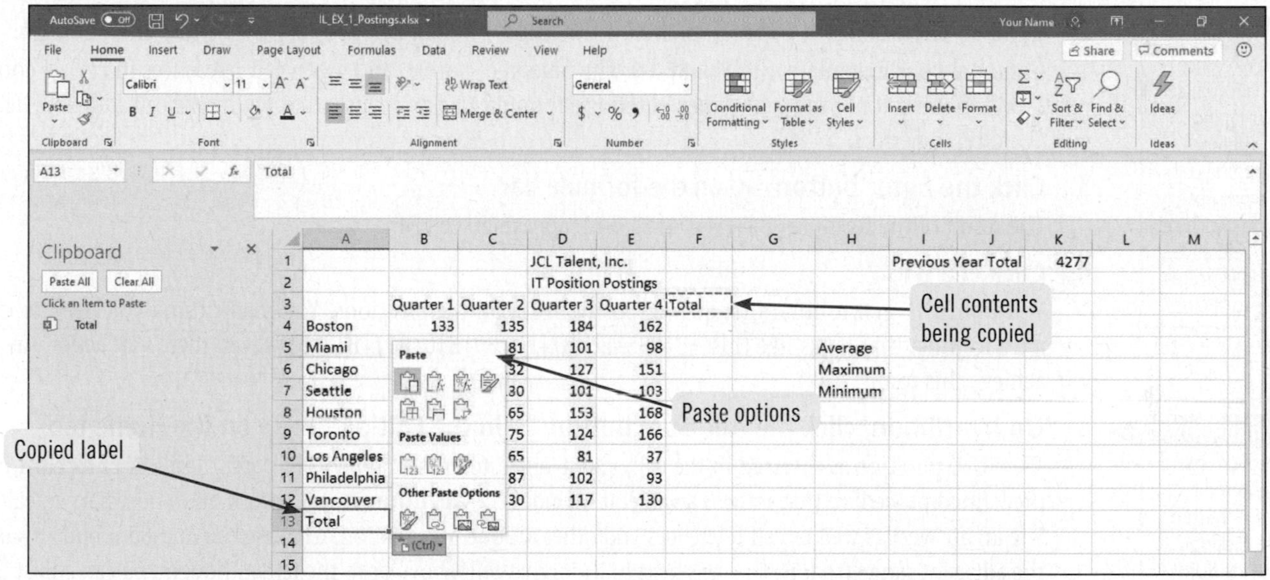

Using Paste Options and Paste Preview

You can selectively paste copied or cut formulas, values, or other data by using the Paste Options button that opens on the worksheet after you paste data or use the Paste arrow in the Clipboard. The Paste Preview feature shows how the current selection will look when pasted. When you click the Paste Options button (or simply press [Ctrl] or the Paste arrow), a gallery of paste option icons opens, organized by category. The Paste category includes pasting formulas, pasting formulas and number formatting, pasting using the source formatting, pasting with no borders (to remove any borders around pasted cells), pasting with the source column widths, and pasting transposed data so that column data appears in rows and row data appears in columns. The Paste Values category includes pasting values only (without formatting), pasting values and number formatting, and pasting values with source formatting. The Other Paste Options category includes pasting formatting, links, pictures, and linked pictures. Clicking Paste Link in this category creates a link to the source data so that in the future, changes to the copied data update the pasted data. Clicking Picture in this category pastes the data as a picture where the picture tools can be used to format it, resize it, or move it.

Excel
Module 1

Learning Outcomes
- Use cell references to create a formula
- Build formulas with the AutoSum button

Enter Formulas and Use AutoSum

Excel is a powerful program because cells can contain formulas rather than simply values like numbers and text. A **formula** is a mathematical statement that calculates a value. Formulas in an Excel worksheet start with the equal sign (=), also called the **formula prefix**, followed by cell addresses, range names, values, and **arithmetic operators**, which are symbols that perform mathematical calculations such as +, –, *, and /. See **TABLE 1-2** for a list of commonly used arithmetic operators. Formulas are automatically recalculated when worksheet data changes. For this reason, use cell references in formulas, rather than values, whenever possible. **CASE** *You want to create formulas in the worksheet that calculate yearly totals for each location.*

STEPS

QUICK TIP
You can reference a cell in a formula by either typing the cell reference or clicking the cell on the worksheet; when you click a cell to add a reference, the Mode indicator changes to "Point."

QUICK TIP
The AutoSum button is also referred to as the Sum button because clicking it inserts the SUM function.

1. **Click cell F4**
   This is the first cell where you want to insert a formula. To calculate the yearly total for the Boston location, you need to add the quarterly totals.
2. **Type =, click cell B4, type +, click cell C4, type +, click cell D4, type +, then click cell E4**
   Compare your formula bar to **FIGURE 1-9**. The blue, red, purple, and green cell references in cell F4 correspond to the color of the cells. When entering a formula, clicking cells rather typing the cell addresses helps avoid typing errors.
3. **Click the Enter button ✓ on the formula bar**
   The result of the formula =B4+C4+D4+E4, 614, appears in cell F4.
4. **Click cell B13**
   You want this cell to total first quarter positions for all the locations. You might think you need to create a formula that looks like this: =B4+B5+B6+B7+B8+B9+B10+B11+B12. However, there's an easier way to achieve this result.
5. **On the ribbon, click the AutoSum button Σ in the Editing group on the Home tab**
   The SUM function is inserted in the cell, and a suggested range appears in parentheses. A **function** is a predefined procedure that returns a value; it includes the **arguments** (the information necessary to calculate an answer) as well as cell references and other unique information. Clicking the AutoSum button sums the adjacent range (that is, the cells next to the active cell) above or to the left, although you can adjust the range if necessary by selecting a different range before accepting the cell entry. Using the SUM function is quicker than entering a formula, and using the range B4:B12 is more efficient than entering individual cell references.
6. **Click ✓ on the formula bar**
   Excel calculates the total contained in cells B4:B12 and displays the result, 1082, in cell B13. The cell actually contains the formula =SUM(B4:B12), but it displays the result. Compare your screen to **FIGURE 1-10**.
7. **Save your work**

FIGURE 1-9: Entering a formula

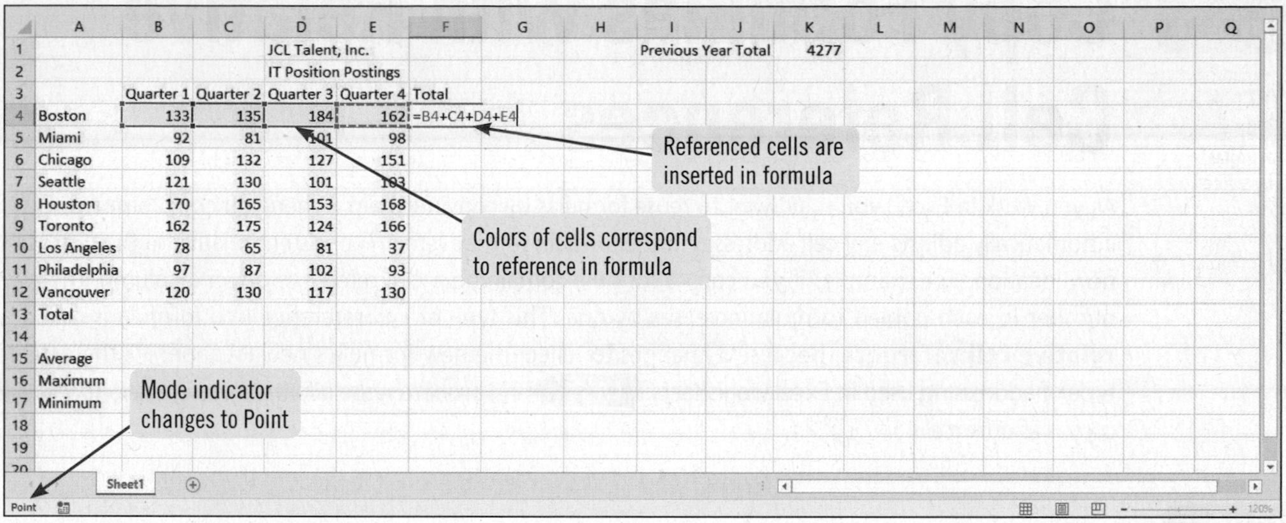

FIGURE 1-10: SUM function in a worksheet

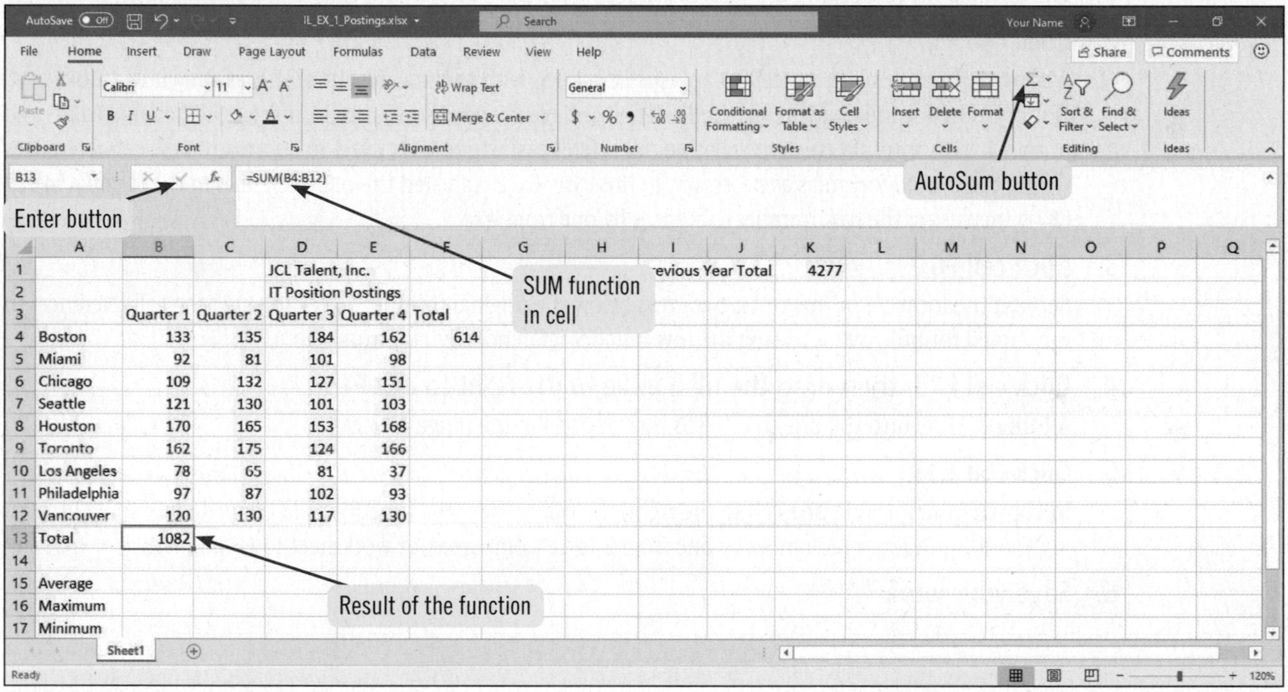

TABLE 1-2: Excel arithmetic operators

operator	purpose	example
+	Addition	=A5+A7
–	Subtraction or negation	=A5–10
*	Multiplication	=A5*A7
/	Division	=A5/A7
%	Percent	=35%
^ (caret)	Exponent	=6^2 (same as 6^2)

Copy Formulas with Relative Cell References

Learning Outcomes
- Copy formulas with relative cell references
- Use the fill handle to copy formulas

As you work in Excel, you may want to reuse formulas by copying them. When you copy formulas, Excel automatically adjusts any cell addresses in the formula so they remain consistent relative to the formula's new location. For example, if you copy a formula containing a cell reference down a column, the row number in each copied formula increases by one. This type of cell reference in a formula is called a **relative cell reference**, because it changes to reflect the new formula's new location; it's the default type of addressing used in Excel worksheets. CASE *You want to reuse a formula you created, so you will copy it to other cells.*

STEPS

1. **Click cell F4, then drag the fill handle down to cell F12**
   The formula for calculating the total for all four quarters is copied into the range F5:F12.
2. **Click cell F5**
   A copy of the formula from cell F4 appears in cell F5, with the new result of 372, as shown in **FIGURE 1-11**. Notice in the formula bar that the cell references have changed so that cells in row 5 are referenced instead of row 4. This formula contains relative cell references, which tells Excel to substitute new cell references within the copied formulas as necessary. In this case, Excel adjusted the cell references in the formula in cell F5 by increasing the row number references by one from 4 to 5.
3. **Click cell F6**
   Because the location of this cell is two rows below the original formula, Excel adjusted the cell references in the copied formula by increasing the row number references by two from 4 to 6.
4. **Click cell B13, then drag the fill handle to the right to cell F13**
   A formula similar to the one in cell B13 now appears in the range C13:F13.
5. **Click cell C13**
   In copying the formula one cell to the right, the cell references in the formula bar are adjusted by increasing the column letter references by one from B to C. Compare your worksheet to **FIGURE 1-12**.
6. **Save your work**

FIGURE 1-11: Formula copied using the fill handle

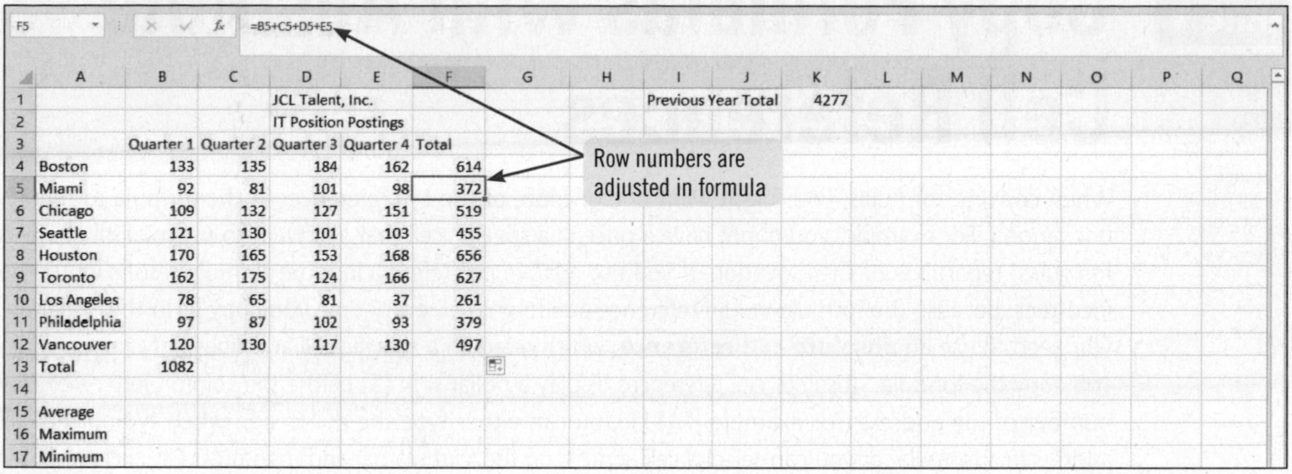

	A	B	C	D	E	F						
	F5		✕ ✓ *fx*	=B5+C5+D5+E5								
1				JCL Talent, Inc.					Previous Year Total	4277		
2				IT Position Postings								
3		Quarter 1	Quarter 2	Quarter 3	Quarter 4	Total						
4	Boston	133	135	184	162	614						
5	Miami	92	81	101	98	372		Row numbers are adjusted in formula				
6	Chicago	109	132	127	151	519						
7	Seattle	121	130	101	103	455						
8	Houston	170	165	153	168	656						
9	Toronto	162	175	124	166	627						
10	Los Angeles	78	65	81	37	261						
11	Philadelphia	97	87	102	93	379						
12	Vancouver	120	130	117	130	497						
13	Total	1082										
14												
15	Average											
16	Maximum											
17	Minimum											

FIGURE 1-12: Formula column references changed

	A	B	C	D	E	F						
	C13		✕ ✓ *fx*	=SUM(C4:C12)								
1				JCL Talent, Inc.					Previous Year Total	4277		
2				IT Position Postings								
3		Quarter 1	Quarter 2	Quarter 3	Quarter 4	Total						
4	Boston	133	135	184	162	614						
5	Miami	92	81	101	98	372		Column references are adjusted in copied formula				
6	Chicago	109	132	127	151	519						
7	Seattle	121	130	101	103	458						
8	Houston	170	165	153	168	656						
9	Toronto	162	175	124	168	627						
10	Los Angeles	78	65	81	37	261						
11	Philadelphia	97	87	102	93	379						
12	Vancouver	120	130	117	130	497						
13	Total	1082	1100	1090	1108	4380						
14												
15	Average											
16	Maximum											
17	Minimum											

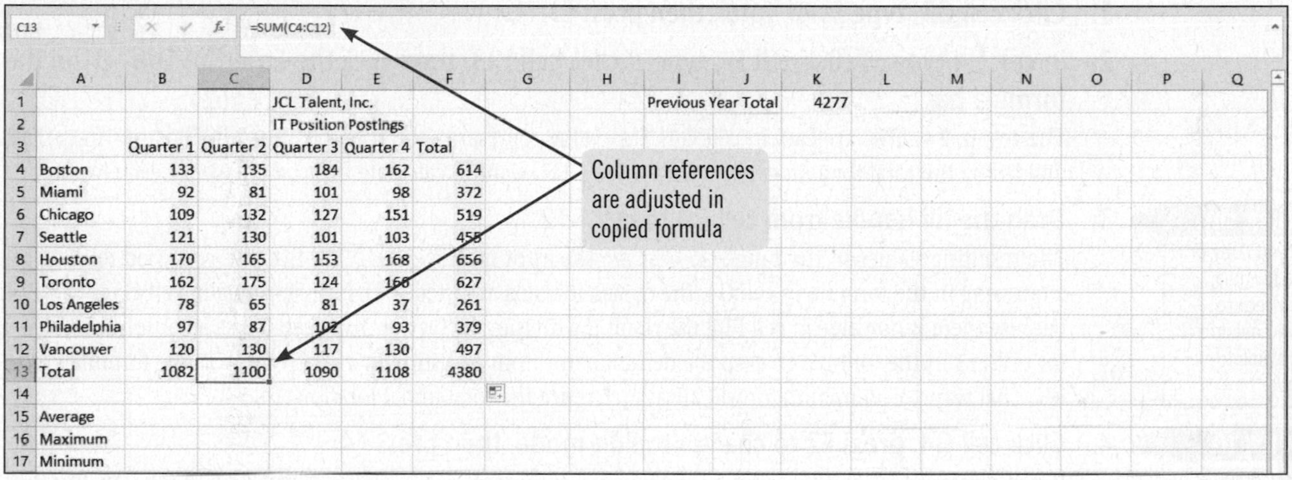

Inserting functions into formulas

You can insert a function on its own or as part of another formula. For example, you have used the SUM function on its own to add a range of cells—for example, =SUM(B5:B9). You could also use the SUM function within a formula that adds a range of cells and then multiplies the total by a decimal—for example, =SUM(B5:B9)*.5.

Excel
Module 1

Learning Outcomes
- Create an absolute cell reference
- Use the fill handle to copy absolute cell references

Copy Formulas with Absolute Cell References

When copying formulas, you might want one or more of the cell references in the formula to remain unchanged. For example, you might have a price in a specific cell that you want to use in all the copied formulas, regardless of their location. If you use relative cell referencing, the formula results would be incorrect, because the formula would reference a different cell every time you copy it. In this situation, you need to use an **absolute cell reference**, which refers to a specific cell and does not change when you copy the formula. Absolute cell references display a dollar sign ($) before the column letter and row number of the address (for example, $A$1). You can either type the dollar sign when typing the cell address in a formula, or you can select a cell address on the formula bar and then press F4, and the dollar signs are added automatically. When copying a formula, absolute cell references remain fixed in the copied formulas. **CASE** *You decide to calculate each location's percentage of the total postings.*

STEPS

1. **Click cell G3, type % of Total, then press ENTER**
2. **In cell G4 type =, click cell F4, type /, click cell F13, then click the Enter button ✓ on the formula bar**

   The result, 14.02%, appears in cell G4. This value represents the total positions for Boston (in cell F4) divided by the total for all locations (in cell F13). You want to calculate this percentage for each location.

3. **Drag the fill handle from cell G4 to cell G12**

   The resulting values in the range G5:G12 are the error messages #DIV/0!. Because you used relative cell addressing in the formula in cell G4, the copied formula adjusted so that the formula in cell G5 is =F5/F14; because there is no value in cell F14, the result is a division by 0 error. You need to use an absolute reference for cell F13 in the formula to keep the denominator from adjusting in a relative way as the formula is copied. That way, the denominator will always reference the total for all locations in cell F13.

4. **Click cell G4, press F2 to change to Edit mode, then press F4**

   When you press F2, the range finder outlines the arguments of the equation in blue and red. The insertion point appears next to the F13 cell reference in cell G4. When you press F4, dollar signs are inserted in the F13 cell reference, making it an absolute reference. See **FIGURE 1-13**.

5. **Click ✓, then drag the fill handle from cell G4 to cell G12**

   Because the formula correctly contains an absolute cell reference, the correct percentage values appear for each location in cells G5:G12. Compare your worksheet to **FIGURE 1-14**.

6. **Save your work**

QUICK TIP
Before you copy or move a formula, always check to see if you need to use an absolute cell reference.

QUICK TIP
When changing a cell reference to an absolute reference, make sure the reference is selected or the insertion point is to the left of the reference you want to change before pressing F4.

FIGURE 1-13: Absolute reference created in formula

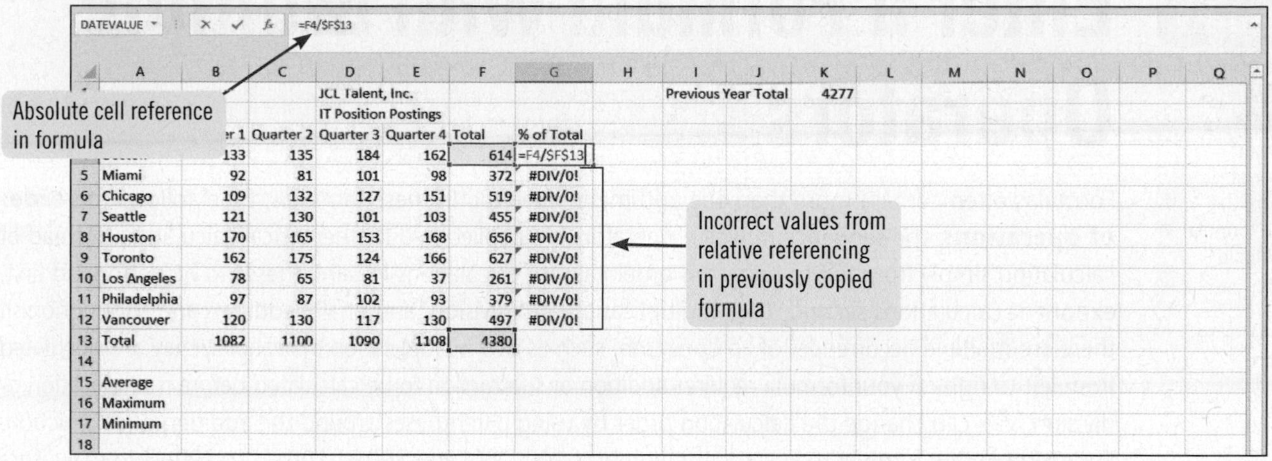

FIGURE 1-14: Correct percentages calculated

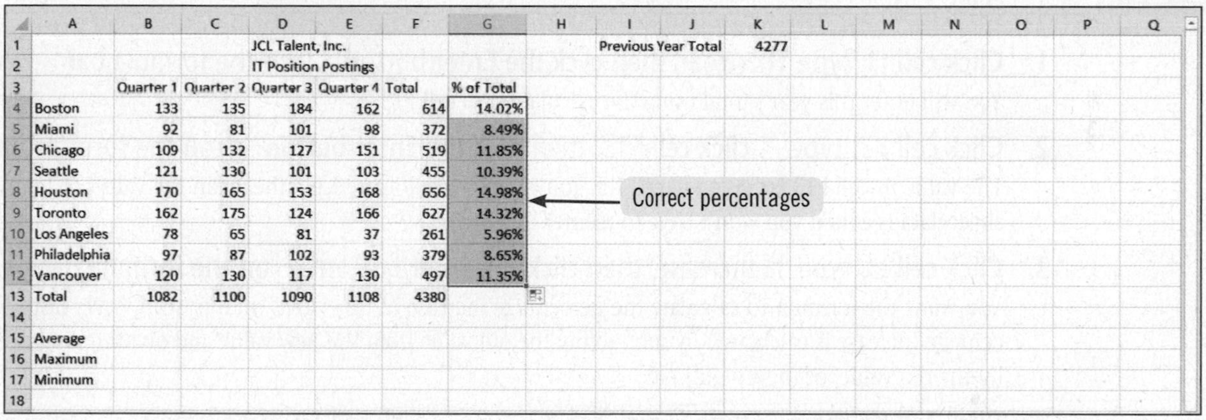

Using a mixed reference

Sometimes when you copy a formula, you want to change the row reference, but keep the column reference the same. This type of cell referencing, where one factor remains constant and the other one varies, is a **mixed reference**. For example, when copied, a formula containing the mixed reference C$14 would change the column letter relative to its new location, but not the row number. In the mixed reference $C14, the column letter would not change, but the row number would be updated relative to its location. Like an absolute reference, a mixed reference can be created by pressing F4 with the cell reference selected. With each press of the F4 key, you cycle through all the possible combinations of relative, absolute, and mixed references (C14, $C$14, C$14, and $C14).

Excel

Excel
Module 1

Learning Outcomes
- Understand the order of operations
- Create a formula with multiple operators

Enter a Formula with Multiple Operators

Formulas often contain more than one arithmetic operator. In these formulas, Excel follows the **order of operations**, the sequence in which operators are applied in a mathematical calculation. Instead of calculating simply from left to right, this order calls for calculations in parentheses to be performed first, exponent calculations second, then multiplication and division, and finally addition and subtraction. If there are multiple occurrences of an operation, such as two multiplication operations, they are calculated from left to right. If your formula requires addition or subtraction to be calculated before multiplication or division, you can change the calculation order by using parentheses around the addition or subtraction. For example, the formula to average the numbers 100, 200, and 300 is (100+200+300)/3 to make sure the numbers are totaled before the division operation. **TABLE 1-3** shows more examples of how calculations are performed in Excel. **CASE** *You need to analyze the percentage increase of this year's total for the North American locations from last year's total.*

STEPS

1. **Click cell J3, type This Year, then click the Enter button ✓ on the formula bar**
   You will enter this year's total using the calculation in cell F13.
2. **Click cell K3, type =, click cell F13, then click the Enter button ✓ on the formula bar**
   The value in cell F13 is copied to cell K3. You entered a cell reference rather than the value, so if any worksheet data is edited you won't have to reenter this total.
3. **Click cell J5, type % Increase, then click the Enter button ✓ on the formula bar**
   You want the formula to calculate the percentage increase of this year's total postings over last year. Percentage increase is calculated by subtracting the old value from the new value and dividing that difference by the old value, or (new – old)/old.
4. **Click cell K5, type =, type (, click cell K3, type -, click cell K1, then type)**
   In this first part of the formula, you are finding the difference in totals between this year and last year. You enclosed this calculation with parentheses so it will be performed before any other calculations, because calculations in parentheses are always calculated first. Compare your screen to **FIGURE 1-15**.
5. **Type /, click cell K1, then click the Enter button ✓ on the formula bar**
   The second part of this formula divides the difference in yearly totals by the total for the previous year to find the percentage of the growth. Because you enclosed the subtraction calculation in parentheses, it was calculated before the division calculation. The value in cell K5 is in decimal format. You want to display this value as a percentage with two decimal places.
6. **Click the Percent Style button % in the Number group on the Home tab, then click the Increase Decimal button in the Number group twice**
   The percentage increase in cell K5 is 2.41%, as shown in **FIGURE 1-16**.
7. **Save your work**

FIGURE 1-15: Formula with parentheses

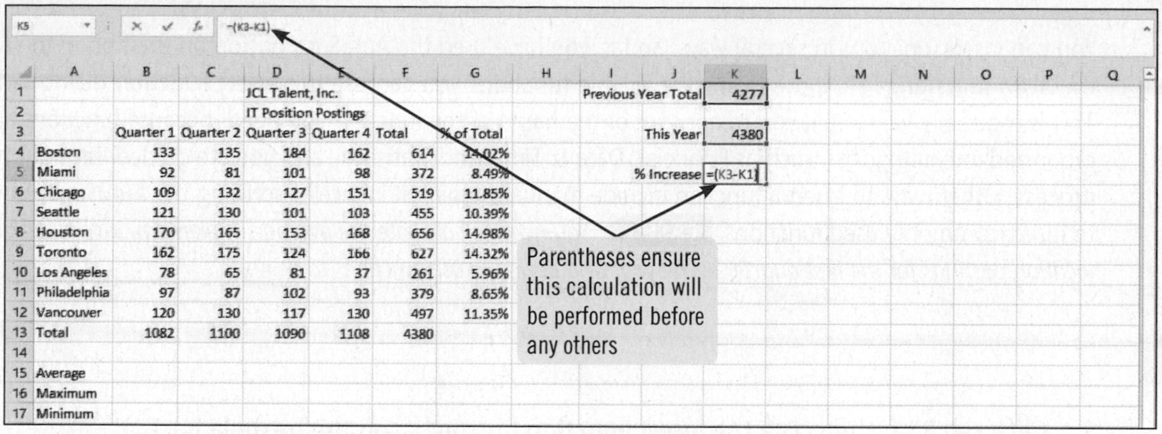

K5 | =(K3-K1)

	A	B	C	D	E	F	G	J	K
1				JCL Talent, Inc.				Previous Year Total	4277
2				IT Position Postings					
3		Quarter 1	Quarter 2	Quarter 3	Quarter 4	Total	% of Total	This Year	4380
4	Boston	133	135	184	162	614	14.02%		
5	Miami	92	81	101	98	372	8.49%	% Increase	=(K3-K1)
6	Chicago	109	132	127	151	519	11.85%		
7	Seattle	121	130	101	103	455	10.39%		
8	Houston	170	165	153	168	656	14.98%		
9	Toronto	162	175	124	166	627	14.32%		
10	Los Angeles	78	65	81	37	261	5.96%		
11	Philadelphia	97	87	102	93	379	8.65%		
12	Vancouver	120	130	117	130	497	11.35%		
13	Total	1082	1100	1090	1108	4380			
14									
15	Average								
16	Maximum								
17	Minimum								

FIGURE 1-16: Formula with percentage increase

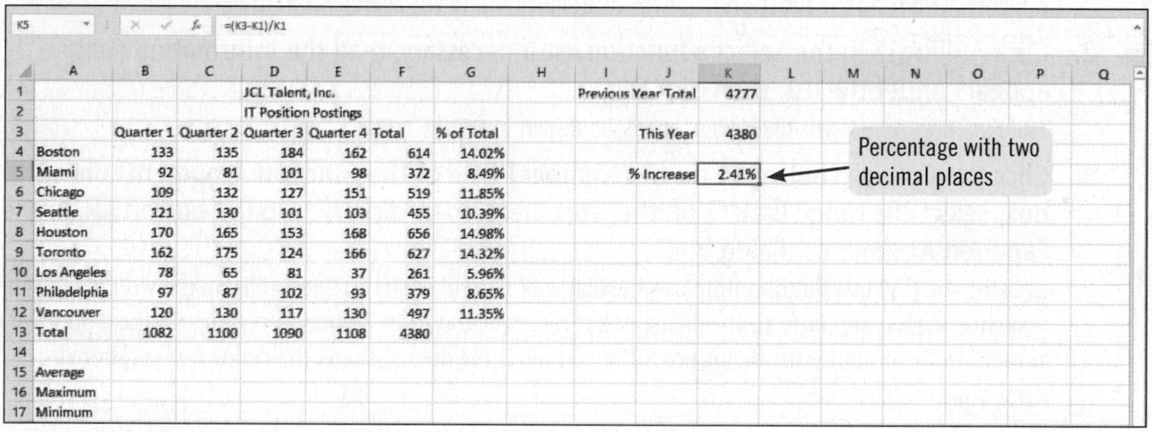

K5 | =(K3-K1)/K1

	A	B	C	D	E	F	G	J	K
1				JCL Talent, Inc.				Previous Year Total	4277
2				IT Position Postings					
3		Quarter 1	Quarter 2	Quarter 3	Quarter 4	Total	% of Total	This Year	4380
4	Boston	133	135	184	162	614	14.02%		
5	Miami	92	81	101	98	372	8.49%	% Increase	2.41%
6	Chicago	109	132	127	151	519	11.85%		
7	Seattle	121	130	101	103	455	10.39%		
8	Houston	170	165	153	168	656	14.98%		
9	Toronto	162	175	124	166	627	14.32%		
10	Los Angeles	78	65	81	37	261	5.96%		
11	Philadelphia	97	87	102	93	379	8.65%		
12	Vancouver	120	130	117	130	497	11.35%		
13	Total	1082	1100	1090	1108	4380			
14									
15	Average								
16	Maximum								
17	Minimum								

TABLE 1-3: Calculation results in Excel formulas

formula	result
10+20+40/2	50
(10+20+40)/2	35
10+5*2	20
(10+5)*2	30
20–10/2	15
(20–10)/2	5

Excel

Excel
Module 1

Insert a Function

Learning Outcomes
- Use the Insert Function button
- Select a range for use in a function
- Insert a function by typing
- Use AutoComplete to enter formulas

You can insert functions in several ways. So far, you have used the AutoSum button on the ribbon to add the SUM function. To choose from all available functions you can use the Insert Function dialog box. This is especially valuable if you're not sure of the name of the function you need, because functions are organized into categories, such as Financial, Date & Time, and Statistical, and you are guided through the process. Other ways to insert a function include manually typing it in a cell and using the AutoSum arrow to insert commonly used functions. **CASE** *You need to calculate the average, maximum, and minimum location postings for the first quarter of the year and decide to use functions to do so.*

STEPS

1. **Click cell B15, then click the Insert Function button on the formula bar**
   An equal sign (=) is inserted in the active cell, and the Insert Function dialog box opens, as shown in **FIGURE 1-17**. In this dialog box, you specify the function you want to use by clicking it in the Select a function list of recently used functions, clicking the Or select a category arrow to choose a desired function category, or typing the function name, or its description, in the Search for a function field.

TROUBLE
If AVERAGE is not in the function list, type AVERAGE in the Search for a function box, then click Go.

2. **Click AVERAGE in the Select a function list if necessary, read the information that appears under the list, then click OK**
   The Function Arguments dialog box opens, as shown in **FIGURE 1-18**.
3. **Click the Collapse button in the Number1 field of the Function Arguments dialog box, select the range B4:B12 on the worksheet, then click the Expand button in the Function Arguments dialog box**
   Clicking the Collapse button minimizes the dialog box so that you can select cells on the worksheet. When you click the Expand button, the dialog box is restored. You can also begin dragging on the worksheet to automatically minimize the dialog box; after you select the desired range, the dialog box is restored.
4. **Click OK**
   The Function Arguments dialog box closes, and the calculated value is displayed in cell B15. The average postings per location for Quarter 1 is 120.222.
5. **Click cell B16, type =, then type m**
   Because you are manually typing this function, you must manually type the opening equal sign (=). Once you type an equal sign in a cell, each letter you type acts as a trigger to activate the Excel **Formula AutoComplete**, a feature that automatically suggests text, numbers, or dates to insert based on previous entries. Because you entered the letter *m*, this feature suggests a list of function names beginning with "M."

QUICK TIP
In the AutoComplete list, if you click a function instead of double-clicking, a ScreenTip displays more detailed information about the function.

6. **Double-click MAX in the list, select the range B4:B12, then click the Enter button on the formula bar**
   The result, 170, appears in cell B16. When you completed the entry, the closing parenthesis was automatically added to the formula.
7. **Click cell B17, type =, type m, double-click MIN in the list of function names, select the range B4:B12, then press ENTER**
   The result, 78, appears in cell B17.
8. **Select the range B15:B17, drag the fill handle to the range C15:E17, then save your work**
   The average, maximum, and minimum values for all the quarters appear in the selected range, as shown in **FIGURE 1-19**.

FIGURE 1-17: Insert Function dialog box

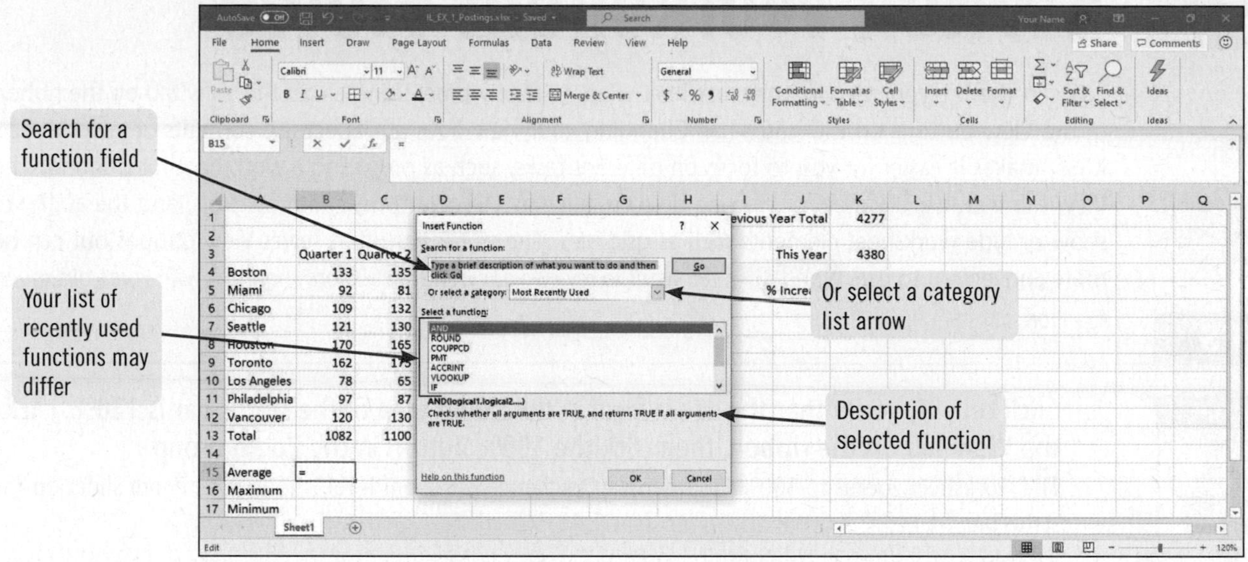

FIGURE 1-18: Function Arguments dialog box

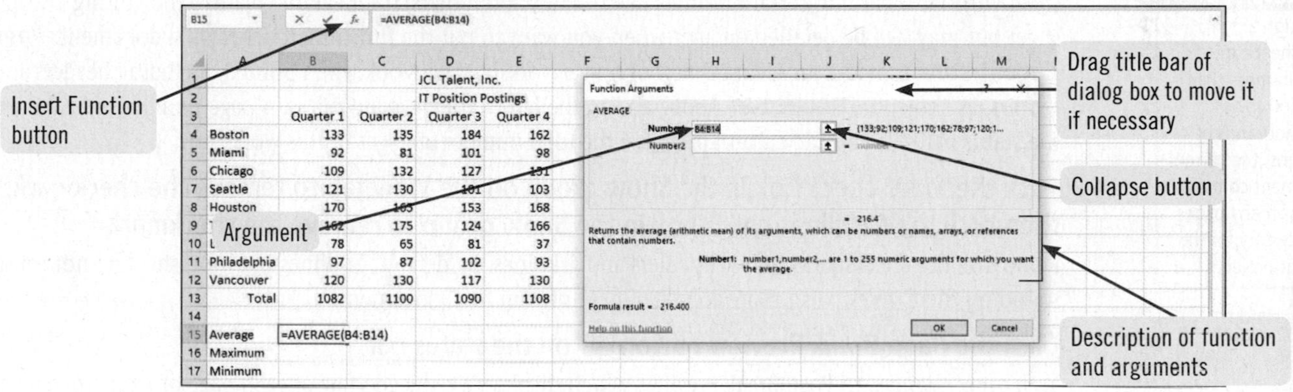

FIGURE 1-19: Completed AVERAGE, MAX, and MIN functions

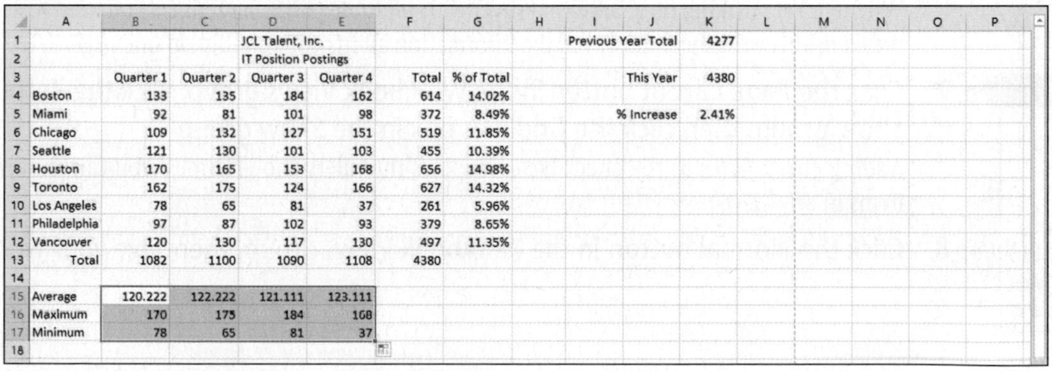

	A	B	C	D	E	F	G	I	K
1				JCL Talent, Inc.				Previous Year Total	4277
2				IT Position Postings					
3		Quarter 1	Quarter 2	Quarter 3	Quarter 4	Total	% of Total	This Year	4380
4	Boston	133	135	184	162	614	14.02%		
5	Miami	92	81	101	98	372	8.49%	% Increase	2.41%
6	Chicago	109	132	127	151	519	11.85%		
7	Seattle	121	130	101	103	455	10.39%		
8	Houston	170	165	153	168	656	14.98%		
9	Toronto	162	175	124	166	627	14.32%		
10	Los Angeles	78	65	81	37	261	5.96%		
11	Philadelphia	97	87	102	93	379	8.65%		
12	Vancouver	120	130	117	130	497	11.35%		
13	Total	1082	1100	1090	1108	4380			
14									
15	Average	120.222	122.222	121.111	123.111				
16	Maximum	170	175	184	168				
17	Minimum	78	65	81	37				
18									

Excel

Excel
Module 1

Switch Worksheet Views

Learning Outcomes
- Change worksheet views
- Zoom a worksheet
- Adjust page breaks in a worksheet

You can change your view of the worksheet window at any time, using either the View tab on the ribbon or the View buttons on the status bar. Changing your view does not affect the contents of a worksheet; it just makes it easier for you to focus on different tasks, such as preparing a worksheet for printing. The View tab includes a variety of viewing options, such as View buttons, zoom controls, and the ability to show or hide worksheet elements such as gridlines. The status bar offers fewer View options but can be more convenient to use. **CASE** *You want to review your worksheet before sharing it with your colleagues.*

STEPS

1. **Click cell A1, verify that the zoom level in the Zoom area of the status bar is 120%, click the View tab on the ribbon, then click the 100% button in the Zoom group**
   The worksheet zooms to 100%. Another way to change the zoom level is to use the Zoom slider on the status bar.

> **QUICK TIP**
> You can use the Zoom button to select the worksheet magnification level or the Zoom to Selection button to zoom into the cell or range that is selected on the worksheet.

2. **Click the Zoom in button [+] on the status bar twice**
   The worksheet zooms in 10% at a time, to 120%.

3. **Click the Page Layout button in the Workbook Views group on the View tab**
   The view switches from the default view, Normal, to Page Layout view. **Normal view** shows the worksheet without including certain features like headers and footers; it's ideal for creating and editing a worksheet but may not be detailed enough when you want to put the finishing touches on a document. **Page Layout view** provides an accurate view of how a worksheet will look when printed, including headers and footers, as shown in FIGURE 1-20. Above and to the left of the page are rulers. A page number indicator on the status bar tells you the current page and the total number of pages in this worksheet.

> **QUICK TIP**
> Although a worksheet can contain more than a million rows and thousands of columns, the current document contains only as many pages as necessary for the current project.

4. **Click the Ruler check box in the Show group on the View tab to remove the checkmark, then click the Gridlines check box in the Show group to remove the checkmark**
   Removing the checkmarks hides the rulers and gridlines. By default, gridlines in a worksheet do not print, so hiding them gives you a more accurate image of your final document.

5. **Click the Page Break Preview button on the status bar**
   Your view changes to Page Break Preview, which displays a reduced view of each page of your worksheet, along with page break indicators that you can drag to include more or less information on a page.

6. **Drag the pointer ↕ from the bottom page break indicator to the bottom of row 20, as shown in FIGURE 1-21**
   When you're working on a large worksheet with multiple pages, sometimes you need to adjust where pages break; in this worksheet, however, the information all fits comfortably on one page.

> **QUICK TIP**
> Once you view a worksheet in Page Break Preview, the page break indicators appear as lines after you switch back to Normal view or Page Layout view.

7. **Click the Page Layout button in the Workbook Views group, click the Ruler box in the Show group, then click the Gridlines box in the Show group**
   Adding checkmarks to the check boxes displays the rulers and gridlines. You can show or hide View tab items in any view.

8. **Click the Normal button in the Workbook Views group, then save your work**

FIGURE 1-20: Page Layout view

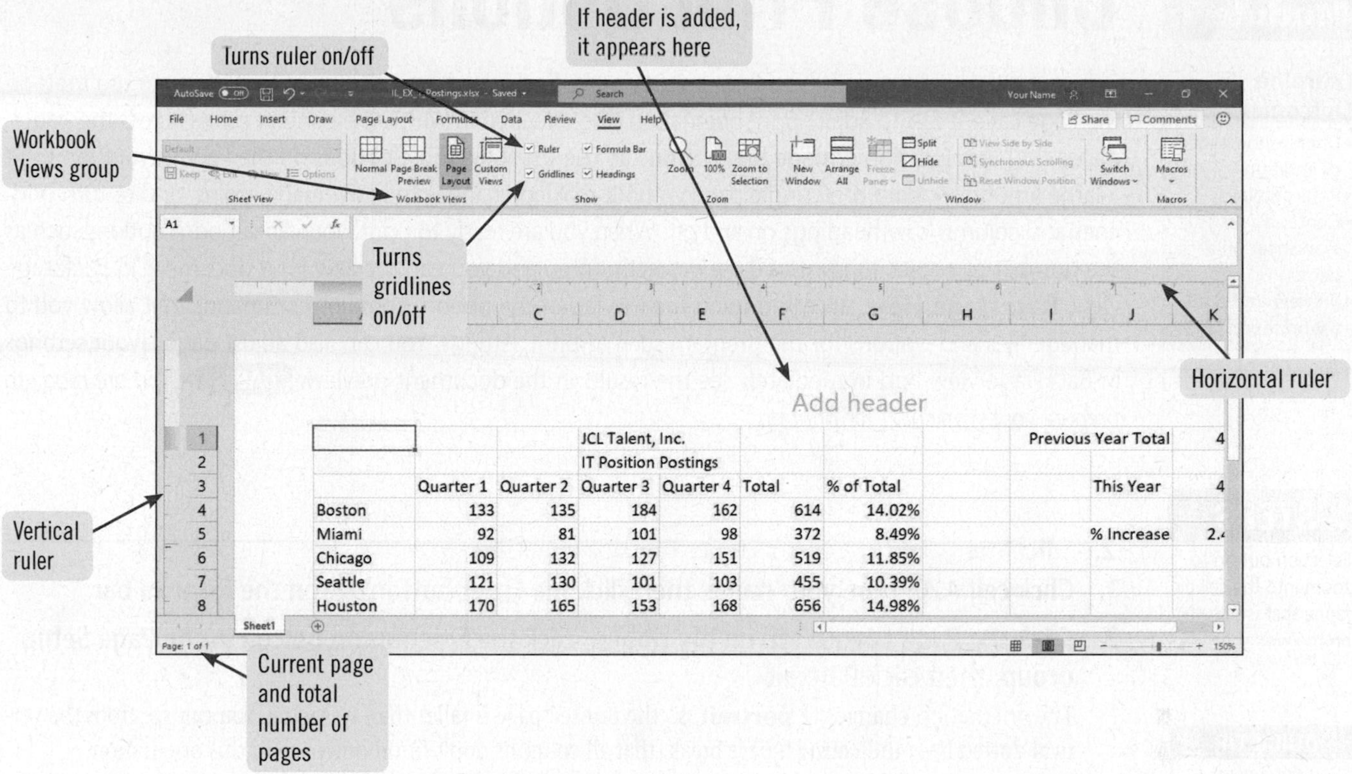

FIGURE 1-21: Page Break Preview

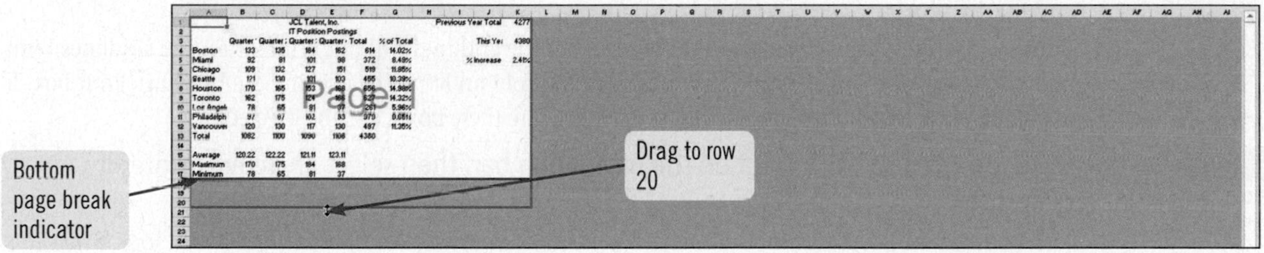

Excel
Module 1

Choose Print Options

Learning Outcomes
- Change the page orientation
- Print gridlines
- Center a worksheet on a page
- Preview and print a worksheet

Before printing a document, you may want to make final adjustments to the output. You can use tools on the Page Layout tab to adjust print orientation (the direction in which the content prints across the page), paper size, and location of page breaks. You can use the Scale to Fit options on the Page Layout tab to fit a large amount of data on a single page without making changes to individual margins, and to turn gridlines and column/row headings on and off. When you are ready to print, you can set print options such as the number of copies to print and the correct printer, and you can preview your document in Backstage view. **Backstage view**, accessed using the File tab of the ribbon, contains commands that allow you to manage files and options for the program such as print settings. You can also adjust page layout settings in Backstage view and immediately see the results in the document preview. CASE *You are ready to prepare your worksheet for printing.*

STEPS

1. **Click cell A20, type your name, then click the Enter button ✓ on the formula bar**
2. **Click the Page Layout tab on the ribbon, click the Orientation button in the Page Setup group, then click Portrait**

   The orientation changes to **portrait**, so the printed page is taller than it is wide. You can see from the vertical dotted line, indicating a page break, that all columns don't fit on one page in this orientation.
3. **Click the Orientation button in the Page Setup group, then click Landscape**

   The paper orientation returns to **landscape**, so the printed page is wider than it is tall. Now all the content fits on one page.
4. **Click the Gridlines Print box in the Sheet Options group on the Page Layout tab, then save your work**

   Printing gridlines makes the data easier to read, but the gridlines will not print unless the Gridlines Print box is selected. You can also print row numbers and column letters by clicking the Headings Print box. If you don't want to print gridlines or headings, make sure these boxes are not selected.
5. **Click the File tab, click Print on the navigation bar, then select an active printer if necessary**

   The Print tab in Backstage view displays a preview of your worksheet exactly as it will look when it is printed. To the left of the preview, you can also change a number of document settings and print options. Compare your screen to **FIGURE 1-22**. You can print from this view by clicking Print, or you can return to the worksheet without printing by clicking the Back button.
6. **Click the Page Setup link in the Settings list, click the Margins tab in the Page Setup dialog box, click the Horizontally check box in the Center on page section, click the Vertically check box in the Center on page section, then compare your screen to FIGURE 1-23**

   The printed worksheet will be centered on the page.
7. **Click OK, then click Print**

   One copy of the worksheet prints.
8. **sam Save your workbook, submit your work to your instructor as directed, click File, click Close, then click the Close button on the title bar**

QUICK TIP
If you don't want to print gridlines or headings, make sure to clear the Print check boxes for both options in the Sheet Options group; clearing the View check boxes does not affect what prints.

QUICK TIP
You can choose to print an entire workbook or a selected area of the worksheet by clicking the Print Active Sheets button in the Settings list, then clicking Print Entire Workbook or Print Selection.

QUICK TIP
You can change the number of printed pages of your worksheet by clicking the Page Layout tab, then clicking the Width and Height arrows in the Scale to Fit group.

FIGURE 1-22: Worksheet in Backstage view

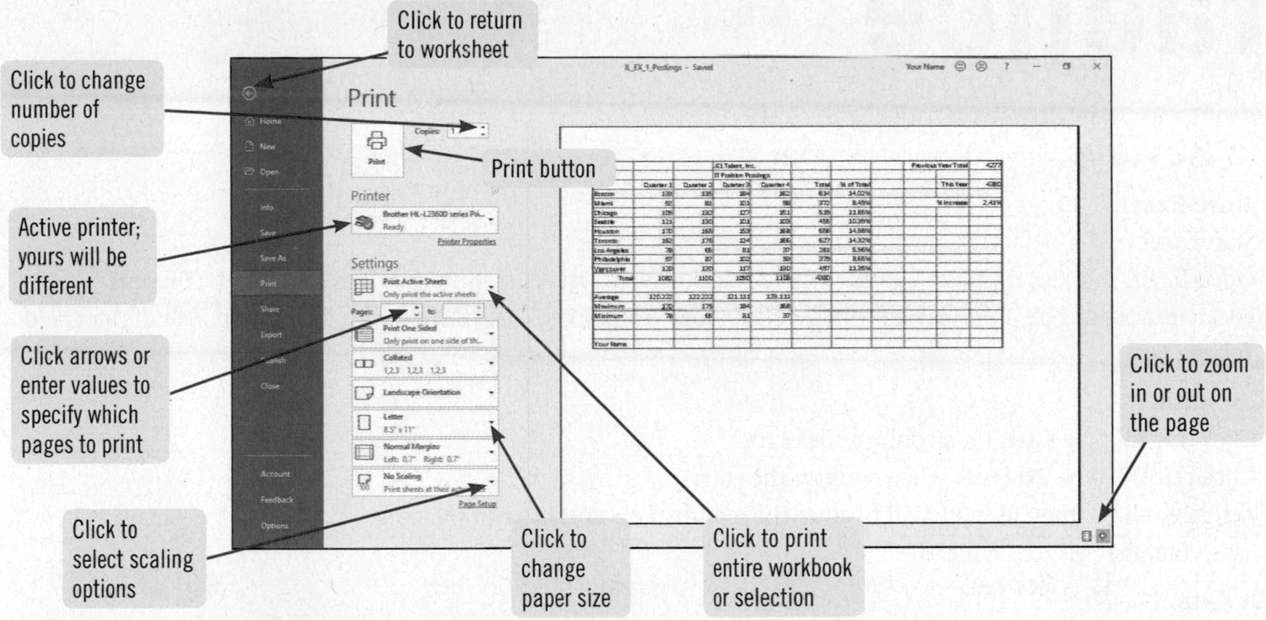

FIGURE 1-23: Page Setup dialog box

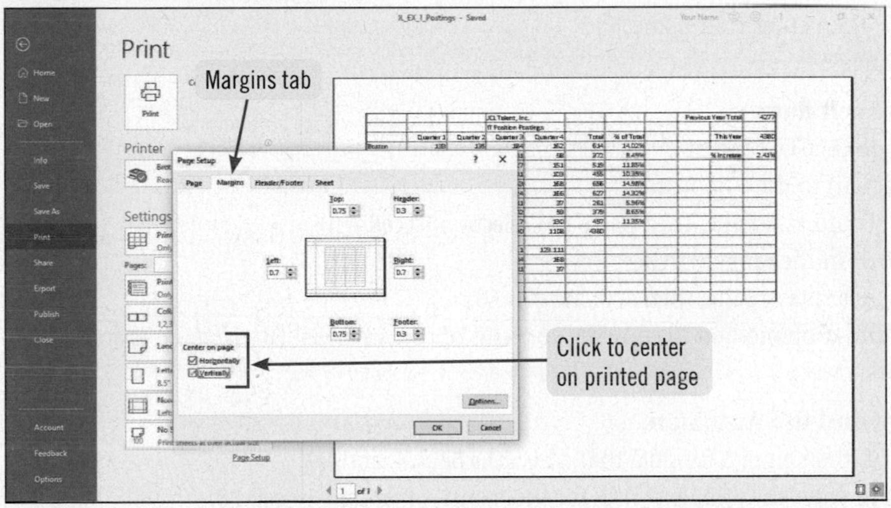

Setting a print area

If you want to print a selected worksheet area repeatedly, it's best to define a **print area**, so that the Quick Print feature prints only that portion of the worksheet area. To define a print area, select the range you want to print on the worksheet, click the Page Layout tab on the ribbon, click the Print Area button in the Page Setup group, then click Set Print Area. A print area can consist of one contiguous range of cells, or multiple ranges in different parts of a worksheet. To clear a print area, click the Page Layout tab on the ribbon, click the Print Area button in the Page Setup group, then click Clear Print Area.

Scaling to fit

If you have a large amount of data that you want to fit to a single sheet of paper, you can control how much of your work to print on a single sheet by clicking the No Scaling arrow in the Settings list in the Print screen in Backstage view, then clicking Fit Sheet on One Page, Fit All Columns on One Page, or Fit All Rows on One Page. Another method for fitting worksheet content onto one page is to click the Page Layout tab on the ribbon, then change the Width and Height settings in the Scale to Fit group to 1 page each. You can also click the Page Setup link in the Print screen in Backstage view, click the Page tab if necessary in the Page Setup dialog box, click the Fit to option button, then enter 1 in the page(s) wide by and tall fields.

Practice

Skills Review

1. Explore Excel.
- **a.** Start Excel.
- **b.** Open IL_EX_1-2.xlsx from the location where you store your Data Files, then save it as **IL_EX_1_Travel**.
- **c.** Locate the Name box, formula bar, worksheet window, cell pointer, sheet tab scrolling buttons, mode indicator, and Tell me box.

2. Enter data.
- **a.** Click cell B3, type **Jan**, then confirm the entry.
- **b.** Click cell D7, type **202497**, then confirm the entry.
- **c.** Activate cell B3, then use Auto Fill to enter the months **Feb** and **Mar** in the range C3:D3.
- **d.** Save your changes to the file.

3. Edit data.
- **a.** Use F2 to correct the spelling of Maimi in cell A6 (the correct spelling is Miami).
- **b.** Click cell C7, then use the formula bar to change the value to **188270**.
- **c.** Click cell A17, then enter your name.
- **d.** Save your changes.

4. Copy and move cell data.
- **a.** Select the range G4:G6.
- **b.** Copy the selection to the Clipboard.
- **c.** Open the Clipboard task pane, then paste the selection to cell A10.
- **d.** Delete the labels in the range G4:G6.
- **e.** Close the Clipboard task pane, then activate cell A8.
- **f.** Use the drag-and-drop method to copy the contents of cell A8 to cell E3. (*Hint:* Press and hold CTRL while dragging.)
- **g.** Save your work.

5. Enter formulas and use AutoSum.
- **a.** Activate cell E4, then enter a formula that adds cells B4, C4, and D4.
- **b.** Use AutoSum to enter the total expenses for the month of January in cell B8.
- **c.** Save your changes.

6. Copy formulas with relative cell references.
- **a.** Activate cell E4, then use the fill handle to copy the formula in cell E4 to the range E5:E7.
- **b.** Activate cell B8, then use the fill handle to copy the formula in cell B8 to the range C8:E8.
- **c.** Save your work.

7. Copy formulas with absolute cell references.
- **a.** Enter **% of Total** in cell F3.
- **b.** In cell F4, create a formula that divides the value in cell E4 by the value in cell E8 using an absolute reference to cell E8.
- **c.** Use the fill handle to copy the formula in cell F4 to the range F5:F7.
- **d.** Save your work.

Skills Review (continued)

8. Enter a formula with multiple operators.

- **a.** Enter a formula in cell B10 that calculates the average travel expenses for the month of January. Use a formula that contains cell references and not a function. (*Hint:* The formula is =(B4+B5+B6+B7)/4.)
- **b.** Review the use of the parentheses in the formula.
- **c.** Save your work.

9. Insert a function.

- **a.** Use the Insert Function button to create a formula in cell B11 that calculates the maximum travel expense for January.
- **b.** In cell B12, enter a function to calculate the minimum travel expenses for January.
- **c.** Select the range B10:B12, then use the fill handle to copy the functions into the range C10:D12.
- **d.** Save your work.

10. Switch worksheet views.

- **a.** Click the View tab on the ribbon, then switch to Page Layout view.
- **b.** Verify that the Ruler and Gridlines check boxes contain checkmarks.
- **c.** Switch to Page Break view and adjust the page break so it comes at the bottom of row 20.
- **d.** Switch to Normal View, use a button in the Zoom group of the View tab to zoom the worksheet to 100%, then use the Zoom buttons in the Status bar to zoom the worksheet back to 120%.
- **e.** Save your changes.

11. Choose print options.

- **a.** Use the Page Layout tab to change the orientation to Portrait.
- **b.** Turn on gridlines for printing using a check box in the Sheet Options group of the Page Layout tab.
- **c.** Preview the worksheet in Backstage view, then use the Page Setup dialog box to center the worksheet vertically and horizontally on the page. (*Hint:* The commands are located on the Margins tab.) Compare your screen to **FIGURE 1-24**.
- **d.** Save your changes, submit your work to your instructor as directed, close the workbook, then exit Excel.

FIGURE 1-24

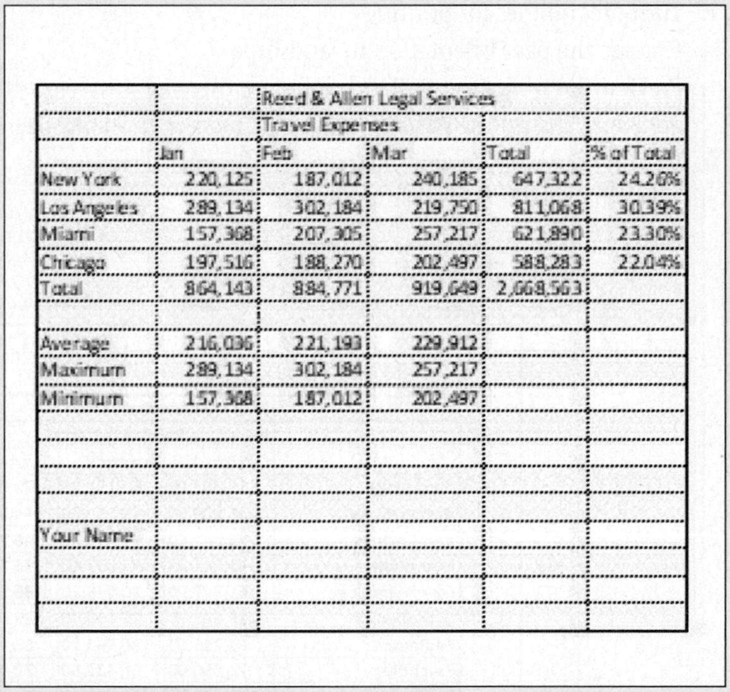

		Reed & Allen Legal Services			
		Travel Expenses			
	Jan	Feb	Mar	Total	% of Total
New York	220,125	187,012	240,185	647,322	24.26%
Los Angeles	289,134	302,184	219,750	811,068	30.39%
Miami	157,368	207,305	257,217	621,890	23.30%
Chicago	197,516	188,270	202,497	588,283	22.04%
Total	864,143	884,771	919,649	2,668,563	
Average	216,036	221,193	229,912		
Maximum	289,134	302,184	257,217		
Minimum	157,368	187,012	202,497		
Your Name					

Independent Challenge 1

The CFO at Riverwalk Medical Clinic has hired you to help him analyze departmental insurance reimbursements. He also would like to see what quarterly revenues would look like with a 20% increase in quarterly reimbursements. You've been given a worksheet for this project that contains some but not all of the data.

- **a.** Open IL_EX_1-3.xlsx from the location where you store your Data Files, then save it as **IL_EX_1_Reimbursements**.
- **b.** Enter the data shown in **TABLE 1-4** in the range E4:E11.
- **c.** Type your name in cell A17.
- **d.** Move the label in cell F2 to cell A15.

Excel

Independent Challenge 1 (continued)

TABLE 1-4

cell address	value
E4	67247.90
E5	45581.20
E6	43000.60
E7	48539.20
E8	38125.00
E9	28909.50
E10	39216.90
E11	71189.10

e. Use the Clipboard to copy and paste the label in cell F3 to cell A12.

f. Use the formula bar to correct the spelling error in the label in cell A6. (*Hint:* The correct spelling is Immunology.)

g. Edit cell A8 to correct the spelling error in the label. (*Hint:* The correct spelling is Ophthalmology.)

h. Type **Quarter 1** in cell B3, then use Auto Fill to enter Quarter 2, Quarter 3, and Quarter 4 in the range C3:E3.

i. Create a formula in cell F4 that uses cell references and totals the quarterly reimbursements for the Cardiology department.

j. Use the fill handle to copy the formula in cell F4 to the range F5:F11.

k. Using AutoSum, create a formula in cell B12 that totals the first quarter reimbursements for all the departments.

l. Copy the formula in cell B12 to the range C12:E12.

m. Enter a formula in cell B14 to calculate a 20% increase in the first quarter reimbursement total in cell B12. (*Hint:* You need to add B12 to B12 multiplied by .20. Use parentheses if necessary to follow the order of operations.)

n. Enter a function, using the help of AutoComplete, in cell B15 that calculates the average first quarter reimbursement amount for the departments.

o. Copy the formulas in the range B14:B15 to the range C14:E15.

p. Switch to Page Break view and adjust the page break to the bottom of row 18.

q. Switch to Normal View, then zoom the worksheet to 120%.

r. Turn on gridlines for printing.

s. Change the page orientation to landscape.

t. Preview the worksheet in Backstage view, then use the Page Setup dialog box to center the worksheet horizontally and vertically on the page. Compare your screen to **FIGURE 1-25**.

u. Submit your work to your instructor as directed.

v. Close the workbook, then exit Excel.

FIGURE 1-25

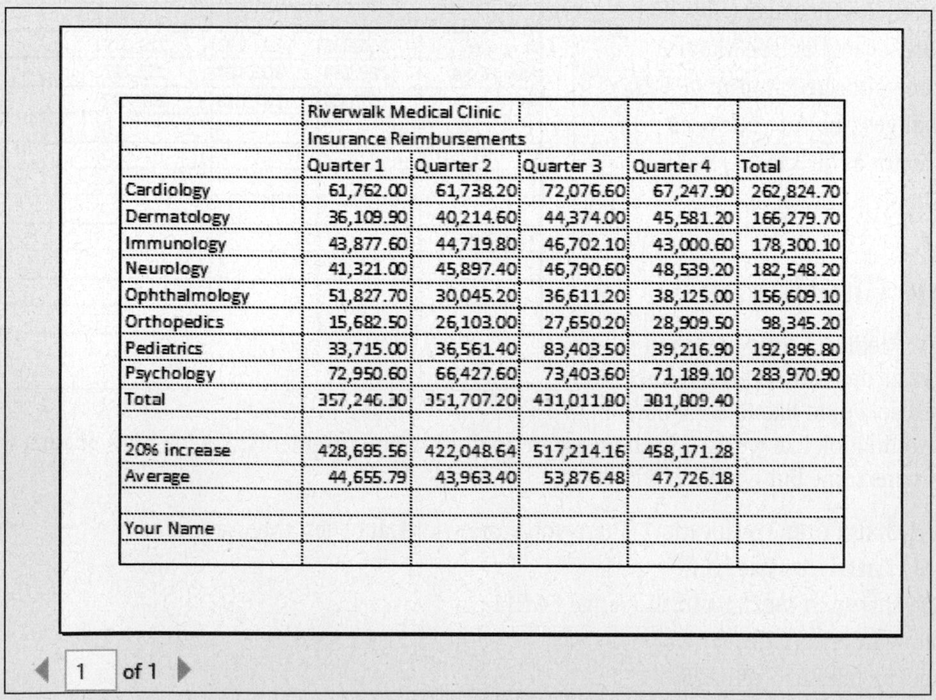

	Riverwalk Medical Clinic				
	Insurance Reimbursements				
	Quarter 1	Quarter 2	Quarter 3	Quarter 4	Total
Cardiology	61,762.00	61,738.20	72,076.60	67,247.90	262,824.70
Dermatology	36,109.90	40,214.60	44,374.00	45,581.20	166,279.70
Immunology	43,877.60	44,719.80	46,702.10	43,000.60	178,300.10
Neurology	41,321.00	45,897.40	46,790.60	48,539.20	182,548.20
Ophthalmology	51,827.70	30,045.20	36,611.20	38,125.00	156,609.10
Orthopedics	15,682.50	26,103.00	27,650.20	28,909.50	98,345.20
Pediatrics	33,715.00	36,561.40	83,403.50	39,216.90	192,896.80
Psychology	72,950.60	66,427.60	73,403.60	71,189.10	283,970.90
Total	357,246.30	351,707.20	431,011.80	381,809.40	
20% increase	428,695.56	422,048.64	517,214.16	458,171.28	
Average	44,655.79	43,963.40	53,876.48	47,726.18	
Your Name					

1 of 1

Independent Challenge 2

As the assistant to the Dean of STEM (science, technology, engineering, and mathematics) at West Shore Community College, it is your responsibility to review the budgets for the departments in the division and help with a budget forecast for the upcoming academic year. You've decided to use Excel formulas and functions to help with this analysis.

- **a.** Open IL_EX_1-4.xlsx from the location where you store your Data Files, then save it as **IL_EX_1_Budgets**.
- **b.** Move the labels in the range A6:A11 to the range A5:A10.
- **c.** Enter **Total** in cell A11, then use AutoSum to calculate the total 2020 expenses for all departments in cell B11.
- **d.** Enter **Average** in cell A12, then use the AutoSum arrow to enter a function in cell B12 that calculates the average 2020 expenses for all departments. (*Hint:* make sure you include only the department data.)
- **e.** Use the fill handle to copy the formulas in the range B11:B12 to the range C11:C12.
- **f.** Using cell references, enter a formula in cell D5 that calculates the 2022 Budget for the engineering department, using the increase shown in cell F2 over the 2021 expenses in cell C5. Use absolute cell references where necessary. (*Hint:* Multiply the percentage in cell F2 by the 2021 expenses in cell C5, then add that amount to the 2021 expenses in cell C5.)
- **g.** Use the fill handle to copy the formula in cell D5 to the range D6:D10.
- **h.** Use the fill handle to copy the formulas in the range C11:C12 to the range D11:D12.
- **i.** Enter a formula in cell F5 that calculates the percentage increase in total expenses from 2020 to 2021. (*Hint:* The 2020 total is in cell B11 and the 2021 total is in cell C11.)
- **j.** Change the page orientation to landscape, then turn on gridlines for printing.
- **k.** Enter your name in cell A14.
- **l.** Preview the worksheet in Backstage view. Compare your screen to **FIGURE 1-26**.
- **m.** Save your work, then submit the worksheet to your instructor as directed.
- **n.** Close the workbook and exit Excel.

FIGURE 1-26

West Shore Community College					2022 Budget Increase		
STEM Division					2.15%		
Departmental Budgets							
Department	2020 Expenses	2021 Expenses	2022 Budget		% Increase in Expenses 2020 to 2021		
Engineering	$50,124.17	$52,457.65	$53,585.49		6.01%		
Computer Science	$45,287.23	$55,214.98	$56,402.10				
Biology	$36,784.98	$36,799.88	$37,591.08				
Chemistry	$58,214.78	$59,847.47	$61,134.19				
Physics	$61,002.27	$62,178.78	$63,515.62				
Math	$37,512.32	$39,781.33	$40,636.63				
Total	$288,925.75	$306,280.09	$312,865.11				
Average	$48,154.29	$51,046.68	$52,144.19				
Your Name							

Excel

Visual Workshop

Open IL_EX_1-5.xlsx from the location where you store your Data Files, then save it as **IL_EX_1_Royalties**. Complete the worksheet shown in **FIGURE 1-27** using the skills you learned in this module. Use functions to calculate the values in B8:B11 and C8. The values in column C are calculated by multiplying the gross revenues in column B by the percentage in cell E2. Adjust your zoom level as necessary to match the figure. Enter your name in cell A14. Submit your work to your instructor as directed.

FIGURE 1-27

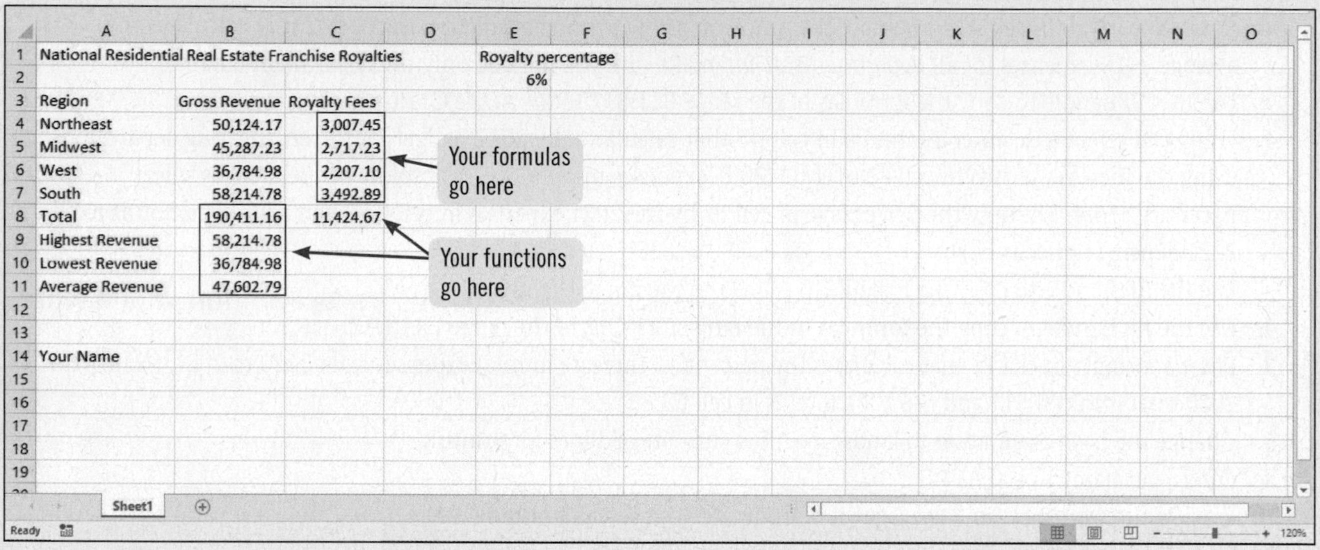

Formatting a Worksheet

CASE Cheri McNeil, the manager of the Boston office at JCL Talent, has gathered data from all JCL recruiters on technology position postings for the first quarter of the year. Cheri has created a worksheet listing this information, and she asks you to format the worksheet to make it easier to read and understand.

Module Objectives

After completing this module, you will be able to:

- Format values
- Change font and font size
- Change font styles and alignment
- Adjust column width
- Insert and delete rows and columns
- Apply colors, borders, and documentation
- Apply conditional formatting
- Rename and move a worksheet
- Check spelling

Files You Will Need

IL_EX_2-1.xlsx
IL_EX_2-2.xlsx
IL_EX_2-3.xlsx
IL_EX_2-4.xlsx
IL_EX_2-5.xlsx

Excel
Module 2

Format Values

Learning Outcomes
- Format a number
- Format a date
- Increase/decrease decimals

When you **format** a cell, you enhance the appearance of information by changing its font, size, color, or alignment. Formatting changes only the appearance of a value or label; it does not alter the actual data in any way. To format a cell or range, first you select it, then you apply the formatting using the ribbon, Mini toolbar, or a keyboard shortcut. You can apply formatting before or after you enter data in a cell or range. **CASE** *Cheri has provided you with a worksheet that details technology postings, and you're ready to improve its appearance. You start by formatting some cells to better reflect the type of information they contain, such as currency, percentages, and dates.*

STEPS

QUICK TIP
You can format values with a custom number format using format symbols. Right-click a cell range, click Format Cells on the shortcut menu, in the Category box of the Format Cells dialog box click Custom, select the number format you want to use in the Type list, make changes to the format symbols in the Type box, then click OK.

QUICK TIP
You can copy formatting into adjacent cells using the fill handle. After dragging the fill handle to select adjacent cells, click the AutoFill Options arrow, then click Fill Formatting Only from the shortcut menu. Values won't be copied, but the formatting will be applied to the selected cells.

QUICK TIP
If you want numeric values to be treated as text, click Text in the Category list. Cells formatted in this way are treated as text even if they contain numeric data. You can also precede a number with an apostrophe to treat the value as text.

1. **sam Start Excel, open IL_EX_2-1.xlsx from the location where you store your Data Files, then save it as IL_EX_2_Tech**
   This worksheet is difficult to interpret because all the information is crowded and looks the same. In some columns, such as D, the contents appear cut off because there is too much data to fit given the current column width. You decide not to widen the columns yet, because the other changes you plan to make might affect column width and row height.
2. **Select the range G3:G15, then click the Accounting Number Format button $ in the Number group on the Home tab**
   A **number format** is applied to values to express numeric concepts, such as currency, date, and percentage. The default Accounting number format adds dollar signs and two decimal places to the expense data, as shown in FIGURE 2-1.
3. **Select the range H3:H15, then click the Comma Style button , in the Number group**
   The values in column H display the Comma Style format, which does not include a dollar sign but can be useful for some types of accounting data.
4. **Click cell M1, click the Number Format arrow, click Percentage, then click the Increase Decimal button in the Number group**
   The revenue rate is now formatted with a percent sign (%) and three decimal places. The Number Format arrow lets you choose from popular number formats and shows an example of what the selected cell or cells would look like (when multiple cells are selected, the example is based on the first cell in the range). Each time you click the Increase Decimal button, you add one decimal place; clicking the button twice would add two decimal places.
5. **Click the Decrease Decimal button in the Number group three times**
   All three decimal places are removed from the revenue rate value.
6. **Select the range C3:C15, then click the launcher in the Number group**
   The Format Cells dialog box opens with the Date category already selected on the Number tab.
7. **Click the 14-Mar format in the Type list box, as shown in FIGURE 2-2, then click OK**
   The dates in column C appear in the 14-Mar format.
8. **Select the range I3:J15, right-click the range, click Format Cells on the shortcut menu, in the Category list click Currency, in the Decimal places box type 2 if necessary, then click OK**
   This number format looks similar to the Accounting format but aligns currency symbols and decimal points slightly differently. Compare your worksheet to FIGURE 2-3.
9. **Select the range G3:I15, click the Decrease Decimal button in the Number group twice, press CTRL+HOME, then save your work**
   The cell values in this range now use a custom format that doesn't display decimal places. This format is applied to all cells in the range, including the cells in column H that display the $ symbol.

FIGURE 2-1: Accounting number format applied to range

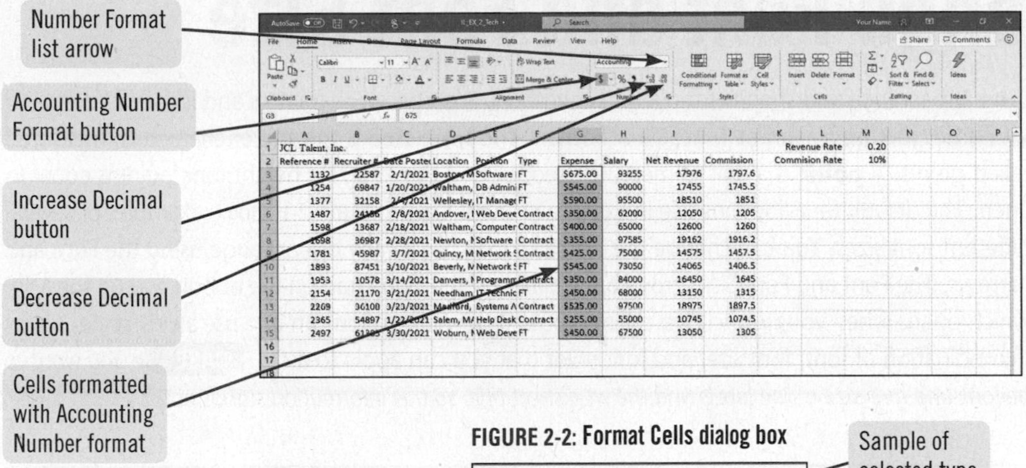

FIGURE 2-2: Format Cells dialog box

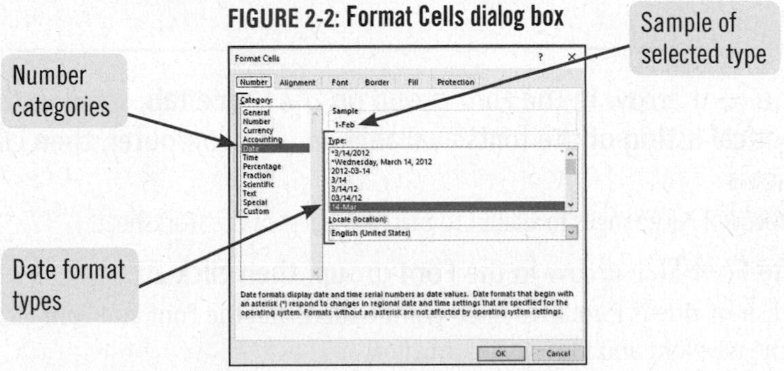

FIGURE 2-3: Worksheet with formatted values

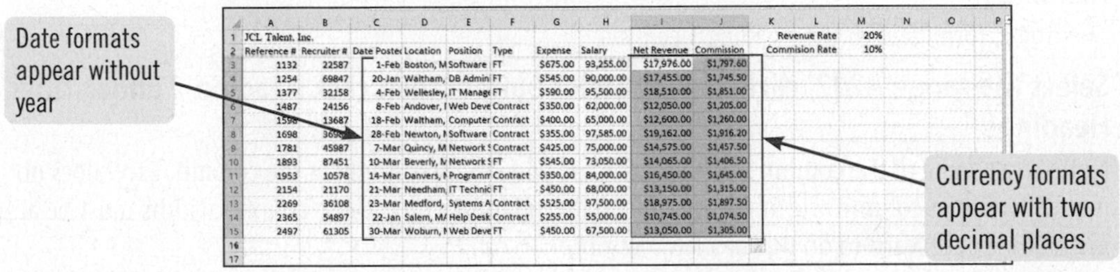

Working with online pictures, other images, and symbols

You can illustrate your worksheets using online pictures and other images. To add a picture to a worksheet, click the Illustrations button on the Insert tab, click Pictures, then click Online Pictures. The Online Pictures dialog box opens. Here you can search for online pictures from the Bing search engine or OneDrive, as shown in **FIGURE 2-4**. To search, type one or more keywords in the search box, then press ENTER. When you double-click an image in the Search Results window, the image is inserted at the location of the active cell. Clicking an image selects it and adds resizing handles. To resize an image proportionally, drag any corner sizing handle. If you drag an edge sizing handle, the image will be resized nonproportionally. You can add alternative text to an image by right-clicking it, clicking Edit Alt Text on the shortcut menu, then entering the text in the Alt Text pane. To move an image, point inside the image until the pointer changes to ✥, then drag it to a new location. To delete a picture, select it, then press DEL. To work with an image it must be selected. You can select an image, or any object, by clicking it. To work with multiple images at once, hold CTRL while clicking each image. You can insert a symbol in a worksheet by clicking the Insert tab, clicking the Symbols button in the Symbols group, clicking Symbol, clicking a symbol from the Symbols tab in the Symbol dialog box, clicking Insert, then clicking Close to close the Symbol dialog box.

FIGURE 2-4: Results of Online Picture search

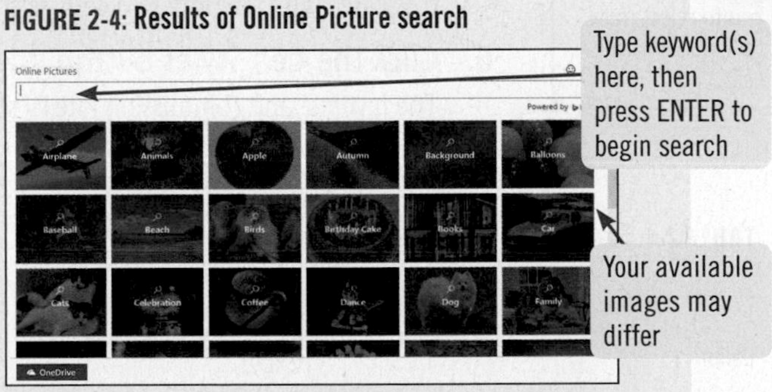

Excel

Change Font and Font Size

Learning Outcomes
- Change a font
- Change a font size

A **font** is the appearance and shape of the letters, numbers, and special characters and is usually designed with a font name, such as Calibri or Times New Roman. The **font size** is the size of characters, measured in units called points. A **point** is a unit of measure used for font size and row height; one point is equal to 1/72 of an inch. The default font and font size in Excel is 11-point Calibri. **TABLE 2-1** shows examples of several fonts in different font sizes. You can change the font and font size of any cell or range using the Font and Font Size arrows. The Font and Font Size arrows are located on the Home tab on the ribbon and on the Mini toolbar, which opens when you right-click a cell or range. To save time, you can also use a **cell style**, a predesigned combination of font, font size, and font color that you can apply to a cell. **CASE** *You want to change the font and font size of the labels and the worksheet title, so this information stands out.*

STEPS

1. **Click the Font arrow in the Font group on the Home tab, scroll in the Font list to see an alphabetical listing of the fonts available on your computer, then click Calibri, as shown in FIGURE 2-5**
   The font in cell A1 changes to Calibri to match the rest of the worksheet.

QUICK TIP
You can also use the Increase Font Size button A^ to increase the font size by one point or the Decrease Font Size button to decrease it by one point. You specify an exact size by entering the size in the Font Size box.

2. **Click the Font Size arrow in the Font group, then click 20**
   The worksheet title is formatted in 20-point Calibri, and the Font and Font Size boxes on the Home tab display the new font and font size information.
3. **Click the Cell Styles button in the Styles group, then click Heading 1 under Titles and Headings**
   The title is formatted in the Heading 1 cell style.
4. **Select the range A2:J2, click the Cell Styles button, then click Heading 2 under Titles and Headings**
   Notice that some of the column labels are now too wide to appear fully in the column. Excel does not automatically adjust column widths to accommodate cell formatting; these column widths must be adjusted manually. You'll learn to do this in a later lesson.

QUICK TIP
Holding CTRL while selecting cells allows you to select multiple nonadjacent cells.

5. **Click cell L1, hold SHIFT, then click cell L2**
   Holding SHIFT while clicking a cell selects that cell and any cells between it and the cell first selected. In this case there are only two cells selected.
6. **Click the Cell Styles button, then click Heading 4 under Titles and Headings**
   The revenue and commission rate labels are now formatted consistently. Compare your worksheet to **FIGURE 2-6**.
7. **Save your work**

TABLE 2-1: Examples of fonts and font sizes

font name	12 point	24 point
Calibri	Excel	Excel
Playbill	Excel	Excel
Comic Sans MS	Excel	Excel
Times New Roman	Excel	Excel

FIGURE 2-5: Font list

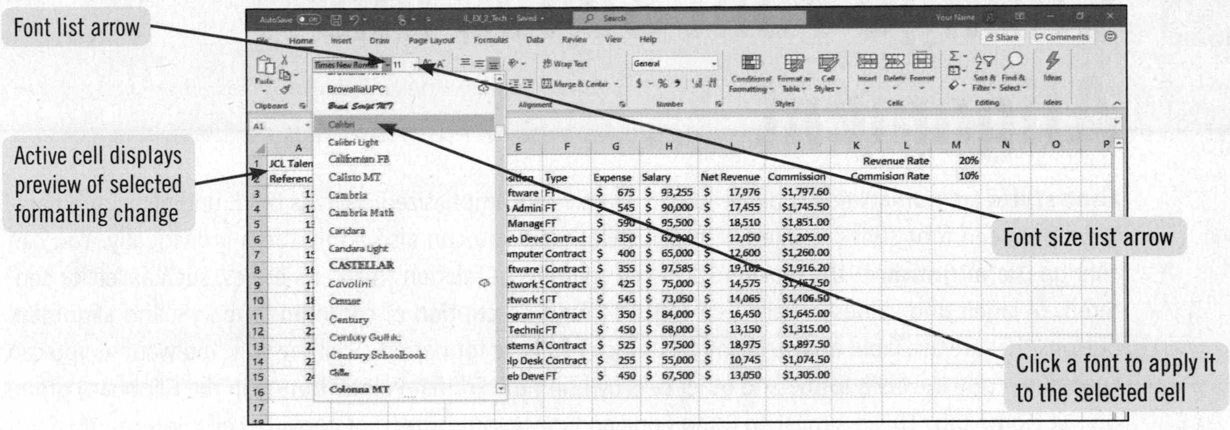

FIGURE 2-6: Worksheet with formatted headings and column labels

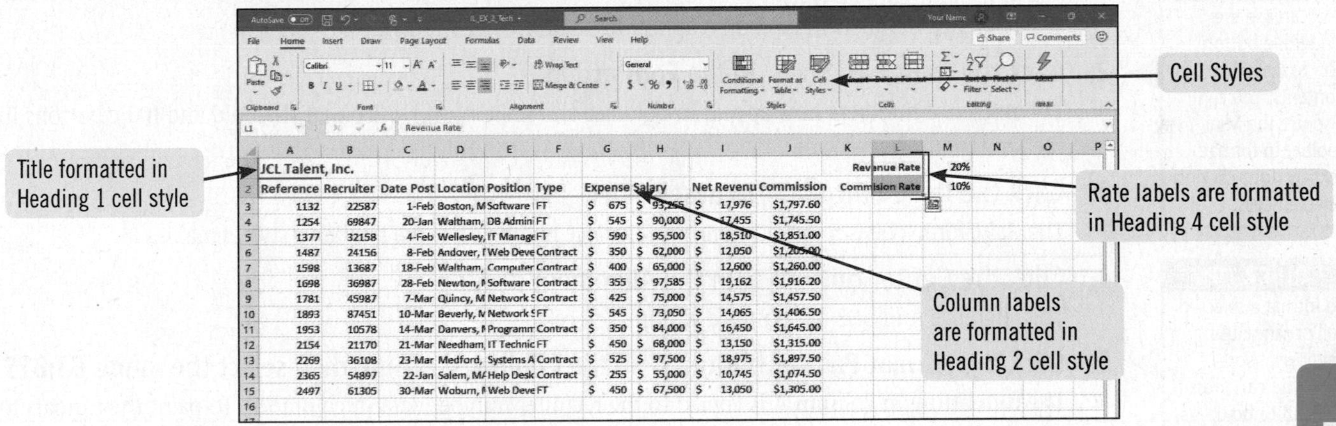

Working with cell styles

You can modify any style in the Cell Styles gallery. In the Cell Styles gallery, right-click the cell style that you want to modify, on the shortcut menu shown in **FIGURE 2-7**, click Modify, select the style options from the Style Includes list in the Style dialog box, click the Format button to choose new customized formatting, then click OK twice. To create a new cell style, click New Cell Style at the bottom of the Cell Styles gallery, enter a name in the Style name box, select style options from the Style Includes list, click the Format button to choose customized formatting for your style, then click OK twice. You can merge styles from a different workbook by opening the workbook that contains the cell styles that you want to copy, clicking Merge Styles at the bottom of the Cell Styles gallery, clicking the workbook in the Merge styles from list, then clicking OK. If styles in the workbooks have the same name, you will be asked if you want to merge those styles.

FIGURE 2-7: Shortcut menu in Cell Styles gallery

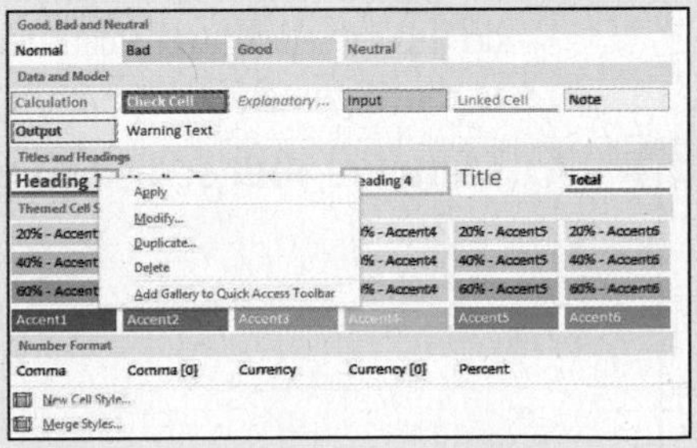

Excel
Module 2

Learning Outcomes
- Apply formatting
- Use the Format Painter
- Change cell alignment

Change Font Styles and Alignment

Font styles are formats that indicate how characters are emphasized, such as bold, underline, and italic. You have seen font styles applied with cell styles, and you can also apply them individually. You can change the **alignment**, the placement of cell contents in relation to a cell's edges, such as left or centered, of labels and values in cells. See **TABLE 2-2** for a description of common font style and alignment buttons that are available on the Home tab. Once you have formatted a cell the way you want it, you can "paint" or copy the cell's formats to other cells by using the Format Painter button in the Clipboard group on the Home tab. This is similar to using copy and paste, but instead of copying cell contents, it copies only the cell's formatting. **CASE** *You want to further enhance the worksheet's appearance by adding bold and underline formatting and centering some of the labels.*

STEPS

QUICK TIP
You can use the Underline button U to underline cell contents. You can also use the Mini toolbar to format text by right-clicking selected cells.

QUICK TIP
To format a selected cell or range using keyboard shortcuts, you can press CTRL+B to bold, CTRL+I to italicize, and CTRL+U to underline.

QUICK TIP
To clear all formatting from a selected range, click the Clear button in the Editing group on the Home tab, then click Clear Formats.

1. **Select the range A3:A15, then click the Bold button B in the Font group on the Home tab**
   The reference numbers in column A appear in bold.
2. **Click the Italic button I in the Font group**
   The reference numbers now appear in boldface and italic type. Notice that the Bold and Italic buttons in the Font group are selected.
3. **Click the Italic button I to deselect it**
   The italic font style is removed from the reference numbers but the bold font style remains.
4. **Click the Center button in the Alignment group**
   The reference numbers are centered within their cells.
5. **Click the Format Painter button in the Clipboard group, then select the range B3:B15**
   The formatting in column A is copied to the recruiter number data in column B. To paint the formats to more than one selection, double-click the Format Painter button to keep it activated until you turn it off. You can turn off the Format Painter by pressing ESC or by clicking .
6. **Click cell A1, select the range A1:J1, then click the Merge & Center button in the Alignment group**
   The Merge & Center button creates one cell out of the ten cells across the row, then centers the text in that newly created, merged cell. The title "JCL Talent, Inc." is centered across the ten columns you selected. To split a merged cell into its original components, select the merged cell, then click the Merge & Center button to deselect it. Occasionally, you may find that you want cell contents to wrap within a cell. You can do this by selecting the cells containing the text you want to wrap, then clicking the Wrap Text button in the Alignment group on the Home tab on the ribbon.
7. **Compare your screen to FIGURE 2-8, then save your work**

FIGURE 2-8: Worksheet with font styles and alignment applied

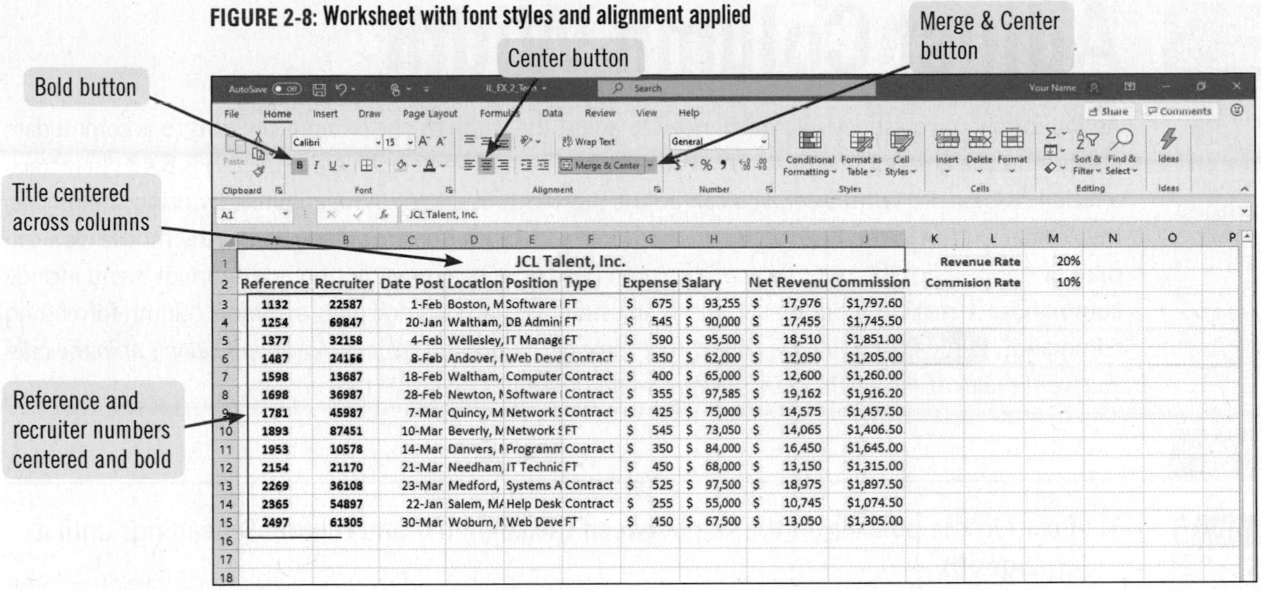

TABLE 2-2: Common font style and alignment buttons

button	description
B	Bolds cell content
I	Italicizes cell content
U	Underlines cell content
	Centers content across columns; also merges two or more selected, adjacent cells into one cell; also unmerges previously merged cells
	Aligns content at the left edge of the cell
	Centers content horizontally within the cell
	Aligns content at the right edge of the cell
	Wraps long text into multiple lines to fit within a column
	Aligns content at the top of a cell
	Aligns content at the bottom of a cell
	Aligns content in the middle of a cell

Rotating and indenting cell entries

In addition to applying fonts and font styles, you can rotate or indent data within a cell. To rotate text within a cell, click the Home tab, select the cells you want to modify, then click the dialog box launcher in the Alignment group to open the Alignment tab of the Format Cells dialog box. Click a position in the Orientation box or type a number in the Degrees box to rotate text from its default horizontal orientation, then click OK. You can indent cell contents by clicking the Increase Indent button in the Alignment group, which moves cell contents to the right one space, or the Decrease Indent button, which moves cell contents to the left one space.

Adjust Column Width

Learning Outcomes
- Change a column width by dragging
- Resize a column with AutoFit
- Change the width of multiple columns

As you format a worksheet, you might need to adjust the width of one or more columns to accommodate changes in the amount of text, the font size, or font style. The default column width is 8.43 characters, a little less than 1". With Excel, you can adjust the width of one or more columns by using the mouse, the Format button in the Cells group on the Home tab, or the shortcut menu. Using the mouse, you can drag or double-click the right edge of a column heading. The Format button and shortcut menu include commands for making more precise width adjustments. **TABLE 2-3** describes common column formatting commands. **CASE** *You have noticed that some of the labels in columns A through L don't fit in the cells. You want to adjust the widths of the columns so that the labels appear in their entirety.*

STEPS

QUICK TIP
If "#######" appears after you adjust a column of values, the column is too narrow to display the values completely; increase the column width until the values appear.

1. **Position the pointer on the line between the column C and column D headings until it changes to ✛**
   See **FIGURE 2-9**. A **column heading** is a box that appears above each worksheet column and identifies it by a letter. You positioned the mouse pointer here because in order to adjust column width using the mouse, you need to position the pointer on the right edge of the column heading for the column you want to adjust.
2. **Click and drag ✛ to the right until the column fully displays the column label Date Posted (approximately 12.71 characters or 94 pixels)**
   As you change the column width, a ScreenTip opens listing the column width.
3. **Position the pointer on the line between columns D and E until it changes to ✛, then double-click**
   Column D automatically widens to fit the widest entry. Double-clicking the right edge of a column heading activates **AutoFit**. This feature adjusts column width or row height to accommodate its widest or tallest entry.
4. **Use AutoFit to resize columns E, F, G, H, and L**
5. **Position the pointer in the column heading area for column I until it changes to ⬇, then drag to select columns I and J**
6. **Click the Format button in the Cells group, then click Column Width**
   The Column Width dialog box opens. Column width measurement is based on the number of characters that will fit in the column when formatted in the Normal font and font size (in this case, 11-point Calibri).
7. **Type 14 in the Column width box, then click OK**
   The widths of columns I and J change to reflect the new setting. See **FIGURE 2-10**.
8. **Click cell A1, then save your work**

QUICK TIP
You can paste copied cell data with the same column width by clicking Keep Source Column Widths in the Paste menu.

QUICK TIP
If an entire column rather than a column cell is selected, you can change the width of the column by right-clicking the selection, then clicking Column Width on the shortcut menu.

FIGURE 2-9: Preparing to change the column width

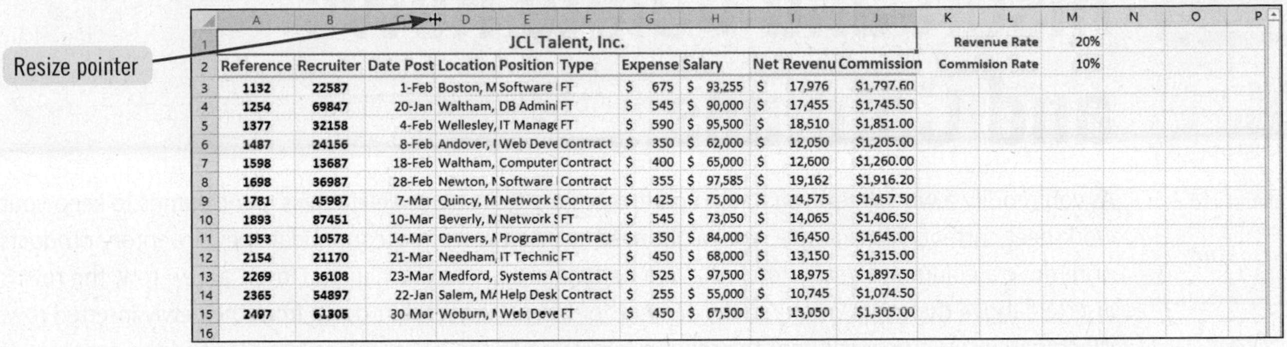

JCL Talent, Inc.									Revenue Rate	20%
Reference	Recruiter	Date Post	Location	Position	Type	Expense	Salary	Net Revenu	Commission	Commision Rate	10%
1132	22587	1-Feb	Boston, M	Software	FT	$ 675	$ 93,255	$ 17,976	$1,797.60		
1254	69847	20-Jan	Waltham,	DB Admini	FT	$ 545	$ 90,000	$ 17,455	$1,745.50		
1377	32158	4-Feb	Wellesley,	IT Manage	FT	$ 590	$ 95,500	$ 18,510	$1,851.00		
1487	24156	8-Feb	Andover, I	Web Deve	Contract	$ 350	$ 62,000	$ 12,050	$1,205.00		
1598	13687	18-Feb	Waltham,	Computer	Contract	$ 400	$ 65,000	$ 12,600	$1,260.00		
1698	36987	28-Feb	Newton, M	Software	Contract	$ 355	$ 97,585	$ 19,162	$1,916.20		
1781	45987	7-Mar	Quincy, M	Network S	Contract	$ 425	$ 75,000	$ 14,575	$1,457.50		
1893	87451	10-Mar	Beverly, M	Network S	FT	$ 545	$ 73,050	$ 14,065	$1,406.50		
1953	10578	14-Mar	Danvers, M	Programm	Contract	$ 350	$ 84,000	$ 16,450	$1,645.00		
2154	21170	21-Mar	Needham,	IT Technic	FT	$ 450	$ 68,000	$ 13,150	$1,315.00		
2269	36108	23-Mar	Medford,	Systems A	Contract	$ 525	$ 97,500	$ 18,975	$1,897.50		
2365	54897	22-Jan	Salem, MA	Help Desk	Contract	$ 255	$ 55,000	$ 10,745	$1,074.50		
2497	61305	30-Mar	Woburn, M	Web Deve	FT	$ 450	$ 67,500	$ 13,050	$1,305.00		

FIGURE 2-10: Worksheet with column widths adjusted

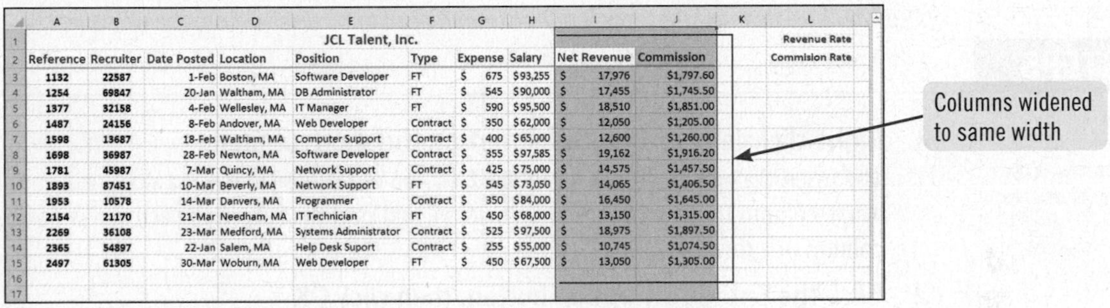

JCL Talent, Inc.										Revenue Rate
Reference	Recruiter	Date Posted	Location	Position	Type	Expense	Salary	Net Revenue	Commission	Commision Rate
1132	22587	1-Feb	Boston, MA	Software Developer	FT	$ 675	$93,255	$ 17,976	$1,797.60	
1254	69847	20-Jan	Waltham, MA	DB Administrator	FT	$ 545	$90,000	$ 17,455	$1,745.50	
1377	32158	4-Feb	Wellesley, MA	IT Manager	FT	$ 590	$95,500	$ 18,510	$1,851.00	
1487	24156	8-Feb	Andover, MA	Web Developer	Contract	$ 350	$62,000	$ 12,050	$1,205.00	
1598	13687	18-Feb	Waltham, MA	Computer Support	Contract	$ 400	$65,000	$ 12,600	$1,260.00	
1698	36987	28-Feb	Newton, MA	Software Developer	Contract	$ 355	$97,585	$ 19,162	$1,916.20	
1781	45987	7-Mar	Quincy, MA	Network Support	Contract	$ 425	$75,000	$ 14,575	$1,457.50	
1893	87451	10-Mar	Beverly, MA	Network Support	FT	$ 545	$73,050	$ 14,065	$1,406.50	
1953	10578	14-Mar	Danvers, MA	Programmer	Contract	$ 350	$84,000	$ 16,450	$1,645.00	
2154	21170	21-Mar	Needham, MA	IT Technician	FT	$ 450	$68,000	$ 13,150	$1,315.00	
2269	36108	23-Mar	Medford, MA	Systems Administrator	Contract	$ 525	$97,500	$ 18,975	$1,897.50	
2365	54897	22-Jan	Salem, MA	Help Desk Suport	Contract	$ 255	$55,000	$ 10,745	$1,074.50	
2497	61305	30-Mar	Woburn, MA	Web Developer	FT	$ 450	$67,500	$ 13,050	$1,305.00	

TABLE 2-3: Common column formatting commands

command	description	available using
Column Width	Sets the width to a specific number of characters	Format button; shortcut menu
AutoFit Column Width	Fits to the widest entry in a column	Format button; mouse
Hide & Unhide	Hides or displays selected column(s)	Format button; shortcut menu
Default Width	Resets column to worksheet's default column width	Format button

Changing row height

Changing row height is as easy as changing column width. Row height is calculated in points, the same unit of measure used for fonts. The row height must exceed the size of the font you are using. Normally, you don't need to adjust row height manually, because row heights adjust automatically to accommodate font size changes. If you format something in a row to be a larger point size, Excel adjusts the row to fit the largest point size in the row. However, you have just as many options for changing row height as you do column width. Using the mouse, you can place the ╪ pointer on the line dividing a row heading from the heading below it, and then drag to the desired height; double-clicking the line AutoFits the row height where necessary. You can also select one or more rows, then use the Row Height command on the shortcut menu, or click the Format button on the Home tab, then click the Row Height or AutoFit Row Height command.

Insert and Delete Rows and Columns

Learning Outcomes
- Use the Insert dialog box
- Use column and row heading buttons to insert and delete

As you modify a worksheet, you might find it necessary to insert or delete rows and columns to keep your worksheet current. For example, you might need to insert rows to accommodate new inventory products or remove a column of yearly totals that are no longer necessary. When you insert a new row, the row is inserted above the cell pointer and the contents of the worksheet shift down from the newly inserted row. When you insert a new column, the column is inserted to the left of the cell pointer and the contents of the worksheet shift to the right of the new column. To insert multiple rows, select the same number of row headings as you want to insert before using the Insert command. **CASE** *You want to improve the overall appearance of the worksheet by inserting a row between the company name and the column labels. Also, you have learned that row 9 and column K need to be deleted from the worksheet.*

STEPS

1. **Right-click cell F2, then click Insert on the shortcut menu**
   The Insert dialog box opens. See **FIGURE 2-11**. You can choose to insert a single cell and shift the cells in the active column to the right, insert a single cell and shift the cells in the active row down, or insert an entire column or a row.
2. **Click the Entire row option button, then click OK**
   A blank row appears between the company name and the column labels, visually separating the worksheet data, and the Insert Options button opens next to cell F3.
3. **Click the Insert Options button, then review your choices**
   This menu lets you format the inserted row in Format Same As Above (the default setting, already selected), Format Same As Below, or Clear Formatting.
4. **Click to close the menu without making changes, then click the row 9 heading**
   All of row 9 is selected, as shown in **FIGURE 2-12**.
5. **Click the Delete button in the Cells group; do not click the Delete arrow**
   Excel deletes row 9, and all rows below it shift up one row. You must use the Delete button or the Delete command on the shortcut menu to delete a row or column; pressing DEL on the keyboard removes only the *contents* of a selected row or column.
6. **Click the column K heading**
   The column is empty and isn't necessary in this worksheet.
7. **Click the Delete button in the Cells group**
   Excel deletes column K. The remaining columns to the right shift left one column.
8. **Save your work**

QUICK TIP
To insert a column, right-click the column heading to the right of where you want the new column, then click Insert on the shortcut menu.

FIGURE 2-11: Insert dialog box

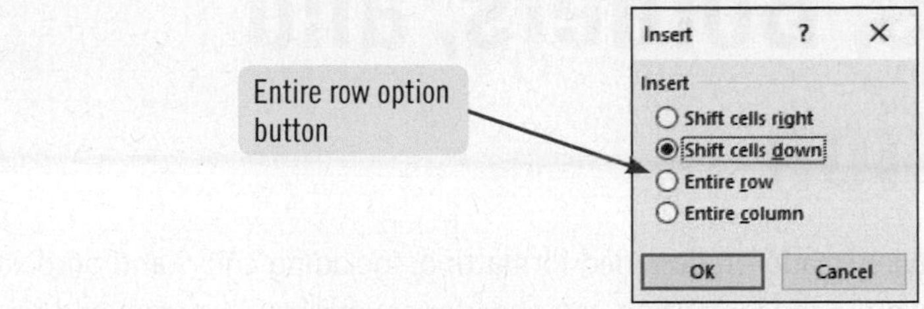

FIGURE 2-12: Worksheet with row 9 selected

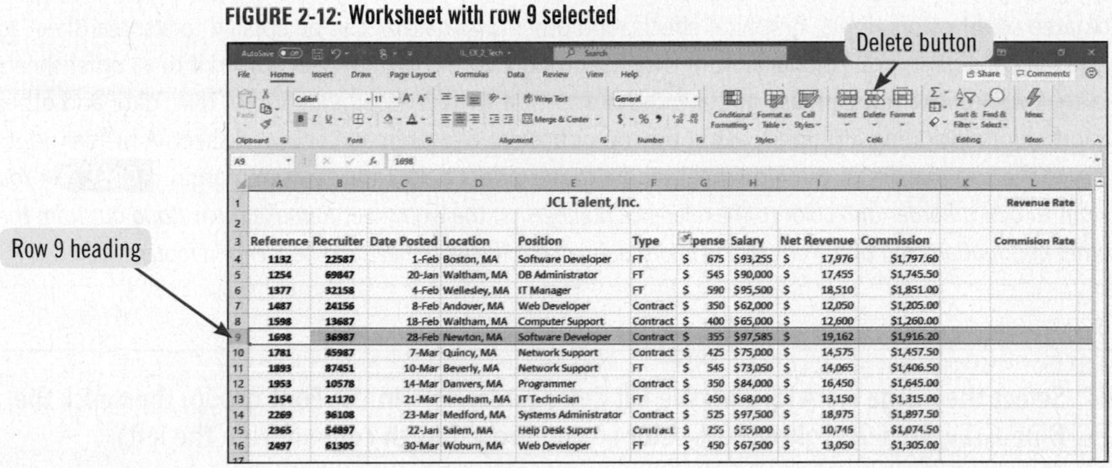

Hiding and unhiding columns and rows

When you don't want data in a column or row to be visible, but you don't want to delete it, you can hide the column or row. To hide a selected column, click the Format button in the Cells group on the Home tab, point to Hide & Unhide, then click Hide Columns. A hidden column is indicated by a dark green vertical line in its original position. This green line is removed when you click elsewhere on the worksheet, but a thin double line remains between the column headings to remind you that one or more columns are hidden. You can display a hidden column by selecting the column headings on either side of the hidden column, clicking the Format button in the Cells group, pointing to Hide & Unhide, then clicking Unhide Columns. (To hide or unhide one or more rows, substitute Hide Rows and Unhide Rows for the Hide Columns and Unhide Columns instructions.)

Excel

Create and apply a template

A **template** is a predesigned, preformatted Office file that contains default text formats, themes, placeholder text, headers and footers, and graphics that you can replace with your own information for hundreds of purposes, including budgets, flyers, and resumes. Template files have a file extension of .xltx. You can create your own template to provide a model for creating a new workbook by saving a workbook with this extension. To use a template, you apply it, which means you create a workbook based on the template. A workbook based on a template has the same content, formulas, and formatting defined in the template but is saved in the standard workbook format, .xlsx. The template file itself remains unchanged. To save a file as a template, click the File tab, click Save As, click This PC if necessary, click More options, click the Save as type arrow, click Excel Template in the list of file types, as shown in **FIGURE 2-13**, type a name for the new template in the File name box (the default save location is the Custom Office Templates folder), then click Save.

FIGURE 2-13: Save menu file types

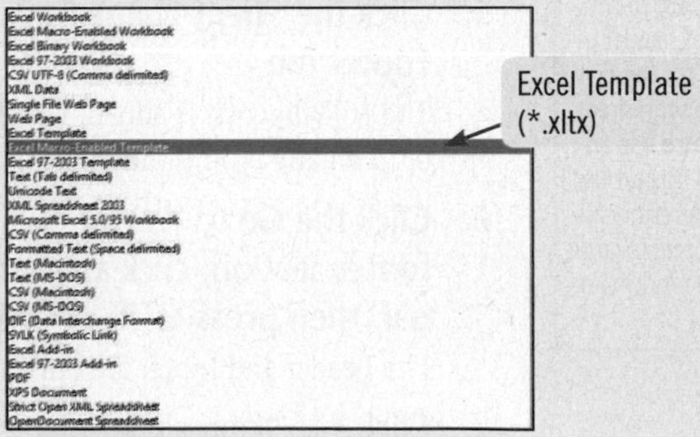

Excel Module 2

Learning Outcomes
- Change text and fill color
- Apply a border to a cell
- Add a header and footer to a worksheet

Apply Colors, Borders, and Documentation

You have seen how you can use cell styles to add predesigned formatting, including colors and borders to a worksheet. If a cell style doesn't capture the formatting you need for a worksheet, you can add this formatting individually. Color options are based on the worksheet theme. A **theme** is a predefined, coordinated set of colors, fonts, graphical effects, and other formats that can be applied to a spreadsheet to give it a consistent, professional look. In Excel, applying a theme to one sheet applies it to all other sheets in that workbook. You can also add a **header** and/or a **footer** to provide useful text, date and other information, including a graphic, along the top or bottom of every page of a worksheet. A header prints above the top margin of the worksheet, and a footer prints below the bottom margin. **CASE** *You want to add a border and color to the reference numbers on the worksheet to make them stand out from the other information. You also want to add information about the worksheet in a header and footer.*

STEPS

QUICK TIP
Themes can be changed by clicking the Page Layout tab, clicking the Themes button, and selecting a Theme from the Themes gallery.

1. **Select the range A4:A15, click the Fill Color arrow in the Font group, then click the Blue-Gray, Text 2, Lighter 80% color (second row, fourth column from the left)**
   The color is applied to the background (or fill) of this range. When you change fill or font color, the color on the Fill Color or Font Color button changes to the last color you selected.
2. **Click the Borders arrow in the Font group, review the Borders menu, as shown in FIGURE 2-14, then click Right Border**
   You can use the options at the bottom of the Borders menu to draw a border or to change a border line color or style.
3. **Click the Font Color arrow in the Font group, then click the Blue-Gray, Text 2 color (first row, fourth column from the left)**
   The new color is applied to the labels in the selected range. This color will make the first column reference numbers stand out.

QUICK TIP
You can use the settings in the Options group on the Header & Footer tab to set a different header or footer for the first page of a worksheet. You can also use an option in this group to set different headers or footers for odd and even worksheet pages.

4. **Click the Insert tab, click the Text button, then click the Header & Footer button**
   The header is divided into three sections, as shown in **FIGURE 2-15**, where you can enter or edit text. The Header & Footer tab includes elements and options for customizing the header or footer.
5. **Click the Sheet Name button in the Header & Footer Elements group on the Header & Footer tab**
   The & [Tab] code is added, which will display the current sheet name in this location. Using codes instead of manually typing the information ensures this information is always up to date.
6. **Click the Go to Footer button in the Navigation group, enter your name in the center footer section, click any cell on the worksheet, click the Normal button in the status bar, then press CTRL+HOME**
   The header and footer are only visible in Page Layout view and Print Preview.
7. **Click File, then click Print**
   Your header and footer will provide useful information to others viewing the worksheet.
8. **Click the Back button to return to your worksheet, then save your work**

FIGURE 2-14: Borders menu

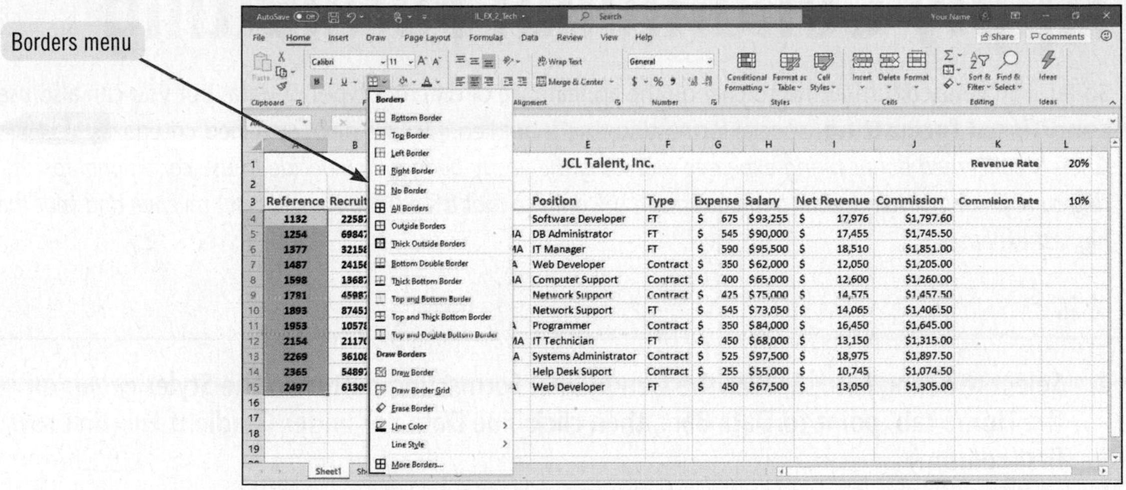

FIGURE 2-15: Header & Footer tab

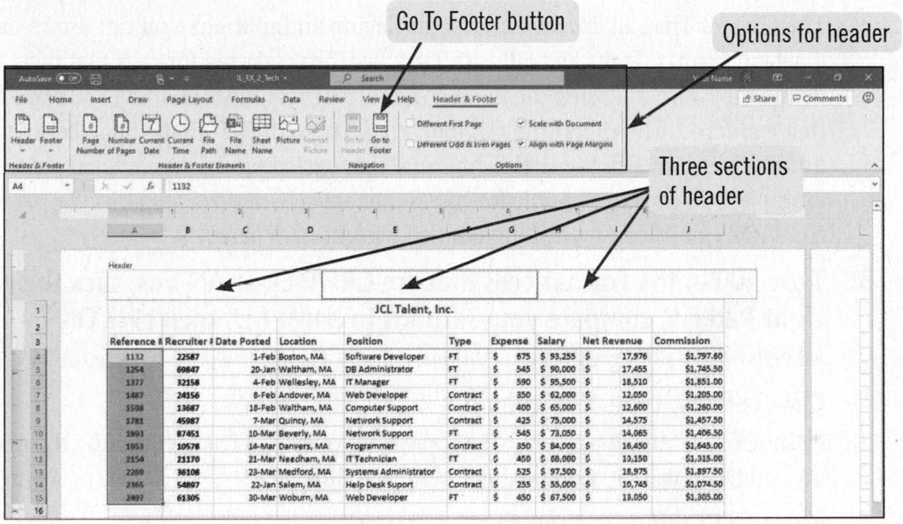

Checking worksheet accessibility

Part of successfully formatting your worksheets includes checking to see if any format presents accessibility problems. **Accessibility** is the quality of removing barriers that may prevent individuals with disabilities from interacting with data or an app. You can check for accessibility issues by clicking the Check Accessibility button in the Accessibility group on the Review tab. The Accessibility pane opens and displays an Inspection Results listing, as shown in **FIGURE 2-16**. You can click the errors and/or warnings to see additional information below the results, as well as steps to take to fix the issue.

FIGURE 2-16: Accessibility Checker pane

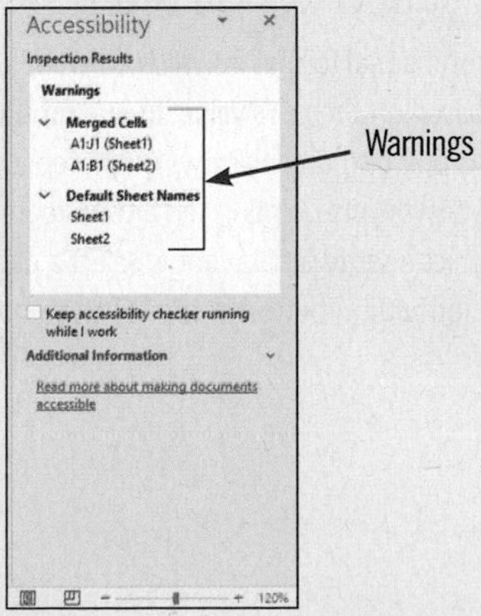

Excel

Excel **Module 2**

Apply Conditional Formatting

Learning Outcomes
- Create a Data Bars rule
- Create a Highlight Cells rule

So far, you've used formatting to change the appearance of different types of data, but you can also use **conditional formatting**, special formatting that is applied if values meet specified criteria. **CASE** *Cheri is concerned about hiring expenses exceeding the yearly budget. You decide to use conditional formatting to highlight certain trends and patterns in the data so that it's easy to compare net revenue and spot the highest expenses.*

STEPS

QUICK TIP
You can create a custom data bar rule by clicking the Conditional Formatting button, pointing to Data Bars, clicking More Rules, adjusting the options in the New Formatting Rule dialog box, then clicking OK.

1. **Select the range I4:I15, click the Conditional Formatting button in the Styles group on the Home tab, point to Data Bars, then click Blue Data Bar under Gradient Fill (first row, first column)**

   Data bars are colored horizontal bars that visually illustrate differences between values in a range of cells.

2. **Select the range G4:G15, click the Quick Analysis button that opens next to the selection, then click the Greater Than button on the Formatting tab**

   The Greater Than dialog box opens, displaying an input box you can use to define the condition and a default format (Light Red Fill with Dark Red Text) selected for cells that meet that condition. You can define the condition using the input box and assigning the formatting you want to use for cells that meet that condition. The Quick Analysis tool offers a powerful but limited number of options. To set more conditions, you can click the Highlight Cells Rules option on the Conditional Formatting menu instead. For example, you can create a rule for values that are between two amounts. Values used in input boxes for a condition can be constants, formulas, cell references, or dates.

QUICK TIP
You can highlight duplicate values in a selected range by clicking the Conditional Formatting button in the Styles group, pointing to Highlight Cells Rules, clicking Duplicate Values, then selecting a formatting option.

3. **Type 500 in the Format cells that are GREATER THAN box, click the with list arrow, click Light Red Fill, compare your settings to FIGURE 2-17, then click OK**

   All cells with values greater than $500 in column G appear with a light red fill.

4. **Click cell G4, type 499, then press ENTER**

   Because of the rule you created, the appearance of cell G4 changes because the new value no longer meets the condition you set. Compare your results to **FIGURE 2-18**.

5. **Press CTRL+HOME, then save your work**

Formatting data with icon sets

Icon sets are a conditional format in which different icons are displayed in a cell based on the cell's value. In one group of cells, for example, upward-pointing green arrows might represent the highest values, while downward-pointing red arrows represent the lower values. To add an icon set to a data range, select a data range, click the Conditional Formatting button in the Styles group, point to Icon Sets, then click an icon set. You can customize the values that are used as thresholds for color scales and icon sets by clicking the Conditional Formatting button in the Styles group, clicking Manage Rules, clicking the rule in the Conditional Formatting Rules Manager dialog box, clicking Edit Rule, entering new values, clicking OK, clicking Apply, then clicking OK to close the dialog box.

FIGURE 2-17: Greater Than dialog box

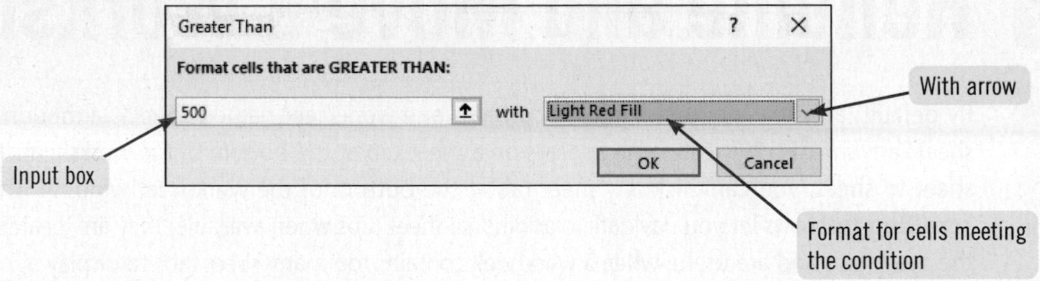

FIGURE 2-18: Worksheet with conditional formatting

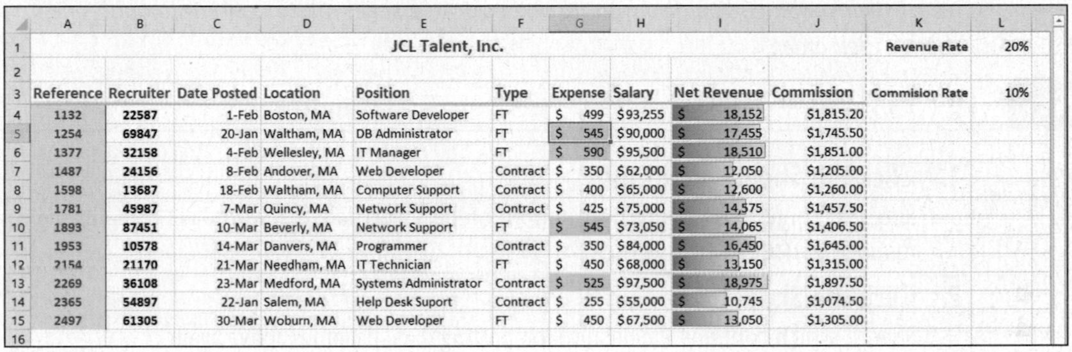

	A	B	C	D	E	F	G	H	I	J	K	L
1					JCL Talent, Inc.						Revenue Rate	20%
2												
3	Reference	Recruiter	Date Posted	Location	Position	Type	Expense	Salary	Net Revenue	Commission	Commision Rate	10%
4	1132	22587	1-Feb	Boston, MA	Software Developer	FT	$ 499	$93,255	$ 18,152	$1,815.20		
5	1254	69847	20-Jan	Waltham, MA	DB Administrator	FT	$ 545	$90,000	$ 17,455	$1,745.50		
6	1377	32158	4-Feb	Wellesley, MA	IT Manager	FT	$ 590	$95,500	$ 18,510	$1,851.00		
7	1487	24156	8-Feb	Andover, MA	Web Developer	Contract	$ 350	$62,000	$ 12,050	$1,205.00		
8	1598	13687	18-Feb	Waltham, MA	Computer Support	Contract	$ 400	$65,000	$ 12,600	$1,260.00		
9	1781	45987	7-Mar	Quincy, MA	Network Support	Contract	$ 425	$75,000	$ 14,575	$1,457.50		
10	1893	87451	10-Mar	Beverly, MA	Network Support	FT	$ 545	$73,050	$ 14,065	$1,406.50		
11	1953	10578	14-Mar	Danvers, MA	Programmer	Contract	$ 350	$84,000	$ 16,450	$1,645.00		
12	2154	21170	21-Mar	Needham, MA	IT Technician	FT	$ 450	$68,000	$ 13,150	$1,315.00		
13	2269	36108	23-Mar	Medford, MA	Systems Administrator	Contract	$ 525	$97,500	$ 18,975	$1,897.50		
14	2365	54897	22-Jan	Salem, MA	Help Desk Suport	Contract	$ 255	$55,000	$ 10,745	$1,074.50		
15	2497	61305	30-Mar	Woburn, MA	Web Developer	FT	$ 450	$67,500	$ 13,050	$1,305.00		
16												

Managing conditional formatting rules

If you create a conditional formatting rule and then want to change a condition, you don't need to create a new rule; instead, you can edit the rule using the Rules Manager. Click the Conditional Formatting button in the Styles group, then click Manage Rules. The Conditional Formatting Rules Manager dialog box opens, as shown in **FIGURE 2-19**, listing any rules you have set. Use the Show Formatting rules for arrow to see rules for other parts of a worksheet or for other sheets in the workbook. Select the rule you want to edit, click Edit Rule, then modify the settings in the Edit the Rule Description area in the Edit Formatting Rule dialog box. To change the formatting for a rule, click the Format button in the Edit the Rule Description area, select the formatting styles you want the cells to have, then click OK three times to close the Format Cells dialog box, the Edit Formatting Rule dialog box, and the Conditional Formatting Rules Manager dialog box. To delete a rule, select the rule in the Conditional Formatting Rules Manager dialog box, then click the Delete Rule button. You can quickly clear conditional formatting rules by clicking the Conditional Formatting button in the Styles group, pointing to Clear Rules, then clicking Clear Rules from Selected Cells or Clear Rules from Entire Worksheet.

FIGURE 2-19: Conditional Formatting Rules Manager dialog box

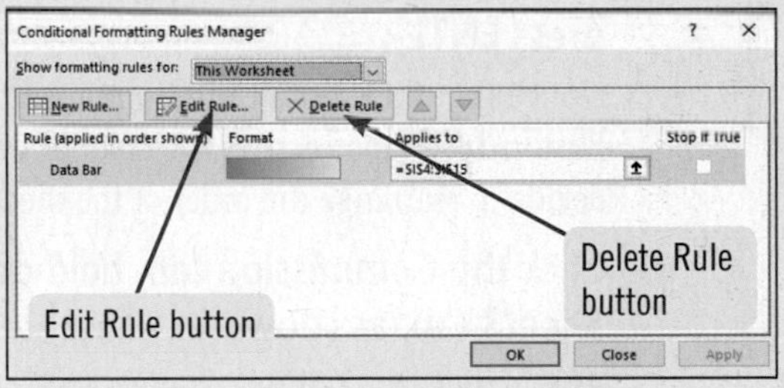

Excel

Rename and Move a Worksheet

Learning Outcomes
- Rename a sheet
- Apply color to a sheet tab
- Reorder sheets in a workbook

By default, an Excel workbook initially contains one worksheet named Sheet1, although you can add sheets anytime. Each sheet name appears on a sheet tab at the bottom of the worksheet. To move from sheet to sheet, you can click any sheet tab at the bottom of the worksheet window. The **sheet tab scrolling buttons** let you navigate to additional sheet tabs when available; they are located to the left of the sheet tabs and are useful when a workbook contains too many sheet tabs to display at once. To make a workbook more accessible, you can rename worksheets with descriptive names. Worksheets are easier to identify if you add color to the tabs. You can also organize worksheets in a logical order. **CASE** *In the current worksheet, Sheet1 contains detailed information about technical job postings in the Boston office. Sheet2 contains commission information, and Sheet3 contains no data. You want to rename these sheets to reflect their contents. You also want to add color to a sheet tab to easily distinguish one from the other and change their order.*

STEPS

1. **Click the Sheet2 sheet tab**
   Sheet2 becomes active, appearing in front of the Sheet1 tab; this worksheet contains the commission information. See **FIGURE 2-20**.
2. **Click the Sheet1 tab**
   Sheet1, which contains the detailed job posting data, becomes active again.
3. **Double-click the Sheet2 tab, type Commission, then press ENTER**
   The new name for Sheet2 automatically replaces the default name on the tab. Worksheet names can have up to 31 characters, including spaces and punctuation.
4. **Right-click the Commission tab, point to Tab Color on the shortcut menu, then click the Blue, Accent 5, Darker 25% color (fifth row, second column from the right), as shown in FIGURE 2-21**
5. **Right-click the Sheet1 tab, click Rename on the shortcut menu, type Boston Tech, then press ENTER**
   Notice that the color of the Commission tab changes depending on whether it is the active tab; when the Boston Tech tab is active, the color of the Commission tab changes to the blue tab color you selected. You decide to rearrange the order of the sheets so that the Commission tab is to the right of the Sheet3 tab.
6. **Click the Commission tab, hold down the mouse button, drag it to the right of the Sheet3 tab, as shown in FIGURE 2-22, then release the mouse button**
   As you drag, the pointer changes to the sheet relocation pointer, and a small black triangle just above the tabs shows the position where the moved sheet will be when you release the mouse button. The last sheet in the workbook is now the Commission sheet. See **FIGURE 2-23**. You can move multiple sheets by pressing and holding SHIFT while clicking the sheets you want to move, then dragging the sheets to their new location.
7. **Right-click the Sheet3 tab, click Delete on the shortcut menu, press CTRL+HOME, then save your work**
   The sheet is deleted.

QUICK TIP
If a workbook contains more sheet tabs than are visible, you can navigate between sheets by using the tab scrolling buttons to the left of the sheet tabs: the Previous Worksheet button ◀ and the Next Worksheet button ▶.

QUICK TIP
To insert a worksheet, click the New sheet button ⊕ to the right of the sheet tabs.

FIGURE 2-20: Sheet tabs in workbook

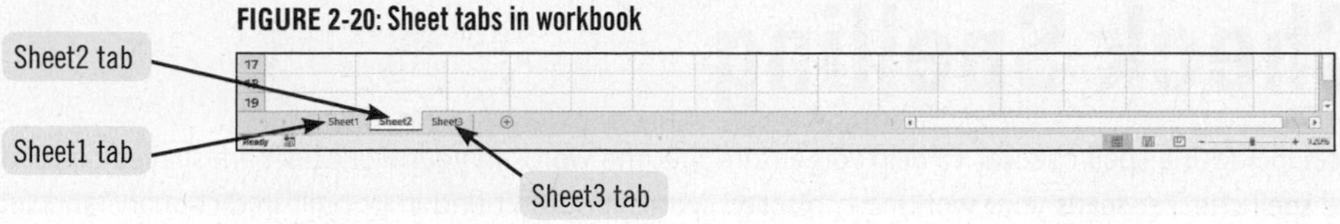

FIGURE 2-21: Tab Color palette

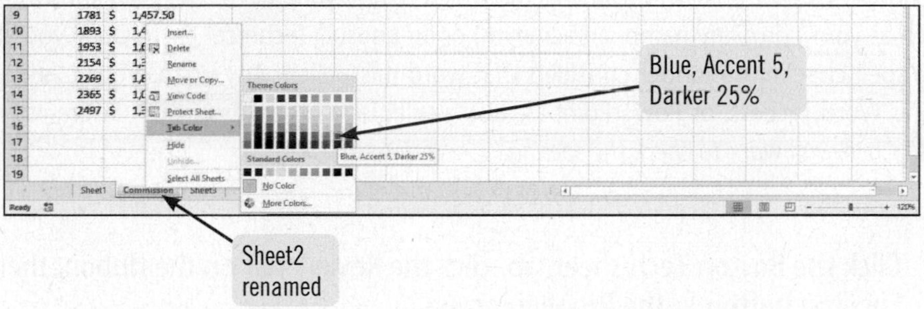

FIGURE 2-22: Moving the Commission sheet

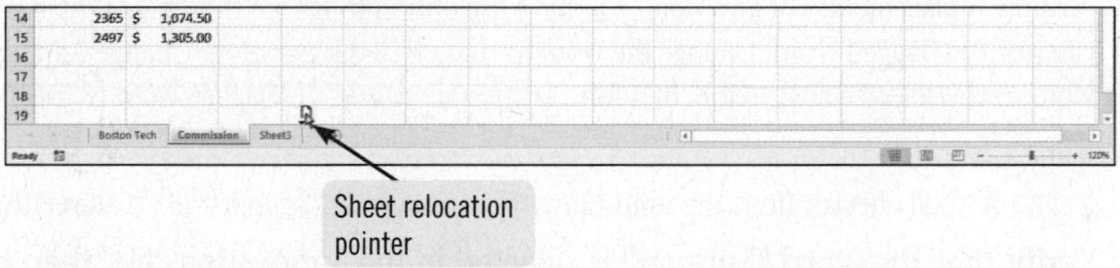

FIGURE 2-23: Reordered sheets

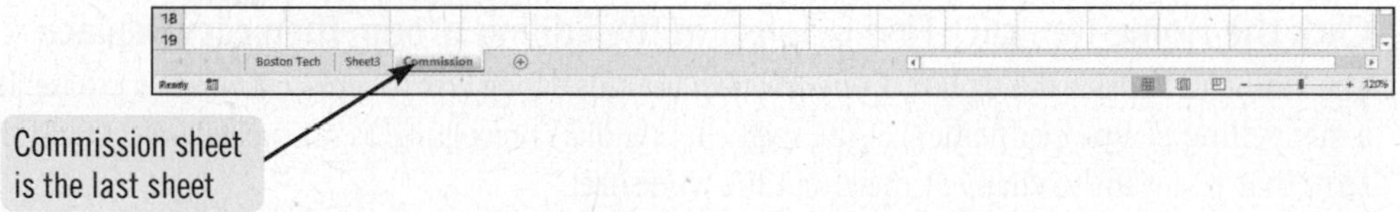

Copying, adding, and deleting worksheets

There are times when you may want to copy a worksheet. For example, a workbook might contain a sheet with Quarter 1 expenses, and you want to use that sheet as the basis for a sheet containing Quarter 2 expenses. To copy a sheet within the same workbook, press and hold CTRL, drag the sheet tab to the desired tab location, release the mouse button, then release CTRL. A duplicate sheet appears with the same name as the copied sheet followed by "(2)" indicating that it is a copy. You can then rename the sheet to a more meaningful name. To copy a sheet to a different workbook, both the source and destination workbooks must be open. Select the sheet to copy or move, right-click the sheet tab, click Move or Copy in the shortcut menu, then complete the information in the Move or Copy dialog box. Be sure to click the Create a copy check box if you want to copy rather than move the worksheet. Carefully check your calculation results whenever you move or copy a worksheet. You can add multiple worksheets quickly by pressing and holding SHIFT, clicking the number of existing worksheet tabs that correspond with the number of sheets you want to add, clicking the Insert arrow in the Cells group on the Home tab, then clicking Insert Sheet. You can delete multiple worksheets from a workbook by clicking the Home tab on the ribbon, pressing and holding SHIFT, clicking the sheet tabs of the worksheets you want to delete, clicking the Delete arrow in the Cells group, then clicking Delete Sheet.

Check Spelling

Learning Outcomes
- Change the spelling using a suggestion
- Replace text using Find & Select

Excel includes a spell checker to help you ensure that the words in your worksheet are spelled correctly. The spell checker scans your worksheet, displays words it doesn't find in its built-in dictionary, and suggests replacements when they are available. To check all the sheets in a multiple-sheet workbook, you need to display each sheet individually and run the spell checker for each one. Because the built-in dictionary cannot possibly include all the words that anyone needs, you can add words to the dictionary, such as your company name, an acronym, or an unusual technical term. Once you add a word or term, the spell checker no longer considers that word misspelled. Any words you've added to the dictionary using Word, Access, or PowerPoint are also available in Excel. **CASE** *Before you share this workbook with Cheri, you want to check the spelling.*

STEPS

QUICK TIP
You can click the Thesaurus button in the Proofing group to open a Thesaurus pane with a list of synonyms for a selected word in a cell.

1. **Click the Boston Tech sheet tab, click the Review tab on the ribbon, then click the Spelling button in the Proofing group**
   The Spelling: English (United States) dialog box opens, as shown in **FIGURE 2-24**, with "Commision" selected as the first misspelled word on the worksheet, and with "Commission" selected in the Suggestions list as a possible replacement. For any word, you have the option to Ignore this case of the flagged word, Ignore All cases of the flagged word, Change the word to the selected suggestion, Change All instances of the flagged word to the selected suggestion, or Add to Dictionary to add the flagged word to the dictionary.
2. **Click Change**
   Next, the spell checker finds the word "Suport" and suggests "Support" as an alternative.
3. **Verify that the word "Support" is selected in the Suggestions list, then click Change**
   When no more incorrect words are found, Excel displays a message indicating that the spell check is complete.
4. **Click OK**

QUICK TIP
If you want to find text, click Find & Select in the Editing group, then click Find.

5. **Click the Home tab, click Find & Select in the Editing group, then click Replace**
   The Find and Replace dialog box opens. You can use this dialog box to replace a word or phrase. It might be a misspelling of a proper name that the spell checker didn't recognize as misspelled, or it could simply be a term that you want to change throughout the worksheet.
6. **Type Contract in the Find what text box, press TAB, then type Temp in the Replace with text box**
   Compare your dialog box to **FIGURE 2-25**.

QUICK TIP
You can find and replace cell formatting by clicking the Options button in the Find and Replace dialog box, then clicking the Format arrows to select the desired formatting.

7. **Click Replace All, click OK to close the Microsoft Excel dialog box, then click Close to close the Find and Replace dialog box**
   Excel made six replacements, changing each instance of "Contract" on the worksheet to "Temp."
8. **Click the File tab, click Print on the navigation bar, click the Custom Scaling setting in the Settings section on the Print tab, then click Fit Sheet on One Page**
9. **sam Click the Back button to return to your worksheet, save your work, submit it to your instructor as directed, close the workbook, then close Excel**
   The completed worksheet is shown in **FIGURE 2-26**.

Translating text

You can translate text in a worksheet by clicking the Review tab, clicking the Translate button in the Language group, then, if necessary, clicking Turn on when asked if you want to use intelligent services. The Translator pane opens and allows you to select the From language and the To language from menus of world languages. The translated text appears in the To language box.

FIGURE 2-24: Spelling: English (United States) dialog box

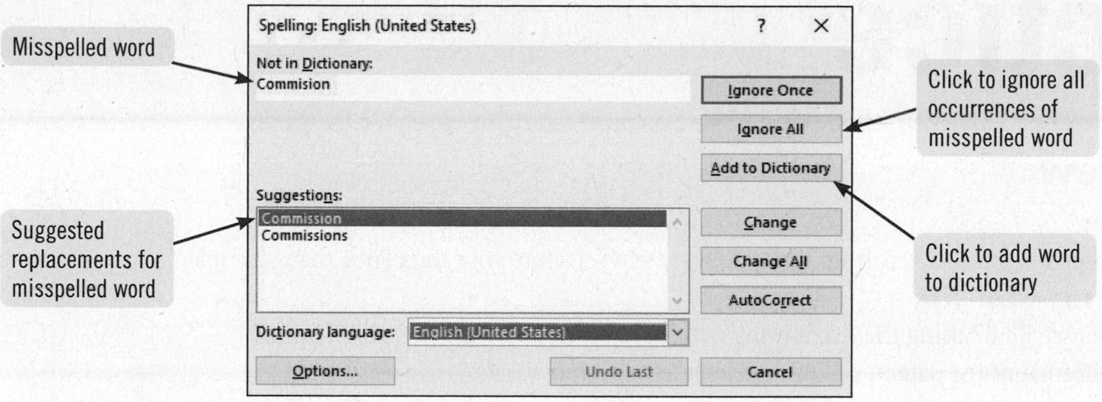

FIGURE 2-25: Find and Replace dialog box

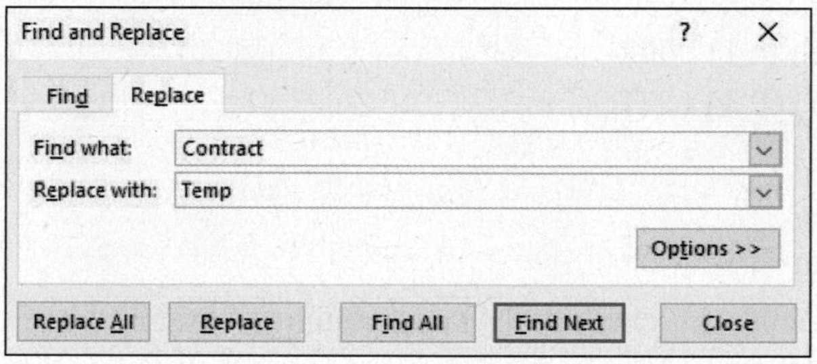

FIGURE 2-26: Completed worksheet

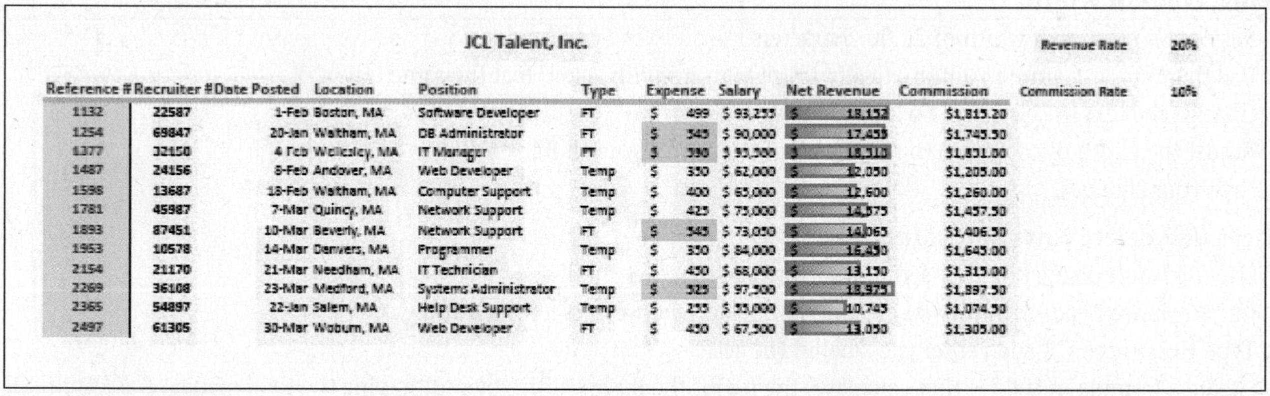

JCL Talent, Inc.

Reference #	Recruiter #	Date Posted	Location	Position	Type	Expense	Salary	Net Revenue	Commission		
										Revenue Rate	20%
										Commission Rate	10%
1132	22587	1-Feb	Boston, MA	Software Developer	FT	$ 499	$ 93,255	$ 18,152	$1,815.20		
1254	69847	20-Jan	Waltham, MA	DB Administrator	FT	$ 545	$ 90,000	$ 17,455	$1,745.50		
1377	32150	4-Feb	Wellesley, MA	IT Manager	FT	$ 390	$ 94,500	$ 18,510	$1,851.00		
1487	24156	8-Feb	Andover, MA	Web Developer	Temp	$ 350	$ 62,000	$ 12,050	$1,205.00		
1598	13687	18-Feb	Waltham, MA	Computer Support	Temp	$ 400	$ 65,000	$ 12,600	$1,260.00		
1781	45987	7-Mar	Quincy, MA	Network Support	Temp	$ 425	$ 75,000	$ 14,575	$1,457.50		
1893	87451	10-Mar	Beverly, MA	Network Support	FT	$ 545	$ 73,050	$ 14,065	$1,406.50		
1953	10578	14-Mar	Danvers, MA	Programmer	Temp	$ 350	$ 84,000	$ 16,450	$1,645.00		
2154	21170	21-Mar	Needham, MA	IT Technician	FT	$ 450	$ 68,000	$ 13,150	$1,315.00		
2269	36108	23-Mar	Medford, MA	Systems Administrator	Temp	$ 525	$ 97,500	$ 18,975	$1,897.50		
2365	54897	22-Jan	Salem, MA	Help Desk Support	Temp	$ 255	$ 55,000	$ 10,745	$1,074.50		
2497	61305	30-Mar	Woburn, MA	Web Developer	FT	$ 450	$ 67,500	$ 13,050	$1,305.00		

Using Find & Select features

You can navigate to a specific place in a workbook by clicking the Find & Select button in the Editing group on the Home tab, clicking Go To, typing a cell address, then clicking OK. Clicking the Find & Select button also allows you to quickly go to notes, formulas, constants, data validation, and conditional formatting in a worksheet. You can use the Go to Special dialog box to navigate to cells with special elements such as different types of formulas or objects. Some Go to Special commands also appear on the Find & Select menu. Using this menu, you can also change the mouse pointer shape to the Select Objects pointer so you can quickly select drawing objects when necessary. To return to the standard Excel pointer, press ESC.

Practice

Skills Review

1. Format values.

a. Start Excel, open IL_EX_2-2.xlsx from the location where you store your Data Files, then save it as **IL_EX_2_Investments**.
b. Format the range B3:B7 using the Accounting number format.
c. Change the format of the date in cell B9 so it appears as 18-Jun.
d. Increase the number of decimals in cell D1 to 1, using a button in the Number group on the Home tab.
e. Save your work.

2. Change font and font size.

a. Select the range A3:A7.
b. Change the font of the selection to Calibri.
c. Increase the font size of the selection to 11 point.
d. Increase the font size of the label in cell A1 to 11 point.
e. Save your changes.

3. Change font styles and alignment.

a. Apply the Heading 2 cell style to cell A1.
b. Use the Merge & Center button to center the label in cell A1 over columns A and B.
c. Apply the italic and bold font formats to the label in cell C1.
d. Use the Format Painter to copy the format in cell C1 to the label in cell A9.
e. Change the alignment of cell B2 to Align Right using a button in the Alignment group on the Home tab.
f. Save your changes.

4. Adjust column width.

a. Resize column C to a width of 21.00 characters.
b. Use the AutoFit feature to automatically resize both columns A and B at the same time.
c. Change the text in cell B2 to **Total Managed Assets**.
d. Adjust the width of column B to display all of the content in cell B2.
e. Save your changes.

5. Insert and delete rows and columns.

a. Use the Insert dialog box to insert a new row between rows 1 and 2.
b. Use a column heading button to insert a new column between columns B and C.
c. Type **Fee** in cell C3 and center the label in the cell.
d. Create a formula in cell C4 that calculates the fee for the Boston office by multiplying the total managed assets in cell B4 by the annual fee percentage in cell E1. (*Hint:* Make sure you use the correct type of cell references in the formula.)
e. Copy the formula in cell C4 to the range C5:C8.
f. Use a row heading button to delete the Philadelphia row from the worksheet.
g. Save your changes.

6. Apply colors, borders, and documentation.

a. Add an outside border around the range A3:C7.
b. Apply the Green, Accent 6, Lighter 80% fill color (second row, last column) to the range D1:E1.
c. Change the color of the font in the range A9:B9 to Green, Accent 6, Darker 50% (last row, last column under Theme Colors).
d. Add a header in the center section of the worksheet that contains the sheet name.

Skills Review (continued)

  e. Enter your name in the center section of the worksheet footer.
  f. Save your changes.

7. **Apply conditional formatting.**
  a. Select the range C4:C7, then create a Highlight Cells rule that changes cell contents to green fill with dark green text if the value is greater than 50000.
  b. Select the range B4:B7, then apply Gradient Fill green data bars. (*Hint:* Click Green Data Bar in the Gradient Fill section.)
  c. Open the Conditional Formatting Rules Manager dialog box and view the conditional formatting rules for the worksheet. (*Hint:* Click Manage Rules on the Conditional Formatting menu, then click the Show formatting rules for arrow.)
  d. Review the rules for the worksheet, making sure your rules are correct, then close the dialog box.
  e. Save your changes.

8. **Rename and move a worksheet.**
  a. Rename the Sheet1 tab to **Active Management** and rename the Sheet2 tab to **Passive Management**.
  b. Add a sheet to the workbook, then name the new sheet **Total Fees**.
  c. Change the Active Management tab color to Green, Accent 6, Darker 50%.
  d. Change the Passive Management tab color to Blue, Accent 5, Darker 50%.
  e. Reorder the sheets so that the Total Fees sheet comes before (to the left of) the Active Management sheet.
  f. Delete the Total Fees sheet.
  g. Activate the Active Management sheet, then save your work.

9. **Check spelling.**
  a. Move the cell pointer to cell A1.
  b. Use the Find & Select feature to replace the word "Boston" with **New York**.
  c. Use the Spelling tool to check the spelling on the worksheet and correct any spelling errors, using suggestions as appropriate.
  d. Save your changes, then compare your Active Management sheet to **FIGURE 2-27**.
  e. Preview the Active Management sheet in Backstage view, submit your work to your instructor as directed, then close the workbook and close Excel.

FIGURE 2-27

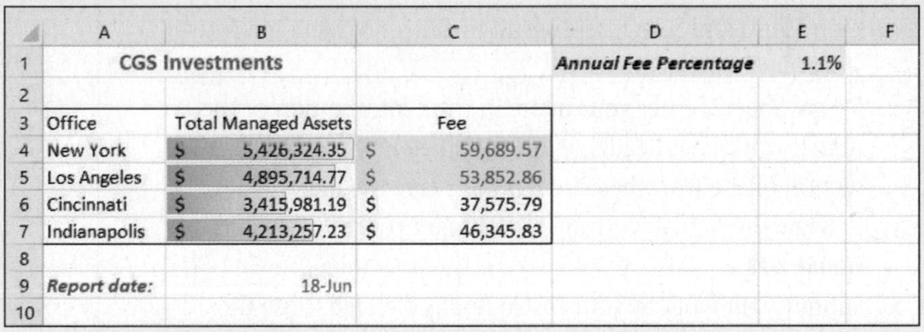

	A	B	C	D	E	F
1	CGS Investments			*Annual Fee Percentage*	1.1%	
2						
3	Office	Total Managed Assets	Fee			
4	New York	$ 5,426,324.35	$ 59,689.57			
5	Los Angeles	$ 4,895,714.77	$ 53,852.86			
6	Cincinnati	$ 3,415,981.19	$ 37,575.79			
7	Indianapolis	$ 4,213,257.23	$ 46,345.83			
8						
9	*Report date:*	18-Jun				
10						

Excel

Independent Challenge 1

As an accountant for Riverwalk medical clinic, you have been asked to review the expenses for the emergency room. You've organized the data in an Excel workbook, and now you want to format the data to improve its readability and highlight trends in expenses.

  a. Start Excel, open IL_EX_2-3.xlsx from the location where you store your Data Files, then save it as **IL_EX_2_Riverwalk**.
  b. Format the values in the Total column in the Accounting number format with two decimal places.
  c. Format the values in the % of Total column as Percent format with two decimal places.
  d. Format the values in the Inv. Date column with the Date format 14-Mar.

Independent Challenge 1 (continued)

e. Apply bold formatting to the column labels and increase the font size of the labels to 12.
f. Italicize the inventory Type items in column A.
g. Change the font of the Sales Tax label in cell K1 to Calibri.
h. Apply the Title cell style to cell A1.
i. Delete column I, then delete row 13.
j. Merge and center the title in cell A1 over columns A1:I1.
k. Resize column widths as necessary, using AutoFit or by dragging, so that all columns are wide enough to display the data and labels.
l. Use the Format Painter to copy the date format in the Inv. Date column to the values in the Inv. Due column.
m. Change the fill color of the sales tax information in the range J1:K1 to the Light Gray, Background 2 color (first row, third column from the left).
n. Change the font color of the sales tax information in the range J1:K1 to the Blue-Gray, Text 2 color (first row, fourth column from the left).
o. Add a bottom border to the column labels.
p. Use conditional formatting to apply blue gradient data bars to the Total column data. Do not include the total in cell H38 at the bottom of the column.
q. Add the 3 Arrows (Colored) (first set in the Directional group) icon set to the Quantity column to illustrate the relative differences between quantities. Do not include the total in cell E38 at the bottom of the column in this format.
r. Rename Sheet3 to **Budget** and rename Sheet1 to **Actual**. Change the color of the Budget sheet to Red in the Standard colors. Change the color of the Actual sheet to Purple in the Standard colors.
s. Move Sheet2 to the right of the Budget sheet.
t. Activate the Actual Sheet and spell check the worksheet. Correct any spelling errors.
u. Using Find and Select, replace all instances of Maxi on the worksheet with ACE.
v. Delete Sheet2, enter your name in the center section of the Actual worksheet header, enter the sheet name in the center section of the worksheet footer, then save the file.
w. Preview the Actual worksheet. Compare your worksheet to **FIGURE 2-28**.
x. Submit your work to your instructor as directed, close the workbook, then close Excel.

FIGURE 2-28

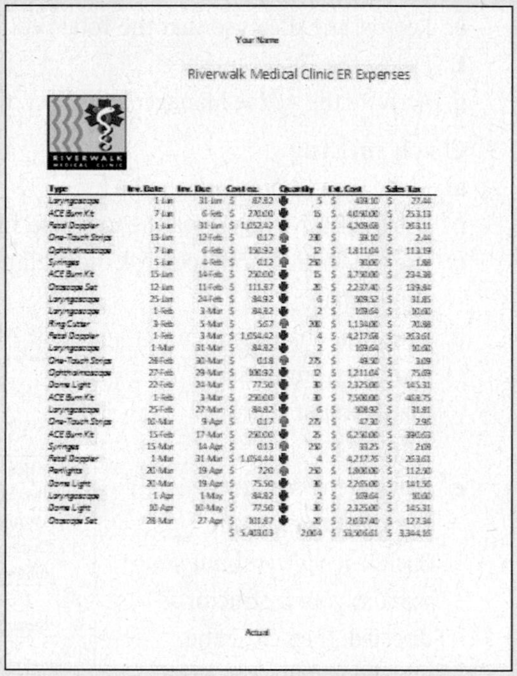

Independent Challenge 2

You are assisting the head of business operations at First Financial Services. You have been asked to format a worksheet showing the first-quarter business services for the company's five branches. As part of this effort, you want to illustrate service trends among the branches.

a. Start Excel, open IL_EX_2-4.xlsx from the location where you store your Data Files, then save it as **IL_EX_2_FinancialServices**.
b. Enter a formula in cell B8 for the Main total, then copy the formula to the range C8:F8.
c. Enter a formula in cell G3 for the Credit card processing total, then copy the formula to the range G4:G8.
d. Apply the Title cell style to cell A1, apply the Heading 4 cell style to the column headings in row 2, and apply the Total cell style to the range A8:G8.
e. Merge and center the title in cell A1 across the range A1:G1.
f. Format the range B3:G8 using the Accounting number format. AutoFit the widths of all columns and format the range with no decimal places.
g. Format the date in cell B9 using the first 14-Mar-12 date format.
h. Rotate the label in cell A2 up by 45 degrees. Copy this rotated format to the other column headings.
i. Format the range A9:B9 with a Blue-Gray, Text 2, Lighter 80% (second row, fourth column from the left) fill.
j. Format the range A9:B9 with a Blue, Accent 1, Darker 50% (last row, fifth column from the left, under Theme Colors) font color.
k. Create a conditional format in the range G3:G8 so that entries less than 25,000,000 appear in light red fill with dark red text.
l. Create a conditional format in the range B8:F8 to add the 3 Stars Ratings icon set. Widen the columns as necessary to fully display the data and formatting.
m. Use the Spelling tool to check spelling in the sheet.
n. Rename Sheet1 to **First Quarter**. Copy the First Quarter sheet and rename the copied sheet **Second Quarter**. Move the Second Quarter sheet if necessary so it is to the right of the First Quarter sheet.
o. On the Second Quarter sheet, delete the data in the range B3:F7 and delete the date in cell B9.
p. Activate the First Quarter sheet. Compare your worksheet to **FIGURE 2-29**.
q. Enter your name in the center header section, change the worksheet orientation to landscape, then save your work.
r. Preview the worksheet, make any final changes you think are necessary, then submit your work to your instructor as directed.
s. Close the workbook, then close Excel.

FIGURE 2-29

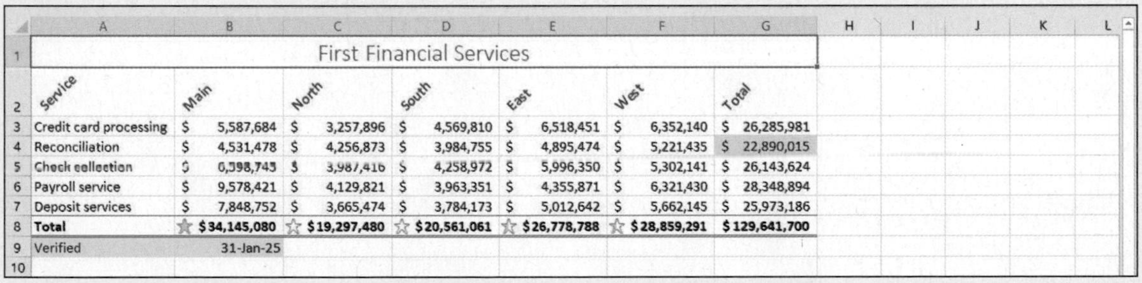

	A	B	C	D	E	F	G
1	First Financial Services						
2	Service	Main	North	South	East	West	Total
3	Credit card processing	$ 5,587,684	$ 3,257,896	$ 4,569,810	$ 6,518,451	$ 6,352,140	$ 26,285,981
4	Reconciliation	$ 4,531,478	$ 4,256,873	$ 3,984,755	$ 4,895,474	$ 5,221,435	$ 22,890,015
5	Check collection	$ 6,598,745	$ 3,987,416	$ 4,258,972	$ 5,996,350	$ 5,302,141	$ 26,143,624
6	Payroll service	$ 9,578,421	$ 4,129,821	$ 3,963,351	$ 4,355,871	$ 6,321,430	$ 28,348,894
7	Deposit services	$ 7,848,752	$ 3,665,474	$ 3,784,173	$ 5,012,642	$ 5,662,145	$ 25,973,186
8	Total	$34,145,080	$19,297,480	$20,561,061	$26,778,788	$28,859,291	$129,641,700
9	Verified	31-Jan-25					
10							

Visual Workshop

Open IL_EX_2-5.xlsx from the location where you store your Data Files, then save it as **IL_EX_2_EngineeringServices**. Use the skills you learned in this module to format the worksheet so it looks like the one shown in **FIGURE 2-30**. (Note that cell A1 is selected in the figure.) Use the blue gradient fill for the data bars in the Total column. Use the Title cell style for the company name in cell A1, the Heading 1 cell style for the column labels in row 2, and the Total cell style for the total values in the last row. The font color for the service packages listed in column A is Dark Blue in the standard colors. (*Hint:* A row has been deleted from the worksheet.) Enter your name in the upper-left section of the header, check the spelling on the worksheet, save your changes, then submit your work to your instructor as directed.

FIGURE 2-30

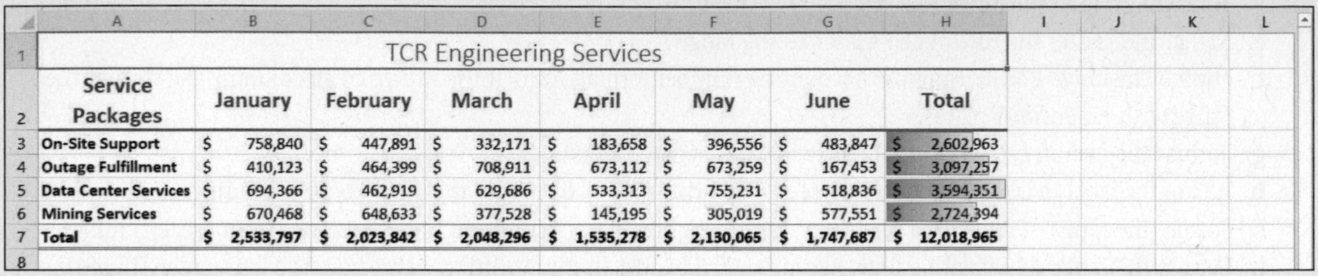

	A	B	C	D	E	F	G	H
1	TCR Engineering Services							
2	Service Packages	January	February	March	April	May	June	Total
3	On-Site Support	$ 758,840	$ 447,891	$ 332,171	$ 183,658	$ 396,556	$ 483,847	$ 2,602,963
4	Outage Fulfillment	$ 410,123	$ 464,399	$ 708,911	$ 673,112	$ 673,259	$ 167,453	$ 3,097,257
5	Data Center Services	$ 694,366	$ 462,919	$ 629,686	$ 533,313	$ 755,231	$ 518,836	$ 3,594,351
6	Mining Services	$ 670,468	$ 648,633	$ 377,528	$ 145,195	$ 305,019	$ 577,551	$ 2,724,394
7	Total	$ 2,533,797	$ 2,023,842	$ 2,048,296	$ 1,535,278	$ 2,130,065	$ 1,747,687	$ 12,018,965
8								

Analyzing Data Using Formulas

CASE Ellie Schwartz, the vice president of Finance at JCL, wants to know how North American revenues have performed compared to last year and relative to projected targets. She asks you to prepare a worksheet that summarizes and analyzes this revenue data.

Module Objectives

After completing this module, you will be able to:

- Enter a formula using the Quick Analysis tool
- Build a logical formula with the IF function
- Build a logical formula with the AND function
- Round a value with a function
- Build a statistical formula with the COUNTA function
- Enter a date function
- Work with equation tools
- Control worksheet calculations

Files You Will Need

IL_EX_3-1.xlsx
IL_EX_3-2.xlsx
IL_EX_3-3.xlsx
IL_EX_3-4.xlsx
IL_EX_3-5.xlsx

Enter a Formula Using the Quick Analysis Tool

Learning Outcomes
- Create a formula using the Quick Analysis tool
- Create a formula to find a percentage increase

So far, you have used the AutoSum button on the ribbon to quickly add simple formulas that sum and average selected data. You can also add formulas using the Quick Analysis tool, which opens when you select a range of cells. This tool allows you to quickly format, chart, or analyze data by calculating sums, averages, and other selected totals. **CASE** *To help Ellie evaluate revenues at JCL, you want to calculate yearly revenue totals for each North American office and compare the yearly performance of each office to the previous year.*

STEPS

1. **sam Start Excel, open IL_EX_3-1.xlsx from the location where you store your Data Files, then save it as IL_EX_3_Revenue**
2. **Select the range B3:E12, click the Quick Analysis button that appears below the selection, then click the Totals tab**

   The Totals tab in the Quick Analysis tool displays commonly used functions, as shown in **FIGURE 3-1**. This tab includes two Sum buttons, one that inserts the SUM function in a row beneath the selected range, and one that inserts the SUM function in the column to the right of the range.
3. **Click the Sum button displaying the gold column**

   The newly calculated totals display in the column to the right of the selected range, in cells F3:F12.

   QUICK TIP Clicking the first AutoSum button enters totals in a row below a selected range.
4. **Click cell H3, type =(, click cell F3, type -, click cell G3, then type)**

   This first part of the formula finds the difference in total revenue from the previous year to this year. You enclosed this operation in parentheses to make sure this difference is calculated first.
5. **Type /, then click cell G3**

   The second part of this formula divides the difference in revenue by the total revenue for the previous year, to calculate the increase or decrease.
6. **Click the Enter button on the formula bar**

   The result, .75405003, appears in cell H3. The column isn't wide enough to fully display this value but the number of decimal places will be adjusted in the next formatting step.
7. **Click the Percent Style button in the Number group, then click the Increase Decimal button in the Number group twice**

   The formatted percentage, 75.41%, appears in cell H3.
8. **Drag the fill handle from cell H3 to cell H12, then save your work**

   The percentage changes in annual revenue for each office appear in column H, as shown in **FIGURE 3-2**.

FIGURE 3-1: Quick Analysis tool

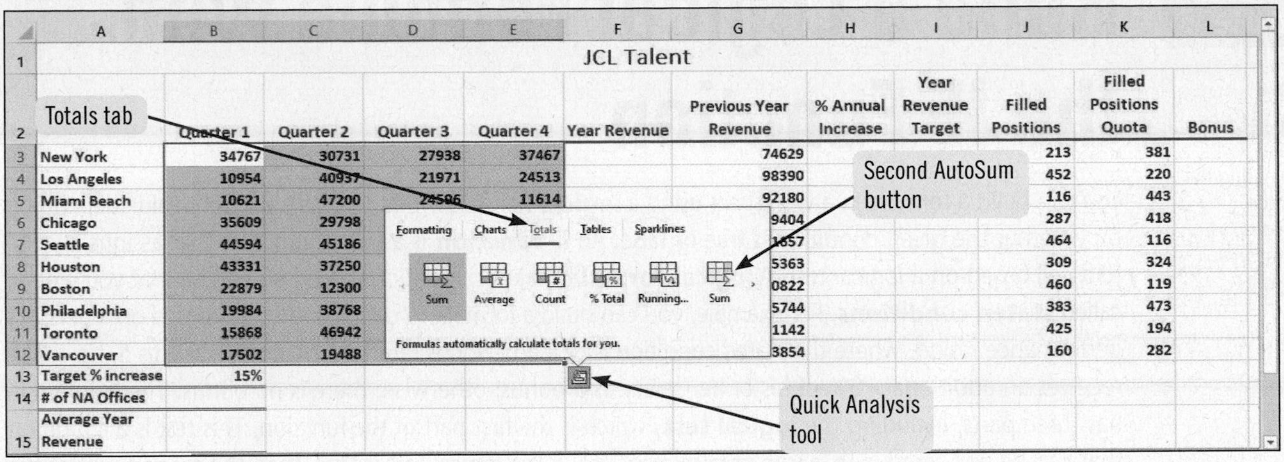

	A	B	C	D	E	F	G	H	I	J	K	L
1						JCL Talent						
2		Quarter 1	Quarter 2	Quarter 3	Quarter 4	Year Revenue	Previous Year Revenue	% Annual Increase	Year Revenue Target	Filled Positions	Filled Positions Quota	Bonus
3	New York	34767	30731	27938	37467		74629			213	381	
4	Los Angeles	10954	40937	21971	24513		98390			452	220	
5	Miami Beach	10621	47200	24596	11614		92180			116	443	
6	Chicago	35609	29798				9404			287	418	
7	Seattle	44594	45186				1657			464	116	
8	Houston	43331	37250				5363			309	324	
9	Boston	22879	12300				0822			460	119	
10	Philadelphia	19984	38768				5744			383	473	
11	Toronto	15868	46942				1142			425	194	
12	Vancouver	17502	19488				3854			160	282	
13	Target % increase	15%										
14	# of NA Offices											
15	Average Year Revenue											

FIGURE 3-2: Percentage changes

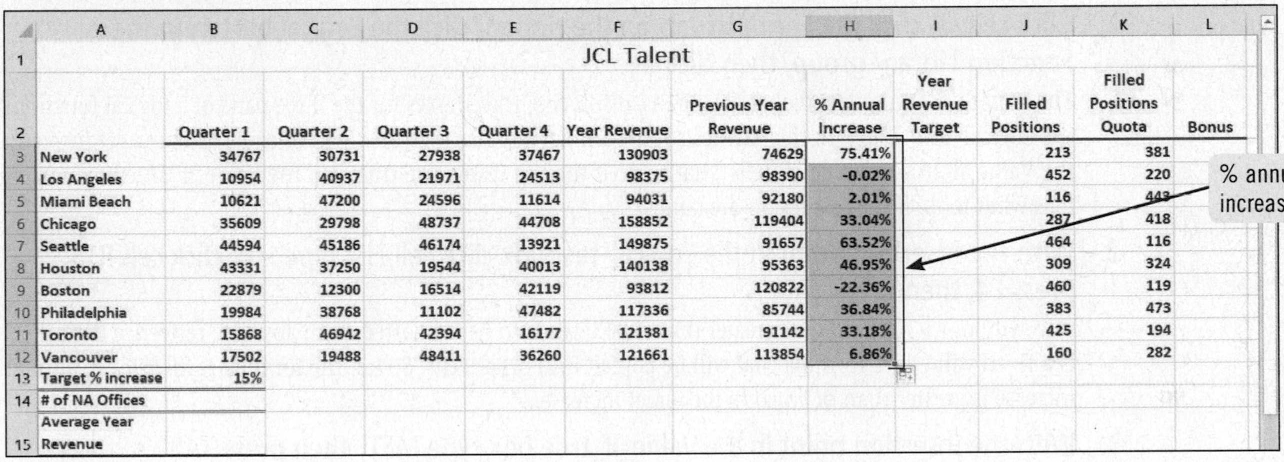

	A	B	C	D	E	F	G	H	I	J	K	L
1						JCL Talent						
2		Quarter 1	Quarter 2	Quarter 3	Quarter 4	Year Revenue	Previous Year Revenue	% Annual Increase	Year Revenue Target	Filled Positions	Filled Positions Quota	Bonus
3	New York	34767	30731	27938	37467	130903	74629	75.41%		213	381	
4	Los Angeles	10954	40937	21971	24513	98375	98390	-0.02%		452	220	
5	Miami Beach	10621	47200	24596	11614	94031	92180	2.01%		116	443	
6	Chicago	35609	29798	48737	44708	158852	119404	33.04%		287	418	
7	Seattle	44594	45186	46174	13921	149875	91657	63.52%		464	116	
8	Houston	43331	37250	19544	40013	140138	95363	46.95%		309	324	
9	Boston	22879	12300	16514	42119	93812	120822	-22.36%		460	119	
10	Philadelphia	19984	38768	11102	47482	117336	85744	36.84%		383	473	
11	Toronto	15868	46942	42394	16177	121381	91142	33.18%		425	194	
12	Vancouver	17502	19488	48411	36260	121661	113854	6.86%		160	282	
13	Target % increase	15%										
14	# of NA Offices											
15	Average Year Revenue											

Excel

Build a Logical Formula with the IF Function

Learning Outcomes
- Build a logical formula using the IF function
- Apply comparison operators in a logical test

You can build a formula in a worksheet using a **logical function** that returns a different value depending on whether the given condition is true or false. An **IF function** is a logical function that assigns a value to a cell based on a logical test. A **logical formula** makes calculations based on criteria that you create, called **stated conditions**. For example, you can build a formula to calculate bonuses based on a person's performance rating, where the stated condition is 5. If a person is rated a 5 on a scale of 1 to 5, he or she receives an additional 10% of his or her salary as a bonus; otherwise, there is no bonus. The IF function has three parts, including the **logical test**, which is the first part of the function. This test is a condition that can be answered with a true or false response. If the logical test is true, then the second part of the function is applied; if it is false, then the third part of the function is applied. When entering the logical test portion of an IF statement, you often use some combination of the comparison operators listed in **TABLE 3-1**.

CASE *Ellie asks you to calculate whether each office met or missed its revenue target for the year.*

STEPS

1. **Click cell I3, click the Formulas tab on the ribbon, click the Logical button in the Function Library group, then click IF**

   The Function Arguments dialog box opens, displaying three boxes for the three parts of a logical function: the Logical_test, which in this case tests if the annual increase is greater than or equal to the target increase; the Value_if_true box, which tells what to do if the test results are true; and the Value_if_false box, which tells what to do if the test results are false.

2. **With the insertion point in the Logical_test box click cell H3, type > =, click cell B13, press F4, then press TAB**

   The symbol (>) represents "greater than." B13 needs to be formatted as an absolute reference because it is a fixed value in a formula that will be copied into other cells. So far, the formula reads, "If the annual increase is greater than or equal to the target increase..."

3. **With the insertion point in the Value_if_true box type MET, then press TAB**

   This part of the function tells Excel to display the text MET if the annual increase equals or exceeds the target increase of 15%. Quotation marks are automatically added around the text you entered.

4. **Type MISSED in the Value_if_false box, then click OK**

   This part tells Excel to display the text MISSED if the results of the logical test are false—that is, if the increase does not equal or exceed the target. The function is complete, and the result, MET, appears in cell I3, as shown in **FIGURE 3-3**.

5. **Drag the fill handle to copy the formula in cell I3 into the range I4:I12**

   Compare your results with **FIGURE 3-4**. Most offices met their target increase but four offices did not.

6. **Save the workbook**

FIGURE 3-3: Worksheet with IF function

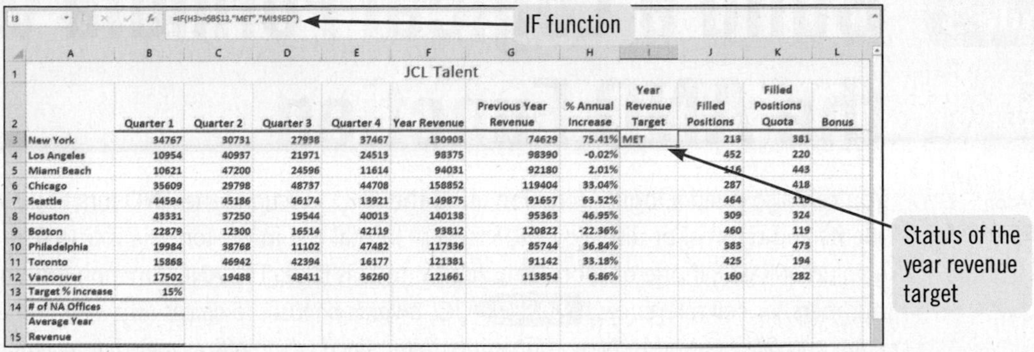

FIGURE 3-4: Worksheet showing yearly revenue status

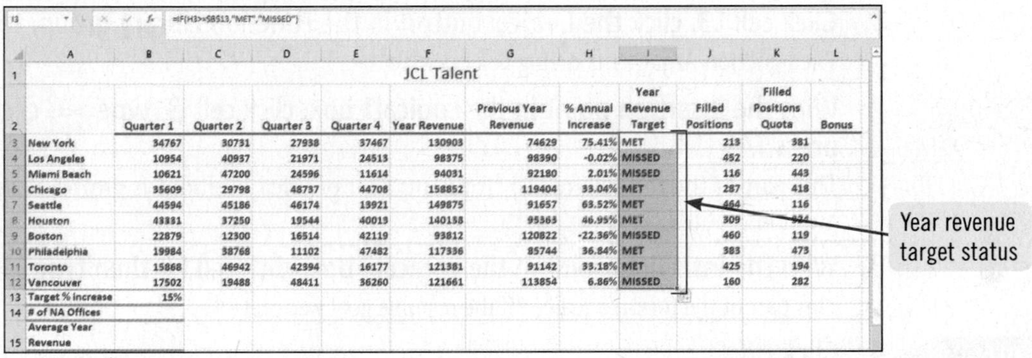

TABLE 3-1: Comparison operators

operator	meaning	operator	meaning
<	Less than	<=	Less than or equal to
>	Greater than	>=	Greater than or equal to
=	Equal to	<>	Not equal to

Nesting IF functions

You can nest IF functions to test several conditions in a formula. A nested IF function contains IF functions inside other IF functions to test these multiple conditions. To create a nested IF function, enter the second IF statement in the value_if_false argument of the first IF statement. For example, the nested statement =IF(H3<0%,"Warning",IF(H3<50%,"No Bonus","Bonus")) tests whether a warning should be issued based on the percentage increases for an office. Assuming the percentage increase of an office is in cell H3, the nested IF statement first checks to see if the increase was less than 0. If that first test is true, the text "Warning" will appear. If the first test is false, a second test will be performed to check to see if the increase is less than 50%. If that second test is true (values are less than 50%), the text "No Bonus" will appear. If that second test is false, the text "Bonus" will be displayed.

Excel

Build a Logical Formula with the AND Function

Learning Outcomes
- Build a logical formula using the AND function
- Apply logical tests

You can also build a logical function using the AND function. The AND function evaluates all of its arguments and returns, or displays, TRUE if every logical test in the formula is true. The AND function returns a value of FALSE if one or more of its logical tests is false. The AND function arguments can include text, numbers, or cell references. **CASE** *JCL awards bonuses to offices that meet targets for both annual revenue and filled positions. Now that you've determined which offices met their revenue goal, you need to see which offices are eligible for a bonus by meeting both this target and the filled positions target.*

STEPS

1. **Click cell L3, click the Logical button in the Function Library group, then click AND**
   The Function Arguments dialog box opens.
2. **With the insertion point in the Logical1 box, click cell J3, type >=, click cell K3, then press TAB**
   This part of the formula reads, "If the number of filled positions is greater than or equal to the filled positions quota..."
3. **With the insertion point in the Logical2 box, click cell I3, then type = "MET"**
   This part of the formula reads, "If the revenue goal was met..."
4. **Click OK**
   The function is complete, and the result, FALSE, appears in cell L3, as shown in **FIGURE 3-5**, because both stated conditions were not met. Although the revenue target was met, the number of filled positions was not greater than or equal to the quota.
5. **Drag the fill handle to copy the formula in cell L3 into the range L4:L12**
   Compare your results with **FIGURE 3-6**.
6. **Enter your name in the center section of the footer, preview the worksheet, then save your work**

TROUBLE
If you get a formula error, check to be sure that you typed the quotation marks around MET.

QUICK TIP
You can place one function, such as an AND function, inside a formula containing another function, such as an IF function. For example, you could replace the formulas in cell I3 and L3 with one formula in L3 that reads =IF(AND(H3>=$B$13, J3>=K3), "TRUE", "FALSE").

Using the OR and NOT logical functions

The OR logical function follows the same syntax as the AND function, but rather than returning TRUE if every argument is true, the OR function will return TRUE if any of its arguments are true. It will only return FALSE if all of its arguments are false. The NOT logical function reverses the value of its argument. For example, NOT(TRUE) reverses its argument of TRUE and returns FALSE. You might want to use this function in a worksheet to ensure that a cell is not equal to a particular value. See **TABLE 3-2** for examples of the AND, OR, and NOT functions.

FIGURE 3-5: Worksheet with AND function

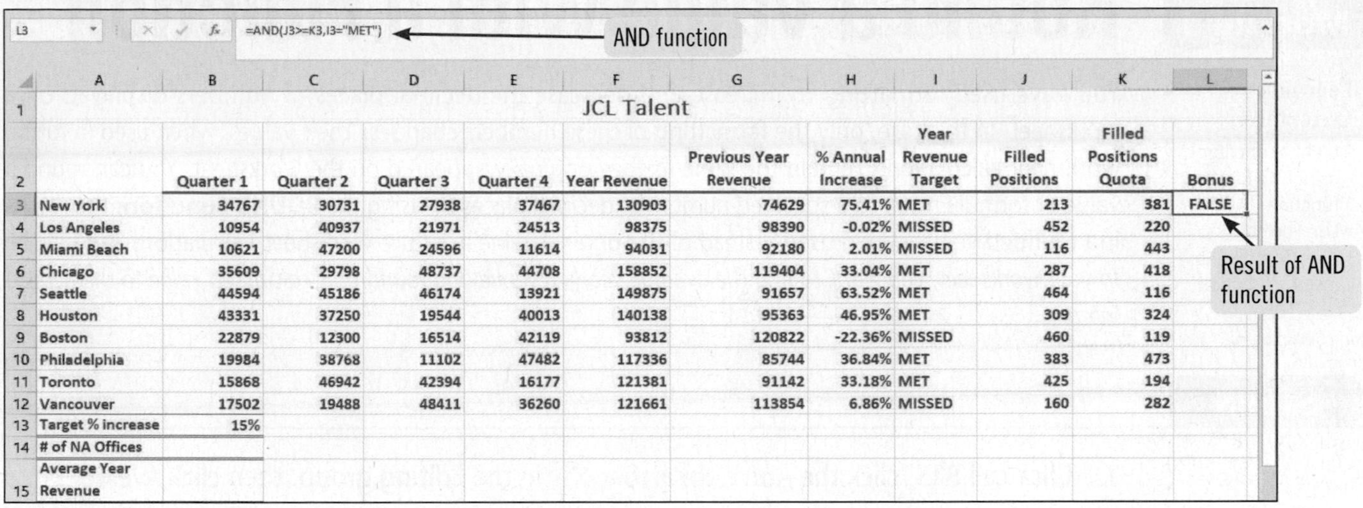

	A	B	C	D	E	F	G	H	I	J	K	L
1						JCL Talent						
2		Quarter 1	Quarter 2	Quarter 3	Quarter 4	Year Revenue	Previous Year Revenue	% Annual Increase	Year Revenue Target	Filled Positions	Filled Positions Quota	Bonus
3	New York	34767	30731	27938	37467	130903	74629	75.41%	MET	213	381	FALSE
4	Los Angeles	10954	40937	21971	24513	98375	98390	-0.02%	MISSED	452	220	
5	Miami Beach	10621	47200	24596	11614	94031	92180	2.01%	MISSED	116	443	
6	Chicago	35609	29798	48737	44708	158852	119404	33.04%	MET	287	418	
7	Seattle	44594	45186	46174	13921	149875	91657	63.52%	MET	464	116	
8	Houston	43331	37250	19544	40013	140138	95363	46.95%	MET	309	324	
9	Boston	22879	12300	16514	42119	93812	120822	-22.36%	MISSED	460	119	
10	Philadelphia	19984	38768	11102	47482	117336	85744	36.84%	MET	383	473	
11	Toronto	15868	46942	42394	16177	121381	91142	33.18%	MET	425	194	
12	Vancouver	17502	19488	48411	36260	121661	113854	6.86%	MISSED	160	282	
13	Target % increase	15%										
14	# of NA Offices											
15	Average Year Revenue											

FIGURE 3-6: Worksheet with bonus status evaluated for all offices

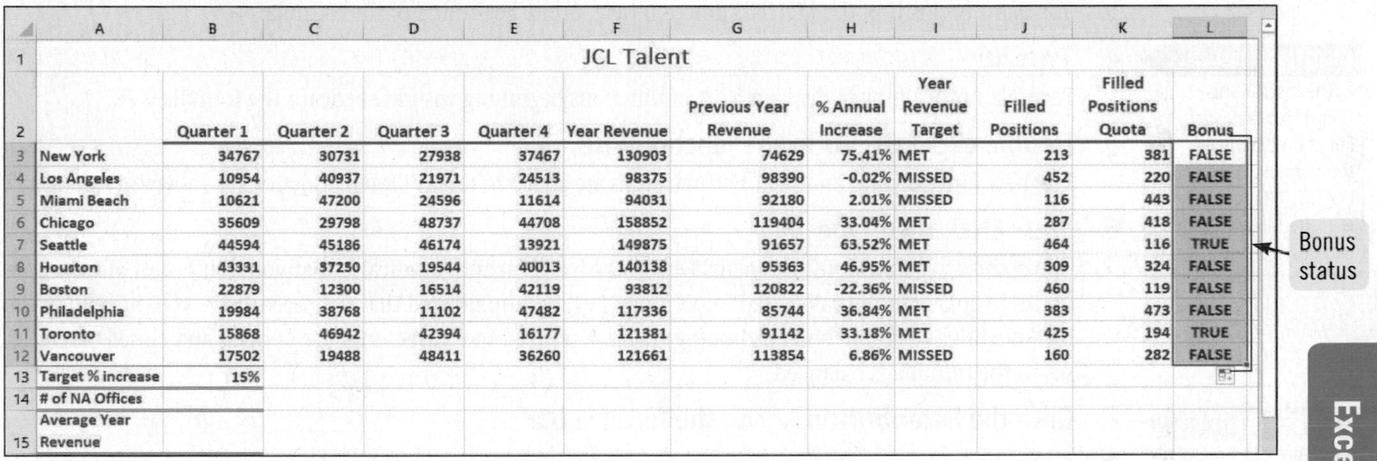

	A	B	C	D	E	F	G	H	I	J	K	L
1						JCL Talent						
2		Quarter 1	Quarter 2	Quarter 3	Quarter 4	Year Revenue	Previous Year Revenue	% Annual Increase	Year Revenue Target	Filled Positions	Filled Positions Quota	Bonus
3	New York	34767	30731	27938	37467	130903	74629	75.41%	MET	213	381	FALSE
4	Los Angeles	10954	40937	21971	24513	98375	98390	-0.02%	MISSED	452	220	FALSE
5	Miami Beach	10621	47200	24596	11614	94031	92180	2.01%	MISSED	116	443	FALSE
6	Chicago	35609	29798	48737	44708	158852	119404	33.04%	MET	287	418	FALSE
7	Seattle	44594	45186	46174	13921	149875	91657	63.52%	MET	464	116	TRUE
8	Houston	43331	37250	19544	40013	140138	95363	46.95%	MET	309	324	FALSE
9	Boston	22879	12300	16514	42119	93812	120822	-22.36%	MISSED	460	119	FALSE
10	Philadelphia	19984	38768	11102	47482	117336	85744	36.84%	MET	383	473	FALSE
11	Toronto	15868	46942	42394	16177	121381	91142	33.18%	MET	425	194	TRUE
12	Vancouver	17502	19488	48411	36260	121661	113854	6.86%	MISSED	160	282	FALSE
13	Target % increase	15%										
14	# of NA Offices											
15	Average Year Revenue											

Excel

TABLE 3-2: Examples of AND, OR, and NOT functions (cell A1=10, cell B1=20)

function	formula	result
AND	=AND(A1>5,B1>25)	FALSE
OR	=OR(A1>5,B1>25)	TRUE
NOT	=NOT(A1=0)	TRUE

Excel
Module 3

Round a Value with a Function

Learning Outcomes
- Build a function using the ROUND function
- Use Formula AutoComplete to insert a function

You have used formatting to increase and decrease the decimal places of numbers displayed on a worksheet. In this case, only the formatting of these numbers changes. Their values, when used in future worksheet calculations, remain the same as they originally appeared on the worksheet. You can round a value or formula result to a specified number of decimal places by using the **ROUND function**; the resulting rounded value is then used instead of the original value in future worksheet calculations. **CASE** *In your worksheet, you want to find the average yearly revenue and round that calculated value to the nearest integer.*

STEPS

QUICK TIP
In the Insert Function dialog box and Function Library on the Formulas tab, the ROUND function is in the Math & Trig category.

TROUBLE
If you have too many or too few parentheses, the extraneous parenthesis is displayed in red, or a warning dialog box opens with a suggested solution to the error.

1. **Click cell B15, click the AutoSum arrow [Σ ▾] in the Editing group, then click Average**
2. **Select the range F3:F12, then click the Enter button [✓] on the formula bar**
   The result, 122636.4, appears in cell B15.
3. **Click to the right of = in the formula bar**
   You want to position the ROUND function here, at the beginning of the formula.
4. **Type RO**
   Formula AutoComplete displays a list of functions beginning with RO beneath the formula bar.
5. **Double-click ROUND in the functions list**
   The new function and an opening parenthesis are added to the AVERAGE function, as shown in **FIGURE 3-7**.
6. **Press END, then type ,0)**
   The comma separates the arguments within the formula, and 0 indicates that you don't want any decimal places to appear in the calculated value. You may have also noticed that the parentheses at either end of the formula briefly became bold, indicating that you entered the correct number of open and closed parentheses so the formula is balanced.
7. **Click the Enter button [✓] on the formula bar**
8. **Compare your worksheet to FIGURE 3-8, then save your work**

FIGURE 3-7: ROUND function added to an existing function

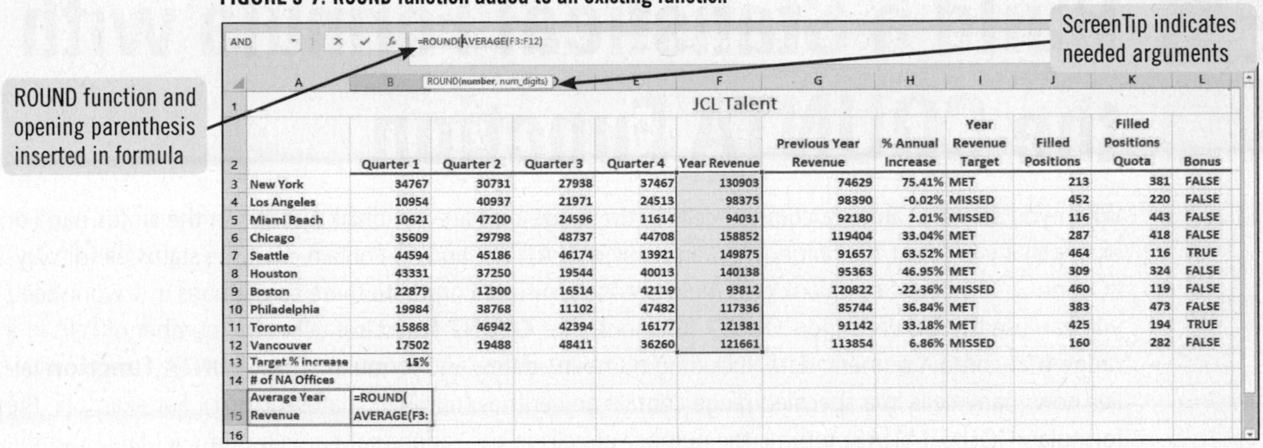

	A	B	C	D	E	F	G	H	I	J	K	L
1						JCL Talent						
2		Quarter 1	Quarter 2	Quarter 3	Quarter 4	Year Revenue	Previous Year Revenue	% Annual Increase	Year Revenue Target	Filled Positions	Filled Positions Quota	Bonus
3	New York	34767	30731	27938	37467	130903	74629	75.41%	MET	213	381	FALSE
4	Los Angeles	10954	40937	21971	24513	98375	98390	-0.02%	MISSED	452	220	FALSE
5	Miami Beach	10621	47200	24596	11614	94031	92180	2.01%	MISSED	116	443	FALSE
6	Chicago	35609	29798	48737	44708	158852	119404	33.04%	MET	287	418	FALSE
7	Seattle	44594	45186	46174	13921	149875	91657	63.52%	MET	464	116	TRUE
8	Houston	43331	37250	19544	40013	140138	95363	46.95%	MET	309	324	FALSE
9	Boston	22879	12300	16514	42119	93812	120822	-22.36%	MISSED	460	119	FALSE
10	Philadelphia	19984	38768	11102	47482	117336	85744	36.84%	MET	383	473	FALSE
11	Toronto	15868	46942	42394	16177	121381	91142	33.18%	MET	425	194	TRUE
12	Vancouver	17502	19488	48411	36260	121661	113854	6.86%	MISSED	160	282	FALSE
13	Target % increase	15%										
14	# of NA Offices											
15	Average Year Revenue	=ROUND(AVERAGE(F3:										
16												

FIGURE 3-8: Rounded year average

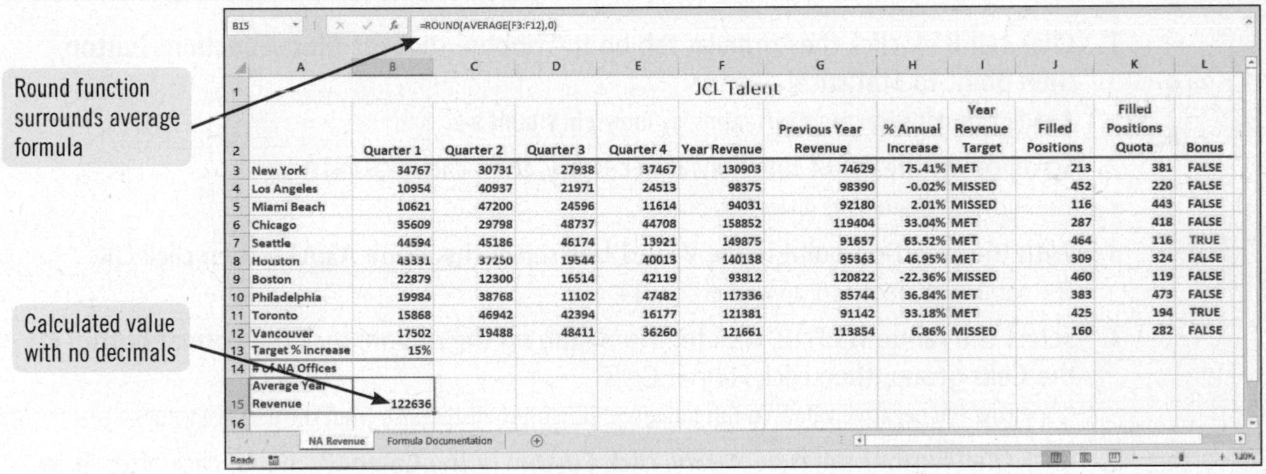

	A	B	C	D	E	F	G	H	I	J	K	L
1						JCL Talent						
2		Quarter 1	Quarter 2	Quarter 3	Quarter 4	Year Revenue	Previous Year Revenue	% Annual Increase	Year Revenue Target	Filled Positions	Filled Positions Quota	Bonus
3	New York	34767	30731	27938	37467	130903	74629	75.41%	MET	213	381	FALSE
4	Los Angeles	10954	40937	21971	24513	98375	98390	-0.02%	MISSED	452	220	FALSE
5	Miami Beach	10621	47200	24596	11614	94031	92180	2.01%	MISSED	116	443	FALSE
6	Chicago	35609	29798	48737	44708	158852	119404	33.04%	MET	287	418	FALSE
7	Seattle	44594	45186	46174	13921	149875	91657	63.52%	MET	464	116	TRUE
8	Houston	43331	37250	19544	40013	140138	95363	46.95%	MET	309	324	FALSE
9	Boston	22879	12300	16514	42119	93812	120822	-22.36%	MISSED	460	119	FALSE
10	Philadelphia	19984	38768	11102	47482	117336	85744	36.84%	MET	383	473	FALSE
11	Toronto	15868	46942	42394	16177	121381	91142	33.18%	MET	425	194	TRUE
12	Vancouver	17502	19488	48411	36260	121661	113854	6.86%	MISSED	160	282	FALSE
13	Target % increase	15%										
14	# of NA Offices											
15	Average Year Revenue	122636										
16												

Using Excel rounding functions

You can use other rounding functions besides ROUND to fine-tune the rounding results you want to see. The **MROUND function** rounds a number to the nearest multiple of another number. The syntax is: MROUND(number, multiple). For example, MROUND(14,3) returns the value 15 because 15 is the nearest multiple of 3 to 14. The **ROUNDDOWN function** works like the ROUND function except that rather than rounding a number to the next closest value, it always rounds down. The syntax is ROUNDDOWN(number, num_digits). For example, =ROUNDDOWN(15.778, 2) returns a value of 15.77 because this is the nearest two-digit number below 15.778. The **ROUNDUP function** works similarly but rounds a number up. The syntax is ROUNDUP(number, num_digits). For example, =ROUNDUP(15.778, 2) returns a value of 15.78.

Excel
Module 3

Build a Statistical Formula with the COUNTA Function

Learning Outcomes
- Insert a statistical function
- Build a function using the COUNTA function
- Create a number format

When you select a range, a count of cells in the range that are not blank appears in the status bar. For example, if you select the range A1:A5 and only cells A1, A4, and A5 contain data, the status bar displays "Count: 3." To count nonblank cells more precisely, or to incorporate these calculations in a worksheet, you can use the COUNT and COUNTA functions. The **COUNT function** tallies the number of cells in a range that contain numeric data, including numbers, dates, and formulas. The **COUNTA function** tallies how many cells in a specified range contain any entries (numbers, dates, or text). For example, the formula =COUNT(A1:A5) returns the number of cells in the range that contain numeric data, and the formula =COUNTA(A1:A5) returns the number of cells in the range that are not empty. **CASE** *In your worksheet, you want to calculate the number of offices in the North America region. You also want to format some worksheet values using a custom format, so that the data looks exactly the way you want.*

STEPS

1. **Click cell B14, click the Formulas tab on the ribbon, click the More Functions button, then point to Statistical**
   A gallery of statistical functions opens, as shown in **FIGURE 3-9**.
2. **Scroll down the list of functions if necessary, then click COUNTA**
   The Function Arguments dialog box opens.
3. **With the insertion point in the Value1 box select the range A3:A12, then click OK**
   The number of offices, 10, appears in cell B14.
4. **Select the range H3:H12, click the Home tab on the ribbon, click the Format button in the Cells group, then click Format Cells**
   Currently, the negative values in this range are difficult to distinguish from the positive values.
5. **Click the Number tab if necessary, click Custom in the Category menu, click after % in the Type box, type ;[Red](0.00%) as shown in FIGURE 3-10, then click OK**
   The negative percentages in cells H4 and H9 now appear in red with parentheses.
6. **Select the range B3:G12, press and hold CTRL, then click cell B15**
   Holding CTRL allows you to select multiple ranges and cells.
7. **Click the Accounting Number Format button $ in the Number group, then click the Decrease Decimal button twice**
   Formatting these revenue figures makes them easier to read. Compare your worksheet to **FIGURE 3-11**.

FIGURE 3-9: Statistical functions

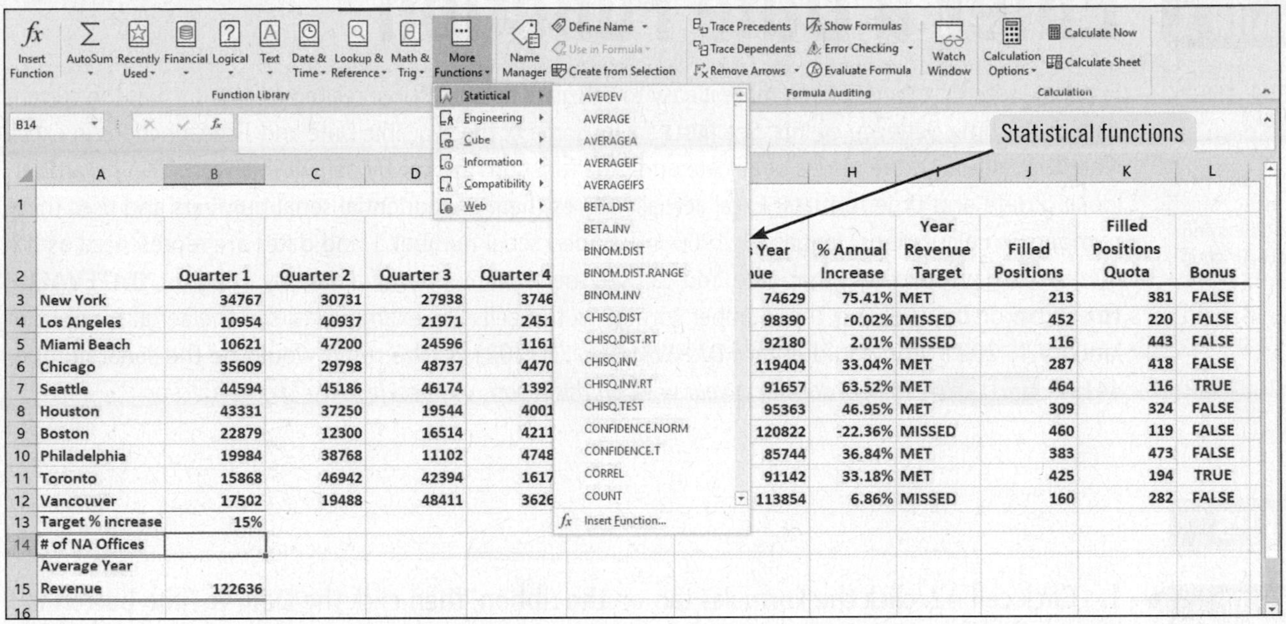

FIGURE 3-10: Custom number format

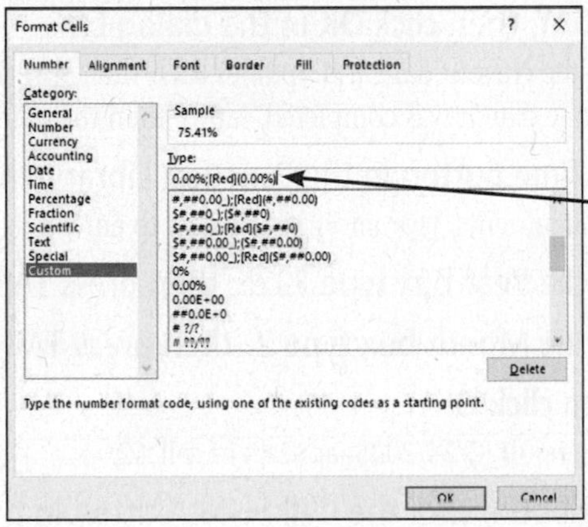

FIGURE 3-11: Formatted worksheet

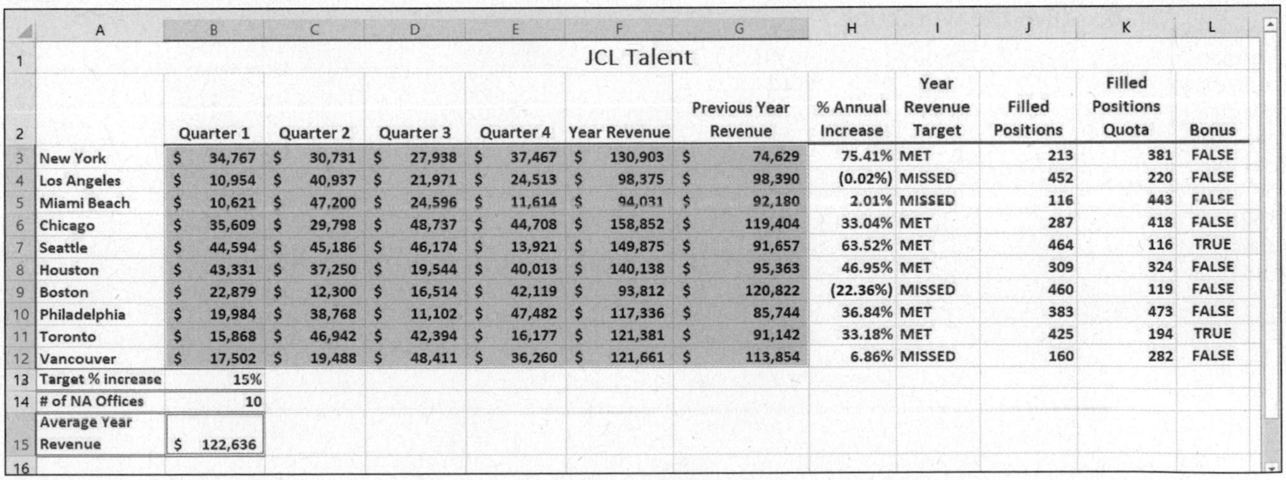

Excel

Enter a Date Function

Learning Outcomes
- Enter a date using the TODAY function
- Enter a date using the DATE function

Excel includes date functions to make it easy to calculate date and time related results, such as the current date or the time between events. See **TABLE 3-3** for some of the available Date and Time functions in Excel. Note that although the results of all date and time functions appear by default in a worksheet in familiar-looking date and time formats, Excel actually stores them as sequential serial numbers and uses these numbers in calculations. January 1, 1900 is assigned serial number 1 and dates are represented as the number of days following that date. You can see the serial number of a date by using the **DATEVALUE function** or by applying the Number format to the cell. For example, to see the serial number of January 1, 2021 you would enter =DATEVALUE("1/1/2021"). The result would be the serial number 44197. **CASE** *To help document your work on this report, you decide to use a date function.*

STEPS

QUICK TIP
You can type = and the first few characters of a date or time function, then use AutoComplete to enter the function.

1. **Click cell A2, click the Formulas tab on the ribbon, then click the Date & Time button in the Function library**
   A list of date and time functions opens, as shown in **FIGURE 3-12**.
2. **Scroll if necessary, click TODAY, then click OK in the dialog box**
   The **TODAY function** displays the current date and updates each time a worksheet is opened. However, you want the workbook to show the date it was completed, rather than the date the workbook is opened.
3. **Press DEL, click the Date & Time button in the Function Library, then click DATE**
   The **DATE function** uses three arguments, year, month, and day, to enter a date.
4. **With the insertion point in the Year box type 2025, then press TAB**
5. **With the insertion point in the Month box type 2, then press TAB**
6. **Type 24 in the Day box, then click OK**
   The function is complete, and the result, 2/24/2025, appears in cell A2.

QUICK TIP
To apply a format to a selection of time data, you can click the Format button in the Cells group, click Format Cells, click Time in the Category list, select the time format in the Type list, then click OK. For example, choosing the 13:30 type would display the time of 11:15 PM as 23:15.

7. **Click the Home tab on the ribbon, click the Cell Styles button in the Styles group, then click 20% Accent1 in the Themed Cell Styles group**
   Compare your worksheet to **FIGURE 3-13**.
8. **Save the workbook**

FIGURE 3-12: Date & Time functions

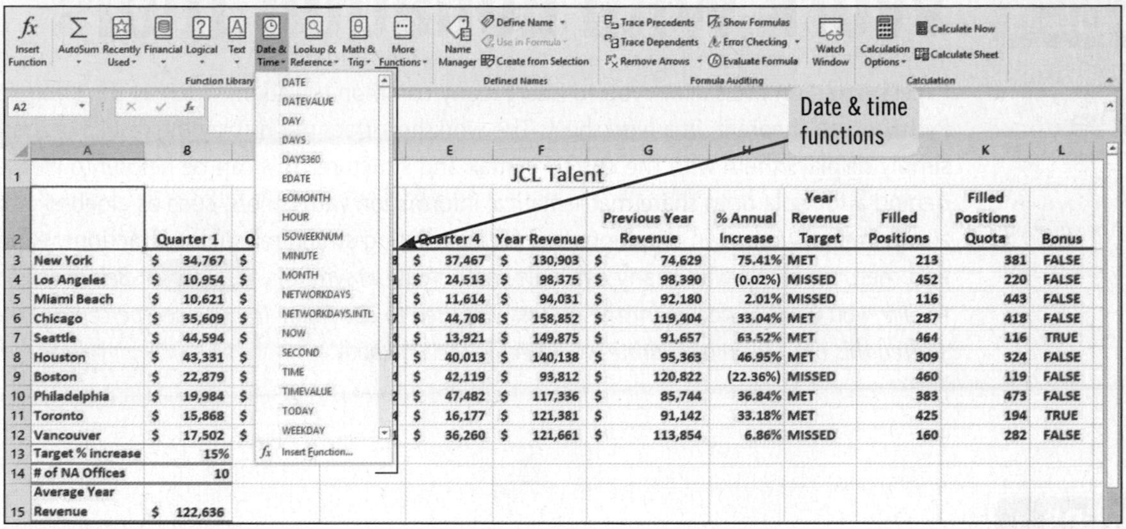

FIGURE 3-13: Formatted date

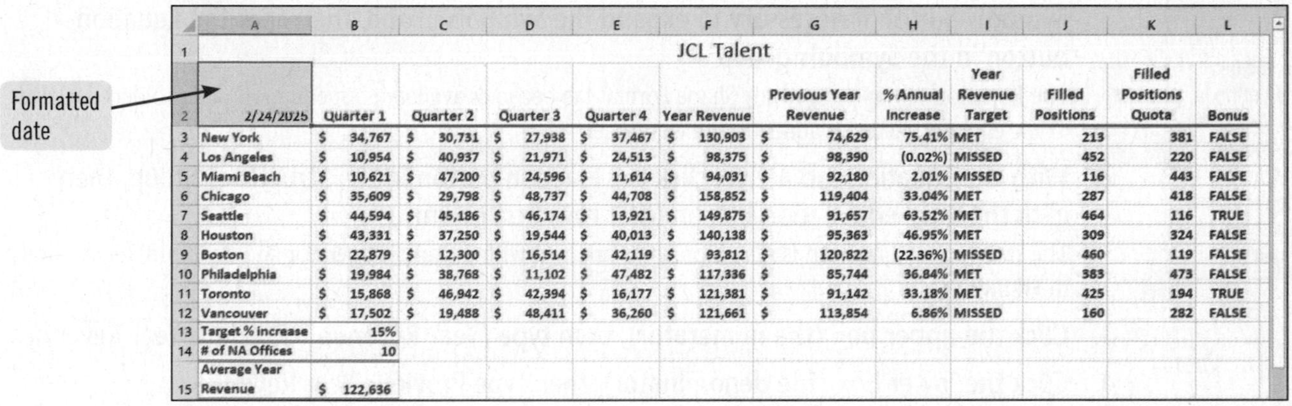

TABLE 3-3: Date and Time functions

function	calculates	example formula	example result
DAY	The day of the month using a date serial number	=DAY(44197)	1
NOW	The current date and time	=NOW()	1/1/2021 10:00
MONTH	The month number using a date serial number	=MONTH(44197)	1
TIME	A serial number in time format from hours, minutes, and seconds	=TIME(5,12,20)	0.216898
TIMEVALUE	A serial time in text format	=TIMEVALUE("5:15:24")	.219028
YEAR	The year portion of a date	=YEAR(44197)	2021
HOUR	The hour portion of a time	=HOUR("6:45:21 PM")	18
MINUTE	The minute portion of a time	=MINUTE("6:45:21 PM")	45
SECOND	The second portion of a time	=SECOND("6:45:21 PM")	21
WEEKDAY	The day of the week from a serial date (1 =Sunday, 2 = Monday…)	=WEEKDAY("6/21/2021")	2
WORKDAY	A serial number in date format after a certain number of working days	=WORKDAY(44198,5)	44204 (When formatted as a date: 1/8/2021)

Excel
Module 3

Work with Equation Tools

Learning Outcomes
- Select an equation structure
- Enter an equation using the equation tools

Excel's equation tools allow you to insert many common equations, such as the area of a circle and the Pythagorean theorem, in a worksheet. The worksheet does not display the results of these expressions, it simply displays them with the correct syntax and structure. This can be helpful to illustrate the thinking behind a formula or to share mathematical information with others, such as algebraic formulas. You can also compose your own equations and formulas using structures such as fractions, exponents, radicals, and matrices along with many available mathematical symbols. **CASE** *Before sending the workbook to Ellie, you want to document the process you used to determine the revenue percentage increase. You have started this process on a separate worksheet in the workbook.*

STEPS

QUICK TIP
If your device is touch-enabled, you can click the Ink Equation button in the Tools group of the Equation tab to write a math equation using your mouse, a stylus, or your fingertip.

1. **Click the Formula Documentation sheet tab, click the Insert tab on the ribbon, click the Symbols button if necessary to expand the Symbols group, then click the Equation button in the Symbols group**
   The Equation tab opens and the Shape Format tab becomes available. An equation placeholder that reads, "Type equation here," is added to the worksheet.
2. **With the Equation tab active, click the Fraction button in the Structures group, then click the Stacked Fraction button (first row, first column)**
   The structure of a fraction is placed on the worksheet with a blank numerator and denominator, as shown in **FIGURE 3-14**.
3. **Click the upper box (the numerator), then type (Year Revenue – Previous Year Revenue)**
4. **Click the lower box (the denominator), then type Previous Year Revenue**
5. **Select the equation if necessary, place the Move pointer on the edge of the equation, drag the equation so the upper-left corner is in cell A9, then click cell A1**
6. **Compare your worksheet to FIGURE 3-15, then save your work**

FIGURE 3-14: Fraction structure added to worksheet

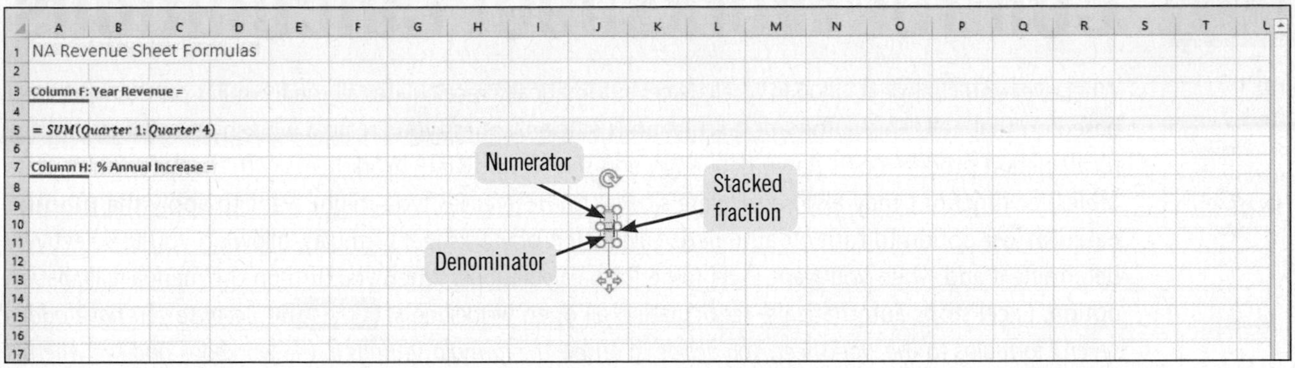

FIGURE 3-15: Completed equation

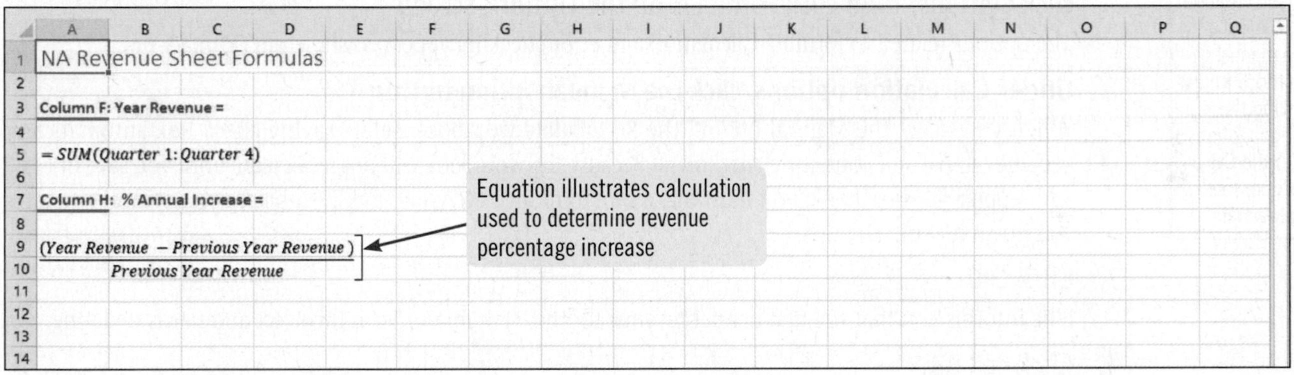

Using Draw tools

On a touch-enabled device you can use your mouse, a stylus, or even your finger to draw or write. If your device is touch-enabled, the Touch/Mouse Mode button appears on the Quick Access toolbar and the Draw tab automatically becomes available on the ribbon. You can add or remove the Touch/Mouse Mode button by clicking the Customize Quick Access Toolbar button, then clicking Touch/Mouse Mode. Touch mode adds space between the buttons on the ribbon, making them easier to access with your fingertip. You can manually turn on the Draw tab by clicking the File tab, clicking Options, clicking Customize Ribbon in the Excel Options dialog box, selecting the Draw box in the Main Tabs list, then clicking OK.

Clicking the Draw button in the Input Mode group of the Draw tab allows you to select a pen, pencil, or highlighter. If you click the selected instrument you can change its thickness and color. As you work, you can correct drawing mistakes using the Eraser tool, also in the Drawing Tools group. Clicking the Ink to Shape button in the Convert group before beginning to draw converts your completed drawing to a geometric shape. The Ink to Shape feature works with pens and pencils but not highlighters. The Convert group includes an Ink to Math button that converts a handwritten mathematical expression to text. If you wish to see the steps followed in creating drawings on the worksheet, use the Ink Replay button in the Replay group to replay each step.

To modify an ink shape, you must select it, either by using the lasso button in the Drawing Tools group to enclose it or by using the lasso tool or arrow tool to click the shape. Once a shape is selected, you can format it using the Shape Format tab.

Excel

Control Worksheet Calculations

Learning Outcomes
- Control formula calculations
- Calculate worksheet formulas

Whenever you change a value in a cell, Excel automatically recalculates all the formulas on the worksheet based on that cell. This automatic calculation is efficient unless you create a worksheet so large that the recalculation process slows down data entry and screen updating. Worksheets with many formulas, data tables, or functions may also recalculate slowly. In these cases, you might want to apply the **manual calculation** option to turn off automatic calculation of worksheet formulas, allowing you to selectively determine if and when you want Excel to perform calculations. When you turn on the manual calculation option, Excel stops automatically recalculating all open worksheets. **CASE** *Because you have added several formulas to the worksheet, you decide to review the formula settings in the workbook and see whether changing from automatic to manual calculation improves performance.*

STEPS

QUICK TIP
You can also change the formula calculation to manual by clicking the Formulas tab, clicking the Calculation Options button in the Calculation group, then clicking Manual.

1. **Click the NA Revenue sheet tab, click the File tab on the ribbon to open Backstage view, click Options, then click Formulas on the Options screen**
   The options related to formula calculation and error checking appear, as shown in **FIGURE 3-16**.
2. **Under Calculation options, click the Manual option button**
   When you select the Manual option, the Recalculate workbook before saving check box automatically becomes active and contains a checkmark. Because the workbook will not recalculate until you save or close and reopen the workbook, you must make sure to recalculate your worksheet before you print it and after you finish making changes.
3. **Click OK**
   Ellie informs you that the first quarter revenue for the New York office is incorrect and needs updating.
4. **Click cell B3**
   Before proceeding, notice that in cell F3 the year revenue for the New York office is $130,903.
5. **Type 34305, then click the Enter button ✓ on the formula bar**
   Notice that the year revenue in cell F3 does not adjust to reflect the change in cell B3. The word "Calculate" appears in the status bar to indicate that a specific value on the worksheet did indeed change and reminding you that the worksheet must be recalculated.

QUICK TIP
The Calculate Now command calculates the entire workbook, not just the worksheet. You can also manually recalculate a workbook by pressing F9. Pressing SHIFT+F9 recalculates only the current worksheet.

6. **Click the Formulas tab, click the Calculate Sheet button in the Calculation group, click cell A1, then save the workbook**
   The year revenue in cell F3 is now $130,441. The other formulas on the worksheet affected by the value in cell B3 changed as well, as shown in **FIGURE 3-17**. Because this is a relatively small worksheet that recalculates quickly, you decide that the manual calculation option is not necessary.

QUICK TIP
If your worksheet contains a table, such as a complex payment schedule, you may want to use manual recalculation just for the table. To do so, click the Automatic Except for Data Tables option.

7. **Click the Calculation Options button in the Calculation group, then click Automatic**
   Now Excel will automatically recalculate the worksheet formulas any time you make changes.
8. **sam Save your changes, activate cell A1, submit the workbook to your instructor as directed, close the workbook, then close Excel**

FIGURE 3-16: Excel formula options

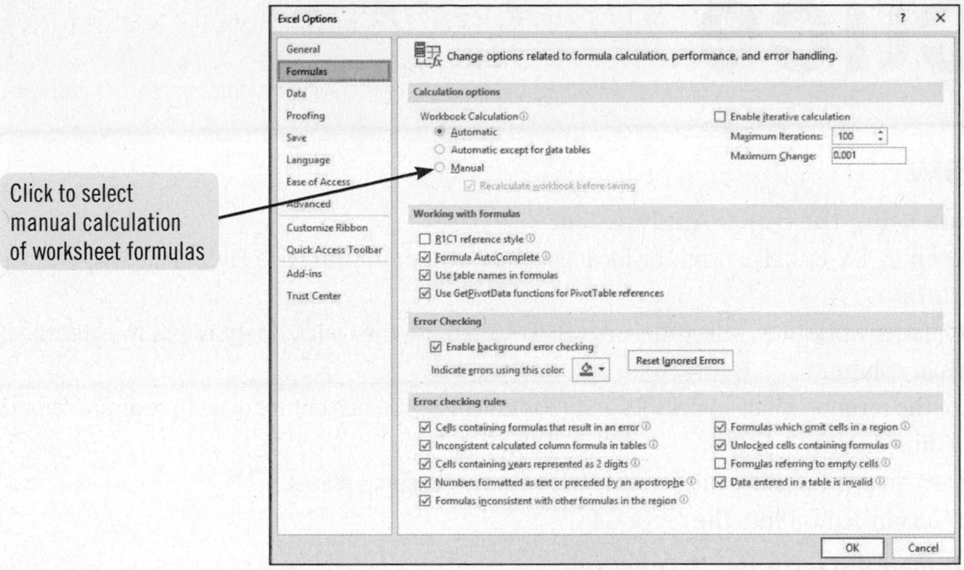

FIGURE 3-17: Worksheet with updated values

	A	B	C	D	E	F	G	H	I	J	K	L
1	JCL Talent											
2	2/24/2025	Quarter 1	Quarter 2	Quarter 3	Quarter 4	Year Revenue	Previous Year Revenue	% Annual Increase	Year Revenue Target	Filled Positions	Filled Positions Quota	Bonus
3	New York	$ 34,305	$ 30,731	$ 27,938	$ 37,467	$ 130,441	$ 74,629	74.79%	MET	213	381	FALSE
4	Los Angeles	$ 10,954	$ 40,937	$ 21,971	$ 24,513	$ 98,375	$ 98,390	(0.02%)	MISSED	452	220	FALSE
5	Miami Beach	$ 10,621	$ 47,200	$ 24,596	$ 11,614	$ 94,031	$ 92,180	2.01%	MISSED	116	443	FALSE
6	Chicago	$ 35,609	$ 29,798	$ 48,737	$ 44,708	$ 158,852	$ 119,404	33.04%	MET	287	418	FALSE
7	Seattle	$ 44,594	$ 45,186	$ 46,174	$ 13,921	$ 149,875	$ 91,657	63.52%	MET	464	116	TRUE
8	Houston	$ 43,331	$ 37,250	$ 19,544	$ 40,013	$ 140,138	$ 95,363	46.95%	MET	309	324	FALSE
9	Boston	$ 22,879	$ 12,300	$ 16,514	$ 42,119	$ 93,812	$ 120,822	(22.36%)	MISSED	460	119	FALSE
10	Philadelphia	$ 19,984	$ 38,768	$ 11,102	$ 47,482	$ 117,336	$ 85,744	36.84%	MET	383	473	FALSE
11	Toronto	$ 15,868	$ 46,942	$ 42,394	$ 16,177	$ 121,381	$ 91,142	33.18%	MET	425	194	TRUE
12	Vancouver	$ 17,502	$ 19,488	$ 48,411	$ 36,260	$ 121,661	$ 113,854	6.86%	MISSED	160	282	FALSE
13	Target % increase	15%										
14	# of NA Offices	10										
15	Average Year Revenue	$ 122,590										

Updated values

Showing and printing worksheet formulas

Sometimes you need to show or keep a record of all the formulas in a worksheet. You might want to do this to show exactly how you came up with a complex calculation, so you can explain it to others. To display formulas rather than results in a worksheet, first open the workbook. Click the Formulas tab on the ribbon, then click the Show Formulas button in the Formula Auditing group to select it. When the Show Formulas button is selected, formulas rather than resulting values are displayed on the worksheet, and any entered values appear without number formatting. You can print the worksheet to save a record of all the formulas. The Show Formulas button is a toggle: click it again to show the values, rather than the formulas, on the worksheet.

Practice

Skills Review

1. **Enter a formula using the Quick Analysis tool.**
   - **a.** Start Excel, open IL_EX_3-2.xlsx from the location where you store your Data Files, then save it as **IL_EX_3_Labs**.
   - **b.** On the First Quarter worksheet, select the range B3:D9, then use the Quick Analysis tool to enter the first quarter revenue totals in column E.
   - **c.** In cell G3, use the revenue totals in cells E3 and F3 to calculate the percent increase in revenue from the previous quarter to the first quarter.
   - **d.** Format the value in cell G3 using the percent style with two decimal places.
   - **e.** Copy the formula in cell G3 into the range G4:G9.
2. **Build a logical formula with the IF function.**
   - **a.** In cell H3, use the Function Arguments dialog box to enter the formula **=IF(G3>=$B$10,"Met","Missed")**.
   - **b.** Copy the formula in cell H3 into the range H4:H9.
   - **c.** Save your work.
3. **Build a logical formula with the AND function.**
   - **a.** In cell J3, use the Function Arguments dialog box to enter the formula **=AND(H3="Met",I3>=4)**.
   - **b.** Copy the formula in cell J3 into the range J4:J9.
   - **c.** Enter your name in the center section of the footer for the First Quarter sheet.
   - **d.** Save your work.
4. **Round a value with a function.**
   - **a.** In cell B12, use the AutoSum list arrow to enter a function to average the first quarter revenue values in column E.
   - **b.** Use Formula AutoComplete to edit this formula to include the ROUND function showing zero decimal places.
   - **c.** Correct any errors in the formula.
   - **d.** Save your work.
5. **Build a statistical formula with the COUNTA function.**
   - **a.** In cell B11, use a statistical formula to calculate the number of lab locations in column A.
   - **b.** Create a custom format for the percentages in column G so that the negative values appear in red with parentheses.
   - **c.** Format the revenue values in the range B3:F9 and in cell B12 using the Accounting Number Format with no decimal places.
   - **d.** Save your work.
6. **Enter a date function.**
   - **a.** In cell D12, enter **Report Date**.
   - **b.** In cell E12, use the TODAY function to enter today's date.
   - **c.** Delete the TODAY function in cell E12, then use the DATE function to enter the date 4/3/2025.
   - **d.** Use the Cell Style Rose, 20% - Accent 1 (the first row and first column in the Themed Cell Styles group) to format the range D12:E12.
   - **e.** Activate cell A1, then save your work.
7. **Work with equation tools.**
   - **a.** Activate the Formula Documentation sheet.
   - **b.** Add a stacked fraction to the worksheet.
   - **c.** Enter **(First Quarter Revenue – Previous Quarter Revenue)** as the numerator.
   - **d.** Enter **Previous Quarter Revenue** as the denominator.

Skills Review (continued)

e. Move the equation to place its upper-left corner in cell A9.

f. Activate cell A1, then save your work.

8. Control worksheet calculations.

a. Activate the First Quarter sheet.

b. Open the Formulas category of the Excel Options dialog box.

c. Change the worksheet calculations to manual.

d. Change the value in cell B3 to **72000**.

e. Recalculate the worksheet manually.

f. Change the worksheet calculation back to automatic using the Calculation Options button on the Formulas tab of the ribbon, then save the workbook.

g. Preview the worksheet. Compare your screen to **FIGURE 3-18**.

h. Save your changes, submit your work to your instructor as directed, close the workbook, then close Excel.

FIGURE 3-18

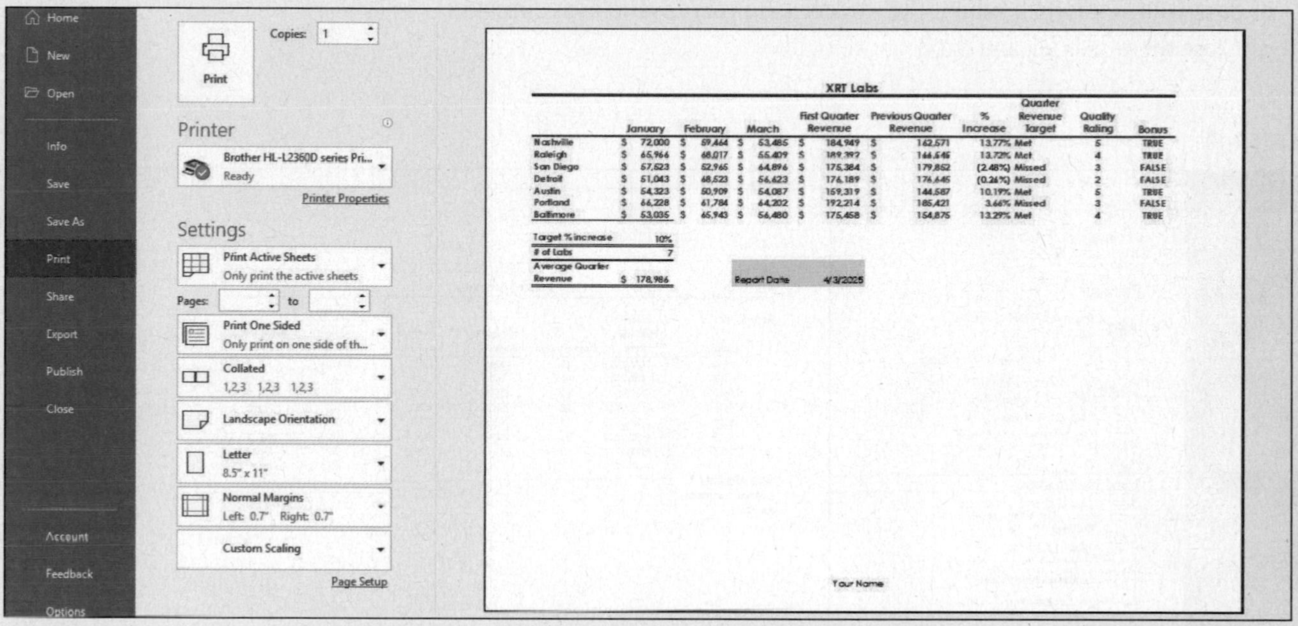

Independent Challenge 1

The manager at Riverwalk Medical Clinic has hired you to analyze patient accounts and insurance reimbursements for their Boston imaging facility. He would like you to flag overdue accounts and calculate the average procedure amount.

a. Open IL_EX_3-3.xlsx from the location where you store your Data Files, then save it as **IL_EX_3_Accounts**.

b. Use the DATE function to return the date 5/18/2021 in cell B3.

c. Enter a formula in cell C5 that calculates the statement age by subtracting the statement date in cell B5 from the report date in cell B3. (*Hint:* The formula needs to use an absolute reference for the report date in cell B3 so this cell address doesn't change when copied.)

d. Copy the formula in cell C5 to the range C6:C11.

Excel

Independent Challenge 1 (continued)

e. In cell F5, enter an IF function that calculates the patient responsibility. (*Hint:* The Logical_test should check to see if the procedure amount is greater than the insurance payment, the Value_if_true should calculate the procedure amount minus the insurance payment, and the Value_if_false should be 0.)
f. Copy the IF function in cell F5 to the range F6:F11.
g. In cell G5, enter an AND function to find accounts that are past due. Accounts are past due if a patient is responsible for a balance due and the statement age is over 30 days. (*Hint:* The Logical1 condition should check to see if the statement age is more than 30, and the Logical2 condition should check if the patient responsibility is greater than 0.)
h. Use the fill handle to copy the AND function in cell G5 into the range G6:G11.
i. In cell B13, enter a COUNTA function to calculate the number of accounts in column A.
j. Enter a function in cell B14 that averages the procedure amounts in column D.
k. Use Formula AutoComplete to enter a function to round the average in cell B14 to zero decimal places.
l. Enter your name in the center section of the footer.
m. Preview the worksheet. Compare your screen to **FIGURE 3-19**.
n. Save your work, then submit the worksheet to your instructor as directed.
o. Close the workbook and Excel.

FIGURE 3-19

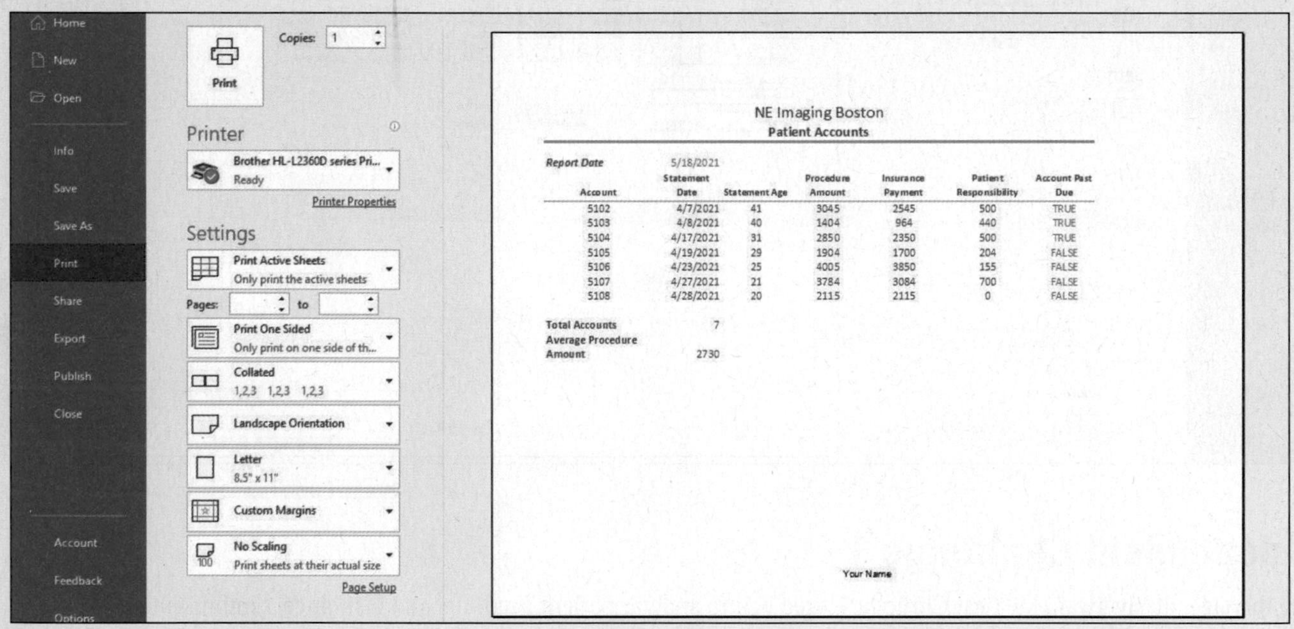

Independent Challenge 2

As the senior loan officer at North Shore Bank, one of your responsibilities is reviewing the quarterly loan portfolios for the four branches. This includes adding statistics including total loan amounts, average total loans, and the growth in loans issued at each branch. You are preparing a portfolio review for the 4th quarter, which you plan to issue on December 31.

a. Open IL_EX_3-4.xlsx from the location where you store your Data Files, then save it as **IL_EX_3_Loans**.
b. Use the TODAY function to enter today's date in cell B12. Verify today's date is displayed.
c. Delete the date in cell B12 and replace it with the date 12/31/2025 using the DATE function.
d. Use the Quick Analysis button to enter totals in the range F4:F7 and B8:E8. (*Hint:* You need to use two buttons on the Totals tab to accomplish this.)
e. Enter a formula in cell H4 to find the percentage increase for the total 4th quarter loans over the 3rd quarter total for the Main Street branch. Format the percentage increase using the percent style with two decimal places.
f. Copy the percentage increase formula in cell H4 to the range H5:H7.
g. In cell J4, enter an AND function to determine if the Main Street branch is eligible for a bonus. To be eligible, the 4th quarter percentage increase must be over 10% and the customer ratings must be higher than 85%.
h. Use the fill handle to copy the AND function in cell J4 into the range J5:J7.
i. Enter a function in cell B10 that averages the total 4th quarter loan amounts in column F, then round the average to zero decimal places.
j. In cell B11, enter a function to calculate the number of branches in column A.
k. Create a custom format for the percentages in column H so that the negative values appear in red with parentheses.
l. Format the loan values in the ranges B4:G7, B8:E8, and cell B10 using the Accounting Number Format with no decimals. Widen the columns as necessary to fully display all of the worksheet data.
m. Activate the Documentation tab and use a stacked fraction to document the 4th quarter % increase formula in cell A3.
n. Activate the 4th Quarter Report sheet. Switch to manual calculation for formulas. Change the personal loan amount for the Main Street branch in cell B4 to **1306500**. Calculate the worksheet formula manually. Turn on automatic calculation again.
o. Enter your name in the center footer section.
p. Preview the worksheet. Compare your screen to **FIGURE 3-20**.
q. Save your work, then submit the worksheet to your instructor as directed.
r. Close the workbook and Excel.

Excel

FIGURE 3-20

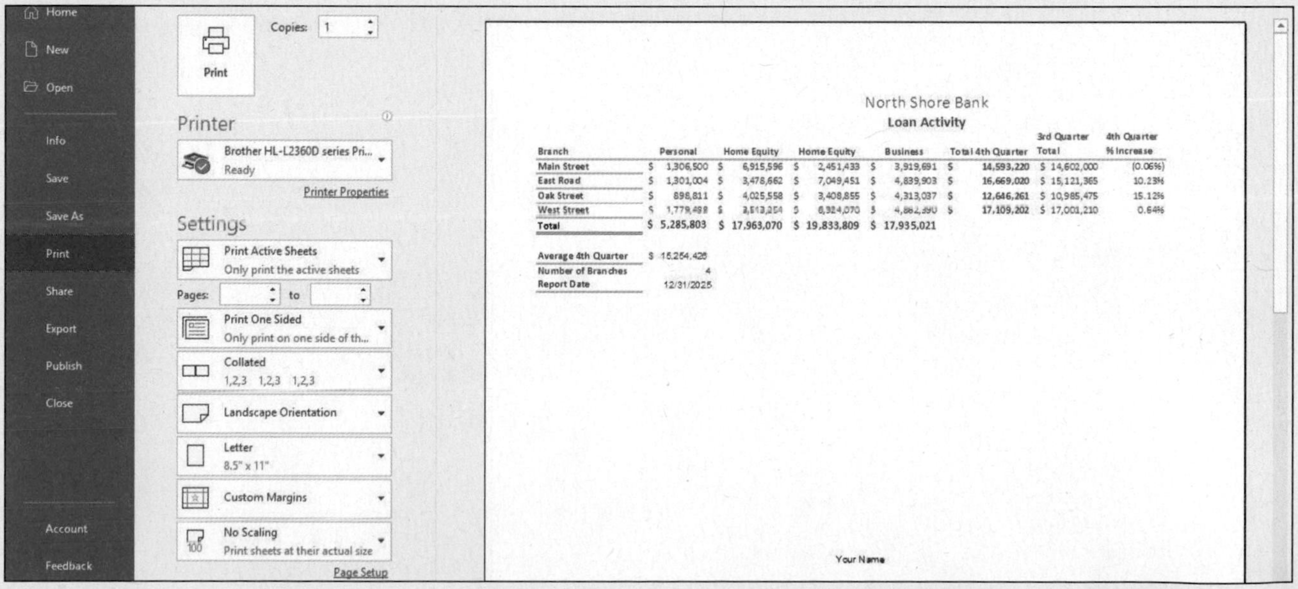

Visual Workshop

Open IL_EX_3-5.xlsx from the location where you store your Data Files, then save it as **IL_EX_3_Freight**. Use the skills you learned in this module to complete the worksheet so it looks like the one shown in **FIGURE 3-21**. To build the formulas in column G, calculate the percentage increase of the second quarter revenue over the first quarter revenue. (*Hint:* The percentage increases in column G must be calculated before calculating the average increase in cell B10.) To build the formulas in column I, a warning should be issued if the percentage increase is less than the average increase shown in cell B10 AND the on-time delivery is less than 75%. (*Hint:* Remember to use an absolute cell reference where necessary.) When you are finished, enter your name in the center footer section, then submit your work to your instructor as directed.

FIGURE 3-21

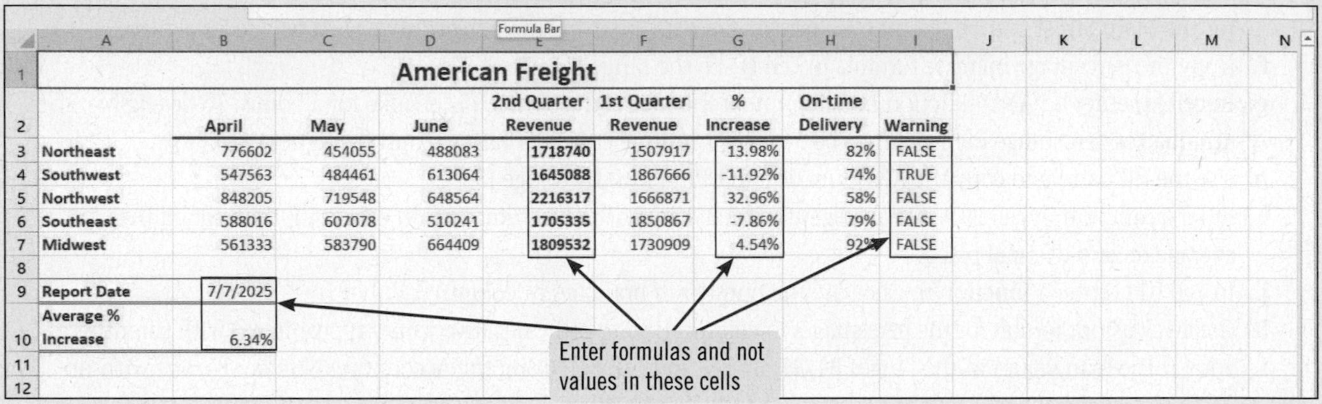

Excel **Module 4**

Working with Charts

CASE At the upcoming annual meeting, Ellie Schwartz, the vice president of finance, wants to review expenses at JCL Talent's U.S. offices. She asks you to create charts showing the expense trends in these offices over the past four quarters.

Module Objectives

After completing this module, you will be able to:

- Plan a chart
- Create a chart
- Move and resize a chart
- Change the chart design
- Change the chart layout
- Format a chart
- Create a pie chart
- Summarize data with sparklines
- Identify data trends

Files You Will Need

IL_EX_4-1.xlsx
IL_EX_4-2.xlsx
IL_EX_4-3.xlsx
IL_EX_4-4.xlsx
IL_EX_4-5.xlsx

Plan a Chart

Learning Outcomes
- Identify chart elements
- Explore common chart types

The process of creating a chart involves deciding which data to use and what type of chart best highlights the trends or patterns that are most important, such as steady increases over time or stellar performance by one sales rep compared to others in the same division. Understanding the parts of a chart makes it easier to evaluate specific elements to make sure the chart effectively illustrates your data. **CASE** *In preparation for creating the charts for Ellie's presentation, you review the purpose of the charts and decide how to organize the data.*

DETAILS

Use the following guidelines to plan the chart:

QUICK TIP
To see the available charts in Excel, select the worksheet data, click the Insert tab on the ribbon, click the Recommended Charts button in the Charts group, then click the All Charts tab.

- **Determine the purpose of the chart, and identify the data relationships you want to graphically communicate**
  You want to create a chart that shows quarterly expenses for JCL U.S. offices. You also want to illustrate whether the quarterly expenses for each office increased or decreased from quarter to quarter.
- **Determine the results you want to see, and decide which chart type is most appropriate**
  Different chart types display data in distinctive ways. For example, a pie chart compares parts of a whole, whereas a line chart is best for showing trends over time. To choose the best chart type for your data, first decide how you want your data to be interpreted. **FIGURE 4-1** shows the available chart types in Excel, listed by category on the All Charts tab of the Insert Chart dialog box. **TABLE 4-1** describes several of these charts. Because you want to compare JCL expenses in multiple offices over a period of four quarters, you decide to use a column chart.
- **Identify the worksheet data you want the chart to illustrate**
  Sometimes you use all the data in a worksheet to create a chart, while at other times you may need to select a range within the sheet. The worksheet from which you are creating your chart contains expense data for each of the past four quarters and the totals for the past year. To create a column chart, you will need to use all the quarterly data except the quarterly totals.
- **Understand the elements of a chart**
  The chart shown in **FIGURE 4-2** contains basic elements of a chart. In the figure, JCL offices are on the category axis and expense dollar amounts are on the value axis. The **category axis**, also called the *x*-axis, is the horizontal axis in a chart, usually containing the names of data categories. The **value axis**, also called the vertical axis, contains numerical values. In a two-dimensional chart, it is also known as the *y*-axis. (Three-dimensional charts contain a ***z*-axis**, for comparing data across both categories and values.) The area inside the horizontal and vertical axes that contains the graphical representation of the data series is the **plot area**. **Gridlines**, the horizontal and vertical lines, make a chart easier to read. Each individual piece of data plotted in a chart is a **data point**. In any chart, a **data marker** is a graphical representation of a data point, such as a bar or column. A set of values represented in a chart is a **data series**. In this chart, there are four data series: Quarter 1, Quarter 2, Quarter 3, and Quarter 4. Each is made up of columns of a different color. To differentiate each data series, information called a **legend** or a legend key identifies how the data is represented using colors and/or patterns.

FIGURE 4-1: Insert Chart dialog box lists available charts by category

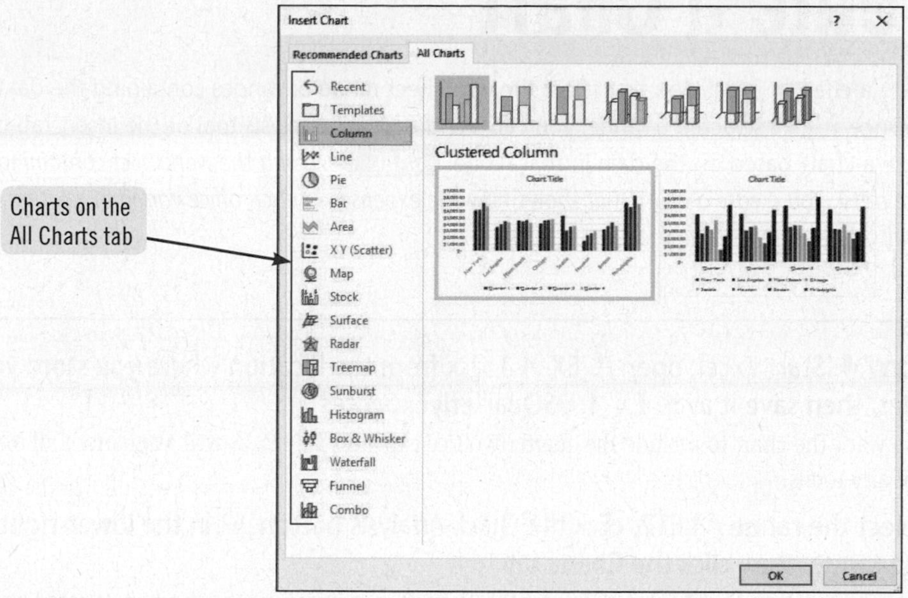

FIGURE 4-2: Chart elements

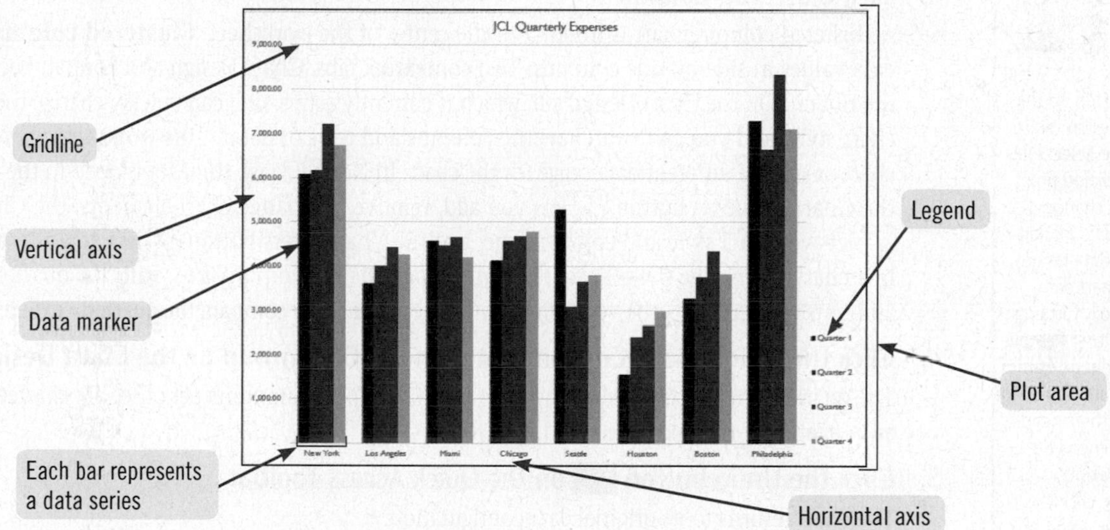

TABLE 4-1: Common chart types

type	description
Column	A chart that displays data values as columns; column height represents its value
Line	A chart or visualization that displays data as separate lines across categories
Pie	A chart in the shape of a circle divided into slices like a pie, which shows data values as percentages of the whole
Bar	A column chart turned on its side so that the length of each bar is based on its value
Area	Shows how individual volume changes over time in relation to total volume
Line with Markers	Compares trends over time by showing data markers that represent worksheet data values

Create a Chart

Learning Outcomes
- Create a chart
- Add a title to a chart

To create a chart in Excel, you first select the worksheet range or ranges containing the data you want to chart. Once you've selected a range, you can use the Quick Analysis tool or the Insert tab on the ribbon to create a chart based on the data in that range. **CASE** *Using the worksheet containing the quarterly expense data, you create a chart that shows how the expenses in each office varied in relation to each other, across all four quarters of the year.*

STEPS

1. **sam Start Excel, open IL_EX_4-1.xlsx from the location where you store your Data Files, then save it as IL_EX_4_USQuarterlyExpenses**
   You want the chart to include the quarterly office expenses values, as well as quarter and office labels, but not any totals.
2. **Select the range A4:E12, click the Quick Analysis button in the lower-right corner of the range, then click the Charts tab**
   The Charts tab on the Quick Analysis tool recommends commonly used chart types based on the range you have selected. It also includes a More Charts button for additional chart types.
3. **On the Charts tab, verify that Clustered Column is selected, as shown in FIGURE 4-3, then click Clustered Column**
   A clustered column chart is inserted in the center of the worksheet. **Clustered column charts** display data values in side-by-side columns. Two contextual tabs, Chart Design and Format, become available on the ribbon. On the Chart Design tab, which is currently active, you can quickly change the chart layout and chart style, and you can swap how the columns and rows of data in the worksheet are represented in the chart or select a different data range for the chart. In Normal view, three tools open to the right of the chart: the Chart Elements button lets you add, remove, or change chart elements; the Chart Styles button lets you set a style and color scheme; and the Chart Filters button lets you filter the results shown in a chart. Currently, the offices are charted along the horizontal *x*-axis, with the quarterly expense dollar amounts charted along the vertical *y*-axis. This lets you easily compare the quarterly expenses for each office.

> **QUICK TIP**
> You can change either the data source or the legend by clicking the Select Data button on the Chart Design tab to open the Select Data Source dialog box. You can change the source data by editing the data range in the chart data range box. Clicking Add, Edit, or Remove under Legend Entries (Series) allows you to change the legend labels. When you finish making changes, click OK to close the dialog box.

4. **Click the Switch Row/Column button in the Data group on the Chart Design tab**
   The quarters are now charted along the x-axis. The expense amounts per office are charted along the y-axis, as indicated by the updated legend. See FIGURE 4-4.
5. **Click the Undo button on the Quick Access Toolbar**
   The chart returns to its original data configuration.
6. **Click the Chart Title placeholder, type JCL Quarterly Expenses, click the Enter button, then click anywhere in the chart to deselect the title**
   Adding a title helps identify the chart. The border around the chart, along with the **sizing handles**, the small circles at the corners and the edges, indicates that the chart is selected. See FIGURE 4-5. Your chart might be in a different location on the worksheet and may look slightly different; you will move and resize it in the next lesson. Any time a chart is selected, as it is now, a blue border surrounds the worksheet data range on which the chart is based, a purple border surrounds the cells containing the category axis labels, and a red border surrounds the cells containing the data series labels. This chart is known as an **embedded chart** because it is displayed as an object in the worksheet. Embedding a chart in the current sheet is the default selection when creating a chart, but you can also embed a chart on a different sheet in the workbook, or on a newly created chart sheet. A **chart sheet** is a separate sheet in a workbook that contains only a chart that is linked to the workbook data.
7. **Save your work**

FIGURE 4-3: Charts tab in Quick Analysis tool

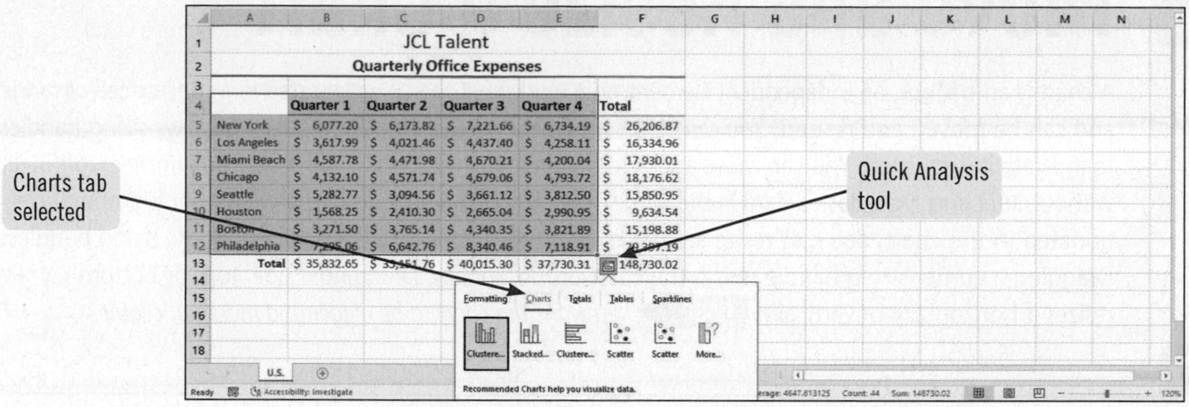

FIGURE 4-4: Clustered Column chart with different configuration of rows and columns

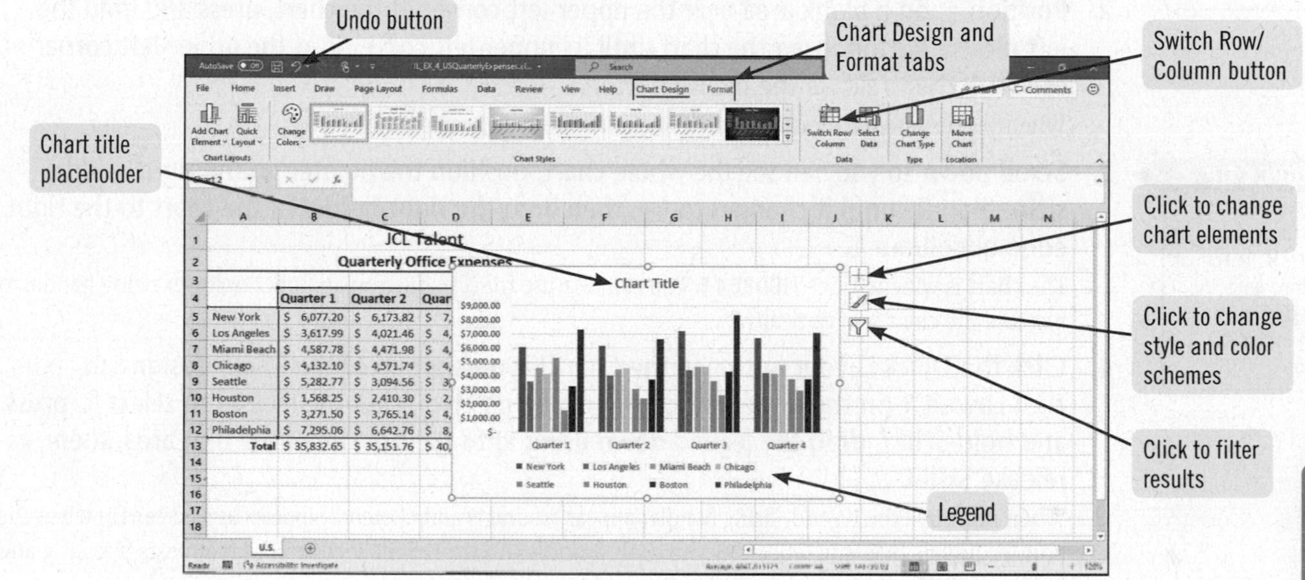

FIGURE 4-5: Chart with original configuration restored and title added

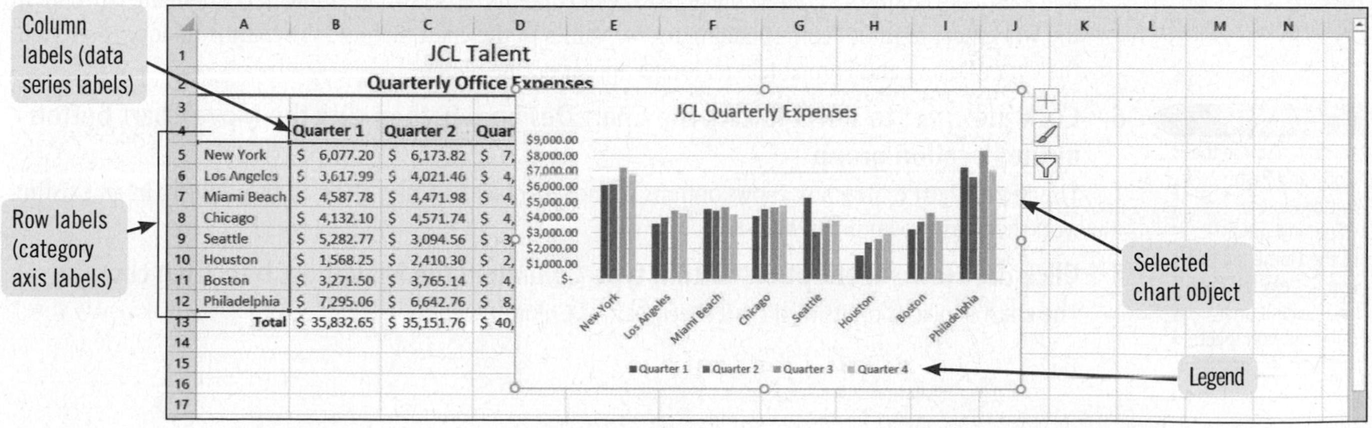

Move and Resize a Chart

Learning Outcomes
- Reposition a chart
- Resize a chart

A chart is an **object**, an independent element on a worksheet that is not located in a specific cell or range and can be moved and resized. You can select an object by clicking it; the object displays sizing handles to indicate it is selected. You can move a selected chart anywhere on a worksheet or to another worksheet without affecting formulas or data in the worksheet. Any data changed in the worksheet is automatically updated in the chart. You can resize a chart to improve its appearance by dragging its sizing handles. Dragging a corner sizing handle resizes the chart proportionally. Dragging a side, top, or bottom handle resizes it horizontally or vertically. **CASE** *You want the chart to be bigger and more noticeable.*

STEPS

QUICK TIP
To delete a selected chart, press DEL.

1. **Make sure the chart is still selected, then position the pointer over the chart**
   The pointer shape ✥ indicates that you can move the chart.
2. **Position ✥ on a blank area near the upper-left corner of the chart, press and hold the left mouse button, drag the chart until its upper-left corner is at the upper-left corner of cell A16, then release the mouse button**
   When you release the mouse button, the chart appears in the new location.

QUICK TIP
To resize a selected chart to an exact size, click the Format tab, then enter the desired height and width in the Size group.

3. **Scroll down so you can see the whole chart, position the pointer on the right-middle sizing handle until it changes to ⇔, then drag the right border of the chart to the right edge of column G**
   The chart is widened. See **FIGURE 4-6**. You can also use the ⇕ pointer on an upper or lower sizing handle to increase the chart size vertically.
4. **Click the Quick Layout button in the Chart Layouts group of the Chart Design tab, click Layout 1 (in the upper-left corner of the palette), click the legend to select it, press and hold SHIFT, drag the legend down using ✥ to the bottom of the plot area, then release SHIFT**
   When you click the legend, sizing handles appear around it and "Legend" appears as a ScreenTip when the pointer hovers over the object. As you drag, a dotted outline of the legend border appears. Pressing and holding SHIFT holds the horizontal position of the legend as you move it vertically.
5. **Scroll up if necessary, click cell A7, type Miami, then click the Enter button ✓ on the formula bar**
   The axis label changes to reflect the updated cell contents, as shown in **FIGURE 4-7**. Changing any data in the worksheet modifies corresponding text or values in the chart. Because the chart is no longer selected, the Chart Design and Format tabs no longer appear on the ribbon.

QUICK TIP
You can also use the Copy and Paste buttons in the Clipboard group of the Home tab to copy a selected chart and paste it on a different worksheet.

6. **Click the chart to select it, click the Chart Design tab, then click the Move Chart button in the Location group**
   The Move chart dialog box shows options to move a chart to a new sheet or as an object in an existing worksheet, as shown in **FIGURE 4-8**.
7. **Click the New sheet option button, type Column in the New sheet box, then click OK**
   The chart is placed on its own chart sheet, named Column.

FIGURE 4-6: Moved and resized chart

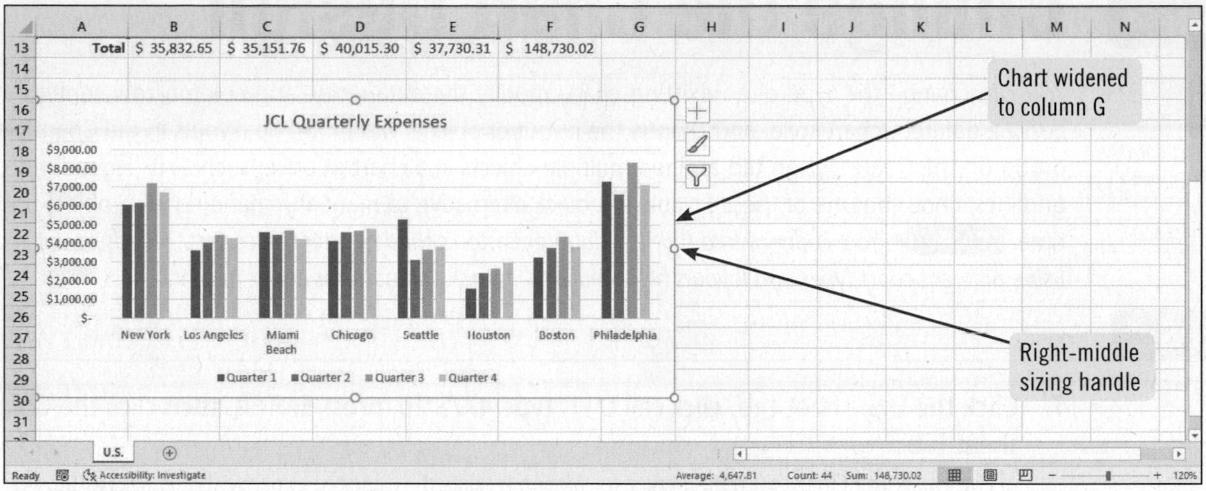

FIGURE 4-7: Worksheet with modified legend and label

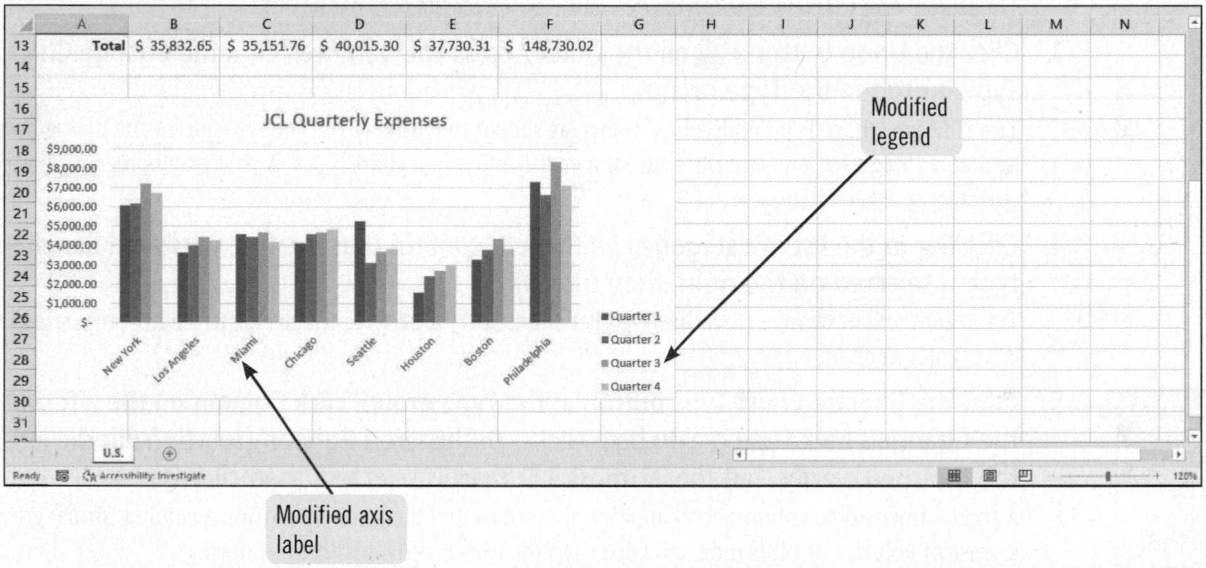

FIGURE 4-8: Move Chart dialog box

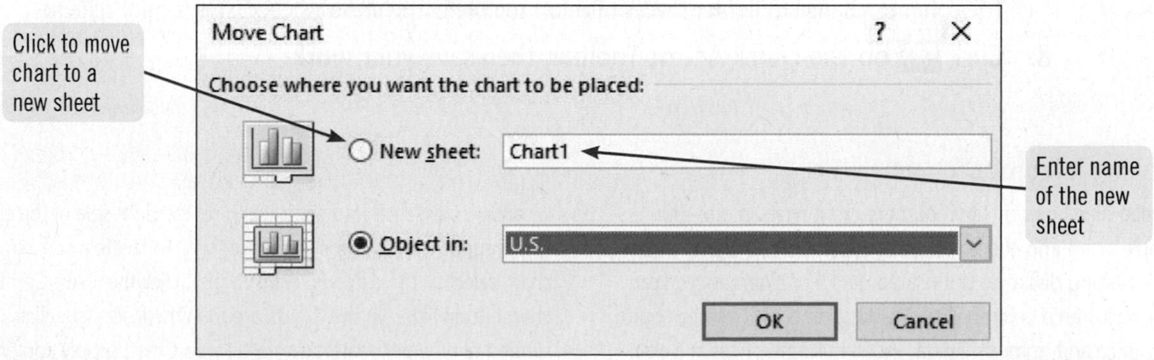

Excel
Module 4

Change the Chart Design

Learning Outcomes
- Modify chart data
- Change the chart type
- Apply a chart style

You can change the type of an existing chart, modify the data range and column/row configuration, apply a different chart style, and change the layout of objects within it. The layouts in the Chart Layouts group on the Chart Design tab arrange multiple objects in a chart at once, such as its legend, title, and gridlines; choosing one of these layouts is a quick alternative to manually changing each object one at a time. **CASE** *You've discovered that the data for Boston's third quarter is incorrect. You also want to see if using different chart types and layouts helps make the trends and patterns easier to spot.*

STEPS

1. **Click the U.S. sheet tab, click cell D11, type 4775.20, press ENTER, then click the Column sheet tab**
   In the chart, the Quarter 3 data marker for Boston reflects the adjusted expense figure. See **FIGURE 4-9**.
2. **Select the chart, if necessary, by clicking a blank area within the chart border, click the Chart Design tab on the ribbon, click the Quick Layout button in the Chart Layouts group, then click Layout 3**
   The legend moves to the bottom of the chart. You prefer the original layout.
3. **Click the Undo button on the Quick Access Toolbar, then click the Change Chart Type button in the Type group**
   The Change Chart Type dialog box opens, as shown in **FIGURE 4-10**. The left side of the dialog box lists available categories, and the right side shows the individual chart types. A pale gray border surrounds the currently selected chart type.
4. **Click Bar in the list of categories on the left, confirm that the first Clustered Bar chart type is selected on the right, then click OK**
   The column chart changes to a Clustered Bar chart. See **FIGURE 4-11**. You decide to see how the data looks in a 3-D column chart.
5. **Click the Change Chart Type button in the Type group, click Column on the left side of the Change Chart Type dialog box, click 3-D Clustered Column (fourth from the left in the top row), verify that the leftmost 3-D chart is selected, then click OK**
   A three-dimensional column chart appears. You notice that the three-dimensional column format gives you a sense of volume, but it is more crowded than the two-dimensional column format.
6. **Click the Change Chart Type button in the Type group, click Clustered Column (first from the left in the top row), then click OK**
7. **Click the Style 3 chart style in the Chart Styles group**
   The columns change to lighter shades of color. You prefer the previous chart style's color scheme.
8. **Click on the Quick Access Toolbar, then save your work**

QUICK TIP
You can add a 3-D effect to a 3-D chart by selecting the chart, clicking the Format tab, clicking the Shape Effects button in the Shape Styles group, clicking 3-D Rotation, then selecting the desired effect.

Creating a combo chart

A **combo chart** presents two or more chart types in one—for example, a column chart with a line chart. Combo charts are useful when charting dissimilar but related data. For example, you can create a clustered column–line combination chart based on both home price and home size data, showing home prices in a clustered column chart and related home sizes in a line chart. Here, a secondary axis (such as a vertical axis on the right side of the chart) would supply the scale for the home sizes. To create a combo chart, select all the data you want to plot, click the Insert Combo chart button in the Charts group in the Insert tab, click a suggested type or Create Custom Combo Chart, supply additional series information if necessary, then click OK.

FIGURE 4-9: Chart with modified data

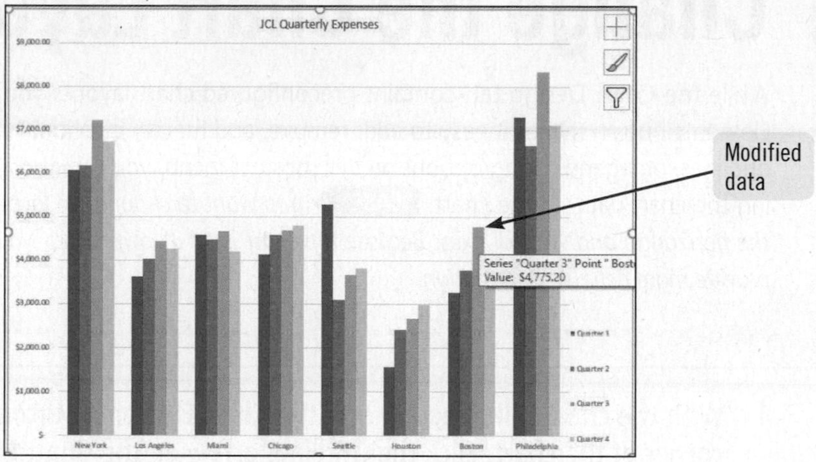

FIGURE 4-10: Change Chart Type dialog box

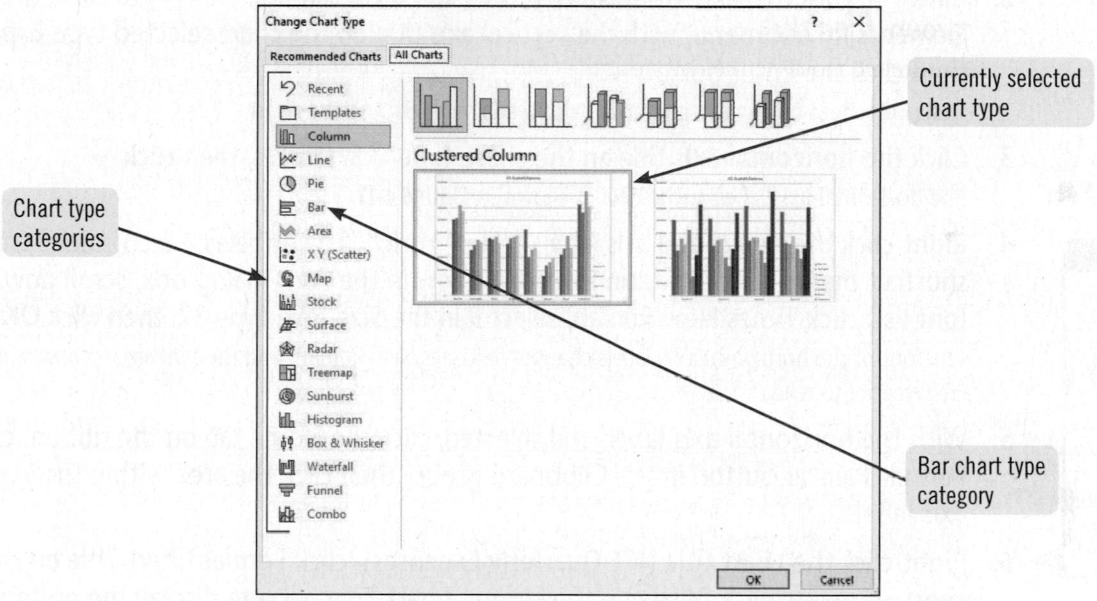

FIGURE 4-11: Column chart changed to bar chart

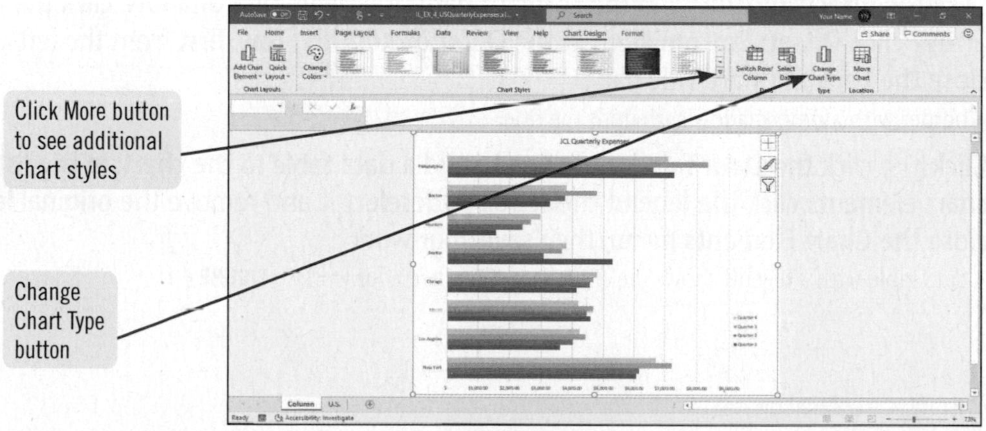

Excel

Change the Chart Layout

Learning Outcomes
- Change the gridlines display
- Add axis titles
- Add a data table

While the Chart Design tab contains preconfigured chart layouts you can apply to a chart, the Chart Elements button makes it easy to add, remove, and modify individual chart objects such as a chart title, gridlines, or legend. Using options on this shortcut menu, you can also add a **data table**, a grid containing the chart data, to the chart. CASE *You want to change the layout of the chart by creating titles for the horizontal and vertical axes. Because the chart is on its own sheet, you also want to add a data table to provide more detailed information.*

STEPS

1. **With the chart still selected, click the Chart Elements button ⊞ in the upper-right corner of the chart, click the Gridlines arrow on the Chart Elements fly-out menu, click Primary Major Horizontal to deselect it, then click ⊞ to close the menu**
   The gridlines that extend across the chart's plot area are removed, as shown in **FIGURE 4-12**.
2. **Click ⊞, click the Axis Titles check box to add a checkmark, click ⊞ to close the Chart Elements fly-out menu, with the vertical axis title on the chart selected type Expenses, then click the Enter button ✓**
   Descriptive text on the category axis helps readers understand the chart.
3. **Click the horizontal axis title on the chart, type U.S. Offices, then click ✓**
   The horizontal axis labels are added, as shown in **FIGURE 4-13**.
4. **Right-click the horizontal axis labels ("New York," "Los Angeles," etc.), click Font on the shortcut menu, click the Latin text font arrow in the Font dialog box, scroll down the font list, click Times New Roman, select 9 in the Size box, type 12, then click OK**
   The font of the horizontal axis labels changes to Times New Roman, and the font size increases, making the labels easier to read.
5. **With the horizontal axis labels still selected, click the Home tab on the ribbon, click the Format Painter button in the Clipboard group, then click the area within the vertical axis labels**
6. **Right-click the chart title (JCL Quarterly Expenses), click Format Chart Title on the shortcut menu, click Border in the Format Chart Title pane to display the options if necessary, then click the Solid line option button in the pane**
   A solid border in the default blue color appears around the chart title.
7. **Click the Effects button in the Format Chart Title pane, click Shadow, click the Presets arrow, click Offset: Bottom Right in the Outer group (first row, first from the left), then close the Format Chart Title pane**
   A border with a drop shadow surrounds the title.
8. **Click ⊞, click the Data Table check box to add a data table to the chart, in the list of chart elements click the legend check box to deselect it and remove the original legend, close the Chart Elements menu, then save your work**
   A data table with a legend shows the chart data. Compare your work to **FIGURE 4-14**.

QUICK TIP
You can also apply a border to a chart by double-clicking the Chart Area, clicking Format Chart Area on the shortcut menu, then selecting from the available border options in the Format Chart Area pane.

QUICK TIP
You can apply a shadow, glow, or outline to title text by clicking Text Options in the Format Chart Title pane. Clicking the Text Effects button allows you to select from the available shadow and glow options; clicking the Text Fill & Outline button displays outline options for chart text.

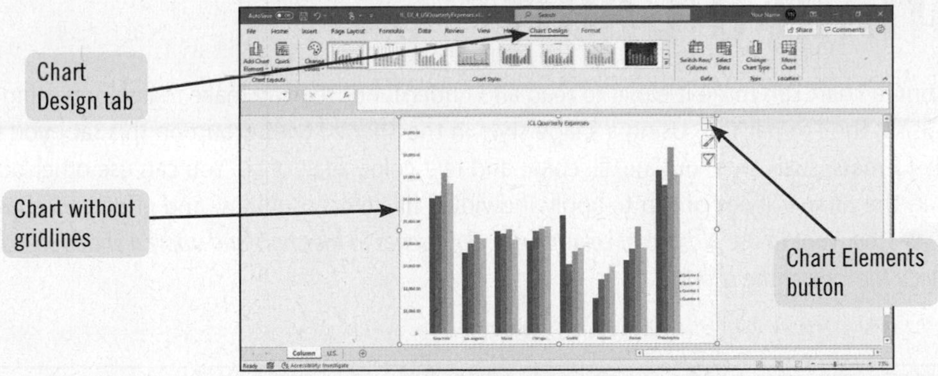

FIGURE 4-12: Gridlines removed from chart

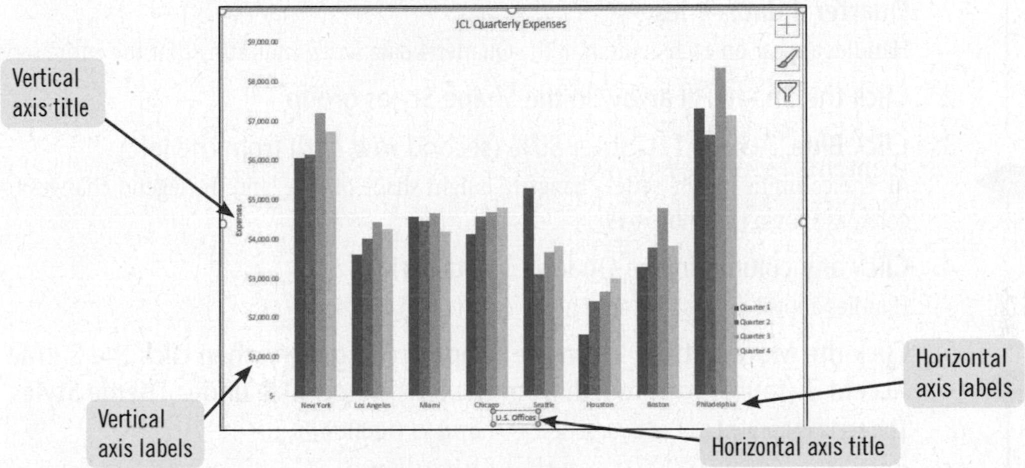

FIGURE 4-13: Axis titles added to chart

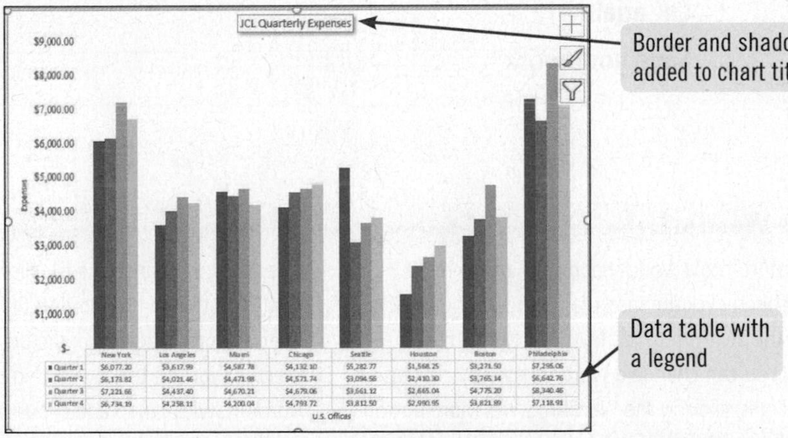

FIGURE 4-14: Enhanced chart

Working with chart axes

You can change both the number format and text formatting of a chart's axes. For example, you may want to change the starting and ending values of an axis. You can do this by double-clicking the axis, selecting Format Axis from the shortcut menu, clicking Axis Options in the Format Axis pane if necessary, then entering values in the Minimum and Maximum boxes. To change the number format of the values on an axis, scroll down in the Axis Options, click Number to display the options if necessary, then select from the available number formats. In the Number area, you can also create a number format code by typing a code in the Format Code box and clicking Add. In addition to these axis options, you can work with axis text by clicking the Text Options button at the top of the pane, then clicking the Textbox button [A≡]. The Text Box group includes options for changing the vertical alignment of the data labels on the axis and the text direction of axis data labels from horizontal to stacked or rotated.

Format a Chart

Learning Outcomes
- Change the fill of a data series
- Apply a style to a data series

Formatting a chart can make it easier to read and understand. You can make many formatting enhancements using the Format tab. Using a shape style in the Shape Styles group on this tab, you can apply multiple formats, such as an outline, fill color, and text color, all at once. You can use other buttons and arrows in the Shape Styles group to apply individual fill colors, outlines, and effects to chart objects. **CASE** *You want to use a different color for one data series in the chart and apply a shape style to another, to enhance the look of the chart.*

STEPS

QUICK TIP
You can remove a data series from a chart by selecting the data series, then pressing DEL.

QUICK TIP
You can add a texture fill by pointing to Texture in the Shape Fill menu and selecting a texture.

QUICK TIP
You can change the colors used in a chart by clicking the Chart Design tab, clicking the Change Colors button in the Chart Styles group, then clicking a color palette in the gallery.

1. **With the chart selected, click the Format tab on the ribbon, then click any column in the Quarter 4 data series**
   Handles appear on each column in the Quarter 4 data series, indicating that the entire series is selected.
2. **Click the Shape Fill arrow in the Shape Styles group**
3. **Click Blue, Accent 1, Lighter 80% (second row, fifth from the left)**
   All the columns for the series change to a light shade of blue, and the legend changes to match the new color, as shown in **FIGURE 4-15**.
4. **Click any column in the Quarter 3 data series**
   Handles appear on each column in the Quarter 3 data series.
5. **Click the More button on the Shape Styles gallery, then click the Subtle Effect – Gray, Accent 3 (fourth row, fourth from the left) shape style under Theme Styles**
   The style is applied to the data series, as shown in **FIGURE 4-16**.
6. **Click the Insert tab on the ribbon, click the Text button, click the Header & Footer button, click Custom Footer, type your name in the center section, click OK, then click OK again**
7. **Save your work**

Working with WordArt

You can insert WordArt into a worksheet or a chart. To insert WordArt in a worksheet, click the Insert tab on the ribbon, click the Text button in the Text group, click WordArt, then click a style in the gallery. You can change a WordArt style by clicking the WordArt to select it, clicking the WordArt Styles More button on the Shape Format tab, then selecting a new WordArt style. You can change the fill color of the WordArt by clicking the Text Fill button in the WordArt Styles group and choosing a fill color, texture, gradient, or picture. You can change the outline of selected WordArt text by clicking the Text Outline button in the the WordArt Styles group and choosing an outline color, weight, and/or dashes.

FIGURE 4-15: New shape fill applied to data series

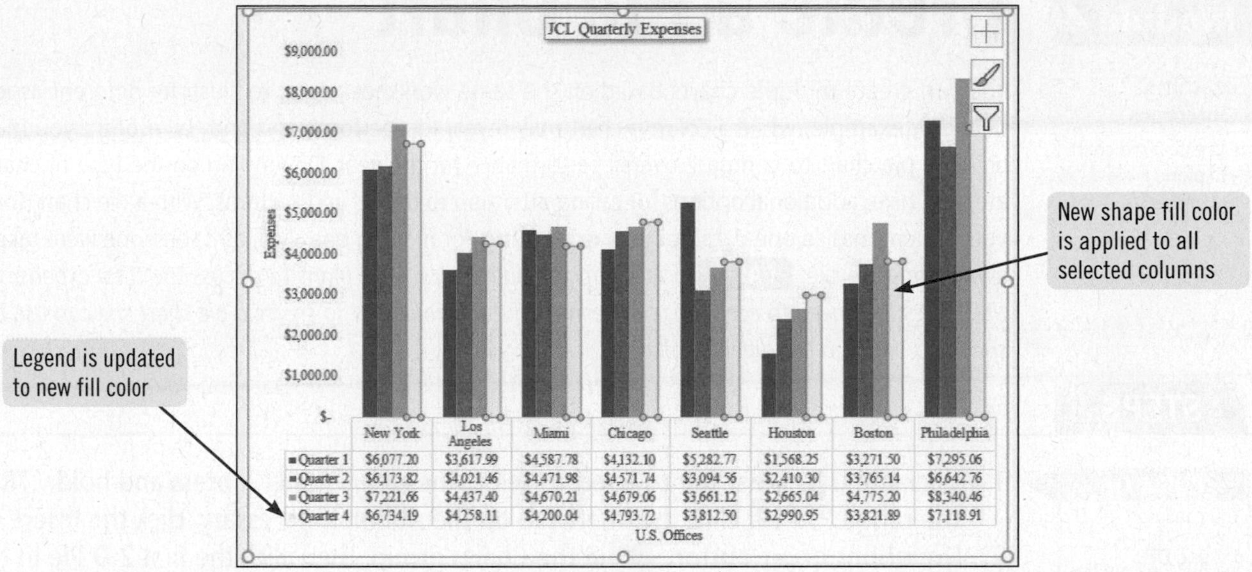

FIGURE 4-16: Style applied to data series

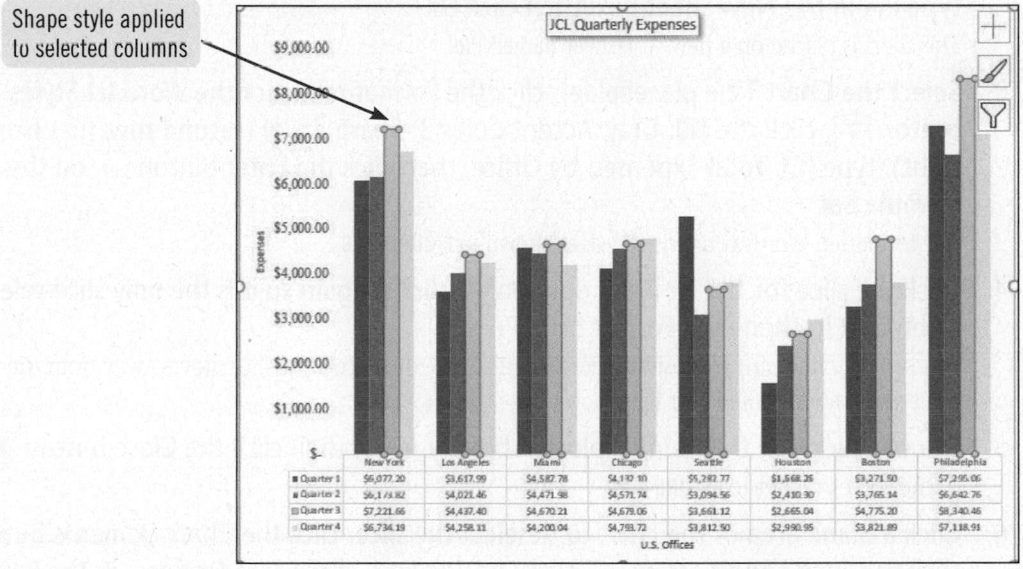

Aligning charts

If you have two or more embedded charts on a worksheet, you can line them up to make them easier to view. First, select the charts by clicking the first chart and holding SHIFT, then click the other chart(s). With the charts selected, click the Shape Format tab, click the Align button in the Arrange group, then choose the alignment position for the charts. The chart shown in **FIGURE 4-17** uses the Align Top option.

FIGURE 4-17: Charts aligned at the top

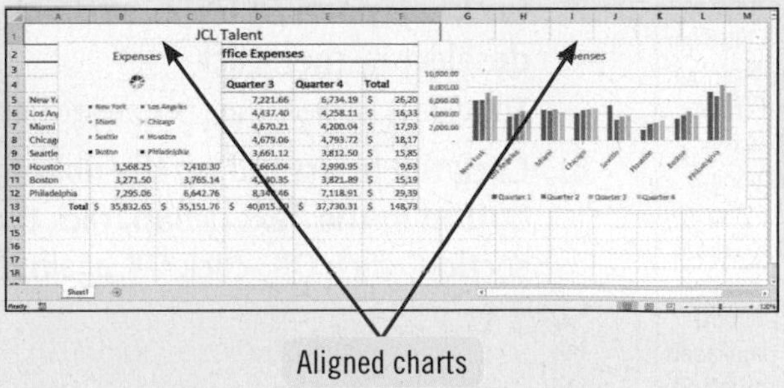

Excel

Excel
Module 4

Create a Pie Chart

Learning Outcomes
- Create a pie chart
- Explode a pie chart slice

You can create multiple charts based on the same worksheet data, to illustrate different aspects of the data. For example, while a column chart may reveal top performers month by month, you may want to create a pie chart to compare overall performance for the year. Depending on the type of chart you create, you have additional options for calling attention to trends and patterns. With a pie chart, for example, you can emphasize one data point by **exploding**, or moving one slice, as if someone were taking a piece away from the pie. CASE *At an upcoming meeting, Ellie plans to discuss the total expenses and identify offices that need to economize more in the future. You want to create a pie chart she can use to compare spending between the different offices.*

STEPS

QUICK TIP
You can insert a 3-D pie chart by choosing 3-D Pie from the chart gallery.

1. **Click the U.S. sheet tab to select it, select the range A5:A12, press and hold CTRL, select the range F5:F12, click the Insert tab on the ribbon if necessary, click the Insert Pie or Doughnut Chart button in the Charts group, then click the first 2-D Pie in the chart gallery**
2. **Click the Move Chart button in the Location group, click the New sheet option button, type Pie in the New sheet box, then click OK**
   The chart is placed on a new worksheet named Pie.
3. **Select the Chart Title placeholder, click the Format tab, click the WordArt Styles More button, click the Fill: Gray, Accent Color 3; Sharp Bevel (second row, first from the right), type JCL Total Expenses, by Office, then click the Enter button on the formula bar**
   The formatted WordArt title is added, as shown in **FIGURE 4-18**.
4. **Click the slice for the Houston data point, click it again so it is the only slice selected, right-click it, then click Format Data Point**
   You can use the Point Explosion slider to control the distance a pie slice moves away from the pie, or you can type a value in the Point Explosion box.
5. **Double-click 0 in the Point Explosion box, type 10, then click the Close button**
   Compare your chart to **FIGURE 4-19**.
6. **Click a blank area of the chart to deselect the slice, click the Chart Elements button, click the Data Labels arrow, click Outside End, click More Options, in the Format Data Labels pane click the Percentage check box to add a checkmark, click the Value box to deselect it, then close the Format Data Labels pane**
   The data labels identify the pie slices by percentage.
7. **Click, point to Data Labels, click, click Data Callout, click the Legend check box to deselect it, then click**
   The data is labeled using percentage callouts, as shown in **FIGURE 4-20**.
8. **Click the Insert tab on the ribbon, click the Text button, click the Header & Footer button in the Text group, click the Custom Footer button, enter your name in the center section, click OK, click OK again, then save your work**

QUICK TIP
You can change the number format of the data labels by clicking the Label Options button in the Format Data Labels pane if necessary, clicking Number to show the Number options, and choosing the desired category or entering a format code. Also in this pane are options under Label Position to change the position of the data labels to Center, Inside End, and Best Fit.

FIGURE 4-18: Title formatted using WordArt

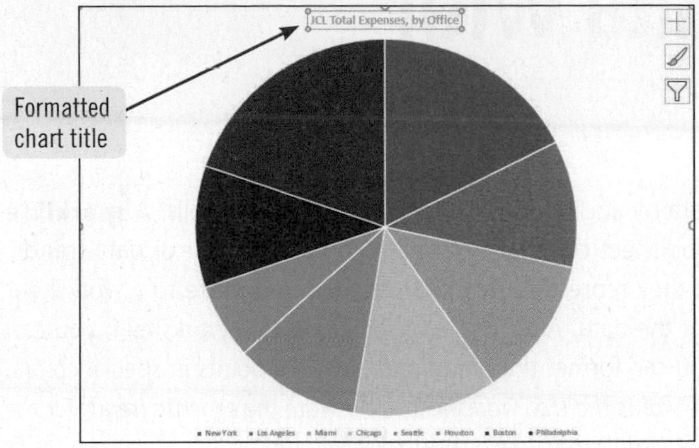

FIGURE 4-19: Exploded pie slice

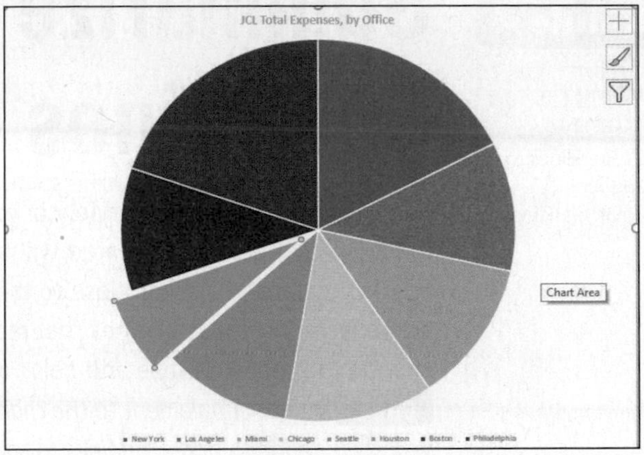

FIGURE 4-20: Pie chart with percentages

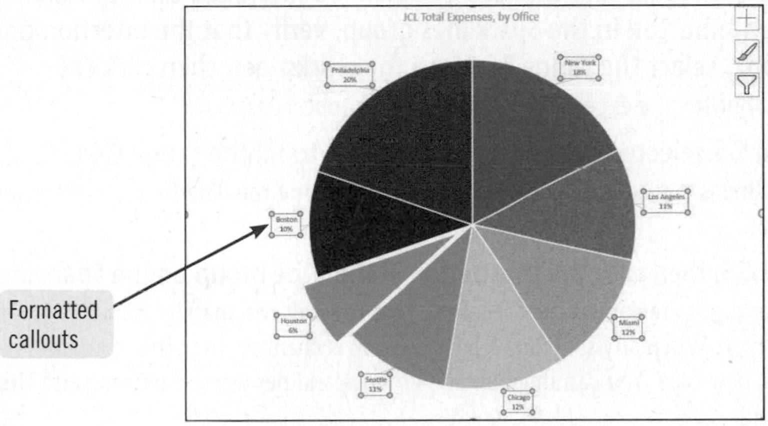

Working with other chart types

Excel includes chart types that are useful for illustrating highly specific types of data. These include Waterfall, Histogram, Pareto, Box & Whisker, Treemap, Scatter, and Sunburst. A **treemap chart** is a hierarchy chart in which each category is placed within a rectangle and subcategories are nested as rectangles within those rectangles. A **sunburst chart** is also a hierarchy chart, but it groups categories within a series of concentric rings, with the upper levels of the hierarchy placed in the innermost rings. To insert one of these chart types, click the Insert tab, click the Insert Hierarchy Chart button in the Charts group, then click the chart type. **Waterfall charts** are used to track the addition and subtraction of values within a sum. To insert a Waterfall chart, click the Insert tab, click the Insert Waterfall, Funnel, Stock, Surface, or Radar Chart button in the Charts group, then click Waterfall. A **histogram chart** shows the distribution of data grouped in bins. These charts look similar to column charts, but each column (or bin) represents a range of values. To insert a histogram chart, click the Insert tab on the ribbon, click the Insert Statistic Chart button in the Charts group, then click the Histogram chart button. You can edit the bins in a histogram chart by double-clicking the x-axis, clicking to expand the Axis Options group on the Format Axis pane, then choosing options under Bins.

A **scatter chart** displays the correlation between two numeric variables. It is a type of **XY scatter chart**, which shows the pattern or relationship between two or more sets of values. Scatter charts look similar to line charts but have two value axes. The data points on a scatter chart show the intersection of the horizontal and vertical axes values. To insert a scatter chart, select the data you want to chart, click the Insert tab, click the Insert Scatter (X,Y) or Bubble Chart button in the Charts group, then choose a scatter chart type.

Excel
Module 4

Learning Outcomes
- Add sparklines to a worksheet
- Format sparklines

Summarize Data with Sparklines

You can create a quick overview of your data by adding sparklines to the worksheet cells. A **sparkline** is a small, simple chart located within a worksheet cell that serves as a visual indicator of data trends. Sparklines usually appear close to the data they represent. Any changes that you make to a worksheet are reflected in the sparklines that represent the data. After you add sparklines to a worksheet, you can change the sparkline style and color, and you can format their high and low data points in special colors. **CASE** *As a supplement to the charts, Ellie wants the U.S. worksheet to illustrate the expense trends for the year. You decide to add sparklines to tell a quick visual story within the worksheet cells.*

STEPS

QUICK TIP
If you have an empty cell directly to the right of a range, you can use the Quick Access tool to insert a sparkline into the empty cell.

QUICK TIP
To insert Win/Loss sparklines, which show upward column symbols for positive values and downward symbols for negative values, click the Win/Loss button in the Type group.

QUICK TIP
To clear sparklines, select the sparklines, then click the Clear button in the Group group.

1. **Click the U.S. sheet tab, click cell G5, click the Insert tab on the ribbon if necessary, click the Column button in the Sparklines group, verify that the insertion point is in the Data Range box, select the range B5:E5 on the worksheet, then click OK**
   Columns showing the expense trend for New York appear in cell G5.
2. **With cell G5 selected, drag the fill handle + to fill the range G6:G12**
   The sparkline is copied, and column sparklines reflecting the data for each office are added, as shown in **FIGURE 4-21**.
3. **Click cell G5, then click the Line button in the Type group on the Sparkline tab**
   When sparklines are copied they become a group, so all the sparklines in this group change to the Line sparkline type. When any sparkline type in a group is changed, the other sparklines in the group change to match the new type. You can ungroup and group sparklines using the Group and Ungroup buttons in the Group group.
4. **Click the Sparkline Color button in the Style group, then click Green, Accent 6, Darker 50% (last row, first color from the right)**
5. **Click the More button in the Style group, then click Brown, Sparkline Style Accent 2, Darker 50% (second from the left in the first row)**
   The sparkline colors and styles are consistent with the colors on the worksheet.
6. **Click the Marker Color button in the Style group, point to High Point, select Orange Accent 2, Darker 50% (sixth from left, sixth row), click the Marker Color button in the Style group, point to Markers, select Green, Accent 6 (last in Theme Colors), then click the Markers check box in the Show group to add a checkmark if necessary**
   Data markers indicate each quarter's expenses, with the highest quarter value in a different color.
7. **Click cell C5, type 6,742.13, click the Enter button ✓, then compare your screen to FIGURE 4-22**
   The sparklines update to reflect the new worksheet data.
8. **Click the Insert tab on the ribbon, click the Text button, click the Header & Footer button in the Text group, click the Go to Footer button in the Navigation group, enter your name in the center footer section, click any cell on the worksheet, click the Normal button on the status bar, then press CTRL+HOME**
9. **Save your changes**

FIGURE 4-21: Expense trend sparklines

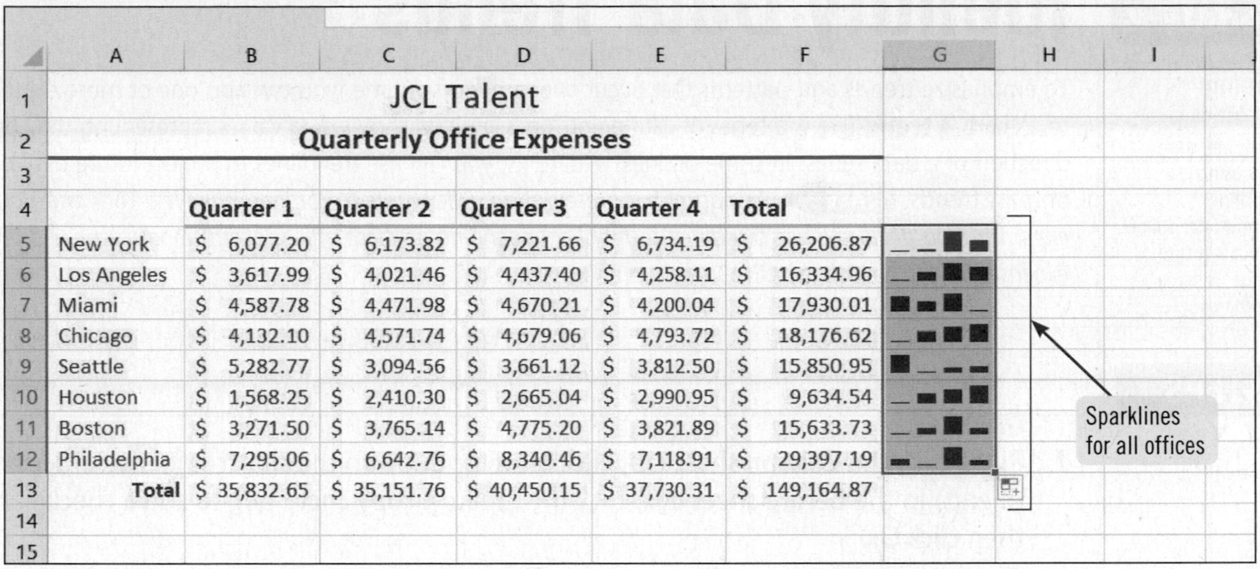

	A	B	C	D	E	F
1	JCL Talent					
2	Quarterly Office Expenses					
3						
4		Quarter 1	Quarter 2	Quarter 3	Quarter 4	Total
5	New York	$ 6,077.20	$ 6,173.82	$ 7,221.66	$ 6,734.19	$ 26,206.87
6	Los Angeles	$ 3,617.99	$ 4,021.46	$ 4,437.40	$ 4,258.11	$ 16,334.96
7	Miami	$ 4,587.78	$ 4,471.98	$ 4,670.21	$ 4,200.04	$ 17,930.01
8	Chicago	$ 4,132.10	$ 4,571.74	$ 4,679.06	$ 4,793.72	$ 18,176.62
9	Seattle	$ 5,282.77	$ 3,094.56	$ 3,661.12	$ 3,812.50	$ 15,850.95
10	Houston	$ 1,568.25	$ 2,410.30	$ 2,665.04	$ 2,990.95	$ 9,634.54
11	Boston	$ 3,271.50	$ 3,765.14	$ 4,775.20	$ 3,821.89	$ 15,633.73
12	Philadelphia	$ 7,295.06	$ 6,642.76	$ 8,340.46	$ 7,118.91	$ 29,397.19
13	Total	$ 35,832.65	$ 35,151.76	$ 40,450.15	$ 37,730.31	$ 149,164.87
14						
15						

FIGURE 4-22: Formatted sparklines

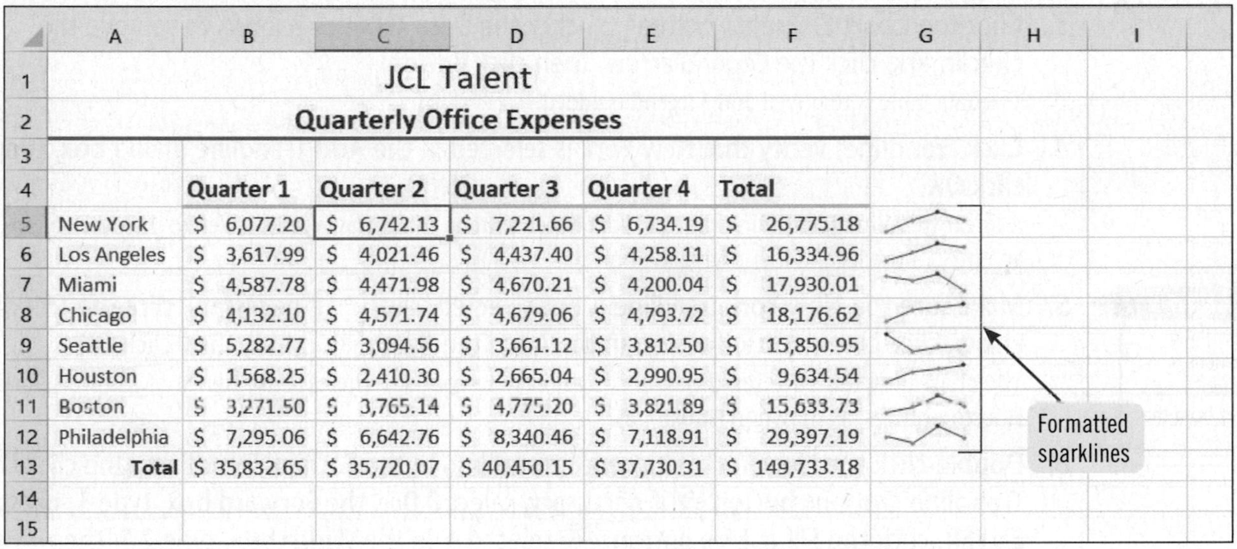

	A	B	C	D	E	F
1	JCL Talent					
2	Quarterly Office Expenses					
3						
4		Quarter 1	Quarter 2	Quarter 3	Quarter 4	Total
5	New York	$ 6,077.20	$ 6,742.13	$ 7,221.66	$ 6,734.19	$ 26,775.18
6	Los Angeles	$ 3,617.99	$ 4,021.46	$ 4,437.40	$ 4,258.11	$ 16,334.96
7	Miami	$ 4,587.78	$ 4,471.98	$ 4,670.21	$ 4,200.04	$ 17,930.01
8	Chicago	$ 4,132.10	$ 4,571.74	$ 4,679.06	$ 4,793.72	$ 18,176.62
9	Seattle	$ 5,282.77	$ 3,094.56	$ 3,661.12	$ 3,812.50	$ 15,850.95
10	Houston	$ 1,568.25	$ 2,410.30	$ 2,665.04	$ 2,990.95	$ 9,634.54
11	Boston	$ 3,271.50	$ 3,765.14	$ 4,775.20	$ 3,821.89	$ 15,633.73
12	Philadelphia	$ 7,295.06	$ 6,642.76	$ 8,340.46	$ 7,118.91	$ 29,397.19
13	Total	$ 35,832.65	$ 35,720.07	$ 40,450.15	$ 37,730.31	$ 149,733.18
14						
15						

Excel

Identify Data Trends

Learning Outcomes
- Compare chart data using trendlines
- Format a trendline
- Forecast future trends using trendlines

To emphasize trends and patterns that occur over a period of time, you can add one or more trendlines to a chart. A **trendline** is a series of data points on a line that shows data values representing the general direction of a data series. In some business situations, you can use trendlines to project future data based on past trends. **CASE** *As part of her presentation, Ellie wants to compare the New York and Houston expenses. You decide to use trendlines to highlight spending at these offices over the past year and project expenses for the next six months, if past trends continue.*

STEPS

1. **Right-click the Column sheet tab, click Move or Copy on the shortcut menu, click (move to end) in the Before sheet box, click the Create a copy check box to add a checkmark, then click OK**
   The new worksheet Column (2) is a copy of the Column sheet.
2. **Right-click the Column (2) sheet tab, click Rename on the shortcut menu, type Trends, click the chart to select it, click the Chart Design tab, then click the Switch Row/Column button in the Data group**
   The chart displays quarters, a time measure, on the x-axis.
3. **Click the Chart Elements button [+], click the Data Table check box to remove the checkmark, click the Legend arrow, then click Bottom**
   The data table is removed and a legend is added.
4. **Click Trendline, verify that New York is selected in the Add Trendline dialog box, then click OK**
   A linear trendline identifying the New York expense trend in the past year is added to the chart, along with an entry in the legend identifying the line.
5. **Make sure the New York trendline is not selected, click [+] if necessary, click the Trendline arrow, click Linear, click Houston in the Add Trendline dialog box, then click OK**
   The chart now has two trendlines, making it easy to compare the expense trends of the New York and Houston offices, as shown in **FIGURE 4-23**.

QUICK TIP
To ensure that a chart element is not selected, simply click away from the element.

6. **Double-click the New York data series trendline, in the Format Trendline pane click the Trendline Options button if necessary, select 0.0 in the Forward box, type 1, press ENTER, click the Fill & Line button, select 1.5 in the Width box, type 2.5, then close the Format Trendline pane**
   Trendlines are often used to project future trends. The formatted New York trendline projects an additional quarter of future expenses trends for the office, assuming past trends continue.
7. **Double-click the Houston data series trendline, select 0.0 in the Forward box, type 1, press ENTER, click [Fill & Line], select 1.5 in the Width box, type 2.5, then close the Format Trendline pane**
   The formatted Houston trendline also projects an additional quarter of future expenses, if past trends continue.
8. **sam Save your work, preview the Trends sheet, compare your chart to FIGURE 4-24, close the workbook, submit the workbook to your instructor, then close Excel**

FIGURE 4-23: Chart with two trendlines

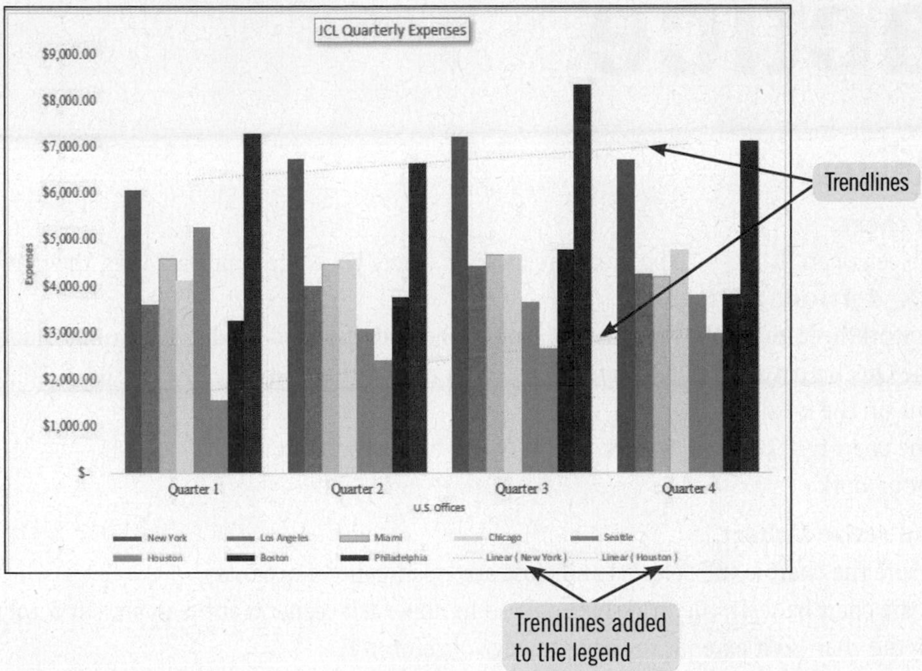

FIGURE 4-24: Expense chart with trendlines for New York and Houston data

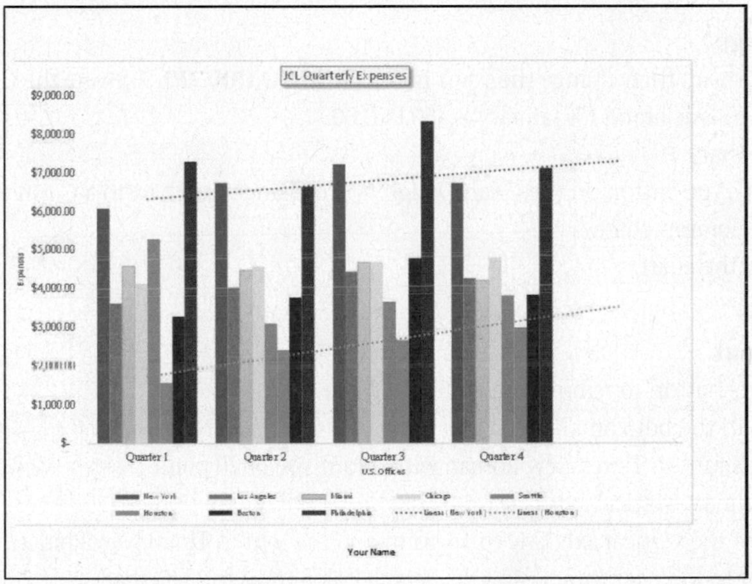

Choosing the right trendline options for your chart

When choosing a trendline, it is important to know which one is best for the information you want to communicate. If the data progression follows a straight line, using a linear trendline helps to emphasize that. If the pattern of a chart's data is linear but the data points don't follow a straight line, you can use a linear forecast trendline to chart a best-fit straight line. When data values increase or decrease in an arc shape, consider using an exponential or power trendline to illustrate this. A two-period moving average smooths out fluctuations in data by averaging the data points.

Excel

Practice

Skills Review

1. Create a chart.

a. Start Excel, open IL_EX_4-2.xlsx from the location where you store your Data Files, then save it as **IL_EX_4_FoodServices**.

b. In the worksheet, select the range containing all the sales data and headings. Do not include the totals.

c. Use the Quick Analysis tool to create a Clustered Column chart. Use the first Clustered Column option, placing the months on the x-axis.

d. Add the chart title **Brand Sales, by Month** above the chart.

e. Save your work.

2. Move and resize a chart.

a. Make sure the chart is still selected and close any open panes if necessary.

b. Move the chart beneath the worksheet data so its upper-left corner is at the upper-left corner of cell A11.

c. Widen the chart so it extends to the right edge of column H.

d. Use the Quick Layout button in the Chart Layouts group on the Chart Design tab to move the legend to the right of the charted data. (*Hint:* Use Layout 1.)

e. Move the chart to a new worksheet that you name **Column**.

f. Save your work.

3. Change the chart design.

a. Activate the Q1 & Q2 sheet, then change the value in cell B4 to **80,000.00**. Activate the Column sheet and verify that the value for the Classic brand for January is $80,000.00.

b. Select the chart if necessary.

c. Use the Change Chart Type button on the Chart Design tab to change the chart to a Clustered Bar chart, then change it back to a Clustered Column chart.

d. Apply Chart Style 6 to the chart.

e. Save your work.

4. Change the chart layout.

a. Use the Chart Elements button to remove the gridlines in the chart.

b. Change the font used in the horizontal and vertical axis labels to Times New Roman.

c. Change the chart title's font to Times New Roman with a font size of 20 point.

d. Insert **Sales** as the primary vertical axis title.

e. Change the font size of the vertical axis title to 16 point and the font to Times New Roman.

f. Add a solid line border to the chart title, using the default color and a (preset) shadow of Outer Offset: Bottom Right.

g. Add a data table to the chart with a legend key, then remove the legend from the chart.

h. Save your work.

5. Format a chart.

a. Use the Format tab to change the shape fill of the Classic data series to Olive Green, Accent 3, Darker 50% (last row of the theme colors, seventh from the left).

b. Change the shape style of the Classic data series to Intense Effect – Blue, Accent 1 (sixth row, second from the left), then click the chart area to deselect the Classic data series.

c. Save your work.

Skills Review (continued)

6. Create a pie chart.

- **a.** Switch to the Q1 & Q2 sheet, then select the range A4:A8 and H4:H8. (*Hint:* Holding CTRL allows you to select multiple nonadjacent ranges.)
- **b.** Create a 2-D pie chart and move the chart beneath the worksheet data so the upper-left corner is at the upper-left corner of cell A11.
- **c.** Add data callout labels and do not display the legend.
- **d.** Change the chart title to **Q1 & Q2 Sales** and format the title using the WordArt style Fill: Blue, Accent color 1, Shadow (second style in the first row).
- **e.** Explode the Artisan slice from the pie chart at **20%**.
- **f.** Enter your name in the center footer section of the worksheet, then save your work.

7. Summarize data with sparklines.

- **a.** Add a Line sparkline to cell I4 that represents the data in the range B4:G4.
- **b.** Copy the sparkline in cell I4 into the range I5:I8.
- **c.** Change the sparklines to columns.
- **d.** Apply the Sparkline style Blue Sparkline Style Dark #1 (fifth row, first column) to the group.
- **e.** Add high point markers with the color of Red, Accent 2 (first row, sixth from the left).
- **f.** Preview the worksheet and compare it to **FIGURE 4-25**.
- **g.** Save the workbook.

FIGURE 4-25

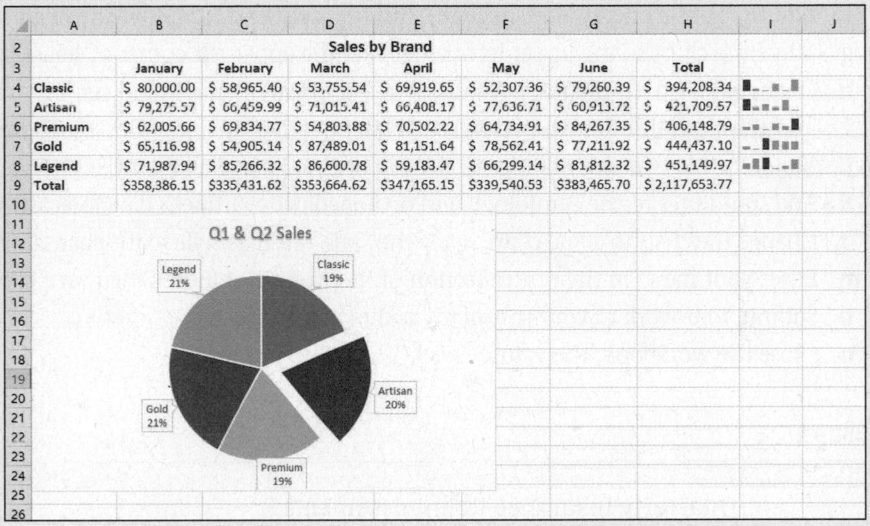

8. Identify data trends.

- **a.** Switch to the Column sheet.
- **b.** Add linear trendlines to the Premium and Gold data series.
- **c.** Set the forward option to 2 periods for both trendlines.
- **d.** Change the width of both trendlines to 3, then compare your screen to **FIGURE 4-26**.
- **e.** Add your name to the center footer section of the Column sheet, save the workbook, close the workbook, then submit the workbook to your instructor.
- **f.** Close Excel.

FIGURE 4-26

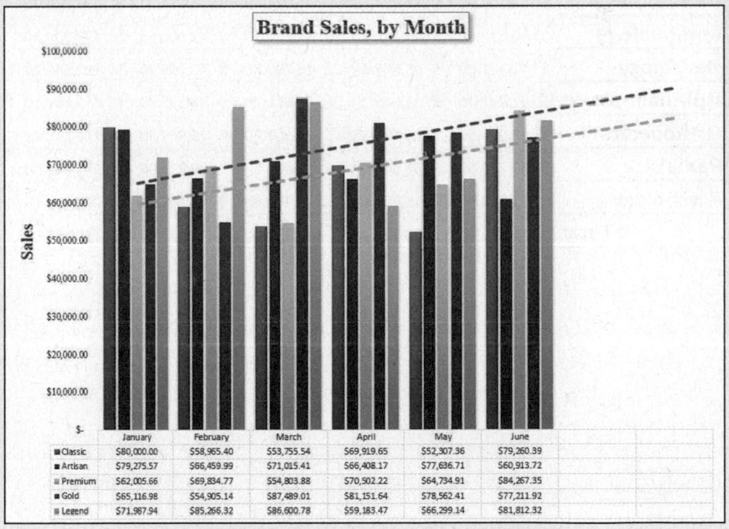

Excel

Independent Challenge 1

As an insurance manager for Riverwalk Medical Clinic, you have been asked to review the reimbursements for the clinic's departments. You will create a chart showing the insurance reimbursement over the past four quarters and predict future trends based on this history.

a. Start Excel, open IL_EX_4-3.xlsx from the location where you store your Data Files, then save it as **IL_EX_4_Reimbursements**.

b. Create a Clustered Column chart using the reimbursement amounts for the quarters and departments. (*Hint:* Do not include the totals.)

c. Switch the placement of the rows and columns, if necessary, to place the quarters on the x-axis.

d. Remove the chart gridlines.

e. Change the fill of the Psychology data series to Orange, Accent 6, Darker 50% (last row, last column of the Theme colors).

f. Add the Subtle effect – Red, Accent 2 (fourth row, third from the left) shape style to the Psychology data series.

g. Move the chart so the upper-left corner is at the upper-left corner of cell G2.

h. Change the fourth-quarter psychology reimbursement amount in cell E10 to **60,254.20**.

i. Add the chart title **Reimbursements** and format the title with a solid line blue border from the Standard Colors.

j. Move the bottom chart border to the top of row 20, add a data table, then remove the chart legend.

k. Add trendlines to the cardiology and orthopedics department data forecasting 2 periods ahead.

l. Change the chart to a line chart, apply the Style 12 Chart Style to the chart, then compare your worksheet to **FIGURE 4-27**.

m. Enter your name in the center section of the worksheet footer, then save your work.

n. Submit your work to your instructor as directed.

o. Close the workbook, then close Excel.

FIGURE 4-27

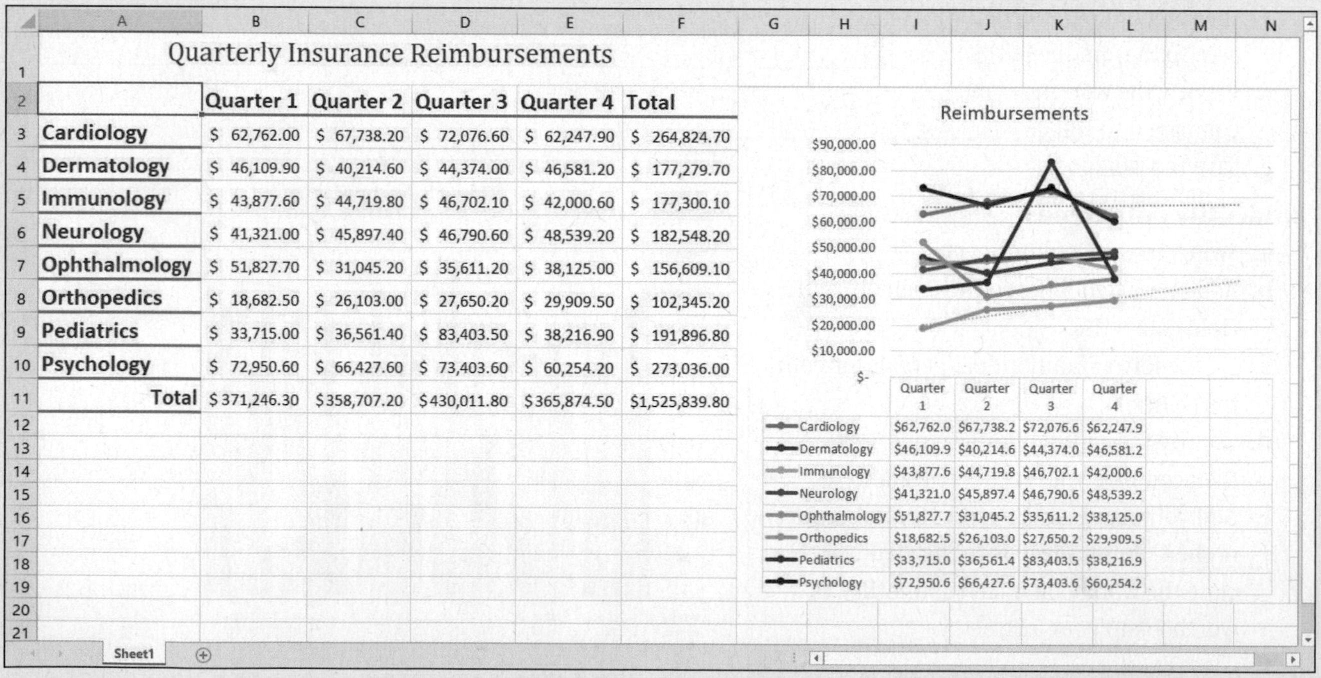

Independent Challenge 2

One of your responsibilities as the director of enrollment at Oceanview College is to present enrollment data to the executive staff at the end of the academic year. Your assistant has organized the college's enrollment data by division in a worksheet. You will review the data and create charts to visually represent the enrollment for the year.

a. Start Excel, open IL_EX_4-4.xlsx from the location where you store your Data Files, then save it as **IL_EX_4_Enrollments**.

b. Create a 3-D Clustered Column chart in the worksheet showing the enrollment data for all four terms. (*Hint:* The divisions, such as STEM, Business, and so forth, should appear on the x-axis.)

c. Add the chart title **Enrollment, by Division**, then format the title with the WordArt style of Fill: Blue, Accent color 1; Shadow (first row, second from left).

d. Move the chart so its upper-left corner is at the upper-left corner of cell H3.

e. On the worksheet, type **Average** in cell F3, then enter a formula in cell F4 to calculate the average STEM enrollment for the year.

f. Copy the average formula in cell F4 to the range F5:F9.

g. Add the average data from column F to the chart. (*Hint:* Use the Select Data button on the Chart Design tab to select the new chart data, including the average data.)

h. Change the chart type to Combo Clustered Column – Line chart (first option of combo charts) with the average data series charted as a line. (*Hint:* After selecting the chart type in the Change Chart Type dialog box, scroll down to make sure the Fall, Spring, Summer, and Intersession series are charted as clustered columns and the Average data series is charted as a line. You may need to change the Intersession chart type. Do not use the secondary axis options.)

i. Using **FIGURE 4-28** as a guide, resize the chart, then add data labels to the Average data series only. (*Hint:* Select the Average data series on the chart before adding data labels.)

j. Save your work.

k. Enter your name in the center footer section of the chart sheet, then preview the worksheet.

l. Submit your work to your instructor as directed, close the workbook, then close Excel.

FIGURE 4-28

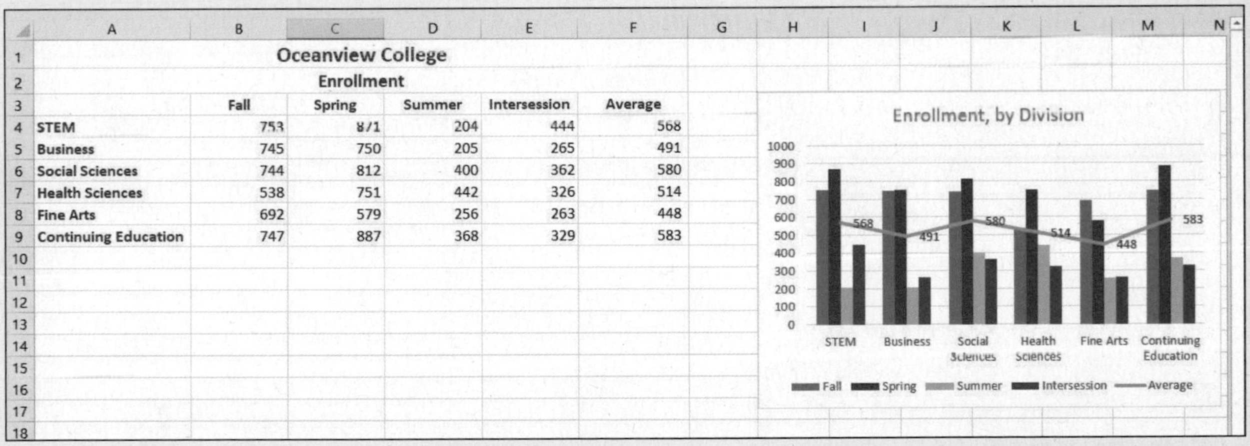

Oceanview College
Enrollment

	Fall	Spring	Summer	Intersession	Average
STEM	753	871	204	444	568
Business	745	750	205	265	491
Social Sciences	744	812	400	362	580
Health Sciences	538	751	442	326	514
Fine Arts	692	579	256	263	448
Continuing Education	747	887	368	329	583

Visual Workshop

Open IL_EX_4-5.xlsx from the location where you store your Data Files, then save it as **IL_EX_4_Insurance**. Create, modify, and position charts, including the sparklines, as shown in **FIGURE 4-29**. (*Hint:* Use the CTRL key as needed to select nonadjacent ranges.) You will need to make formatting, layout, and design changes once you create the charts. (*Hints:* The WordArt Style used in the pie chart title is Fill: Gold, Accent color 4: Soft Bevel. The WordArt Style used in the column chart title is Fill: Blue, Accent color 1: Shadow. The Life data point in the pie chart is exploded 30 degrees.) Enter your name in the center section of the footer, then save and preview the worksheet. Submit your work to your instructor as directed, then close the workbook and close Excel.

FIGURE 4-29

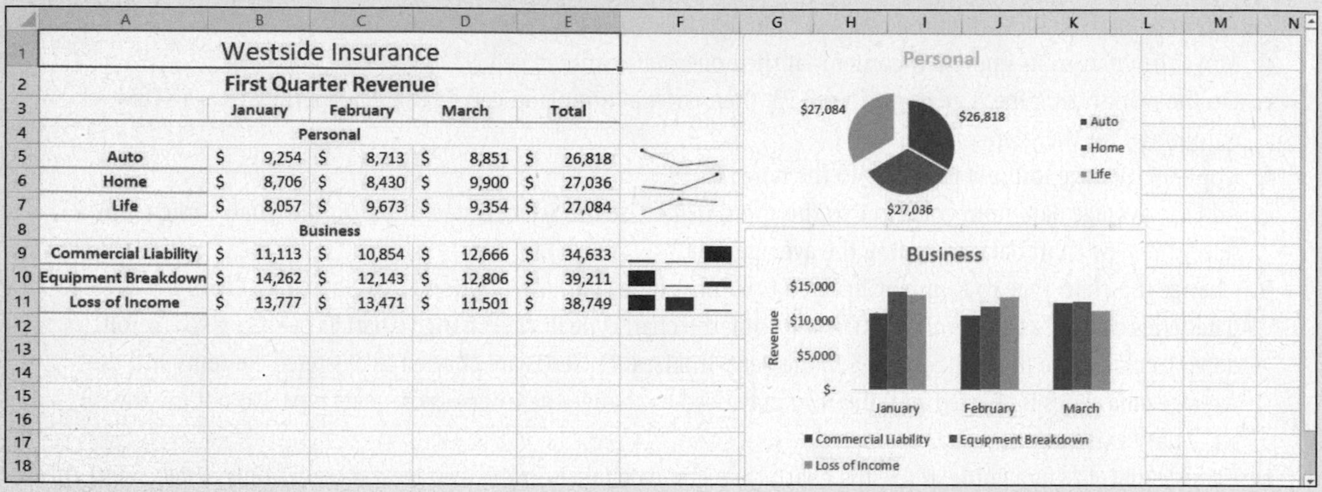

Westside Insurance				
First Quarter Revenue				
	January	February	March	Total
Personal				
Auto	$ 9,254	$ 8,713	$ 8,851	$ 26,818
Home	$ 8,706	$ 8,430	$ 9,900	$ 27,036
Life	$ 8,057	$ 9,673	$ 9,354	$ 27,084
Business				
Commercial Liability	$ 11,113	$ 10,854	$ 12,666	$ 34,633
Equipment Breakdown	$ 14,262	$ 12,143	$ 12,806	$ 39,211
Loss of Income	$ 13,777	$ 13,471	$ 11,501	$ 38,749

Integrating Word and Excel

CASE You are working with Lydia Snyder, the vice president of Operations for JCL Talent, Inc. Lydia has asked you to explore the integration capabilities of Microsoft Office. First, you create a report in Word that includes values and a chart that are created in Excel, and then you embed a paragraph of text that is created in Word into an Excel worksheet.

Module Objectives

After completing this module, you will be able to:

- Integrate data between Word and Excel
- Copy data from Excel to Word
- Copy a chart from Excel to Word
- Create linked objects
- Embed a Word file in Excel

Files You Will Need

IL_INT_1-1.xlsx	IL_INT_1-8.docx
IL_INT_1-2.docx	IL_INT_1-9.xlsx
IL_INT_1-3.xlsx	IL_INT_1-10.docx
IL_INT_1-4.docx	IL_INT_1-11.docx
IL_INT_1-5.xlsx	IL_INT_1-12.xlsx
IL_INT_1-6.docx	IL_INT_1-13.xlsx
IL_INT_1-7.xlsx	IL_INT_1-14.docx

Integration
Module 1

Learning Outcome
- Define copy/paste, link, and embed integration options

Integrate Data between Word and Excel

Office programs are designed to work together through a process called integration. **Integration** is the combining of objects and data from two or more applications using linking or embedding. When you integrate data from multiple Office programs, you work with both a source file and a destination file. The **source file** is the file in which you create an object that you will place in a destination file. The **destination file** is the file that displays an object from a source file. You can choose from three integration methods: pasting, linking, and embedding. **CASE** *Your work in the Operations division of JCL Talent often requires you to create documents such as reports and price lists that include data from both Word and Excel. You decide to review some of the ways in which you integrate data between the two programs.*

DETAILS

You can integrate Word and Excel by:

- **Copying and pasting data from the Clipboard**
  You use the Copy and Paste commands to duplicate objects such as text selections, numbers (called values in Excel), and pictures from one program and place them into another program. An **object** is the data to be exchanged between another document or program. After you copy and paste an object, changes that you make to the object in the source file do not appear in the destination file. The report shown in **FIGURE 1-1** was created in Word and includes two objects that were copied from Excel—the photograph that appears to the right of the document title and the shaded table under the document subtitle.

- **Linking data**
  Sometimes you want to connect the data that is included in two or more files. For example, suppose you copy the contents of a cell containing a formula from an Excel worksheet and paste it into a Word document. When you change the formula values in Excel, you want the corresponding values to change in the Word document. To create a **link**, or a connection between data in a source file and a destination file, you select one of the link options that appears when you either click the Paste button arrow or view options in the Paste Special dialog box. You use the term **linked object** to refer to a text selection, value, or picture that is contained in a destination file and linked to a source file. In the report shown in **FIGURE 1-1**, the value "90%" is a linked object. If this percentage changes in the Excel worksheet, the linked percentage in the Word document also changes.

- **Copying and pasting charts**
  When you copy a chart from Excel and paste it into Word using the Paste command, Word automatically creates a link between the pasted chart and the original chart. In the report shown in **FIGURE 1-1**, the column chart was copied from Excel and pasted into the Word document. When the chart values are updated in Excel, the same chart values are updated in the chart copied to Word. You can also copy a chart from the source file and then paste it into the destination file as an object that is not linked.

- **Embedding a Word file in Excel**
  You can **embed**, or place an unlinked copy of, the contents of a Word file into an Excel worksheet. You edit the embedded object by double-clicking it and using Word program tools to change text and formatting. This process changes the embedded copy of the Word object in Excel but does not affect the original source document you created in Word. Similarly, any changes to the source Word document are not reflected in the embedded copy in Excel. In the list shown in **FIGURE 1-2**, the text that describes current job trends was inserted in Excel as an embedded Word file.

FIGURE 1-1: Word report with objects copied from Excel

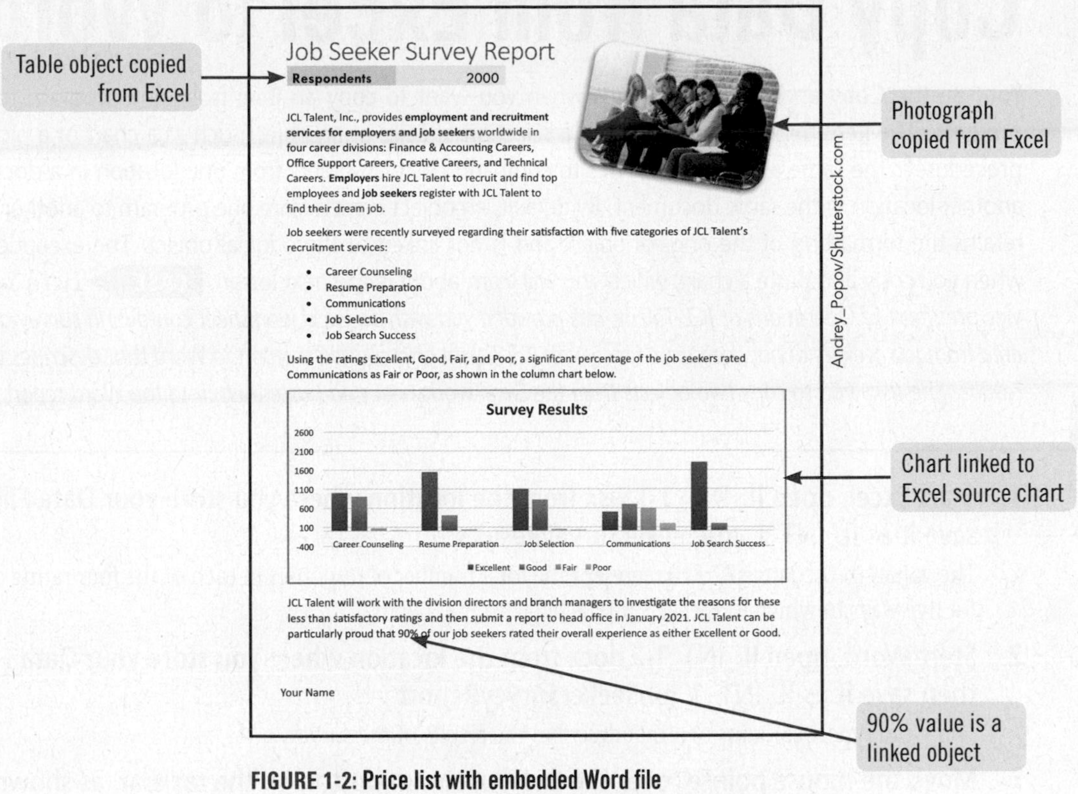

FIGURE 1-2: Price list with embedded Word file

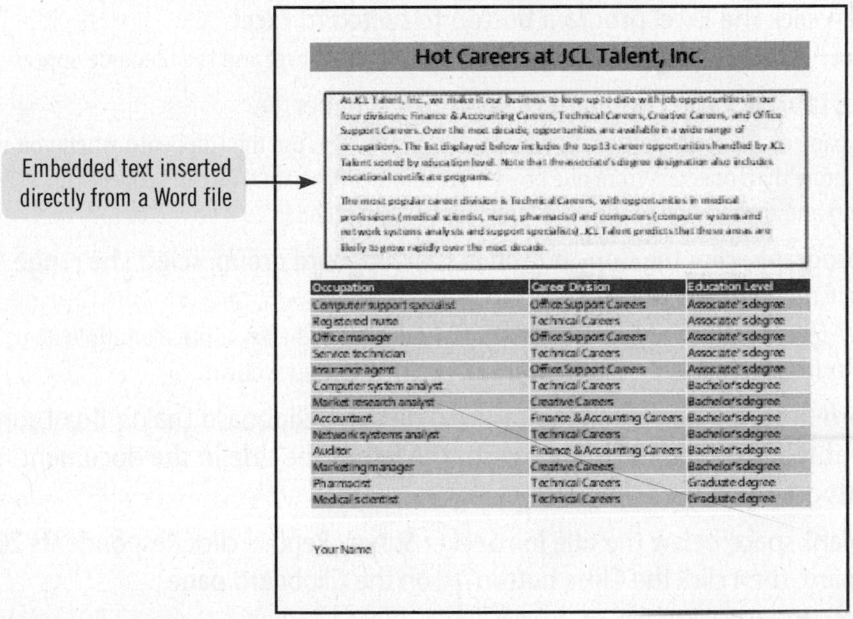

Occupation	Career Division	Education Level
Computer support specialist	Office Support Careers	Associate's degree
Registered nurse	Technical Careers	Associate's degree
Office manager	Office Support Careers	Associate's degree
Service technician	Technical Careers	Associate's degree
Insurance agent	Office Support Careers	Associate's degree
Computer system analyst	Technical Careers	Bachelor's degree
Market research analyst	Creative Careers	Bachelor's degree
Accountant	Finance & Accounting Careers	Bachelor's degree
Network systems analyst	Technical Careers	Bachelor's degree
Auditor	Finance & Accounting Careers	Bachelor's degree
Marketing manager	Creative Careers	Bachelor's degree
Pharmacist	Technical Careers	Graduate degree
Medical scientist	Technical Careers	Graduate degree

Understanding object linking and embedding (OLE)

The term **object linking and embedding (OLE)** refers to a technology that lets you share information among the Office programs. You create an object in one program, and then you can choose to either link the object to or embed it in another program. The difference between linking and embedding relates to where the object is stored and how you update the object after you place it in a document. A linked object in a destination file is an image of an object contained in a source file, not a copy of it. Both objects share a single source, which means you make changes to an object only in the source file.

When you embed an object that you created in another program, you include a copy of the object in a destination file. To update the object, you double-click it in the destination file and then use the tools of the source program to make changes. You cannot edit the source object using the tools of the destination program.

Copy Data from Excel to Word

Learning Outcomes
- Switch between Word and Excel
- Copy objects to the clipboard
- Paste Excel objects into Word

You use the Copy and Paste commands when you want to copy an item from one program to another program. The item might be a line of text, a selection of cells, or an object such as a chart or a picture. The procedure is the same as the one you use to copy and paste an object from one location in a document to another location in the same document. By default, an object copied from one program to another program retains the formatting of the original object and is not linked to the original object. The exception occurs when you copy and paste a chart, which you will learn about in the next lesson. **CASE** *Lydia Snyder, the vice president of Operations at JCL Talent, has provided you with an Excel worksheet containing survey data gathered from job seekers about their experience with JCL Talent and created a report in Word that describes the survey results. She asks you to copy two objects from the Excel worksheet and paste them into the Word report.*

STEPS

1. **Start Excel, open IL_INT_1-1.xlsx from the location where you store your Data Files, then save it as IL_INT_1_JobSeekerSurveyResults**

   The values in the range B7:F10 represent the total number of responses in each of the four rating categories for five ways in which job seekers interacted with JCL Talent.

2. **Start Word, open IL_INT_1-2.docx from the location where you store your Data Files, then save it as IL_INT_1_JobSeekerSurveyReport**

   The Word report contains text that describes the results of the survey.

3. **Move the mouse pointer over the Excel program button on the taskbar, as shown in FIGURE 1-3, then click the Excel program button to switch to Excel**

   When you point to the Excel program button, a picture of the worksheet and the filename appear.

TROUBLE
If items already appear in the Clipboard pane, click Clear All.

4. **On the Home tab, click the Clipboard Dialog Box Launcher**

   The Clipboard pane opens to the left of the worksheet window. You use the Clipboard when you want to copy and paste more than one item from one program to another program. You can "collect" up to 24 items on the Clipboard and then switch to the other program to paste them.

5. **Click the photograph, click the Copy button in the Clipboard group, select the range A4:B4, then click the Copy button**

   Both items now appear on the Clipboard, as shown in **FIGURE 1-4**. When you place multiple items on the Clipboard, newer items appear at the top of the list and older items move down.

6. **Click the Word program button on the taskbar, click the Clipboard Dialog Box Launcher, verify that the insertion point appears to the left of the title in the document, then click the photograph on the Clipboard**

7. **Click in the blank space below the title Job Seeker Survey Report, click Respondents 2000 on the Clipboard, then click the Close button on the Clipboard pane**

   You pasted the object as a table below the document title. When you use the Copy and Paste commands, the default setting is for the copied object to retain the formatting applied to it in the source file.

TROUBLE
If the alignment guides are not showing, click the Align button in the Arrange group, then click Use Alignment Guides.

8. **Click the photograph in the Word document, click the Layout Options button in the upper-right corner of the photograph, click the Square option, close the Layout Options window, then drag the photograph to the right of the first paragraph using the green alignment guides, as shown in FIGURE 1-5**

9. **Click anywhere in the document to deselect the photograph, then save the document**

FIGURE 1-3: Word and Excel on the taskbar

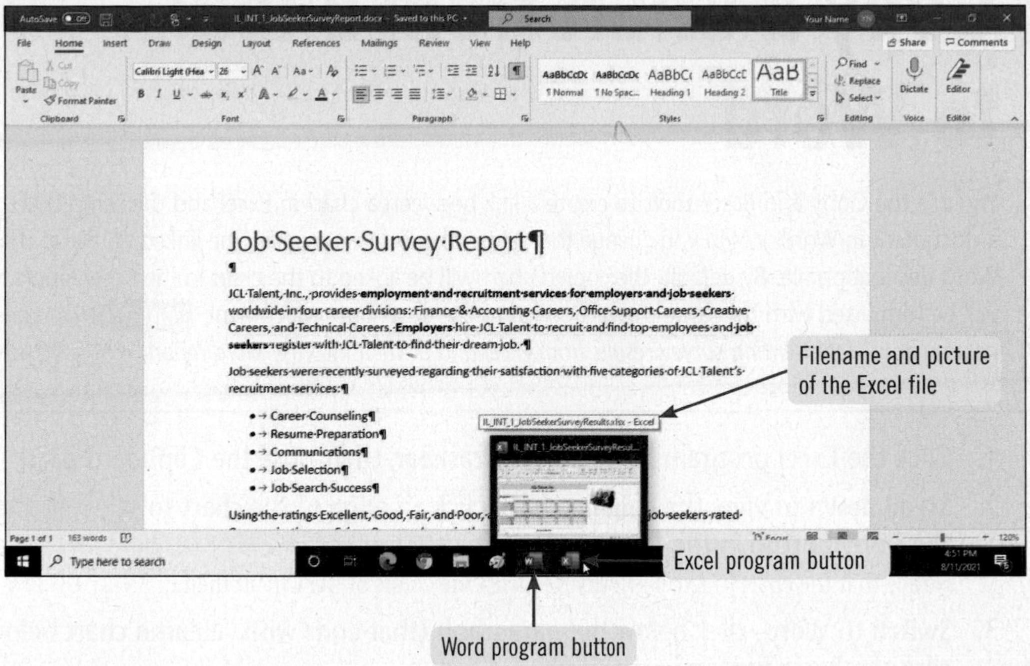

FIGURE 1-4: Two items collected on the Clipboard

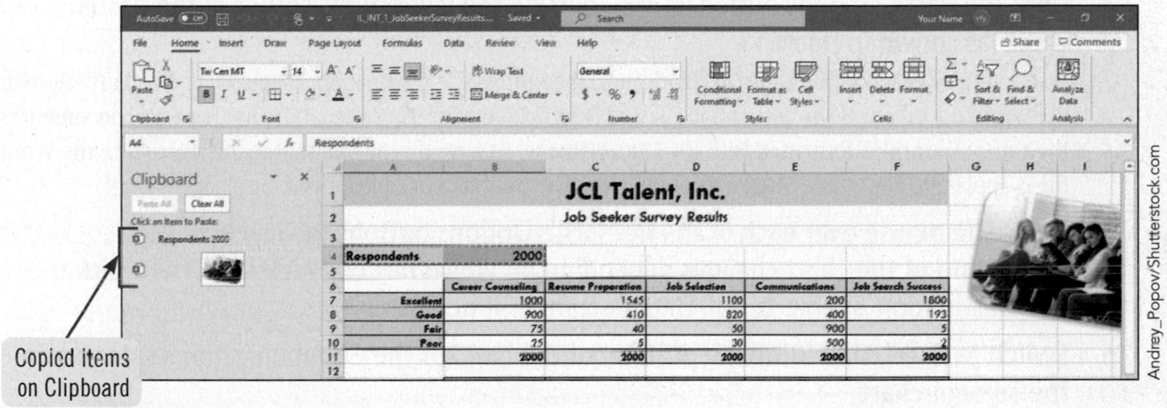

FIGURE 1-5: Picture positioned in the Word report

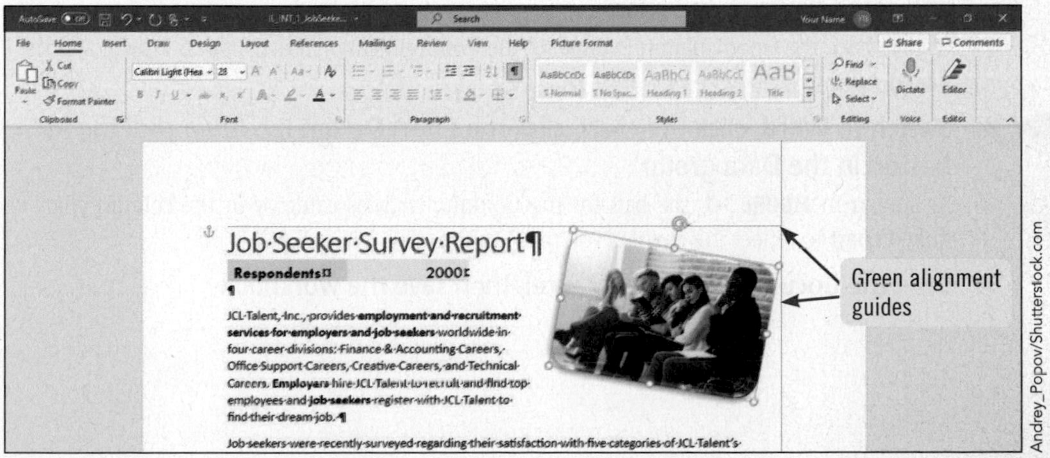

Integration
Module 1

Learning Outcomes
- Copy a chart
- View Paste options
- Update a linked chart

Copy a Chart from Excel to Word

You use the Copy and Paste tools to create a link between a chart in Excel and the same chart pasted into a document in Word. When you change the data in the Excel source file, the linked data also changes in the Word destination file. By default, the copied chart will be linked to the chart in the Excel report. However, it will be formatted with the same theme applied to the destination document. **CASE** *You need to copy a column chart representing survey results from Excel and paste it into the Word report.*

STEPS

1. **Click the Excel program button on the taskbar, then close the Clipboard pane**
2. **Scroll down to view the column chart, click an edge of the chart to select it, then click the Copy button in the Clipboard group**
   Notice that the chart in Excel is formatted with the colors of the Circuit theme.
3. **Switch to Word, click below the paragraph (that ends with "column chart below"), then click the Paste button in the Clipboard group**
   The chart appears in the Word document formatted with the colors of the Celestial theme because this theme was already applied to the Word document. The Paste Options button appears in the lower-right corner of the chart.
4. **Click the Paste Options button (Ctrl) outside the lower-right corner of the pasted chart, as shown in FIGURE 1-6**
   A selection of paste options appears. By default, the option Use Destination Theme & Link Data is selected. The Word document is the destination file and is formatted with the Celestial theme. The Excel document is the source file and is formatted with the Circuit theme. As a result, the Celestial theme applied to the Word file is applied to the chart. **TABLE 1-1** describes the five options available for pasting a copied chart.
5. **Move the mouse over each of the five Paste Options buttons to view how the formatting of the chart changes depending on which button is selected, then click the Use Destination Theme & Link Data button if necessary**
6. **Switch to Excel, then note the position of the bars for the Communications category in the column chart**
   At present, the Poor column (purple) is quite high compared to the Poor columns for the other categories.
7. **Scroll up, click cell E8, type 700, press ENTER, click cell E10, type 200, then press ENTER and scroll down to the chart**
   In the chart, the Good column (orange) in the Communications category has grown, and the Poor column has shrunk.
8. **Switch to Word, click the chart, click the Chart Design tab, then click the Refresh Data button in the Data group**
   As shown in **FIGURE 1-7**, the bars for the Communications category in the column chart change in the linked chart to reflect the changes you made to the chart in Excel.
9. **Save the document, switch to Excel, then save the workbook**

TROUBLE
You may not need to refresh the chart data.

FIGURE 1-6: Paste Options

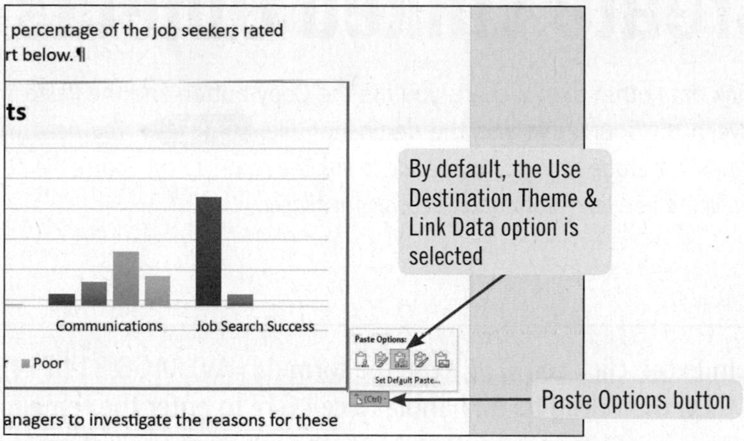

FIGURE 1-7: Linked chart updated in Word

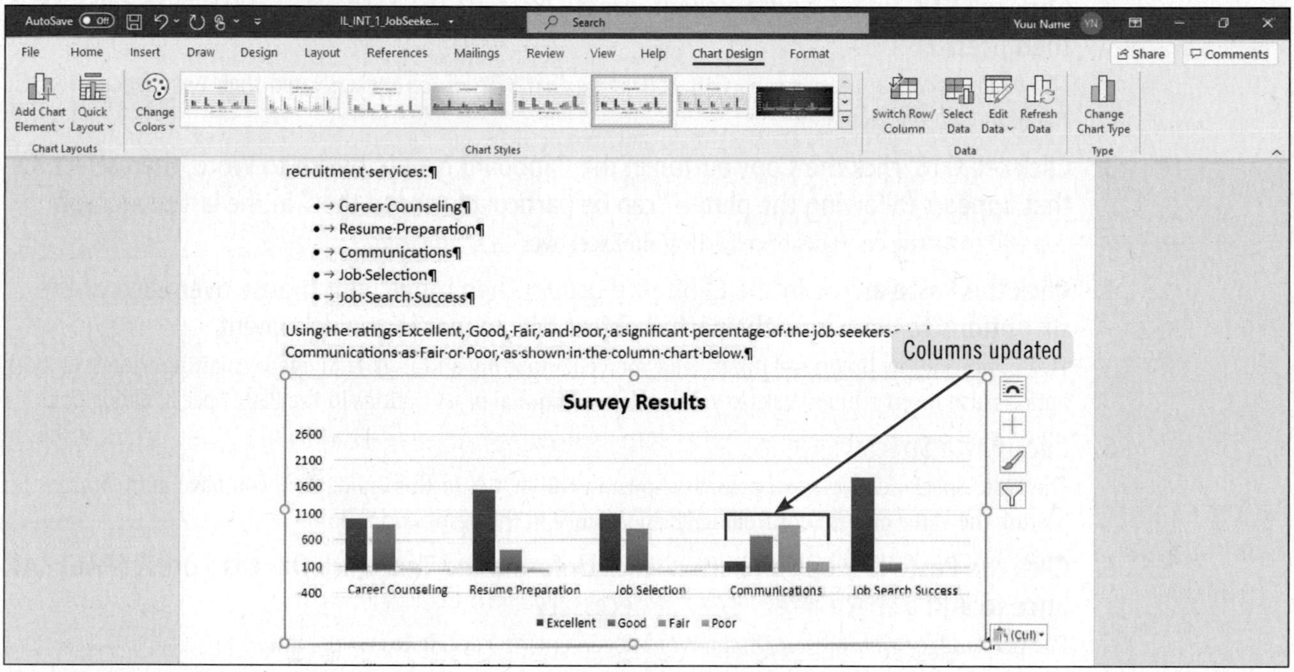

TABLE 1-1: Paste options for charts

Paste Options button	button name	description
	Use Destination Theme & Embed Workbook	The pasted chart is not linked to the source document, and the pasted chart assumes the formatting of the destination document
	Keep Source Formatting & Embed Workbook	The pasted chart is not linked to the source document, and the pasted chart keeps the same formatting as the source document
	Use Destination Theme & Link Data	This button is selected by default when a chart is pasted into the destination document; the theme of the destination document is applied to the chart, and the chart is linked to the object in the source document
	Keep Source Formatting & Link Data	The pasted chart is linked to the source document, so any changes made to the chart in the source document will be made to the copied chart in the Word document; in addition, the formatting of the source document is retained
	Picture	The chart is pasted as a picture that cannot be modified, and uses the same formatting as the chart in the source document

Create Linked Objects

Learning Outcomes
- Use Paste Special to create a link
- Update a linked object

To link data other than a chart, you use the Copy button and the Paste Special command to create a link between the source file and the destination file. **CASE** *You need your report to include a value that represents average ratings. You decide to link the report to the source file data so you can update the data in both files when new information becomes available.*

STEPS

1. **In Excel, click cell G14, type the formula =AVERAGE(B14:F14), press ENTER, click cell G14, then drag its fill handle to cell G17 to enter the remaining three percentages**
   The value "56%" appears in cell G14. This value indicates that, on average, 56% of the responses were Excellent. Only 3% of the responses were Poor.
2. **Click cell F18, type Good/Excellent, press TAB, type the formula =G14+G15 in cell G18, then press ENTER**
   The value "87%" appears in cell G18, indicating that 87% of job seekers rated their experience with JCL Talent as Good or Excellent.
3. **Click cell G18, click the Copy button in the Clipboard group, switch to Word, then select XX that appears following the phrase "can be particularly proud that" in the last paragraph**
   You will paste the contents of cell G18 from Excel over "XX" in Word.
4. **Click the Paste arrow in the Clipboard group, then move your mouse over each of the six options to view how the pasted object will appear in the document**
   Two options allow linking—Link & Keep Source Formatting and Link & Merge Formatting. However, both options also insert a line break, so you look for additional paste options in the Paste Special dialog box.
5. **Click Paste Special**
   The Paste Special dialog box opens, as shown in **FIGURE 1-8**. In this dialog box, you have more options for pasting the value and for controlling its appearance in the destination file.
6. **Click the Paste link option button, click Unformatted Text, click OK, then press SPACEBAR once to add a space after "87%" if necessary**
   The percentage, 87%, appears in the Word document. You decide to test the link.
7. **Switch to Excel, click cell E7, type 500, press ENTER, click cell E9, type 600, then press ENTER**
   The Good/Excellent rating in cell G18 is now 90%.
8. **Switch to Word, right-click 87%, then click Update Link**
   The value 90% appears. The final document is shown in **FIGURE 1-9**.
9. **Type your name where indicated in the Word footer, save the document, switch to Excel, type your name where indicated in cell A37, save the workbook, submit your files to your instructor, then close the files**
   If you print the Excel workbook, make sure you fit it on one page.

FIGURE 1-8: Paste Special dialog box

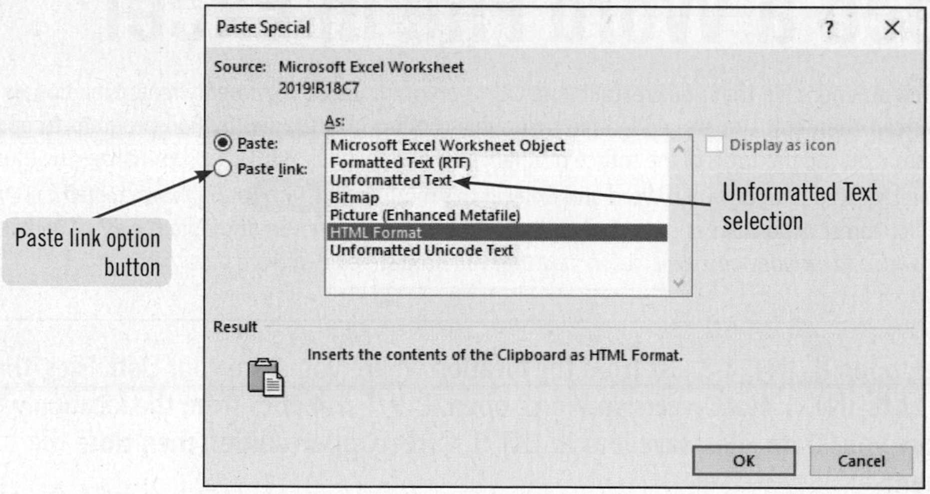

FIGURE 1-9: Completed report

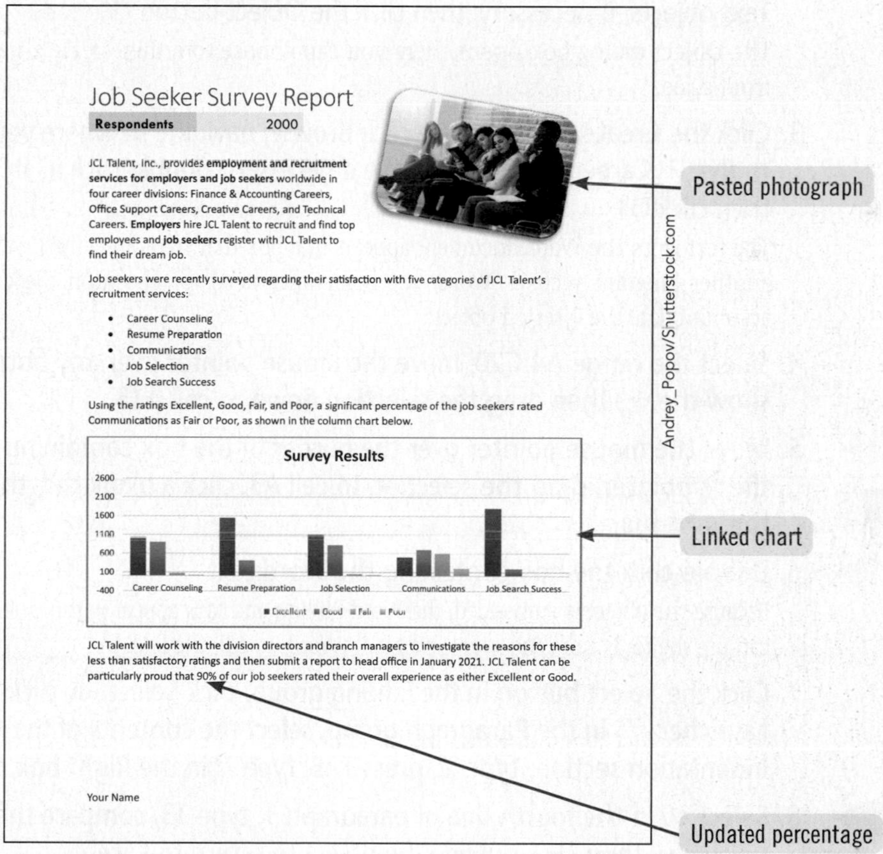

Opening linked files and reestablishing links to charts

When you open a Word file that contains links from an Excel file, a dialog box opens with a message telling you that the document contains links that may refer to other files. The message also asks if you want to update this document with the data from the linked file. Click Yes to update the document with data from the linked file. If you want to change information in both the Excel file and the Word file, you need to open the Excel workbook first, followed by the Word document.

If you make a change to a linked chart in the Excel file, you need to refresh the chart data in Word. To do so, click the chart in Word, click the Chart Design tab, then click the Refresh Data button in the Data group. You also need to manually update any other links by right-clicking the link in Word and then clicking Update Link.

Integration
Module 1

Embed a Word File in Excel

Learning Outcomes
- Insert a Word file as an object
- Edit the Word file in Excel

You can embed an entire file that you create in one Office program into a document created in another Office program. You can then edit the embedded file by double-clicking it in the destination program to open the source program. You use the tools of the source program to make changes. **TABLE 1-2** summarizes the four ways in which you integrated data between Word and Excel in this module. **CASE** *You have created a list in Excel that includes hot career opportunities currently handled by JCL Talent. Before you distribute the list at an upcoming meeting, you decide to include some explanatory text that you have stored in a Word document.*

STEPS

1. **In Excel, open IL_INT_1-3.xlsx from the location where you store your Data Files, then save it as IL_INT_1_HotCareers; in Word, open IL_INT_1-4.docx from the location where you store your Data Files, save it as IL_INT_1_CareerOpportunities, then close the document**
2. **In Excel, click cell E3, click the Insert tab, click the Text button to display the selection of Text objects, if necessary, then click the Object button**
   The Object dialog box opens. Here you can choose to either create a new object or insert an object from a file.
3. **Click the Create from File tab, click Browse, navigate to where you stored the IL_INT_1_CareerOpportunities file if necessary, double-click IL_INT_1_CareerOpportunities, then click OK**
   The text from the Word document appears in a box that starts in cell E3. When you insert an object from another program such as Word, you sometimes need to reposition the current worksheet contents to accommodate the inserted object.
4. **Select the range A4:C20, move the mouse pointer over any border of the selection to show the , then drag the selection down to cell A15**
5. **Move the mouse pointer over the border of the box containing the Word text to show the pointer, drag the selection to cell A3, click a blank cell, then compare your screen to FIGURE 1-10**
6. **Double-click the box containing the Word text**
   Because the object is embedded, the Word Ribbon and tabs appear within the Excel window. As a result, you can use the tools from the source program (Word) to edit the text.
7. **Click the Select button in the Editing group, click Select All, click the Dialog Box Launcher in the Paragraph group, select the contents of the Left box in the Indentation section, type .2, press TAB, type .2 in the Right box, then click OK**
8. **Select 10 in the fourth line of paragraph 1, type 13, compare the edited object to FIGURE 1-11, then click outside the object to return to Excel**
   The embedded object is updated in Excel. The text in the source file is not updated because the source file is not linked to the destination file.
9. **Click the File tab, click Print, click Page Setup, (you may need to scroll down the Print dialog box), click the Margins tab, click the Horizontally check box, click OK, then click to return to the workbook**
   The embedded Word object and Excel data are centered between the left and right margins of the page.
10. **Type your name where indicated in cell A31, save the workbook, submit your files to your instructor, then close the workbook and close Word and Excel**

TROUBLE
If your embedded Word document opens in a separate window, proceed with the steps, and at the end of Step 8, close the Word window.

TROUBLE
If a space does not appear between "top" and "13" in the embedded object, return to Word and add an extra space.

FIGURE 1-10: Embedded Word file positioned in Excel

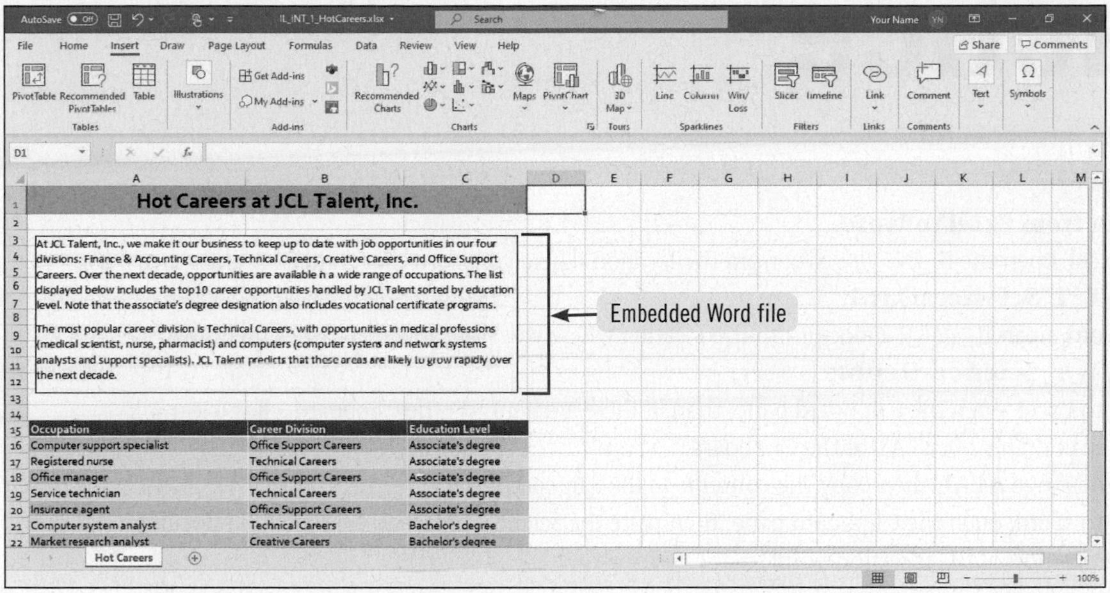

FIGURE 1-11: Embedded object updated in Excel

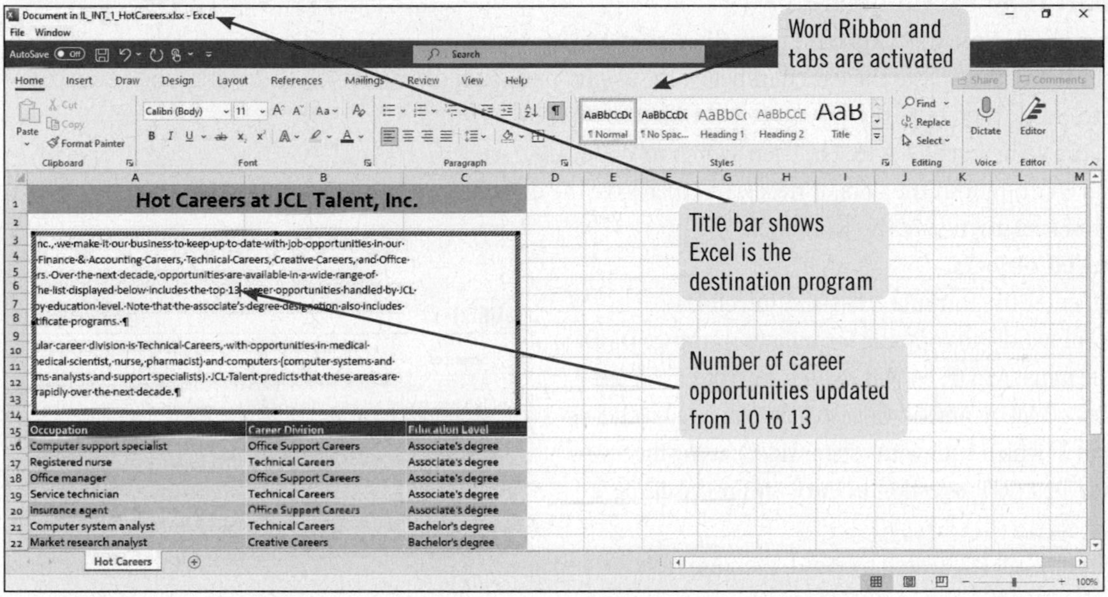

TABLE 1-2: Module 1 integration tasks

object	command	source program	destination program	result	connection	page no.
Cells	Copy/Paste	Excel	Word	Object with Excel formatting	Pasted: no link	4
Chart	Copy/Paste	Excel	Word	Object with Word formatting	Linked	6
Cell	Copy/Paste Special/Paste link	Excel	Word	Formatting varies depending on the formatting option chosen in the Paste Special dialog box	Linked	8
File	Insert/Object/ Create from File	Word	Excel	Text box containing the Word file: to update, double-click and use Word tools within the Excel destination file	Embedded: no link	10

Practice

Skills Review

1. Copy data from Excel to Word.

a. Start Excel, open the IL_INT_1-5.xlsx from the location where you store your Data Files, then save it as **IL_INT_1_SciencesData**.

b. Start Word, open IL_INT_1-6.docx from the location where you store your Data Files, then save it as **IL_INT_1_SciencesReport**.

c. Switch to Excel, open the Clipboard pane, then, if there are items on the Clipboard, click Clear All.

d. Copy the contents of cell A1 to the Clipboard.

e. Select the range A4:A7, then copy the contents to the Clipboard.

f. Switch to Word, open the Clipboard pane, then paste the Sciences object at the top of the document (at the current position of the insertion point).

g. Paste the subject areas object on the blank line below the first paragraph.

h. Close the Clipboard pane, then save the document.

2. Copy a chart from Excel to Word.

a. Switch to Excel, close the Clipboard pane, then copy the bar chart.

b. Switch to Word, then paste the bar chart below the second paragraph of text (which ends with "and State scores").

c. Switch to Excel, then note the position of the bars for Physics.

d. Change the value in cell C4 to **70**, then switch to Word.

e. Click the chart, refresh the data, if necessary, then save the document.

f. Switch to Excel, then save the workbook.

3. Create linked objects.

a. In Excel, enter the formula **=B4-C4** in cell D4.

b. Use the Fill handle to copy the formula to the range D5:D7.

c. Select the range A3:D7, copy it, switch to Word, then use the Paste Special command to paste the cells as a link below paragraph 3 (which ends with "state-wide"), using the Formatted Text (RTF) selection in the Paste Special dialog box.

d. In Excel, copy cell D7, switch to Word, then use Paste Special to paste the cell over "XX" in the last paragraph as a link using the Unformatted Text option in the Paste Special dialog box. Add a space after the linked object if necessary.

e. In Excel, change the value in cell B7 to **90**.

f. In Word, refresh the chart if necessary.

g. Update the link in the table and the link in the last paragraph so that "20" appears in both places.

h. Enter your name where indicated in the footer in Word, compare your document to **FIGURE 1-12** and adjust spacing if necessary, save the Word report, submit your file to your instructor, then close the document.

i. In Excel, enter your name in cell A26, save the workbook, submit the file to your instructor, then close the workbook.

FIGURE 1-12

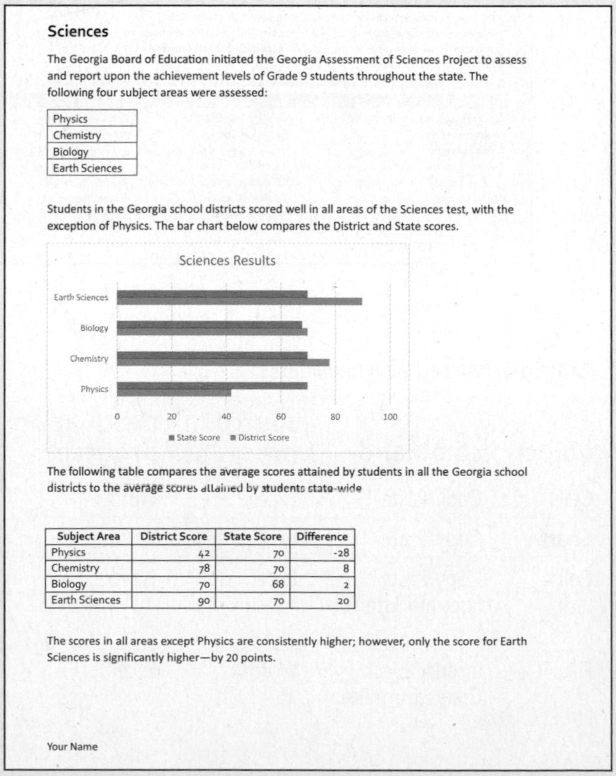

Sciences

The Georgia Board of Education initiated the Georgia Assessment of Sciences Project to assess and report upon the achievement levels of Grade 9 students throughout the state. The following four subject areas were assessed:

Physics
Chemistry
Biology
Earth Sciences

Students in the Georgia school districts scored well in all areas of the Sciences test, with the exception of Physics. The bar chart below compares the District and State scores.

The following table compares the average scores attained by students in all the Georgia school districts to the average scores attained by students state-wide

Subject Area	District Score	State Score	Difference
Physics	42	70	-28
Chemistry	78	70	8
Biology	70	68	2
Earth Sciences	90	70	20

The scores in all areas except Physics are consistently higher; however, only the score for Earth Sciences is significantly higher—by 20 points.

Your Name

Skills Review (continued)

4. Embed a Word file in Excel.

a. In Excel, open IL_INT_1-7.xlsx from the location where you store your Data Files, then save it as **IL_INT_1_LanguageCourseRevenue**.

b. In Word, open IL_INT_1-8.docx from the location where you store your Data Files, save it as **IL_INT_1_LanguageCourses**, then close it.

c. In Excel, in cell H4, insert the Word file IL_INT_1_LanguageCourses.docx as an embedded file.

d. Select the range A6:F16, then move it to cell A12.

e. Position the box containing the Word text so its upper-left corner is in cell A4.

f. Change "XX" to **$65** in paragraph 1 and add two spaces between "just" and "$65" if necessary, then change "ZZ" in paragraph 1 to **80%**.

g. Click outside the embedded object to return to Excel, adjust the size of the embedded file if necessary, compare your screen to **FIGURE 1-13**, enter your name in cell A22, save the workbook, submit the file to your instructor, then close the workbook and close Word and Excel.

FIGURE 1-13

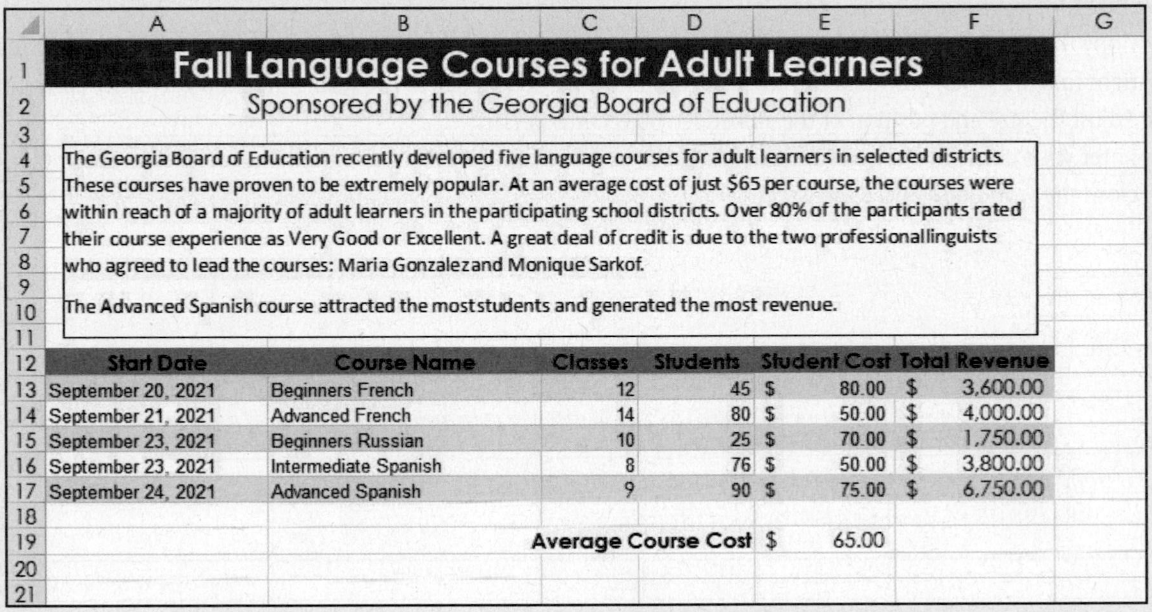

Fall Language Courses for Adult Learners

Sponsored by the Georgia Board of Education

The Georgia Board of Education recently developed five language courses for adult learners in selected districts. These courses have proven to be extremely popular. At an average cost of just $65 per course, the courses were within reach of a majority of adult learners in the participating school districts. Over 80% of the participants rated their course experience as Very Good or Excellent. A great deal of credit is due to the two professionallinguists who agreed to lead the courses: Maria Gonzalezand Monique Sarkof.

The Advanced Spanish course attracted the moststudents and generated the most revenue.

Start Date	Course Name	Classes	Students	Student Cost	Total Revenue
September 20, 2021	Beginners French	12	45	$ 80.00	$ 3,600.00
September 21, 2021	Advanced French	14	80	$ 50.00	$ 4,000.00
September 23, 2021	Beginners Russian	10	25	$ 70.00	$ 1,750.00
September 23, 2021	Intermediate Spanish	8	76	$ 50.00	$ 3,800.00
September 24, 2021	Advanced Spanish	9	90	$ 75.00	$ 6,750.00
		Average Course Cost		$ 65.00	

Integration

Independent Challenge 1

You assist the office manager at Riverwalk Medical Clinic, a large outpatient medical facility that provides a wide range of medical and health services and programs to community members. One of the programs trains young volunteers to assist with patient care. You have collected data about two volunteer programs in an Excel workbook. Now you need to prepare the workbook for distribution at an upcoming meeting of management staff at the clinic who are interested in expanding the programs. You want to include text in the workbook that you have stored in a Word document.

a. Start Excel, open IL_INT_1-9.xlsx from the location where you store your Data Files, then save it as **IL_INT_1_RiverwalkClinicVolunteerProgram**.

b. Start Word, open IL_INT_1-10.docx from the location where you store your Data Files, save it as **IL_INT_1_VolunteerInformation**, then close it.

c. In a blank area of the Excel worksheet, insert the Volunteer Information file as an embedded object.

d. Adjust the positions of the Excel data and the box containing the Word text so the Word text appears above the Excel data and below the title.

e. In Excel, calculate the total enrollment for the Patient Care and Nutrition programs in the appropriate cells.

f. To the right of the "Nutrition Program" cell, enter and format **Total** to match the formatting for "Patient Care Program" and "Nutrition Program," then calculate the total enrollment for both programs for each year and the total for all programs in all years.

g. Copy the Total enrollment value, edit the embedded Word document so the text is indented by .3" from the left and right margins, then paste the correct total enrollment figure to replace "XX" using the Keep Text Only paste option. Adjust the size and position of the embedded object as necessary.

h. Enter your name in the cell indicated in Excel, save the Excel workbook, submit the file to your instructor, then close the workbook and close Excel.

Independent Challenge 2

As a member of the Beaver Island Arts Commission in Washington State, you are responsible for compiling the minutes of the commission's quarterly meetings. You have already written most of the text required for the minutes. Now you need to insert data from Excel that shows how much money was raised from various fundraising activities.

- **a.** Start Word, open IL_INT_1-11.docx from the location where you store your Data Files, save it as **IL_INT_1_BeaverIslandArtsCommissionMinutes**, start Excel, open IL_INT_1-12.xlsx from the location where you store your Data Files, then save it as **IL_INT_1_BeaverIslandData**.
- **b.** In Excel, open the Clipboard pane, clear all items if necessary, then copy the photograph and cell A2.
- **c.** In Word, open the Clipboard pane, paste the photograph at the top of the Word document, change the text wrapping of the picture to Square, then position the photograph to the right of the first paragraph, keeping within the green guidelines.
- **d.** Click to the left of "Approval of Minutes," then paste cell A2.
- **e.** Copy the Fundraising Revenue chart from Excel, then paste it in the appropriate area in the Word document.
- **f.** In Excel, change the number of participants in the bake sale to **1000**; then in Word, refresh the data in the chart if necessary. The Bake Sale slice should be 60%.
- **g.** In Excel, copy the figure representing the funds raised for the Bake Sale in cell E7, switch to Word, select "XX" in the paragraph below the chart, view the paste options, then paste the value as a link using the Unformatted Text selection in the Paste Special dialog box. Add a space if necessary.
- **h.** In Excel, click cell G7, then calculate the total funds raised by adding the contents of the range B7:F7.
- **i.** In cell B8, enter the formula **=B7/G7**, use [F4] to make cell G7 absolute, then copy the formula to the range C8:F8.
- **j.** Copy cell E8, switch to Word, select "ZZ" in the paragraph below the chart, then paste the value as a link using the Unformatted Text selection, adding a space if necessary.
- **k.** In Excel, change the number of participants in the bake sale to **1200**; then in Word, verify the Bake Sale slice changed to 64% and the links updated to $60,000 and 64%. If the links do not update automatically, right-click them and click Update Link in the Word document.
- **l.** Type your name in the Word footer, then save the Word document and Excel workbook, submit the files to your instructor, then close them.

Visual Workshop

Using the Data Files IL_INT_1-13.xlsx and IL_INT_1-14.docx, create the price list shown in **FIGURE 1-14**. Use formulas to calculate the prices for two-packs and four-packs. Save the workbook as **IL_INT_1_GardenGourmetPriceList**, and save the Word document as **IL_INT_1_GardenGourmetInformation**. Embed the Word document into the Excel worksheet, position the inserted file and the price list in Excel as shown in **FIGURE 1-14**, then format the embedded Word object as shown in **FIGURE 1-14**. (*Hint*: The indentation on both sides of the text is .3, and the font size is 12 point.) Add your name to the Excel worksheet in the cell indicated, save all files, submit them to your instructor, then close all files.

FIGURE 1-14

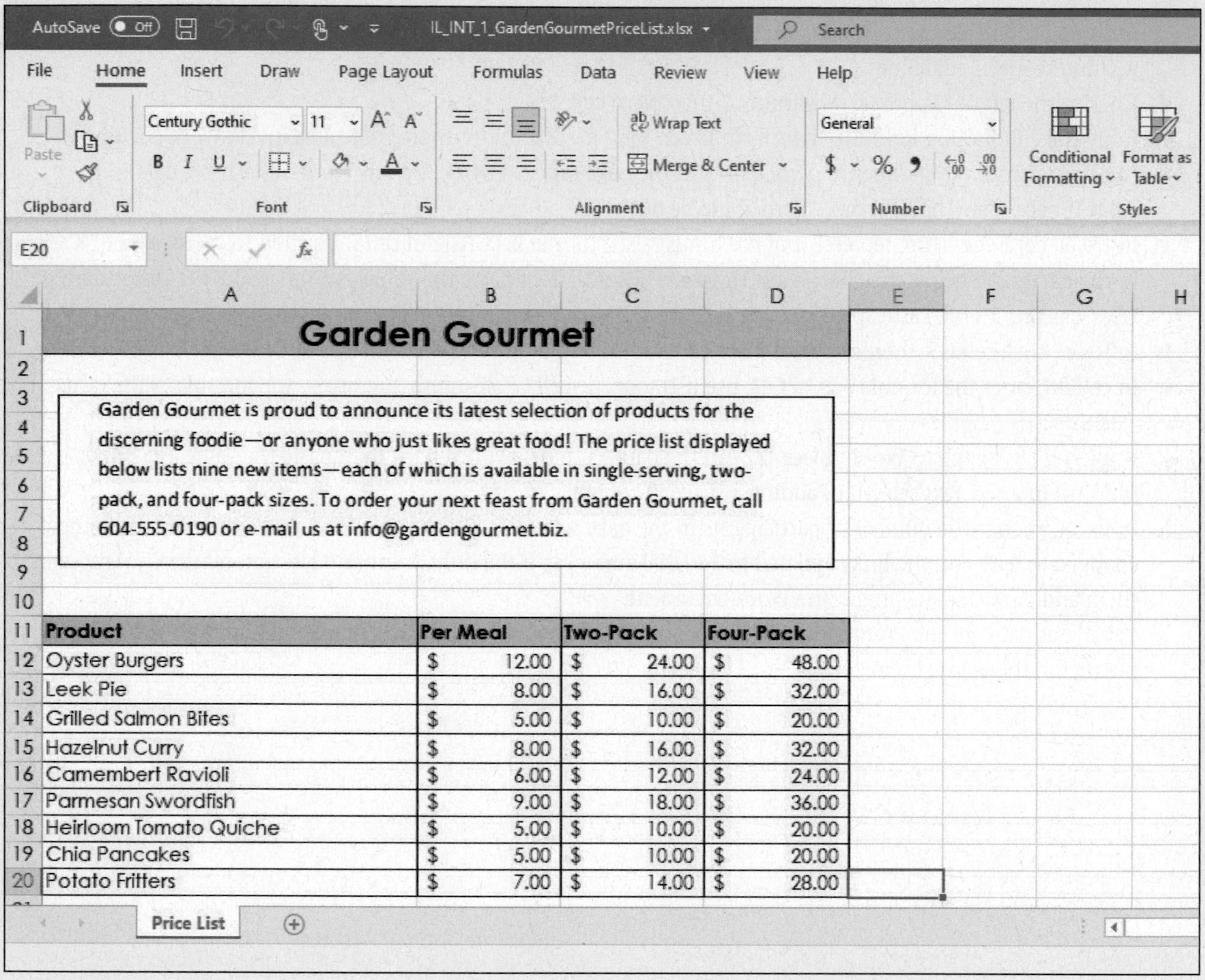

Getting Started with Access

CASE Lydia Snyder is the vice president of operations for JCL Talent, a company that provides recruitment and employment services for employers and job seekers. You will work with Lydia to use Microsoft Access 2019 to store, maintain, and analyze job placement data.

Module Objectives

After completing this module, you will be able to:

- Understand relational databases
- Open and explore a database
- Navigate and enter data
- Edit existing data
- Create a table
- Modify fields
- Create a query
- Create a form
- Create a report
- Save and share a database with OneDrive
- Create a new database
- Compact and back up a database

Files You Will Need

IL_AC_1-1.accdb
Support_IL_AC_1_Employees.xlsx
IL_AC_1-2.accdb
Support_IL_AC_1_StatesAndProvs.xlsx
IL_AC_1-3.accdb
IL_AC_1-4.accdb

Understand Relational Databases

Learning Outcomes
- Describe relational database concepts
- Explain when to use a database
- Compare a relational database to a spreadsheet

Microsoft Access 2019 is relational database software that runs on the Windows operating system. You use **relational database software** to manage data organized into lists, such as information about customers, products, vendors, employees, projects, or sales. Some companies track lists of information in a spreadsheet program such as Microsoft Excel. Although Excel offers some list management features, Access provides many more tools and advantages for managing data. Access uses a relational database model to manage data, whereas Excel manages data as a single list. **TABLE 1-1** compares the two programs. **CASE** *Lydia has noticed that JCL Talent manages multiple copies of several lists of data in Excel. She asks you to help her review the advantages of managing data in a relational database model used by Access as compared to the single list spreadsheet approach used by Excel.*

DETAILS

The advantages of using Access for database management include the following:

- **Duplicate data is minimized**

  FIGURES 1-1 and **1-2** compare how you might store data in a single list in an Excel spreadsheet versus managing the same data using three tables in an Access relational database. With Access, you enter company data only once no matter how many jobs that company has to offer.

- **Information is more accurate, reliable, and consistent because duplicate data is minimized**

  When data is not duplicated, it is more accurate, reliable, and consistent.

- **Data entry is faster and easier using Access forms**

  Data entry forms (screen layouts) make data entry faster, easier, and more accurate than entering data in a spreadsheet.

- **Information can be viewed and sorted in many ways using Access queries, forms, and reports**

  In Access, you can save multiple queries (questions about the data), data entry forms, and reports, allowing different users to view the same data in different ways.

- **Information is more secure using Access forms, passwords, and security features**

  Access databases can be encrypted and password protected. Forms can be created to protect and display specific data.

- **Several users can share and edit information at the same time**

  Unlike spreadsheets or word-processing documents, more than one person can enter, update, and analyze data in an Access database at the same time. This also means that you are not tempted to create copies that inevitably become inaccurate because of the difficulties of updating multiple copies of the same data. Having all users work on the same, single set of data at the same time is enormously accurate and reliable.

FIGURE 1-1: Using a spreadsheet to organize data

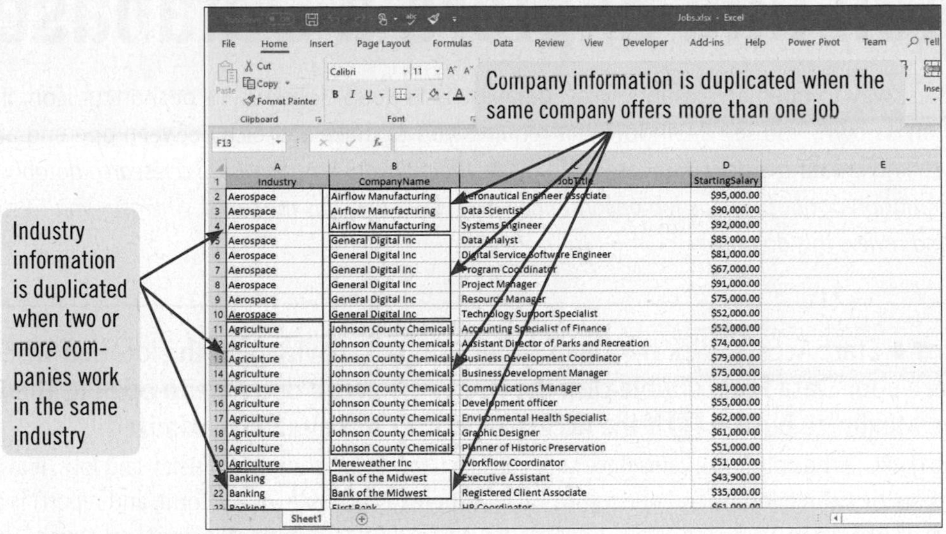
Company information is duplicated when the same company offers more than one job
Industry information is duplicated when two or more companies work in the same industry

FIGURE 1-2: Using a relational database to organize data

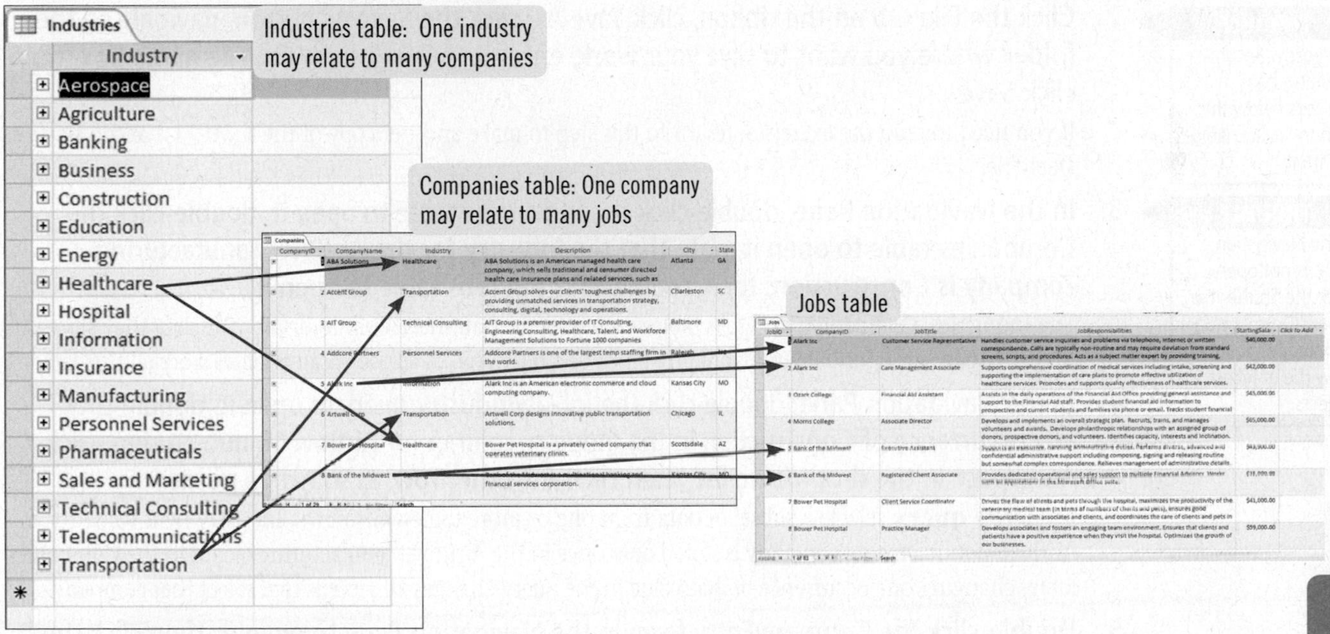
Industries table: One industry may relate to many companies
Companies table: One company may relate to many jobs
Jobs table

TABLE 1-1: Comparing Excel with Access

feature	Excel	Access
Data entry	Provides only one spreadsheet layout	Provides the ability to create an unlimited number of data entry forms
Storage	Restricted to a single file's limitations	Virtually unlimited when coupled with the ability to use Microsoft SQL Server to store data
Data model	Manages single lists of information	Manages data in a relational database with related tables, which tremendously reduces data redundancy and improves data integrity
Reporting	Provides a printout of the spreadsheet	Provides the ability to create and save an unlimited number of reports that summarize and organize data in different ways
Security	Limited to file security options such as marking the file "read-only" or protecting a range of cells	When used with SQL Server, provides extensive security down to the user and data level
Multiuser capabilities	Limited to one user at a time	Allows multiple users to simultaneously enter and update data

Open and Explore a Database

Learning Outcomes
- Start Access
- Save a database
- Explore objects

The fastest way to open an existing Access database is to double-click its file or shortcut icon. If you start Access on its own, you see a window that requires you to make a choice between opening an existing database and creating a new database. **CASE** *Lydia Snyder has developed a research database containing information about previous job opportunities that JCL Talent has managed. She asks you to start Access 2019 and review this database.*

STEPS

1. **sam Start Access, click the Open Other Files link, navigate to the location where you store your Data Files, double-click the IL_AC_1-1.accdb database to open it, then click the Maximize button if the Access window is not already maximized**

   The IL_AC_1-1 database contains three tables of data named Companies, Industries, and Jobs. It also includes two queries, three forms, and one report. Each of these items (table, query, form, and report) is a different type of **object** in an Access database application and is displayed in the **Navigation Pane**. The purpose of each object is defined in TABLE 1-2.

> **TROUBLE**
> If a yellow Security Warning bar appears below the ribbon, click Enable Content.

2. **Click the File tab on the ribbon, click Save As, click the Save As button, navigate to the folder where you want to save your work, enter IL_AC_1_Jobs in the File name box, then click Save**

   If you need to redo the exercises, return to this step to make another copy of the IL_AC_1-1.accdb starting Data File.

> **TROUBLE**
> If the Navigation Pane is not open, click the Shutter Bar Open/Close button « to open it and view the database objects.

3. **In the Navigation Pane, double-click the Industries table to open it, double-click the Companies table to open it, note that the Industry for the Airflow Manufacturing company is Construction, then double-click the Jobs table to open it**

   The Industries, Companies, and Jobs tables each open in Datasheet View to display the data they store. An Access **table** is the fundamental building block of a relational database because tables store all the data.

4. **In the Navigation Pane, double-click the JobsByIndustry query to open it, double-click any occurrence of Construction in the Industry column for Airflow Manufacturing, click Aerospace in the drop-down list, then click any other row, as shown in FIGURE 1-3**

   An Access **query** selects a subset of data from one or more tables. Given the Industry field value for the Airflow Manufacturing company is stored only once in the Airflow Manufacturing record in the Companies table, changing one occurrence of that value in the query changes all records that select that company.

5. **Double-click the CompanyEntry form in the Navigation Pane to open it, then click the Next button in the upper-right corner of the form three times**

   An Access **form** is a data entry screen that often includes command buttons to make common tasks such as moving between records easy to perform. Forms are the most common way to enter and edit data. Note that Airflow Manufacturing's Industry value is Aerospace, which reflects the change you made to Airflow Manufacturing in the JobsByIndustry query.

6. **Double-click the JobsByHighestSalary report in the Navigation Pane to open it, then scroll down to see Airflow Manufacturing**

   An Access **report** is a professional printout that can be distributed electronically or on paper. The Aerospace update to Airflow Manufacturing carried through to the report, demonstrating the power and productivity of a relational database.

7. **Right-click each object tab (except for the Companies table), click Close on the shortcut menu, notice that the Industry for Airflow Manufacturing is now set to Aerospace in the Companies table, then close it**

   Changes to data are automatically saved as you work.

FIGURE 1-3: IL_AC_1_Jobs.accdb database

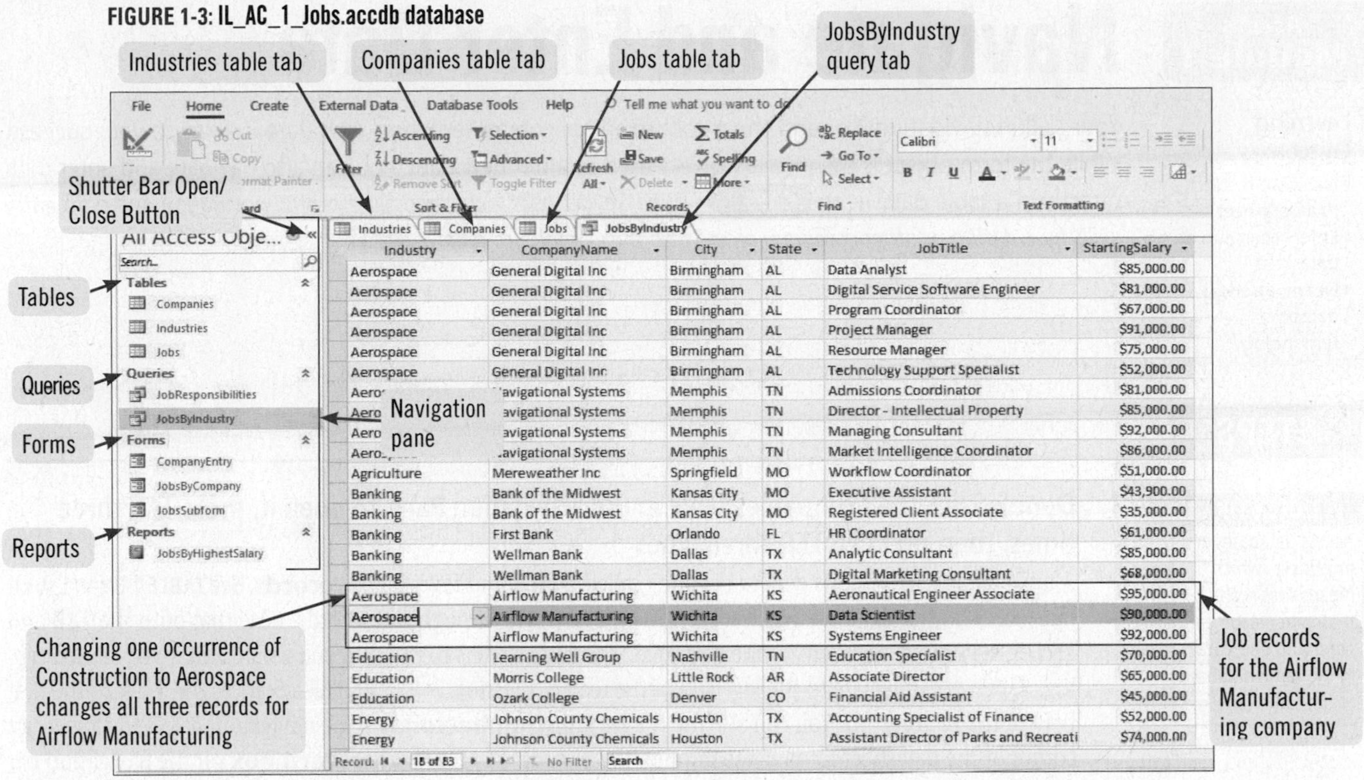

TABLE 1-2: Access objects and their purpose

object	icon	purpose
Table		Contains all the data within the database in a spreadsheet-like view called **Datasheet View**; tables are linked with a common field to create a relational database
Query		Allows you to select a subset of fields or records from one or more tables; create a query when you have a question about the data
Form		Provides an easy-to-use data entry screen
Report		Provides a professional presentation of data with headers, footers, graphics, and calculations on groups of records

Navigate and Enter Data

Learning Outcomes
- Navigate records in a datasheet
- Enter records in a datasheet
- Define essential database terminology

Your skill in navigating through the database and accurately entering new data is a key to your success. While the form object is the primary object used to enter new data, you can also navigate and enter data directly in a table datasheet. **CASE** *Lydia Snyder asks you to master essential navigation and data entry skills by entering another company record into the Companies table.*

STEPS

QUICK TIP
Access databases are **multiuser**, which means that more than one person can enter and edit data in the same database at the same time!

1. **Double-click the Companies table in the Navigation Pane to open it, press TAB three times, then press ENTER three times**
   A table datasheet presents data in columns called **fields** and rows called **records**. See **TABLE 1-3** for a summary of essential database terminology. As you navigate through the records, note that both the TAB and ENTER keys move the focus to the next field. The **focus** refers to the data you would edit if you started typing. When you navigate to the last field of the record, pressing TAB or ENTER advances the focus to the first field of the next record. You can also use the **navigation buttons** on the navigation bar in the lower-left corner of the datasheet to navigate through the records. The **Current record box** on the navigation bar tells you the number of the current record as well as the total number of records in the datasheet. You use the navigation bar to practice record navigation.

2. **Click the Next record button ▶ on the navigation bar, click the Previous record button ◀, click the Last record button ▶|, click the First record button |◀, then click the New (blank) record button ▶* on the navigation bar to move to a new record**
   You navigate to and enter new records at the end of the datasheet. A complete list of navigation keystrokes is shown in **TABLE 1-4**.

QUICK TIP
Press TAB in the CompanyID AutoNumber field.

3. **At the end of the datasheet, enter the new record, as shown in FIGURE 1-4**
   The CompanyName is Jigsaw Company, the Industry is Information, the Description is Jigsaw provides big data mining, analytics, and forecasting tools and services, the City is Dayton, and the State is OH
   The **edit record symbol** ✎ appears to the left of the record you are currently editing. When you move to a different record, Access automatically saves the data.

   Your CompanyID value might differ from the one in **FIGURE 1-4**. The CompanyID field is an **AutoNumber** field, which means that Access automatically enters the next consecutive number into the field as it creates the record. If you delete a record or are interrupted when entering a record, Access discards the value in the AutoNumber field and does not reuse it. Therefore, AutoNumber values do not represent the number of records in your table. Instead, they only provide a unique value per record.

Changing from Navigation mode to Edit mode

If you navigate to another area of the datasheet by clicking with the mouse pointer instead of pressing TAB or ENTER, you change from Navigation mode to Edit mode. In Edit mode, Access assumes that you are making changes to the current field value, so keystrokes such as CTRL+END, CTRL+HOME, ←, and → move the insertion point within the field. To return to Navigation mode, press TAB or ENTER (thus moving the focus to the next field), or press ↑ or ↓ (thus moving the focus to a different record).

FIGURE 1-4: Adding a new record to the Companies table

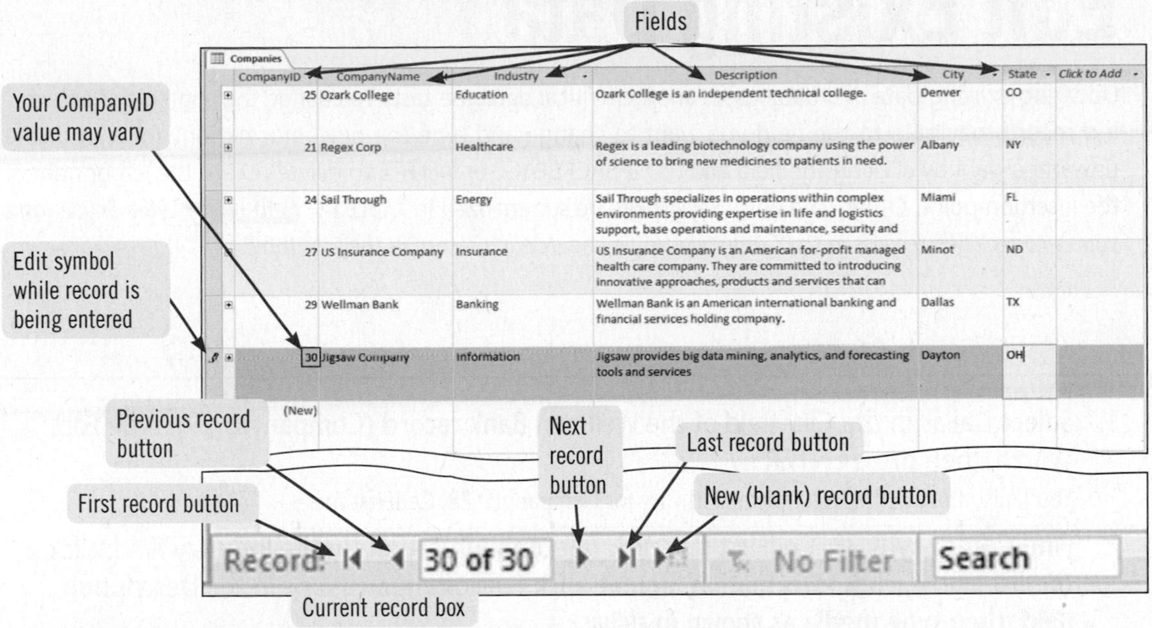

TABLE 1-3: Essential database terminology

term	description
Field	A specific piece or category of data such as a company name, first name, last name, city, state, or phone number
Record	A group of related fields that describes a person, place, thing, or transaction such as a company or job
Primary key field	A field that contains unique information for each record, such as a CompanyID value for a company
Table	A collection of records for a single subject such as Industries, Companies, or Jobs
Relational database	Multiple tables that are linked together to address a business process such as managing industries, companies, and jobs at JCL Talent
Objects	The parts of an Access database that help you view, edit, manage, and analyze the data; Access has six major objects: tables, queries, forms, reports, macros, and modules

TABLE 1-4: Navigation mode keyboard shortcuts

shortcut key	moves to the
TAB, ENTER, or →	Next field of the current record
SHIFT+TAB or ←	Previous field of the current record
HOME	First field of the current record
END	Last field of the current record
CTRL+HOME or F5	First field of the first record
CTRL+END	Last field of the last record
↑	Current field of the previous record
↓	Current field of the next record

Resizing and moving datasheet columns

You can resize the width of a field in a datasheet by dragging the column separator, the thin line that separates the field names to the left or right. The pointer changes to ↔ as you make the field wider or narrower. Release the mouse button when you have resized the field. To adjust the column width to accommodate the widest entry in the field, double-click the column separator. To move a column, click the field name to select the entire column, then drag the field name left or right.

Access

Edit Existing Data

Learning Outcomes
- Edit data in a datasheet
- Delete records in a datasheet
- Preview and print a datasheet

Updating existing data in a database is another critical database task. To change the contents of an existing record, navigate to the field you want to change and type the new information. You can delete unwanted data by clicking the field and using BACKSPACE or DELETE to delete text to the left or right of the insertion point. Other data entry keystrokes are summarized in **TABLE 1-5**. **CASE** *Lydia Snyder asks you to correct two records in the Companies table and delete a record in the Jobs table.*

STEPS

1. **Select Dallas in the City field of the Wellman Bank record (CompanyID 29), type Fort Worth, then press ENTER**

   You'll also update the Description and City for CompanyID 28, CellFirst Inc.

2. **Find CompanyID 28, CellFirst Inc, click Telecommunications in the Industry field, click the list arrow, click Information, double-click telecommunications in the Description field, then type media as shown in FIGURE 1-5**

   While editing a field value, you press ESC once to remove the current field's editing changes, and twice to remove all changes to the current record. When you move to another record, Access saves your edits, so you can no longer use ESC to remove editing changes to the current record. You can, however, click the Undo button on the Quick Access Toolbar to undo the last saved action.

3. **Double-click the Jobs table in the Navigation Pane to open it in Datasheet View, click the record selector for the second record (JobID 2, Alark Inc, Care Management Associate), click the Delete button in the Records group, then click Yes**

   A message warns that you cannot undo a record deletion. The Undo button is dimmed, indicating that you cannot use it. The Jobs table now has 82 records. The first four are shown in **FIGURE 1-6**.

4. **Click the File tab, click Print, then click Print Preview to preview the printout of the Jobs table before printing**

5. **Click the Close Print Preview button, then right-click each table tab and click Close**

QUICK TIP
The ScreenTip for the Undo button displays the action you can undo.

QUICK TIP
If requested to print the Companies or Jobs datasheet by your instructor, click the Print button, then click OK.

QUICK TIP
It's a good idea to close the objects if you are not currently working with them.

FIGURE 1-5: Editing records in the Companies table

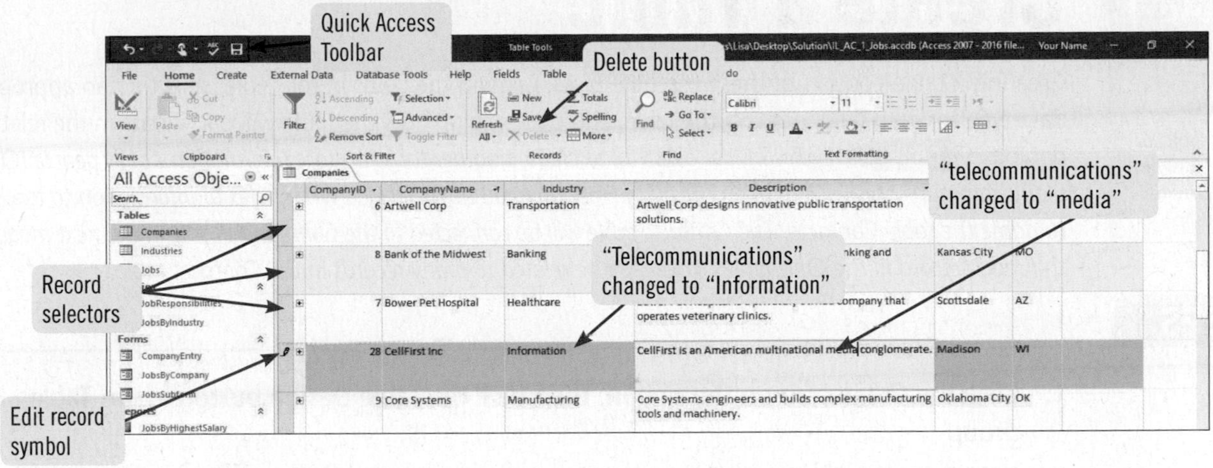

FIGURE 1-6: Deleting a record in the Jobs table

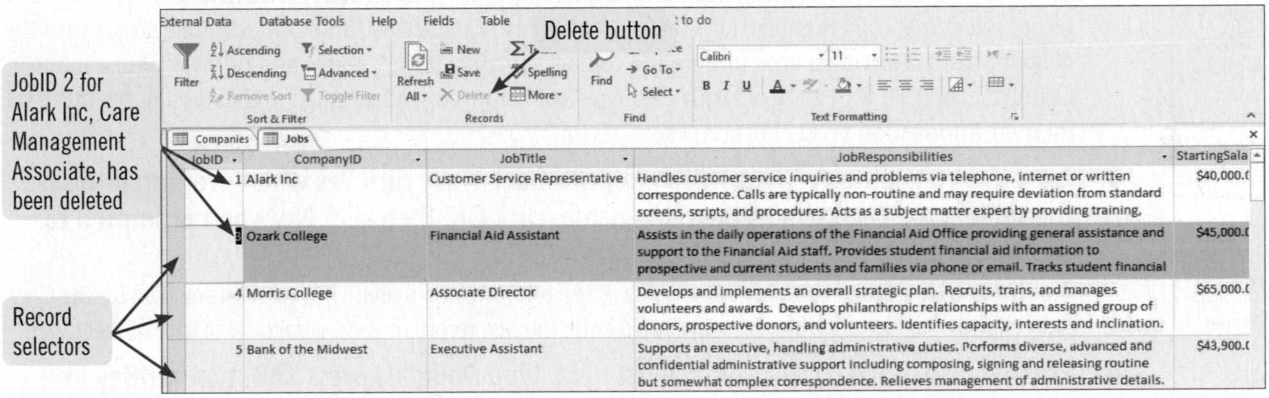

TABLE 1-5: Edit mode keyboard shortcuts

editing keystroke	action
BACKSPACE	Deletes one character to the left of the insertion point
DELETE	Deletes one character to the right of the insertion point
F2	Switches between Edit and Navigation mode
ESC	Undoes the change to the current field
ESC, ESC	Undoes all changes to the current record
F7	Starts the spell-check feature
CTRL+'	Inserts the value from the same field in the previous record into the current field
CTRL+;	Inserts the current date in a Date field

Access Module 1

Create a Table

Learning Outcomes
- Create a table in Table Design View
- Set appropriate data types for fields

Creating a table consists of these essential tasks: naming the fields in the table, selecting an appropriate data type for each field, naming the table, and determining how the table will participate in the relational database. **CASE** *Lydia Snyder asks you to create another table to store information about people JCL regularly communicates with at each company. Together you have decided what fields of information to track and to name the table Contacts. The Contacts table will be connected to the Companies table in the next module so that each record in the Companies table may be related to many records in the Contacts table.*

STEPS

1. **Click the Create tab on the ribbon, then click the Table Design button in the Tables group**

   You can create a table in either Datasheet View or Design View, but **Design View** gives you more control over the characteristics called **field properties** of each field in the table.

2. **Enter the Field Names and Data Types for each field as shown in FIGURE 1-7**

   The Contacts table will contain five fields. ContactID is set with an **AutoNumber** data type so each record is automatically numbered by Access. ContactFirst, ContactLast, and ContactPhone are set with the default **Short Text** data type to store the contact's first name, last name, and primary phone number. ContactEmail is set with a **Hyperlink** data type that helps you send an email to that person. See TABLE 1-6 for more information on field data types.

3. **Click the View button to switch to Datasheet View, click Yes when prompted to save the table, type Contacts as the table name, click OK, then click No when prompted to create a primary key**

   A **primary key field** contains unique data for each record. You'll identify a primary key field for the Contacts table in the next module. For now, you'll enter the first record in the Contacts table in Datasheet View.

4. **Press TAB to move to the ContactFirst field, type Douglas, press TAB, type Griffey in the ContactLast field, type 5554443333 in the ContactPhone field, press TAB, then type dgriffey@accentgroup.com**

   Right now, you have not identified Douglas Griffey's company affiliation. After you relate the tables in the next module, Access will make it easy to relate each contact to the correct company.

5. **Point to the divider line after the ContactEmail field name, then double-click the column resize pointer ↔ to widen the ContactEmail field to read the entire email value, as shown in FIGURE 1-8**

6. **Right-click the Contacts table tab, then click Save to save the table**

QUICK TIP

Fields that contain numbers but are not used in calculations such as a telephone number or postal code should be set as a Short Text data type.

TROUBLE

The ContactID field is an AutoNumber field, which will automatically increment to provide a unique value. If the number has already incremented beyond 1 for the first record, it doesn't matter.

Creating a table in Datasheet View

You can also create a new table in Datasheet View using the commands on the Fields tab of the ribbon. However, if you use Design View to design your table before entering data, you will probably avoid some common data entry errors because Design View helps you focus on the appropriate data type for each field.

Selecting the best data type for each field before entering any data into that field helps prevent incorrect data and unintended typos. For example, if a field has a Number, Currency, or Date/Time data type, you will not be able to enter text into that field by mistake.

FIGURE 1-7: Creating a table in Design View

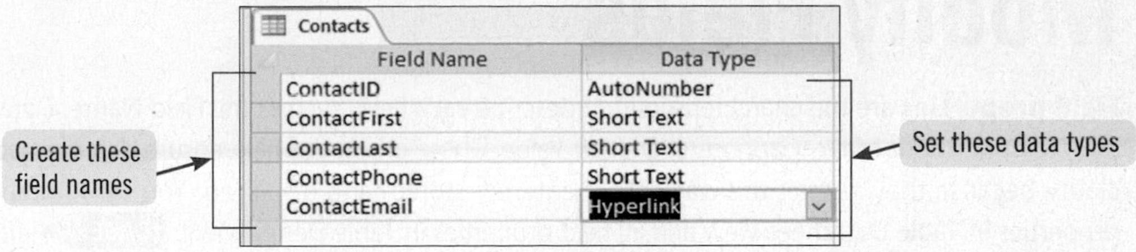

FIGURE 1-8: Entering a new record in Datasheet View

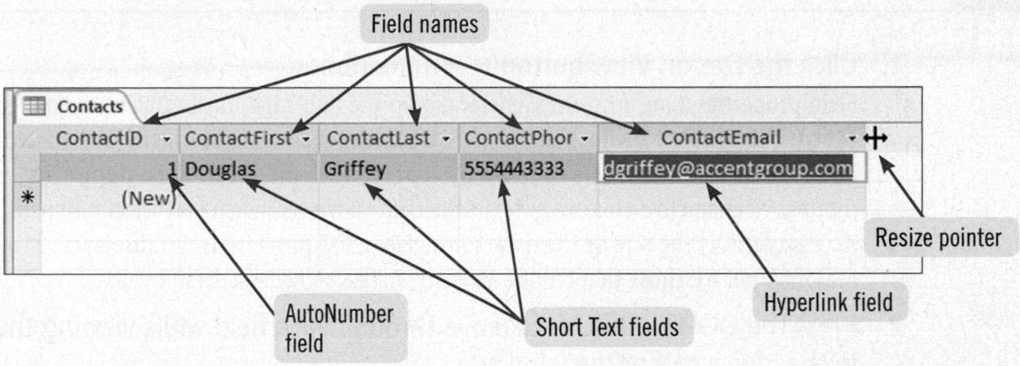

TABLE 1-6: Data types

data type	description of data
Short Text	Text or numbers not used in calculations such as a name, postal code, or phone number fewer than 255 characters
Long Text	Lengthy text greater than 255 characters, such as comments or notes
Number	Numeric data that can be used in calculations, such as quantities
Large Number	Provides additional analytical capability and deepens the integration experience when users are importing or linking to BigInt data
Date/Time	Dates and times
Currency	Monetary values
AutoNumber	Sequential integers controlled by Access
Yes/No	Yes or No or Null (neither Yes nor No)
OLE Object	OLE (Object Linking and Embedding) objects such as an Excel spreadsheet or Word document
Hyperlink	Web and email addresses or links to local files
Attachment	Files such as .jpg images, spreadsheets, and documents
Calculated	Result of a calculation based on other fields in the table
Lookup Wizard	The Lookup Wizard is not a data type even though it is on the Data Type list. It helps you set Lookup properties, which display a drop-down list of values for the field. After using the Lookup Wizard, the final data type for the field is either Short Text or Number depending on the type of data in the drop-down list.

Object views

Each object has a number of views that allow you to complete different tasks. For example, to enter and edit data into the database using a table or query, use Datasheet View. To enter and edit data in a form, use Form View. To see how a report will appear on a physical piece of paper, use Print Preview. To see all the available views for an object, click the arrow at the bottom of the View button on the Home tab.

Access

Access
Module 1

Modify Fields

Learning Outcomes
- Rename a field
- Understand field properties

Field properties are the characteristics that describe each field, such as the Field Name, Data Type, Field Size, Format, Input Mask, Caption, or Default Value. These properties help ensure database accuracy and clarity because they restrict the way data is entered, stored, and displayed. You can modify most field properties in Table Datasheet View and all field properties in Table Design View. CASE *After reviewing the Contacts table with Lydia Snyder, you decide to change several Short Text field properties.*

STEPS

1. **Click the Design View button on the ribbon**
   Field properties appear on the General tab on the lower half of the Table Design View window called the **Field Properties pane**. Field properties change depending on the field's data type. For example, when you select a field with a Short Text data type, you see the **Field Size property**, which determines the number of characters you can enter in the field. However, when you select a Hyperlink or Date/Time field, Access controls the size of the data, so the Field Size property is not displayed. Many field properties are optional, but for those that require an entry, Access provides a default value.
2. **Press the DOWN ARROW to move through each field while viewing the field properties in the lower half of the window**
   The **field selector** button to the left of the field indicates which field is currently selected.
3. **Click the ContactFirst field name, double-click 255 in the Field Size property text box, type 20, right-click the Contacts tab, click Save on the shortcut menu, then click Yes**
   The default value for the Field Size property for a Short Text field is 255, but you want to make the Field Size property for Short Text fields only as large as needed to accommodate the longest reasonable entry. In some cases, shortening the Field Size property helps prevent typographical errors. For example, you should set the Field Size property for a State field that stores two-letter state abbreviations to 2 to prevent typos such as TXX.
4. **Click the ContactLast field name, double-click 255 in the Field Size property text box, type 20, right-click the Contacts tab, click Save on the shortcut menu, then click Yes**
   No existing entries are greater than the new Field Size values, so no data is lost. Table Design View of the Contacts table should look like FIGURE 1-9.
5. **Right-click the Contacts table tab, then click Close**

FIGURE 1-9: Modifying field properties

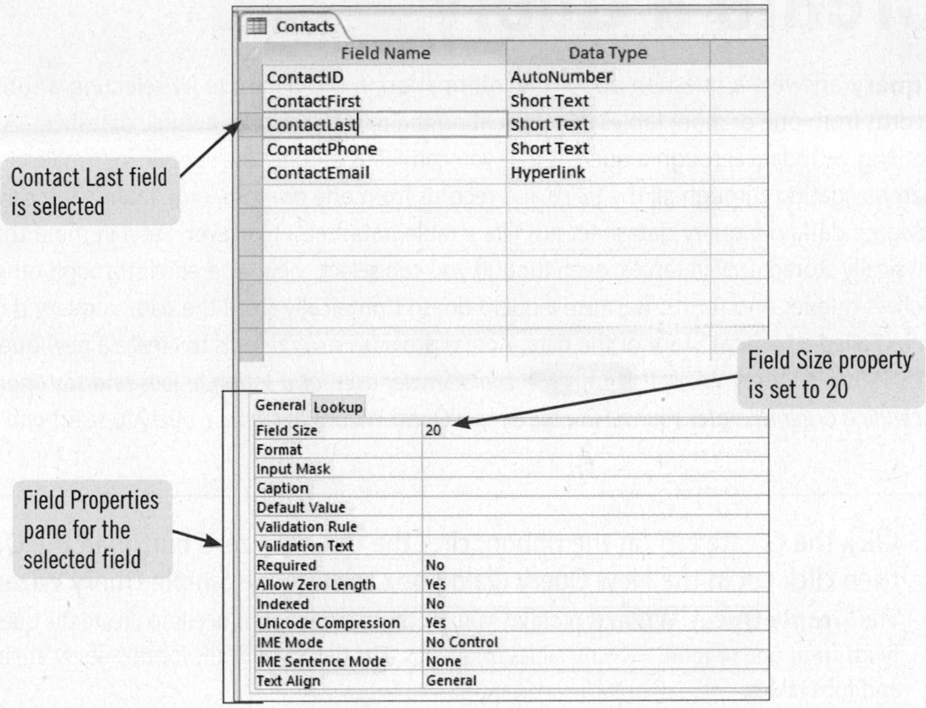

Field properties

Properties are the characteristics that define the field. Two properties are required for every field: Field Name and Data Type. Many other properties, such as Field Size, Format, Caption, and Default Value, are defined in the Field Properties pane in the lower half of a table's Design View. Many common properties can also be accessed on the Fields tab of the ribbon in Table Datasheet View. As you add more property entries, you are generally restricting the amount or type of data that can be entered in the field, which increases data entry accuracy. For example, you might change the Field Size property for a State field to 2 to eliminate an incorrect entry such as FLL. Field properties change depending on the data type of the selected field. For example, Date/Time, Currency, and Yes/No fields do not have a Field Size property because Access controls the size of fields with those data types.

Access

Create a Query

Learning Outcomes
- Describe the purpose for a query
- Create a query with the Simple Query Wizard

A **query** answers a question about the information in the database by selecting a subset of fields and records from one or more tables and presenting the selected data as a single datasheet. A major benefit of working with data through a query is that you can focus on only the specific information you need, rather than navigating through all the fields and records from one or more large tables. You can enter, edit, and navigate data in a query datasheet just like a table datasheet. However, keep in mind that Access data is physically stored only in tables, even though you can select, view, and edit it through other Access objects such as queries and forms. Because a query doesn't physically store the data, a query datasheet is sometimes called a **logical view** of the data. Access provides several tools to create a new query, one of which is the Simple Query Wizard. CASE *Lydia Snyder asks for a listing of jobs and starting salaries sorted in ascending order by state. You will use the Simple Query Wizard to create a query to select and display this data.*

STEPS

1. **Click the Create tab on the ribbon, click the Query Wizard button in the Queries group, then click OK in the New Query dialog box to start the Simple Query Wizard**

   The **Simple Query Wizard** prompts you for the information it needs to create the query. You can select fields from one or more existing tables or queries. The fields you want for this query are in the Companies and Jobs tables.

TROUBLE
Click the Remove Single Field button [<] if you need to remove a field from the Selected Fields list.

2. **Click the Tables/Queries list arrow, click Table: Companies, double-click State in the Available Fields list to move it to the Selected Fields list, click the Tables/Queries list arrow, click Table: Jobs, double-click JobTitle, then double-click StartingSalary as shown in FIGURE 1-10**

   You've selected three fields for this query from two different tables.

TROUBLE
Click Back if you need to move to a previous dialog box in the Simple Query Wizard.

3. **Click Next, click Next to select Detail, select Companies Query in the title text box, type JobsByState as the name of the query, then click Finish**

   The JobsByState datasheet opens, displaying one field from the Companies table (State) and two from the Jobs table (JobTitle and StartingSalary). To sort the records by JobTitle within State, you'll select those two fields and use the Ascending button on the Home tab.

4. **Use the column selector pointer ⬇ to drag across the field names of State and JobTitle to select both columns, click the Home tab on the ribbon, then click the Ascending button in the Sort & Filter group**

   The JobsByState datasheet is sorted in ascending order by the State field, and then in ascending order by the JobTitle field within each state, as shown in **FIGURE 1-11**.

5. **Right-click the JobsByState tab, click Close, then click Yes when prompted to save the query**

Simple Query Wizard

The **Simple Query Wizard** is a series of dialog boxes that prompt you for the information needed to create a Select query. A **Select query** selects fields from one or more tables in your database and is by far the most common type of query.

The other query wizards—Crosstab, Find Duplicates, and Find Unmatched—are used to create queries that do specialized types of data analysis and are covered in Module 5.

FIGURE 1-10: Using the Simple Query Wizard

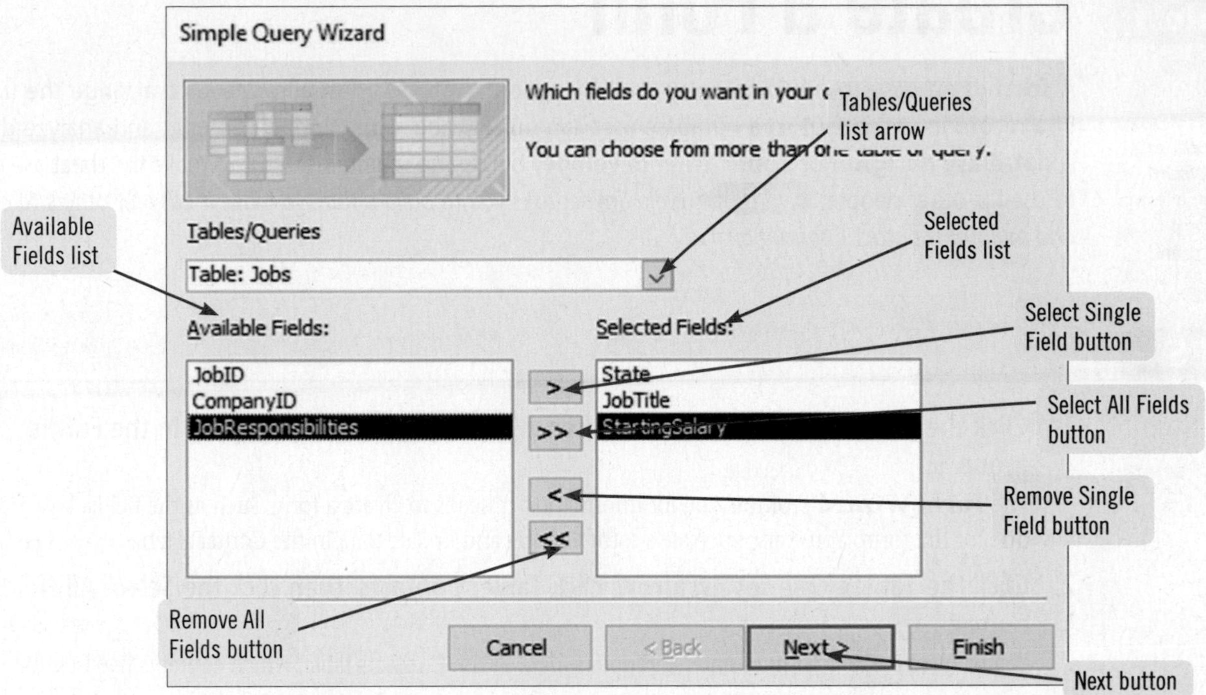

FIGURE 1-11: Sorting a query datasheet

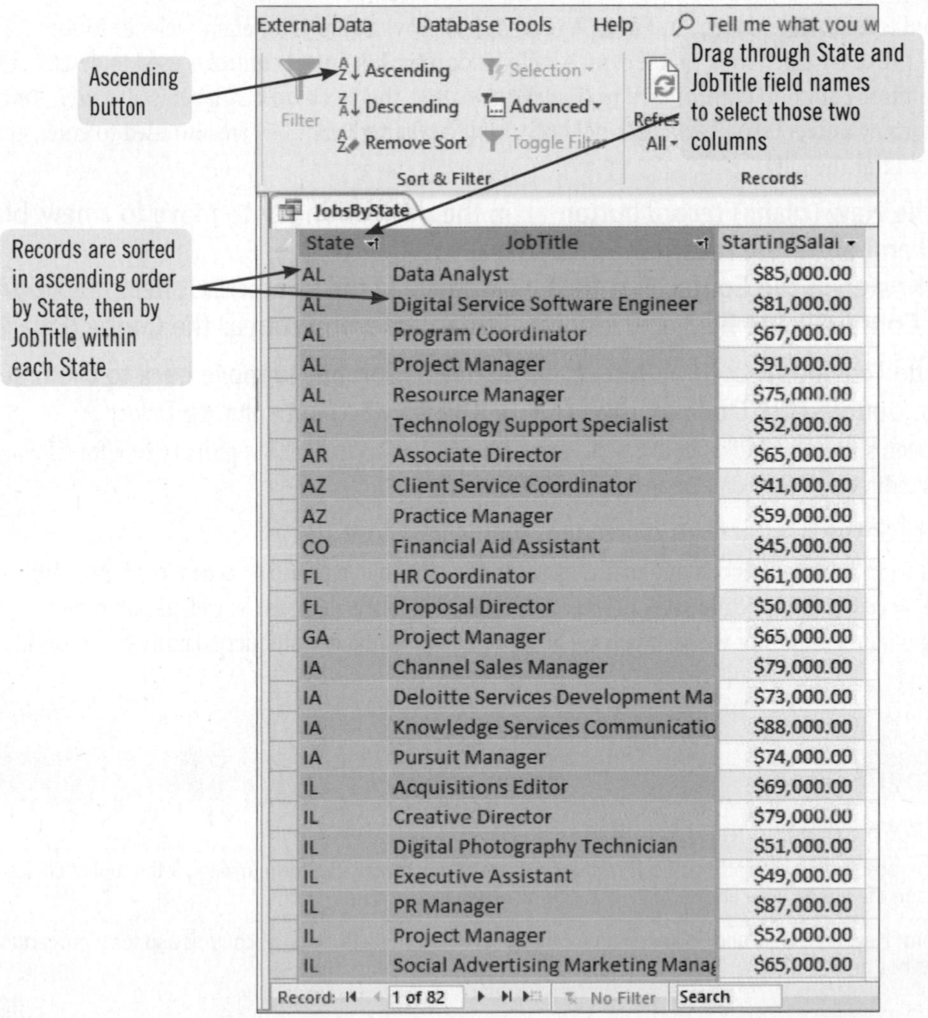

Access

Create a Form

Learning Outcomes
- Create a form with the Form Wizard
- Sort data in a form
- Describe form terminology and views

A **form** is an easy-to-use data entry and navigation screen. A form allows you to arrange the fields of a record in any layout so a database user can quickly and easily find, enter, edit, and analyze data. A **database designer** or **application developer** builds and maintains forms to make the database easy to use for other people. CASE *Lydia Snyder asks you to build a form to make it easy for others to enter and maintain contact information.*

STEPS

TROUBLE
To rename a form, or any object, close it, right-click it in the Navigation Pane, and then click Rename.

QUICK TIP
Tab through the AutoNumber ContactID field, which automatically increments.

TROUBLE
If you click an email hyperlink in the form, Outlook starts. Close Outlook or click Cancel to stop the process.

1. **Click the Create tab on the ribbon, then click the Form Wizard button in the Forms group**
   The **Form Wizard** prompts you for information it needs to create a form, such as the fields, layout, and title for the form. You want to create a form to enter and update data in the Contacts table.
2. **Click the Tables/Queries list arrow, click Table: Contacts, then click the Select All Fields button >>**
   You want to create a form to enter and update data in the Contacts table, which contains five fields.
3. **Click Next, click the Columnar option button, click Next, modify Contacts to ContactEntry for the title, then click Finish**
   The ContactEntry form opens in **Form View**. Access provides three different views of forms, as summarized in TABLE 1-7. Each item on the form is called a **control**. A **label** control is used to describe the data, and the most common control used to display the data is the **text box**. A label is also used for the title of the form, ContactEntry. Text boxes not only display existing data, they are also used to enter, edit, find, sort, and filter the data.
4. **Click the New (blank) record button in the navigation bar to move to a new, blank record and enter the record shown in FIGURE 1-12**
   Enter Kristen in the ContactFirst field, Fontanelle in the ContactLast field, 5556667777 in the ContactPhone field, and kfontanelle@accentgroup.com as the ContactEmail value
5. **Click the Previous record button in the navigation bar to move back to the first record, double-click Douglas, then change the ContactFirst value to Doug**
   Your screen should look like FIGURE 1-13. Forms open in Form View are the primary tool for database users to enter, edit, and delete data in an Access database.
6. **Right-click the ContactEntry form tab, then click Close**
   When a form is closed, Access automatically saves any edits made to the current record. As you have experienced, Access automatically saves new records entered into the database as well as any edits you make to existing data regardless of whether you are working in a table datasheet, query datasheet, or form.

TABLE 1-7: Form views

view	primary purpose
Form	To find, sort, enter, and edit data
Layout	To modify the size, position, or formatting of controls; shows data as you modify the form, making it the tool of choice when you want to change the appearance and usability of the form while viewing data
Design	To modify the Form Header, Detail, and Footer section, or to access the complete range of controls and form properties; Design View does not display data

FIGURE 1-12: Entering a new record in a form

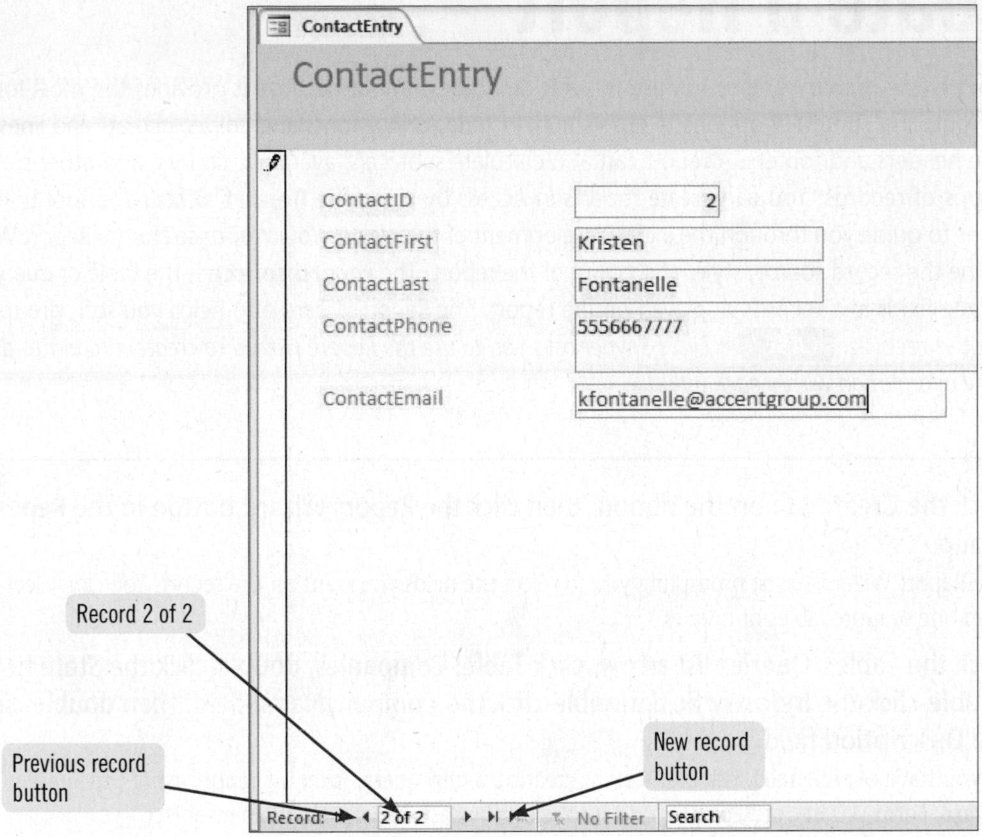

FIGURE 1-13: Editing an existing record in a form

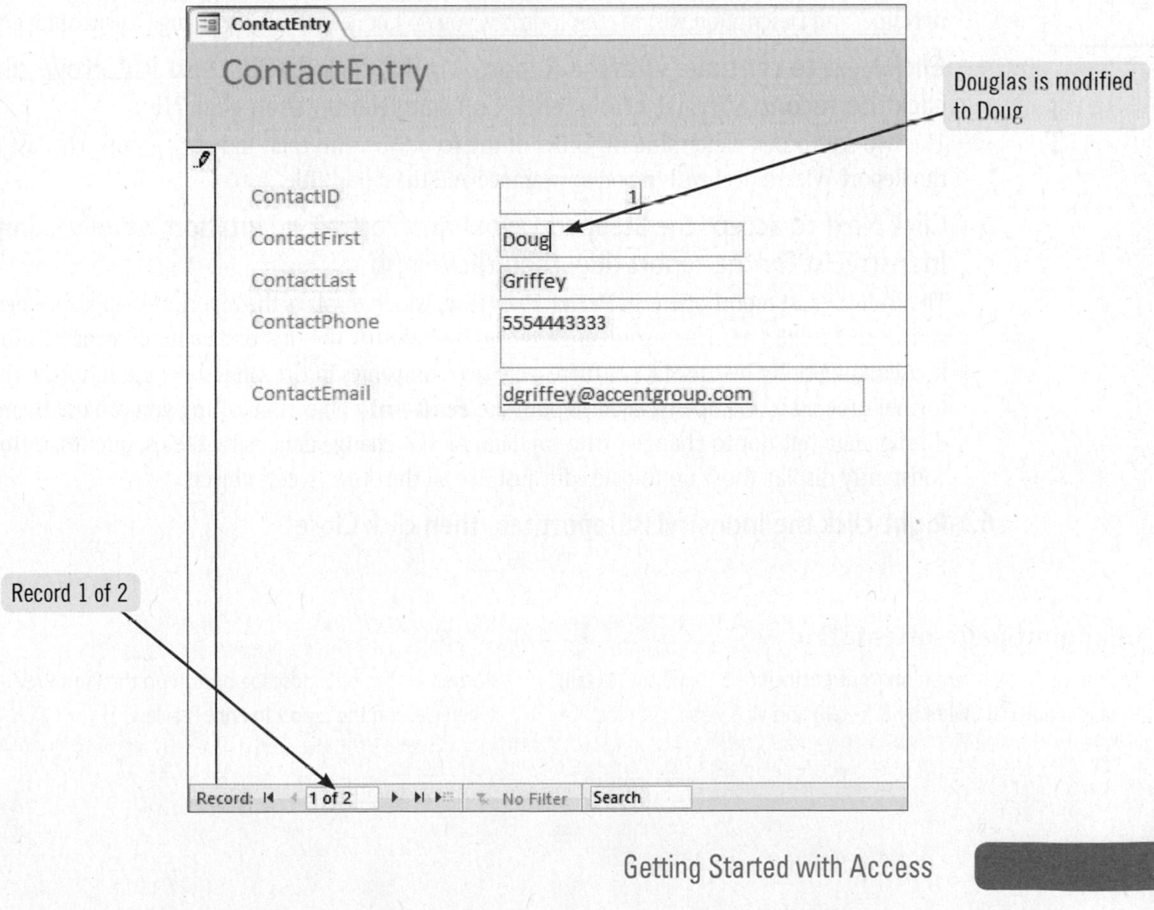

Create a Report

Learning Outcomes
- Create a report with the Report Wizard
- Change page orientation

A **report** is the primary object you use to print database content because it provides the most formatting, layout, and summary options. A report may include various fonts and colors, clip art and lines, and multiple headers and footers. A report can also calculate subtotals, averages, counts, and other statistics for groups of records. You can create reports in Access by using the **Report Wizard**, a tool that asks questions to guide you through the initial development of the report. Your responses to the Report Wizard determine the record source, style, and layout of the report. The **record source** is the table or query that defines the fields and records displayed on the report. The Report Wizard also helps you sort, group, and analyze the records. CASE *Lydia Snyder asks you to use the Report Wizard to create a report to display company information within each industry.*

STEPS

1. **Click the Create tab on the ribbon, then click the Report Wizard button in the Reports group**

   The Report Wizard starts, prompting you to select the fields you want on the report. You can select fields from one or more tables or queries.

2. **Click the Tables/Queries list arrow, click Table: Companies, double-click the State field, double-click the Industry field, double-click the CompanyName field, then double-click the Description field**

   As you have experienced, the first step of creating a new query, form, or report using the Simple Query Wizard, Form Wizard, or Report Wizard is to select the desired fields for the new object.

QUICK TIP
Click Back to review previous dialog boxes within a wizard.

3. **Click Next to advance to the report grouping options, as shown in FIGURE 1-14**

   The Report Wizard automatically wants to group the records by Industry and gives you the opportunity to specify additional grouping levels if desired. Given you are creating a report displaying the State, CompanyName, and Description within each Industry, you do not need to add or change the existing grouping level.

4. **Click Next to continue with the Report Wizard, click the first sort list arrow, click State, click the second sort list arrow, click CompanyName, then click Next**

   The two sort orders determine the order of the records within each Industry group. The last questions in the Report Wizard deal with report appearance and the report title.

5. **Click Next to accept the Stepped Layout and Portrait orientation, modify Companies to IndustryList for the report title, then click Finish**

   The IndustryList report opens in **Print Preview**, which displays the report as it appears when printed, as shown in FIGURE 1-15. The records are grouped by Industry, the first one being Aerospace, and then sorted in ascending order by the State. If there were two companies in the same state and industry, they would be further ordered by CompanyName. Reports are **read-only** objects, meaning you can use them to read and display data but not to change (write to) data. As you change data using tables, queries, or forms, reports constantly display those up-to-date edits just like all the other Access objects.

6. **Right-click the IndustryList report tab, then click Close**

Changing page orientation

To change page orientation from **portrait** (8.5" wide by 11" tall) to **landscape** (11" wide by 8.5" tall) and vice versa, click the Portrait button or Landscape button on the Print Preview tab when viewing the report in Print Preview.

FIGURE 1-14: Setting report grouping fields

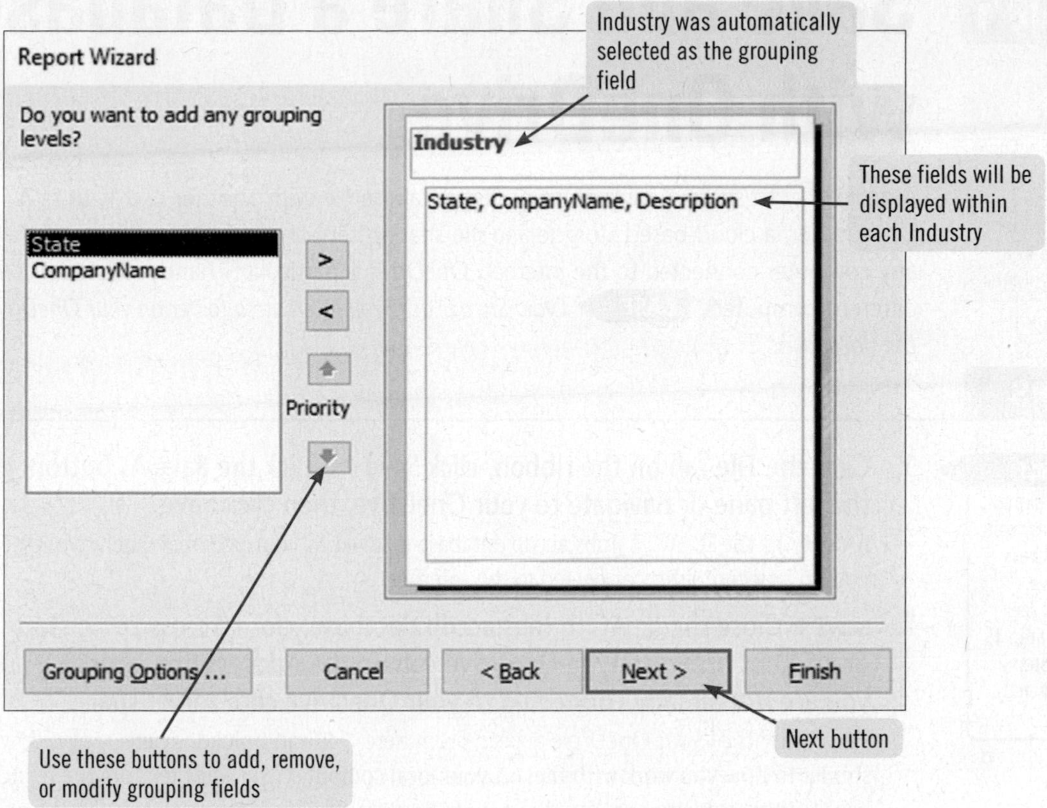

FIGURE 1-15: Previewing a report

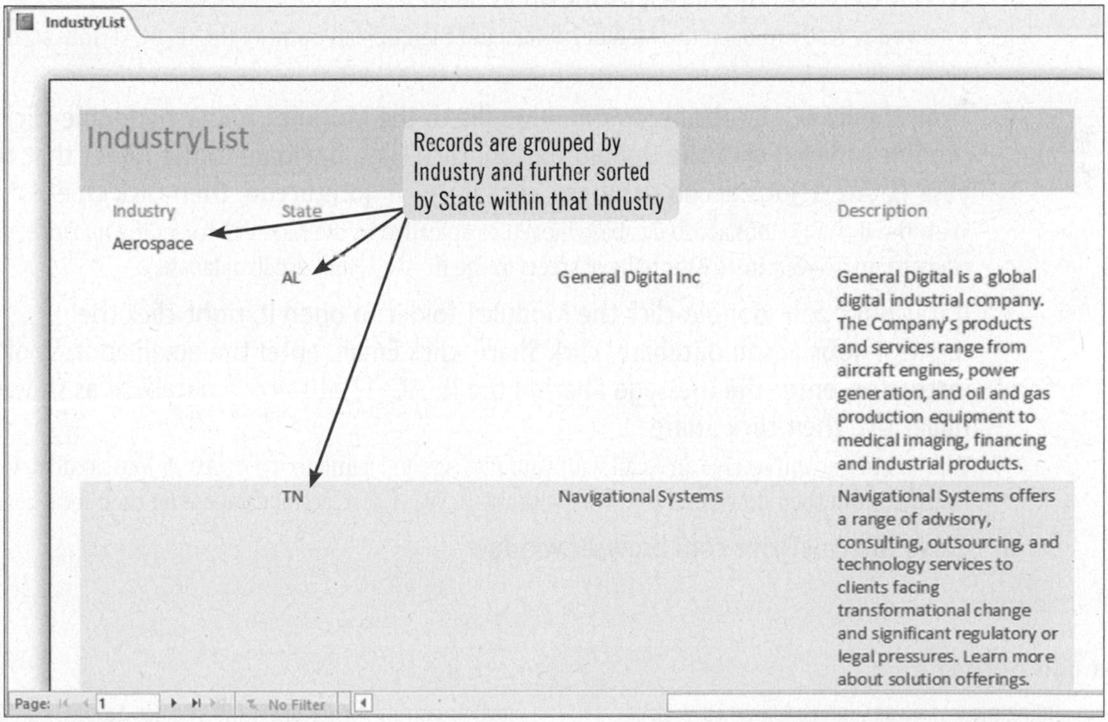

Access

Save and Share a Database with OneDrive

Learning Outcomes
- Create a OneDrive folder
- Save a file to a OneDrive folder
- Share a file in a OneDrive folder

A good way to share a copy of an Access database file with another user is to save it to a shared OneDrive folder, a cloud-based storage and file-sharing service provided by Microsoft that is accessible from any computer connected to the Internet. OneDrive is particularly handy for students who work on many different computers. **CASE** *Lydia Snyder asks you to create a folder on your OneDrive to save and share the database.*

STEPS

TROUBLE
You must be signed in to your Microsoft account to access your OneDrive. If you do not see OneDrive in Step 1, continue to Step 2 to access it directly and sign in.

1. **Click the File tab on the ribbon, click Save As, click the Save As button, click OneDrive in the left pane or navigate to your OneDrive, then click Save**
   A **copy** of the IL_AC_1_Jobs.accdb database is saved to your personal OneDrive. OneDrive is available to you on any computer connected to the Internet.
2. **sam Close the IL_AC_1_Jobs.accdb database, close Access 2019, start Microsoft Edge or another browser, type OneDrive.com in the Address box, press ENTER, then sign in if you are not already connected to your OneDrive.com server space**
   The contents of your OneDrive appear. From here, you can upload, delete, move, download, or copy files, similar to how you work with files on your local computer. You want to share the IL_AC_1_Jobs.accdb database with your instructor. You decide to first create a folder for the database. That way, your OneDrive will stay more organized.
3. **Click the New button, click Folder, type Module1 as the new folder name, then press ENTER to create the folder, as shown in FIGURE 1-16**
   Now you're ready to open the Module1 folder and then upload or move the IL_AC_1_Jobs.accdb database file into it.
4. **Drag the IL_AC_1_Jobs.accdb database file to the Module1 folder *or* double-click the Module1 folder, click the Upload button, click Files, navigate to the folder that contains your IL_AC_1_Jobs.accdb database, click IL_AC_1_Jobs.accdb, then click Open**
   With the IL_AC_1_Jobs.accdb database moved or uploaded to the Module1 folder in OneDrive, you're now ready to invite your instructor to have access to the IL_AC_1_Jobs.accdb database.
5. **If it is not open, double-click the Module1 folder to open it, right-click the IL_AC_1_Jobs.accdb database, click Share, click Email, enter the email address of your instructor, enter the message Sharing the IL_AC_1_Jobs.accdb database as shown in FIGURE 1-17, then click Share**
   Your instructor will receive an email with your message and a link to the IL_AC_1_Jobs.accdb database. Your instructor can then download and work with the IL_AC_1_Jobs.accdb database on their local computer.
6. **Close the OneDrive.com browser window**

Cloud computing

Cloud computing means you are using an Internet resource to complete your work. Using **OneDrive**, a free service from Microsoft, you can store files in the "cloud" and retrieve them anytime you are connected to the Internet. Saving your files to the OneDrive is one example of cloud computing.

FIGURE 1-16: Creating a new folder in OneDrive

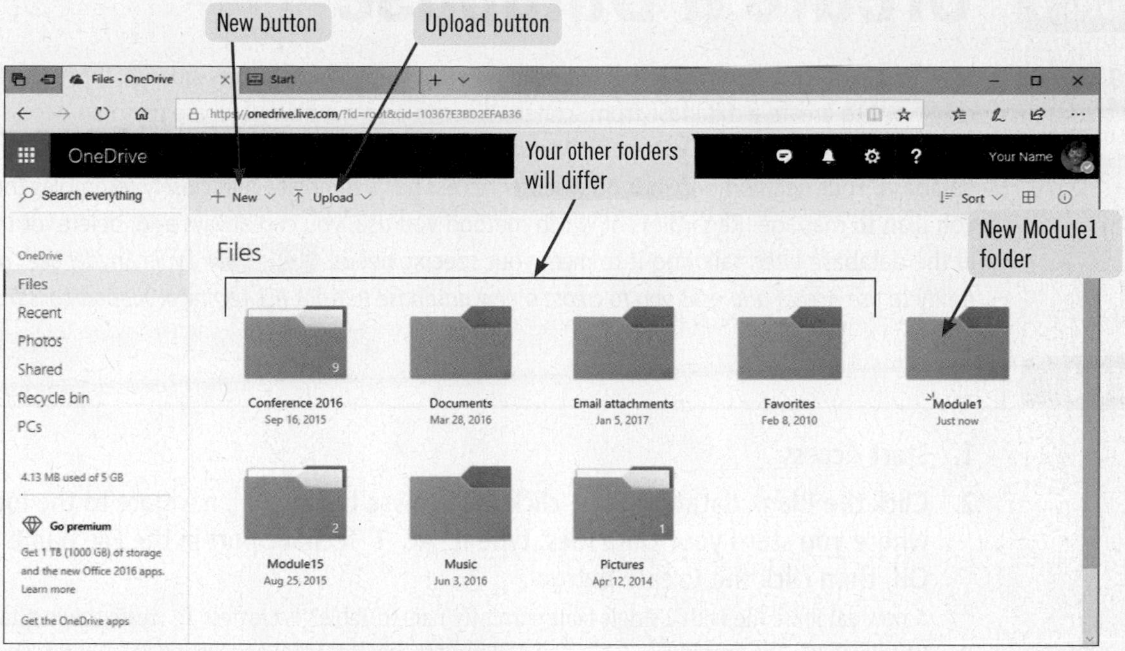

FIGURE 1-17: Sharing a database with OneDrive

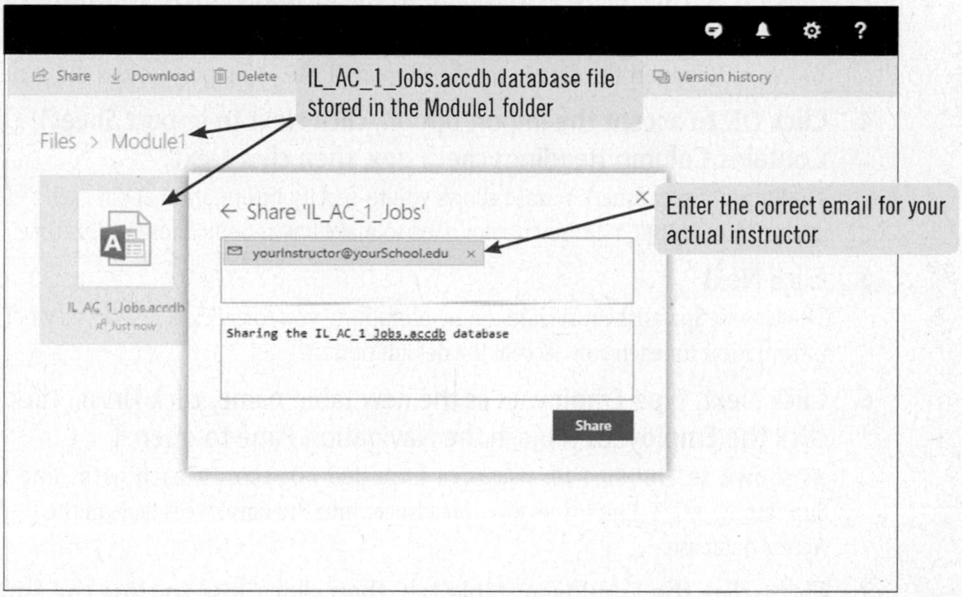

Access is a local application

Unlike Word and Excel, Access does not have an online version of itself. Access is a **local application** that runs from the hard drive of a local Windows machine. You can share a copy of a database with others using OneDrive, but remember that saving a database to OneDrive creates a **copy** of the database. For multiple people to work in the same database at the same time, the database must be located in a shared folder on a local file server.

Access

Access Module 1

Create a Database

Learning Outcomes
- Create a database
- Import data from Excel

Now that you are familiar with the four main objects of a database (tables, queries, forms, and reports), you may want to create a database from scratch. You can create a new database using an Access **template**, a sample database provided within the Microsoft Access program, or you can start with a completely blank database. Your decision depends on whether Access has a template that closely resembles the type of data you plan to manage. Regardless of which method you use, you can always add, delete, or modify objects in the database later, tailoring it to meet your specific needs. **CASE** *Lydia Snyder sees another opportunity to use Access and asks you to create a new database to track JCL technical support calls from employees.*

STEPS

1. **Start Access**
2. **Click the Blank database icon, click the Browse button, navigate to the location where you store your Data Files, type IL_AC_1_TechSupport in the File name box, click OK, then click the Create button**

   A new database file with a single table currently named Table1 is created. To create the first table needed for this database, the Employees table, you will import the data from an existing Excel spreadsheet.
3. **Right-click the Table1 tab, click Close, click the External Data tab on the ribbon, click the New Data Source button in the Import & Link group, point to From File, click Excel, click Browse, navigate to the location where you store your Data Files, click Support_IL_AC_1_Employees.xlsx, then click Open**

   You want to import the data in the file Support_IL_AC_1_Employees.xlsx into a new table.
4. **Click OK to accept the import option, click Next to import Sheet1, click the First Row Contains Column Headings check box, then click Next**

   The Import Spreadsheet Wizard allows you to specify information about each field that you are importing as shown in **FIGURE 1-18**. You do not need to make any modifications at this time.
5. **Click Next**

   The Import Spreadsheet Wizard is now prompting you to define a primary key field which contains unique information for each row. Accept the default option.
6. **Click Next, type Employees as the new table name, click Finish, click Close, then double-click the Employees table in the Navigation Pane to open it**

   As shown in **FIGURE 1-19**, you have imported 60 records, each with nine fields of data from the Support_IL_AC_1_Employees.xlsx spreadsheet into the Employees table in the IL_AC_1_TechSupport.accdb Access database.
7. **Right-click the Employees table tab, then click Close to close the Employees table**

FIGURE 1-18: Using the Import Spreadsheet Wizard

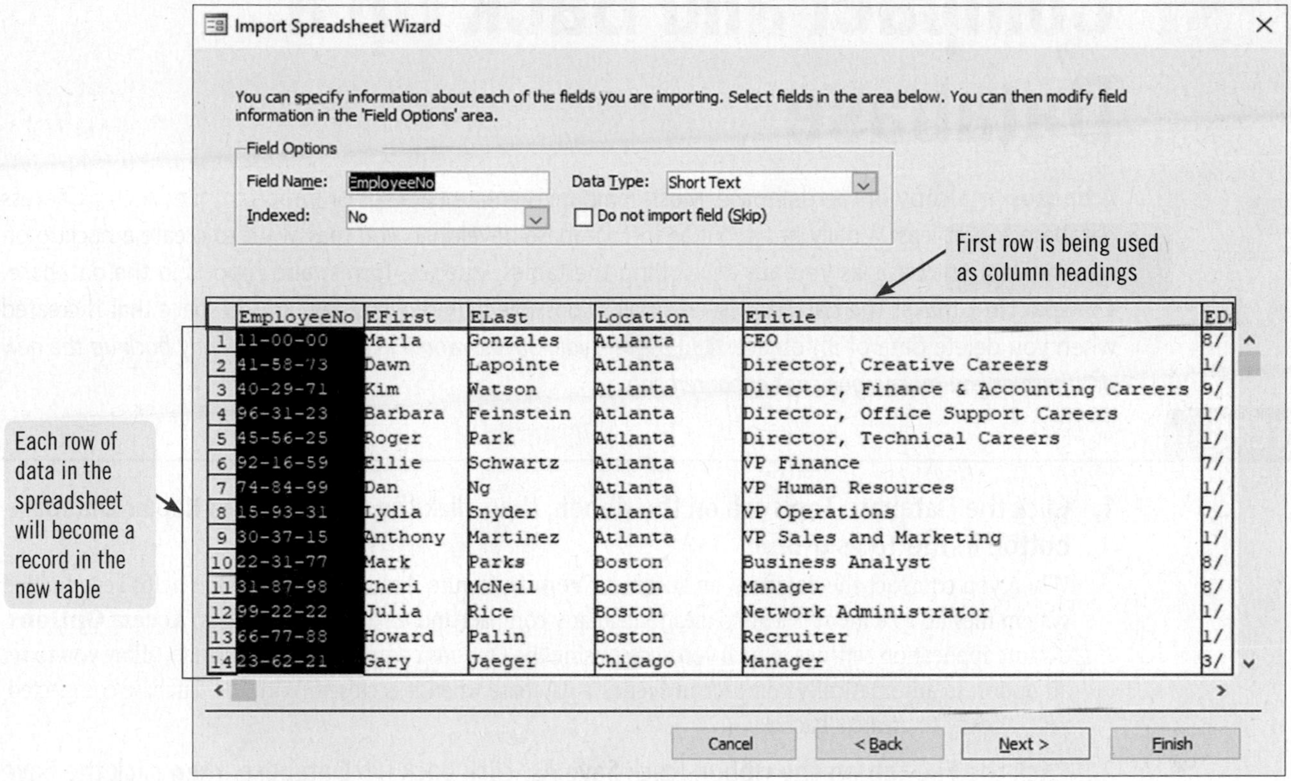

FIGURE 1-19: Employees table in Datasheet View

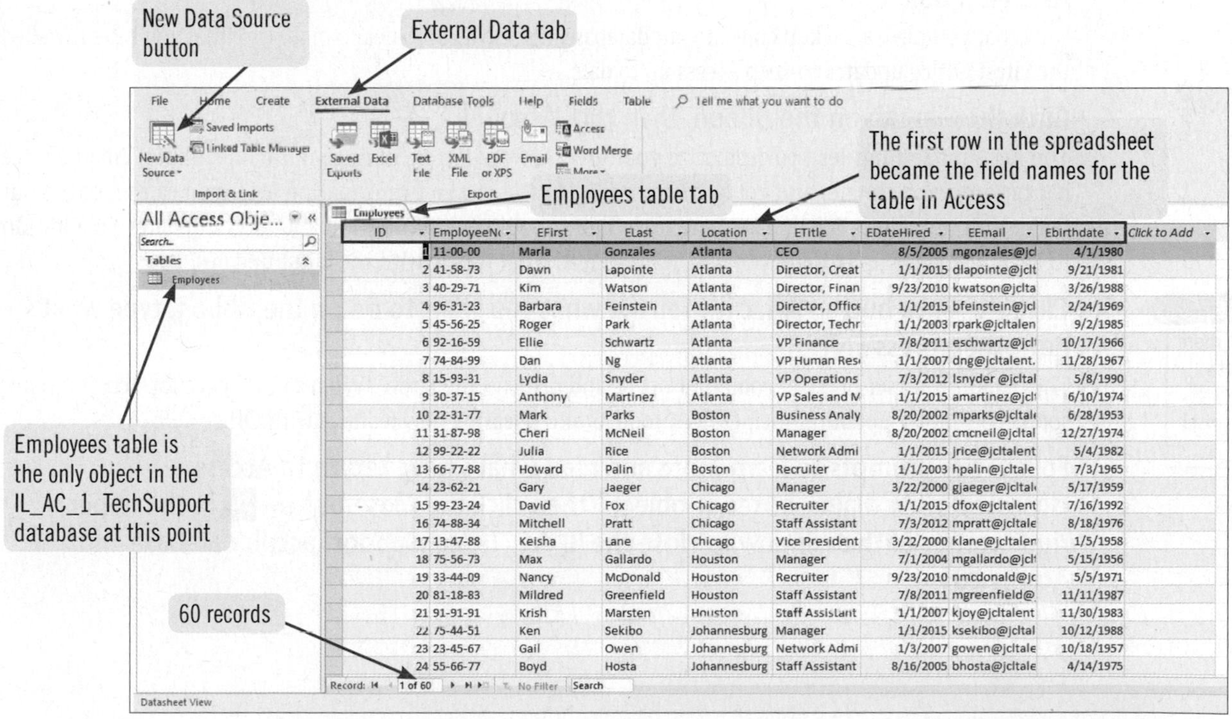

Access
Module 1

Compact and Back Up a Database

Learning Outcomes
- Compact and repair a database
- Back up a database
- View Account settings
- Use the Tell Me box

A **backup** is a copy of the database. Most companies create backups of important files such as Access databases on at least a daily basis, but as the database developer, you may want to create a backup on a more frequent basis as you are developing the tables, queries, forms, and reports in the database. **Compacting** makes the database file as small as possible by removing any unused space that is created when you delete data or an object. CASE *Lydia Snyder would like you to frequently back up the new database as you make significant enhancements.*

STEPS

1. **Click the Database Tools tab on the ribbon, then click the Compact and Repair Database button in the Tools group**

   When you compact the database, an automatic **repair** feature is also initiated, which helps keep hidden system files up to date. It is a good idea to regularly compact and repair your databases. **Access Options**, default application settings, which you access using the Options command on the File tab, allow you to set an option to automatically compact and repair a database when it is closed. With the database compacted, you're ready to create a backup.

2. **Click the File tab on the ribbon, click Save As, click Back Up Database, then click the Save As button**

   Although any copy of the database can serve as a backup, when you use the Back Up Database option, the database file is automatically saved with a filename that includes the date the backup was made.

3. **Navigate to the folder where you want to store the backup, then click Save in the Save As dialog box**

   Now that you have a backup copy of your database, it's also a good idea to make sure that you have installed the latest Office updates to keep Access up to date.

4. **Click the File tab on the ribbon, then click Account**

   The Account settings let you customize your user information including your name, photo, email, Office background and theme, and connected services. In the Product Information area, you can manage your Office account, check for updates, and learn more about your application and recent updates. In addition to keeping Access up to date, you may want to read what is new with the latest updates.

TROUBLE
Click the Learn more link in the What's New in Access window if a browser doesn't open.

5. **Click the Back button, click Tell me what you want to do on the ribbon, type what's new, then press ENTER**

   The default browser on your computer opens and displays the latest "What's new" page for Access. Microsoft is constantly updating their Office products and releasing new features with Office 365.

6. **Follow the prompts to learn more and read what's new, return to Access, close any open dialog boxes or objects, then click the Close button in the upper-right corner of the window to close the IL_AC_1_TechSupport.accdb database and Access 2019**

Practice

Concepts Review

Label each element of the Access window shown in FIGURE 1-20.

FIGURE 1-20

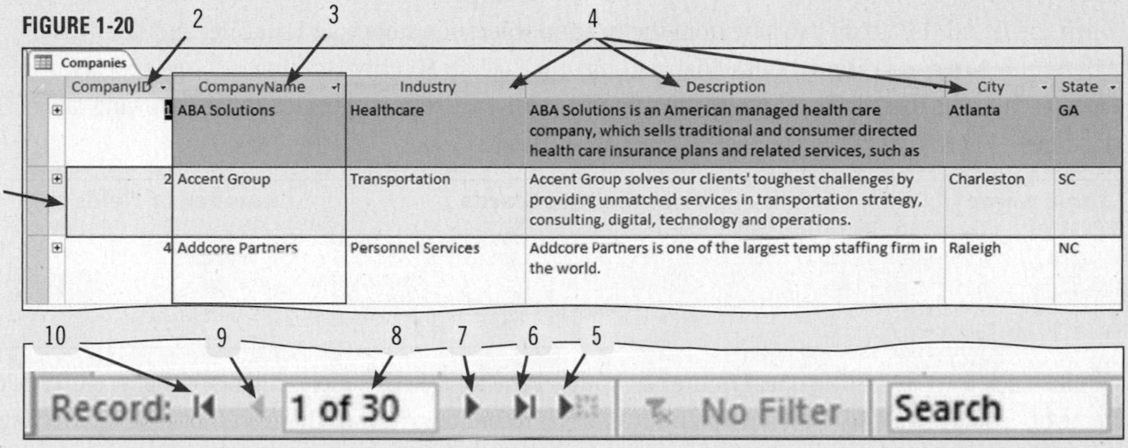

Match each term with the statement that best describes it.

11. Field
12. Record
13. Table
14. Datasheet
15. Query
16. Form
17. Report

a. A subset of data from one or more tables
b. A collection of records for a single subject, such as all the customer records
c. A professional printout of database information
d. A spreadsheet-like grid that displays fields as columns and records as rows
e. A group of related fields for one item, such as all the information for one customer
f. A category of information in a table, such as a company name, city, or state
g. An easy-to-use data entry screen

Select the best answer from the list of choices.

18. Which Access object cannot be used to enter or edit data?

a. Report
b. Table
c. Query
d. Form

19. Which of the following is *not* an advantage of managing data with relational database software such as Access versus spreadsheet software such as Excel?

a. Allows multiple users to enter data simultaneously
b. Uses a single table to store all data
c. Reduces duplicate data entry
d. Provides data entry forms

20. Which of the following is *not* a typical benefit of relational databases?

a. Minimized duplicate data entry
b. Tables automatically create needed relationships
c. More accurate data
d. More consistent data

Skills Review

1. **Understand relational databases.**
   - **a.** In a Word document, enter your name and the current date.
   - **b.** Using a bulleted list, identify five advantages of managing database information in Access versus using a spreadsheet.
   - **c.** Write a sentence to explain how the terms *field*, *record*, *table*, and *relational database* relate to one another.
   - **d.** Save the document with the name **IL_AC_1_Database** then close it and close Word.
2. **Open and explore a database.**
   - **a.** Start Access.
   - **b.** Open the IL_AC_1-2.accdb database from the location where you store your Data Files and save it as **IL_AC_1_SupportDesk**. Click Enable Content if a yellow Security Warning message appears.
   - **c.** Open each of the three tables to study the data they contain. Create and complete the following table in the document you started in the previous step, IL_AC_1_Database.docx.

table name	number of records	number of fields

   - **d.** Double-click the CaseListing query in the Navigation Pane to open the query. Change either occurrence of the last name of "Poole" to **Fredrick** then move to another record to save your changes. Close the CaseListing query.
   - **e.** Double-click the EmployeeEntry form in the Navigation Pane to open the form. Use the navigation buttons to navigate through the 20 records to observe each employee's cases. When you reach the Lisa Fredrick record (record 17 of 20), change her extension value to **8686**. Close the EmployeeEntry form.
   - **f.** Double-click the CallLog report in the Navigation Pane to open the report. The records are listed in ascending order by employee last name. Scroll through the report to find the "Fredrick, Lisa" record. Close the CallLog report. Note that both the edit to Lisa's last name and the change to her extension value in previous steps are reflected in the report.
   - **g.** In your IL_AC_1_Database.docx document, add one more sentence to explain why the edits to Lisa's record in previous steps carried through to the CallLog report. Check the spelling, save your changes, then close the IL_AC_1_Database.docx document.
3. **Navigate and enter data.**
   - **a.** Double-click the Employees table to open it, then enter the following record for a new employee:
     EmployeeID: (AutoNumber)
     LastName: Curtiss
     FirstName: Pamela
     Extension: 8181
     Department: Marketing
   - **b.** Close the Employees table.
4. **Edit existing data.**
   - **a.** Double-click the Cases table to open it, click the ResolvedDate field for CaseID 1, then enter **4/3/21**. Note that you can use the automatic Calendar Picker that assists you when you are entering or updating data in a field with a Date/Time data type. You can also type a date using a month/day/year format.
   - **b.** Click the ResolvedDate field for the record with CaseID 5 and enter today's date. Note that you can enter today's date from the keyboard or use the CTRL+; shortcut. (*Hint*: Press and hold the CTRL key while pressing the semicolon ; key.)
   - **c.** Edit the CaseTitle value for CaseID 23 to include the word **automatically** as in "Excel formulas are not automatically updating".
   - **d.** Close the Cases table.

5. **Create a table.**
   a. Click the Create tab on the ribbon, click the Table Design button in the Tables group, then create a new table with the following three fields and data types:

field name	data type
StateName	Short Text
StateAbbreviation	Short Text
Capital	Short Text

   b. Save the table with the name **States**. Click No when asked if you want Access to create the primary key field.

6. **Modify fields.**
   a. In Design View of the States table, change the Field Size property for the StateName and Capital fields to **25**, and the StateAbbreviation field to **2**.
   b. Enter an Input Mask property of **LL;;*** for the StateAbbreviation field. (*Hint*: Do not use the Input Mask Wizard. Enter the property directly into the Input Mask property box.)
   c. Change the Field Name of the StateAbbreviation field to **StateAbbrev**.
   d. Save the States table, then test the Input Mask by entering the first record into the table for Alabama using the following information:

StateName	StateAbbrev	Capital
Alabama	AL	Montgomery

   e. Use the Tell Me (Search) box to read about the three parts of an Input Mask property and the meaning of the L character.
   f. Close the States table.

7. **Create a query.**
   a. Use the Simple Query Wizard to create a new query with the following fields in the following order: LastName and FirstName from the Employees table, CaseTitle from the Cases table, and CallDateTime from the Calls table.
   b. Select a detail query, and title the query **CallListing**.
   c. Display the query datasheet, and change the last name of Mindi Meyers to **Perez**. Notice that both records that display Mindi's name change to Perez when you move to a new record. Her name was stored only once in the Employees table but selected twice for this query because she has taken two calls.
   d. Save and close the CallListing query.

8. **Create a form.**
   a. Use the Form Wizard to create a new form based on all the fields in the Employees table. Use a Columnar layout and title the form **EmployeeMaster**.
   b. Use the record navigation buttons to navigate to the third record to confirm that Mindi Meyers has been changed to Mindi Perez.
   c. Save and close the EmployeeMaster form.

9. **Create a report.**
   a. Use the Report Wizard to create a new report based on all the fields of the Employees table.
   b. Group the records by Department, and sort them in ascending order by LastName and then FirstName.
   c. Use a stepped layout and a landscape orientation.
   d. Title the report **EmployeeMasterList**, and preview it as shown in **FIGURE 1-21**.
   e. Use the navigation buttons to locate the Mindi Perez record (in the Research department) to confirm that the report is also based on the updated data.
   f. Save and close the EmployeeMasterList report.

Skills Review (continued)

FIGURE 1-21

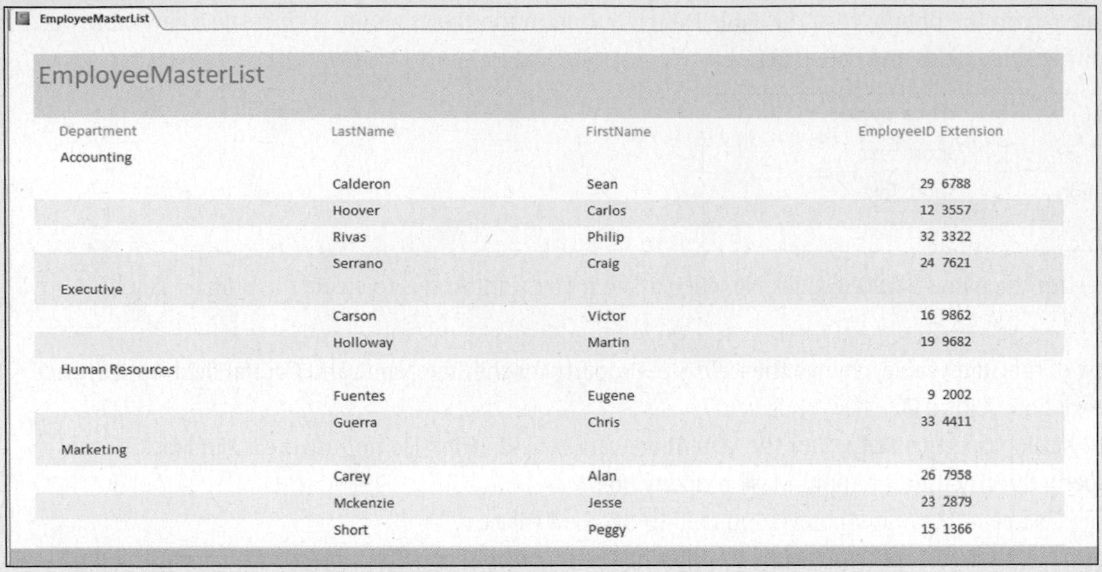

EmployeeMasterList

Department	LastName	FirstName	EmployeeID	Extension
Accounting				
	Calderon	Sean	29	6788
	Hoover	Carlos	12	3557
	Rivas	Philip	32	3322
	Serrano	Craig	24	7621
Executive				
	Carson	Victor	16	9862
	Holloway	Martin	19	9682
Human Resources				
	Fuentes	Eugene	9	2002
	Guerra	Chris	33	4411
Marketing				
	Carey	Alan	26	7958
	Mckenzie	Jesse	23	2879
	Short	Peggy	15	1366

10. Save and share a database with OneDrive.

- **a.** Close the IL_AC_1_SupportDesk.accdb database.
- **b.** Log into your Microsoft OneDrive.com account.
- **c.** Create a Module1 folder (if you have not already done so).
- **d.** Upload the IL_AC_1_SupportDesk.accdb database to the Module1 folder.
- **e.** Through email, share the IL_AC_1_SupportDesk.accdb database with your instructor.

11. Create a new database.

- **a.** Start Access and use the Blank desktop database to create a new database named **IL_AC_1_CustomerSurvey** in the folder where you store your Data Files.
- **b.** Close the Table1 table without saving it.
- **c.** Build the first table by importing a listing of states and provinces from an existing Excel spreadsheet named **Support_IL_AC_1_StatesAndProvs**.
- **d.** The first row contains column headings. Accept the default field options, but choose StateAbbrev as the primary key field.
- **e.** Name the new table **StatesAndProvs**, and do not save the import steps.
- **f.** Open the StatesAndProvs table in Datasheet View to confirm that 64 records were imported, then close the StatesAndProvs table.

12. Compact and back up a database.

- **a.** On the Database Tools tab, compact and repair the IL_AC_1_CustomerSurvey.accdb database.
- **b.** Create a backup of the IL_AC_1_CustomerSurvey.accdb database in the folder where you store your Data Files. Be sure to use the Back Up Database option so that the current date is automatically appended to the filename.
- **c.** View your Account settings, and in a Word document, note your existing Connected Services.
- **d.** Using the Tell me what you want to do feature, research Connected Services and pick one of the services to explore further. Identify which Connected Service you chose in your Word document, write at least one sentence explaining why you chose it and one sentence describing the features it offers. Save the document with the name **IL_AC_1_AccessConnectedServices**.
- **e.** Close the IL_AC_1_CustomerSurvey.accdb database and Access.

Independent Challenge 1

It's important to think about how to set up proper fields for a table before working in Access. Consider the following twelve subject areas:

- Contacts
- Islands of the Caribbean
- Members of the U.S. House of Representatives
- College course offerings
- Physical activities
- Ancient wonders of the world
- Restaurant menu
- Shopping catalog items
- Vehicles
- Conventions
- Party guest list
- Movie listings

a. For each subject, create a table in a single Word document named **IL_AC_1_SampleTables**. The table should contain four to seven columns and three rows. In the first row, enter appropriate field names that you would expect to see in a table used to manage that subject. Note the guidelines for proper field construction below.

b. In the second and third rows of each table, enter two realistic records. The first subject, Contacts, is completed as an example to follow.

TABLE: Contacts

FirstName	LastName	Street	Zip	Phone
Marco	Lopez	100 Main Street	88715	555-612-3312
Christopher	Stafford	253 Maple Lane	77824	555-612-1179

c. Use the following guidelines as you build each table in Word:

- Make sure each record represents one item in that table. For example, in the Restaurant Menu table, the following table is a random list of categories of food. These records do not represent one item in a restaurant menu.

Beverage	Appetizer	Meat	Vegetable	Dessert
Milk	Chicken wings	Steak	Carrots	Chocolate cake
Tea	Onion rings	Salmon	Potato	Cheesecake

A better example of records that describe an item in the restaurant menu would be the following:

Category	Description	Price	Calories	Spicy
Appetizer	Chicken wings	$10	800	Yes
Beverage	Milk	$2	250	No

- Do not put first and last names in the same field. This prevents you from easily sorting, filtering, or searching on either part of the name later.
- Break street, city, state, zip, and country data into separate fields for the same reasons.
- Do not put values and units of measure such as 5 minutes, 4 lbs., or 6 square miles in the same field. This also prevents you from sorting and calculating on the numeric part of the information.
- Make your field names descriptive such as TimeInMinutes or AreaInSquareMiles so that each record's entries are consistent.
- Remember that this exercise is a conceptual exercise on creating proper fields for a particular subject. Putting all these tables in one Access database would be analogous to putting a letter to your Congressman, a creative poem, and a cover letter to a future employer all in the same Word file. Use Word for this exercise to focus on the concepts of creating appropriate fields and records for a subject.

d. Save and close the IL_AC_1_SampleTables Word document.

Independent Challenge 2

You are working for a city to coordinate a series of community-wide preparedness activities. You have started a database to track the activities and volunteers who are attending them.

a. Start Access, then open the IL_AC_1-3.accdb database from the location where you store your Data Files. Save it with the name **IL_AC_1_Volunteers** and then enable content if prompted.

b. Open each table's datasheet to study the number of fields and records per table.

c. In a Word document named **IL_AC_1_VolunteerTables**, re-create the following table and fill in the blanks:

table name	number of records	number of fields

d. Close all open tables, then use the Simple Query Wizard to create a query using the following fields in the following order: FirstName and LastName from the Volunteers table, and ActivityName, ActvityDate, and ActivityHours from the Activities table. Show detail records, name the query **VolunteerActivity**, then open it in Datasheet View.

e. In the ActivityName field, change any occurrence of Shelter Fundamentals to **Outdoor Shelter Fundamentals**, then click any other record to save the change, as shown in **FIGURE 1-22**. Save and close the VolunteerActivity query.

f. Use the Form Wizard to create a new form based on all the fields in the Activities table. Use a columnar layout, title the form **ActivityEntry**, and view it in Form View. The Outdoor Shelter Fundamentals record should be the first record in the form. Save and close the ActivityEntry form.

FIGURE 1-22

VolunteerActivity

FirstNa	LastNar	ActivityName	ActivityDate	ActivityHour
Rhea	Alman	Outdoor Shelter Fundamentals	7/31/2021	8
Micah	Ati	Managing Volunteers	8/27/2021	8
Young	Bogard	Outdoor Shelter Fundamentals	7/31/2021	8
Andrea	Collins	First Aid	8/1/2021	8
Gabriel	Hammer	Outdoor Shelter Fundamentals	7/31/2021	8
Evan	Bouchart	Forklift Training	8/14/2021	6
Ann	Bovier	Outdoor Shelter Fundamentals	7/31/2021	8
Gabriel	Hammer	Warehouse Logistics	8/19/2021	4
Forrest	Browning	Forklift Training	8/14/2021	6
Patch	Bullock	Cardiopulmonary resuscitation CPR	8/28/2021	4
Student Fi	Student Lː	Community Preparedness	8/7/2021	16
Denice	Custard	Water Safety	8/4/2021	6
Angela	Cabriella	Water Safety	8/4/2021	6
Gina	Daniels	Livestock in Disasters	8/22/2021	0
Quentin	Garden	Personal Safety and Security	8/15/2021	6
Heidi	Kalvert	Grief Counseling	8/6/2021	8
Helen	Hubert	Automated External Defibrillator AED	8/5/2021	4
Jeremiah	Hopper	Hurricane Preparedness	8/26/2021	6
Loraine	Goode	Outdoor Shelter Fundamentals	7/31/2021	8
Karla	Larson	Animals in Disasters	8/8/2021	4
Katrina	Margolis	Incident Management	8/11/2021	4
Harvey	McCord	Food Service	8/13/2021	6
Sally	Olingback	Community Preparedness	8/7/2021	16
Mallory	Olson	Basic Life Support BLS	8/25/2021	4

Record: 2 of 76 No Filter Search

Independent Challenge 2 (continued)

g. Use the Report Wizard to create a new report based on the following fields in the following order: ActivityName from the Activities table and LastName from the Volunteers table. View the data by ActivityName then sort the records in ascending order by the LastName. Use a stepped layout and a portrait orientation. Title the report **ActivityRoster** and preview the report.

h. Close the IL_AC_1_Volunteer.accdb database, then exit Access.

Visual Workshop

Open the IL_AC_1-4.accdb database from the location where you store your Data Files and save it as **IL_AC_1_CollegeCourses**, then enable content if prompted. Use the Simple Query Wizard to create the query shown in **FIGURE 1-23** that contains the ClassNo, Description, and Credits fields from the Classes table, and the SectionNo, MeetingDay, and Time fields from the Sections table. Name the query **DepartmentOfferings**.

FIGURE 1-23

DepartmentOfferings

ClassNo	Description	Credits	SectionNo	MeetingDay	Time
ACCT109	Basics of Income Taxes	3	52	M	10:00 AM
ACCT111	Small Business Accounting	3	51	T	8:00 AM
ACCT121	Accounting I	3	48	W	10:00 AM
ACCT121	Accounting I	3	49	H	12:00 PM
ACCT121	Accounting I	3	50	M	1:00 PM
ACCT122	Accounting II	3	47	T	11:00 AM
ACCT135	Computerized Accounting Applications	3	44	W	9:00 AM
ACCT135	Computerized Accounting Applications	3	45	W	8:00 AM
ACCT135	Computerized Accounting Applications	3	46	M	9:00 AM
ACCT145	Accounting for Nonprofits	3	43	H	8:00 AM
ACCT155	Cost Accounting	3	42	T	9:00 AM
ACCT165	Managerial Accounting	3	41	W	1:00 PM
ACCT201	Fraud Examination	3	40	H	9:00 AM
BUS120	Managerial Attitudes	3	39	M	2:00 PM
BUS121	Introduction to Business	3	38	T	2:00 PM
BUS123	Personal Finance	3	37	H	1:00 PM
BUS123	Personal Finance	3	36	W	10:00 AM
BUS140	Principles of Supervision	3	34	T	9:00 AM
BUS140	Principles of Supervision	3	35	M	8:00 AM
CIS134	Programming Fundamentals	4	6	M	3:00 PM
CIS134	Programming Fundamentals	4	7	T	6:00 PM
CIS134	Programming Fundamentals	4	8	M	8:00 AM
CIS134	Programming Fundamentals	4	9	T	8:00 AM
CIS162	Database Programming	4	5	W	8:00 AM

Record: 1 of 59 No Filter Search

Building Tables and Relationships

CASE At JCL Talent, you are working with Lydia Snyder, vice president of operations, to continue developing the Access database that tracks job placement data. You will improve the individual tables in the database and then link them together to create a relational database.

Module Objectives

After completing this module, you will be able to:

- Import data from Excel
- Modify fields in Datasheet View
- Modify Number and Currency fields
- Modify Short Text fields
- Modify Date/Time fields
- Create primary key fields
- Design related tables
- Create one-to-many relationships
- Work with subdatasheets

Files You Will Need

IL_AC_2-1.accdb
Support_IL_AC_2_States.xlsx
Support_IL_AC_2_Provs.xlsx
IL_AC_2-2.accdb
Support_IL_AC_2_Departments.xlsx
Support_IL_AC_2_Employees.xlsx
IL_AC_2-3.accdb
IL_AC_2-4.accdb
IL_AC_2-5.accdb
Support_IL_AC_2_Majors.xlsx
Support_IL_AC_2_Classes.xlsx
Support_IL_AC_2_Enrollments.xlsx
Support_IL_AC_2_Sections.xlsx
Support_IL_AC_2_Students.xlsx

Access
Module 2

Import Data from Excel

Learning Outcomes
- Import data from Excel
- Describe other file formats that work with Access

Importing enables you to quickly copy data from an external file into an Access database. You can import data from many sources, such as another Access database; Excel spreadsheet; SharePoint site; Outlook email; or text files in an HTML, XML, or delimited text file format. In a **delimited text file**, data is separated by a common character, the **delimiter**, such as a comma, tab, or dash. A **CSV (comma-separated value)** file is a common example of a delimited text file. An **XML file** contains the data surrounded by **Extensible Markup Language (XML)** tags that identify field names and data. The most common file format for importing data into an Access database is **Microsoft Excel**, the spreadsheet program in the Microsoft Office suite. CASE *Lydia Snyder gives you two Excel spreadsheets that list information for USA states and Canadian provinces and asks you to import the data into the database.*

STEPS

QUICK TIP
Updates to linked data made in the original data source are reflected in the Access database, but linked data cannot be changed in Access.

1. **sam Start Access, open the IL_AC_2-1.accdb database from the location where you store your Data Files, save it as IL_AC_2_Jobs, enable content if prompted, click the External Data tab, click the New Data Source button in the Import & Link group, point to From File, click Excel, click the Browse button, navigate to the location where you store your Data Files, then double-click Support_IL_AC_2_States.xlsx**

   The **Get External Data - Excel Spreadsheet** dialog box opens, as shown in FIGURE 2-1. You can **import** the records to a new table, **append** the records to an existing table, or **link** to the data source. Both importing and appending create a copy of the data in the database. **Linking** means that the data is not copied into Access; it is only stored in the original data source. See TABLE 2-1 for more information on file formats that can share data with Access.

2. **Click OK**

   The **Import Spreadsheet Wizard** helps you import data from Excel into Access and presents a sample of the data to be imported, as shown in FIGURE 2-2.

QUICK TIP
You can save the choices you made while importing if you need to repeat the steps regularly.

3. **Click the First Row Contains Column Headings check box, click Next, click Next to accept the default field options, click the Choose my own primary key option button, click the StateName list arrow, click StateAbbrev to choose it as the primary key field, click Next, type States as the new table name, click Finish, then click Close**

   The **primary key field** stores unique data for each record. The two-character state abbreviation is unique for each state and will be used later to connect to other tables. You also want to import more data that represents the 13 provinces in Canada.

4. **Click the New Data Source button, point to From File, click Excel, click the Browse button, navigate to the location where you store your Data Files, then double-click Support_IL_AC_2_Provs.xlsx**

TROUBLE
If a "Subscript out of range" error message appears, close the database, reopen it, then repeat Steps 4 and 5.

5. **Click the Append option button in the Get External Data – Excel Spreadsheet dialog box, click the Companies list arrow, click States, click OK, click Next, click Finish, then click Close**

   In order to append data to an existing table, the column names of the Excel spreadsheet must match the field names in the Access table.

6. **Double-click the States table to view the imported data, note 64 in the record selector box at the bottom of the datasheet, then close the States table**

   A better name for the table would be StatesAndProvinces.

TROUBLE
An object must be closed before you can rename it.

7. **Right-click the States table in the Navigation Pane, click Rename, type StatesAndProvinces as the new name, then press ENTER**

FIGURE 2-1: Get External Data – Excel Spreadsheet dialog box

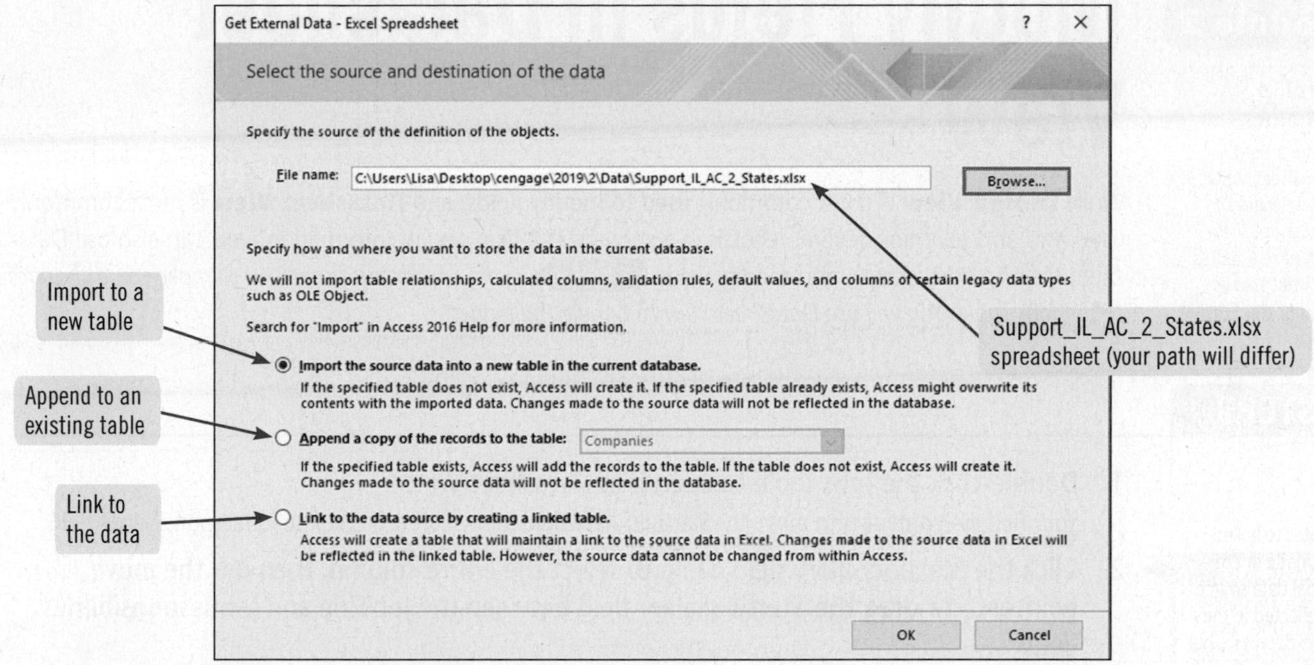

FIGURE 2-2: Import Spreadsheet Wizard

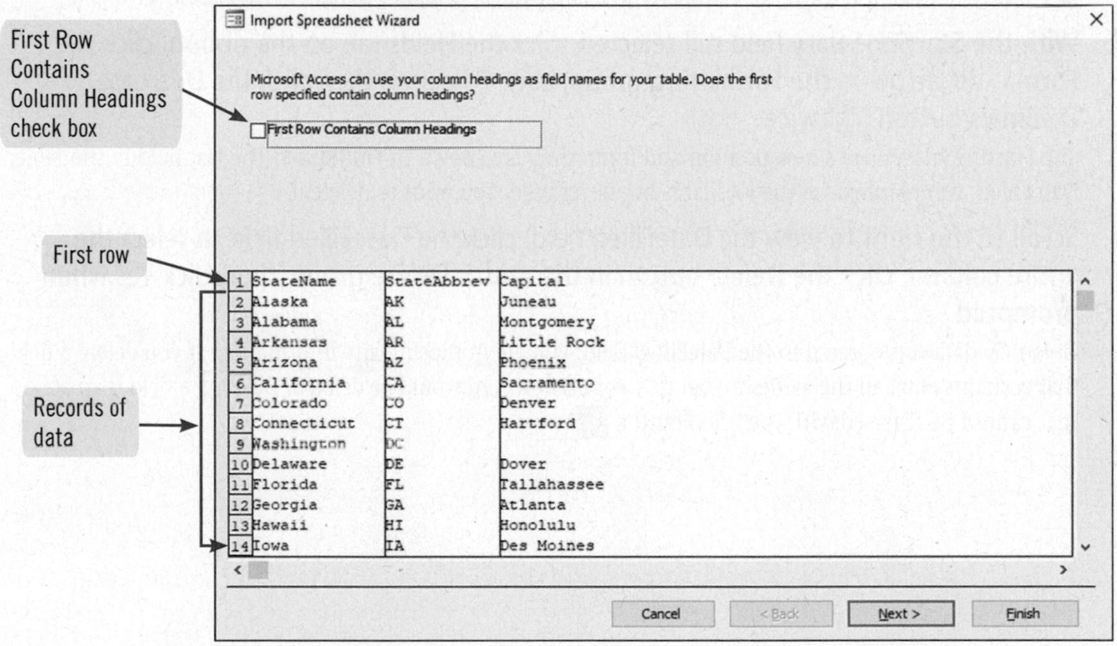

TABLE 2-1: File formats that Access can link to, import, and export

file format	import	link	export
Access	✓	✓	✓
Excel	✓	✓	✓
Word			✓
SharePoint site	✓	✓	✓
Email file attachments			✓
Outlook folder	✓	✓	
ODBC database (such as SQL Server)	✓	✓	✓

file format	import	link	export
dBASE	✓	✓	✓
HTML document	✓	✓	✓
PDF or XPS file			✓
Text file (delimited or fixed width)	✓	✓	✓
XML file	✓		✓

Access
Module 2

Learning Outcomes
- Move a field in Datasheet View
- Delete a field in Datasheet View
- Decrease a field's decimal places
- Modify the Format property

Modify Fields in Datasheet View

While **Design View** is most commonly used to modify fields, and **Datasheet View** is most commonly used find and examine several records in a spreadsheet-like view of information, you can also use Datasheet View to add, delete, and modify fields. **CASE** *Lydia Snyder has asked you to make some changes to the Jobs table. You will use Datasheet View to handle the request.*

STEPS

QUICK TIP
A vertical black line indicates the new position for the field.

1. **Double-click the Jobs table to open it in Datasheet View**
   Your first assignment is to move the StartingSalary field immediately before the JobResponsibilties field.
2. **Click the StartingSalary field name to select the entire column, then use the move pointer to drag the StartingSalary field between the JobTitle and JobResponsibilties fields**
   The StartingSalary field was created using a Number data type, but you want to display the data as a monetary value. You can use the Format property to change the appearance of data in the datasheet.
3. **With the StartingSalary field still selected, click the Fields tab on the ribbon, click the Format list arrow in the Formatting group, click Currency, then click the Decrease Decimals button twice**
   The StartingSalary field's new position and formatting are shown in **FIGURE 2-3**. The last field in the table, DateFilled, was planned for the Jobs table but never used. You want to delete it.
4. **Scroll to the right to view the DateFilled field, click the DateFilled field to select the entire column, click the Delete button in the Add & Delete group, then click Yes when prompted**
   Given no data was entered in the DateFilled field, you are not losing any information. If you delete a field that contains data, all the values in that field for every record would be deleted. Deleting a field is an action that cannot be reversed with the Undo button.

FIGURE 2-3: StartingSalary field in the Jobs table has been moved and formatted

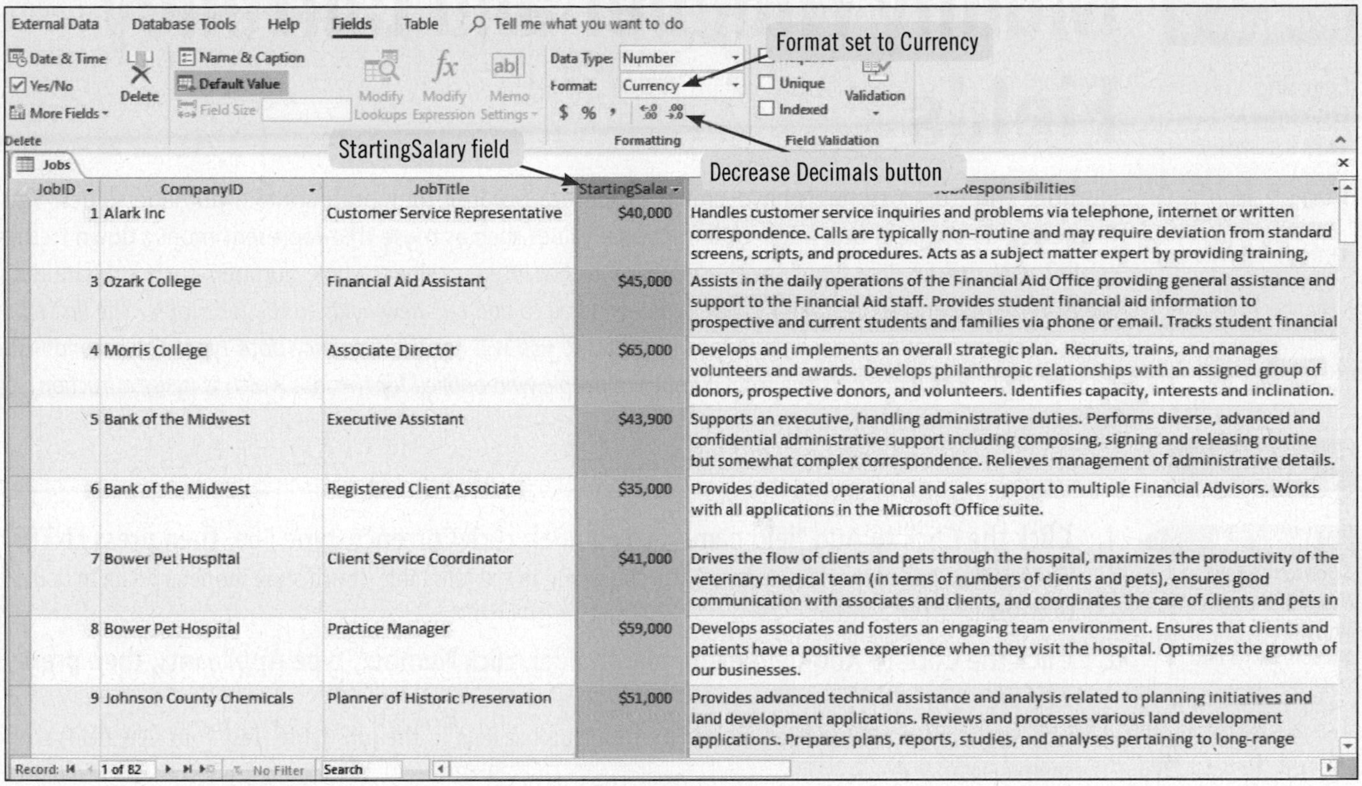

Currency versus Number data type

In general, if a number represents a **fractional** value (such as dollars and cents, not a whole number), choose Currency for its data type. The underlying reason that all fractional values should be given a Currency data type is that a computer works with numbers using a binary system (1s and 0s), which cannot accurately store decimal fractions such as 0.1 or 0.01. The system can lead to rounding errors that all programming languages must address. In Access, the Currency data type includes special code to avoid these errors. If you are working with **integer** (a whole number, not a fraction) data, however, the Number data type provides faster performance. Whether you choose the Currency or Number data type, you can format the data to look as desired.

Modify Number and Currency Fields

Learning Outcomes
- Add a Currency field
- Add a Number field
- Modify the Field Size property for a Number field
- Modify the Decimal Places property

Number and Currency fields have similar properties because they both contain numeric values. The **Currency** data type is best applied to fractional values such as those that represent money down to the cent. The **Number** data type is best used to represent integer values, whole numbers such as quantities, measurements, and scores. CASE *Lydia asks you to add two new fields to the Jobs table. The first field named Fee represents money in dollars and cents, so you will use the Currency data type. The second field named Applicants represents the total number of people who applied for the job, which is never a fraction, so you will use the Number data type.*

STEPS

QUICK TIP
Scroll to the right side of the datasheet to find the Click to Add field name placeholder.

1. **Click the Click to Add field name placeholder, click Currency, type Fee, then press ENTER**
   The Fee field has been added as a new Currency field in the Jobs table. It will store monetary data in dollars and cents.
2. **Click the Click to Add field name placeholder, click Number, type Applicants, then press ENTER**
   The Applicants field has been added as a new Number field in the Jobs table. Test your new fields with sample data.
3. **Click the Fee field for the first record, type 25.25, press TAB, type 50, then click the second record to see the data you've entered, as shown in FIGURE 2-4**
   Access automatically formatted the value in the Fee field as $25.25. Some field properties can be set in both Datasheet View and Design View.
4. **Click the Fee field, click the Fields tab on the ribbon if not already selected, click the Default Value button in the Properties group, type 50.25, click OK in the Expression Builder dialog box, click the Applicants field, then click the Increase Decimals button in the Formatting group**
   The **Default Value** property automatically enters the property value, in this case 50.25, for all new records. The **Decimal Places** property displays the value with the given number of digits to the right of the decimal point. Because the Applicants field will store only whole numbers, showing the decimal place does not make good sense. You will switch to Table Design View to see how the same property can be modified in both views, then change the Decimal Places property value for the Applicants field back to 0.
5. **Right-click the Jobs table tab, click Design View, make sure the Applicants field is selected, click the Decimal Places property box, change the value to 0, then press ENTER**
   Table Design View gives you access to *all* field properties and as such, is generally the preferred way of changing field properties.

   The **Field Size** property determines the size or length of the maximum value for that field. Choosing the smallest Field Size for your Number fields helps improve database performance. See TABLE 2-2 for more information on Number Field Size property options. The Integer Field Size is large enough to hold any potential entry in the Applicants field.

QUICK TIP
Double-click a property name to toggle through the choices.

6. **With the Applicants field still selected, click the Field Size property, click the Field Size list arrow, then click Integer**
   Your Table Design View should look like FIGURE 2-5.
7. **Save the Jobs table then close it**

FIGURE 2-4: Adding a Currency field and a Number field

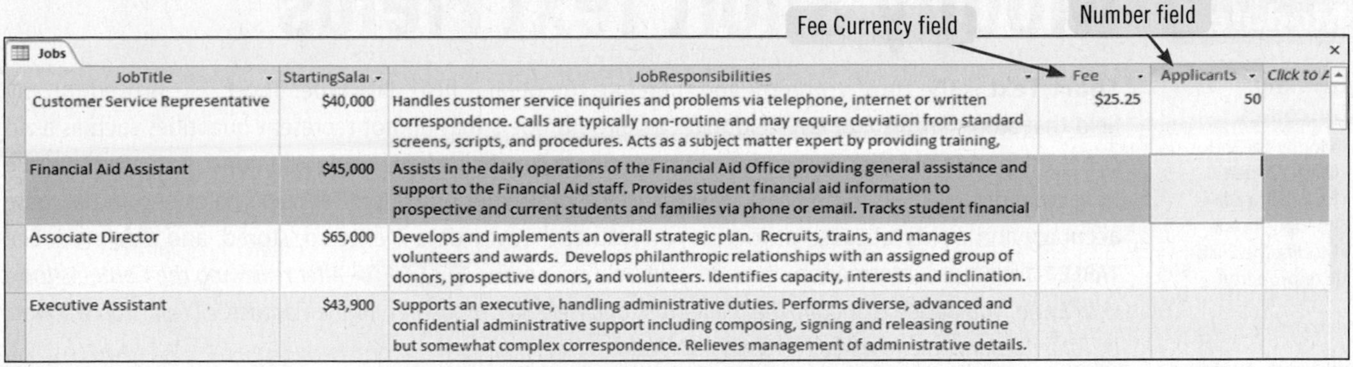

Applicants Number field
Fee Currency field
Jobs
JobTitle
StartingSalai
JobResponsibilities
Fee
Applicants
Click to A
Customer Service Representative
$40,000
Handles customer service inquiries and problems via telephone, internet or written correspondence. Calls are typically non-routine and may require deviation from standard screens, scripts, and procedures. Acts as a subject matter expert by providing training,
$25.25
50
Financial Aid Assistant
$45,000
Assists in the daily operations of the Financial Aid Office providing general assistance and support to the Financial Aid staff. Provides student financial aid information to prospective and current students and families via phone or email. Tracks student financial
Associate Director
$65,000
Develops and implements an overall strategic plan. Recruits, trains, and manages volunteers and awards. Develops philanthropic relationships with an assigned group of donors, prospective donors, and volunteers. Identifies capacity, interests and inclination.
Executive Assistant
$43,900
Supports an executive, handling administrative duties. Performs diverse, advanced and confidential administrative support including composing, signing and releasing routine but somewhat complex correspondence. Relieves management of administrative details.

FIGURE 2-5: Modifying Number Field properties in Table Design View

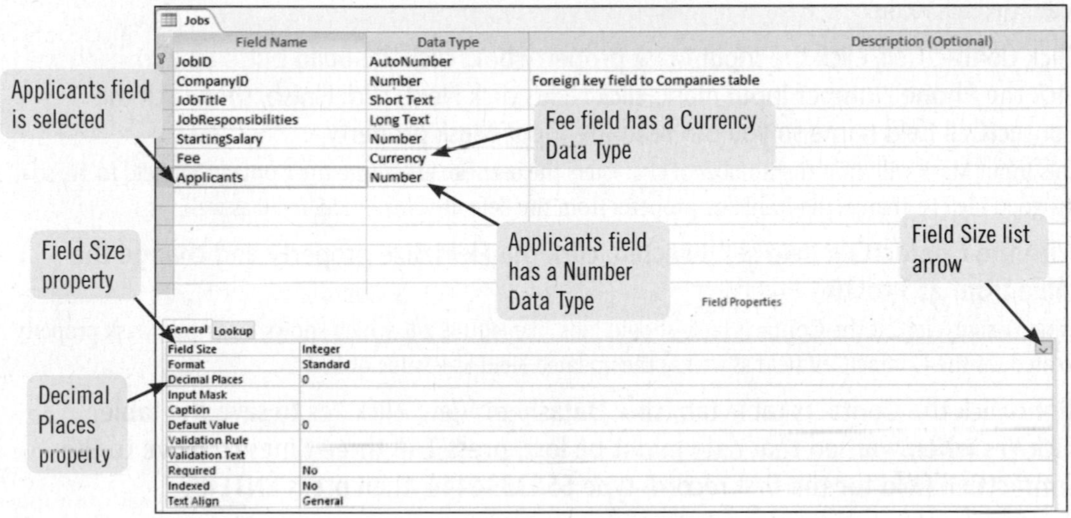

TABLE 2-2: Number Field Size property options

property	description
Byte	Stores numbers from 0 to 255 (no fractions)
Integer	Stores numbers from –32,768 to 32,767 (no fractions)
Long Integer	Stores numbers from –2,147,483,648 to 2,147,483,647 (no fractions)
Single	Stores numbers (including fractions with six digits to the right of the decimal point) times 10 to the –38th to +38th power
Double	Stores numbers (including fractions with more than 10 digits to the right of the decimal point) in the range of 10 to the –324th to +324th power

Modify Short Text Fields

Learning Outcomes
- Modify the Input Mask property
- Enter data using an input mask
- Modify the Field Size property

Short Text is the most common and therefore the default field data type. Short Text is used for any field that stores letters and any field that contains numbers that do not represent quantities such as a zip code, telephone number, or product number. Short Text fields have some additional properties unique to textual data such as Input Mask. Modifying the properties of a Short Text field helps ensure database accuracy and clarity because properties can restrict the way data is entered, stored, and displayed. See **TABLE 2-3** for more information on Short Text field properties. **CASE** *After reviewing the Contacts table with Lydia, you decide to modify the Input Mask and Field Size properties for the ContactCell field. You will work in Table Design View to make the changes.*

STEPS

1. **Right-click the Contacts table in the Navigation Pane, then click Design View on the shortcut menu**

   The **Input Mask** property provides a visual guide for users as they enter data. The ContactCell field is a good candidate for an Input Mask because phone numbers are consistently entered with 10 numeric characters for each record.

> **TROUBLE**
> The Build button [...] is located on the right side of the Input Mask property box.

2. **Click ContactCell, click the Input Mask property box, click the Build button [...], click the Phone Number input mask, click Next, click Next, click Finish, then click the ContactCell field name so you can read the Input Mask property**

   This Input Mask will limit the number of characters the user can enter into the ContactCell field to 10, so it is a good idea to change the Field Size property from the default value of 255 to 10 as well.

3. **With the ContactCell field still selected, click the Field Size property and change the value from 255 to 10**

   Table Design View of the Contacts table should look like **FIGURE 2-6**, which shows the Input Mask property created for the ContactCell field as well as the updated Field Size value of 10.

4. **Right-click the Contacts table tab, click Datasheet View, click Yes to save the table, click Yes when warned that data might be lost, press TAB three times to move to the ContactCell field for the first record, type 5553334444, then press ENTER**

   No data was lost because no existing value in the ContactCell field is greater than 10 characters. The Input Mask property creates an easy-to-use visual guide to facilitate accurate and consistent data entry for the ContactCell field.

   Your screen should look like **FIGURE 2-7**.

5. **Right-click the Contacts table tab, then click Close**

FIGURE 2-6: Modifying the Input Mask property

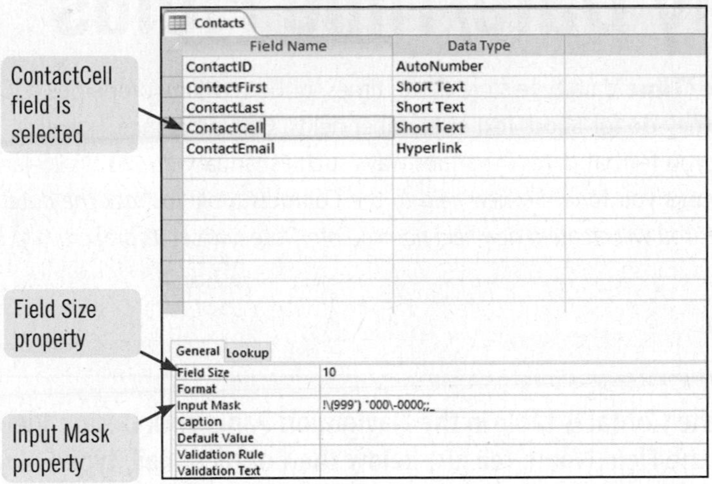

FIGURE 2-7: Entering data with an input mask

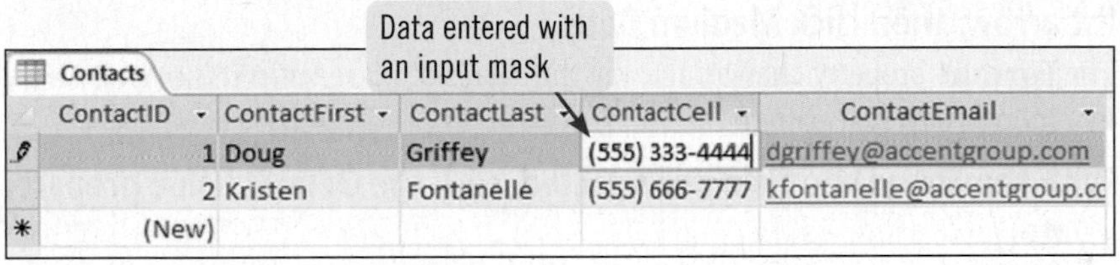

TABLE 2-3: Common Short Text field properties

property	description	sample field	sample property entry
Field Size	Controls how many characters can be entered into the field	State	2
Format	Controls how information will be displayed and printed	State	> (displays all characters in uppercase)
Input Mask	Provides a pattern for data to be entered	Phone	!(999) 000-0000;1;_
Caption	Describes the field in the first row of a datasheet, form, or report; if the Caption property is not entered, the field name is used to label the field	EmpNo	Employee Number
Default Value	Displays a value that is automatically entered in the given field for new records	City	Des Moines
Required	Determines if an entry is required for this field	LastName	Yes

Working with the Input Mask property

The Input Mask property provides a **pattern** for data to be entered, using three parts, each separated by a ; (semicolon). The first part provides a pattern for what type of data can be entered. For example, **9** represents an optional number, **0** a required number, **?** an optional letter, and **L** a required letter. The second part determines whether all displayed characters (such as dashes in a phone number) are stored in the field. For the second part of the input mask, a 0 entry stores all characters, such as 555-1199, and a 1 entry stores only the entered data, 5551199. The third part of the input mask determines which character Access uses to guide the user through the mask. Common choices are the asterisk (*), underscore (_), or pound sign (#).

Modify Date/Time Fields

Learning Outcomes
- Modify the Format property
- Modify the Default Value property
- Modify the Required property

Fields with a **Date/Time** data type store dates, times, or both. Many properties of Date/Time fields work the same way as they do for Short Text or Number fields. One difference, however, is the **Format** property, which helps you format dates in various ways such as January 25, 2021; 25-Jan-21; or 01/25/2021. CASE *Lydia asks you to add a new field to the Contacts table to track the date that the contact was added to the table. You will create a new field named EntryDate and set its properties to handle this request.*

STEPS

1. **Right-click the Contacts table in the Navigation Pane, click Design View on the shortcut menu, click the Field Name cell just below the ContactEmail, type EntryDate, press TAB, click the Data Type list arrow, then click Date/Time**
   With the field name and data type set, you use field properties to further describe the field.
2. **With the EntryDate field still selected, click the Format property box, click the Format list arrow, then click Medium Date**
   The **Format** property changes the way the data is displayed *after it is entered.* All dates in Access are *entered* in a month/day/year pattern.
3. **With the EntryDate field still selected, click the Default Value property box, then type =Date()**
   The Default Value property automatically enters a value in all new records. The equal sign = indicates that you are using a calculated expression, and **Date()** is an Access function that returns the current date.
   The updated Table Design View for the Contacts table is shown in FIGURE 2-8.
4. **Right-click the Contacts table tab, click Save, right-click the Contacts table tab again, then click Datasheet View**
   Note that the current date is already entered in the EntryDate field for the new record. To change the value, you can enter dates from the keyboard using a month/day/year pattern or pick a date from a pop-up calendar using the **Date Picker**.

   TROUBLE The current date will obviously be the date you perform these steps.
5. **Press TAB five times to move to the EntryDate field, click the Date Picker icon, click the current date on the pop-up calendar, click the EntryDate field for the second record, click the Date Picker icon, then click the current date on the calendar for the second record as well**
   With valid dates in the EntryDate field of both records, you can set the Required property to Yes for the EntryDate field.
6. **Click the EntryDate field name, click the Fields tab on the ribbon, then click the Required check box as shown in FIGURE 2-9**
   The **Required** property will create an error message if the user attempts to enter a record in the database without a date in the EntryDate field.
7. **Close the Contacts table**

FIGURE 2-8: Creating a Date/Time field

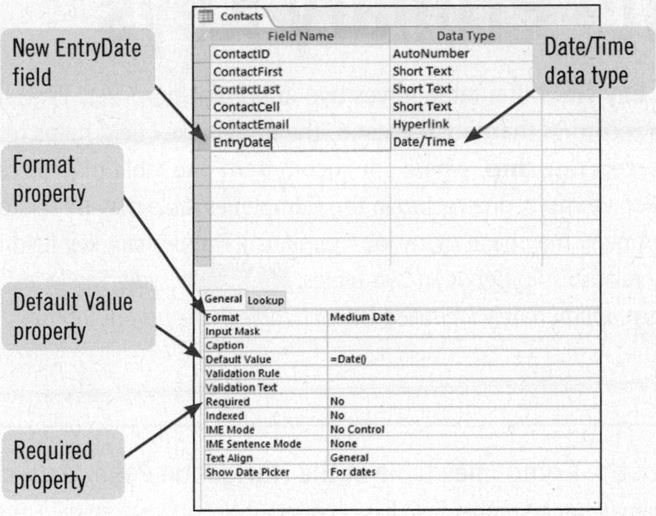

FIGURE 2-9: Working with dates

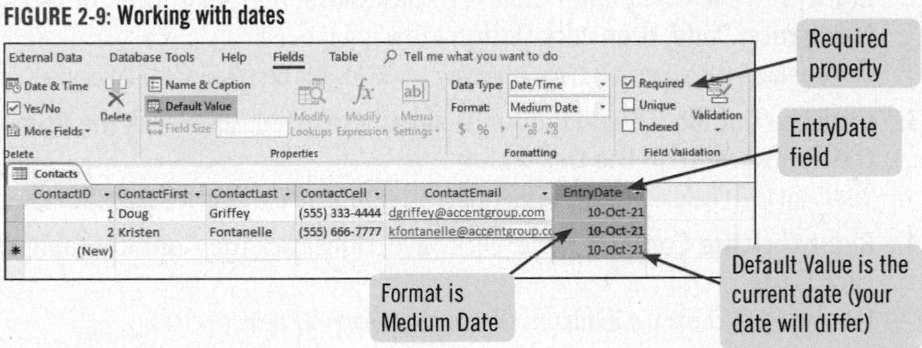

Entering dates

If you type the date for a Date/Type field instead of choosing a date from the pop-up calendar, Access assumes that years entered with two digits from 30 to 99 refer to the years 1930 through 1999, and 00 to 29 refers to the years 2000 through 2029. To enter a year before 1930 or after 2029, you must type all four digits of the year.

Using Smart Tags

Smart Tags are buttons that automatically appear in certain conditions. They provide a small menu of options to help you work with the task at hand. For example, in Table Design View, Access provides the **Property Update Options** Smart Tag to help you quickly apply property changes to other objects of the database that use the field. Another Smart Tag, the **Error Indicator** helps identify potential errors.

Create Primary Keys

Learning Outcome
- Create a primary key field

The **primary key field** of a table serves two important purposes. First, it contains data that uniquely identifies each record in that table. Second, the primary key field helps relate one table to another in a **one-to-many relationship**, where one record from one table may be related to many records in the second table. For example, one record in the Companies table may be related to many records in the Jobs table. (One company may have many job openings.) The primary key field is always on the "one" side of a one-to-many relationship between two tables. **CASE** *Lydia Snyder asks you to confirm that a primary key field has been appropriately identified for each table in the new database.*

STEPS

1. **Right-click the Companies table in the Navigation Pane, then click Design View**
   The CompanyID AutoNumber field has been set as the primary key field as evidenced by the **key symbol** to the left of the field name. A field with the AutoNumber data type is a good candidate for the primary key field in a table because it automatically contains a unique number for each record.
2. **Right-click the Companies table tab, click Close, right-click the Contacts table in the Navigation Pane, then click Design View**
   The Contacts table does not have a primary key field. The best choice would be the ContactID field.
3. **Click the ContactID field if it is not already selected, then click the Primary Key button in the Tools group on the Design tab**
   The ContactID field is now set as the primary key field for the Contacts table, as shown in FIGURE 2-10.
4. **Right-click the Contacts table, click Save, right-click the Contacts table tab again, then click Close**
   Next, you will check the Industries table for a primary key field.
5. **Right-click the Industries table in the Navigation Pane, click Design View, observe that the Short Text Industry field is set as the primary key field, right-click the Industries table tab, then click Close**
   Next, check the Jobs table.
6. **Right-click the Jobs table in the Navigation Pane, click Design View, observe that the AutoNumber JobID field is set as the primary key field, right-click the Jobs table tab, then click Close**
   Next, check the StatesAndProvinces table.
7. **Right-click the StatesAndProvinces table in the Navigation Pane, click Design View, observe that the Short Text StateAbbrev field is set as the primary key field as shown in FIGURE 2-11, right-click the StatesAndProvinces table tab, then click Close**
   Often, the primary key field is the first field in the table, but that is not a requirement. If you do not make any design changes to an object, you are not prompted to save it when you close it.

   Now that you have confirmed that each table in the database has an appropriate primary key field, you are ready to link the tables together to create a relational database. The primary key field plays a critical role in this process.

FIGURE 2-10: Setting the primary key field in Design View of the Contacts table

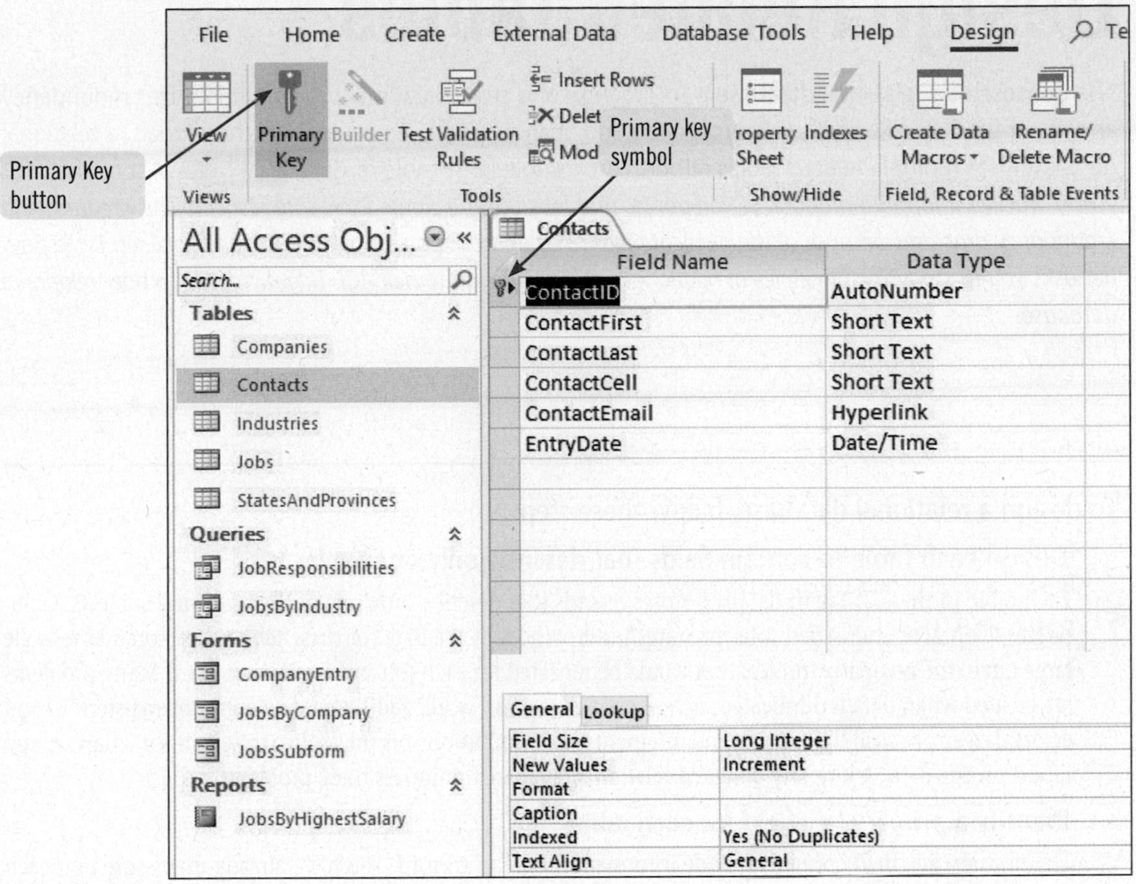

FIGURE 2-11: Design View of the StatesAndProvinces table

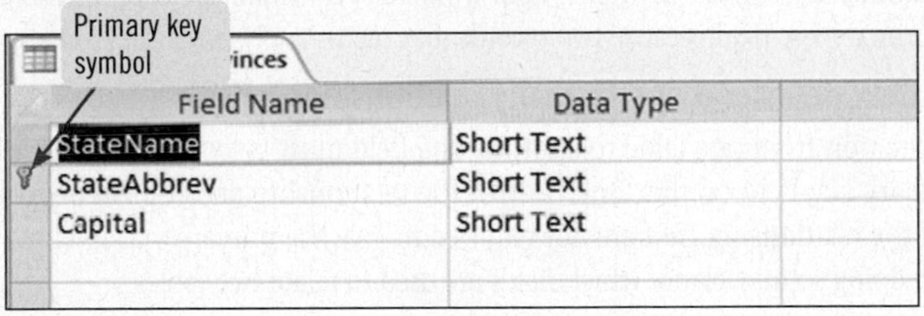

Access

Design Related Tables

Learning Outcomes
- Understand the terminology used when creating a relational database
- Understand the steps to create a relational database
- Analyze one-to-many relationships

The purpose of a relational database is to organize and store data in a way that minimizes redundancy and maximizes your flexibility when querying and analyzing data. To accomplish these goals, a relational database uses multiple related tables rather than a single large table of data. **CASE** *At one time, JCL Talent tracked information about its companies and jobs using a single Excel spreadsheet. This created data redundancy problems because of the duplicate industries and companies for each job and contact. Lydia Snyder asks you to study the principles of relational database design to help JCL Talent create a proper relational database.*

DETAILS

To design a relational database, follow these steps:

- **Design each table to contain fields that describe only one subject**

  Each table in the JCL Talent database stores records that describe only one of the following subjects: Companies, Contacts, Industries, Jobs, or StatesAndProvinces. If the data for these tables was stored in a single large table, the company information would be repeated for each job and for each contact. Many problems are created when data is duplicated such as extra data entry work; additional data entry inconsistencies and errors; larger physical data storage requirements; and limitations on the ability to search for, analyze, and report on the data. A properly designed relational database minimizes these problems.

- **Identify a primary key field for each table**

  The primary key field contains unique information for each record. You have already made sure that each of the five tables has a proper primary key field. Generally the primary key field has a numeric data type such as AutoNumber (automatically increments) or Number (user controlled), but sometimes Short Text fields serve this purpose such as the StateAbbrev field in the StatesAndProvinces table. Although using a contact's last name as the primary key field might work in a very small database, names are generally a poor choice for the primary key field because two records may legitimately have the same name.

- **Build foreign key fields and one-to-many relationships**

  To tie the information from one table to another, one field must be common to each table. This linking field is the primary key field on the "one" side of the relationship and the **foreign key field** on the "many" side of the relationship. You are not required to give the primary and foreign key fields the same name, although doing so may clarify which fields are used to relate two tables.

  The current relational database design for the Jobs database is shown in **FIGURE 2-12**. It is only partially completed. Currently, one record in the Industries table is related to many records in the Companies table using the common Industry field. One record in the Companies table is related to many records in the Jobs tables using the common CompanyID field. The StatesAndProvinces as well as the Contacts tables are not currently participating in the relational database, but you will correct that in the next lesson. See **TABLE 2-4** for a summary of important relational database terminology.

TABLE 2-4: Terminology used when creating a relational database

term	definition
Field	An individual column of information in a table. A field should not contain more than one piece of data. For example, always separate first and last names into two fields to preserve your ability to sort, filter, or find either name. Do not enter numbers and units of measurement such as *10 minutes* or *5 hours* into a single field. Doing so prevents you from easily sorting and calculating on the numeric part of the information.
Record	A group of related fields that describes a person, place, thing, or transaction such as a company or a job; a row

term	definition
Table	A collection of records for a single subject such as Industries, Companies, Jobs, Contacts, or StatesAndProvinces
Primary key field	A field that contains unique data for each record. Often an AutoNumber or Number field, a primary key field may also have a Short Text data type. The primary key field may also be used on the parent table ("one" table) side of a one-to-many relationship.
Foreign key field	A field in the child table ("many" table) that connects each record to the appropriate record in the parent table ("one" table)
Parent table	The table on the "one" side of a "one-to-many" relationship
Parent record	A record in the parent table
Child table	The table on the "many" side of a "one-to-many" relationship
Child record	A record in the child table
One-to-many relationship	A link between two tables that relates one record in the parent table to many records in the child table. For example, one record in the Industries table can be related to many records in the Companies table. One record in the Companies table can be related to many records in the Jobs table. One record in the Companies table can be related to many records in the Contacts table.
One-to-one relationship	A link between two tables that relates one record in the parent table to one record in the child table. One-to-one relationships are rare because this relationship can be simplified by moving all the fields into a single table.
Many-to-many relationship	If two tables have a many-to-many relationship, it means that one record in one table may be related to many records in the other table and vice versa. You cannot directly create a many-to-many relationship between two tables in Access. To connect two tables with this relationship, you must establish a third table called a **junction table** and create two one-to-many relationships from the original two tables using the junction table as the child table for both relationships. For example, at a school, the Students and Classes tables have a many-to-many relationship because one student can be in many classes and one class can have many students. To connect the Students and Classes tables, you would have to create a third table, perhaps called Enrollments, as the junction table. One student can be enrolled in many classes. One class can have many enrollments.
Junction table	The table between two tables that have a many-to-many relationship; the junction table is a child table to both of the other two tables.
Referential integrity	A set of rules that helps eliminate the creation of orphan records in a child ("many") table. For example, with referential integrity enforced, you cannot enter a value in a foreign key field of the child ("many") table that does not have a match in the linking field of the parent ("one") table. Referential integrity also prevents you from deleting a record in the parent ("one") table if a matching entry exists in the foreign key field of the child ("many") table.
Orphan record	A record in a child ("many") table that has no match in the parent ("one") table. Orphan records cannot be created in a child table if referential integrity is enforced.
Scrubbing or data cleansing	The process of removing and fixing orphan records in a relational database

Access

FIGURE 2-12: Initial relational design for the Jobs database

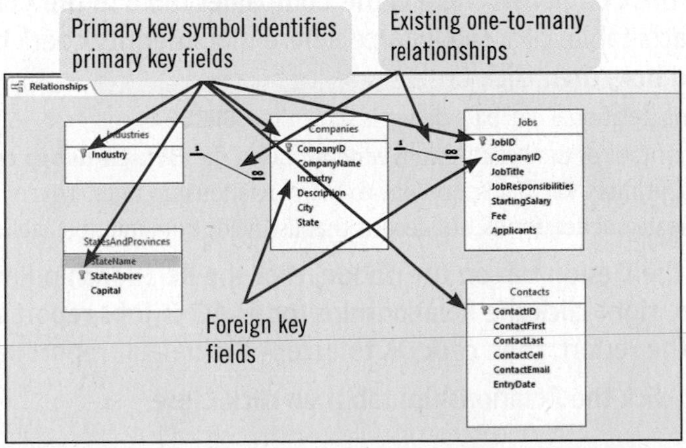

Create One-to-Many Relationships

Learning Outcomes
- Create a foreign key field
- Create one-to-many relationships
- Set referential integrity
- Create a Relationship report

You must connect the tables in your database in proper one-to-many relationships to enjoy the benefits of a relational database. You use a common field in each table to create one-to-many relationships between the tables. The common field is always the primary key field in the parent ("one") table and is called the foreign key field in the child ("many") table. **TABLE 2-5** includes a few common one-to-many relationships.

CASE *Lydia Snyder asks you to complete the relational database by connecting the StatesAndProvinces and Contacts tables with one-to-many relationships.*

STEPS

1. **Click the Database Tools tab on the ribbon, click the Relationships button, then drag the StatesAndProvinces table from the Navigation Pane to the Relationships window**

   Each table in the database is represented by a small **field list** window that displays the table's field names. A **key symbol** identifies the primary key field in each table. To relate the two tables in a one-to-many relationship, you connect them using a common field, which is always the primary key field on the parent ("one") side of the relationship.

QUICK TIP
Drag a table's title bar to move the field list.

2. **Drag the StateAbbrev field in the StatesAndProvinces table to the State field in the Companies table**

   The Edit Relationships dialog box opens, as shown in **FIGURE 2-13**, which provides information about the tables and fields that will participate in the relationship and the option to enforce referential integrity.

3. **Click the Enforce Referential Integrity check box, then click Create**

   A **one-to-many line** appears between the StatesAndProvinces table and the Companies table. The parent ("one") side, as indicated by the "1" symbol on the line, identifies the primary key field used in the relationship. The child ("many") side, as indicated by the **infinity symbol**, identifies the foreign key field used in the relationship.

   The Contacts table does not have a corresponding foreign key field, which you need to create a one-to-many relationship.

TROUBLE
If you need to delete a relationship, right-click a relationship line, then click Delete.

4. **Right-click the Contacts table field list, click Table Design, click the blank Field Name cell just below the EntryDate field, type CompanyID, click the Data Type list arrow, click Number, right-click the Contacts table tab, click Save, right-click the Contacts table tab again, then click Close**

   Now you are ready to connect the Contacts table to the Companies table.

5. **Drag the CompanyID field in the Companies table to the CompanyID field in the Contacts table, click the Enforce Referential Integrity check box in the Edit Relationships dialog box, then click Create**

   The final relational database design is shown in **FIGURE 2-14**.

   A printout of the Relationships window, called the **Relationship report**, includes table names, field names, primary key fields, and one-to-many relationship lines. This printout is a helpful resource as you later create queries, forms, and reports that use fields from multiple tables.

6. **Click the Design tab on the ribbon, click the Relationship Report button in the Tools group, right-click the Relationships for IL_AC_2_Jobs report tab, click Close, click Yes to save the report, then click OK to accept the default report name**

7. **Right-click the Relationships tab then click Close**

FIGURE 2-13: Edit Relationships dialog box

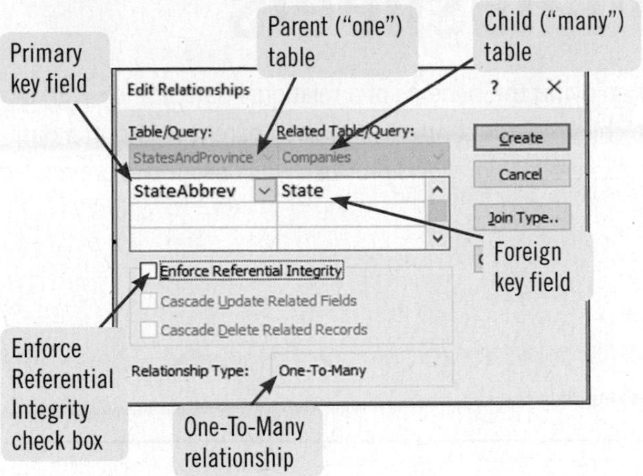

FIGURE 2-14: Final Relationships window

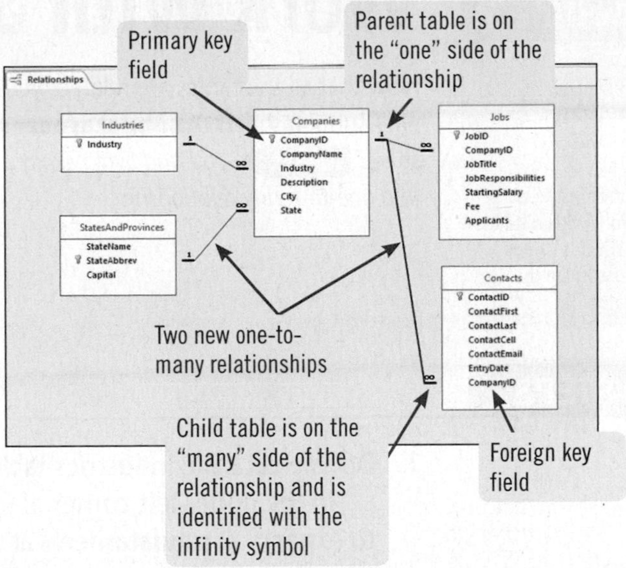

TABLE 2-5: Common one-to-many relationships

table on "one" side	table on "many" side	linking field	description
Products	Sales	ProductID	A ProductID field must have a unique entry in a Products table, but it is listed many times in a Sales table
Students	Enrollments	StudentID	A StudentID field must have a unique entry in a Students table, but it is listed many times in an Enrollments table as the student enrolls in multiple classes
Employees	Promotions	EmployeeID	An EmployeeID field must have a unique entry in an Employees table, but it is listed many times in a Promotions table as the employee is promoted to new job positions over time

Specifying the data type of the foreign key field

The foreign key field in the child table must have the same data type (Short Text or Number) as the primary key it is related to in the parent table. An exception to this rule is when the primary key field in the parent table has an AutoNumber data type. In this case, the linking foreign key field in the child table must have a Number data type. Also note that a Number field used as a foreign key field must have a Long Integer Field Size property to match the Field Size property of the AutoNumber primary key field.

Cascade options

Cascade Update Related Fields means that if a value in the primary key field (the field on the "one" side of a one-to-many relationship) is modified, all values in the foreign key field (the field on the child ("many") side of a one-to-many relationship) are automatically updated as well. **Cascade Delete Related Records** means that if a record on the parent ("one") side of a one-to-many relationship is deleted, all related records in the child ("many") table are also deleted. Because both of these options automatically change or delete data in the child ("many") table behind the scenes, they should be used with caution.

Access
Module 2

Work with Subdatasheets

Learning Outcomes
- Expand and collapse subdatasheets
- Work with data in a subdatasheet
- Customize the status bar

Now that all the tables are related, you can start enjoying the benefits of a relational database by working with subdatasheets. A **subdatasheet** shows the child records connected to each parent record in a datasheet. CASE *You and Lydia explore the subdatasheet feature that is provided when two tables are related in a one-to-many relationship.*

STEPS

1. **Double-click the Industries table to open it in Datasheet View, click the Select All button in the upper-left corner of the Industries datasheet, then click any Expand button to expand all subdatasheets at the same time, as shown in FIGURE 2-15**

   The Industries and Companies tables are linked in a one-to-many relationship, so the subdatasheet for each industry record displays related child records from the Companies table.

   Note that the records in the subdatasheet also have Expand buttons.

2. **Click the Expand button to the left of the Navigational Systems record (the second record in the Aerospace subdatasheet)**

   The Companies table participates as the parent table in two different one-to-many relationships, so you are presented with the Insert Subdatasheet dialog box, asking which child table you want to select.

3. **Click Jobs in the Insert Subdatasheet dialog box**

   Notice that the CompanyID field is automatically added to the Link Child Fields and Link Master Fields boxes, as shown in **FIGURE 2-16**, because it is the field that connects the Companies and Jobs tables.

4. **Click OK in the Insert Subdatasheet dialog box**

   The four records in the Jobs table are linked to the Navigational Systems record in the Companies table and are now displayed in the Navigational Systems subdatasheet. You can use subdatasheets to enter and edit data.

5. **Enter 50.25 as the Fee field value for each of the four job records in the Navigational Systems subdatasheet, click the Select All button in the upper-left corner of the Industries datasheet, click the Collapse button to the left of the Aerospace record, right-click the Industries table tab, click Close, then click No when asked to save changes to the Companies table**

6. **Double-click the Jobs table to open it in Datasheet View, scroll down to the records for the Navigational Systems company (JobIDs 23 through 26), then scroll to the right to view the 50.25 entries you previously made to the Fee field in a subdatasheet**

   When working with data in Datasheet View, subdatasheets make it easy to view child records.

   As you are working with Access, you may notice messages and indicators that appear in the status bar, the bottom bar in the application window. See **TABLE 2-6** for information on status bar indicators. You may turn these indicators on and off by right-clicking the status bar and selecting the indicator that you want to change. Most of the indicator messages appear in the right corner of the status bar.

7. **sam Right-click the Jobs table tab, click Close, click the Database Tools tab, click the Compact and Repair Database button, then close Access**

FIGURE 2-15: Expanding subdatasheets for the Industries table

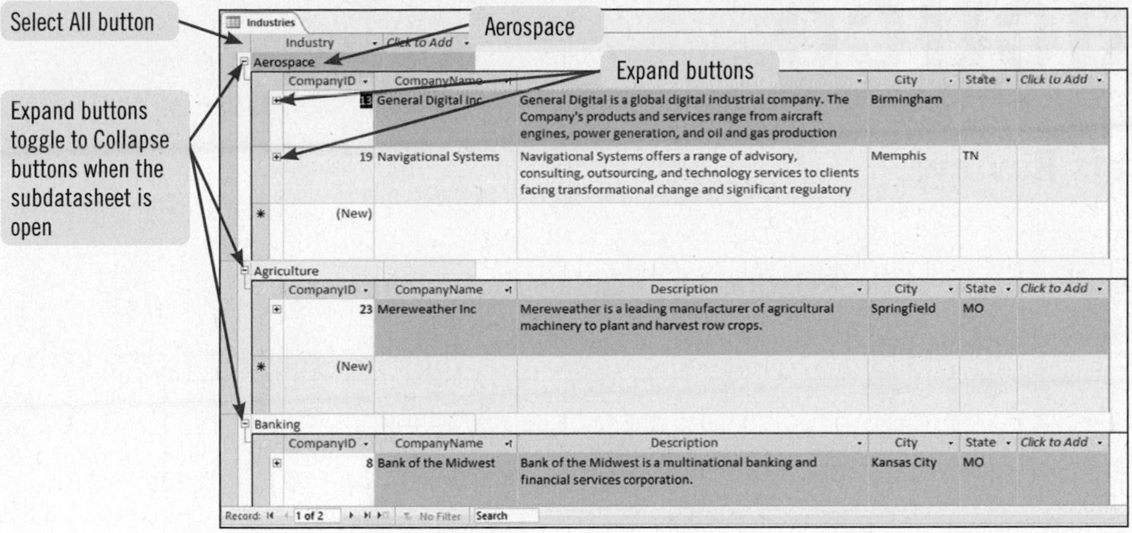

FIGURE 2-16: Insert Subdatasheet dialog box

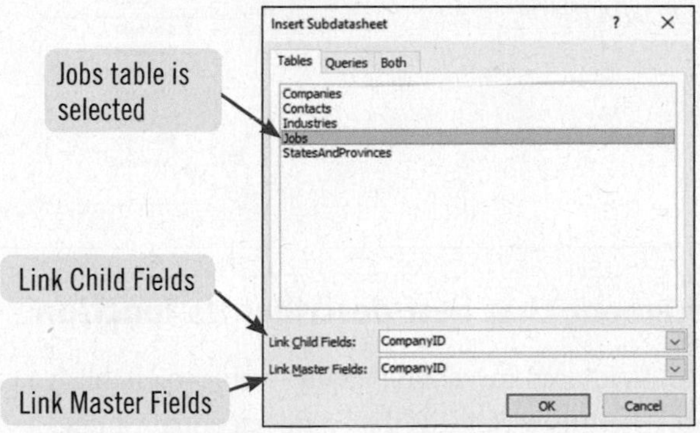

TABLE 2-6: Status bar indicators

status bar indicator	displays
Caps Lock	**Caps Lock** in the status bar when the Caps Lock is toggled on
Kana Mode	Short for Katakana, which is a Japanese language; you must have a special installation of Access to enter these characters
Num Lock	**Num Lock** in the status bar when the Num Lock is toggled on.
Scroll Lock	**Scroll Lock** in the status bar when the Scroll Lock is toggled on
Overtype	**Overtype** in the status bar when Overtype mode (vs. Insert mode) is toggled on
Filtered	**Filtered** in the status bar when using the filter features
Move Mode	**Move Mode** in the status bar when using customized insertion point and key behaviors
Extended Selection	**Extended Selection** in the status bar when using extend mode, a feature that allows you to more easily select text without using a mouse
View Shortcuts	**View shortcut icons**

Practice

Concepts Review

Identify each element of the Relationships window shown in FIGURE 2-17.

FIGURE 2-17

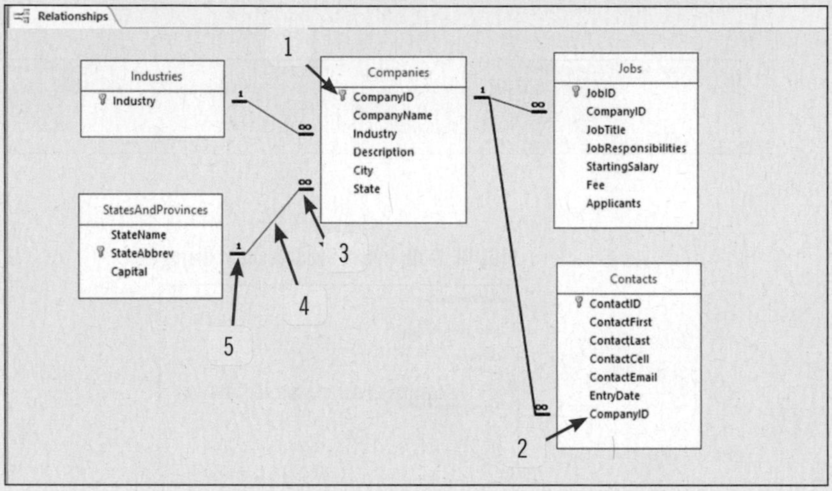

Match each term with the statement that best describes its function.

6. **Subdatasheet**
7. **Currency data type**
8. **Importing**
9. **Foreign key field**
10. **Referential integrity**
11. **Primary key field**
12. **Number data type**
13. **Integer**
14. **Linking**

a. Field used in a child ("many") table to establish a one-to-many relationship
b. Use this with fields that store fractional values.
c. A whole number
d. A way to copy information from another database, spreadsheet, or file format into an Access database
e. Use this with fields that store integers.
f. A way to connect to data in an external source without copying it
g. A field that contains unique information for each record in that table
h. Shows related records from a child ("many") table
i. A set of rules that prevent the creation of orphan records in the child ("many") table

Select the best answer from the list of choices.

15. What would be the best data type for a field that stores prices in dollars and cents?

a. Short Text
b. Currency
c. Number
d. AutoNumber

16. What would be the best data type for a field that stores the quantity of various car parts in inventory?

a. Short Text
b. Currency
c. Number
d. AutoNumber

17. Which of the following is *not* a file format that Access can import?

a. Access
b. Word
c. Excel
d. HTML

18. Which of the following properties would you use to create a visual guide for data entry?

a. Format
b. Default Value
c. Field Size
d. Input Mask

19. Which is *not* true about enforcing referential integrity?

a. It is required for all one-to-many relationships.
b. It prevents orphan records.
c. It prevents records from being deleted on the "one" side of a one-to-many relationship that have matching records on the "many" side.
d. It prevents records from being created on the "many" side of a one-to-many relationship that do not have a matching record on the "one" side.

20. Which of the following is *not* true about linking?

a. Access can link to data in an Excel spreadsheet.
b. Linking copies data from one data file to another.
c. Access can link to data in an HTML file.
d. You can edit linked data in Access.

Skills Review

1. Import data from Excel.

a. Start Access.
b. Open the IL_AC_2-2.accdb database from the location where you store your Data Files and save it as **IL_AC_2_SupportDesk**. Click Enable Content if a yellow Security Warning message appears.
c. Import the **Support_IL_AC_2_Departments.xlsx** spreadsheet, located where you store your Data Files, to a new table in the current database using the Import Spreadsheet Wizard. Make sure that the first row is specified as a column heading, and do not create or select a primary key field. Name the table **Departments** and do not save the import steps.
d. Open the Departments table in Table Datasheet View to confirm that the import worked properly. The Departments table should have seven records. Close the Departments table.
e. Append the records from the **Support_IL_AC_2_Employees.xlsx** spreadsheet, located where you store your Data Files, to the existing Employees table. (*Hint*: If a "Subscript out of range" error appears, close the database, reopen it, then repeat Step 1e.)
f. Open the Employees table in Table Datasheet View to confirm that the append process worked properly. The Employees table should have 26 records. Close the Employees table.

2. Modify Datasheet View.

a. Open the Calls table in Datasheet View and delete the last field, CallPriority, which currently has no data.
b. Move the CallMinutes field between the CallDateTime and CallNotes fields.
c. Decrease decimals on the CallMinutes field to **0** and make sure the Format property is set to **Standard**.
d. Save and close the Calls table.

3. Modify Number and Currency fields.

a. Open the Employees table in Datasheet View and after the Department field, add a new field named **Salary** with a Currency data type.
b. After the Salary field, add another field named **Dependents** with a Number data type.
c. Enter **55000** for the Salary field and **3** for the Dependents field for the first employee (Aaron Cabrera, EmployeeID 3).
d. Decrease the decimals for the Salary field to **0**.
e. Make the Default Value for the Dependents field **1**.
f. Save and close the Employees table.

4. **Modify Short Text fields.**
   a. Open the Employees table in Design View and after the Dependents field, add a new field named **EmergencyPhone** with a Short Text data type.
   b. Use the Input Mask Wizard to add a Phone Number input mask. Use the asterisk (*) as the Placeholder character and accept the other default settings.
   c. Change the Field Size property of the EmergencyPhone field to **10**.
   d. Change the Field Size property of the Department field to **15**.
   e. Save the Employees table and click **Yes** when prompted. No data will be lost because no existing entries exceed the new Field Size property limits you have set.
   f. Display the Employees table in Datasheet View, tab to the EmergencyPhone field for the first record (Aaron Cabrera EmployeeID 3), then type **5552227777** to experience the value of the Input Mask property.
   g. Close the Employees table.
5. **Modify Date/Time fields.**
   a. Open the Cases table in Design View and change the Format property for both the OpenedDate and the ResolvedDate fields to **Short Date**.
   b. Change the Default Value for the OpenedDate field to **=Date()** to provide today's date.
   c. Change the Required Value for the OpenedDate field to **Yes**.
   d. Save the table, click Yes when prompted to test the data, then close the Cases table.
6. **Create primary key fields.**
   a. Open the Departments table in Table Design View and set the Department field as the primary key field. Save and close the Departments table.
   b. Open each of the other tables, Calls, Cases, and Employees, in Design View to view and confirm that they have a primary key field. In each case, the first field is designated as the primary key field and has an AutoNumber data type. A field with an AutoNumber data type will automatically increment to the next number as new records are entered into that table.
7. **Design related tables.**
   a. Open the Relationships window to study the existing relationships between the tables.
   b. Drag the edges of the field lists so that all fields are clearly visible and drag the field list title bars as needed to clearly position the tables so that the Calls table is to the right of the Cases table and the Cases table is to the right of the Employees table.
   c. Be ready to discuss these issues in class or in an online discussion thread.
      - Why is it important to relate tables in the first place?
      - What relationships exist in this database?
      - What role does the primary key field in each table play in the relationships identified in Step 7a?
      - What is the foreign key field in each of the relationships?
      - What parent ("one") tables exist in this database?
      - What child ("many") tables exist in this database?
      - What do the "1" and infinity symbols tell you about the relationship?
   d. Save the Relationships window.
8. **Create one-to-many relationships.**
   a. Add the Departments table to the Relationships window. Position it to the left of the Employees table.
   b. Create a one-to-many relationship between the Departments table and the Employees table using the common Department field.
   c. Enforce referential integrity on the relationship.
   d. Save the Relationships window, as shown in **FIGURE 2-18**, then close it.

Skills Review (continued)

9. Work with subdatasheets.

a. Open the Departments table in Datasheet View. Expand the Accounting Department's subdatasheet to display the employees who work in that department.

b. Change the Extension value of EmployeeID 24 (Craig Serrano) from 7621 to **7766** in the subdatasheet.

c. Expand the subdatasheet for EmployeeID 24 (Craig Serrano) to see the cases that are linked to that employee.

d. Expand the subdatasheet for CaseID 22 (Email attachment problem) to see what calls are linked to that case.

e. Collapse all subdatasheets and close the Departments table.

f. Compact and repair the database and close Access.

FIGURE 2-18

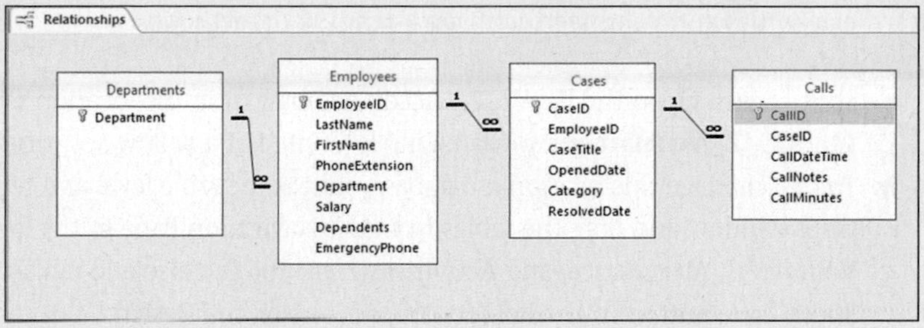

Independent Challenge 1

As the manager of Riverwalk, a multi-specialty health clinic, you have created a database to manage the schedules that connect each healthcare provider with the nurses that provider needs to efficiently handle patient visits. In this exercise, you create the primary keys and relationships required to create a relational database.

a. Start Access. Open the IL_AC_2-3.accdb database from the location where you store your Data Files and save it as **IL_AC_2_Riverwalk**. Click Enable Content if a yellow Security Warning message appears.

b. Open the Relationships window. Drag the ScheduleItems table from the Navigation Pane to the Relationships window, positioning it between the existing four tables. (*Hint*: You can also add tables to the Relationships window by clicking the Show Table button in the Relationships group on the Design tab.)

c. Now that all four tables are in the Relationships window, notice that each table has a primary key field except for the ScheduleItems table. Open the ScheduleItems table in Design View, set the TransactionNo field as the primary key field, then save and close the table to return to the Relationships window.

d. To connect the tables, you have to decide how "one" record in a parent table relates to "many" records in a child table. In this case, the ScheduleItems table is the child table to each of the four other tables. Therefore, build four one-to-many relationships with referential integrity as follows:

- Drag the ScheduleNo field from the ScheduleDate table to the ScheduleNo field of the ScheduleItems table.
- Drag the LocationNo field from the Locations table to the LocationNo field of the ScheduleItems table.
- Drag the DoctorNo field from the Providers table to the DoctorNo field of the ScheduleItems table.
- Drag the NurseNo field from the Nurses table to the NurseNo field of the ScheduleItems table.

e. Be sure to enforce referential integrity on each relationship. Doing so will add the "1" and "infinity" symbols to the relationship line. If they are missing, double-click the relationship line to open the Edit Relationships dialog box, where you can check the Enforce Referential Integrity check box.

f. Click the Relationship Report button in the Tools group on the Design tab to create a relationships report, as shown in **FIGURE 2-19**.

g. Save and close the report with the default name of **Relationships for IL_AC_2_Riverwalk**, then save and close the Relationships window.

h. Compact and repair the database then close Access.

FIGURE 2-19

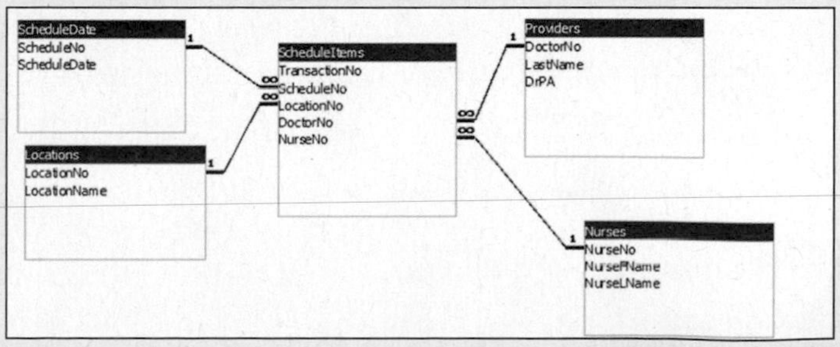

Independent Challenge 2

You are working for a city to coordinate a series of community-wide preparedness activities. You have started a database to track the activities and volunteers who are attending the activities.

- **a.** Start Access. Open the IL_AC_2-4.accdb database from the location where you store your Data Files and save it as **IL_AC_2_Volunteers**. Click Enable Content if a yellow Security Warning message appears.
- **b.** To best manage this relational database, start at the table level and review the table relationships. Open the Relationships window and drag the tables from the Navigation Pane to the Relationships window in this order: Zipcodes, Volunteers, Attendance, and Activities. (*Hint*: You can also add tables to the Relationships window by clicking the Show Table button in the Relationships group on the Design tab.)
- **c.** Some of the relationships are more obvious than others. For example, one record in the Zipcodes table may be related to many records in the Volunteers table. To establish this relationship, drag the Zip field from the Zipcodes table to the Zipcode field in the Volunteers table and enforce referential integrity on the relationship.
- **d.** The Volunteers, Attendance, and Activities tables are more difficult to analyze because one volunteer may be related to many activities and one activity may have many volunteers. This many-to-many relationship is resolved with the Attendance table, which serves as the junction table between the Volunteers and Activities tables. Open the Attendance table in Design view and add two foreign key fields named **VolunteerID** and **ActivityID**, each with a Number data type. Save and close the Attendance table and return to the Relationships window.
- **e.** With the foreign key fields in the Attendance table established, you are ready to link the Volunteers, Attendance, and Activities tables by building these two relationships:
  - Drag the VolunteerID field from the Volunteers table to the VolunteerID field in the Attendance table. Enforce referential integrity on the relationship.
  - Drag the ActivityID field from the Activities table to the ActivityID field in the Attendance table. Enforce referential integrity on the relationship.
- **f.** The final Relationships window should look like **FIGURE 2-20**. Save and close the Relationships window.
- **g.** Open the Zipcodes table to review its one-to-many relationship with the Volunteers table by working in Table Datasheet View.
- **h.** Expand the subdatasheet for the 64145 Springfield KS record, change Micah Ati's name to *your name*, then close the Zipcodes table.
- **i.** Compact and repair the database and close Access.

FIGURE 2-20

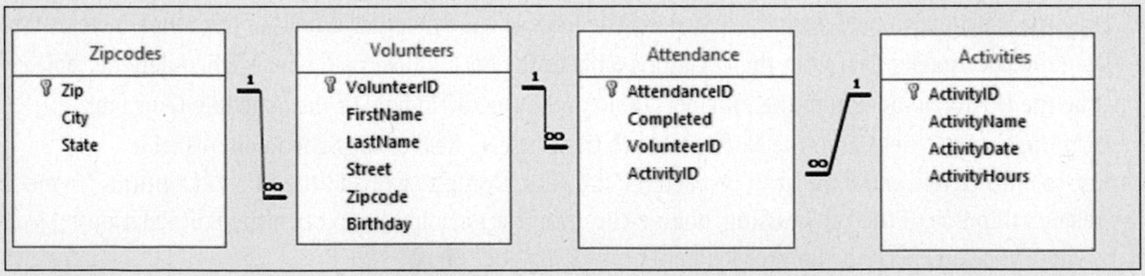

Visual Workshop

Open the IL_AC_2-5.accdb database from the location where you store your Data Files and save it as **IL_AC_2_CollegeCourses**, then enable content if prompted. Import the **Support_IL_AC_2_Majors.xlsx** Excel spreadsheet and append the records to the Departments table. Do not save the import steps.

Import the following spreadsheets as new tables with the following names. For each import, use the first row as the column headings and other default options of the Import Spreadsheet Wizard. Do not save the import steps.

Import **Support_IL_AC_2_Classes.xlsx** as **Classes** and set ClassNo as the primary key field.

Import **Support_IL_AC_2_Enrollments.xlsx** as **Enrollments** and set EnrollmentID as the primary key field.

Import **Support_IL_AC_2_Sections.xlsx** as **Sections** and set SectionNo as the primary key field.

Import **Support_IL_AC_2_Students.xlsx** as **Students** and set StudentID as the primary key field.

In the Relationships window, relate the tables in one-to-many relationships using **FIGURE 2-21** as a guide. Enforce referential integrity on each relationship. Save and close the Relationships window.

FIGURE 2-21

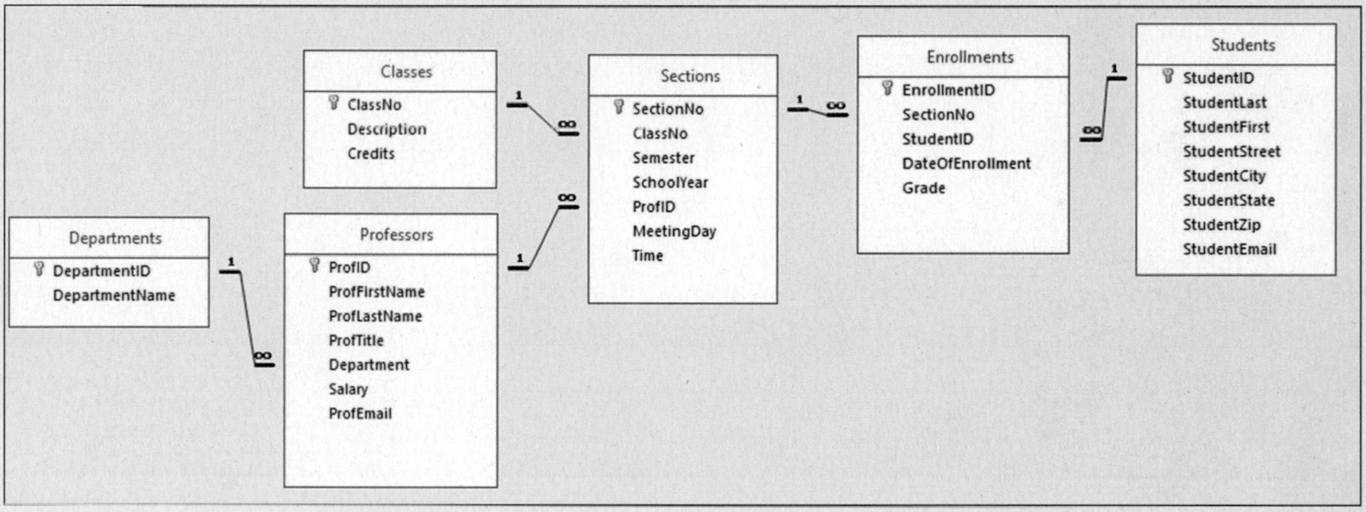

Access

Creating Queries

CASE Now that you've updated the tables in the database for JCL Talent and linked them in one-to-many relationships to create a relational database, you're ready to mine the data for information. You'll develop queries to provide Lydia Snyder, vice president of operations, with fast and accurate answers.

Module Objectives

After completing this module, you will be able to:

- Work in Query Datasheet View
- Work in Query Design View
- Work in SQL View
- Sort data
- Find and replace data
- Filter data
- Enter and save criteria
- Apply AND criteria
- Apply OR criteria
- Create calculated fields
- Format a datasheet

Files You Will Need

IL_AC_3-1.accdb
IL_AC_3-2.accdb
IL_AC_3-3.accdb
IL_AC_3-4.accdb
IL_AC_3-5.accdb

Work in Query Datasheet View

Learning Outcomes
- Edit and delete records
- Hide and unhide columns
- Freeze and unfreeze columns

A **query** answers a question about the information in the database by allowing you to select a subset of fields and records from one or more tables and present them in a single datasheet. You can enter, edit, and navigate data in **Query Datasheet View**, which displays each field as a column and each record as a row just like Table Datasheet View. Given all data is stored only in tables, any edits, additions, or deletions made in Query Datasheet View are automatically reflected elsewhere in the database. **CASE** *Lydia asks you to change some data that is currently organized in a query. You'll work in Query Datasheet View to make the updates.*

STEPS

1. **sam Start Access, open the IL_AC_3-1.accdb database from the location where you store your Data Files, save it as IL_AC_3_Jobs, enable content if prompted, then double-click the JobsByIndustry query to open it in Datasheet View**

   Each time a query is opened, it shows a current view of the data. Notice that the datasheet displays one record for every job and that one company may be connected to many jobs.

   The records for General Digital Inc in Birmingham do not have a value in the State field. Although data is stored in tables, you can edit data in Query Datasheet View.

2. **Click the State field cell for any General Digital Inc record, type AL, then click any other record**

   All records for General Digital Inc in this query update to show AL (Alabama) in the State field because General Digital Inc is related to six records in the Jobs table.

3. **Click the record selector to the left of the twelfth record (CompanyID 8 and JobTitle of Executive Assistant), click the Delete button in the Records group, then click Yes**

   You can delete records from a query datasheet the same way you delete them from a table datasheet. Notice that the navigation bar now indicates that you have 81 records in the datasheet as shown in **FIGURE 3-1**.

   In large datasheets, you may want to freeze certain fields so that they remain on the screen at all times.

> **QUICK TIP**
> To unfreeze a field, right-click any field name, then click Unfreeze All Fields on the shortcut menu.

4. **Right-click the CompanyName field name to select the entire column, click Freeze Fields on the shortcut menu, press TAB as needed to move to the Applicants field for the first record, then type 15**

   Notice that the CompanyName field is now positioned as the first field in the datasheet and doesn't scroll off the screen as you press TAB.

   In large datasheets, you may also want to hide fields.

> **QUICK TIP**
> To unhide a field, right-click any field name, click Unhide Fields on the shortcut menu, click the check box beside the field that you want to unhide, then click Close.

5. **Press TAB as needed to move to the Description field, right-click the Description field name to select the entire column, as shown in FIGURE 3-2, then click Hide Fields on the shortcut menu**

   Hiding a field in a query datasheet doesn't remove it from the query, it merely hides it on the datasheet.

6. **Right-click the JobsByIndustry tab, click Save, right-click the JobsByIndustry tab, then click Close**

   Saving your changes to this query saves the changes you made to freeze the CompanyName field and to hide the Description field. Edits to data are automatically saved as you work.

FIGURE 3-1: Editing data in Query Datasheet View

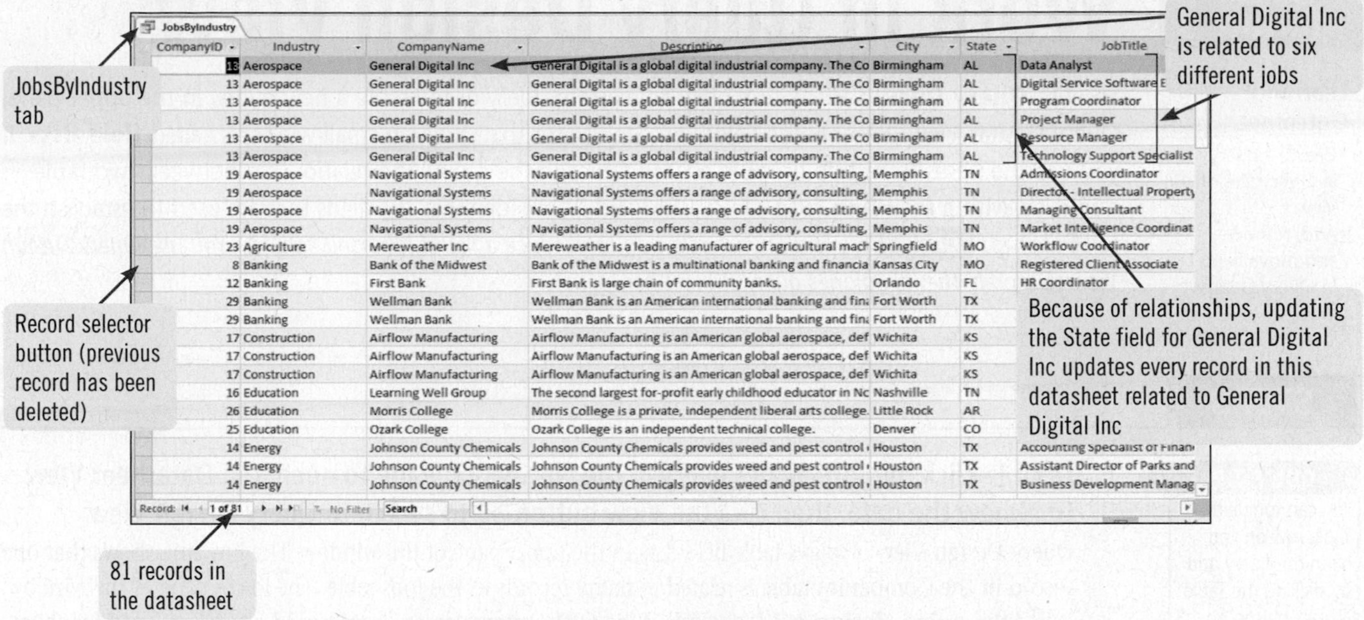

FIGURE 3-2: Freezing and hiding columns in Query Datasheet View

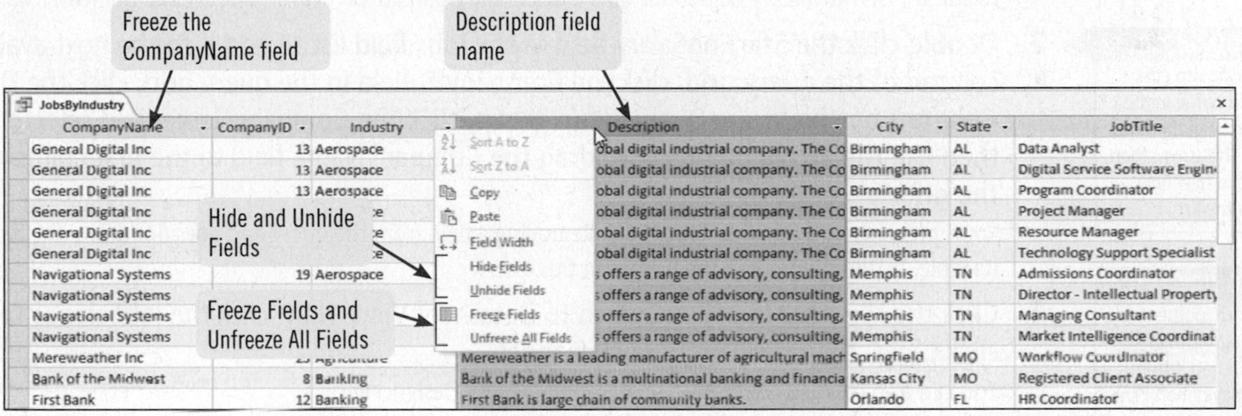

Access

Access
Module 3

Work in Query Design View

Learning Outcomes
- Create a query in Query Design View
- Add, remove, and move fields in Query Design View

You use **Query Design View** to modify an existing query or to create a new query. In the upper pane, Query Design View presents the fields you can use for that query in small windows called **field lists.** If you use the fields from two or more related tables in the query, the relationship between two tables is displayed with a **join line** (also called a **link line**) that identifies the fields that are used to establish the relationship. CASE *Lydia Snyder asks you to produce a list of jobs and salaries. You use Query Design View to modify the JobSalaries query to meet her request.*

STEPS

QUICK TIP
You can toggle the Table row on and off in the query grid by clicking the Table Names button on the ribbon.

QUICK TIP
You can also click a field name in the first row of the grid, click the arrow, then select a new field from the list.

QUICK TIP
To add another table to Query Design View, drag it from the Navigation Pane to Query Design View or click the Show Table button in the Query Setup group.

QUICK TIP
You can also add a new column to the grid by clicking the Insert Columns button in the Query Setup group.

1. **Double-click the JobSalaries query in the Navigation Pane to open it in Datasheet View to review the data, then click the View button to switch to Query Design View**
   Query Design View displays table field lists in the upper pane of the window. The link line shows that one record in the Companies table is related to many records in the Jobs table. The lower pane of the window, called the **query design grid** (also called the **QBE**, **query by example grid**, or **query grid** for short), displays the field names, sort orders, and criteria used within the query. The JobSalaries query selects the Industry and CompanyName fields from the Companies table and three fields from the Jobs table. You want to add the StartingSalary field to the query, delete the CompanyID field, and move the CompanyName field.

2. **Double-click the StartingSalary field in the Jobs field list to add it to the next available column of the query grid, click the CompanyID field in the query grid, click the Delete Columns button in the Query Setup group, click the CompanyName field selector, then use the arrow pointer to drag the CompanyName field to the first column of the grid**
   Your screen should look like **FIGURE 3-3**. Removing a field from the query grid does not delete the field from its table. It simply removes the field from this query.

3. **Click the View button to switch to Datasheet View, right-click the JobSalaries tab, click Close, then click Yes to save changes**
   You can also create a query from scratch using Query Design View.

4. **Click the Create tab on the ribbon, click the Query Design button in the Queries group, double-click Jobs in the Show Table dialog box, double-click Companies, then click Close**
   For this query, you want to include three fields. You can drag fields from the field lists to any column to position them in the query. Any existing fields will move to the right to accommodate the new field.

5. **Drag the StartingSalary field to the first column of the grid, drag the JobTitle field to the first column of the grid, then drag the CompanyName field to the first column of the grid**
   Your screen should look like **FIGURE 3-4**.

6. **Click the Datasheet View button to run the query**
   For a **select query**, a query that selects fields and records, you can **run** the query by clicking either the Datasheet View button or the Run button. In an **action query**, clicking the Run button starts a process that modifies all of the selected records. Because the Datasheet View button never changes data regardless of what type of query you are building, it is a safe way to run a select query or view selected fields and records for an action query. In later modules, you will learn about action queries that change data.

7. **Right-click the Query1 tab, click Save, type CompanyJobs as the new query name, then click OK**

FIGURE 3-3: Adding and removing fields in Query Design View

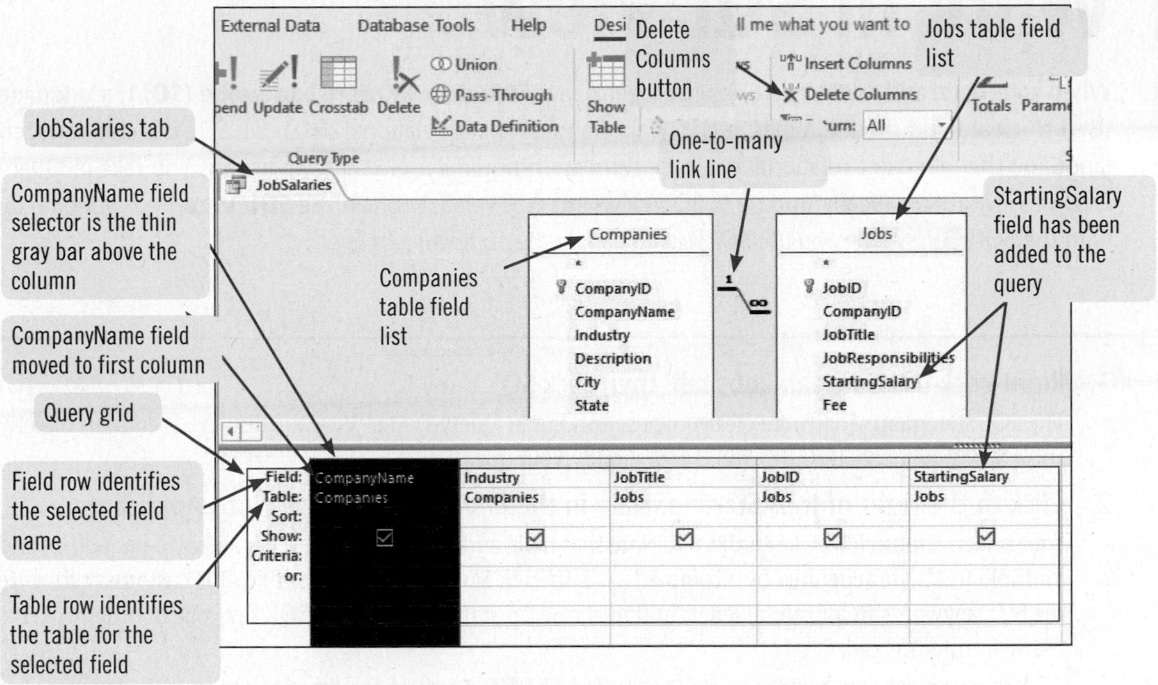

FIGURE 3-4: Creating a new query in Query Design View

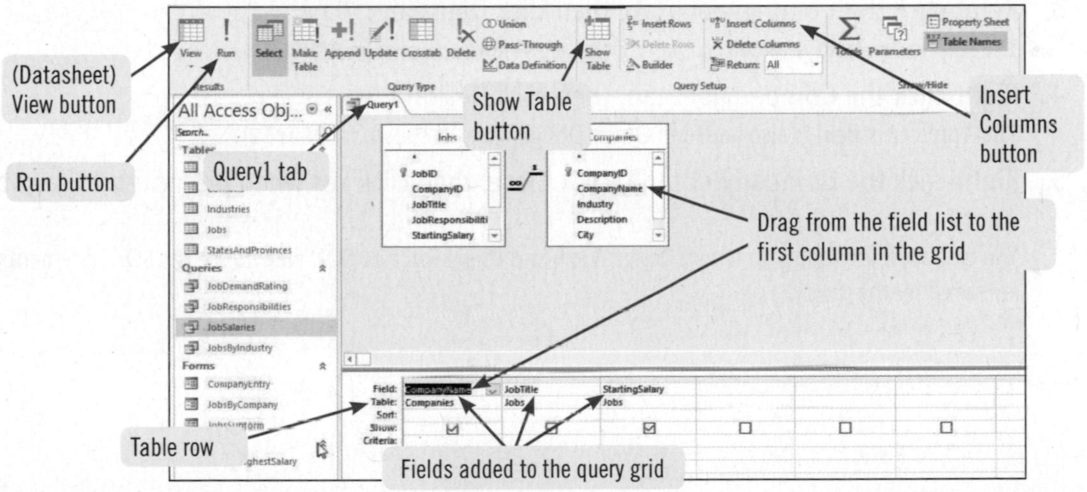

Adding or deleting a table in Query Design View

You might want to add a table's field list to the upper pane of Query Design View to select fields from that table for the query. To add a new table to Query Design View, drag it from the Navigation Pane to Query Design View, or click the Show Table button in the Query Setup group on the Design tab. To delete an unneeded table from Query Design View, click its title bar, then press DELETE.

Linking tables in Query Design View

If tables are joined in the Relationships window, they are automatically joined in Query Design View. If tables are not joined in the Relationships window, you can join them in Query Design View by dragging the linking field from one field list to another. However, you cannot enforce referential integrity on a relationship created in Query Design View. Also, a relationship created in Query Design View is established for that query only. Creating one-to-many relationships for the database in the Relationships window provides tremendous productivity and application performance benefits over relating tables within individual queries.

Access
Module 3

Work in SQL View

Learning Outcomes
- Modify a query in SQL View
- Learn common SQL keywords

When you create and save a query, you create and save **Structured Query Language (SQL)**, a language used to create and modify tables, relationships, and data in a relational database. SQL is a standardized language that all major relational database software programs use. Whatever actions you take in Query Design View automatically update in SQL View and vice versa. You can use **SQL View** to work directly with the SQL. **CASE** *You use SQL View to update the CompanyJobs query.*

STEPS

1. **Right-click the CompanyJobs tab, then click SQL View**
   The SQL statements that were created when working in Query Design View are displayed. You can directly enter SQL statements into this window to modify your query.
2. **Click to the right of Jobs.StartingSalary in the first line, then type , Jobs.Applicants**
   Your screen should look like **FIGURE 3-5**. Note that table and field names are separated by a period (.) and multiple fields are separated by a comma (,). Although SQL is not case sensitive, it is customary to write the SQL keywords in all capital letters and to start each statement with an SQL keyword in order to make the SQL easier to read.
   A select query starts with the SQL keyword **SELECT**. Some of the most common SQL keywords are shown in **TABLE 3-1**.
3. **Right-click the CompanyJobs tab, then click Datasheet View**
   The Applicants field is added to Query Datasheet View as shown in **FIGURE 3-6**.
4. **Right-click the CompanyJobs tab, then click Design View**
   The Applicants field is also added to Query Design View as shown in **FIGURE 3-7**.
5. **Right-click the CompanyJobs tab, click Close, then click Yes when prompted to save the query**
   You can open any query in Query Design View and then switch to SQL View to see the SQL statements that are saved by the query.

TROUBLE
If you receive an error message, make sure you have used a comma (,) to separate the new field name and spelled the table and field name correctly.

FIGURE 3-5: Adding the Applicants field in SQL View

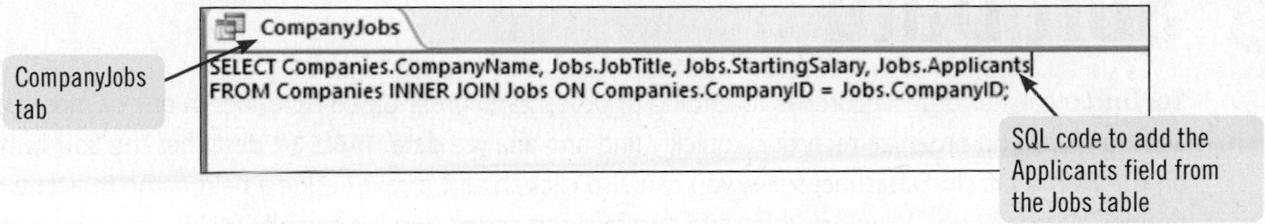

FIGURE 3-6: Viewing the Applicants field in Query Datasheet View

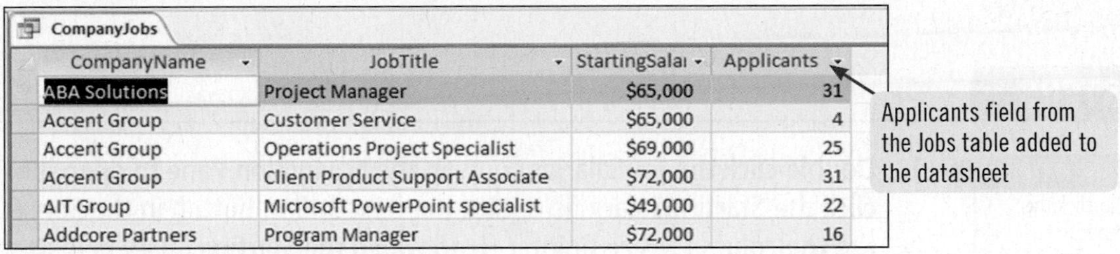

CompanyName	JobTitle	StartingSalai	Applicants
ABA Solutions	Project Manager	$65,000	31
Accent Group	Customer Service	$65,000	4
Accent Group	Operations Project Specialist	$69,000	25
Accent Group	Client Product Support Associate	$72,000	31
AIT Group	Microsoft PowerPoint specialist	$49,000	22
Addcore Partners	Program Manager	$72,000	16

FIGURE 3-7: Viewing the Applicants field in Query Design View

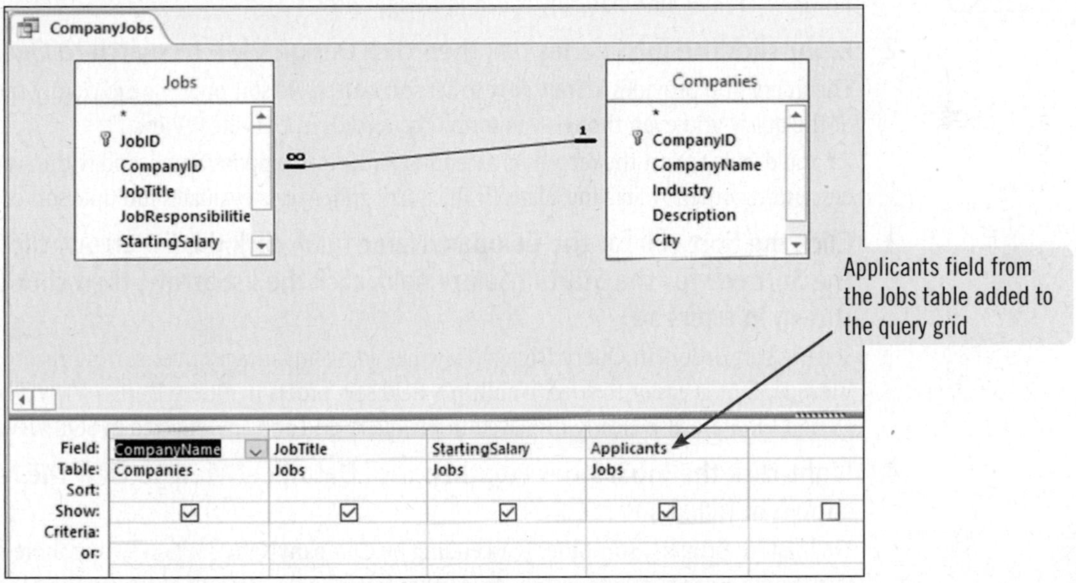

TABLE 3-1: Common SQL keywords

keyword	identifies...
SELECT	which fields you want to include in a select query
FROM	what tables contain the fields you have selected
WHERE	criteria used to limit the number of records selected
ORDER BY ... ASC (DESC)	sort order for the records; **ASC** means ascending, **DESC** means descending
INNER JOIN ... ON	which records will be selected when choosing fields from more than one table (there must be a match in both tables)
INSERT	the data and fields used when adding a new record
UPDATE...SET	the data and fields used when updating specific records
DELETE	records to delete

Access
Module 3

Sort Data

Learning Outcomes
- Sort records in Query Datasheet View
- Sort records in Query Design View

Sorting means to order records in ascending or descending order based on values in one or more fields. Sorting helps you organize records to quickly find and analyze data. **TABLE 3-2** describes the Sort buttons on the Home tab. In Datasheet View, you can also click the list arrow beside a field name to access sort options. Query Design View helps you add and save sort orders and is especially useful when you want to sort on multiple fields. **CASE** *Lydia Snyder asks you to sort the JobSalaries query to more clearly show the records with a high starting salary.*

STEPS

QUICK TIP
Double-click the column resize pointer ✛ to widen a field to display the widest entry.

1. **Double-click the JobSalaries query in the Navigation Pane to open it in Datasheet View, click the StartingSalary field, click the Descending button in the Sort & Filter group, then use the column resize pointer ✛ to widen the StartingSalary field as shown in FIGURE 3-8**
   The JobSalaries query now displays the records from highest StartingSalary to lowest, and the StartingSalary field displays a small descending sort indicator by the field name. Sort orders applied to Datasheet View, however, are not automatically added to Design View.
2. **Right-click the JobSalaries tab, then click Design View to switch to Query Design View**
   The query grid provides a **Sort row** to set sort orders. No sort orders are currently specified in the Sort row of the query grid even though you sorted the records in Datasheet View.
   You decide to sort the records in ascending order by CompanyName, and within each CompanyName, in descending order by StartingSalary. In the query grid, Access evaluates multiple sort orders from left to right.
3. **Click the Sort cell for the CompanyName field, click the list arrow, click Ascending, click the Sort cell for the StartingSalary field, click the list arrow, then click Descending as shown in FIGURE 3-9**
   Setting sort orders in Query Design View has some advantages over sorting records in Query Datasheet View. First, it is easier to specify multiple field sort orders in Query Design View. Sort orders set in Query Design View are also clearly displayed in the query grid and are reflected in SQL View.
4. **Right-click the JobSalaries tab, then click Datasheet View to view the resorted records as shown in FIGURE 3-10**
   The first, or primary, sort order is ascending by CompanyName. When two or more records have the same CompanyName value, the records are further sorted in descending order based on the StartingSalary field.
5. **Right-click the JobSalaries tab, click Close, then click Yes when prompted to save changes**
   Sort orders set in Query Design View are always saved with the query.

FIGURE 3-8: Sorting in Query Datasheet View

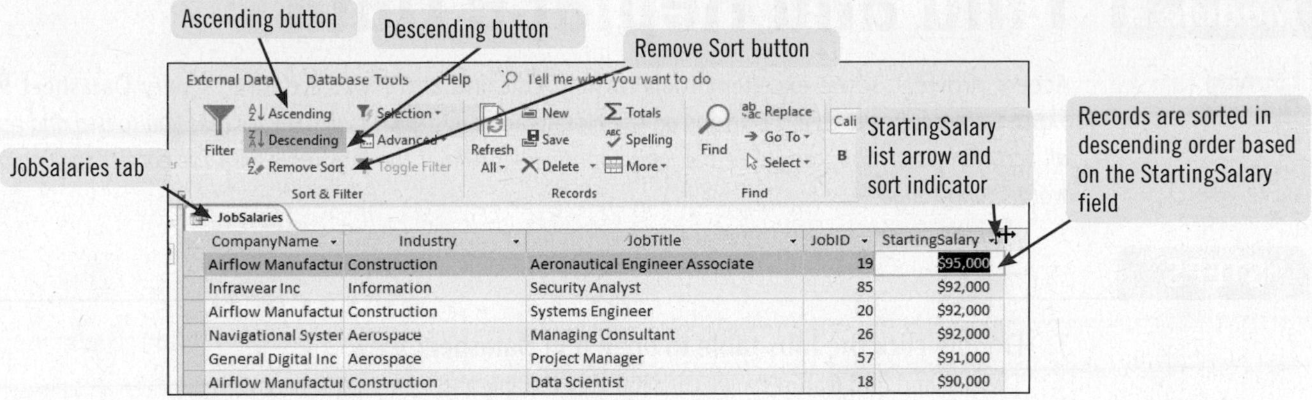
Ascending button
Descending button
Remove Sort button
JobSalaries tab
StartingSalary list arrow and sort indicator
Records are sorted in descending order based on the StartingSalary field

FIGURE 3-9: Sorting by multiple fields in Query Design View

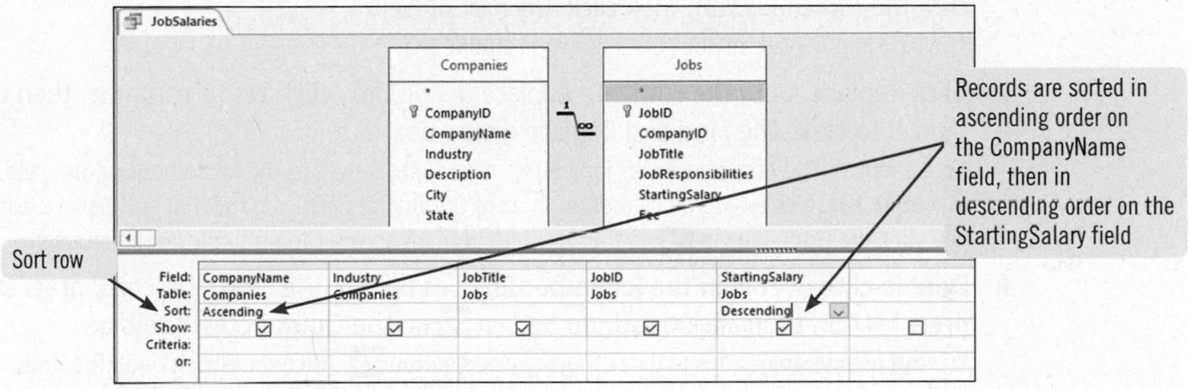
Records are sorted in ascending order on the CompanyName field, then in descending order on the StartingSalary field
Sort row

FIGURE 3-10: Final JobSalaries datasheet

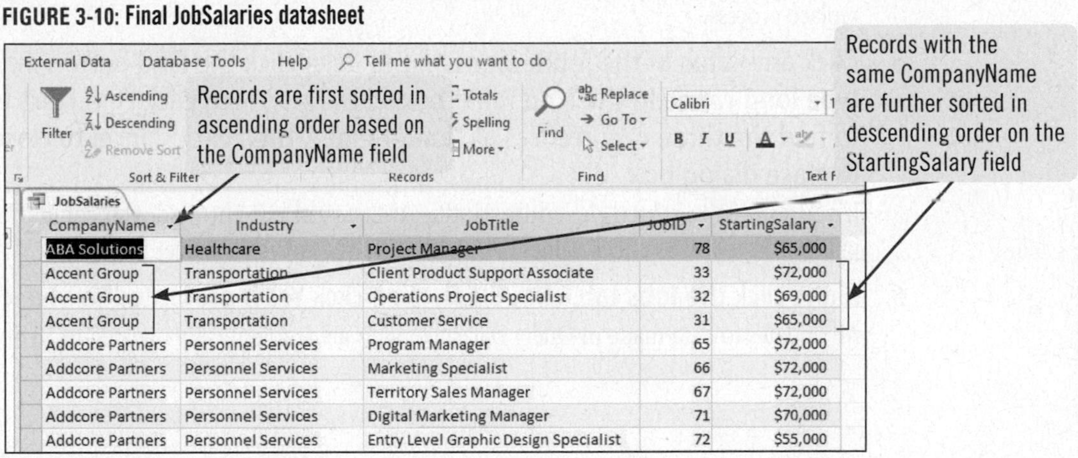
Records are first sorted in ascending order based on the CompanyName field
Records with the same CompanyName are further sorted in descending order on the StartingSalary field

TABLE 3-2: Datasheet View Sort buttons

name	button	purpose
Ascending		Sorts records based on the selected field in ascending order (0 to 9, A to Z)
Descending		Sorts records based on the selected field in descending order (Z to A, 9 to 0)
Remove Sort		Removes the current sort order

Access
Module 3

Find and Replace Data

Learning Outcomes
- Find and replace data
- Undo edits

Access provides some excellent tools to help you find and replace data in Query Datasheet View. **TABLE 3-3** describes the Find buttons on the Home tab. **CASE** *Lydia Snyder asks you to find and replace all occurrences of "longrange" in the JobResponsibilities field of the Jobs table with the correct spelling of the word, "long-range".*

STEPS

1. **Double-click the Jobs table to open it in Datasheet View**
   The sort and find features work the same way in Table and Query Datasheet View.
2. **Click any value in the JobResponsibilities field, click the Replace button in the Find group, type longrange in the Find What box, click in the Replace With box, type long-range, click the Match button, then click Any Part of Field**
   The Find and Replace dialog box is shown in **FIGURE 3-11**.
3. **Click Replace All in the Find and Replace dialog box, click Yes to continue, then click Cancel to close the Find and Replace dialog box**
   Access replaced all occurrences of "longrange" with "long-range" in the JobResponsibilities field, as shown in **FIGURE 3-12**. Note that you cannot undo *all* of the changes made by the find and replace feature, but if you click the Undo button on the Quick Access toolbar, you can undo the last replacement.
4. **Double-click overall in the JobResponsibilities field of the JobID 4 record, press DELETE, press ENTER, then click the Undo button on the Quick Access toolbar**
   You can reverse single edits to data using the Undo button. After you click it once, the Undo button is dim, indicating it is no longer available. When working in Datasheet View, you can undo only the *most recent* edit. Use the Find feature to find and review all of the replacements that were made with the find and replace process.
5. **Click any value in the JobResponsibilities field, click the Find button in the Find group, type long-range in the Find What box, click Find Next, click Find Next two more times to find the three occurrences of "long-range," then click Cancel to close the Find and Replace dialog box**
   If you wanted to search the entire datasheet versus the current field, you could use the Look In option, which allows you to check values in every field in the entire datasheet.
6. **Right-click the Jobs tab, click Close, then click Yes if prompted to save changes**
   All updates to data made in Query Datasheet View are automatically updated in all objects.

FIGURE 3-11: Find and Replace dialog box

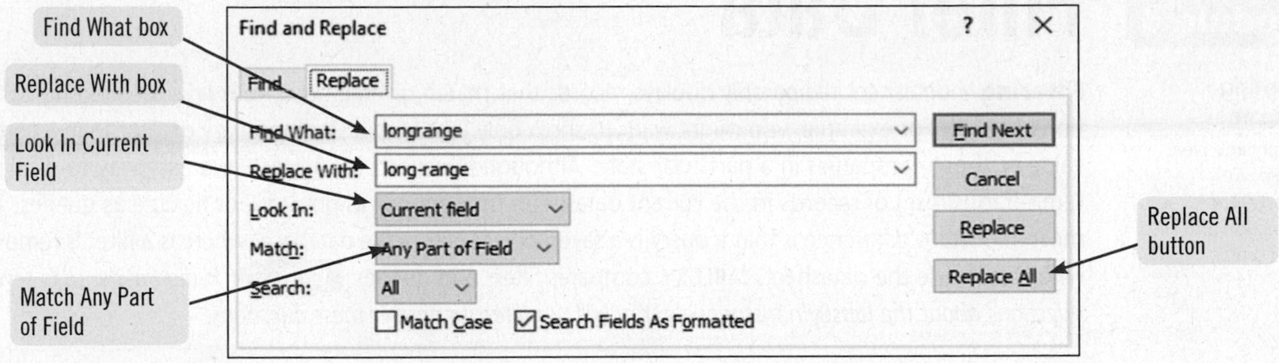

FIGURE 3-12: Jobs table in Datasheet View

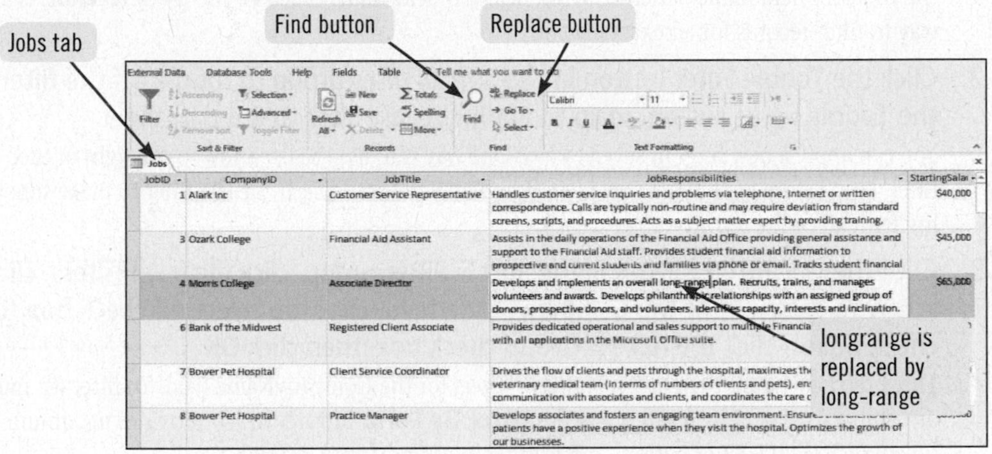

TABLE 3-3: Find buttons

Find		Opens the Find and Replace dialog box to find data
Replace		Opens the Find and Replace dialog box to find and replace data
Go To		Helps you navigate to the first, previous, next, last, or new record
Select		Helps you select a single record or all records in a datasheet

Access
Module 3

Filter Data

Learning Outcomes
- Apply and clear filters
- Use Filter by Selection and Filter by Form

Filtering a datasheet *temporarily* displays records that match given criteria. **Criteria** are limiting conditions you set. For example, you might want to show only jobs with a starting salary greater than a certain value or those companies in a particular state. Although filters provide a quick and easy way to display a temporary subset of records in the current datasheet, they are not as powerful or flexible as queries. The most important difference is that a query is a saved object within the database, whereas a filter is removed when you close the datasheet. **TABLE 3-4** compares filters and queries. **CASE** *Lydia Snyder asks several questions about the JobsByIndustry query. You will use filters to answer these questions.*

STEPS

QUICK TIP
Filters work the same way in Table and Query Datasheet Views.

1. **Double-click the JobsByIndustry query to open it, click any occurrence of Energy in the Industry field, click the Selection button in the Sort & Filter group, then click Equals "Energy"**

   Nine records from two companies are selected, as shown in **FIGURE 3-13**. A filter icon appears to the right of the Industry field name. Filtering by the selected field value, called **Filter By Selection**, is a fast and easy way to filter records for an exact match.

QUICK TIP
The Filtered button to the right of the navigation buttons also toggles the filter.

2. **Click the Toggle Filter button in the Sort & Filter group to toggle off the filter, then click the Toggle Filter button again to apply the last filter to the datasheet**

   You can apply a new filter in several ways. One way is to use the list arrow to the right of each field name to filter data. Before applying a new filter, however, you should clear the last filter to make sure you are working with all of the records in the datasheet.

3. **Click the Advanced button in the Sort & Filter group, click Clear All Filters, click the list arrow to the right of the CompanyName field, click the Select All check box to clear all check boxes, click the Accent Group check box, then click OK**

   Three records match the criteria of *Accent Group* for the CompanyName field. To filter for multiple criteria or comparative data, you might use the **Filter By Form** feature, which provides maximum flexibility for specifying criteria. Filter buttons and features are summarized in **TABLE 3-5**.

4. **Click the Advanced button in the Sort & Filter group, click Clear All Filters, click the Advanced button again, then click Filter By Form**

   After clearing all filters, the Filtered/Unfiltered button to the right of the navigation buttons at the bottom of the datasheet displays "No Filter" to indicate that all previous filters have been cleared. The Filter by Form window opens.

QUICK TIP
You can clear the Filter by Form grid by clicking the Advanced button, then clicking Clear Grid.

5. **Scroll to the right, click the StartingSalary cell, type >=50000, click the Applicants cell, then type <=10 as shown in FIGURE 3-14**

   If more than one criterion is entered, a record must satisfy the requirements for each criterion to be selected.

6. **Click the Toggle Filter button in the Sort & Filter group**

   The datasheet selects 14 records that match both of the filter criteria, as shown in **FIGURE 3-15**. Note that filter icons appear next to the StartingSalary and Applicants field names.

7. **Right-click the JobsByIndustry tab, click Close, then click Yes if prompted**

   Filters are *temporary* views of the data. Filters are *not* saved with a table or query datasheet after you close the datasheet even if you save the datasheet. If you want to save criteria, create a query.

FIGURE 3-13: Filtering the JobsByIndustry query

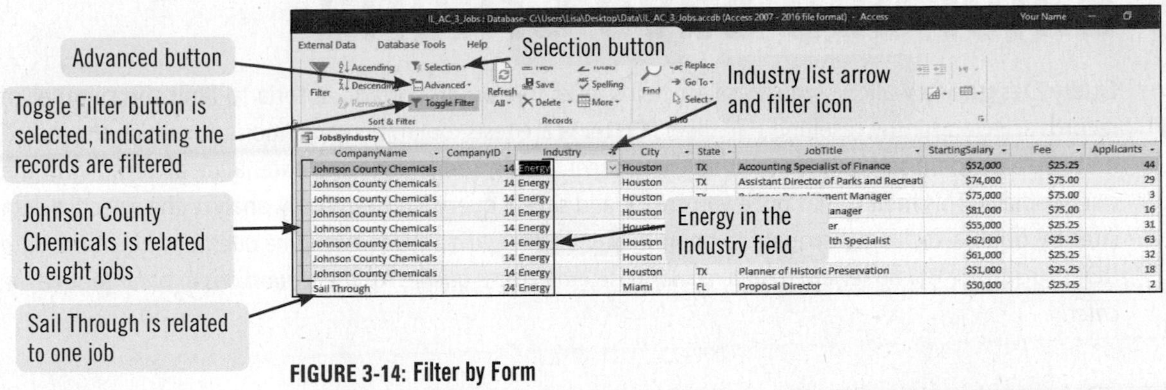

Advanced button
Selection button
Toggle Filter button is selected, indicating the records are filtered
Industry list arrow and filter icon
Johnson County Chemicals is related to eight jobs
Energy in the Industry field
Sail Through is related to one job

FIGURE 3-14: Filter by Form

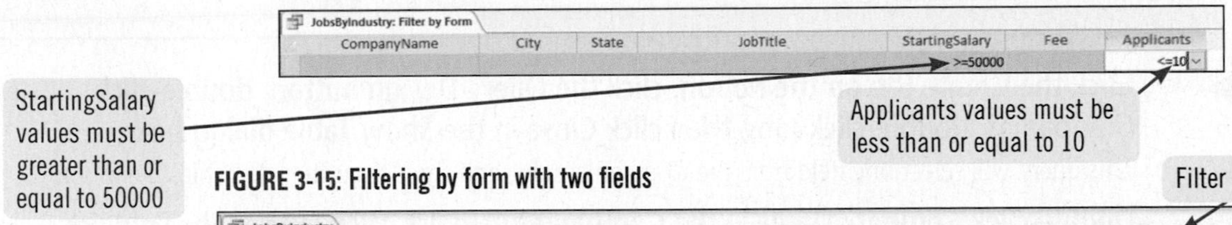

StartingSalary values must be greater than or equal to 50000
Applicants values must be less than or equal to 10

FIGURE 3-15: Filtering by form with two fields

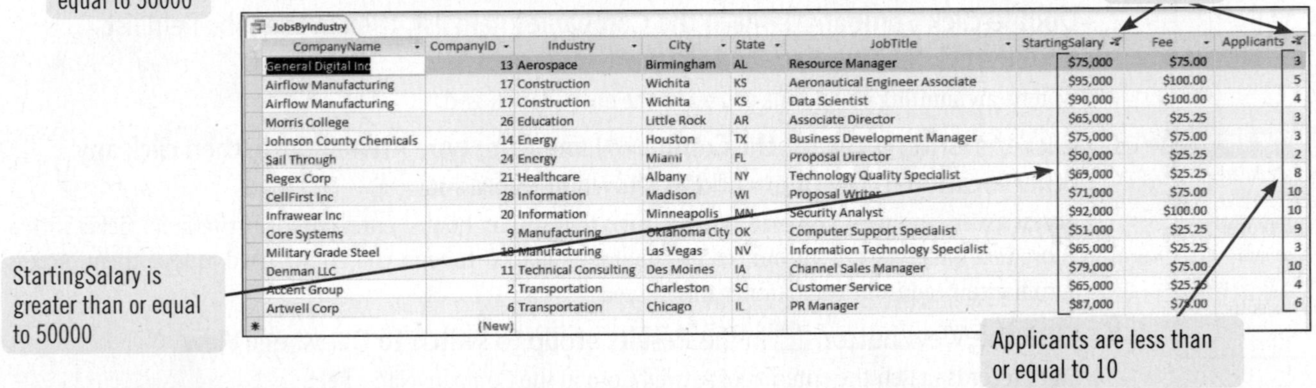

Filter icons
StartingSalary is greater than or equal to 50000
Applicants are less than or equal to 10

TABLE 3-4: Filters vs. queries

characteristic	filters	queries
Are saved as an object in the database		•
Can be used to select a subset of records in a datasheet	•	•
Can be used to select a subset of fields in a datasheet		•
Resulting datasheet used to enter and edit data	•	•
Resulting datasheet used to sort, filter, and find records	•	•
Commonly used as the source of data for a form or report		•
Can calculate sums, averages, counts, and other types of summary statistics across records		•
Can be used to create calculated fields		•

TABLE 3-5: Filter buttons

name	button	purpose
Filter		Provides a list of values in the selected field that can be used to customize a filter
Selection		Filters records that equal, do not equal, or are otherwise compared with the current value
Advanced		Provides advanced filter features such as Filter By Form, Save As Query, and Clear All Filters
Toggle Filter		Applies or removes the current filter

Access

Access Module 3

Enter and Save Criteria

Learning Outcomes

- Add a criterion to a Short Text field
- Add a criterion to a Number field
- Add a criterion to a Date/Time field

Query Design View allows you to select fields, add sort orders, or add criteria to limit the number of records selected for the resulting datasheet. **Criteria** are tests, or limiting conditions, for which the record must be true to be selected for the query datasheet. Fields, sort orders, and criteria are all saved with the query object. This means that once you create and save a query, you can easily analyze the selected data later by double-clicking the query to open it. CASE *Lydia Snyder asks some questions about the data that you suspect will be reviewed on a regular basis. You create queries for these questions in order to save the criteria.*

STEPS

QUICK TIP
Drag the bottom edge of a field list to resize it to display all fields.

1. **Click the Create tab on the ribbon, click the Query Design button, double-click Companies, double-click Jobs, then click Close in the Show Table dialog box**
   This query will select one field from the Companies table and three from the Jobs table.
2. **Double-click CompanyName in the Companies field list, then in the Jobs field list double-click JobTitle, Fee, and FirstPosted**
   Criteria are limiting conditions you set in the query design grid.

QUICK TIP
Query criteria are not case sensitive, but using proper uppercase and lowercase text makes criteria easier to read.

3. **Click the Criteria cell for the CompanyName field, type Artwell Corp, then click any other location in the query grid as shown in FIGURE 3-16**
   Access assists you with **criteria syntax**, rules that specify how to enter criteria. Criteria for fields with a Short Text data type are surrounded by "quotation marks" though you do not need to type them. Access automatically adds the quotation marks for you.
4. **Click the View button in the Results group to switch to Datasheet View**
   Eight records match the criterion of Artwell Corp in the CompanyName field.
5. **Click the View button to switch to Design View, delete the "Artwell Corp" criterion in the CompanyName field, click the Fee Criteria cell, type 75, then click the View button**
   Criteria in Number, Currency, and Yes/No fields are not surrounded by any characters. Thirty records are selected where the Fee field equals 75.
6. **Click the View button, delete the 75 criterion in the Fee field, click the FirstPosted Criteria cell, type 1/4/21, then click in any other location in the query grid as shown in FIGURE 3-17**
   Criteria for fields with a Date/Time data type are surrounded by #pound signs# though you do not need to type them. The pound sign symbol (#) is also known as the number sign, hashtag, and octothorpe.
7. **Click the View button**
   Seven records are selected where the FirstPosted field equals 1/4/21.
8. **Right-click the Query1 tab, click Save, type FirstPostedJan4, click OK, right-click the FirstPostedJan4 tab, then click Close**
   The query is saved with the new name, FirstPostedJan4, as a new query object in the database. Criteria entered in Query Design View are saved with the query.

FIGURE 3-16: Entering text criteria

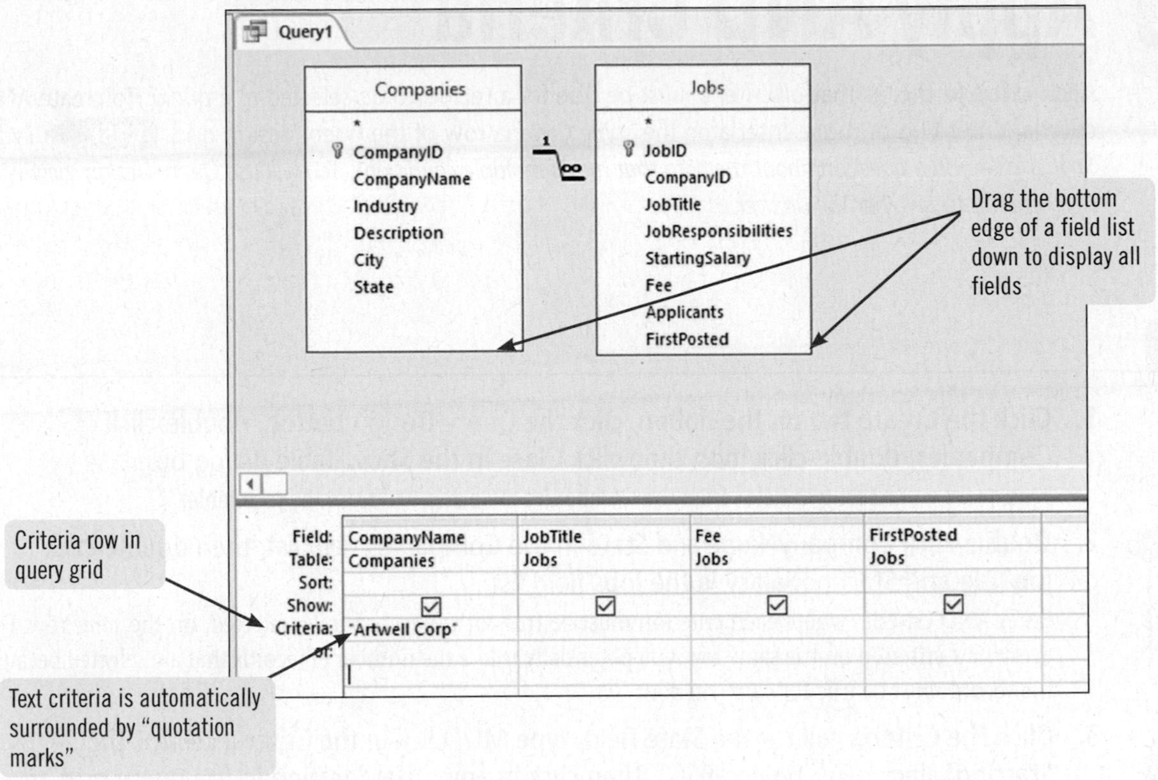

FIGURE 3-17: Entering date criteria

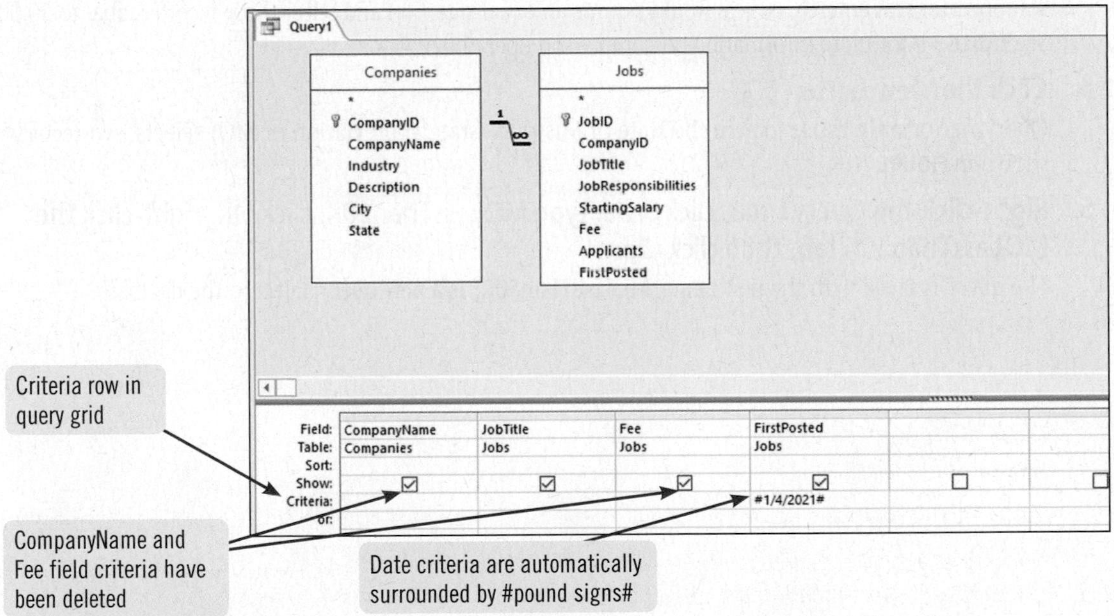

Access

Apply AND Criteria

Learning Outcomes
- Enter AND criteria in a query
- Use comparison operators

AND criteria means that *all* criteria must be true for a record to be selected in a query. To create AND criteria, enter two or more criteria on the *same* Criteria row of the query design grid. CASE *Lydia Snyder asks you a question about the data that meets multiple conditions. You will use Query Design View with AND criteria to give her the answer.*

STEPS

1. **Click the Create tab on the ribbon, click the Query Design button, double-click Companies, double-click Jobs, then click Close in the Show Table dialog box**
   This query will select two fields from the Companies table and two from the Jobs table.

QUICK TIP
Drag the bottom edge of a field list to resize it to display all fields.

2. **Double-click CompanyName and State in the Companies field list, then double-click JobTitle and StartingSalary in the Jobs field list**
   Enter AND criteria, where each criterion must be true for the record to be selected, on the *same* row. For every new criterion on the same row, you potentially *reduce* the number of records that are selected because the record must be true for *each* criterion.

3. **Click the Criteria cell for the State field, type MO, click in the Criteria cell for the StartingSalary field, type <50000, then click in any other location in the query grid as shown in FIGURE 3-18**
   The less than symbol (<) is a **comparison operator** that compares the criterion to the values in the StartingSalary field. In this case, it selects all records with a StartingSalary less than 50,000. If no comparison operator was entered, Access would assume an equal sign (=) and select those records equal to 50,000. See **TABLE 3-6** for more information on comparison operators.

TROUBLE
If your datasheet doesn't match **FIGURE 3-19**, return to Query Design View and compare your criteria with that of **FIGURE 3-18**.

4. **Click the View button**
   Querying for only those jobs in the state of Missouri (state abbreviation of MO) selects two records as shown in **FIGURE 3-19**.

5. **Right-click the Query1 tab, click Save, type MOLessThan50K, click OK, right-click the MOLessThan50K tab, then click Close**
   The query is saved with the new name, MOLessThan50K, as a new query object in the database.

FIGURE 3-18: Query Design View with AND criteria

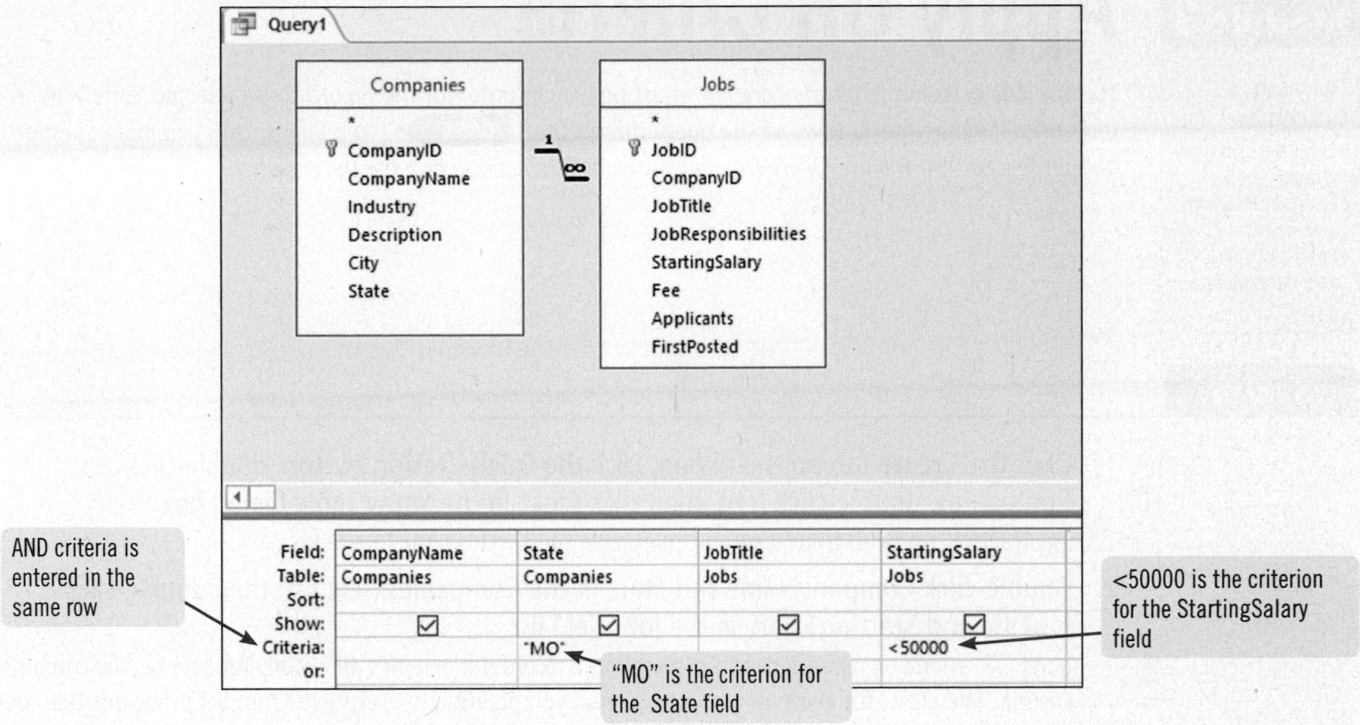

FIGURE 3-19: Final datasheet of MOLessThan50K query

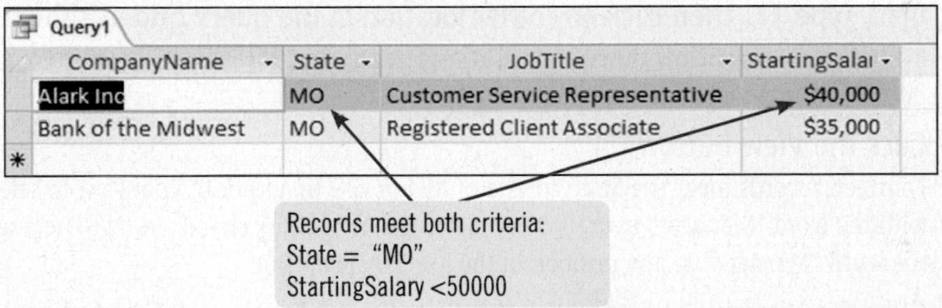

TABLE 3-6: Comparison operators

operator	description	expression	meaning
>	Greater than	>500	Numbers greater than 500
>=	Greater than or equal to	>=500	Numbers greater than or equal to 500
<	Less than	<"Elder"	Names from A to Elder, but not Elder
<=	Less than or equal to	<="Langguth"	Names from A through Langguth, inclusive
<>	Not equal to	<>"Fontanelle"	Any name except for Fontanelle
=	Equal to	="Eagan" =500	Equal to Eagan Equal to 500. Note that the equal sign is assumed when no other comparison operator is used.

Searching for blank fields

Is Null and Is Not Null are two other types of common criteria. The **Is Null** criterion finds all records where no entry has been made in the field. **Is Not Null** finds all records where there is any entry in the field, even if the entry is 0. Primary key fields cannot have a null entry.

Access

Apply OR Criteria

Learning Outcomes
- Enter OR criteria in a query
- Enter criteria with a wildcard
- Enter both AND and OR criteria in a query

You use **OR criteria** when *any one row* must be true in order for the record to be selected. Enter OR criteria on *different* Criteria rows of the query design grid. **CASE** *Lydia Snyder asks you more questions about the jobs. You will use Query Design View with OR criteria to give her the answers.*

STEPS

1. **Click the Create tab on the ribbon, click the Query Design button, double-click Companies, double-click Jobs, then click Close in the Show Table dialog box**
   Again select two fields from the Companies table and two from the Jobs table.
2. **Double-click CompanyName and State in the Companies field list, then double-click JobTitle and StartingSalary in the Jobs field list**
   Enter OR criteria on *different* rows. Access selects a record if it matches the criteria for *any row* that contains criteria. Therefore, for every new row of criteria, you potentially *increase* the number of records that are selected.
3. **Click the Criteria cell for the State field, type MO, click the or Criteria cell for the State field, type TX, then click any other location in the query grid as shown in FIGURE 3-20**
   Every Criteria row below the first row is considered an "or" row. Access selects records that match the criterion in *any* row that contains criteria.
4. **Click the View button**
   Fourteen records meet the State criteria of MO or TX. In addition, you want to select only those records with the word "Manager" in the JobTitle field. You use asterisk characters (*) to help select records that have the word "Manager" in any position in the JobTitle field value.
5. **Click the View button, click the Criteria cell for the JobTitle field, type *Manager*, then click**
   Twelve records meet the State criteria of MO with the word "Manager" in the JobTitle field or the State criteria of TX. But *all* TX records are still selected.
6. **Click, click the second Criteria cell for the JobTitle field, type *Manager*, then click any other location in the query grid as shown in FIGURE 3-21**
   Access adds the **Like** keyword to criteria that contain the asterisk (*) wildcard character.
7. **Click to switch to Datasheet View**
   Three records meet the State criteria of MO or the State criteria of TX with the word "Manager" in the JobTitle field, as shown in **FIGURE 3-22**.
8. **Right-click the Query1 tab, click Save, type MOTXManager, click OK, right-click the MOTXManager tab, then click Close**
   You can also use **AND OR** SQL keywords in your criteria. But a simpler approach is to remember these rules: Criteria on a *single row must all be true* for a record to be selected. Criteria on *different rows constitute separate tests* that the record may satisfy in order to be selected.

QUICK TIP
The query grid provides eight criteria rows by default, but you can add more by clicking the Insert Rows button in the Query Setup group on the Design tab.

FIGURE 3-20: Query Design View with OR criteria

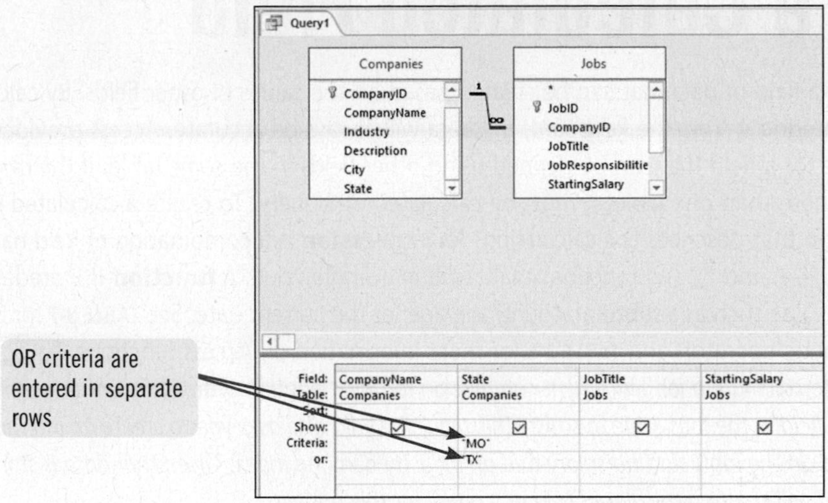

FIGURE 3-21: Query Design View with AND and OR criteria

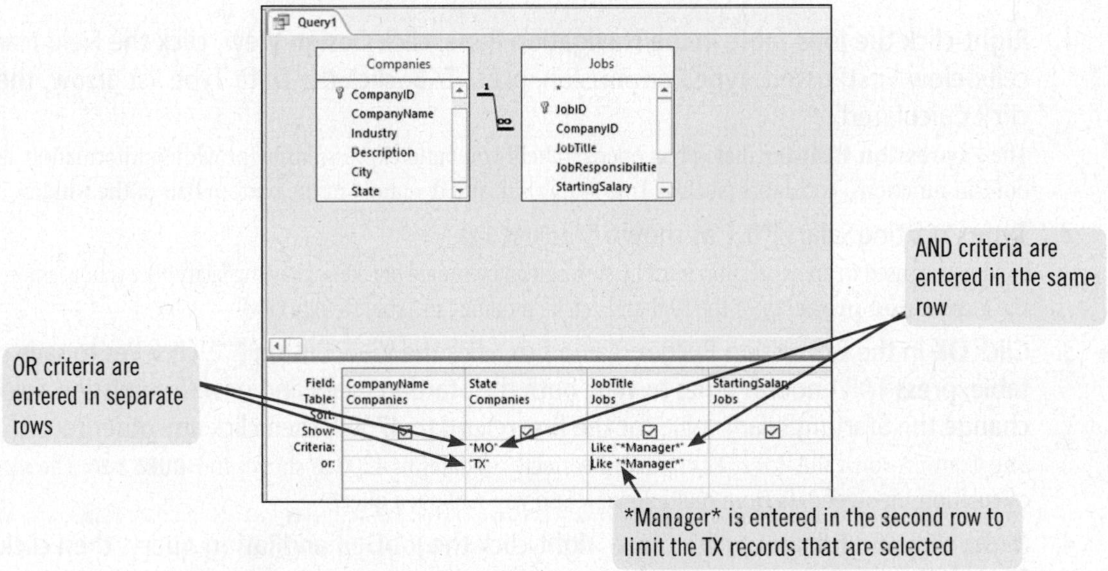

FIGURE 3-22: Final datasheet of MOTXManager query

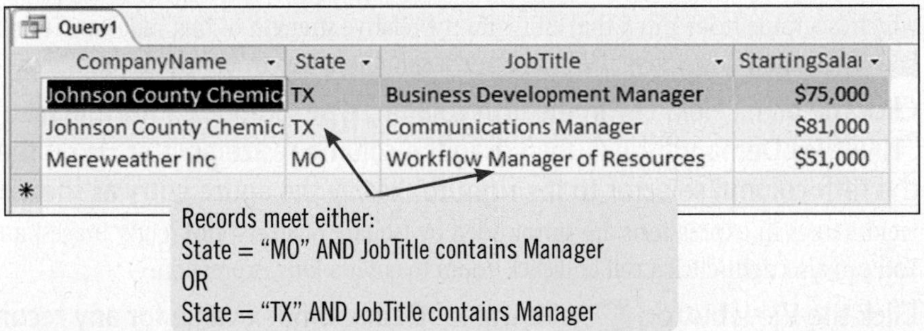

Using wildcard characters

To search for a pattern, you can use a wildcard character to represent any character in the condition entry. Use a question mark (?) to search for any single character and an asterisk (*) to search for any number of characters. Access uses the **Like** keyword when your criterion contains wildcard characters. For example, the criterion Like "12/*/21" finds all dates in December of 2021, and the criterion Like "F*" finds all values that start with the letter F.

Create a Calculated Field

Learning Outcomes
- Create a field with a Calculated data type
- Create calculated fields in queries
- Define functions and expressions

A **calculated field** is a field of data that can be created based on the values of other fields. By calculating the data versus entering it from the keyboard, the data will always be accurate. Access provides the **Calculated** data type for a field that can be defined using other fields in the *same* table. If the calculation uses fields from more than one table, it must be calculated in a query. To create a calculated field, you enter an expression that describes the calculation. An **expression** is a combination of field names, **operators** (such as +, –, /, and *), and functions that result in a single value. A **function** is a predefined formula that returns a value such as a subtotal, count, average, or the current date. See **TABLE 3-7** for more information on arithmetic operators and **TABLE 3-8** for more information on Access functions. **CASE** *Lydia Snyder asks you to calculate a job placement commission for each position that JCL Talent helps fill. You will create a Calculated field in the Jobs table to satisfy this request. Lydia also asks you to create an internal job rating calculation based on the job's starting salary and an industry demand index. Given that data is stored in two different tables, you will create a calculated field in a query for this answer.*

STEPS

1. **Right-click the Jobs table in the Navigation Pane, click Design View, click the Field Name cell below FirstPosted, type Commission, press TAB, click the Data Type list arrow, then click Calculated**

   The **Expression Builder** dialog box opens to help you build expressions by providing information about built-in functions, constants (such as True and False), and operators in the bottom half of the window.

2. **Type [StartingSalary]*0.1 as shown in FIGURE 3-23**

   Field names used in an expression must be surrounded by square brackets. [StartingSalary]*0.1 is now entered in the **Expression property** of the field and can be modified in Table Design View.

3. **Click OK in the Expression Builder dialog box, click the View button, click Yes to save the table, press TAB enough times to view both the StartingSalary and new Commission fields, change the StartingSalary value for the first record to 47000, then click any other record**

   The Commission value for the first record correctly updates to 4700 as shown in **FIGURE 3-24**. The second calculation involves data from multiple tables, so you will use a query.

4. **Right-click the Jobs tab, click Close, right-click the JobDemandRating query, then click Design View**

   The Job Index calculation is defined as the starting salary divided by 1000 times the job demand index, which is a value from 1 to 5 that estimates the relative strength of that industry. To create a calculated field, you enter a new descriptive field name and a colon followed by an expression.

5. **Click the blank Field cell in the fifth column, type JobIndex: [StartingSalary]/1000*[JobDemandIndex], then drag the column resize pointer on the right edge of the fifth column selector to the right to display the entire entry as shown in FIGURE 3-25**

   Field names in expressions are surrounded by [square brackets] not {curly braces} and not (parentheses). You can also right-click a cell and click Zoom to enter a long expression.

6. **Click the View button, edit the JobDemandIndex value for any record with the Industry value of Personnel Services from 3 to 4, then click any other record**

   The JobIndex value for all jobs within the industry of Personnel Services automatically recalculated when you changed the JobDemandIndex value used in the expression for that calculated field.

7. **Click the Save button on the Quick Access toolbar, right-click the JobDemandRating tab, then click Close**

   Some database experts encourage you to create all calculations using queries because the Calculated field data type doesn't convert well to other relational database systems.

QUICK TIP
To modify the expression in a calculated field in Datasheet View, right-click it, then click Modify Expression.

QUICK TIP
You can also use expressions as query criteria.

FIGURE 3-23: Creating a Calculated field in Table Design View

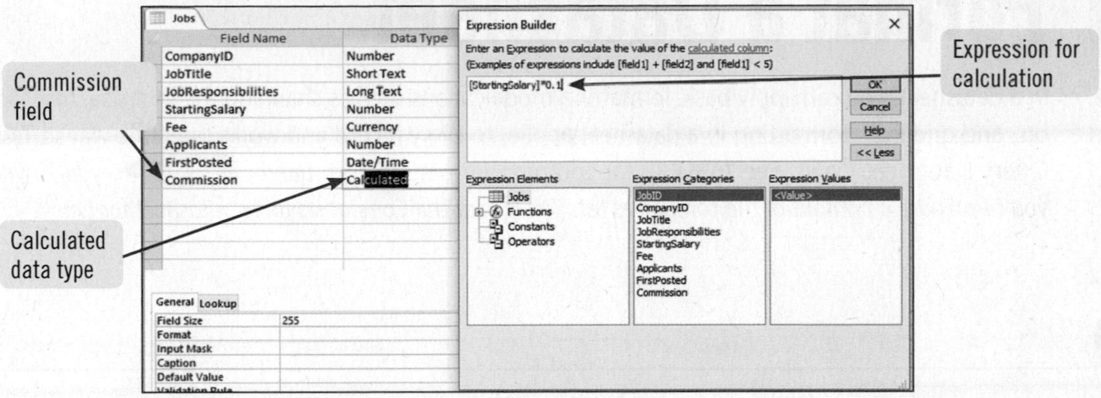

FIGURE 3-24: Calculated field in Table Datasheet View

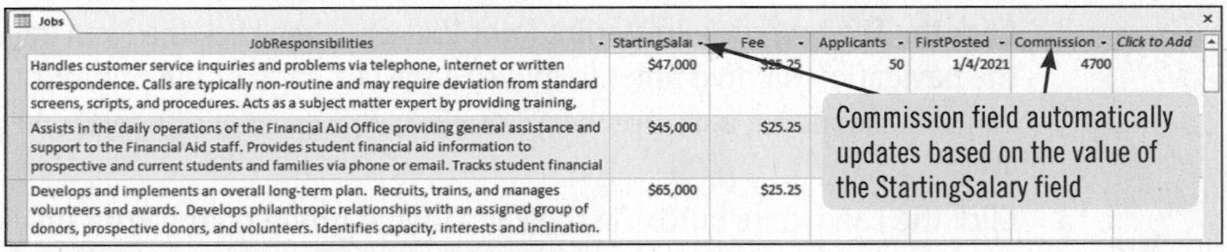

FIGURE 3-25: Creating a calculated field in Query Design View

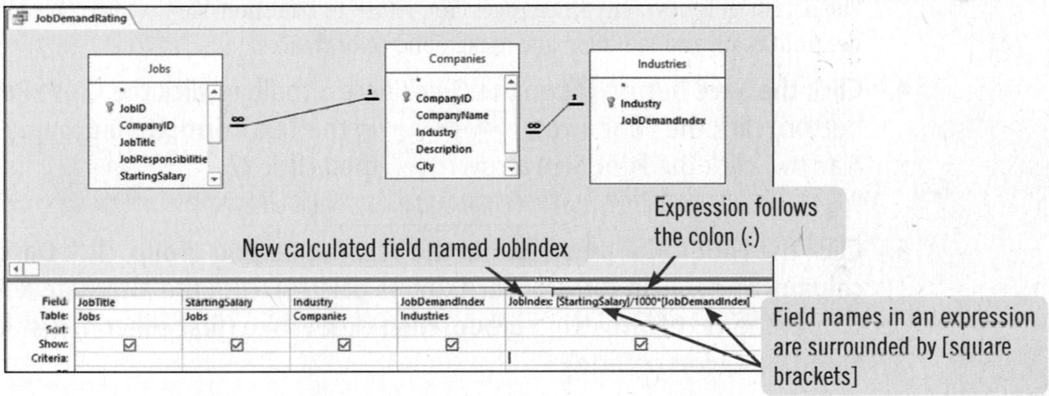

TABLE 3-7: Arithmetic operators

operator	description
+	Addition
–	Subtraction
*	Multiplication
/	Division
^	Exponentiation

TABLE 3-8: Common functions

function	sample expression and description
DATE	DATE()-[BirthDate] Calculates the number of days between today and the date in the BirthDate field; Access expressions are not case sensitive, so DATE()-[BirthDate] is equivalent to date()-[birthdate] and DATE()-[BIRTHDATE]; therefore, use capitalization in expressions in any way that makes the expression easier to read
PMT	PMT([Rate],[Term],[Loan]) Calculates the monthly payment on a loan where the Rate field contains the monthly interest rate, the Term field contains the number of monthly payments, and the Loan field contains the total amount financed
LEFT	LEFT([LastName],2) Returns the first two characters of the entry in the LastName field
RIGHT	RIGHT([PartNo],3) Returns the last three characters of the entry in the PartNo field
LEN	LEN([Description]) Returns the number of characters in the Description field

Access

Access
Module 3

Format a Datasheet

Learning Outcomes
- Change page orientation
- Change margins
- Format a datasheet

In a datasheet, you can apply basic formatting modifications such as changing the font size, font face, colors, and gridlines. Formatting in a datasheet applies to every record and works the same way in Table and Query Datasheet Views. See **TABLE 3-9** for common formatting commands. **CASE** *Lydia Snyder asks you to prepare a printout of the companies list. You format the Companies table datasheet for her.*

STEPS

1. **Double-click the Companies table to open it in Datasheet View**
   Before applying new formatting enhancements, preview the default printout.

2. **Click the File tab, click Print, click Print Preview, then click the Next Page button in the navigation bar five times to move to the last page of the printout**
   Currently, the printout is six pages, but you can reduce that number by changing the page orientation and margin.

3. **Click the Landscape button in the Page Layout group on the Print Preview tab to switch the report to landscape orientation, click the Margins button in the Page Size group, click Narrow, then click the Previous Page button twice to display the first page**
   The datasheet is now only three pages. You return to Datasheet View where you can make font face, font size, font color, gridline color, and background color choices.

4. **Click the Save button on the Quick Access toolbar, click the Close Print Preview button, click the Font arrow Calibri (Body) in the Text Formatting group, click Arial Narrow, click the Font Size arrow 11, then click 12**
   You also decide to change the font color and background color.

5. **Click the Font Color arrow in the Text Formatting group, click Dark Blue (fourth column, first row in the Standard Colors palette), click the Alternate Row Color arrow in the Text Formatting group, then click White (first column, first row in the Standard Colors palette)**

6. **Click the File tab, click Print, click Print Preview, then click the preview to zoom in and out**
   Your Companies datasheet should look like **FIGURE 3-26**. The preview is three pages, and in landscape orientation, it is easier to read.

7. **sam Right-click the Companies tab, click Close, click Yes when prompted to save changes, then click the Close button on the title bar to close the database and Access 2019**

FIGURE 3-26: Formatted Companies datasheet

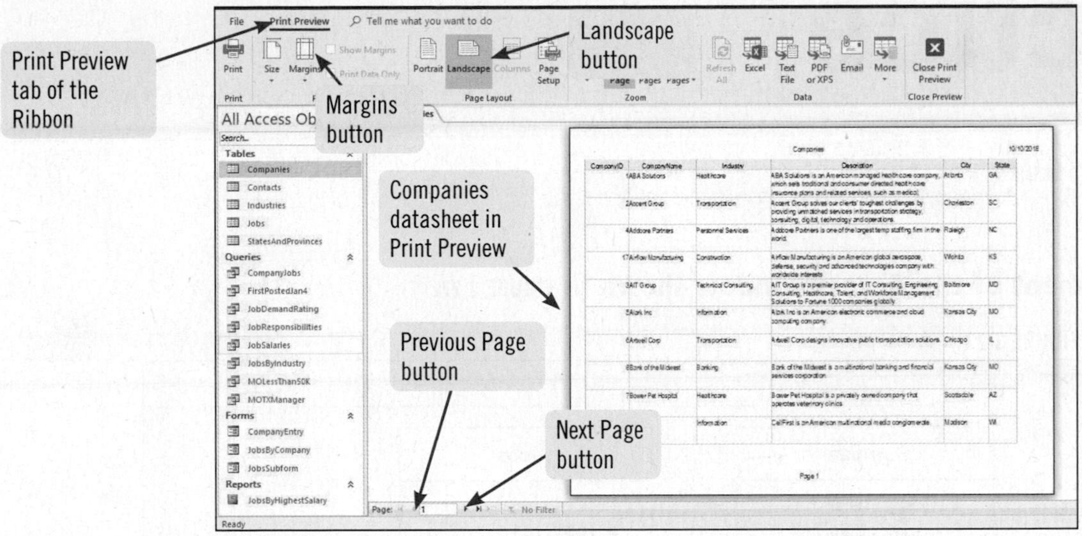

TABLE 3-9: Useful formatting commands

button	button name	description
Calibri (Body)	Font	Changes the font face of the data
11	Font Size	Changes the font size of the data
B	Bold	Toggles bold on or off
I	Italic	Toggles italic on or off
U	Underline	Toggles underline on or off
A	Font Color	Changes the font color of the data
	Background Color	Changes the background color
	Align Left	Left-aligns the data
	Center	Centers the data
	Align Right	Right-aligns the data
	Alternate Row Color	Changes the background color of alternate records
	Gridlines	Changes the gridlines

Access

Practice

Concepts Review

Label each element of the Access window shown in FIGURE 3-27.

FIGURE 3-27

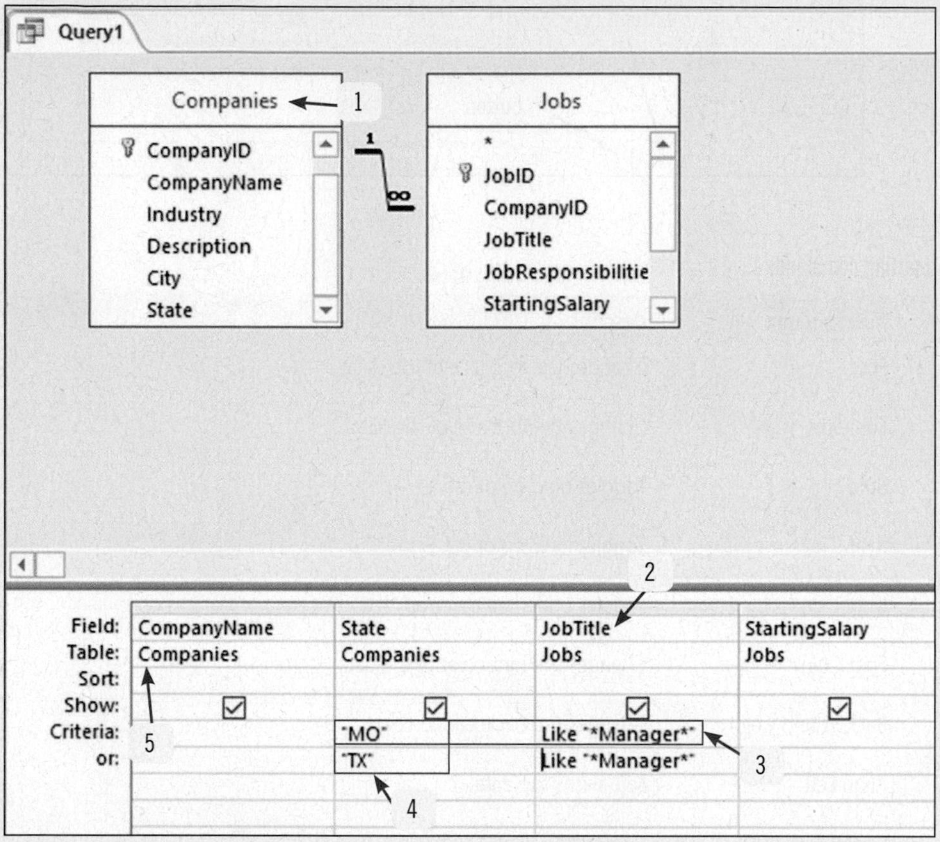

Match each term with the statement that best describes it.

6. Query grid
7. Field selector
8. Filter
9. Filter By Selection
10. Field lists
11. Sorting
12. Join line
13. Criteria
14. Syntax
15. Wildcard

a. A fast and easy way to filter the records for an exact match
b. Limiting conditions used to restrict the number of records that are selected in a query
c. The thin gray bar above each field in the query grid
d. Creates a temporary subset of records
e. Small windows that display field names
f. Rules that determine how criteria are entered
g. Used to search for a pattern of characters
h. The lower pane in Query Design View
i. Identifies which fields are used to establish a relationship between two tables
j. Putting records in ascending or descending order based on the values of a field

Select the best answer from the list of choices.

16. AND criteria:

- **a.** Determine sort orders.
- **b.** Help set link lines between tables in a query.
- **c.** Must all be true for the record to be selected.
- **d.** Determine fields selected for a query.

17. SQL stands for which of the following?

- **a.** Simple Query Listing
- **b.** Structured Query Language
- **c.** Standard Query Language
- **d.** Special Query Listing

18. Which of the following is *not* true about a calculated field?

- **a.** You can create some calculated fields in a table.
- **b.** You can create all calculated fields in a query.
- **c.** Some database experts encourage all calculated fields be created in a query.
- **d.** Once the expression for a calculated field is created, it cannot be changed.

19. Which of the following describes OR criteria?

- **a.** Use two or more rows of the query grid to select only those records that meet given criteria.
- **b.** Select a subset of fields and/or records to view as a datasheet from one or more tables.
- **c.** Reorganize the records in either ascending or descending order based on the contents of one or more fields.
- **d.** Use multiple fields in the query design grid.

20. Which of the following is *not* true about a query?

- **a.** A query can select fields from one or more tables in a relational database.
- **b.** A query is the same thing as a filter.
- **c.** A query can be used to enter and edit data.
- **d.** An existing query can be modified in Query Design View.

Skills Review

1. Work in Query Datasheet View.

- **a.** Open the IL_AC_3-2.accdb database from the location where you store your Data Files and save it as **IL_AC_3_SupportDesk**. Click Enable Content if a yellow Security Warning message appears.
- **b.** Open the CaseDetails query in Datasheet View and change Cabrera to **Douglas** in the LastName field of either the first or second record.
- **c.** Delete the third record (EmployeeID 6, Tony Roth).
- **d.** Hide the Dependents field.
- **e.** Freeze the first three fields: EmployeeID, FirstName, and LastName in their current positions in the datasheet. (*Hint*: Select all three fields by dragging through their field names before selecting the Freeze Fields option.)
- **f.** Save and close the CaseDetails query.

2. Work in Query Design View.

- **a.** Create a new query in Query Design View. Add the Cases and Calls tables.
- **b.** Select the CaseTitle and Category fields from the Cases table. Select the CallDateTime and CallNotes from the Calls table.
- **c.** Save the query with the name **CallListing**, then view it in Datasheet View to observe that one case may have many calls over a period of several dates in the CallDateTime field.

Skills Review (continued)

3. Work in SQL View.

a. Open the CallListing query in SQL View.

b. Add the CallMinutes field to the query after the CallNotes field.

c. Save the query then view it in Datasheet View to make sure your SQL statement was entered correctly. Save and close the CallListing query.

4. Sort data.

a. Open the EmployeeCalls query in Datasheet View, sort the records in ascending order by the LastName field, then save and close the query.

b. Open the EmployeesByDepartment query in Design View, then add an ascending sort order to the Department, LastName, and FirstName fields.

c. Save the EmployeesByDepartment query, then view it in Datasheet View.

d. Be prepared to discuss this question in class on in a discussion thread: Were all three sort fields used to determine the order of the records? If so, where?

e. Close the EmployeesByDepartment query.

5. Find and replace data.

a. In Datasheet View of the Cases table, click any value in the Category field, then search for all occurrences of "Office" and replace it with **Microsoft Office** using the Whole Field match.

b. Click the Undo button on the Quick Access toolbar and note that you can undo your last replacement, but not all replacements.

c. Edit the Category entry in the last record (CaseID 23) to be **Microsoft Office** versus Office.

d. Save and close the Cases table datasheet.

6. Filter data.

a. Open the CaseDetails query and filter for all records where the Department is **Accounting** and the CallMinutes is **greater than or equal to 30**. Your datasheet should show five records that meet this criteria.

b. There are several ways to apply a filter, including the filter buttons in the Sort & Filter group of the ribbon, the Filter by Form feature, and the options listed in the sort and filter menu when you click the list arrow to the right of the field name in the datasheet. In class or in a discussion group, be prepared to explain which technique you chose to apply the filter.

c. Save and close the CaseDetails query. Reopen it to see that all records are shown. In class or in a discussion group be prepared to explain why the filter criteria was not reapplied to the query.

7. Enter and save criteria.

a. Create a query in Query Design View with the Cases and Employees tables.

b. Add the following fields, in this order: CaseID and Category from the Cases table, LastName and FirstName from the Employees table.

c. Add criteria to select only those records with **Internet** in the Category field.

d. Save the query with the name **InternetCases**, display it in Datasheet View to make sure you have selected the correct records, and then close the InternetCases query.

8. Apply AND criteria.

a. Right-click the InternetCases query, copy it, and then paste it as **InternetAccountingCases**.

b. Add the Department field to the InternetAccountingCases query, then add criteria to select all of the records **Internet** in the Category field and **Accounting** in the Department field.

c. Display the results in Datasheet View as shown in **FIGURE 3-28**, then save and close the query.

FIGURE 3-28

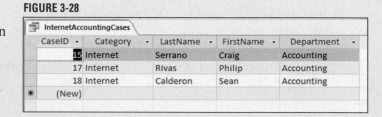

InternetAccountingCases

CaseID	Category	LastName	FirstName	Department
15	Internet	Serrano	Craig	Accounting
17	Internet	Rivas	Philip	Accounting
18	Internet	Calderon	Sean	Accounting
* (New)				

9. Apply OR criteria.

   a. Copy the InternetAccountingCases, then paste it as **InternetAccountingProductionCases**.

   b. Open the InternetAccountingProductionCases query in Design View, then add criteria to select the records in either the Departments of **Accounting** or **Production** with a Category value of **Internet**.

   c. Display the results in Datasheet View as shown in **FIGURE 3-29**, then save and close the query.

FIGURE 3-29

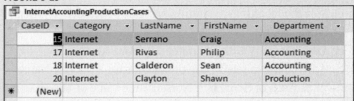

InternetAccountingProductionCases

	CaseID	Category	LastName	FirstName	Department
	15	Internet	Serrano	Craig	Accounting
	17	Internet	Rivas	Philip	Accounting
	18	Internet	Calderon	Sean	Accounting
	20	Internet	Clayton	Shawn	Production
*	(New)				

10. Create Calculated fields.

   a. Open the Employees table in Design View then add field named **Monthly** with a Currency format and Calculated data type.

   b. Use the expression **[Salary]/12** to calculate the values for the new Monthly field.

   c. Save the Employees table and display it in Datasheet View.

   d. Change the salary for Mindi Perez from $70,000 to **80000** then click anywhere else in the datasheet to observe the automatic update to the Monthly field.

   e. Save and close the Employees table.

   f. Create a new query in Query Design View with the Employees, Cases, and Calls tables.

   g. Add the LastName field from the Employees table, the CaseTitle field from the Cases table, and the CallMinutes field from the Calls table.

   h. Add a calculated field to the fourth column of the query grid with the following field name and expression: **TotalTime: [CallMinutes]+10** which estimates the total time required per call for assuming a five-minute gap before and after each call.

   i. Save the query with the name **TotalCallMinutes** and display the datasheet. Change the CallMinutes value for the first "Google doesn't look right" record from 40 minutes to 45 minutes, then click anywhere else in the datasheet. The TotalTime value should automatically update to 55.

   j. Save and close the TotalCallMinutes datasheet.

   k. In class or in a discussion group, be prepared to discuss the TotalTime calculated field in the TotalCallMinutes query. What are the advantages and disadvantages of creating this field in a query versus in the Calls table?

11. Format a datasheet.

   a. In the Cases table datasheet, apply the Georgia font and a **12**-point font size.

   b. Change the alternate row color to Light Blue 1 (fifth column, second row in the Standard Colors palette), and the gridlines to None.

   c. Display the Cases datasheet in Print Preview, then switch the orientation to Landscape, and the margins to Narrow. The datasheet should now fit on a single sheet of paper.

   d. Save the Cases datasheet, and then close it.

   e. Close Access 2019.

Independent Challenge 1

As the manager of Riverwalk, a multi-specialty health clinic, you have created a database to manage the schedules that connect each healthcare provider with the nurses that provider needs to efficiently handle patient visits. In this exercise, you will create a query to answer a special scheduling question at the clinic.

   a. Start Access. Open the IL_AC_3-3.accdb database from the location where you store your Data Files and save it as **IL_AC_3_Riverwalk**. Click Enable Content if a yellow Security Warning message appears.

   b. Create a new query in Query Design View with the Locations, ScheduleItems, ScheduleDate, and Nurses tables.

Independent Challenge 1 (continued)

c. Add the following fields to the query in this order: LocationName from the Locations table, ScheduleDate from the ScheduleDate table, and NurseLName and NurseFName from the Nurses table.

d. Sort the records in ascending order by ScheduleDate, then NurseLName.

e. Save the query with the name **NorthSouth**.

f. Add criteria to select only the records for a LocationName of **North** or **South**, a NurseLName value of **Washington** or **Fredrick**, and a ScheduleDate **on or after 12/1/2021** as shown in **FIGURE 3-30**.

g. Close the NorthSouth query, then close the database and exit Access 2019.

FIGURE 3-30

NorthSouth

LocationNan	ScheduleDat	NurseLName	NurseFName
North	12/6/2021	Fredrick	Sam
South	12/6/2021	Washington	Dana
North	12/9/2021	Fredrick	Sam
South	12/9/2021	Washington	Dana
North	12/10/2021	Fredrick	Sam
South	12/10/2021	Washington	Dana
North	12/11/2021	Fredrick	Sam
North	12/11/2021	Washington	Dana
North	12/12/2021	Fredrick	Sam
South	12/12/2021	Washington	Dana
North	12/13/2021	Fredrick	Sam
South	12/13/2021	Washington	Dana
North	12/16/2021	Fredrick	Sam
South	12/16/2021	Washington	Dana
*			

Independent Challenge 2

You are working for a city to coordinate a series of community-wide preparedness activities. You have created a database to track the activities and volunteers who are attending the activities. In this exercise you will create a query to answer a special activities question at the city.

a. Start Access. Open the IL_AC_3-4.accdb database from the location where you store your Data Files and save it as **IL_AC_3_Volunteers**. Click Enable Content if a yellow Security Warning message appears.

b. Create a new query in Query Design View with the Volunteers, Attendance, and Activities tables.

c. Add the following fields to the query in this order: FirstName and LastName from the Volunteers table, Completed field from the Attendance table, ActivityName and ActivityHours from the Activities table.

d. Sort the records in ascending order on LastName.

e. Add criteria to select only those records with **CPR** anywhere in the ActivityName field and an ActivityHours value **greater than or equal to 7**.

f. Add a calculated field with the following name and expression to estimate the value of the volunteer's time within that activity: **Labor: [ActivityHours]*15**

g. Save the query with the name **LaborCalculation**, display it in Datasheet View, then change the record for William Wilberforce to have your first and last names, as shown in **FIGURE 3-31**.

h. Close the database and exit Access 2019.

FIGURE 3-31

LaborCalculation

FirstNa	LastNar	Completed	ActivityName	ActivityHour	Labor
Rhea	Alman	☑	First Aid and CPR	8	120
Young	Bogard	☑	First Aid and CPR	8	120
Forrest	Browning	☑	First Aid and CPR	8	120
Patch	Bullock	☑	First Aid and CPR	8	120
Angela	Cabriella	☑	First Aid and CPR	8	120
Herman	Cain	☑	First Aid and CPR	8	120
Gina	Daniels	☑	First Aid and CPR	8	120
Quentin	Garden	☑	First Aid and CPR	8	120
Loraine	Goode	☑	First Aid and CPR	8	120
Loraine	Goode	☑	CPR and Automated External Defibrillator AED	7	105
Karla	Larson	☑	First Aid and CPR	8	120
Karla	Larson	☑	CPR and Automated External Defibrillator AED	7	105
Aaron	Love	☑	CPR and Automated External Defibrillator AED	7	105
Aaron	Love	☑	First Aid and CPR	8	120
Katrina	Margolis	☑	CPR and Automated External Defibrillator AED	7	105
Katrina	Margolis	☑	First Aid and CPR	8	120
Jaye	Mati	☑	First Aid and CPR	8	120
Jaye	Mati	☑	CPR and Automated External Defibrillator AED	7	105
Jon	Maxim	☑	First Aid and CPR	8	120
Jon	Maxim	☑	CPR and Automated External Defibrillator AED	7	105
Sindy	Russo	☑	First Aid and CPR	8	120
StudentFi	StudentLa	☑	First Aid and CPR	8	120
*					

Record: 1 of 22 No Filter Search

Visual Workshop

Open the IL_AC_3-5.accdb database from the location where you store your Data Files and save it as **IL_AC_3_CollegeCourses**, then enable content if prompted. Create a query in Query Design View based on the Classes, Professors, Sections, Enrollments, and Students tables with the fields shown in **FIGURE 3-32**. Add criteria to select only those records where Grade field value is **A** or **B** and the Credits field value equals **4**. Display the query in Datasheet View, widen the columns to display all of the data, and save it with the name **4CreditsAB**. Close the 4CreditsAB query then exit Access 2019.

FIGURE 3-32

4CreditsAB

StudentLast	StudentFirst	Description	Credits	Grade	ProfLastName
Mitchell	Irma	Programming Fundamentals	4	B	Zimmerman
Davis	Timothy	Programming Fundamentals	4	A	Zimmerman
Bennet	Domenico	Programming Fundamentals	4	A	Zimmerman
Snow	Frederick	Programming Fundamentals	4	A	Zimmerman
Gregory	Roger	Programming Fundamentals	4	A	Zimmerman
Simmons	Michael	Programming Fundamentals	4	B	Zimmerman
Owen	Leo	Programming Fundamentals	4	B	Zimmerman
Amstell	Mark	Database Programming	4	B	Quinn
Willis	Carl	Database Programming	4	A	Douglas
Cooper	Yehudah	Mobile Application Development	4	B	Quinn
Gallow	Taiichi	Mobile Application Development	4	B	Quinn
Noble	Hector	Database Management	4	B	Zimmerman
Noble	Hector	Engineering Graphics	4	B	Rosenbaum
Cooper	Yehudah	Engineering Graphics	4	B	Rosenbaum
Bennet	Domenico	Engineering Graphics	4	A	Rosenbaum
Dow	Johann	Engineering Graphics	4	A	Rosenbaum
Gregory	Roger	Engineering Graphics	4	A	Rosenbaum
Gallow	Taiichi	Engineering Graphics	4	B	Rosenbaum
Owen	Leo	Engineering Graphics	4	B	Rosenbaum
*					

Record: 1 of 19 No Filter Search

Access

Working with Forms and Reports

CASE Lydia Snyder, vice president of operations at JCL Talent, asks you to create forms to make job and company information easier to access, enter, and update. She also wants you to create some reports that will provide a professional presentation and analysis of selected data.

Module Objectives

After completing this module, you will be able to:

- Work in Form View
- Work in Form Layout View
- Work in Form Design View
- Work in Report Layout View
- Work in Report Design View
- Add conditional formatting
- Use the Format Painter and themes

Files You Will Need

IL_AC_4-1.accdb
IL_AC_4-2.accdb
IL_AC_4-3.accdb
IL_AC_4-4.accdb
IL_AC_4-5.accdb

Access
Module 4

Work in Form View

Learning Outcomes
- Navigate records in a form
- Enter records in a form

A form allows you to arrange the fields of a record in any layout so a database **user** can quickly and easily find, enter, edit, and analyze data. You can use several different tools to create forms, as shown in **TABLE 4-1**. Each form has three views, and each view has a primary purpose, as described in **TABLE 4-2**, although you can complete some tasks in multiple views. **Form View** gives a user an easy-to-use data entry and navigation screen. **CASE** *Lydia Snyder asks you to find and enter company data in the database. You will use a form to complete the work.*

STEPS

1. **sam Start Access, open the IL_AC_4-1.accdb database from the location where you store your Data Files, save it as IL_AC_4_Jobs, enable content if prompted, then double-click the CompanyEntry form to open it in Form View**
   The CompanyEntry form organizes all the fields of the Companies table to clearly display the data from one record at a time. Forms contain **controls** such as labels to describe information, text boxes and combo boxes to help you enter information, and command buttons to help you work with the form. Forms also provide **navigation buttons** in the lower-left corner, which help you navigate through the data.
2. **Click the Next record button ▶ in the navigation bar three times to navigate to the fourth record**
   The **Current Record box** identifies what record you are currently viewing as well as the total number of records. The navigation buttons also provide a way to move to the first or last record in the form very quickly.
3. **Click the Last record button ▶| in the navigation bar**
   To move to a prior record, you use the Previous record and First record buttons.
4. **Click the Previous record button ◀ in the navigation bar, then click the First record button |◀ to return to the first record**
   In addition, you can type any number in the Current Record box to quickly move to that record.
5. **Click the Current Record box, type 17, press ENTER, then change the Industry field value to Aerospace**
   Changes are saved as you move from record to record and new records are always entered at the end.
6. **Click the New (blank) record button ▶*, then enter a new company record, as shown in FIGURE 4-1 and described below**

Company ID:	TAB (AutoNumber field that automatically increments)
Company Name:	**Heritage Computing Inc**
Industry:	**Information**
Description:	**Database modeling, management, warehousing and analytics.**
City:	**Springfield**
State:	**MO**

7. **Right-click the CompanyEntry tab, then click Close**
   When you close a form, Access automatically saves data in the current record.

FIGURE 4-1: Adding a new record to the CompanyEntry form in Form View

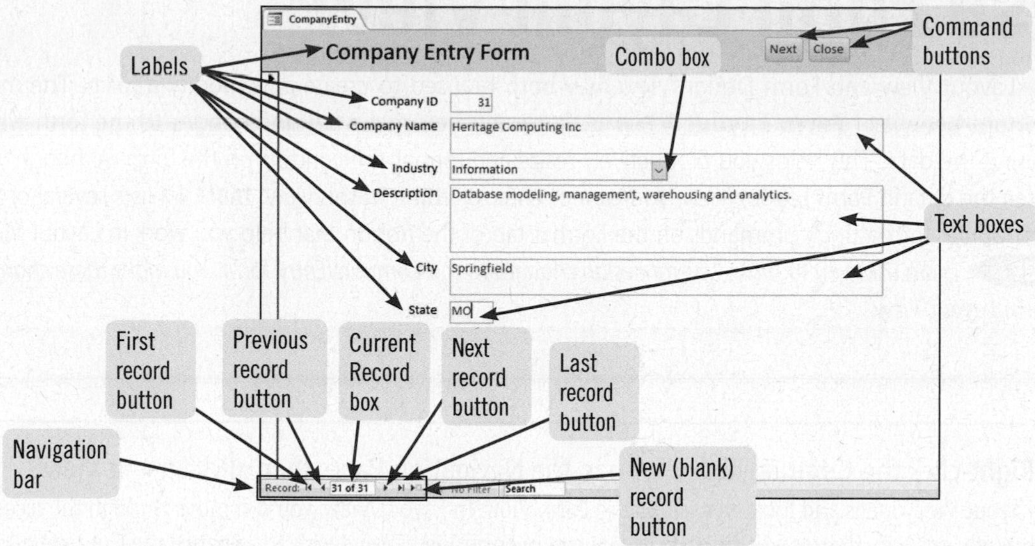

TABLE 4-1: Form creation tools

tool	icon	creates a form
Form		with one click based on the selected table or query
Form Design		from scratch in Form Design View
Blank Form		from scratch in Form Layout View
Form Wizard		by answering a series of questions provided by the Form Wizard dialog boxes
Navigation		to navigate or move between different areas of the database
More Forms		for Multiple Items, Datasheet, Split Form, or Modal Dialog arrangements
Split Form		with two panes, the upper showing one record at a time and the lower displaying a datasheet of many records

TABLE 4-2: Form views

view	primary purpose
Form	To find, sort, enter, and edit data
Layout	To modify the size, position, or formatting of controls; shows data as you modify the form, making it the tool of choice when you want to change the appearance and usability of the form while viewing data
Design	To modify the Form Header, Detail, and Footer section, to work with form rulers and gridlines, or to access the complete range of controls and form properties; Design View does not display data

Access
Module 4

Use Form Layout View

Learning Outcomes
- Format controls in Form Layout View
- Edit labels in Form Layout View

Form Layout View and Form Design View may both be used to create and modify a form. The most important benefit of **Form Layout View** is that it lets you make design changes to the form while browsing the data. This helps you productively resize and format the controls on the form. Although you can see the data in Form Layout View, you cannot enter or edit it in this view. **TABLE 4-3** lists several of the most popular formatting commands on the Format tab of the ribbon that help you work in Layout View.

CASE *Lydia asks you to make several design changes to the CompanyEntry form. You make these changes in Form Layout View.*

STEPS

1. **Right-click the CompanyEntry form in the Navigation Pane, then click Layout View**
   Layout View opens and looks very similar to Form View. In Layout View, you can move through the records, but you cannot enter or edit the data as you can in Form View. You decide to enhance the Company Entry Form label at the top of the form.

2. **Click the Company Entry Form label in the Form Header section, click the Format tab on the ribbon, click the Bold button B, click the Font Color list arrow, click Dark Blue (fourth column, first row of the Standard Colors palette), click the Font Size arrow 11, then click 24**
   You often use Layout View to make minor design changes, such as editing labels and changing formatting characteristics.

QUICK TIP
You can also apply formatting commands in Form Design View.

3. **Click the Industry label to select it, click the Industry label again to position the insertion point within the label, edit the text to be Primary Industry, then press ENTER**
   Your users do not need the Next button because they use the buttons in the navigation bar, so you can delete the Next command button.

4. **Click the Next command button, then press DELETE**
   You change the style, shape, and outline of the Close button.

5. **Click the Close command button, click the Quick Styles button, click the Colored Fill – Blue, Accent 1 option (second column, second row), click the Change Shape button, click the Oval shape, click the Shape Outline button, then click Transparent near the bottom of the menu**
   You decide to make one other small change. You feel that the data in the Company ID text box would be easier to read if it were centered.

QUICK TIP
You can undo multiple formatting actions by clicking the Undo button on the Quick Access toolbar.

6. **Click 1 in the box to the right of the Company ID label, then click the Center button**
   Your CompanyEntry form should look like **FIGURE 4-2**. The form label is more pronounced, the Close button is styled, and the Company ID data is easier to read.

TROUBLE
Be sure to modify the text box instead of the Company ID label on the left.

FIGURE 4-2: Modifying controls in Form Layout View

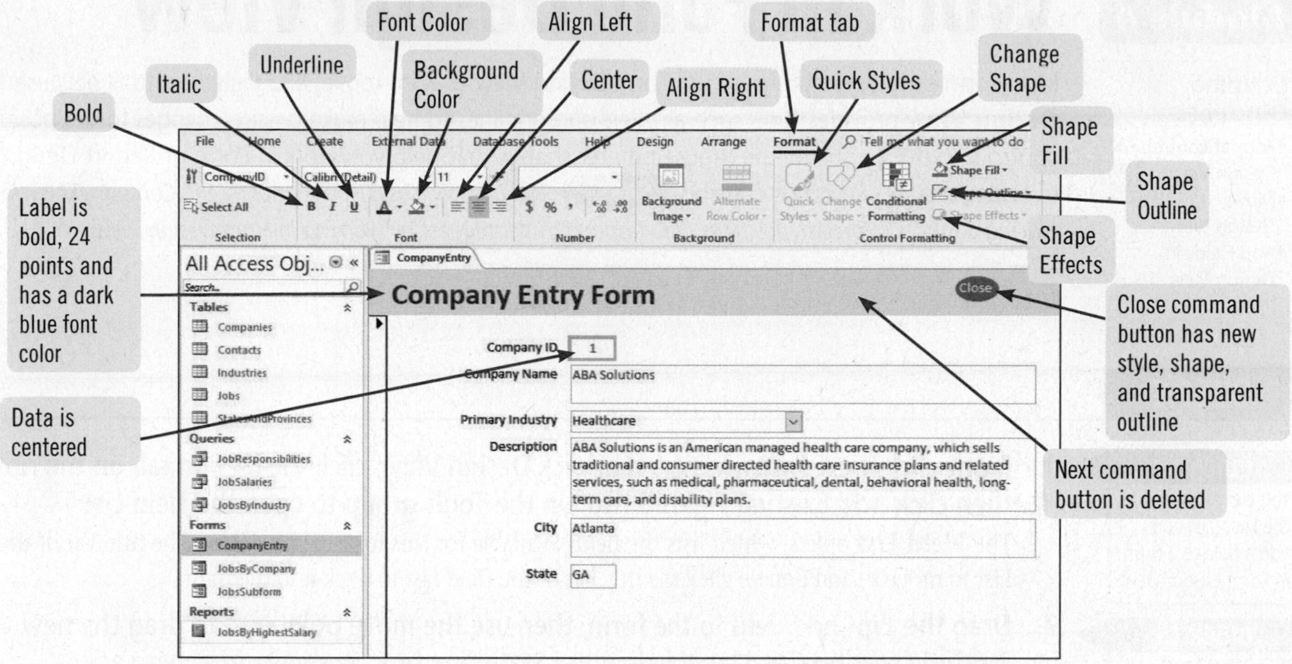

TABLE 4-3: Useful formatting commands

button	button name	description
B	**Bold**	Toggles bold on or off for the selected control(s)
I	**Italic**	Toggles italic on or off for the selected control(s)
U	**Underline**	Toggles underline on or off for the selected control(s)
A	**Font Color**	Changes the text color of the selected control(s)
	Background Color or Shape Fill	Changes the background color of the selected control(s)
	Align Left	Left-aligns the selected control(s) within its own border
	Center	Centers the selected control(s) within its own border
	Align Right	Right-aligns the selected control(s) within its own border
	Alternate Row Color	Changes the background color of alternate records in the selected section
	Shape Outline	Changes the border color, thickness, or style of the selected control(s)
	Shape Effects	Changes the special visual effect of the selected control(s)

Work in Form Design View

Learning Outcomes
- Format controls in Design View
- Move controls in Design View
- Add Fields in Design View

Most form developers prefer to use Form Design View to add, move, and resize controls because **Form Design View** provides tools such as rulers and gridlines to help make precise changes to the position of controls. TABLE 4-4 shows the mouse pointer shapes that help you work in Form or Report Design View to select, resize, and move controls. **CASE** *Lydia Snyder asks you to modify the CompanyEntry form by placing controls in precise positions. You respond to her request by working in Form Design View.*

STEPS

QUICK TIP
You can also open the Field List and add a field to a form in Form Layout View.

1. **Right-click the CompanyEntry tab, click Design View, click the Design tab on the ribbon, then click Add Existing Fields button in the Tools group to open the Field List**
   The **Field List** opens, which lists the fields available for this form. You can drag the title bar of the Field List to move it, and double-click the title bar of the Field List to dock it to the right.

QUICK TIP
If you make a mistake, click the Undo button and try again.

2. **Drag the ZipCode field to the form, then use the move pointer to drag the new ZipCode text box and label below the State text box, as shown in FIGURE 4-3**
   When you add the ZipCode field to the form, two controls are added: a label and a text box. The **label** on the left describes the data. By default, the label displays the field name, though you can modify it as desired. The **text box** on the right displays the data from the field. It *must* contain the actual field name to stay connected (also called "**bound**") to the data.

3. **Click the ZipCode label, click the ZipCode label a second time to place the insertion point in the text, modify the text to be ZIP, press ENTER, click the Format tab on the ribbon, click the Font Color arrow, then click Automatic**
   You also want to align and format the new controls.

TROUBLE
Labels are on the left, and text boxes are on the right.

4. **Click the ZIP label, click the Align Right button, press and hold CTRL, click the State label to select both labels at the same time, click the Arrange tab on the ribbon, click the Align button, then click Right**
   You right-aligned the ZIP text within the label, then you right-aligned the right edges of the ZIP label with the State label above it. Now left-align the edges of the State and ZipCode text boxes.

5. **Click the State text box, press and hold CTRL, click the ZipCode text box, click the Align button, then click Left**
   The new controls for the ZipCode field are now added, moved, and aligned on the form. As a final touch, you want to add a label to the Form Footer section with the text "JCL Talent".

QUICK TIP
You can also add and edit labels in Form Layout View.

6. **Drag the bottom of the Form Footer bar down about 0.5", click the Design tab on the ribbon, click the Label button, click at about the 1" mark in the Form Footer section, type JCL Talent, then press ENTER**
   You are ready to review the final CompanyEntry form in Form View.

7. **Right-click the CompanyEntry tab, click Save, right-click the CompanyEntry tab again, then click Form View as shown in FIGURE 4-4**
   In general, it is common to use Form Layout View for formatting changes and Form Design View to add and position new controls. However, much of the functionality between the two views overlaps.

8. **Right-click the CompanyEntry tab, then click Close**

FIGURE 4-3: Adding, moving, and aligning controls in Form Design View

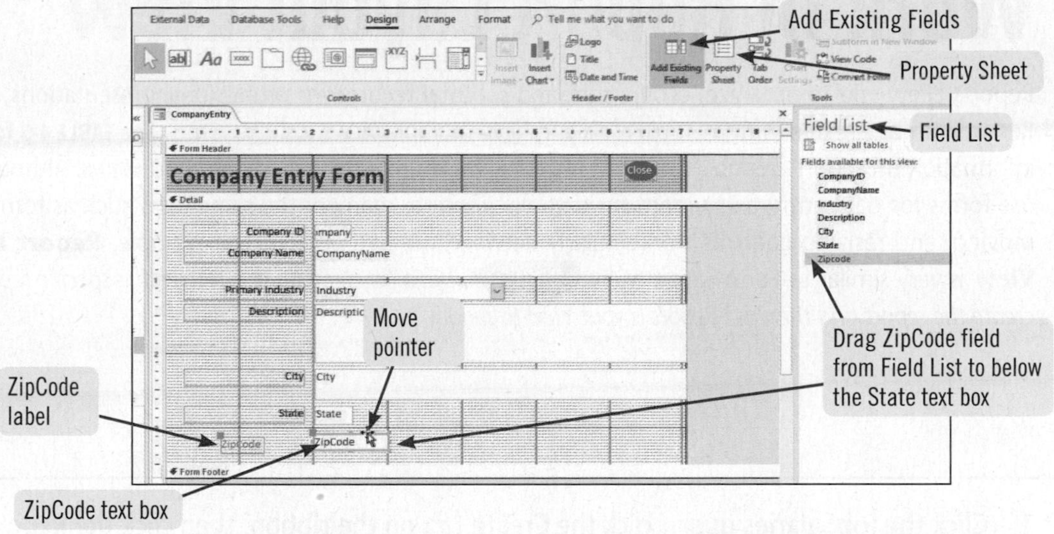

FIGURE 4-4: Final CompanyEntry form in Form View

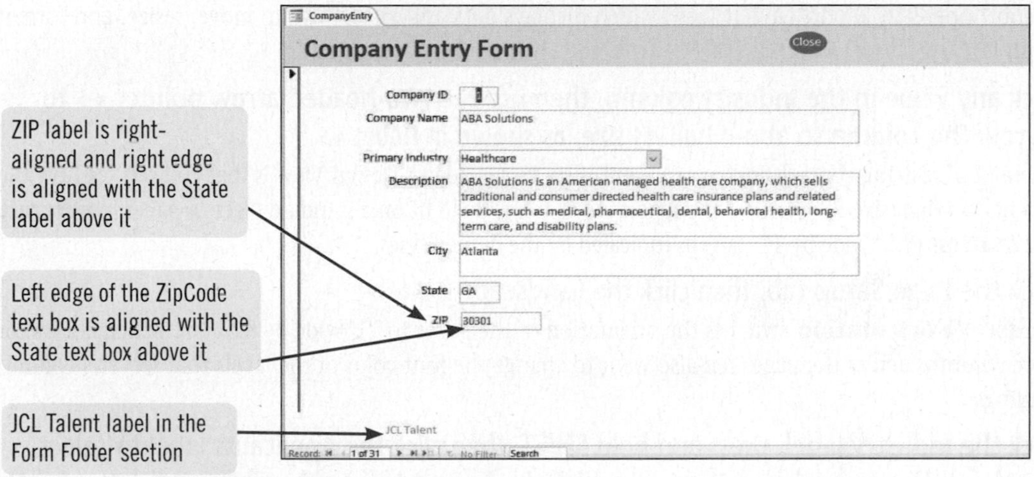

TABLE 4-4: Mouse pointer shapes in Form or Report Design View

shape	when does this shape appear?	action
	When you point to any unselected control on the form (the default mouse pointer)	Single-clicking with this mouse pointer selects a control
	When you point to the upper-left corner or edge of a selected control in Form Design View or the middle of the control in Form Layout View	Dragging with this mouse pointer moves the selected control(s)
	When you point to any sizing handle (except the larger one in the upper-left corner in Form Design View)	Dragging with one of these mouse pointers resizes the control

Bound versus unbound controls

Controls are either bound or unbound. **Bound controls** display values from a field such as text boxes and combo boxes. The most common bound control is the text box. **Unbound controls** describe data or enhance the appearance of the form. Labels are the most common type of unbound control, but other types include lines, images, tabs, and command buttons. Another way to distinguish bound from unbound controls is to observe the form as you move from record to record. Because bound controls display data, their contents change as you move through the records, displaying data from the field of the current record. Unbound controls such as labels, lines, and command buttons do not change as you move through the records in a form.

Access

Work in Report Layout View

Learning Outcomes
- Create a report with the Report tool
- Move, resize, and format controls in Report Layout View
- Change page orientation

Reports allow you to organize, group, sort, and subtotal records for professional presentations of data. Reports can be created with multiple tools and have multiple views just like forms. See **TABLE 4-5** for more information on report creation tools and **TABLE 4-6** for more information on report views. Although you use forms for data entry and reports for data distribution, many of the same tasks such as formatting, moving, and resizing controls work similarly between the two objects. For example, **Report Layout View** is very similar to Form Layout View. CASE *Lydia Snyder asks you to create a specific report. You create the report and then use Report Layout View to modify it.*

STEPS

1. **Click the JobSalaries query, click the Create tab on the ribbon, then click the Report button**

   A report opens in Report Layout View, which displays data and allows you to move, resize, and format controls.

2. **Click any value in the Industry column, then use the two-headed arrow pointer ↔ to narrow the column to about half its size, as shown in FIGURE 4-5**

   A benefit of resizing controls in Report Layout View versus Report Design View is that you can see how the data fits as you resize the control. The report is still too wide to fit on a standard piece of paper in **portrait orientation** (8.5" wide by 11" tall), as indicated by the dashed lines.

3. **Click the Page Setup tab, then click the Landscape button**

   Landscape orientation switches the orientation of the paper to 11" wide by 8.5" tall, which allows for more columns across the page. You also want to change the font color of the labels that serve as column headings.

4. **Click the Industry label, press and hold SHIFT, then click the Applicants label to select all column heading labels in that row, click the Format tab on the ribbon, click the Font Color arrow, then click Automatic**

   Your last change is to move the StartingSalary column to the far right.

5. **Click the StartingSalary label, press and hold SHIFT, click any value in the StartingSalary column, then use the move pointer to drag the column to the right of the Applicants column**

   The final JobSalaries report is shown in **FIGURE 4-6**.

6. **Right-click the JobSalaries tab, click Save, click OK to accept the default name, right-click the JobSalaries tab, click Print Preview to preview the report as it would fit on a piece of paper, right-click the JobSalaries tab, then click Layout View to return to Layout View**

FIGURE 4-5: Resizing a column in Report Layout View

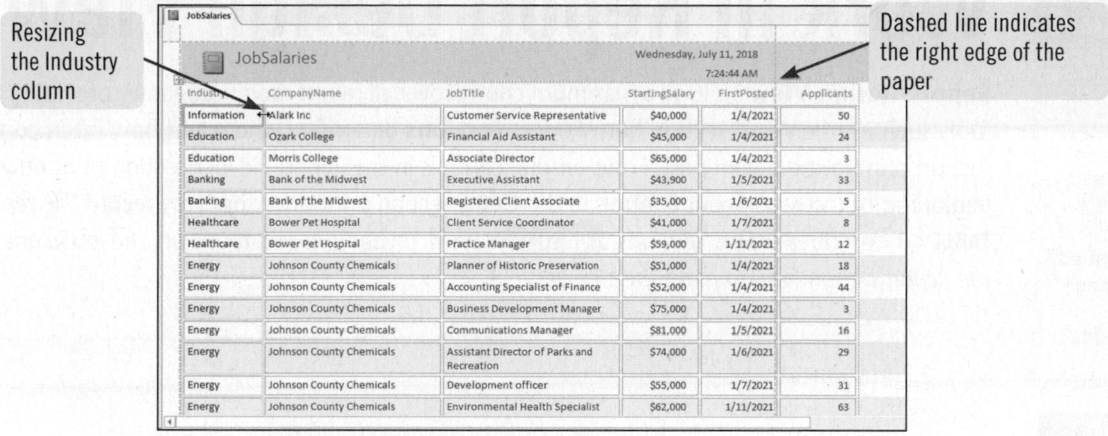

FIGURE 4-6: Final JobSalaries report in Report Layout View

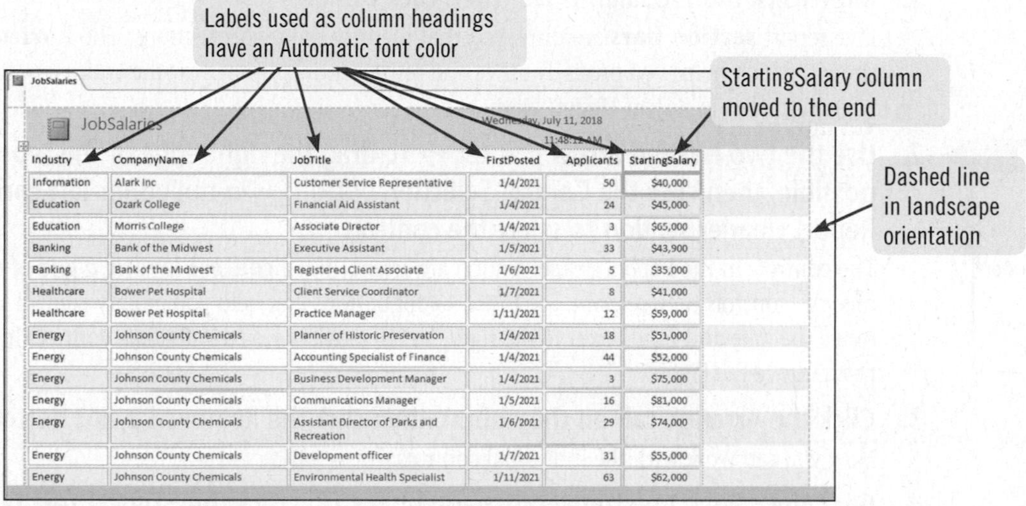

TABLE 4-5: Report creation tools

tool	icon	creates a report
Report		with one click based on the selected table or query
Report Design		from scratch in Report Design View
Blank Report		from scratch in Report Layout View
Report Wizard		by answering a series of questions provided by the Report Wizard dialog boxes
Labels		by answering a series of questions provided by the Label Wizard dialog boxes

TABLE 4-6: Report views

view	primary purpose
Report View	To quickly review the report without page breaks
Print Preview	To review each page of an entire report as it will appear if printed
Layout View	To modify the size, position, or formatting of controls; shows live data as you modify the report, making it the tool of choice when you want to change the appearance and positioning of controls on a report while also reviewing live data
Design View	To work with report sections or to access the complete range of controls and report properties; Design View does not display data

Work in Report Design View

Learning Outcomes
- Modify controls in Report Design View
- Group and ungroup controls in Report Design View
- Change report width

Report Design View gives you maximum control over all report modifications by providing extra design tools such as rulers and section bars. Report **sections** determine where and how often controls in that section print in the final report. For example, controls in the Report Header section print only once at the beginning of the report, but controls in the Detail section print once for every record the report displays. **TABLE 4-7** describes report sections. **CASE** *Lydia Snyder asks you to modify the JobSalaries report. You use Report Design View to make the changes.*

STEPS

1. **Right-click the JobSalaries tab, then click Design View**
   Five report **section bars** are displayed that identify the report sections. The **horizontal ruler** is also shown, which helps you precisely move and resize controls. To narrow the entire report, you drag the right edge to the left in Report Design View.

> **QUICK TIP**
> If a report is too wide to fit on a piece of paper, a green error indicator appears in the upper-left corner of the report.

2. **Use the two-headed arrow pointer ↔ to drag the right edge of the report as far left as possible, then click the Control Selection button in the upper-left corner of the Report Header section to select the controls**
   The controls in the Report Header section are arranged in a **control layout**, a grid of cells that help organize the controls they contain. See **TABLE 4-8** for buttons that help you modify control layouts. You want to move the date and time boxes to the right, but to move or resize individual controls in a layout, you must first remove the layout.
3. **Click the Arrange tab on the ribbon, then click the Remove Layout button**
   Now you can work with the individual controls.
4. **Click the =Date() text box, press and hold CTRL, click the =Time() text box, click the Size/Space button, click Group, then press RIGHT ARROW enough times to position the right edge of the controls at the 9" mark on the horizontal ruler**
   Your screen should look like **FIGURE 4-7**. You can also use the mouse to move controls in Report or Form Design View, though the arrow keys allow you to precisely position the selected controls. You also want to make some formatting changes to the title of the report.
5. **Click the JobSalaries label in the Report Header, click the Format tab on the ribbon, click the Font Color arrow click Automatic, click the Font Size arrow 11, click 24, click the JobSalaries label again to place the insertion pointer in the text, then add a space so that the label reads Job Salaries**
   Your final modification will be to change the background color of the StartingSalary data.

> **QUICK TIP**
> Labels are edited and controls are formatted the same way in Form Design View and Form Layout View.

6. **Click the StartingSalary text box in the Detail section, click the Background Color arrow, then click the Green 2 box (seventh column, third row in the Standard Colors palette)**
   The final Report Design View should look like **FIGURE 4-8**. To review your modifications, show the report in Print Preview.
7. **Right-click the JobSalaries tab, click Save, right-click the JobSalaries tab, click Print Preview, click the Next Page button to navigate through the pages of the report, right-click the JobSalaries tab, then click Close**
   Previewing each page of the report helps you confirm that no blank pages are created and allows you to examine how the different report sections print on each page.

FIGURE 4-7: Working in Report Design View

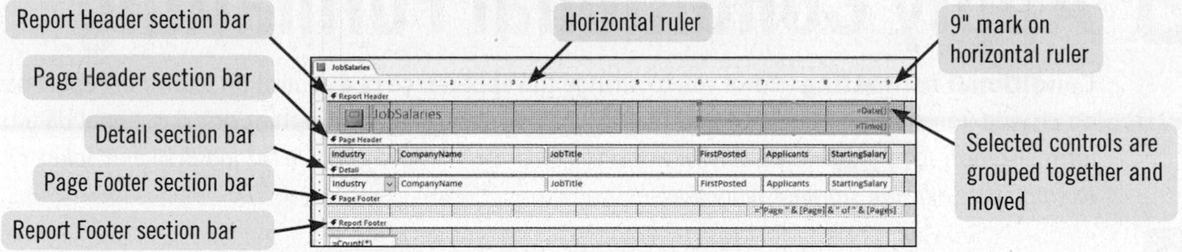

FIGURE 4-8: Final JobSalaries report in Report Design View

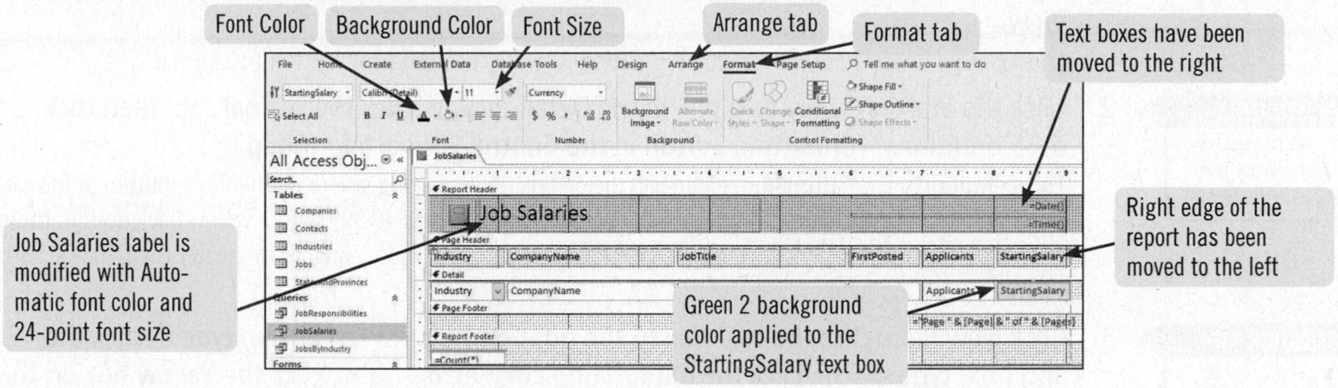

TABLE 4-7: Report sections

section	where does this section print?
Report Header	At the top of the first page
Page Header	At the top of every page (but below the Report Header on the first page)
Detail	Once for every record
Page Footer	At the bottom of every page
Report Footer	At the end of the report

TABLE 4-8: Control layout buttons

button	description
Gridlines	Applies gridlines in different colors, widths, and borders to the cells of the control layout
Stacked	Applies a vertical layout with labels on the left and text boxes on the right
Tabular	Applies a horizontal layout similar to a spreadsheet
Remove Layout	Removes a layout
Insert Above	Inserts a row above the layout
Insert Below	Inserts a row below the layout
Insert Left	Inserts a column to the left of the layout
Insert Right	Inserts a column to the right of the layout

button	description
Select Layout	Selects the entire layout
Select Column	Selects a single column of a layout
Select Row	Selects a single row of a layout
Merge	Merges cells in a layout
Split Vertically	Splits cells into two rows
Split Horizontally	Splits cells into two columns
Move Up	Moves cells into the section above the current section
Move Down	Moves cells into the section below the current section

Apply Conditional Formatting

Learning Outcome
- Apply conditional formats

Conditional formatting allows you to change the appearance of a control on a form or report based on criteria you specify. Conditional formatting helps you highlight important or exceptional data on a form or report. **CASE** *Lydia Snyder wants you to format the salary data in the JobsByHighestSalary report to emphasize different starting salary levels.*

STEPS

1. **Right-click the JobsByHighestSalary report in the Navigation Pane, then click Design View**
   The first step in applying conditional formatting is to select the control you want to format.

TROUBLE
Be sure to select the StartingSalary text box (not the label).

2. **Click the StartingSalary text box in the Detail section, click the Format tab, then click the Conditional Formatting button in the Control Formatting group**
   The Conditional Formatting Rules Manager dialog box opens, asking you to define the conditional formatting rules. You want to format StartingSalary values between 0 and 49,999 with a yellow background, those between 50,000 and 69,999 with a light green background, and those equal to or greater than 70,000 with a light blue background.

QUICK TIP
Between . . . and criteria include both values in the range.

3. **Click New Rule, click the text box to the right of the between arrow, type 0, click the and box, type 49999, click the Background color arrow, click the Yellow box on the bottom row, then click OK**
   You add the second conditional formatting rule.
4. **Click New Rule, click the text box to the right of the between arrow, type 50000, click the and box, type 69999, click the Background color arrow, click the Light Green box on the bottom row, then click OK**
   You add the third conditional formatting rule.
5. **Click New Rule, click the between arrow, click greater than or equal to, click the value box, type 70000, click the Background color arrow, click the Light Blue box on the bottom row, then click OK**
   The Conditional Formatting Rules Manager dialog box with two rules should look like **FIGURE 4-9**.

QUICK TIP
Conditional formatting works the same way in Form and Report Layout and Design Views.

6. **Click OK in the Conditional Formatting Rules Manager dialog box, right-click the JobsByHighestSalary tab, then click Print Preview**
   Conditional formatting rules applied a yellow, light green, or light blue background color to the StartingSalary text box for each record, as shown in **FIGURE 4-10**.
7. **Right-click the JobsByHighestSalary tab, click Save, right-click the JobsByHighestSalary tab, then click Close**

FIGURE 4-9: Conditional Formatting Rules Manager dialog box

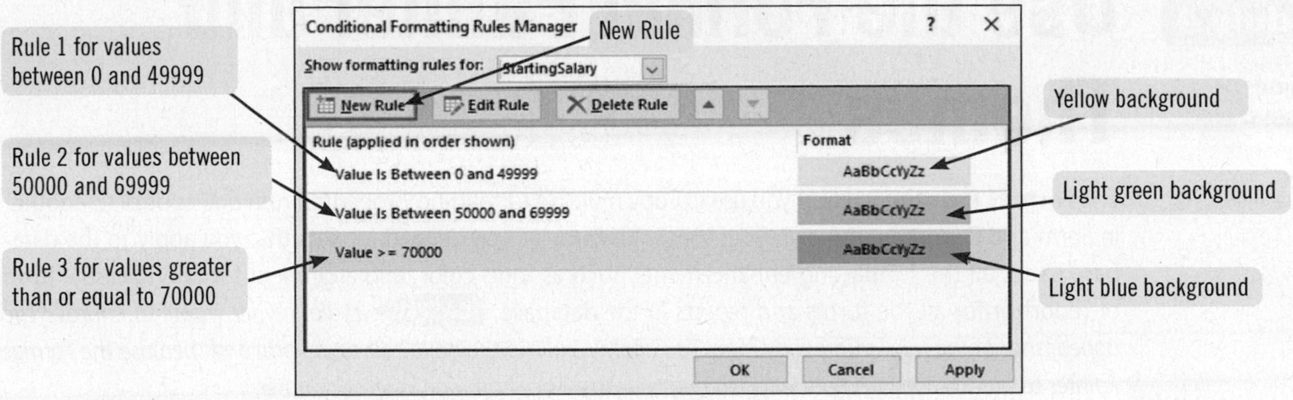

FIGURE 4-10: Conditional formatting applied to the JobsByHighestSalary report

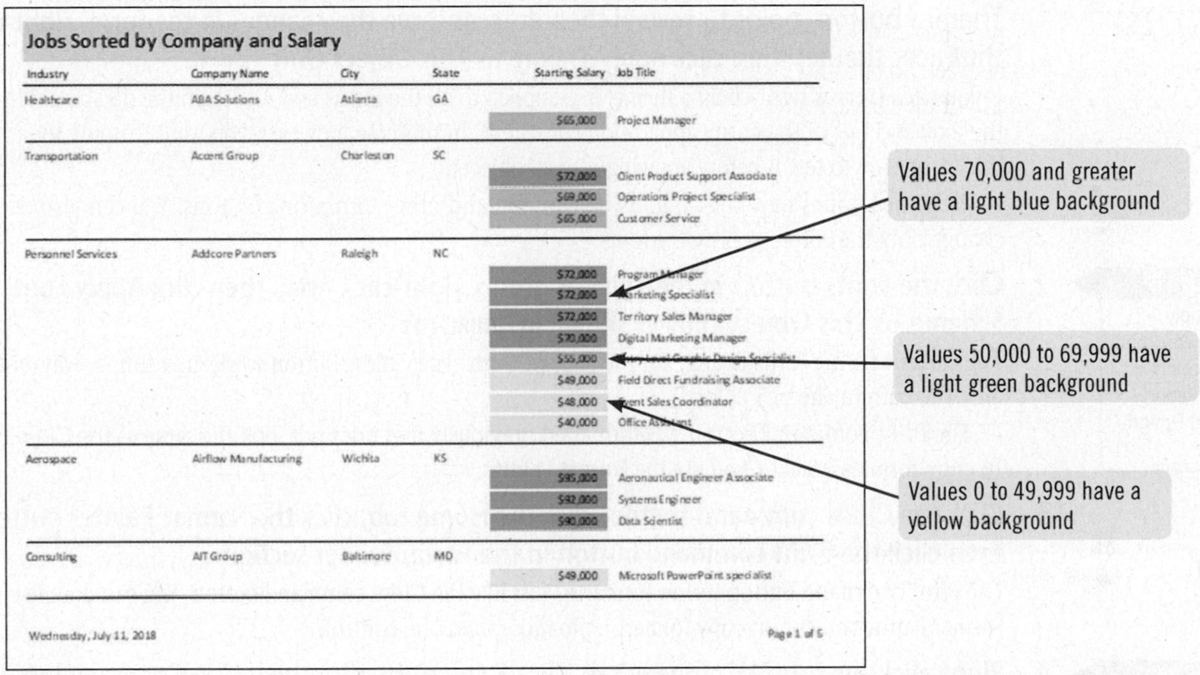

Access

Use the Format Painter and Themes

Learning Outcomes
- Format with Format Painter
- Apply a theme

The **Format Painter** is a tool you use to copy multiple formatting properties from one control to another in Form and Report Design or Layout Views. **Themes** are predefined formats that you apply to the database to set all the formatting enhancements, such as font, color, and alignment for an individual form or report or for all the forms and reports in the database. CASE *Lydia Snyder wants to improve the appearance of the JobsByCompany form. You apply a built-in theme to the entire form and then use the Format Painter to quickly copy and paste formatting characteristics from one label to another.*

STEPS

1. **Right-click the JobsByCompany form in the Navigation Pane, click Design View, click the Themes button, point to several themes to observe the changes in the form, right-click the Facet theme, then click Apply Theme to This Object Only**

   If you click (versus right-click) a theme, it is applied to all the forms and reports in the database. This keeps the look and feel of the entire application consistent. In this case, however, you want to apply the theme to this form only to test it before applying it to all objects.

   A theme applies new colors, fonts, alignment, and other formatting options. You can also choose to change only the colors or only the fonts.

> **QUICK TIP**
> You can apply themes, theme fonts, or theme colors in Form and Report Layout and Design views.

2. **Click the Fonts button in the Themes group, right-click Arial, then click Apply Font Scheme to This Object Only as shown in FIGURE 4-11**

   The current theme fonts change for the current form. The Colors button works in a similar way, changing only the current theme's colors.

   The Print command button was formatted previously and does not look the same as the Close button. To copy formats quickly, you use the Format Painter.

3. **Click the Close command button, click the Home tab, click the Format Painter button, then click the Print command button in the Form Header section**

   The Print command button is now formatted just like the Close command button. You can double-click the Format Painter button to copy formatting to more than one control.

> **QUICK TIP**
> The Format Painter works the same way in Form and Report Layout and Design Views.

4. **Right-click the JobsByCompany tab, click Save, right-click the JobsByCompany tab, then click Form View to review the changes shown in FIGURE 4-12**

5. **Click the Close command button to close the CompanyJobs form, click the Database Tools tab, then click the Compact and Repair Database button**

6. **sam Close the database and exit Access 2019**

FIGURE 4-11: Applying themes

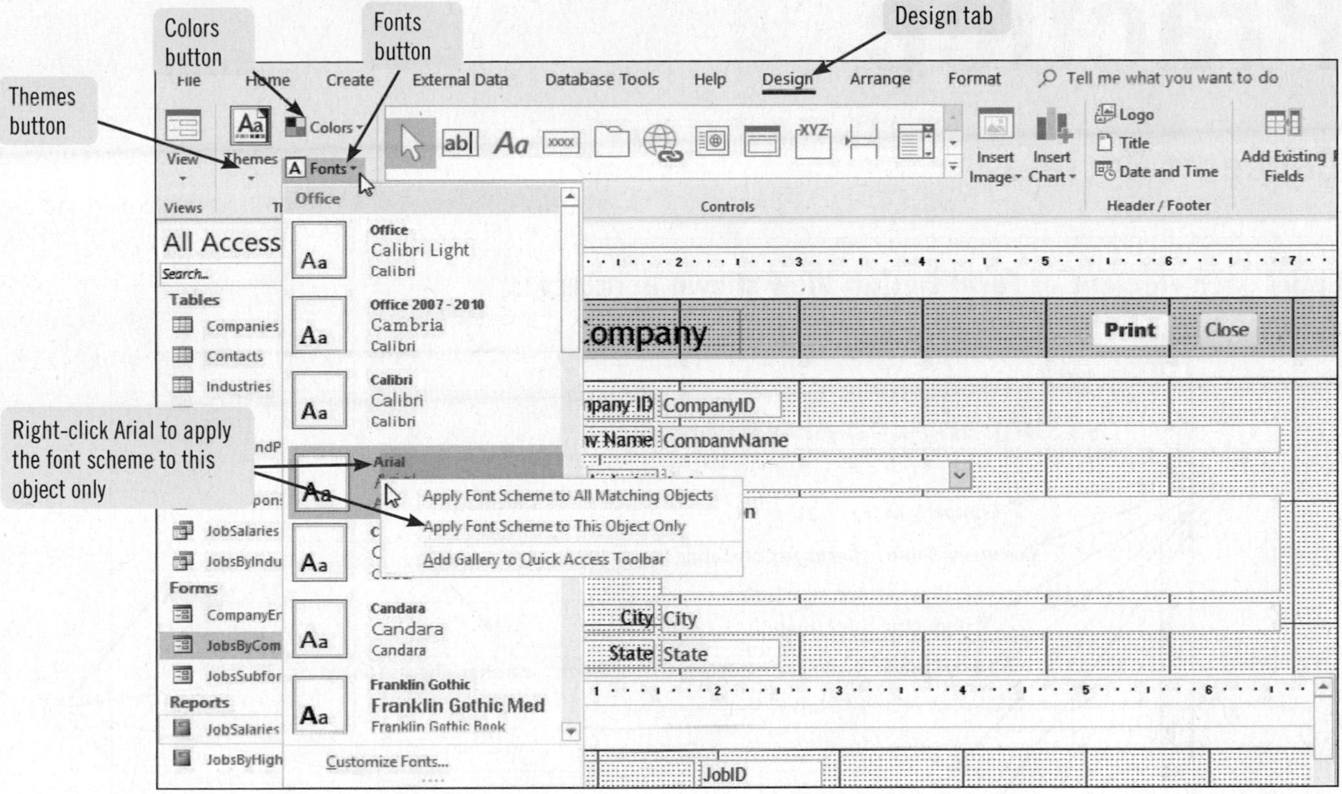

FIGURE 4-12: Final CompanyJobs form

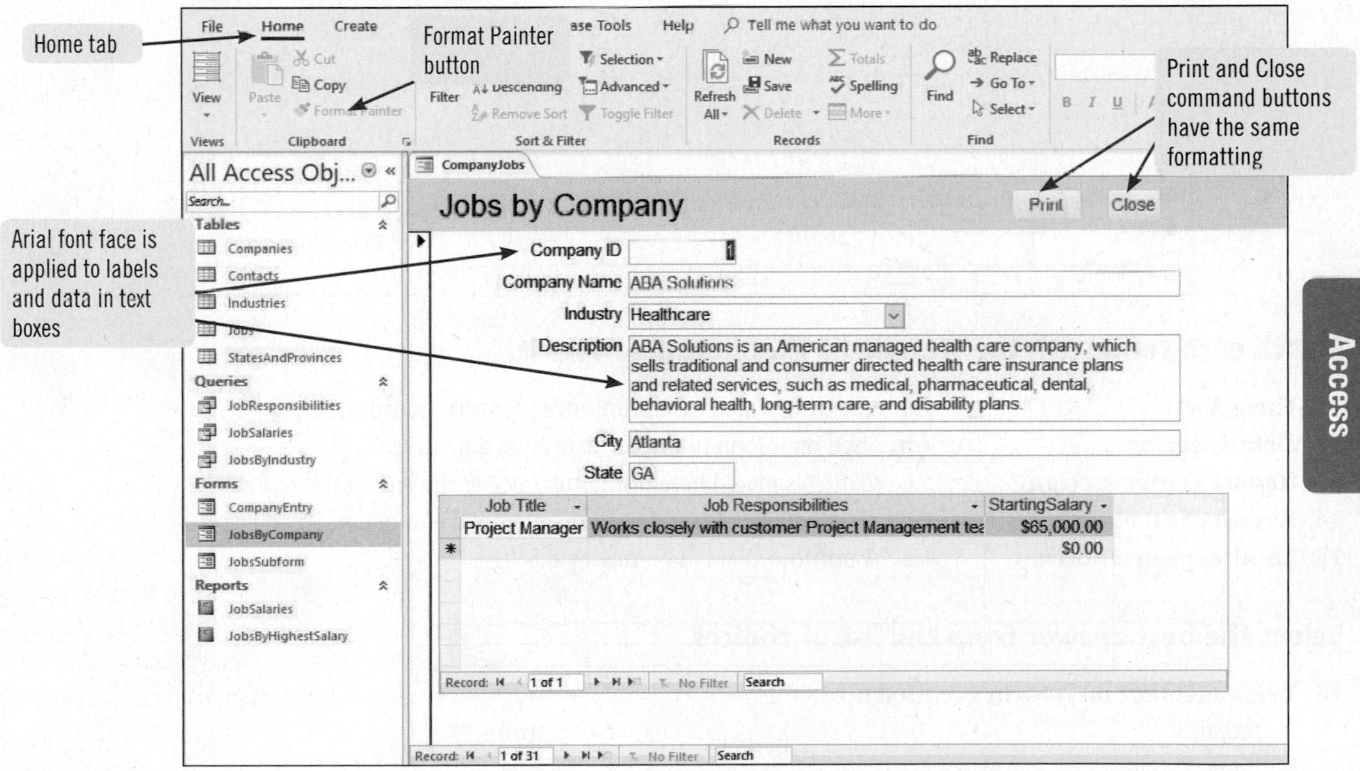

Access

Practice

Concepts Review

Label each element of Form Design View shown in FIGURE 4-13.

FIGURE 4-13

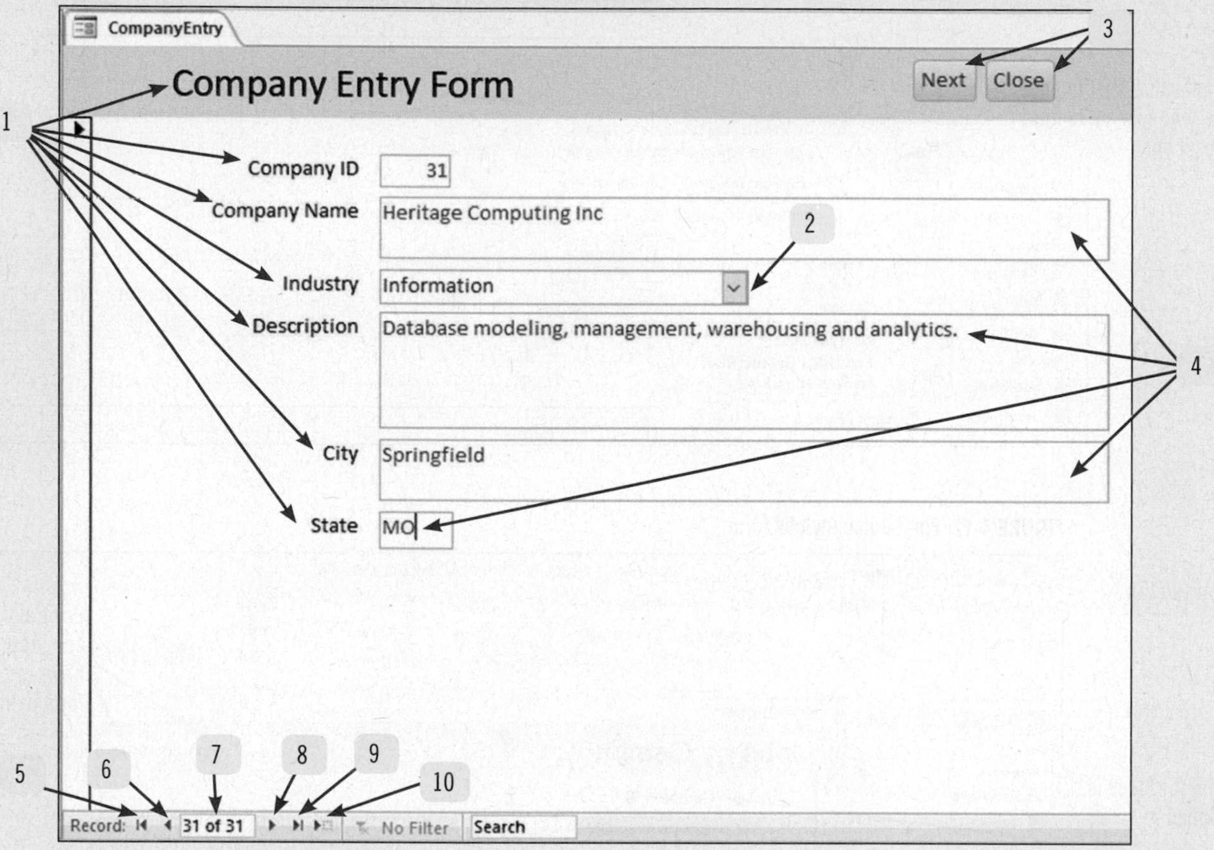

Match each term with the statement that best describes it.

11. Form View
12. Detail section
13. Report Footer section
14. Bound control
15. Landscape orientation

a. Controls placed here print once for every record
b. Used on a form to display data from a field
c. Controls placed here print only once at the end of the report
d. Most commonly used to find, enter, and edit data
e. A printout that is 11" wide by 8.5" tall

Select the best answer from the list of choices.

16. Every element on a form is called a(n):

a. Property.
b. Item.
c. Control.
d. Tool.

17. Which of the following may *not* be used to format controls?

a. Form View
b. Form Layout View
c. Report Design View
d. Report Layout View

18. The most common bound control is the:

a. Combo box.
b. Label.
c. List box.
d. Text box.

19. The most common unbound control is the:

a. Text box.
b. Combo box.
c. Label.
d. Command button.

20. Which view does not show data?

a. Form Layout View
b. Form Design View
c. Print Preview
d. Report Layout View

Skills Review

1. Work in Form View.

a. Start Access, open the IL_AC_4-2.accdb database from the location where you store your Data Files, save it as **IL_AC_4_SupportDesk**, then enable content if prompted.
b. Open the EmployeeMaster form in Form View.
c. Find the record for Peggy Short and change the LastName value to **Hopper**
d. Add a new record with your name in the LastName and FirstName fields, and **Executive** in the Department field.
e. Save the EmployeeMaster form.

2. Work in Form Layout View.

a. Open the EmployeeMaster in Layout View.
b. Modify the label in the Form Header section to have a space between the words to read: **Employee Master**
c. Modify the labels on the left in the Detail section to have spaces between the words to read: **Employee ID**, **Last Name**, and **First Name**
d. Modify the labels on the left in the Detail section to be right-aligned.
e. Change the font color for all labels to Automatic (black).
f. Save the EmployeeMaster form.

3. Work in Form Design View.

a. Open the EmployeeMaster form in Design View.
b. Move the Department label and Department combo box up to fill the blank space after the FirstName controls.
c. Open the Field List, then add the Salary field to the form.
d. Align the right edge of the Salary label with the labels above it and change the font color for the Salary label to Automatic (black).
e. Align the left edge of the Salary text box with the combo box and text boxes above it.
f. Save the EmployeeMaster form and open it in Form View as shown in **FIGURE 4-14**.
g. Close the EmployeeMaster form.

4. Work in Report Layout View.

a. Use the Report tool to create a new report on the Cases table.
b. In Layout View of the new report, resize the Category column to be about half of its current size.
c. In Layout View of the new report, expand the CaseTitle column to be about 50 percent wider than its current size.
d. Switch the report to landscape orientation.
e. Move the OpenedDate column, both the label and the text box, to be the third column in the report.

FIGURE 4-14

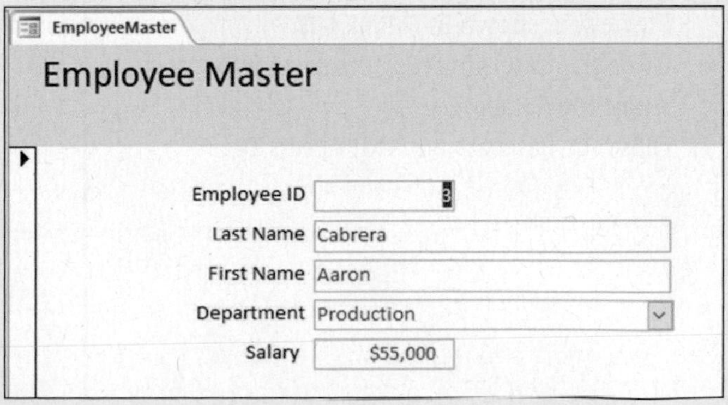

Skills Review (continued)

- **f.** Modify the font color of the Cases label in the Report Header section to Dark Blue (second to the last button in the last row of the Standard Colors palette) and the font size to **24**.
- **g.** Delete the date and time controls in the Report Header section.
- **h.** Modify the font color of the labels that identify every column heading to also be Dark Blue.
- **i.** Save the report with the name **CaseInfo**.

5. Work in Report Design View.

- **a.** Switch the CaseInfo report to Report Design View.
- **b.** Narrow the report to the 10" mark on the horizontal ruler.
- **c.** Remove the control layout from the controls in the Page Header, Detail, Page Footer, and Report Footer sections. (*Hint*: Click the Control Selection button in the upper-left corner of the section to select the control layout.)
- **d.** Resize the =Count(*) text box in the Report Footer to be tall enough so that the entire expression is shown. (*Hint*: This expression was created by the Report tool when the report was initially created. It calculates the total number of records in the report.)
- **e.** Move and align the =Count(*) text box in the Report Footer section so that its top edge is touching the Report Footer section bar and its left edge is aligned with the left edge of the text box in the Page Footer section that contains the page number expression.
- **f.** Delete any extra space in the Report Footer section by dragging the bottom of the report up as far as possible.
- **g.** Select all the labels in the Page Header section and group them together so that they will move as a group should you want to reposition them later.
- **h.** Save the CaseInfo report.

6. Add conditional formatting.

- **a.** With the CaseInfo report still in Report Design View, add a conditional formatting rule to the Category text box. If the field value is equal to **"MS Office"** change the font color to Red (second column, last row of Standard Colors palette).
- **b.** Add a second conditional formatting rule to the Category text box. If the field value is equal to **"Internet"** change the font color to Green (sixth column, last row of Standard Colors palette).
- **c.** Save the CaseInfo report, switch to Print Preview to make sure the conditional formats are applied correctly, then return to Report Design View.

7. Use the Format Painter and themes.

- **a.** In Report Design View, use the Format Painter to copy the format from the page expression text box in the Page Footer section to the =Count(*) control in the Report Footer section.
- **b.** Apply the Franklin Gothic theme font to the CaseInfo report object only.
- **c.** Apply the Blue Warm theme color to the CaseInfo report object only.
- **d.** Save the CaseInfo report and switch to Print Preview, as shown in **FIGURE 4-15**.
- **e.** Close the CaseInfo report, then compact and repair the database.
- **f.** Close the database and exit Access 2019.

FIGURE 4-15

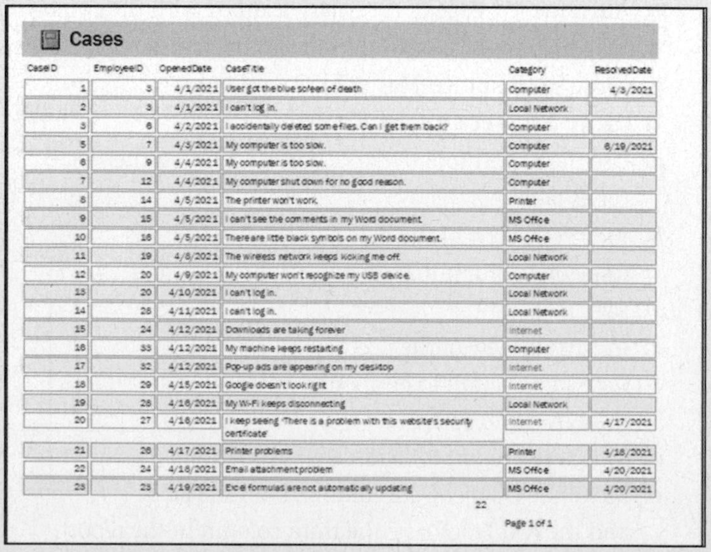

Cases

CaseID	EmployeeID	OpenedDate	CaseTitle	Category	ResolvedDate
1	3	4/1/2021	User got the blue screen of death	Computer	4/3/2021
2	3	4/1/2021	I can't log in.	Local Network	
3	6	4/2/2021	I accidentally deleted some files. Can I get them back?	Computer	
5	7	4/3/2021	My computer is too slow.	Computer	6/19/2021
6	9	4/4/2021	My computer is too slow.	Computer	
7	12	4/4/2021	My computer shut down for no good reason.	Computer	
8	14	4/5/2021	The printer won't work.	Printer	
9	15	4/5/2021	I can't see the comments in my Word document.	MS Office	
10	16	4/5/2021	There are little black symbols on my Word document.	MS Office	
11	19	4/8/2021	The wireless network keeps kicking me off.	Local Network	
12	20	4/9/2021	My computer won't recognize my USB device.	Computer	
13	20	4/10/2021	I can't log in.	Local Network	
14	28	4/11/2021	I can't log in.	Local Network	
15	24	4/12/2021	Downloads are taking forever	Internet	
16	33	4/12/2021	My machine keeps restarting	Computer	
17	32	4/12/2021	Pop-up ads are appearing on my desktop	Internet	
18	29	4/15/2021	Google doesn't look right	Internet	
19	28	4/16/2021	My Wi-Fi keeps disconnecting	Local Network	
20	27	4/16/2021	I keep seeing 'There is a problem with this website's security certificate'	Internet	4/17/2021
21	28	4/17/2021	Printer problems	Printer	4/18/2021
22	24	4/18/2021	Email attachment problem	MS Office	4/20/2021
23	23	4/19/2021	Excel formulas are not automatically updating	MS Office	4/20/2021

22

Page 1 of 1

Independent Challenge 1

As the manager of Riverwalk, a multispecialty health clinic, you have created a database to manage the schedules that connect each healthcare provider with the nurses that provider needs to efficiently handle patient visits. In this exercise, you will modify a form to help users find, enter, and edit data.

a. Start Access. Open the IL_AC_4-3.accdb database from the location where you store your Data Files and save it as **IL_AC_4_Riverwalk**. Click Enable Content if a yellow Security Warning message appears.

b. Open the ScheduleDate form in Form Design View.

c. Change the font face for all controls in the Detail section, including those in the subform, to Calibri (Detail) and a **10**-point font size. (*Hint*: This form contains a subform, the ScheduleItemsSubform. You can change the font face and font size for the controls directly in Form Design View of the ScheduleDate form, or you can close the ScheduleDate form and apply the formats to the ScheduleItemsSubform in Form Design View.)

d. Modify the Work Schedule label in the Form Header section to read **Doctor and Nurse Schedule**. Change the font size to be **16** and resize the label as needed to display it clearly.

e. There are four command buttons in the Detail section with the following Captions: Day, Nurse, by Location, and by Nurse. Format the Day command button with the Rectangle: Rounded Corners shape, and the Colored Fill – Olive Green, Accent 3 quick style.

f. Use the Format Painter to copy the formatting from the Day command button to the Nurse, by Location, and by Nurse command buttons.

g. Save the ScheduleDate form and switch to Form View.

h. Click the Nurse command button, then click the New (blank) record button to position your insertion point at a new record at the end of the form. Enter your name as a new record.

i. Close the Nurse Entry form, then reopen the ScheduleDate form.

j. Move to the first record in the ScheduleDate form, then add a new record in the subform for LocationNo **East**, DoctorNo **Samuelson**, and your name in the NurseNo field, as shown in **FIGURE 4-16**.

k. Save and close the ScheduleDate form, and compact and repair the database.

l. Close the database, then exit Access 2019.

FIGURE 4-16

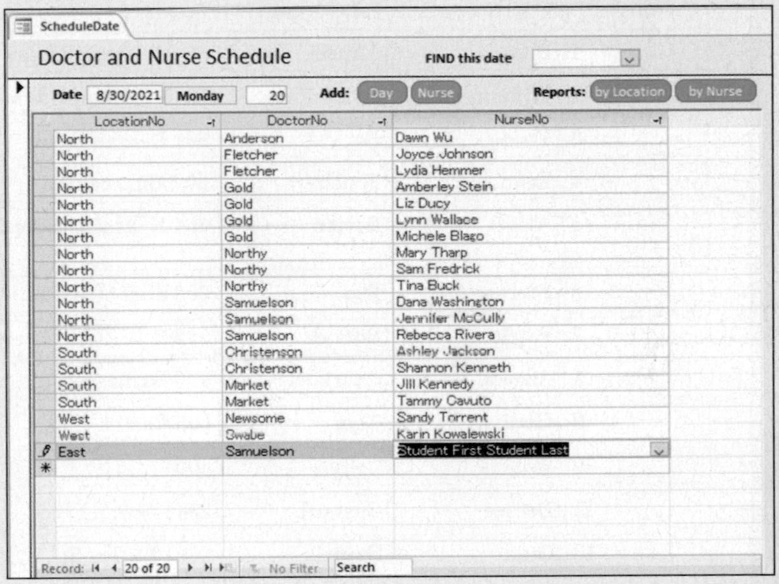

Independent Challenge 2

You are working for a city to coordinate a series of community-wide preparedness activities. You have created a database to track the activities and volunteers who are attending the activities. In this exercise, you will create and modify a report to analyze data.

a. Start Access, open the IL_AC_4-4.accdb database from the location where you store your Data Files, save it as **IL_AC_4_Volunteers**, then enable content if prompted.

b. Use the Report tool to create a new report on the Volunteers table.

c. In Report Layout View, resize the FirstName and LastName columns to be about half as wide.

d. In Report Layout View, resize the Street column to be slightly narrower so that the entire report fits within the dashed line that indicates the right side of the paper in portrait orientation.

Independent Challenge 2 (continued)

- **e.** Switch to Report Design View and remove the control layout from the controls in the Report Header section.
- **f.** Select and then delete the report image to the left of the Volunteers label in the Report Header section. Select and then delete the =Time() text box in the Report Header section.
- **g.** Group the remaining two controls in the Report Header section, then move them to the left edge of the report.
- **h.** Delete the =Count(*) text box in the Report Footer section.
- **i.** Move the text box that contains the page number expression to the left edge of the report.
- **j.** Drag the right edge of the report as far to the left as possible to narrow the report.
- **k.** Apply the Century Schoolbook theme font to this report only.
- **l.** Save the report with the name **VolunteerList**, then display it in Print Preview, as shown in **FIGURE 4-17**.
- **m.** Save and close the VolunteerList report, then compact and repair the database.
- **n.** Close the database and exit Access 2019.

FIGURE 4-17

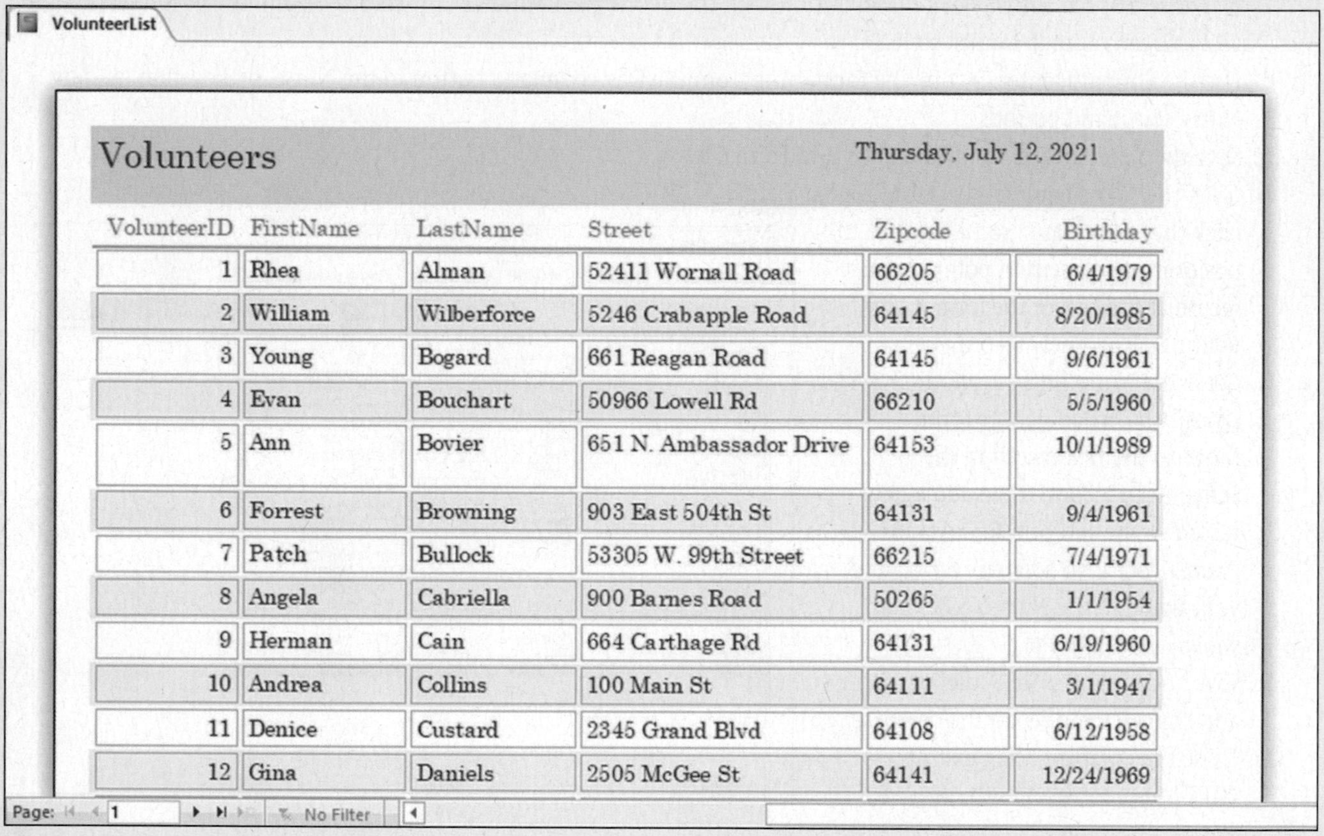

Volunteers — Thursday, July 12, 2021

VolunteerID	FirstName	LastName	Street	Zipcode	Birthday
1	Rhea	Alman	52411 Wornall Road	66205	6/4/1979
2	William	Wilberforce	5246 Crabapple Road	64145	8/20/1985
3	Young	Bogard	661 Reagan Road	64145	9/6/1961
4	Evan	Bouchart	50966 Lowell Rd	66210	5/5/1960
5	Ann	Bovier	651 N. Ambassador Drive	64153	10/1/1989
6	Forrest	Browning	903 East 504th St	64131	9/4/1961
7	Patch	Bullock	53305 W. 99th Street	66215	7/4/1971
8	Angela	Cabriella	900 Barnes Road	50265	1/1/1954
9	Herman	Cain	664 Carthage Rd	64131	6/19/1960
10	Andrea	Collins	100 Main St	64111	3/1/1947
11	Denice	Custard	2345 Grand Blvd	64108	6/12/1958
12	Gina	Daniels	2505 McGee St	64141	12/24/1969

Visual Workshop

Start Access, open the IL_AC_4-5.accdb database from the location where you store your Data Files, save it as **IL_AC_4_CollegeCourses**, then enable content if prompted.

In Query Design View, create a query with the following fields from the following tables:

- Description from the Classes table
- ClassNo from the Sections table
- Grade from the Enrollments table
- StudentFirst and StudentLast from the Students table

Save the query with the name **StudentGrades**, display it in Datasheet View, change any occurrence of Carl Willis to *your name*, then close the StudentGrades query.

Use the Report tool to create a report on this query.

Use Report Layout View to narrow the ClassNo, Grade, StudentFirst, and StudentLast columns. Move the Grade column to be the last. Modify the report title to be **Student Grade Listing**.

Use Report Design View to delete all the controls in the Page Footer and Report Footer sections. Delete the text boxes in the Report Header section that calculate the current date and the current time. Also use Report Design View to narrow the width of the report to 8" or less. Save the report with the name **StudentGradeListing** and preview it in Print Preview, as shown in **FIGURE 4-18**. Compact and repair the database, then close the database and exit Access 2019.

FIGURE 4-18

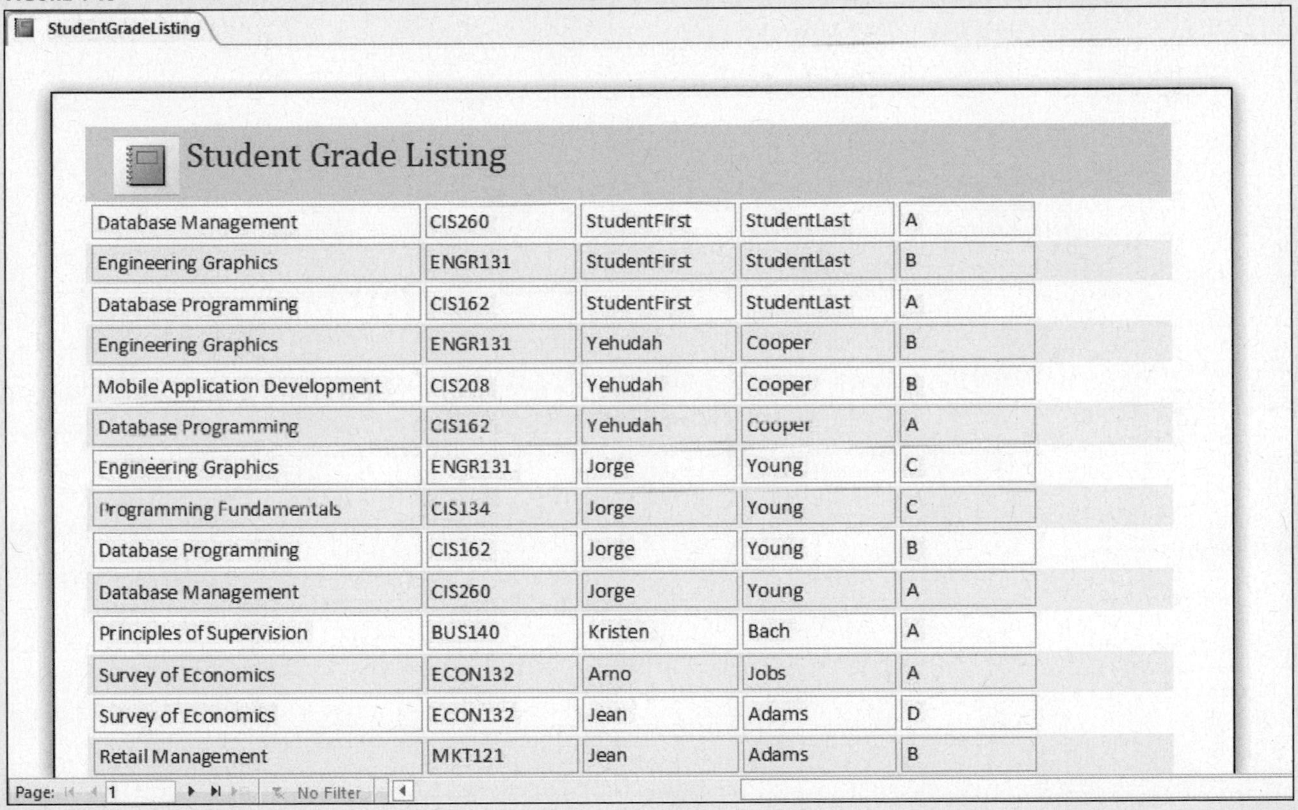
StudentGradeListing

Student Grade Listing

Database Management	CIS260	StudentFirst	StudentLast	A
Engineering Graphics	ENGR131	StudentFirst	StudentLast	B
Database Programming	CIS162	StudentFirst	StudentLast	A
Engineering Graphics	ENGR131	Yehudah	Cooper	B
Mobile Application Development	CIS208	Yehudah	Cooper	B
Database Programming	CIS162	Yehudah	Cooper	A
Engineering Graphics	ENGR131	Jorge	Young	C
Programming Fundamentals	CIS134	Jorge	Young	C
Database Programming	CIS162	Jorge	Young	B
Database Management	CIS260	Jorge	Young	A
Principles of Supervision	BUS140	Kristen	Bach	A
Survey of Economics	ECON132	Arno	Jobs	A
Survey of Economics	ECON132	Jean	Adams	D
Retail Management	MKT121	Jean	Adams	B

Page: 1 No Filter

Integrating Word, Excel, and Access

CASE Anthony Martinez, vice president of Sales and Marketing at the head office of JCL Talent, Inc., in Atlanta, GA, asks you to use Word, Excel, and Access in Office to organize and process data related to the company's top corporate clients.

Module Objectives

After completing this module, you will be able to:

- Integrate data among Word, Excel, and Access
- Import an Excel worksheet into Access
- Copy a Word table to Access
- Link an Access table to Excel and Word
- Copy an Access table to Word

Files You Will Need

IL_INT_2-1.xlsx
Support_INT_2_SalesInformation.docx
IL_INT_2-2.docx
IL_INT_2-3.xlsx
Support_INT_2_EventPlanning.docx
IL_INT_2-4.docx
Support_INT_2_AppsPriceList.docx
IL_INT_2-5.xlsx
Support_INT_2_TimeWiseConsultants.docx
Support_INT_2_ProjectManagerTravel.docx

Integrate Data Among Word, Excel, and Access

Learning Outcome
- Identify integration options for Word, Excel, and Access

You can increase efficiency by integrating the information you create in Word, Excel, and Access so it works together. For example, you can enter data into an Access database, make calculations using that data in Excel, and then create a report in Word that incorporates the Excel data and the Access table. You can also import data from an Excel spreadsheet into Access and copy a table created in Word into an Access table. **CASE** *Anthony Martinez asks you to create a report in Word to describe the company's top corporate clients. The information you need for this report is contained in Excel, Access, and Word files. Before you create the report, you decide to review some of the ways in which information can be shared among Word, Excel, and Access.*

DETAILS

You can integrate Word, Excel, and Access by:

- **Importing an Excel worksheet into Access**
  You can enter data directly into an Access database table, or you can import data from other sources such as an Excel workbook, another Access database, or even a text file. You use the Get External Data command in Access to import data from an outside source. **FIGURE 2-1** shows how data entered in an Excel file appears when imported into a new table in an Access database. During the import process, you can change the field names and the data types of selected fields.

- **Copying a Word table into Access**
  You can also create a table in Word that contains data you want to include in an Access database. To save time, you can copy the table from Word and paste it into a new or existing Access table. By doing so, you save typing time and minimize errors.

- **Linking an Access table to Excel and Word**
  You link an Access table to Excel and then to Word when you want the data in all three applications to always remain current. First, you use the Copy and Paste Special commands to copy an Access table and paste it into Excel as a link. You can then make calculations using Excel tools that are not available in Access. Any changes you make to the data in Access are also reflected in the linked Excel copy. However, you cannot change the structure of the linked Access table in Excel. For example, you cannot delete any of the columns or rows that contain copied data. The data used in the Excel calculations is linked to the source file in Access. When the data in Access is changed, the results of the formulas in Excel also change.

  Once you have made calculations based on the data in Excel, you can then copy the data from Excel and paste it as a link into Word. When you change the data in Access, the data in both the Excel and the Word files also changes. **FIGURE 2-2** shows a Word document that contains two tables. The top table is linked to both Excel and Access. The table was copied from Access and pasted as a link into Excel, additional calculations were made in Excel, and then the table was copied to the Word report and pasted as a link.

- **Copying an Access table to Word**
  You can use the Copy and Paste Special commands to copy a table from Access and then paste it into a Word document. You can then format the table attractively. In **FIGURE 2-2**, the bottom table was copied from Access, pasted into Word, and then reformatted.

FIGURE 2-1: Excel data imported to an Access table

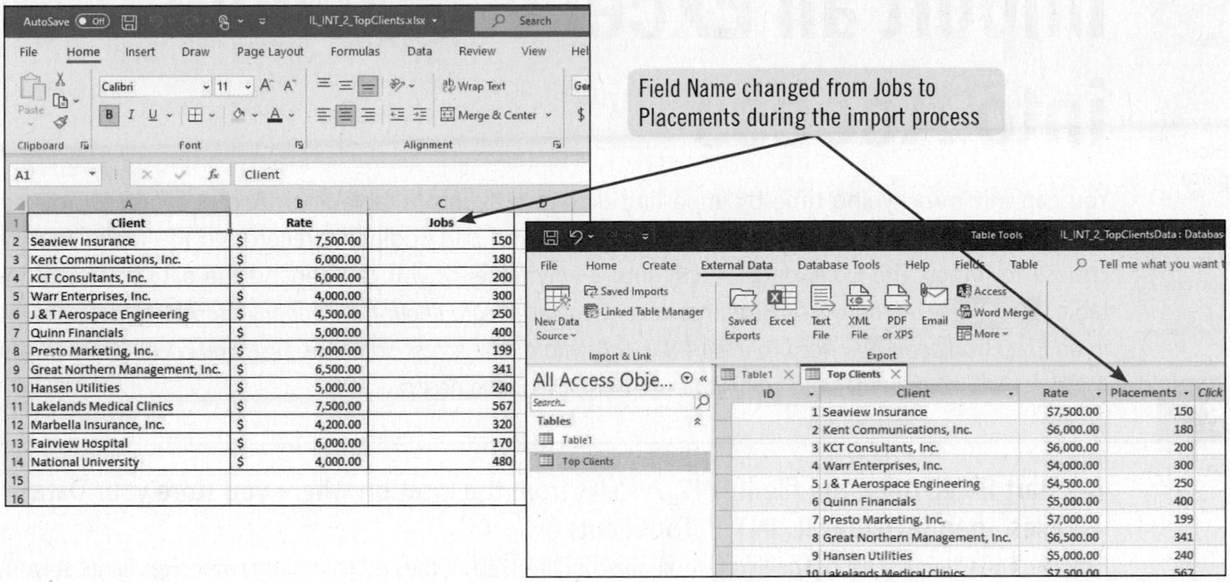

FIGURE 2-2: Word report with links to Excel and Access

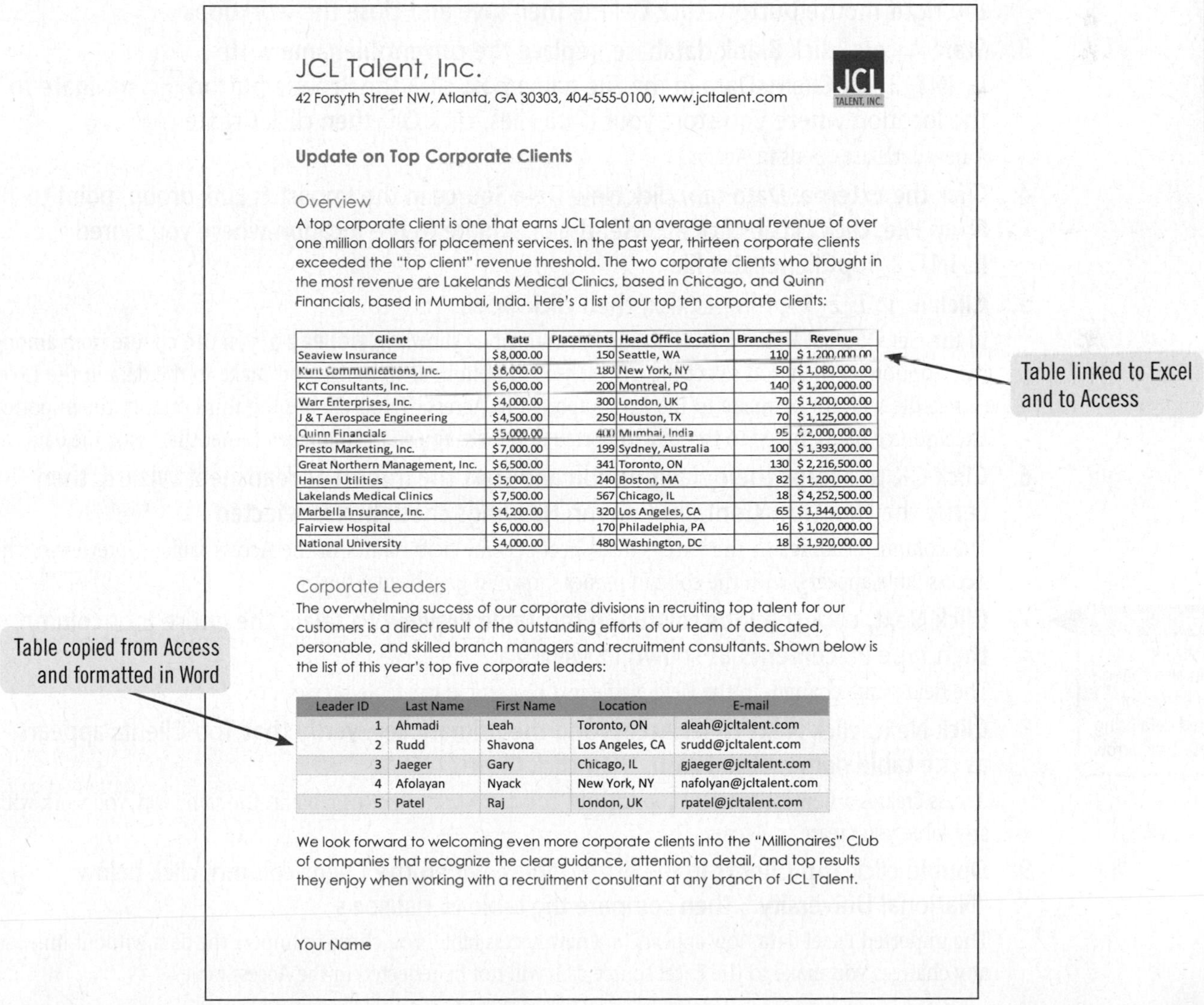

JCL Talent, Inc.

42 Forsyth Street NW, Atlanta, GA 30303, 404-555-0100, www.jcltalent.com

JCL TALENT, INC.

Update on Top Corporate Clients

Overview

A top corporate client is one that earns JCL Talent an average annual revenue of over one million dollars for placement services. In the past year, thirteen corporate clients exceeded the "top client" revenue threshold. The two corporate clients who brought in the most revenue are Lakelands Medical Clinics, based in Chicago, and Quinn Financials, based in Mumbai, India. Here's a list of our top ten corporate clients:

Client	Rate	Placements	Head Office Location	Branches	Revenue
Seaview Insurance	$8,000.00	150	Seattle, WA	110	$ 1,200,000.00
Kent Communications, Inc.	$6,000.00	180	New York, NY	50	$ 1,080,000.00
KCT Consultants, Inc.	$6,000.00	200	Montreal, PQ	140	$ 1,200,000.00
Warr Enterprises, Inc.	$4,000.00	300	London, UK	70	$ 1,200,000.00
J & T Aerospace Engineering	$4,500.00	250	Houston, TX	70	$ 1,125,000.00
Quinn Financials	$5,000.00	400	Mumbai, India	95	$ 2,000,000.00
Presto Marketing, Inc.	$7,000.00	199	Sydney, Australia	100	$ 1,393,000.00
Great Northern Management, Inc.	$6,500.00	341	Toronto, ON	130	$ 2,216,500.00
Hansen Utilities	$5,000.00	240	Boston, MA	82	$ 1,200,000.00
Lakelands Medical Clinics	$7,500.00	567	Chicago, IL	18	$ 4,252,500.00
Marbella Insurance, Inc.	$4,200.00	320	Los Angeles, CA	65	$ 1,344,000.00
Fairview Hospital	$6,000.00	170	Philadelphia, PA	16	$ 1,020,000.00
National University	$4,000.00	480	Washington, DC	18	$ 1,920,000.00

Corporate Leaders

The overwhelming success of our corporate divisions in recruiting top talent for our customers is a direct result of the outstanding efforts of our team of dedicated, personable, and skilled branch managers and recruitment consultants. Shown below is the list of this year's top five corporate leaders:

Leader ID	Last Name	First Name	Location	E-mail
1	Ahmadi	Leah	Toronto, ON	aleah@jcltalent.com
2	Rudd	Shavona	Los Angeles, CA	srudd@jcltalent.com
3	Jaeger	Gary	Chicago, IL	gjaeger@jcltalent.com
4	Afolayan	Nyack	New York, NY	nafolyan@jcltalent.com
5	Patel	Raj	London, UK	rpatel@jcltalent.com

We look forward to welcoming even more corporate clients into the "Millionaires" Club of companies that recognize the clear guidance, attention to detail, and top results they enjoy when working with a recruitment consultant at any branch of JCL Talent.

Your Name

Import an Excel Worksheet into Access

Learning Outcomes
- Prepare an Excel table for export to Access
- Import an Excel table to Access
- Rename imported field names

You can minimize typing time by importing data directly into a table in an Access database. You can then delete field names and data you do not need and add additional records to the table. You can choose to import the Excel data directly into a new table, or you can append the data to an existing table. **CASE** *Anthony's assistant has already compiled data about the company's top 10 corporate clients in an Excel workbook. You need to import this data into a new Access database. First, you open the report that will eventually contain the data compiled from Word, Excel, and Access.*

STEPS

1. **Start Excel, open the file IL_INT_2-1.xlsx from the location where you store your Data Files, then save it as IL_INT_2_TopClients**
   The Top Clients sheet of the Excel workbook contains a list of the company's top corporate clients. A workbook that you plan to export from Excel into Access must contain only the data that you want to appear in the Access table; you need to remove titles, subtitles, charts, and any other extraneous data.
2. **Move the mouse pointer to the left of row 1, click and drag to select rows 1 and 2, click the right mouse button, click Delete, then save and close the workbook**
3. **Start Access, click Blank database, replace the current filename with IL_INT_2_TopClientsData in the File name box, click the Browse button, navigate to the location where you store your Data Files, click OK, then click Create**
   A new database opens in Access.
4. **Click the External Data tab, click New Data Source in the Import & Link group, point to From File, click Excel, click Browse, then navigate to the location where you stored the IL_INT_2_TopClients.xlsx file**
5. **Click IL_INT_2_TopClients.xlsx, then click Open**
   In the Get External Data - Excel Spreadsheet dialog box shown in **FIGURE 2-3**, you can choose from among three options. When you select the first or second option, any change you make to the data in the Excel source file will not be made to the data imported to Access. If you choose the third option, the imported Excel source file is linked to the data imported to Access. You want to import, rather than link, the data.
6. **Click OK to accept the default option and start the Import Spreadsheet Wizard, then verify the First Row Contains Column Headings check box is selected**
   The column headings in the Excel spreadsheet become field names in the Access table. A preview of the Access table appears, with the column names shown in gray header boxes.
7. **Click Next, click the Jobs column in the Table Preview to select the entire Jobs column, then type Placements as shown in FIGURE 2-4**
   The field name changes in the Field Name text box and in the table preview.
8. **Click Next, click Next to let Access add the primary key, verify that Top Clients appears as the table name, click Finish, then click Close**
   Access creates a new table called Top Clients. You can work with this table in the same way you work with any table you create in Access.
9. **Double-click Top Clients in the list of tables, widen the Client column, click below "National University", then compare the table to FIGURE 2-5**
   The imported Excel data now appears in a new Access table. You chose to import the data without links, so any changes you make to the Excel source data will not be reflected in the Access table.

QUICK TIP
In this dialog box, you can also change the data types of imported data using the Data Type arrow.

FIGURE 2-3: Selecting a data source in the Get External Data dialog box

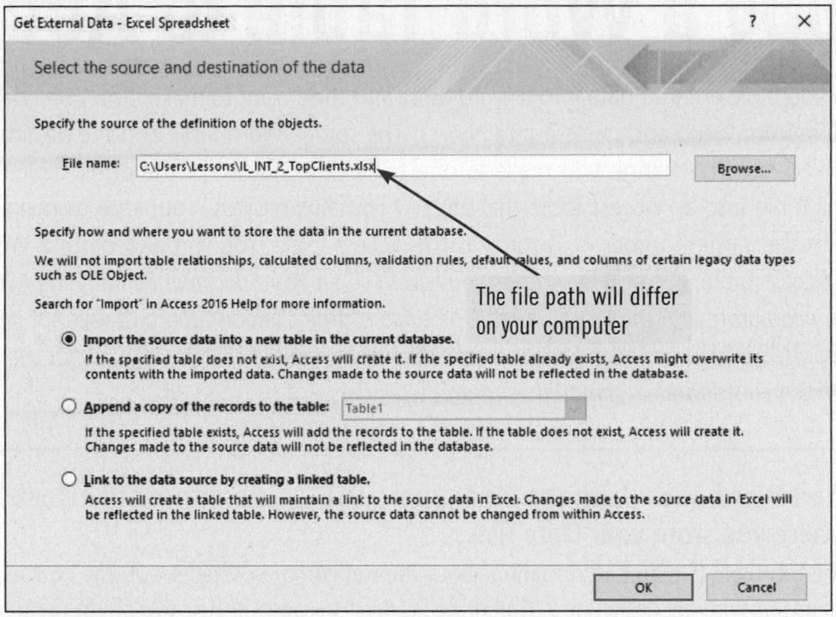

FIGURE 2-4: Changing a field name in an imported table

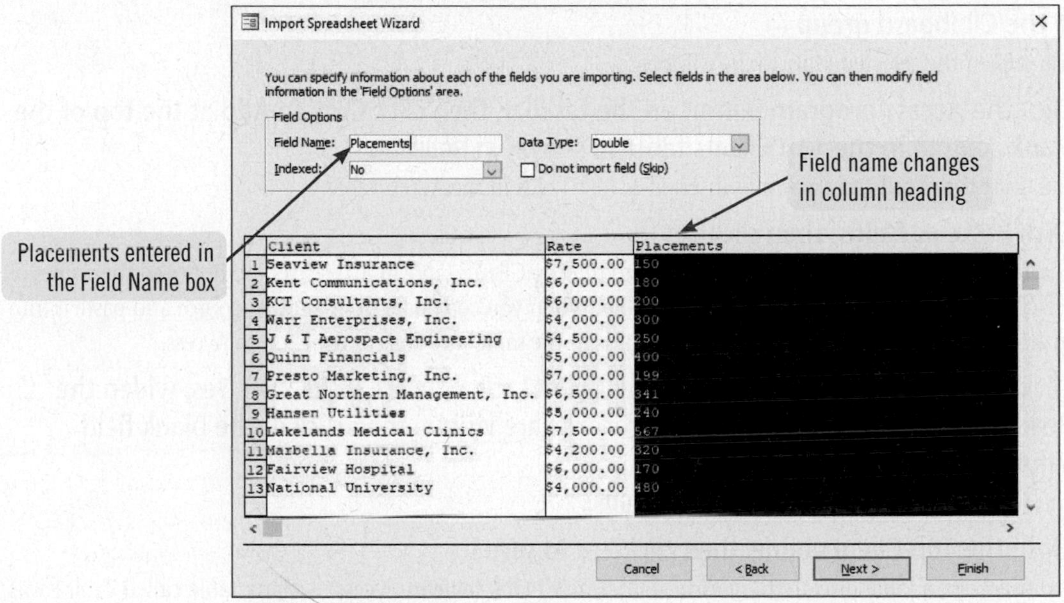

FIGURE 2-5: Excel data imported to an Access table

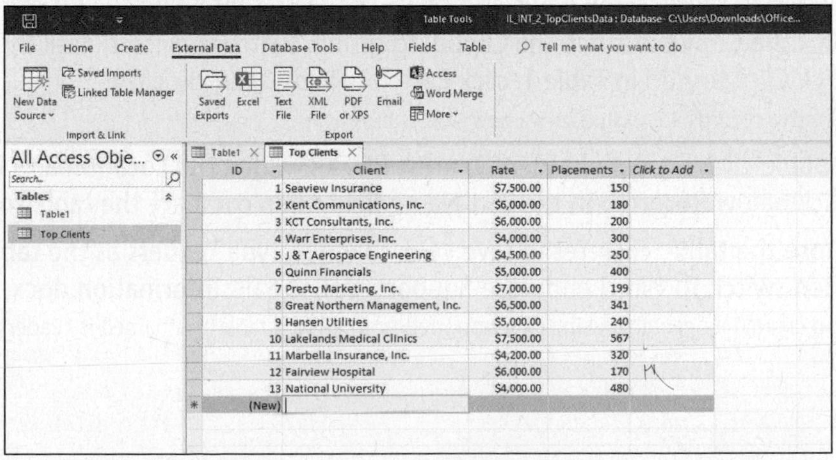

Integration

Copy a Word Table to Access

Learning Outcomes
- Copy a Word table to an existing Access table
- Copy a Word table to a new Access table

When you have entered data into a Word table and then want to make it part of a database, you can copy the table from Word and paste it into Access. The source Word table and the destination Access table are not linked, so any change you make to one table does not affect the other table. If you want to paste a Word table into an Access table that already contains records, you need to make sure the Word table contains the same number of records as the Access table. You can also paste a Word table into a new, blank Access table. **CASE** *Anthony has given you a Word document containing two tables that he wants you to incorporate into the Word report. One table contains information that was not included in the client list you imported into Access from Excel, and the other table contains information about the branch managers and recruitment consultants designated as corporate leaders.*

STEPS

1. **Start Word, then open the file Support_INT_2_SalesInformation.docx from the location where you store your Data Files**
   The top table contains information about the top corporate clients, and the bottom table lists the branch managers who are designated "Corporate Leaders" because of their work with the top clients.
2. **Click Client in the top table, click the table select button ⊞, then click the Copy button in the Clipboard group**
   You copied the selected table to the Clipboard.
3. **Click the Access program button on the taskbar, then click Click to Add at the top of the blank column in the Top Clients table as shown in FIGURE 2-6**
   You want the Word table columns inserted as new fields in the Access table.
4. **Click Paste as Fields, then click Yes**
   Additional data for the 13 records is pasted into the Top Clients table in Access. You do not need the names of the clients to appear twice in the database table. When you copy data from another source and paste it into an Access table, you can delete fields and records in the same way you normally do in Access.
5. **Click anywhere in the table, right-click Client1, click Delete Field, click Yes, widen the Head Office Location field so all the records are visible, then click in the blank field below National University**
   The Top Clients table appears as shown in **FIGURE 2-7**.
6. **Close the Top Clients table, then click Yes to save it**
   You can copy a table directly from Word into a new blank table in Access. A blank table called Table1 was automatically created when you created the database, so you can place the copied information there.
7. **Switch to Word, scroll down and select the table containing the list of corporate leaders, click the Copy button in the Clipboard group, switch to Access, click the Home tab, click Click to Add in Table 1, click Paste as Fields, then click Yes**
   The five records are pasted into a new Access table.
8. **Double-click ID, type Leader ID, press ENTER, widen the Location and E-mail columns, click below Record 5 in the Last Name field, then compare the table to FIGURE 2-8**
9. **Close the table, click Yes to save your changes, type Leaders as the table name, click OK, then switch to Word and close Support_INT_2_SalesInformation.docx**
   You created a new table using data imported from a Word table and named it Leaders.

QUICK TIP
If you want to import additional records to an existing database, make sure the imported Excel data contains the same number of fields (columns) as the database.

FIGURE 2-6: Selecting the location for copied data

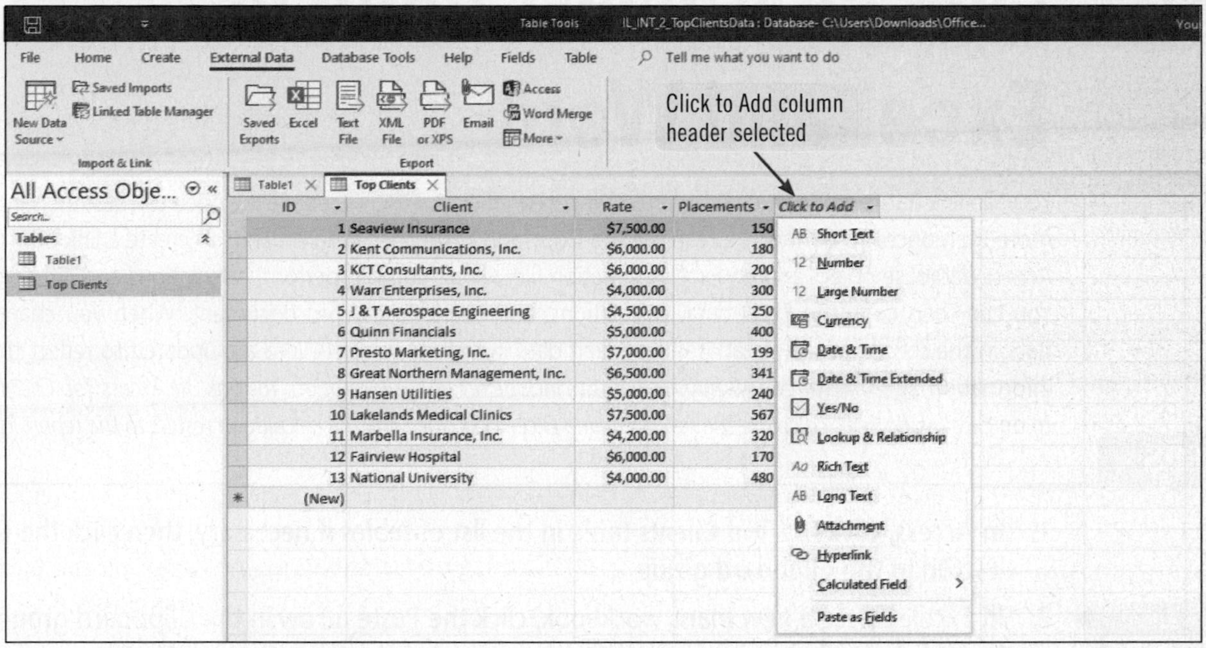

FIGURE 2-7: Table containing data copied from Word

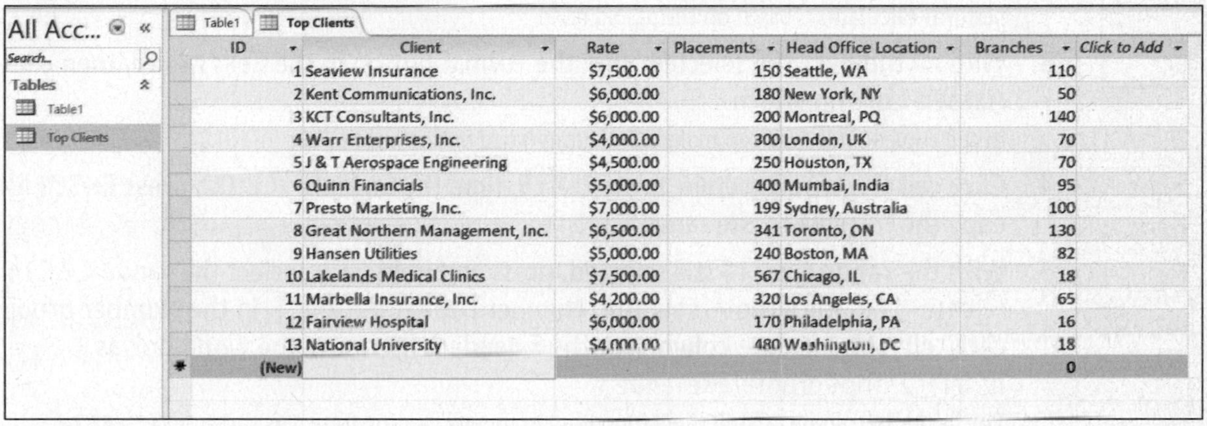

FIGURE 2-8: Renaming the ID field

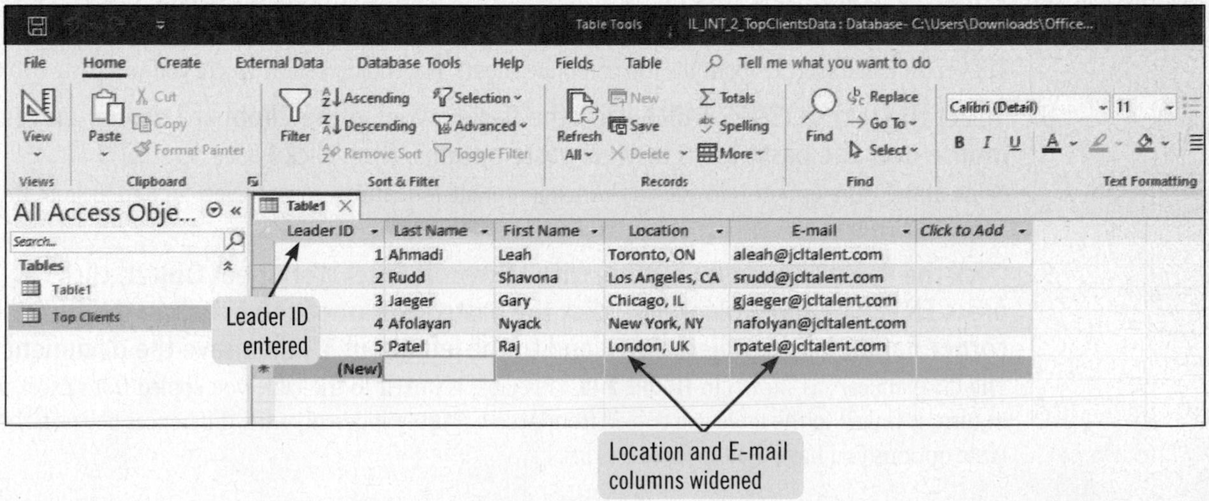

Integration

Link an Access Table to Excel and Word

Learning Outcomes
- Use Copy and Paste Special to create links
- Update linked data

You can link data among three programs to increase efficiency and to reduce the need to enter the same data more than once. To do this, you can use the Copy and Paste Special commands to create a link between an Access database object and an Excel destination file, where you can perform calculations and create charts. You can then copy the Excel data, calculations, and charts to a Word document. When you change the data in the source Access database, the linked data in both Excel and Word are updated to reflect the new information. **CASE** *You want your report to include revenue information. You link the Access Top Clients table to an Excel worksheet, calculate the revenue using Excel tools, then link the calculation results to the report in Word.*

STEPS

1. **In Access, click the Top Clients table in the list of tables if necessary, then click the Copy button in the Clipboard group**

2. **In Excel, create a new blank workbook, click the Paste arrow in the Clipboard group, then click the Paste Link button (the second of the three Paste options)**
   The Top Clients table appears in Excel. You cannot delete any of the rows or columns in the pasted data in Excel because it is linked to the Access source table. However, you can modify cell formatting, and you can perform calculations based on the pasted data.

> **QUICK TIP**
> Click cell A1 if necessary to select it before pasting. If you do not see the Paste Link button, return to Access and copy the table again.

3. **With all the data still selected, click the Format button in the Cells group, then click AutoFit Column Width**
   In the copied table, you can make calculations based on the linked data.

4. **Click cell G1, type Revenue, press ENTER, type the formula =C2*D2, press ENTER, then copy the formula to the range G3:G14**

5. **With the range G2:G14 still selected, press and hold CTRL, select the range C2:C14, release CTRL, click the Accounting Number Format button $ in the Number group, click cell A15, increase column widths if needed, then save the workbook as IL_INT_2_TopCorporateRevenue**
   The values in columns C and G are formatted in the Accounting format as shown in **FIGURE 2-9**.

6. **Select the range B1:G14, then click the Copy button in the Clipboard group**

7. **Switch to Word, open the file IL_INT_2-2.docx from the location where you store your Data Files, then save it as IL_INT_2_TopCorporateClientsReport**
   The report contains text about the top corporate clients. Placeholders show where you will paste two tables.

8. **Select the text CLIENTS TABLE, click the Paste arrow in the Clipboard group, move the mouse over the paste icons to view paste options, then click Paste Special**
   None of the Paste options provide you with appropriate formatting, so you select an option from the Paste Special dialog box.

9. **Click the Paste link option button, click Microsoft Excel Worksheet Object, click OK, press ENTER to add a blank line, click the pasted worksheet object, drag the top-right corner handle of the object down and to the left about 1", then save the document**
   The table appears as shown in **FIGURE 2-10**. This table is linked to the table you copied from Excel, which, in turn, is linked to the table you copied from Access. **TABLE 2-1** describes the differences between the three Paste options you have used in these lessons.

FIGURE 2-9: Copied data formatted in Excel

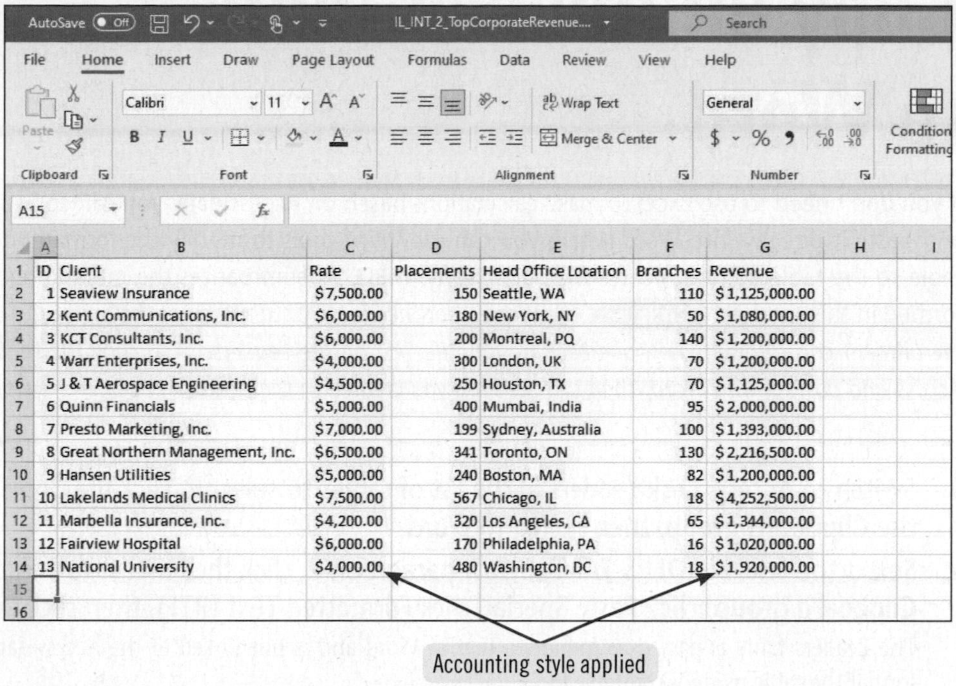

FIGURE 2-10: Excel data pasted and linked in Word

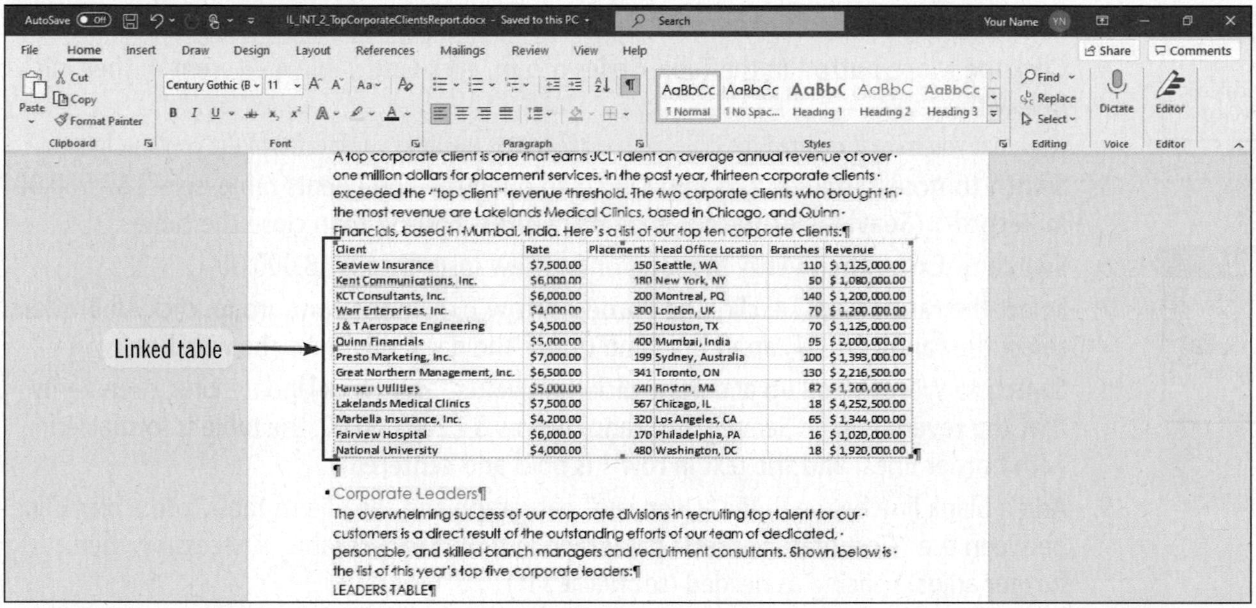

TABLE 2-1: Paste options

command	location	use to
Paste	Paste button in Word and Excel	Paste an object without creating a link; the exception is a chart—when you copy a chart from Excel and paste it into Word, the chart is, by default, linked to the source file in Excel
Paste Special	Paste button list shows Paste Special selection in Word and Excel	Paste an object when you want to create a link or you want to select from a variety of formatting options for the pasted object, whether linked or not
Paste Link	Paste button list shows Paste Link button in Excel	Paste an object such as a copied table from Access into Excel as a link

Integration
Module 2

Learning Outcome
• Copy an Access table to Word

Copy an Access Table to Word

If you don't need to use Excel to make calculations based on Access data, you can copy an Access table and paste it directly into Word where you can use Word tools to modify the formatting of the pasted table so the table communicates the data clearly. **TABLE 2-2** summarizes the integration tasks you performed in this module. **CASE** *The Word report needs to contain a list of the top branch managers and recruitment consultants who have been designated "Corporate Leaders." You copy the Leaders table from Access and paste it into Word, then test the links you created in the previous lesson.*

STEPS

1. **Switch to Access, click Leaders in the list of tables to select it, click the Copy button in the Clipboard group, then switch to Word**
2. **Select the text LEADERS TABLE below paragraph 2, click the Paste arrow in the Clipboard group, click Paste Special, click Formatted Text (RTF), then click OK**
   The Leaders table is pasted as formatted text in Word and is not linked to the Access database. You can format the table using Word table tools.
3. **Click the pasted table, click the table select button ⊞ to select the table, click the Table Design tab, click the Header Row check box in the Table Style Options group to select it, then click the Banded Columns check box to deselect it**
4. **Click the More button in the Table Styles group, click Grid Table 4 - Accent 4, then click below the table**
   Now that you have formatted the table, you decide to test the links you created in the previous lesson.
5. **Switch to Access, double-click Top Clients to open the Top Clients table, select $7,500.00 in Record 1 (Seaview Insurance), type 8000, press ENTER, then close the table**
6. **Switch to Excel, then verify the rate for Seaview Insurance is $8,000.00**
7. **Select the range A1:G14, click the Borders arrow ⊞ in the Font group, click All Borders, select the range A1:G1, apply bold and center the data, then save the workbook**
8. **Switch to Word, scroll up and right-click the Clients table, click Update Link, then verify that the revenue from Seaview Insurance is now $1,200,000.00, the table is formatted with border lines, and the text in row 1 is bold and centered**
9. **Add a blank line between the "Overview" paragraph and the Clients table, add a blank line between the "Corporate Leaders" paragraph and the Leaders table, if necessary, then further adjust spacing as needed (see FIGURE 2-11)**
10. **Type your name in the footer, save and close all files, then submit your files to your instructor**

QUICK TIP
You must always close the table in Access before you check if linked data has been updated in Excel and Word.

TROUBLE
You may need to wait about two minutes for the data to be updated in Excel.

Opening linked files and enabling content

When you open files created in different applications, you need to create them on the same computer logged in as the same user. Open them in the order in which they were created. For example, if you want to change the Word report and need to maintain links, open the Access database first, followed by the Excel workbook. When you open a linked Excel file, click Enable Content if prompted, click Update in response to the message, then, if prompted, click Yes. The exact order of these steps varies depending on how often you have opened the files. In Word, click Yes in response to the message. If all the files were created on the same computer by the same user, the links will all update.

When you email your files to another user, such as your instructor, the links will not work. However, the new user may view the files. After opening the workbook in Excel, they click No, close the workbook without saving it, then reopen the workbook and click Don't Update. In Word, they click No to update links.

FIGURE 2-11: Completed Word report

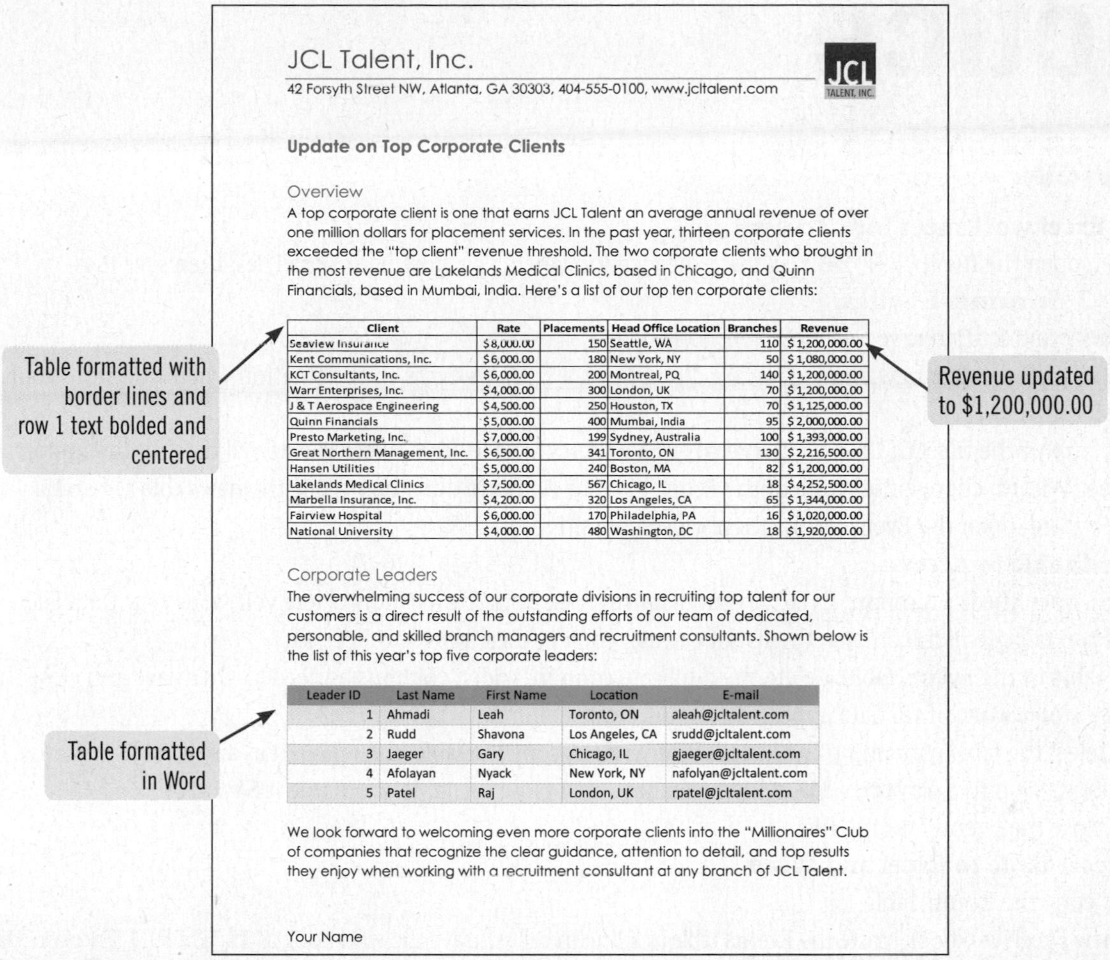

JCL Talent, Inc.

42 Forsyth Street NW, Atlanta, GA 30303, 404-555-0100, www.jcltalent.com

JCL TALENT, INC.

Update on Top Corporate Clients

Overview

A top corporate client is one that earns JCL Talent an average annual revenue of over one million dollars for placement services. In the past year, thirteen corporate clients exceeded the "top client" revenue threshold. The two corporate clients who brought in the most revenue are Lakelands Medical Clinics, based in Chicago, and Quinn Financials, based in Mumbai, India. Here's a list of our top ten corporate clients:

Client	**Rate**	**Placements**	**Head Office Location**	**Branches**	**Revenue**
Seaview Insurance	$8,000.00	150	Seattle, WA	110	$ 1,200,000.00
Kent Communications, Inc.	$6,000.00	180	New York, NY	50	$ 1,080,000.00
KCT Consultants, Inc.	$6,000.00	200	Montreal, PQ	140	$ 1,200,000.00
Warr Enterprises, Inc.	$4,000.00	300	London, UK	70	$ 1,200,000.00
J & T Aerospace Engineering	$4,500.00	250	Houston, TX	70	$ 1,125,000.00
Quinn Financials	$5,000.00	400	Mumbai, India	95	$ 2,000,000.00
Presto Marketing, Inc.	$7,000.00	199	Sydney, Australia	100	$ 1,393,000.00
Great Northern Management, Inc.	$6,500.00	341	Toronto, ON	130	$ 2,216,500.00
Hansen Utilities	$5,000.00	240	Boston, MA	82	$ 1,200,000.00
Lakelands Medical Clinics	$7,500.00	567	Chicago, IL	18	$ 4,252,500.00
Marbella Insurance, Inc.	$4,200.00	320	Los Angeles, CA	65	$ 1,344,000.00
Fairview Hospital	$6,000.00	170	Philadelphia, PA	16	$ 1,020,000.00
National University	$4,000.00	480	Washington, DC	18	$ 1,920,000.00

Corporate Leaders

The overwhelming success of our corporate divisions in recruiting top talent for our customers is a direct result of the outstanding efforts of our team of dedicated, personable, and skilled branch managers and recruitment consultants. Shown below is the list of this year's top five corporate leaders:

Leader ID	Last Name	First Name	Location	E-mail
1	Ahmadi	Leah	Toronto, ON	aleah@jcltalent.com
2	Rudd	Shavona	Los Angeles, CA	srudd@jcltalent.com
3	Jaeger	Gary	Chicago, IL	gjaeger@jcltalent.com
4	Afolayan	Nyack	New York, NY	nafolyan@jcltalent.com
5	Patel	Raj	London, UK	rpatel@jcltalent.com

We look forward to welcoming even more corporate clients into the "Millionaires" Club of companies that recognize the clear guidance, attention to detail, and top results they enjoy when working with a recruitment consultant at any branch of JCL Talent.

Your Name

TABLE 2-2: Module 2 integration tasks

object	commands	source program(s)	destination program	result	connection	page no.
Excel file	External Data/Excel	Excel	Access	Excel spreadsheet is imported into a new table in Access; the spreadsheet must contain only the rows and columns required for the Access table	None	4
Word table	Copy/Paste	Word	Access	Word table is pasted in a new or existing table in Access; if an existing table, the Word table should contain the same number of records as the Access table	None	6
Access table	Copy/Paste Special/ Paste Link	Access	Excel	Access table is pasted into Excel as a link; the linked data can be formatted in Excel and included in formulas but cannot be modified or deleted	Linked	8
Linked Access table in Excel	Copy/Paste Link in Excel Copy/Paste Special/ Paste Link in Word	Access and Excel	Word	Access table is linked to Excel and then to Word; changes made in Access appear in Excel and Word	Linked	8
Access table	Copy/Paste Special	Access	Word	Access table is pasted in Word and can be formatted using Word tools	None	10

Integration

Practice

Skills Review

1. **Import an Excel worksheet into Access.**
   a. Start Excel, open the file IL_INT_2-3.xlsx from the location where you store your Data Files, then save it as **IL_INT_2_SummerEvents**.
   b. Delete rows 1 and 2, then save and close the workbook.
   c. Start Access, then create a new blank database called **IL_INT_2_Events** in the location where you store your Data Files.
   d. In Access, import the file **IL_INT_2_SummerEvents.xlsx** file from Excel as external data. In the Import Spreadsheet Wizard, change the name of the People field to **Attendees**, then name the new table **Events**.
   e. Close the wizard, open the Events table, then widen columns as necessary.
2. **Copy a Word table to Access.**
   a. Start Word, open the file Support_INT_2_EventPlanning.docx from the location where you store your Data Files.
   b. Select the top table (which contains the list of events), copy it, then switch to Access.
   c. Paste the table in the Events table, delete the duplicate column, widen columns as needed, then save and close the table. *Note*: Don't worry if no data appears in the duplicate column.
   d. In Word, select the table containing the list of event services, copy the table, then paste it as a new table in Access.
   e. Change the ID field to **Services ID**, widen columns, then close the table and name it **Services**.
   f. In Word, close the EventPlanning file.
3. **Link an Access table to Excel and Word.**
   a. In Access, copy the Events table.
   b. Create a new Excel workbook, paste the Events table as a link in cell A1, save the workbook as **IL_INT_2_EventsData**, then adjust column widths where necessary.
   c. Enter **Total Revenue** in cell G1, adjust the column width, then in cell G2, enter a formula to multiply the Per Person Rate by the Attendees.
   d. Copy the formula to the range G3:G16, then format the values in columns C and G in the Accounting Number format.
   e. Copy the range B1:G16, switch to Word, open the file IL_INT_2-4.docx from the location where you store your Data Files, then save it as **IL_INT_2_SummerEventsOverview**.
   f. In the Word document, select the text EVENT LIST, paste the copied data as a linked Microsoft Excel Worksheet Object, add a blank line above or below the table if necessary, reduce the width of the table to match the line width, then save the document.
4. **Copy an Access table to Word.**
   a. In Access, copy the Services table, switch to Word, then select the SERVICES LIST placeholder.
   b. Paste the copied table as a Formatted Text (RTF) object, add a blank line above the table, then format the table with the Grid Table 2 - Accent 1 table design with the Header Row selected and the Banded Columns deselected. Adjust column widths so none of the lines wrap.
   c. In Access, open the Events table, change the number of attendees at the Hospital Gala (Record 3) to **700**, then close the table.
   d. In Excel, verify the total revenue value for the Hospital Gala is $560,000.00. You may need to wait a few minutes.
   e. Select the range A1:G16, add border lines to all cells, select the range A1:G1, then apply bold and centering.

Skills Review (continued)

f. In Word, update the link to the table that lists the events, then verify the Hospital Gala total changes to $560,000.00 and the header formats change to the new format.
g. Compare the completed report to **FIGURE 2-12**, make any necessary spacing adjustments, type your name where indicated in the footer, save and close all open files and programs, then submit your files to your instructor.

FIGURE 2-12

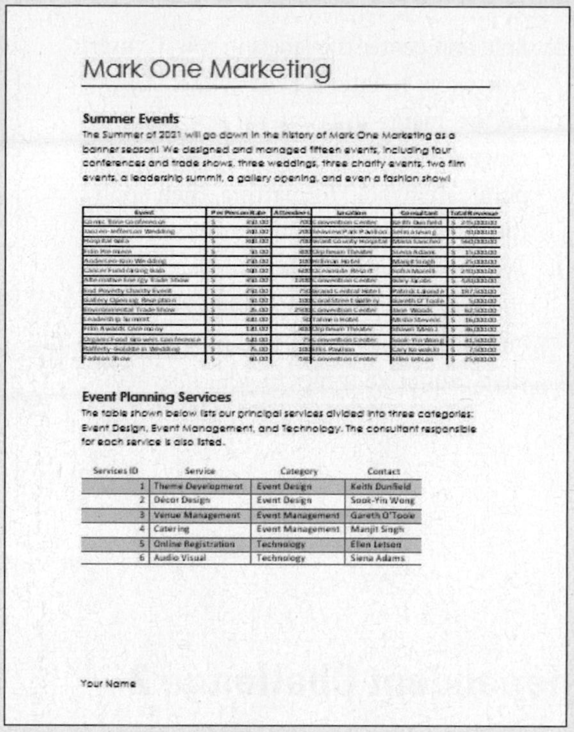

Independent Challenge 1

Riverwalk Medical Clinic in San Antonio, TX, has partnered with a local software developer to create apps that help patients monitor their health and well-being. The demand for the apps is growing rapidly, and you need to develop a system for keeping track of the apps sold. You have a price list saved in a Word document. You transfer the price list into an Access database, then add some new records. You then perform calculations on the data in Excel and verify that when you update data in the Access database, the data in Excel also changes.

a. Start Word, open the file Support_INT_2_AppsPriceList.docx from the location where you store your Data Files.
b. Copy the table, create a new database in Access called **IL_INT_2_RiverwalkApps** in the location where you store your Data Files, then paste the copied table into a new table named **Products**.
c. Add two new records to the Products table with the following information:

App	Category	Price
Blood Sugar Monitor	Medical	$7.00
Yoga for Seniors	Fitness	$5.00

d. Close the table, copy it and paste it as a link into a new Excel workbook, then add a new column in Excel called **Sales**.
e. Enter **200** as the number of sales for the first four products and **300** as the number of sales for the last eight products.
f. Add a new column called **Revenue**, calculate the total revenue for each app, then save the workbook as **IL_INT_2_RiverwalkAppsSales**.
g. Format the Price and Revenue values with the Accounting Number format, then adjust column widths as necessary.
h. Note the current revenue amount for the Heart Health and Fitness Buddy apps ($800 and $1,050).
i. In the Access Products table, change the price of the Heart Health app to $5.00 and the price of the Fitness Buddy app to $4.00, then close the table.
j. In Excel, verify the values have been updated to $1,000 and $1,200. You may need to wait a few minutes.

Independent Challenge 1 (continued)

k. Bold and center the labels in row 1, insert a new row 1, enter **Riverwalk Apps Sales**, merge and center it across the range A1:F1, increase the font size to 16 point, apply bold formatting, then apply the Blue, Accent 5, Lighter 60% fill color.

l. Type your name in cell A16, compare the completed workbook to **FIGURE 2-13**, save and close all open files and programs, then submit your files to your instructor.

FIGURE 2-13

	A	B	C	D	E	F	G
1	Riverwalk Apps Sales						
2	ID	App	Category	Price	Sales	Revenue	
3	1	Tracking Nutrition	Nutrition	$ 7.00	200	$1,400.00	
4	2	Heart Health	Medical	$ 5.00	200	$1,000.00	
5	3	Meditation Helper	Wellness	$ 1.50	200	$ 300.00	
6	4	Meal Planning Pal	Nutrition	$ 6.00	200	$1,200.00	
7	5	First Aid	Emergency	$ 2.00	300	$ 600.00	
8	6	My Records	Medical	$ 3.00	300	$ 900.00	
9	7	Fitness Buddy	Fitness	$ 4.00	300	$1,200.00	
10	8	Rx Helper	Medical	$ 5.50	300	$1,650.00	
11	9	Doctor on Call	Medical	$ 4.50	300	$1,350.00	
12	10	Med Pulse	Medical	$ 3.00	300	$ 900.00	
13	11	Blood Sugar Monitor	Medical	$ 7.00	300	$2,100.00	
14	12	Yoga for Seniors	Fitness	$ 5.00	300	$1,500.00	
15							
16	Your Name						
17							
18							

Independent Challenge 2

Time Wise Media provides social media services to small business owners. You have been asked to build a database that the owner can use to keep track of contracts. The owner would also like you to create a report that analyzes sales trends.

a. Start Excel, open the file **IL_INT_2-5.xlsx** from the location where you store your Data Files, then save it as **IL_INT_2_TimeWiseContracts**.

b. Delete any rows and objects that cannot be imported into Access, then save and close the workbook.

c. Create a database in Access called **IL_INT_2_TimeWiseMedia**, and save it in the location where you store your Data Files.

d. Import the Excel file **IL_INT_2_TimeWiseContracts.xlsx** into the Access database, change the Description field name to **Service**, and accept **Contracts** as the table name.

e. Start Word, open the file Support_INT_2_TimeWiseConsultants.docx from the location where you store your Data Files, copy the table, close the document, then paste the table into the Contracts table in Access.

f. Delete the Client Name1 column from the pasted information, widen columns as needed, then save and close the table.

g. Copy the Contracts table, paste it as a linked file into cell A1 of a new Excel workbook, then adjust the column widths.

h. Calculate the total revenue from each contract total based on an hourly rate of $110. (*Hint*: Add two new columns—one called "Rate" with "110" entered for each record and one called "Total" with the formula entered for each record.)

i. Format the values in columns G and H with the Accounting Number format, then save the Excel workbook as **IL_INT_2_TimeWiseRevenue**.

j. In Word, open a new document and enter the text (but not the table) shown in the completed document in **FIGURE 2-14**, then save it as **IL_INT_2_TimeWiseSpringContracts**. Format the title in 22 point, bold and the subtitle in 14 point, bold.

k. Copy cells B1 to H11 from Excel, paste them as a link using the Microsoft Excel Worksheet Object option in the Paste Special dialog box below the text paragraph in the IL_INT_2_TimeWiseSpringContracts document, resize the object so it fits into the Word document (*Hint*: Drag the bottom-left corner sizing handle up), then save the document.

l. In the Contracts table in Access, change the number of hours for Isabel Cox to **35**, close the table, then verify the revenue for Isabel Cox has changed from $2,200 to $3,850 in the Excel file. Remember, you may need to wait a few minutes for the values to update.

m. Format the range A1:H11 with border lines around all cells, and bold and center column titles.

n. Update the worksheet object in the Word file.

o. Add your name below the worksheet object, compare the completed document to **FIGURE 2-14**, save all files and close all programs, then submit your files to your instructor.

FIGURE 2-14

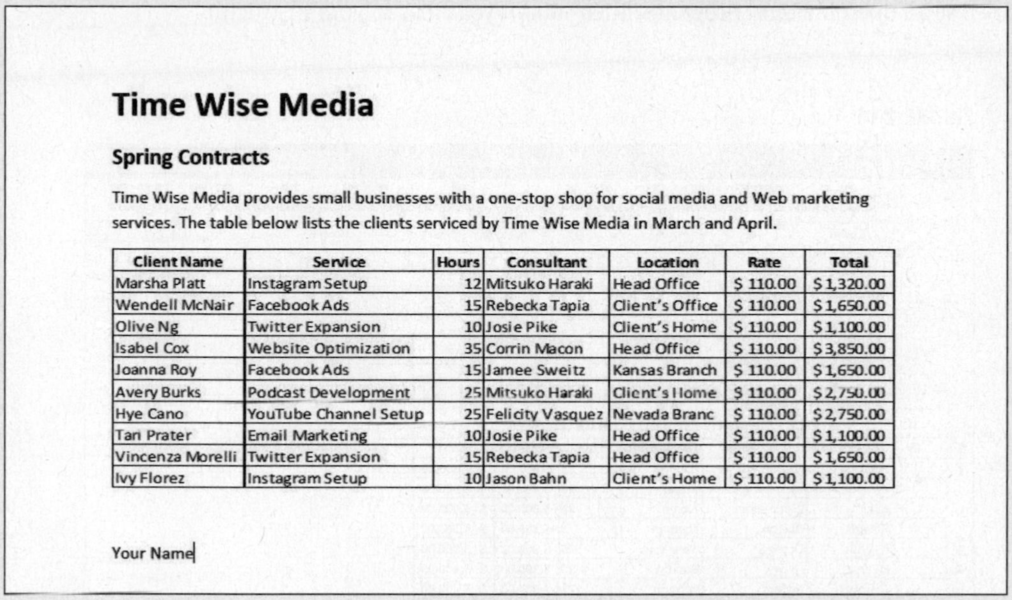

Time Wise Media

Spring Contracts

Time Wise Media provides small businesses with a one-stop shop for social media and Web marketing services. The table below lists the clients serviced by Time Wise Media in March and April.

Client Name	Service	Hours	Consultant	Location	Rate	Total
Marsha Platt	Instagram Setup	12	Mitsuko Haraki	Head Office	$ 110.00	$ 1,320.00
Wendell McNair	Facebook Ads	15	Rebecka Tapia	Client's Office	$ 110.00	$ 1,650.00
Olive Ng	Twitter Expansion	10	Josie Pike	Client's Home	$ 110.00	$ 1,100.00
Isabel Cox	Website Optimization	35	Corrin Macon	Head Office	$ 110.00	$ 3,850.00
Joanna Roy	Facebook Ads	15	Jamee Sweitz	Kansas Branch	$ 110.00	$ 1,650.00
Avery Burks	Podcast Development	25	Mitsuko Haraki	Client's Home	$ 110.00	$ 2,750.00
Hye Cano	YouTube Channel Setup	25	Felicity Vasquez	Nevada Branc	$ 110.00	$ 2,750.00
Tan Prater	Email Marketing	10	Josie Pike	Head Office	$ 110.00	$ 1,100.00
Vincenza Morelli	Twitter Expansion	15	Rebecka Tapia	Head Office	$ 110.00	$ 1,650.00
Ivy Florez	Instagram Setup	10	Jason Bahn	Client's Home	$ 110.00	$ 1,100.00

Your Name

Integration

Visual Workshop

Create a new database called **IL_INT_2_BentonEngineering** in the location where you store your Data Files, then copy the table from the Word file Support_INT_2_ProjectManagerTravel.docx into the database as a new table. Name the table **Manager Travel**. Copy the table, then paste it as linked data in a new Excel workbook. Save the workbook as **IL_INT_2_BentonEngineeringTravelExpenses**. Refer to **FIGURE 2-15** to add two new columns, enter a per diem rate of **$300**, and calculate the total expenses for each staff person. Calculate the total expenses in cell G12 and add and format the Total Expenses label in cell F12. In the Access source table, change the number of days that Jill Zimmerman was away to **20** and the number of days that Alonzo Peters was away to **22**, then close the table. In Excel, verify that the appropriate values are updated, then as shown in **FIGURE 2-15**, add and format a title and subtitle. (*Hint*: The font size of the title is 20 point, and the font size of the subtitle is 16 point.) Format data as shown in the figure. Include your name under the table, save and close all open files and programs, then submit your files to your instructor.

FIGURE 2-15

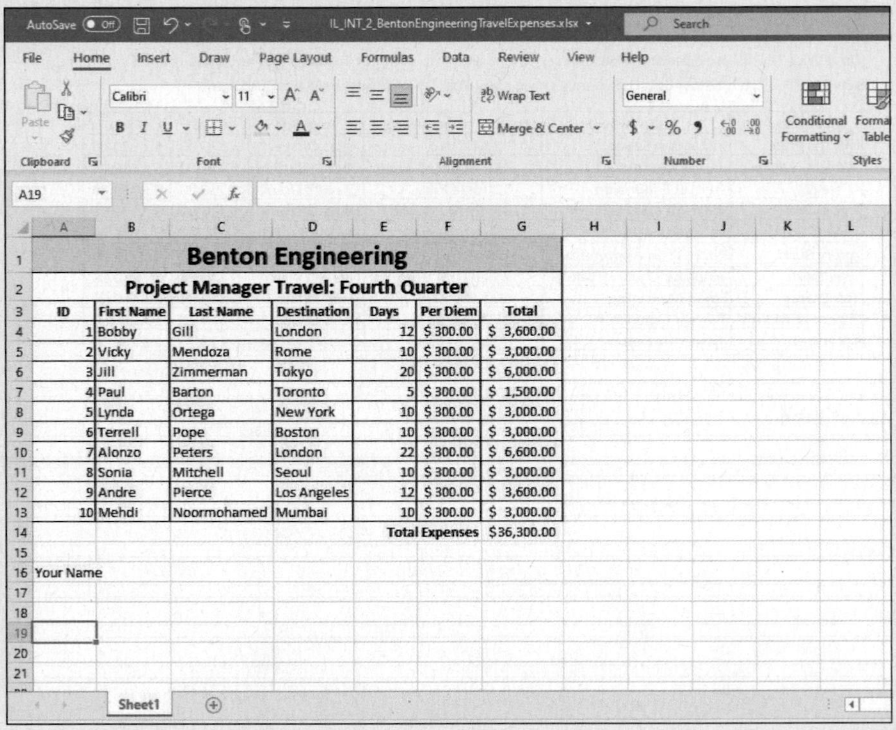

Creating a Presentation in PowerPoint

CASE JCL Talent, based in Atlanta, Georgia, is a company that provides comprehensive recruitment and employment services for employers and job seekers worldwide. You work for Dawn Lapointe in the Technical Careers division. You have been asked to help her create a presentation on global workforce trends that she will give at an upcoming recruiters convention. Use PowerPoint to create the presentation.

Module Objectives

After completing this module, you will be able to:

- Define presentation software
- Plan an effective presentation
- Examine the PowerPoint window
- Enter slide text
- Add a new slide
- Format text
- Apply a design theme
- Compare presentation views
- Insert and resize a picture
- Check spelling
- Print a PowerPoint presentation

Files You Will Need

Support_PPT_1_Woman.jpg
IL_PPT_1-1.pptx
Support_PPT_1_Group.jpg
IL_PPT_1-2.pptx
IL_PPT_1-3.pptx

PowerPoint
Module 1

Define Presentation Software

Learning Outcome
- Describe presentation software

Presentation software (also called presentation graphics software) is a computer program you use to organize and present information to others. Presentations are typically in the form of a slide show. Whether you are explaining a new product or moderating a meeting, presentation software can help you effectively communicate your ideas. You can use PowerPoint to create informational slides that you print or display on a monitor, share in real time on the web, or save as a video for others to watch. **CASE** *You need to start working on the global workforce presentation. Because you are only somewhat familiar with PowerPoint, you get to work exploring its capabilities.* **FIGURE 1-1** *shows how a presentation looks printed as handouts.* **FIGURE 1-2** *shows how the same presentation might look saved as a video.*

DETAILS

You can easily complete the following tasks using PowerPoint:

- **Enter and edit text easily**
  Text editing and formatting commands in PowerPoint are organized by the task you are performing at the time, so you can enter, edit, and format text information simply and efficiently to produce the best results in the least amount of time.
- **Change the appearance of information**
  PowerPoint has many effects that can transform the way text, graphics, and slides appear. By exploring some of these capabilities, you discover how easy it is to change the appearance of your presentation.
- **Organize and arrange information**
  Once you start using PowerPoint, you won't have to spend much time making sure your information is correct and in the right order. With PowerPoint, you can quickly and easily rearrange and modify text, graphics, and slides in your presentation.
- **Include information from other sources**
  Often, when you create presentations, you use information from a variety of sources. With PowerPoint, you can import text, photographs, videos, numerical data, and other information from files created in programs such as Adobe Photoshop, Microsoft Word, Microsoft Excel, and Microsoft Access. You can also import information from other PowerPoint presentations as well as graphic images from a variety of sources such as the Internet, storage devices, computers, a camera, or other graphics programs. Always be sure you have permission to use any work that you did not create yourself.
- **Present information in a variety of ways**
  With PowerPoint, you can present information using a variety of methods. For example, you can print handout pages or an outline of your presentation for audience members. You can display your presentation as an on-screen slide show using your computer, or if you are presenting to a large group, you can use a video projector and a large screen. If you want to reach an even wider audience, you can broadcast the presentation or upload it as a video to the Internet so people anywhere in the world can use a web browser to view your presentation.
- **Collaborate with others on a presentation**
  PowerPoint makes it easy to collaborate or share a presentation with colleagues and coworkers using the Internet. You can use your email program to send a presentation as an attachment to a colleague for feedback. If you have a number of people that need to work together on a presentation, you can save the presentation to a shared workspace such as a network drive or OneDrive so authorized users in your group with an Internet connection can access the presentation.

FIGURE 1-1: PowerPoint handout

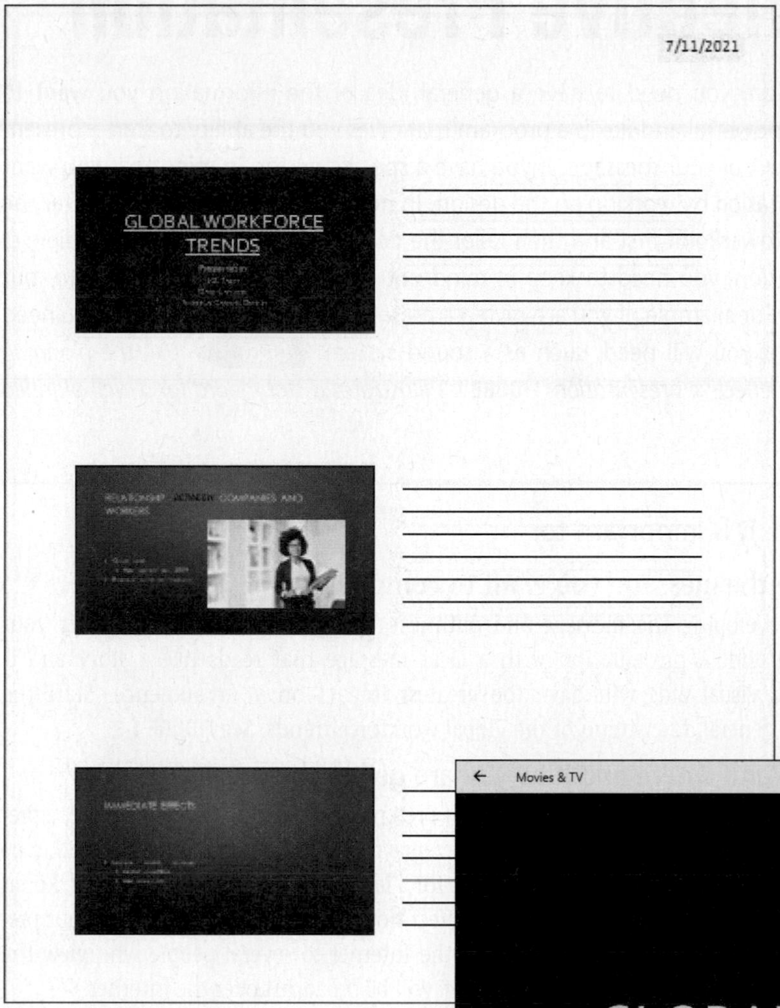

Asier Romero/Shutterstock.com

FIGURE 1-2: Presentation saved as a video

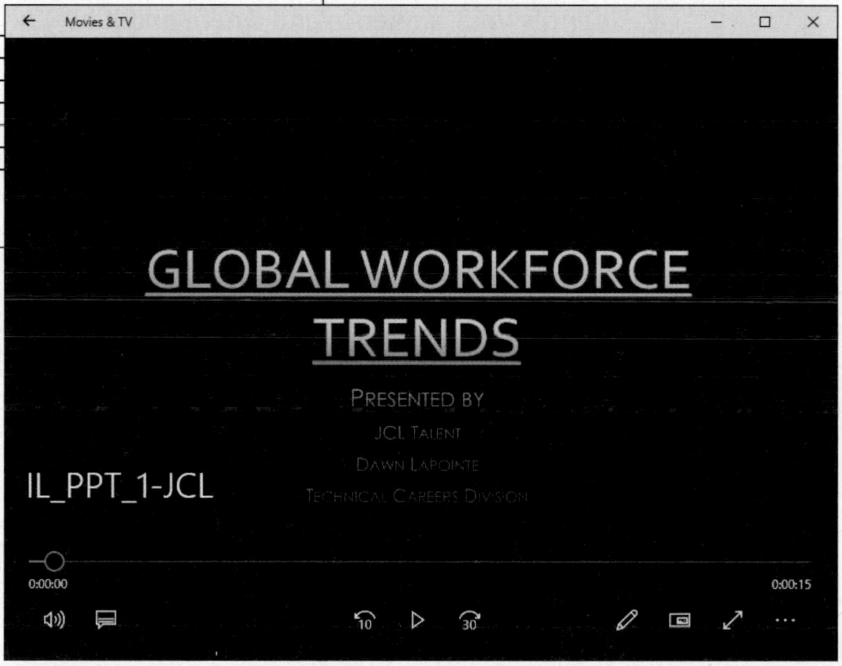

Using PowerPoint on a touch screen

You can use PowerPoint on a Windows computer with a touch-enabled monitor or any other compatible touch screen, such as a tablet. Using your fingers, you can use typical touch gestures to create, modify, and navigate presentations. To enable touch mode capabilities in PowerPoint, you need to add the Touch Mode button to the Quick Access Toolbar. Click the Customize Quick Access Toolbar button, click Touch/Mouse Mode, click the on the Quick Access Toolbar, then click Touch. In Touch mode, additional space is added around all of the buttons and icons in the Ribbon and the status bar to make them easier to touch. Common gestures that you can use in PowerPoint include double-tapping text to edit it and tapping a slide then dragging it to rearrange it in the presentation.

PowerPoint Module 1

Plan an Effective Presentation

Learning Outcome
- Determine presentation content and design

Before you create a presentation, you need to have a general idea of the information you want to communicate. PowerPoint is a powerful and flexible program that gives you the ability to start a presentation simply by entering the text of your message. If you have a specific design in mind that you want to use, you can start the presentation by working on the design. In most cases, you'll probably enter the text of your presentation into PowerPoint first and then tailor the design to the message and audience. When preparing your presentation, you need to keep in mind not only who you are giving it to, but also how you are presenting it. For example, if you are giving a presentation using a projector, you need to know what other equipment you will need, such as a sound system. **CASE** *Use the planning guidelines below to help plan an effective presentation.* **FIGURE 1-3** *illustrates a storyboard for a well-planned presentation.*

DETAILS

In planning a presentation, it is important to:

- **Determine and outline the message you want to communicate**
  The more time you take developing the message and outline of your presentation, the better your presentation will be in the end. A presentation with a clear message that reads like a story and is illustrated with appropriate visual aids will have the greatest impact on your audience. Start the presentation by providing a general description of the global workforce trends. See **FIGURE 1-3**.

- **Identify your audience and where and how you are giving the presentation**
  Audience and delivery location are major factors in the type of presentation you create. For example, a presentation you develop for a staff meeting that is held in a conference room would not necessarily need to be as sophisticated or detailed as a presentation that you develop for a large audience in an auditorium. Room lighting, natural light, screen position, and room layout all affect how the audience responds to your presentation. You might also broadcast your presentation over the Internet to several people who view the presentation on their computers in real time. This presentation will be broadcast over the Internet.

- **Determine the type of output**
  Output choices for a presentation include black-and-white or color handouts for audience members, an on-screen slide show, a video, or an online broadcast. Consider the time demands and computer equipment availability as you decide which output types to produce. Because this presentation will be broadcast over the Internet, the default output settings work just fine.

- **Determine the design**
  Visual appeal, graphics, and presentation design work together to communicate your message. You can choose one of the professionally designed themes that come with PowerPoint, modify one of these themes, or create one of your own. You decide to choose one of PowerPoint's design themes for your presentation.

FIGURE 1-3: Storyboard of the presentation

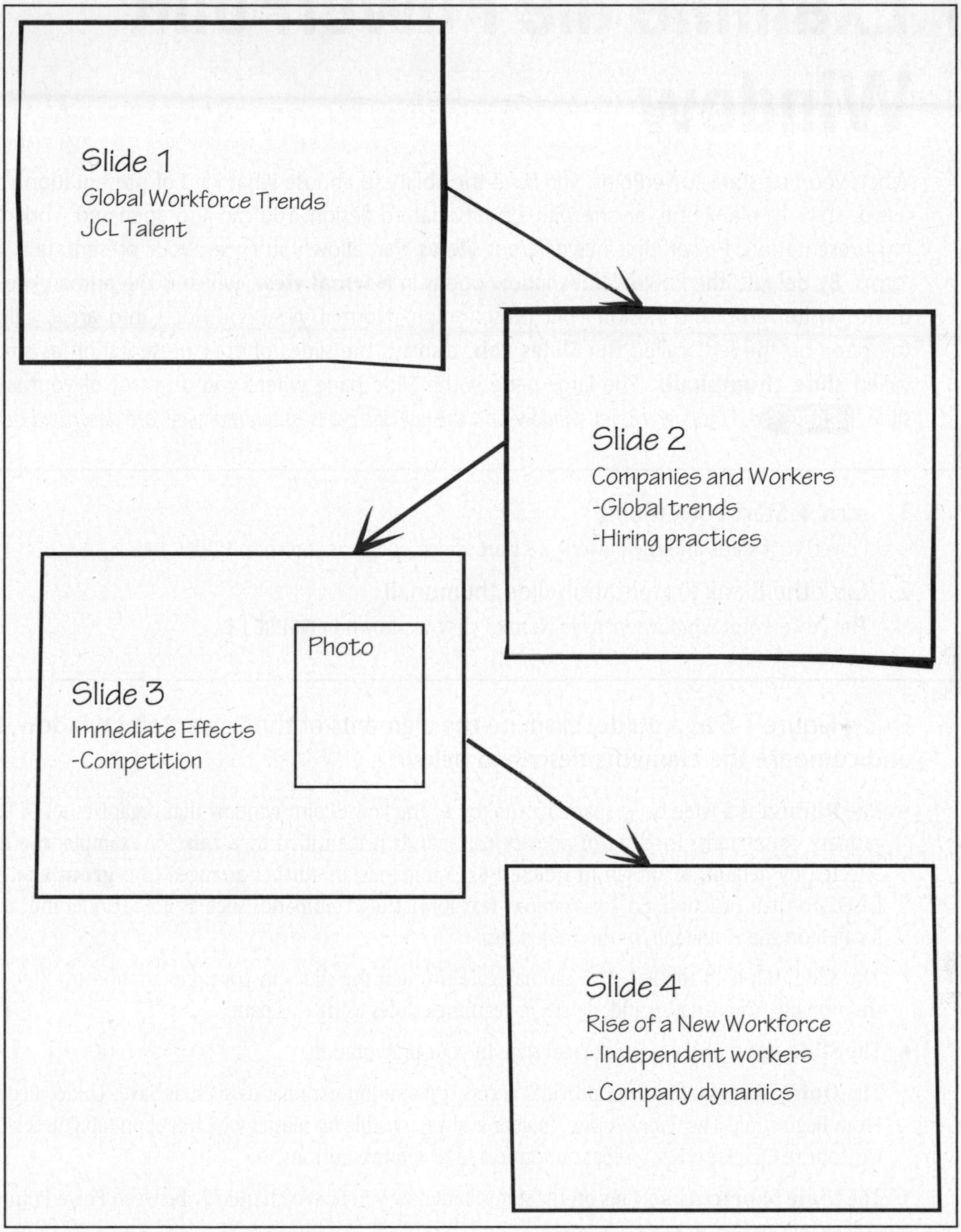
Slide 1
Global Workforce Trends
JCL Talent
Slide 2
Companies and Workers
-Global trends
-Hiring practices
Photo
Slide 3
Immediate Effects
-Competition
Slide 4
Rise of a New Workforce
- Independent workers
- Company dynamics

Understanding copyright

Intellectual property is any idea or creation of the human mind. Copyright law is a type of intellectual property law that protects works of authorship, including books, webpages, computer games, music, artwork, and photographs. Copyright protects the expression of an idea, but not the underlying facts or concepts. In other words, the general subject matter is not protected, but how you express it is, such as when several people photograph the same sunset. Copyright attaches to any original work of authorship as soon as it is created; you do not have to register it with the Copyright Office or display the copyright symbol, ©. Fair use is an exception to copyright and permits the public to use copyrighted material for certain purposes without obtaining prior consent from the owner. Determining whether fair use applies to a work depends on its purpose, the nature of the work, how much of the work you want to copy, and the effect on the work's value. Unauthorized use of protected work (such as downloading a photo or a song from the web) is known as copyright infringement and can lead to legal action.

PowerPoint **Module 1**

Learning Outcome
- Explain PowerPoint window elements

Examine the PowerPoint Window

When you first start PowerPoint, you have the ability to choose what kind of presentation you want to use to start—a blank one, or one with a preformatted design. You can also open and work on an existing presentation. PowerPoint has different **views** that allow you to see your presentation in different forms. By default, the PowerPoint window opens in **Normal view**, which is the primary view that you use to write, edit, and design your presentation. Normal view is divided into areas called **panes**: the pane on the left, called the **Slides tab**, displays the slides of your presentation as small images, called **slide thumbnails**. The large pane is the Slide pane where you do most of your work on the slide. CASE *The PowerPoint window and the specific parts of Normal view are described below.*

STEPS

1. **sam Start PowerPoint**
   PowerPoint starts and the PowerPoint start screen opens, as shown in **FIGURE 1-4**.
2. **Click the Blank Presentation slide thumbnail**
   The PowerPoint window opens in Normal view, as shown in **FIGURE 1-5**.

DETAILS

Using Figure 1-5 as a guide, examine the elements of the PowerPoint window, then find and compare the elements described below:

- The **Ribbon** is a wide band spanning the top of the PowerPoint window that organizes all of PowerPoint's primary commands. Each set of primary commands is identified by a **tab**; for example, the Home tab is selected by default, as shown in **FIGURE 1-5**. Commands are further arranged into **groups** on the Ribbon based on their function. So, for example, text formatting commands such as Bold, Underline, and Italic are located on the Home tab, in the Font group.
- The Slides tab is to the left. You can navigate through the slides in your presentation by clicking the slide thumbnails. You can also add, delete, or rearrange slides using this pane.
- The **Slide pane** displays the current slide in your presentation.
- The **Quick Access Toolbar** provides access to common commands such as Save, Undo, Redo, and Start From Beginning. The Quick Access Toolbar is always visible no matter which Ribbon tab you select. Click the Customize Quick Access Toolbar button to add or remove buttons.
- The **View Shortcuts** buttons on the status bar allow you to switch quickly between PowerPoint views.
- The **Notes button** on the status bar opens the Notes pane and is used to enter text that references a slide's content. You can print these notes and refer to them when you make a presentation or use them as audience handouts. The Notes pane is not visible in Slide Show view.
- The **status bar**, located at the bottom of the PowerPoint window, shows messages about what you are doing and seeing in PowerPoint, including which slide you are viewing and the total number of slides. In addition, the status bar displays the Zoom slider controls, the Fit slide to current window button, and other functionality information.
- The **Zoom slider** on the lower-right corner of the status bar is used to zoom the slide in and out.

FIGURE 1-4: PowerPoint start screen

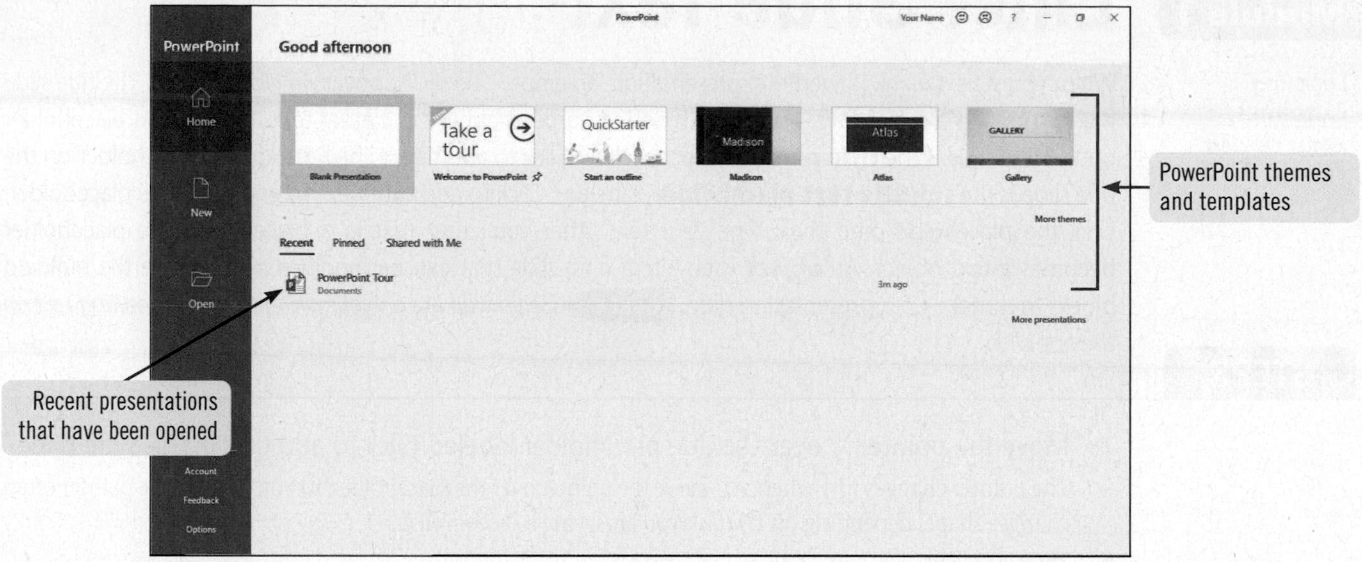

FIGURE 1-5: PowerPoint window in Normal view

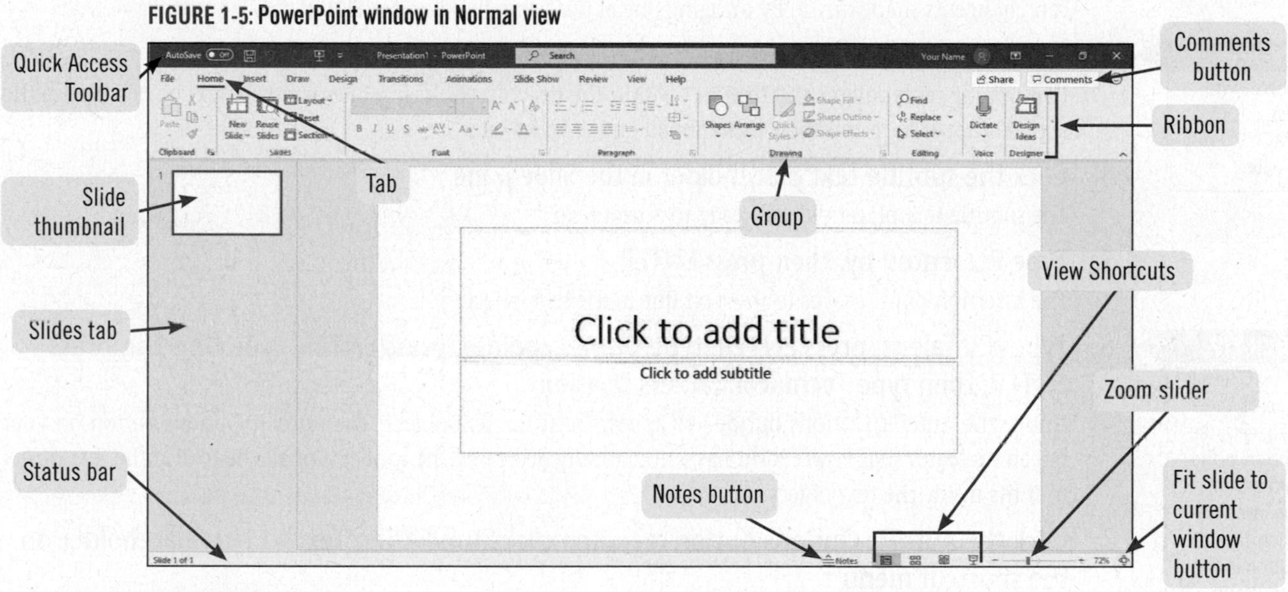

Creating a presentation using a template

PowerPoint offers you a variety of ways to create a presentation, including starting with a blank presentation, a theme, a template, or an existing presentation. A **template** is a type of presentation that contains design information on the slide master and often includes text and design suggestions for information you might want to include in the presentation. You have access to sample templates in PowerPoint and online at the Microsoft.com website. To create a presentation using a template, click the File tab on the Ribbon, click the New tab, locate the template, then click Create.

Enter Slide Text

Learning Outcomes
- Enter slide text
- Change slide text

When you start a blank PowerPoint presentation, an empty title slide appears in Normal view. The title slide has two **text placeholders**—boxes with dotted borders—where you enter text. The top text placeholder on the title slide is the **title placeholder**, labeled "Click to add title." The bottom text placeholder on the title slide is the **subtitle text placeholder**, labeled "Click to add subtitle." To enter text in a placeholder, click the placeholder and then type your text. After you enter text in a placeholder, the placeholder becomes a text object. An **object** is any item on a slide that can be modified. Objects are the building blocks that make up a presentation slide. CASE *Begin working on your presentation by entering text on the title slide.*

STEPS

1. **Move the pointer over the title placeholder labeled Click to add title in the Slide pane**
   The pointer changes to I when you move the pointer over the placeholder. In PowerPoint, the pointer often changes shape, depending on the task you are trying to accomplish.
2. **Click the title placeholder in the Slide pane**
   The **insertion point**, a blinking vertical line, indicates where your text appears when you type in the placeholder. A **selection box** with a dashed line border and **sizing handles** appears around the placeholder, indicating that it is selected and ready to accept text. When a placeholder or object is selected, you can change its shape or size by dragging one of the sizing handles. See **FIGURE 1-6**.
3. **Type Global Workforce Trends**
   PowerPoint center-aligns the title text within the title placeholder, which is now a text object. Notice the text also appears on the Slide 1 thumbnail on the Slides tab.
4. **Click the subtitle text placeholder in the Slide pane**
   The subtitle text placeholder is ready to accept text.
5. **Type Presented by, then press ENTER**
   The insertion point moves to the next line in the text object.
6. **Type JCL Talent, press ENTER, type Dawn Lapointe, press ENTER, type Director, press ENTER, then type Technical Careers Division**
   Notice the AutoFit Options button appears near the text object. The AutoFit Options button on your screen indicates that PowerPoint has automatically decreased the font size of all the text in the text object so it fits inside the text object.
7. **Click the AutoFit Options button, then click Stop Fitting Text to This Placeholder on the shortcut menu**
   The text in the text object changes back to its original size and no longer fits inside the text object.
8. **In the subtitle text object, position I to the right of Director, drag left to select the whole word, press BACKSPACE, then click outside the text object in a blank area of the slide**
   The Director line of text is deleted and the AutoFit Options button menu closes, as shown in **FIGURE 1-7**. Clicking a blank area of the slide deselects all selected objects on the slide.
9. **Click the File tab on the Ribbon to open Backstage view, click Save As, click Browse, then save the presentation as IL_PPT_1_JCL in the location where you store your Data Files**
   In Backstage view, you have the option of saving your presentation to your computer or OneDrive. Notice that PowerPoint automatically entered the title of the presentation as the file name in the Save As dialog box.

TROUBLE
If you press a wrong key, press BACKSPACE to erase the character.

QUICK TIP
To copy text, select the text, click the Home tab, click the Copy button in the Clipboard group, place the insertion point, then click the Paste button in the Clipboard group.

FIGURE 1-6: Title text placeholder selected

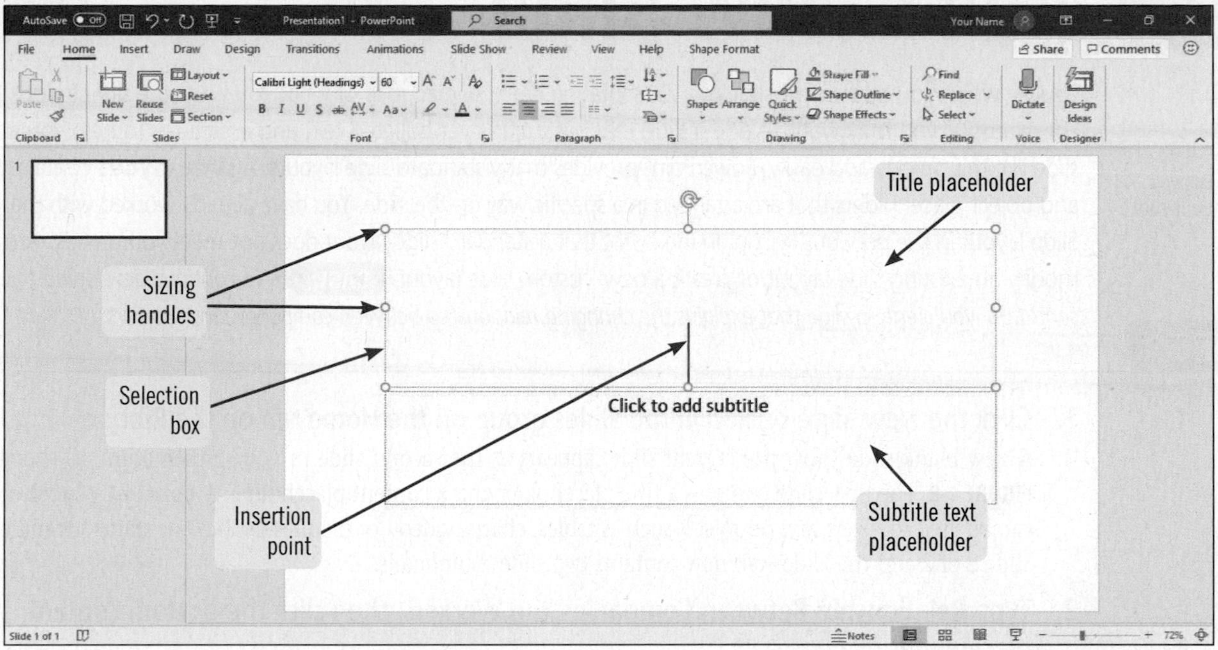

FIGURE 1-7: Text on title slide

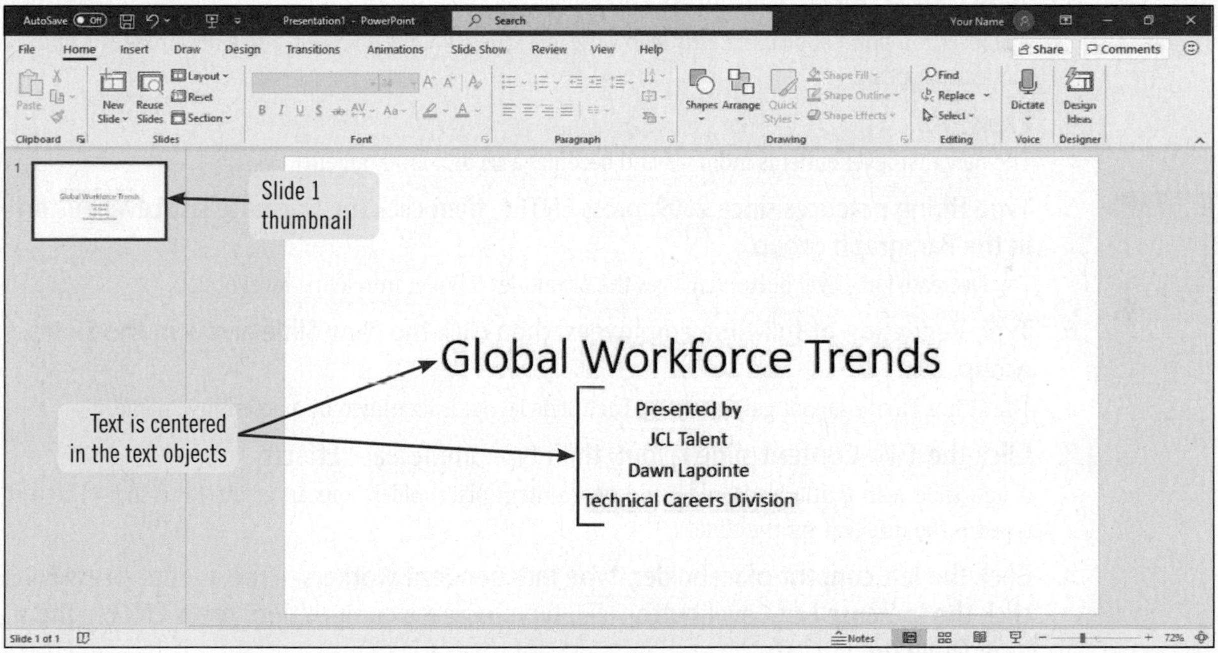

Inking a slide

In Normal view, you can add freehand pen and highlighter marks, also known as **inking**, to the slides of your presentation to emphasize information. To begin inking, go to the slide you want to mark up, click the Draw tab, then click one of the drawing tools in the Drawing Tools group. If you are using a touchscreen, you can use your finger or stylus to mark up a slide. To customize the thickness or color of your pen, click the down arrow on the selected pen. You can also click the Highlighter button in the Drawing Tools group to insert highlighter strokes on your slide. To erase inking on the slide, click the Eraser button in the Drawing Tools group, then click the ink or mark you want to erase.

Add a New Slide

Learning Outcomes
- Add a new slide
- Indent text levels
- Modify slide layout

Usually when you add a new slide to a presentation, you have an idea of what you want the slide to look like. For example, you may want to add a slide that has a title over bulleted text and a picture. To help you add a slide like this quickly and easily, PowerPoint provides many standard slide layouts. A **slide layout** contains text and object placeholders that are arranged in a specific way on the slide. You have already worked with the Title Slide layout in the previous lesson. In the event that a standard slide layout does not meet your needs, you can modify an existing slide layout or create a new, custom slide layout. **CASE** *To continue developing the presentation, you create a slide that explains the changing relationship between companies and workers.*

STEPS

1. **Click the New Slide button in the Slides group on the Home tab on the Ribbon**
   A new blank slide (now the current slide) appears as the second slide in your presentation, as shown in **FIGURE 1-8**. The new slide contains a title placeholder and a content placeholder. A **content placeholder** can be used to insert text or objects such as tables, charts, videos, or pictures. Notice the status bar indicates Slide 2 of 2 and the Slides tab now contains two slide thumbnails.
2. **Type Relationship Between Companies and Workers, then click the bottom content placeholder**
   The text you typed appears in the title placeholder, and the insertion point is now at the top of the bottom content placeholder.
3. **Type Global trends, then press ENTER**
   The insertion point appears directly below the text when you press ENTER, and a new first-level bullet automatically appears.
4. **Press TAB**
   The new first-level bullet is indented and becomes a second-level bullet.
5. **Type Hiring practices since 2009, press ENTER, then click the Decrease List Level button in the Paragraph group**
   The Decrease List Level button changes the second-level bullet into a first-level bullet.

   > **QUICK TIP**
   > You can also press SHIFT+TAB to decrease the indent level.

6. **Type Reduction of full-time employees, then click the New Slide arrow in the Slides group**
   The Office Theme layout gallery opens. Each slide layout is identified by a descriptive name.
7. **Click the Two Content slide layout, then type Immediate Effects**
   A new slide with a title placeholder and two content placeholders appears as the third slide. The text you typed is the title text for the slide.
8. **Click the left content placeholder, type Independent workers—free agents, press ENTER, click the Increase List Level button, type Increase competition, press ENTER, then type Drive down costs**
   The Increase List Level button moves the insertion point one level to the right.
9. **Click a blank area of the slide, then click the Save button on the Quick Access Toolbar**
   The Save button saves all of the changes to the file. Compare your screen with **FIGURE 1-9**.

FIGURE 1-8: New blank slide in Normal view

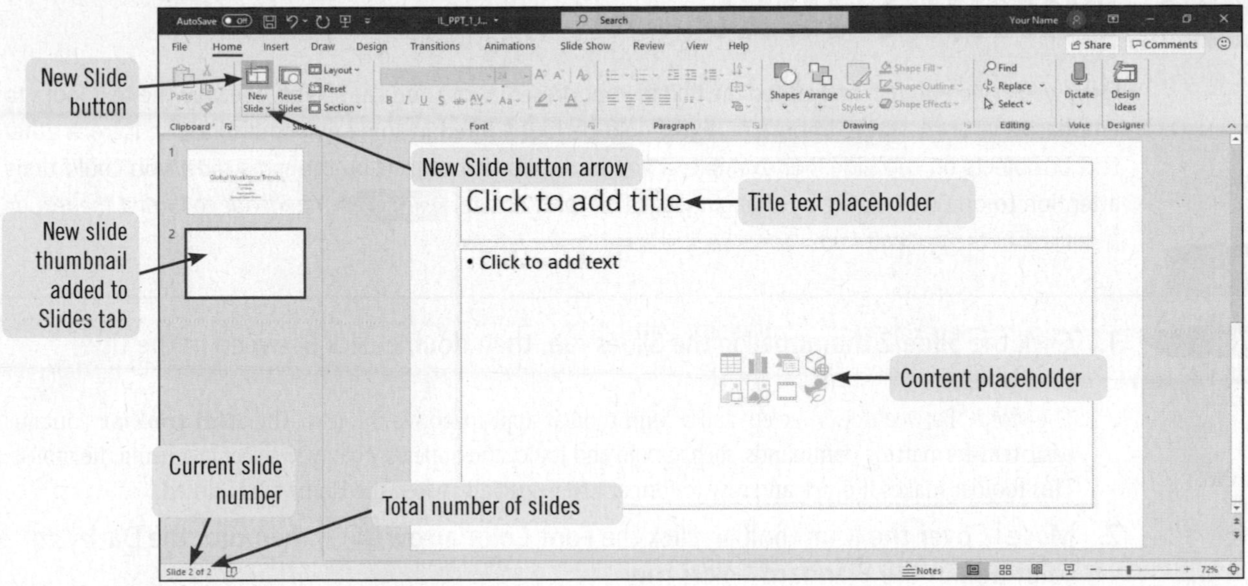

FIGURE 1-9: New slide with Two Content slide layout

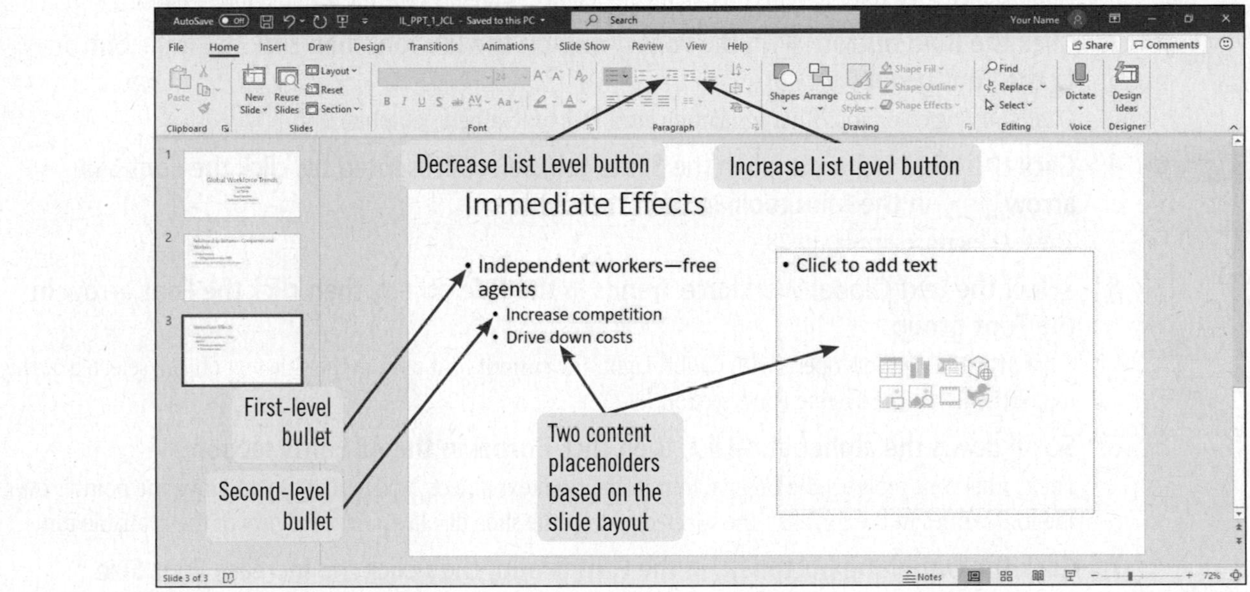

Viewing your presentation in grayscale or black and white

Viewing your presentation in grayscale (using shades of gray) or pure black and white is very useful when you are printing a presentation on a black-and-white printer and you want to make sure your presentation prints correctly. To see how your color presentation looks in grayscale or black and white, click the View tab, then click either the Grayscale or Black and White button in the Color/Grayscale group. Depending on which button you select, the Grayscale or the Black and White tab appears, and the Ribbon displays different settings that you can customize. If you don't like the way an individual object looks in black and white or grayscale, you can change its color. Click the object while still in Grayscale or Black and White view, then choose an option in the Change Selected Object group on the Ribbon.

Format Text

Learning Outcome
- Modify text characteristics

Once you have entered and edited the text in your presentation, you can modify the way the text looks to emphasize your message. Important text should be highlighted in some way to distinguish it from other text or objects on the slide. For example, if you have two text objects on the same slide, you could draw attention to one text object by changing its color, font, or size. **CASE** *You decide to format the text on two slides of the presentation.*

STEPS

QUICK TIP
To show or hide the Mini toolbar, click the File tab on the Ribbon, click Options, then click the Show Mini Toolbar on selection check box.

QUICK TIP
To select an unselected text object, press SHIFT, click the text object, then release SHIFT.

QUICK TIP
For more text formatting options, right-click a text object, then click Format Text Effects to open the Format Shape pane.

1. **Click the Slide 2 thumbnail in the Slides tab, then double-click Between in the title text object**
   The word "Between" is selected, and a Mini toolbar appears above the text. The **Mini toolbar** contains basic text-formatting commands, such as bold and italic, and appears when you select text using the mouse. This toolbar makes it quick and easy to format text, especially when the Home tab is closed.
2. **Move over the Mini toolbar, click the Font Color arrow, then click the Dark Red color box in the Standard Colors row**
   The text changes color to dark red, as shown in **FIGURE 1-10**. When you click the Font Color arrow, the Font Color gallery appears showing the Theme Colors and Standard Colors. ScreenTips help identify font colors. Notice that the Font Color button on the Mini toolbar and the Font Color button in the Font group on the Home tab change color to reflect the new color choice, which is now the active color.
3. **Click the Bold button in the Font group on the Ribbon, then click the Italic button in the Font group**
   Changing the color and other formatting attributes of text helps emphasize it.
4. **Click the Slide 1 thumbnail in the Slides tab, select Presented by, click the Font Size arrow in the Mini toolbar, then click 28**
   The text increases in size to 28.
5. **Select the text Global Workforce Trends in the title object, then click the Font arrow in the Font group**
   A list of available fonts opens with Calibri Light, the current font used in the title text object, selected at the top of the list in the Theme Fonts section.
6. **Scroll down the alphabetical list, then click Corbel in the All Fonts section**
   The Corbel font replaces the original font in the title text object. Notice that as you move the pointer over the font names in the font list, the selected text on the slide displays a Live Preview of the available fonts.
7. **Click the Underline button in the Font group, then click the Increase Font Size button in the Font group**
   All of the text now displays an underline and increases in size to 66.
8. **Click a blank area of the slide outside the text object to deselect it, then save your work**
   Clicking a blank area of the slide deselects all objects that are selected. Compare your screen to **FIGURE 1-11**.

FIGURE 1-10: Selected word with Mini toolbar open

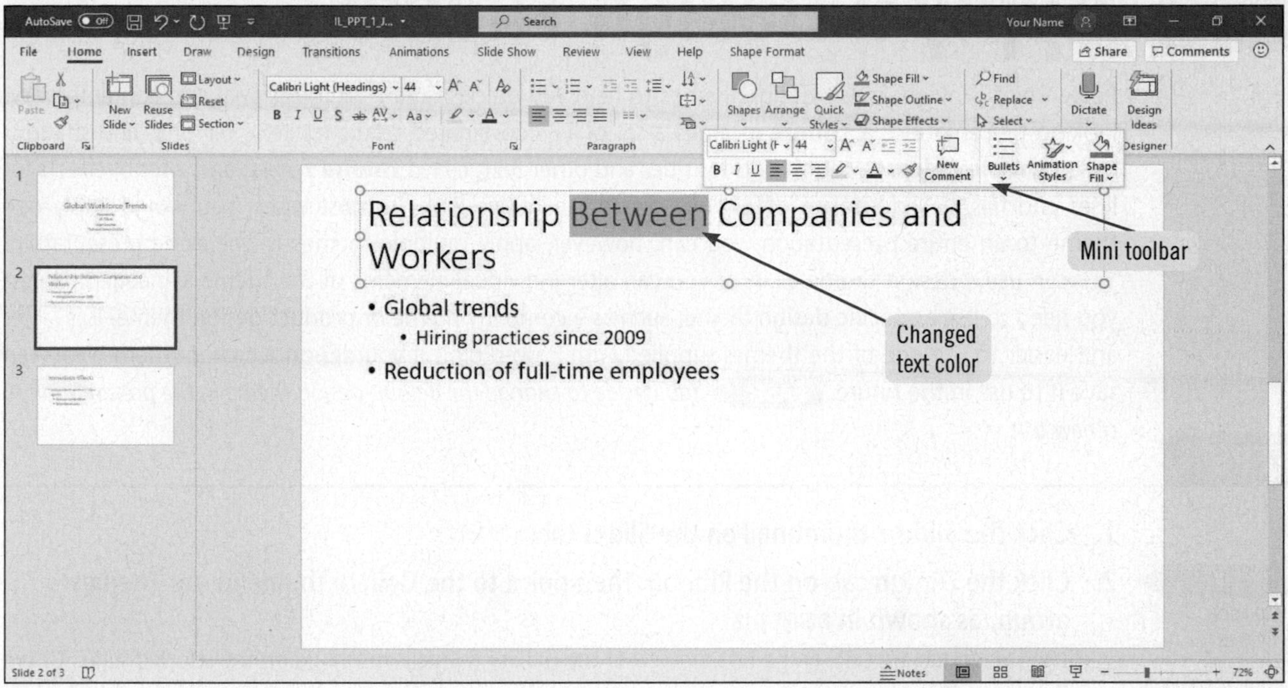

FIGURE 1-11: Formatted text

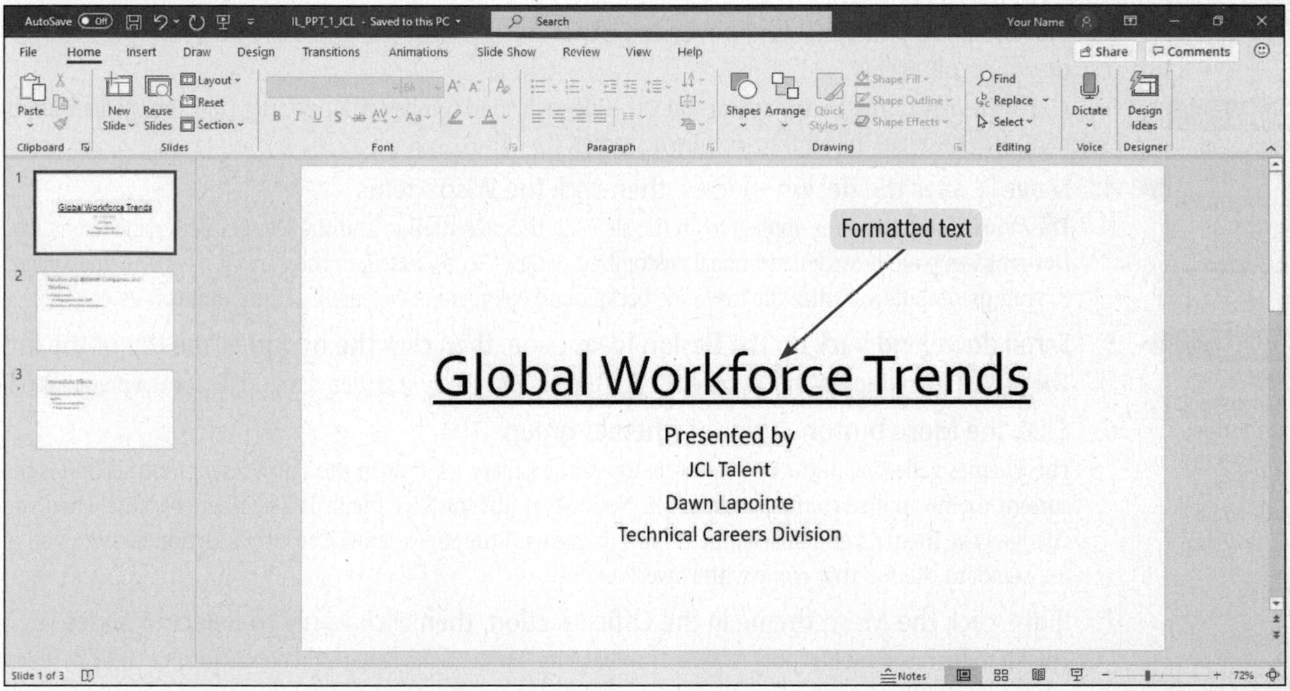

Adding bullets to paragraphs

In PowerPoint, paragraph text is often preceded by either a number or some kind of bullet. Common bullets include graphic images such as arrows, dots, or blocks. To add or change bullets, select the text or text object, click the Bullets arrow in the Paragraph group on the Ribbon, then select a bullet.

PowerPoint Module 1

Apply a Design Theme

Learning Outcome
- Modify the design theme

PowerPoint provides many design themes to help you quickly create a professional and contemporary-looking presentation. A **theme** includes a set of 12 coordinated colors for text, fill, line, and shadow, called **theme colors**; a set of fonts for titles and other text, called **theme fonts**; and a set of effects for lines and fills, called **theme effects** to create a cohesive look. In most cases, you would apply one theme to an entire presentation; you can, however, apply multiple themes to the same presentation. You can use a design theme as is, or you can alter individual elements of the theme as needed. Unless you need to use a specific design theme, such as a company theme or product design theme, it is faster and easier to use one of the themes supplied with PowerPoint. If you design a custom theme, you can save it to use in the future. **CASE** *You decide to change the default design theme in the presentation to a new one.*

STEPS

1. **Click the Slide 1 thumbnail on the Slides tab**
2. **Click the Design tab on the Ribbon, then point to the Gallery theme in the Themes group, as shown in FIGURE 1-12**
   The Design tab appears, and a Live Preview of the Gallery theme is displayed on the selected slide. A **Live Preview** allows you to see how your changes affect the slides before actually making the change. The Live Preview lasts about 1 minute, and then your slide reverts back to its original state. The first (far-left) theme thumbnail identifies the current theme applied to the presentation, in this case, the default design theme called the Office Theme.
3. **Slowly move your pointer over the other design themes, then click the Themes group down scroll arrow**
   A Live Preview of the theme appears on the slide each time you pass your pointer over the theme thumbnails, and a ScreenTip identifies the theme names.
4. **Move over the design themes, then click the Wisp theme**
   The Wisp design theme is applied to all the slides in the presentation and the Design Ideas pane opens. The Design Ideas pane provides additional customized design themes based on the current design theme applied to your presentation. Notice the new slide background color, graphic elements, fonts, and text color.
5. **Scroll down and back up the Design Ideas pane, then click the design at the top of the list**
   The presentation displays the suggested design theme. You decide this theme isn't right for the presentation.
6. **Click the More button in the Themes group**
   The Themes gallery window opens. At the top of the gallery window in the This Presentation section is the current theme applied to the presentation. Notice that just the Slice theme is listed here because when you changed the theme, you replaced the default theme with the Slice theme. The Office section identifies all of the standard themes that come with PowerPoint.
7. **Right-click the Mesh theme in the Office section, then click Apply to Selected Slides**
   The Mesh theme is applied only to Slide 1. You like the Mesh theme better, and decide to apply it to all slides.
8. **Right-click the Mesh theme in the Themes group, then click Apply to All Slides**
   The Mesh theme is applied to all three slides. Preview the next slide in the presentation to see how it looks.
9. **Click the Next Slide button at the bottom of the vertical scroll bar, click the Close button in the Design Ideas pane, then save your changes**
   Compare your screen to **FIGURE 1-13**.

QUICK TIP
One way to apply multiple themes to the same presentation is to click the Slide Sorter button on the status bar, select a slide or a group of slides, then click the theme.

TROUBLE
If the Design Ideas pane doesn't open, click the Design Ideas button on the Ribbon.

TROUBLE
The top slide layout that appears on your screen may be different than the one in **FIGURE 1-13**. If so, select a slide layout the closely resembles the one in **FIGURE 1-13**.

FIGURE 1-12: Slide showing a different design theme

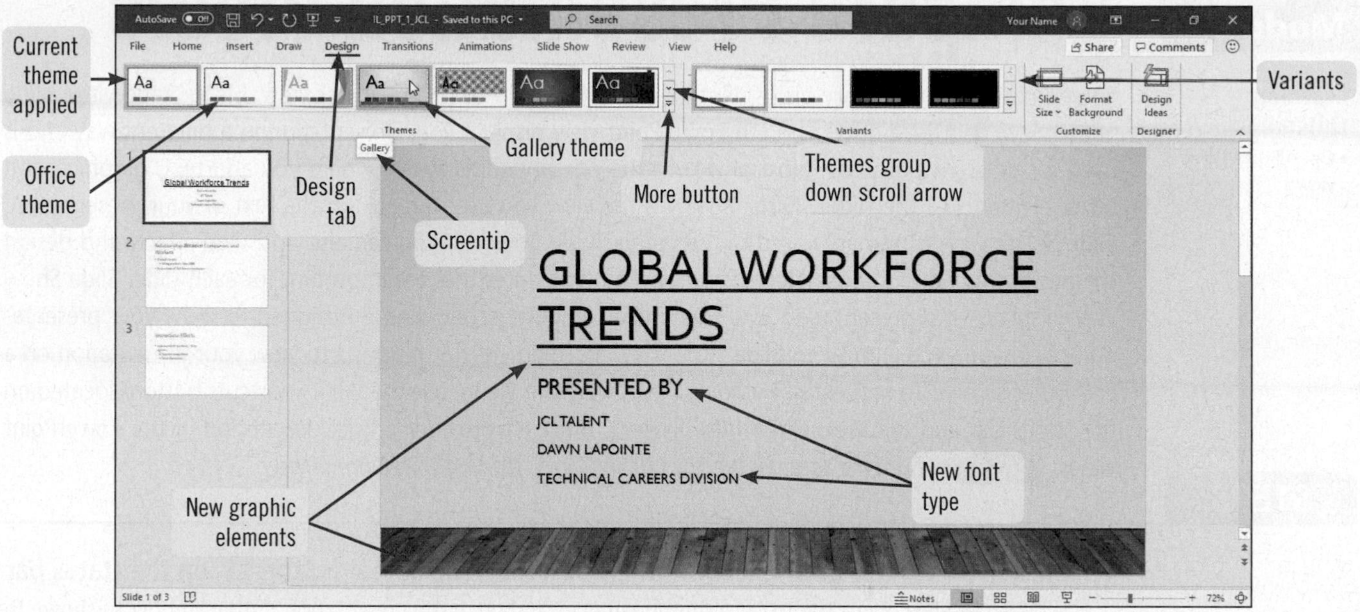

FIGURE 1-13: Presentation with Mesh theme applied

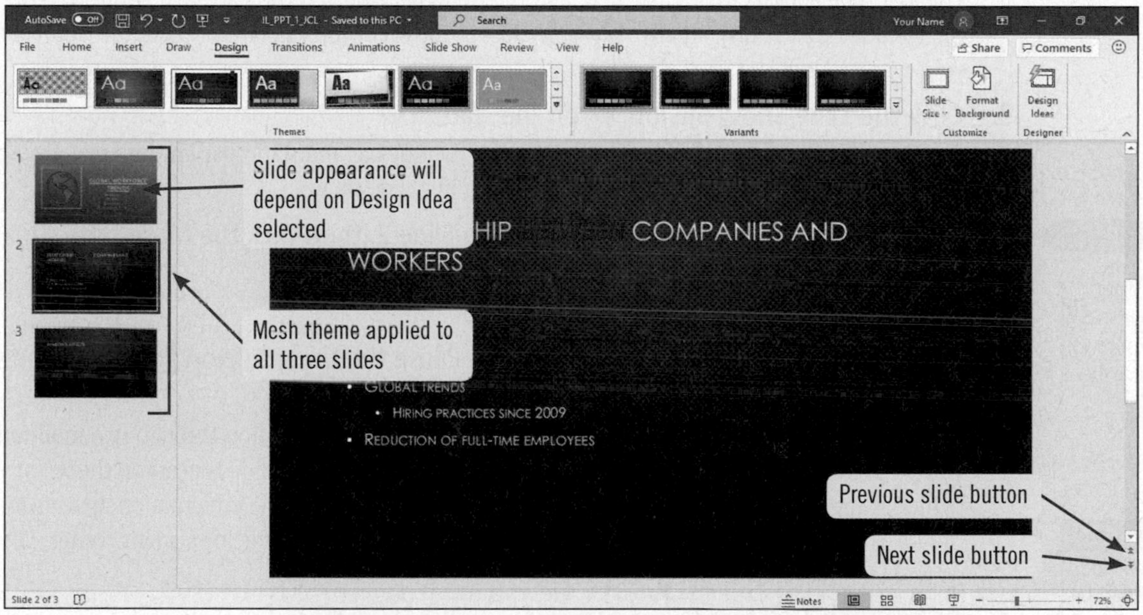

Changing theme colors

You are not limited to using the standard theme colors PowerPoint provides; you can also modify theme colors or create your own custom theme. For example, you might want to incorporate your school's or company's colors on the slide background of the presentation. To change existing theme colors, click the Design tab on the Ribbon, click the More button in the Variants group, point to Colors then select a color theme. You also have the ability to create a new color theme from scratch by clicking the More button in the Variants group, pointing to Colors, then clicking Customize Colors. The Create New Theme Colors dialog box opens where you can select the theme colors you want and then save the color theme with a new name.

Compare Presentation Views

Learning Outcome
- Open PowerPoint views

PowerPoint has six primary views: Normal view, Outline view, Slide Sorter view, Notes Page view, Slide Show view, and Reading view. Each PowerPoint view displays your presentation in a different way and is used for different purposes. Normal view is the primary editing view where you add text, graphics, and other elements to the slides. Outline view is the view you use to focus on the text of your presentation. Slide Sorter view is primarily used to rearrange slides; however, you can also add slide effects and design themes in this view. You use Notes Page view to type notes that are important for each slide. Slide Show view displays your presentation over the whole computer screen and is designed to show your presentation to an audience. Similar to Slide Show view, Reading view is designed to view your presentation on a computer screen. To move easily among the PowerPoint views, use the View Shortcuts buttons located on the status bar and the View tab on the Ribbon. **TABLE 1-1** provides a brief description of the PowerPoint views. **CASE** *Examine some of the PowerPoint views, starting with Normal view.*

STEPS

1. **Click the View tab on the Ribbon, then click the Slide Sorter button on the status bar**
   Slide Sorter view opens to display a thumbnail of each slide in the presentation in the window, as shown in **FIGURE 1-14**. You can examine the flow of your slides and drag any slide or group of slides to rearrange the order of the slides.
2. **Double-click the Slide 1 thumbnail, then click the Notes button on the status bar**
   The first slide appears in Normal view, and the Notes pane opens. The status bar controls at the bottom of the window make it easy to move between slides in this view. You can type notes in the Notes pane to guide your presentation.
3. **Click the Slide Show button on the status bar**
   The first slide fills the entire screen now without the title bar and status bar. In this view, you can practice running through your slides as they would appear in a slide show.
4. **Click the left mouse button to advance to Slide 2, then click the More slide show options button on the Slide Show toolbar**
   The slide show options menu opens.
5. **Click Show Presenter View, then click the Pause the timer button above the slide, as shown in FIGURE 1-15**
   Presenter view is a view that you can use when showing a presentation through two monitors; one that you see as the presenter and one that your audience sees. The current slide appears on the left of your screen (which is the only object your audience sees), and the next slide in the presentation appears in the upper-right corner of the screen. Speaker notes, if you have any, appear in the lower-right corner. The timer you paused identifies how long the slide has been viewed by the audience.
6. **Click , click Hide Presenter View, then click the left mouse button to advance through the slide show until you see a black slide, then press SPACEBAR**
   At the end of a slide show, you return to Normal view and the last slide of the slide show, in this case, Slide 3.
7. **Click the Home tab on the Ribbon**

QUICK TIP
You can also press ENTER, SPACEBAR, Page Up, Page Down, or the arrow keys to advance the slide show.

QUICK TIP
You can start a slide show from Slide 1 by clicking the From Beginning button in the Start Slide Show group on the Slide Show tab.

FIGURE 1-14: Slide Sorter view

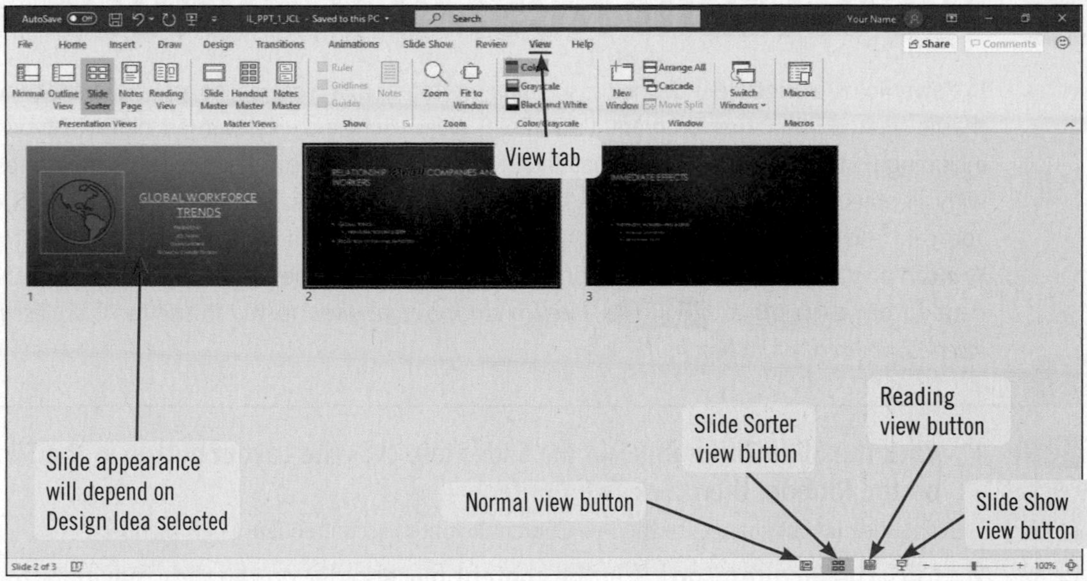

FIGURE 1-15: Slide 2 in Presenter view

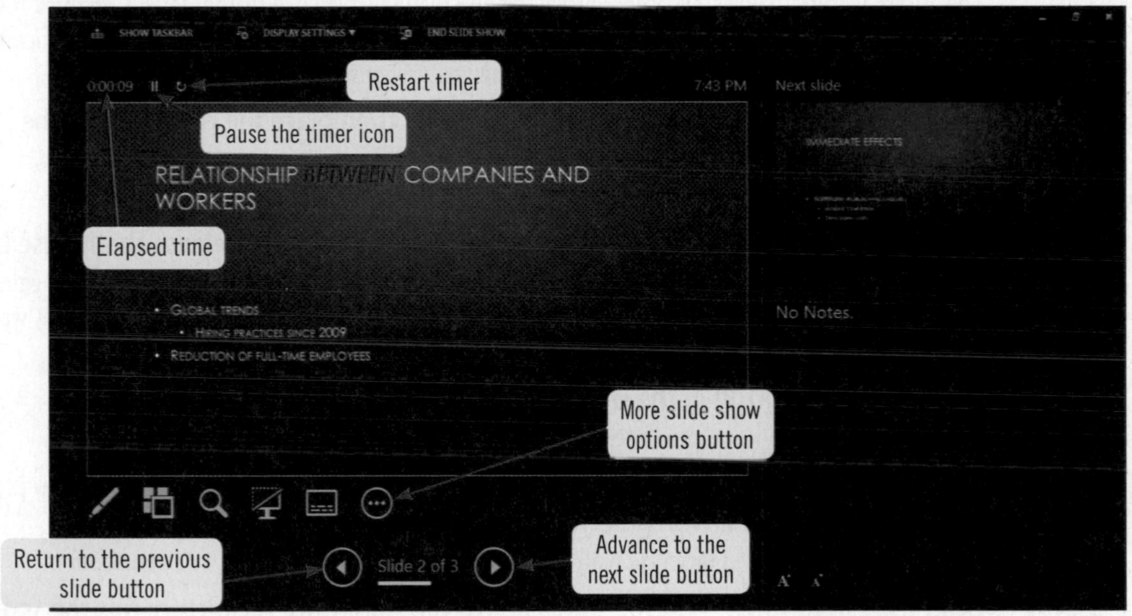

TABLE 1-1: PowerPoint views

view name	button	button name	displays
Normal		Normal	The Slide pane and the Slides tab at the same time
Outline View	(no View Shortcuts button)		An outline of the presentation and the Slide pane at the same time
Slide Sorter		Slide Sorter	Thumbnails of all slides
Slide Show		Slide Show	Your presentation on the whole computer screen
Reading View		Reading View	Your presentation in a large window on your computer screen
Notes Page	(no View Shortcuts button)		A reduced image of the current slide above a large text box

Insert and Resize a Picture

Learning Outcomes
- Insert a picture
- Resize and move a picture

In PowerPoint, a **picture** is defined as a digital photograph, a piece of line art or clip art, or other artwork that is created in another program. PowerPoint gives you the ability to insert different types of pictures, including JPEG File Interchange Format and BMP Windows Bitmap files into a PowerPoint presentation. As with all objects in PowerPoint, you can format and resize inserted pictures to help them fit on the slide. You can resize pictures proportionally, which keeps changes to height and width relative to each other. You can also resize a picture non-proportionally, which allows the height and width to change independently from each other. **CASE** *Insert a stock picture given to you to use for this presentation. Once inserted, you resize it to best fit the slide.*

STEPS

1. **Click the Slide 2 thumbnail in the Slides tab, click the Layout button in the Slides group on the Ribbon, then click Two Content**
   The slide layout changes to the Two Content layout to accommodate a new picture.

> **QUICK TIP**
> You can also insert a picture by clicking the Pictures button in the Images group on the Insert tab.

2. **Click the Pictures icon in the content placeholder on the slide, navigate to the location where you store your Data Files, select the picture file Support_PPT_1_Woman.jpg, then click Insert**
   The Insert Picture dialog box opens displaying the pictures available in the default Pictures folder. The newly inserted picture fills the content placeholder on the slide, and the Picture Format tab opens on the Ribbon. The Design Ideas pane also opens offering you design suggestions for the slide.

> **QUICK TIP**
> To select all the objects on a slide, click the Home tab on the Ribbon, click the Select arrow in the Editing group, then click Select All.

3. **Click the Close button in the Design Ideas pane, then place the pointer over the middle-left sizing handle on the picture**
   The pointer changes to ⇔.
4. **Drag the sizing handle to the left as shown in FIGURE 1-16, then release the mouse button**
   Dragging any of the middle sizing handles resizes the picture non-proportionally, whereas dragging one of the corner sizing handles resizes the picture proportionally. The picture would look better if it was resized proportionally.
5. **Click the Undo button in the Quick Access Toolbar on the title bar**
   The picture reverts to its original size.

> **QUICK TIP**
> You can also resize a picture proportionally by entering specific height or width values in the Height or Width text boxes in the Size group on the Picture Format tab.

6. **Place the pointer over the top-left sizing handle, then drag to the left until the picture edge is just under the word "Between" in the title**
   The picture is now resized proportionally. To see a portion of a slide close up, you can zoom in.
7. **Drag the Zoom slider on the status bar to the right until the picture fills the screen**
   The selected picture fills the screen.
8. **Click the Fit slide to current window button on the status bar, click a blank area of the slide, then save your work**
   The zoom setting returns to its previous position and the slide fits in the PowerPoint window. Compare your screen to **FIGURE 1-17**.
9. **Click the File tab on the Ribbon, then click Close**
   The presentation file closes.

FIGURE 1-16: Picture sized non-proportionally

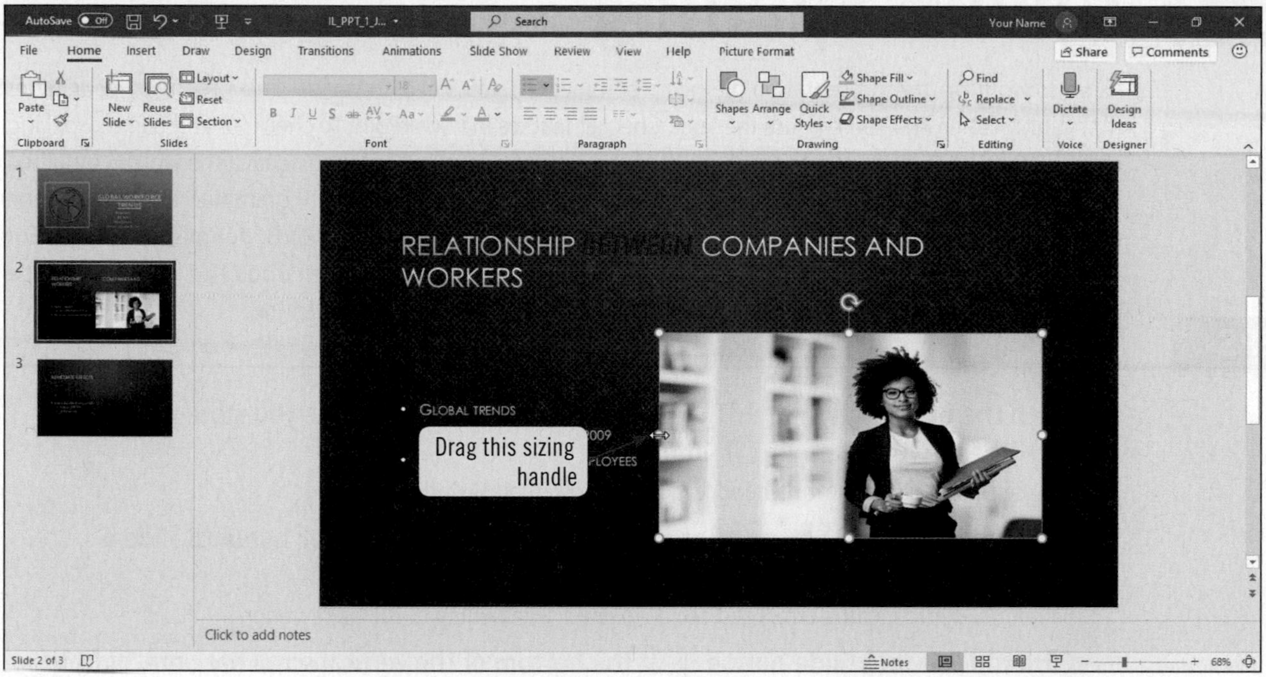

Asier Romero/Shutterstock.com

FIGURE 1-17: Picture sized proportionally

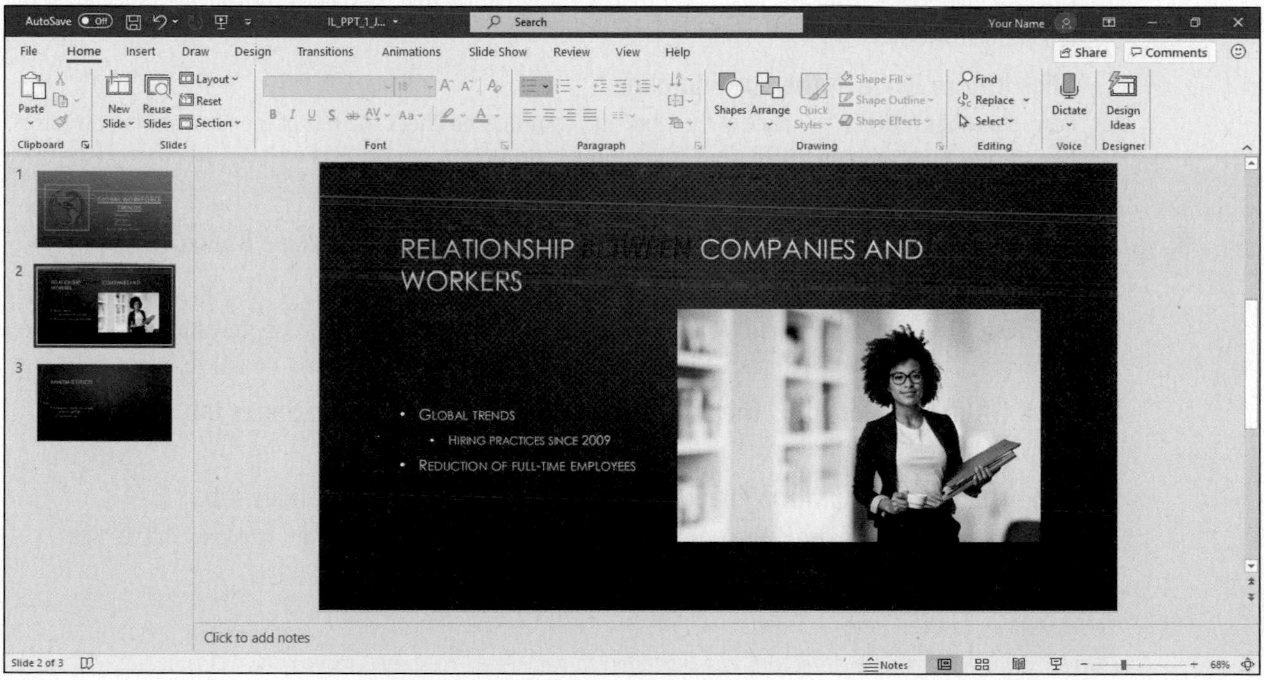

Asier Romero/Shutterstock.com

PowerPoint

Check Spelling

Learning Outcome
- Spell check a presentation

As your work on the presentation file nears completion, you need to review and proofread your slides thoroughly for errors. You can use the Spell Checker feature in PowerPoint to check for and correct spelling errors. This feature compares the spelling of all the words in your presentation against the words contained in the dictionary. You still must proofread your presentation for punctuation, grammar, and word-usage errors because the Spell Checker recognizes only misspelled and unknown words, not misused words. For example, the spell checker would not identify the word "last" as an error, even if you had intended to type the word "past." **CASE** *You've been given a presentation by a colleague to review.*

STEPS

1. **Open the presentation IL_PPT_1-1.pptx from the location where you store your Data Files, then save it as IL_PPT_1_Interview**
   A presentation with a new name appears in the PowerPoint window.
2. **Click the Next Slide button at the bottom of the vertical scroll bar until Slide 4 appears**
   You notice some spelling errors and decide to check the spelling of the presentation.
3. **Click the Previous Slide button at the bottom of the vertical scroll bar until Slide 1 appears, then click the Review tab on the Ribbon**
4. **Click the Spelling button in the Proofing group**
   PowerPoint begins to check the spelling in your presentation. When PowerPoint finds a misspelled word or a word that is not in its dictionary, the Spelling pane opens, as shown in **FIGURE 1-18**. In this case, the Spell Checker identifies a name on Slide 1, but it does not recognize that it's spelled correctly and suggests some replacement words.
5. **Click Ignore Once in the Spelling pane**
   PowerPoint ignores this instance of the word and continues to check the rest of the presentation for errors. PowerPoint finds the misspelled word "professional" on Slide 2.
6. **Click the Change All button in the Spelling pane**
   All instances of this misspelled word are corrected. The word "settings" on Slide 3 is also misspelled.
7. **Click the Change button in the Spelling pane**
   The misspelled word is corrected. When the Spell Checker finishes checking your presentation, the Spelling pane closes, and an alert box opens with a message stating the spelling check is complete.
8. **Click OK in the Alert box, then click the Slide 4 thumbnail in the Slides tab**
   The alert box closes.
9. **Drag the Slide 4 thumbnail between Slide 1 and Slide 2 in the Slides tab.**
   Slide 4 moves and becomes the second slide in the presentation. Compare your screen to **FIGURE 1-19**.

FIGURE 1-18: Window with Spelling pane open

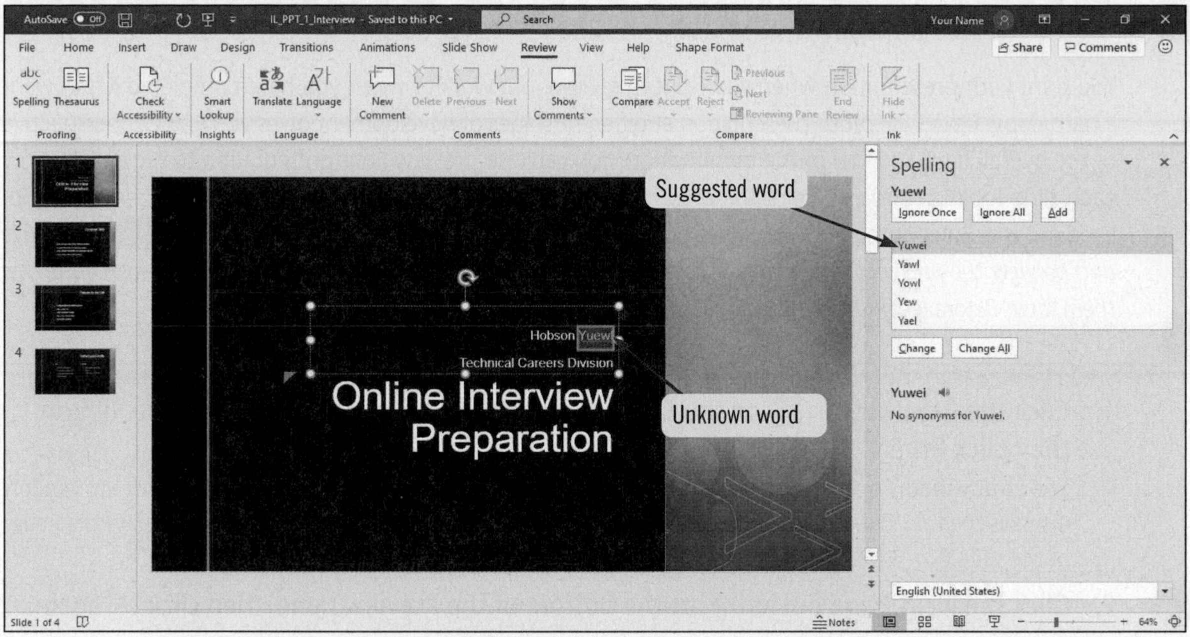

FIGURE 1-19: Moved slide

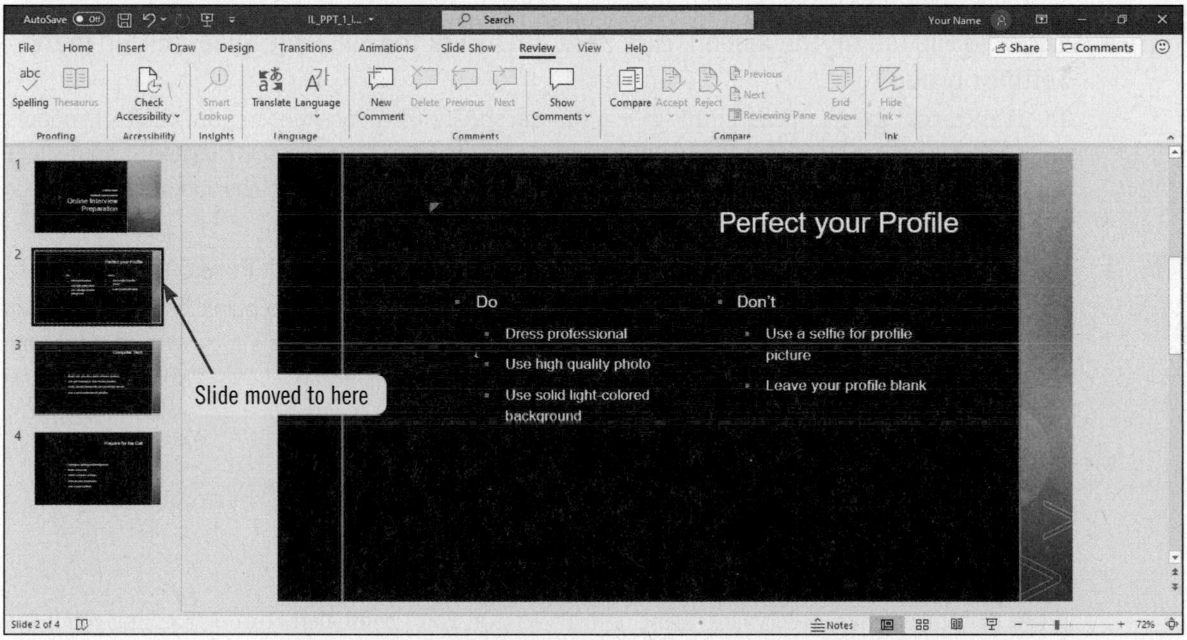

Checking spelling as you type

By default, PowerPoint checks your spelling as you type. If you type a word that is not in the dictionary, a wavy red line appears under it. To correct an error, right-click the misspelled word, then review the suggestions, which appear in the shortcut menu. You can select a suggestion, add the word you typed to your custom dictionary, or ignore it. To turn off automatic spell checking, click the File tab, then click Options to open the PowerPoint Options dialog box. Click Proofing in the left column, then click the Check spelling as you type check box to deselect it. To temporarily hide the wavy red lines, click the Hide spelling and grammar errors check box to select it. Contextual spelling in PowerPoint identifies common grammatically misused words; for example, if you type the word "their" and the correct word is "there," PowerPoint will identify the mistake and place a wavy red line under the word. To turn contextual spelling on or off, click Proofing in the PowerPoint Options dialog box, then click the Check grammar with spelling check box.

Print a PowerPoint Presentation

Learning Outcomes
- Print a presentation
- Set print settings
- Modify color settings

You print your presentation when you want to review your work or when you have completed it and want a hard copy. Reviewing your presentation at different stages of development gives you a better perspective of the overall flow and feel of the presentation. You can also preview your presentation to see exactly how each slide looks before you print the presentation. When you are finished working on your presentation, even if it is not yet complete, you can close the presentation file and exit PowerPoint. **CASE** *You save and preview the presentation, then you print the slides and notes pages of the presentation so you can review them later. Before leaving for the day, you close the file and exit PowerPoint.*

STEPS

1. **Click the Save button on the Quick Access Toolbar, click the File tab on the Ribbon, then click Print**
   The Print window opens, as shown in **FIGURE 1-20**. Notice the Preview pane on the right side of the window displays the first slide of the presentation. If you do not have a color printer, you will see a grayscale image of the slide.
2. **Click the Next Page button at the bottom of the Preview pane, then click again**
   The slides of the presentation appear in the Preview pane.
3. **Click the Print button**
   Each slide in the presentation prints.
4. **Click the File tab on the Ribbon, click Print, then click the Full Page Slides button in the Settings group**
   The Print Layout gallery opens. In this gallery you can specify what you want to print (slides, handouts, notes pages, or outline), as well as other print options. To save paper when you are reviewing your slides, you can print in handout format, which lets you print up to nine slides per page. The options you choose in the Print window remain there until you change them or close the presentation.
5. **Click 3 Slides, click the Color button in the Settings group, then click Pure Black and White**
   PowerPoint removes the color and displays the slides as thumbnails next to blank lines, as shown in **FIGURE 1-21**. Using the Handouts with three slides per page printing option is a great way to print your presentation when you want to provide a way for audience members to take notes. Printing pure black-and-white prints without any gray tones can save printer toner.
6. **Click the Print button**
   The presentation prints one page showing all the slides of the presentation as thumbnails next to blank lines.
7. **Click the File tab on the Ribbon, then click Close**
   If you have made changes to your presentation, a Microsoft PowerPoint alert box opens asking you if you want to save changes you have made to your presentation file.
8. **Click Save, if necessary, to close the alert box**
   Your presentation closes.
9. **sam Click the Close button on the Title bar**
   The PowerPoint program closes, and you return to the Windows desktop.

QUICK TIP
To quickly print the presentation with the current Print options, add the Quick Print button to the Quick Access Toolbar.

QUICK TIP
To print slides appropriate in size for overhead transparencies, click the Design tab, click the Slide Size button in the Customize group, click Custom Slide Size, click the Slides sized for arrow, then click Overhead.

FIGURE 1-20: Print window

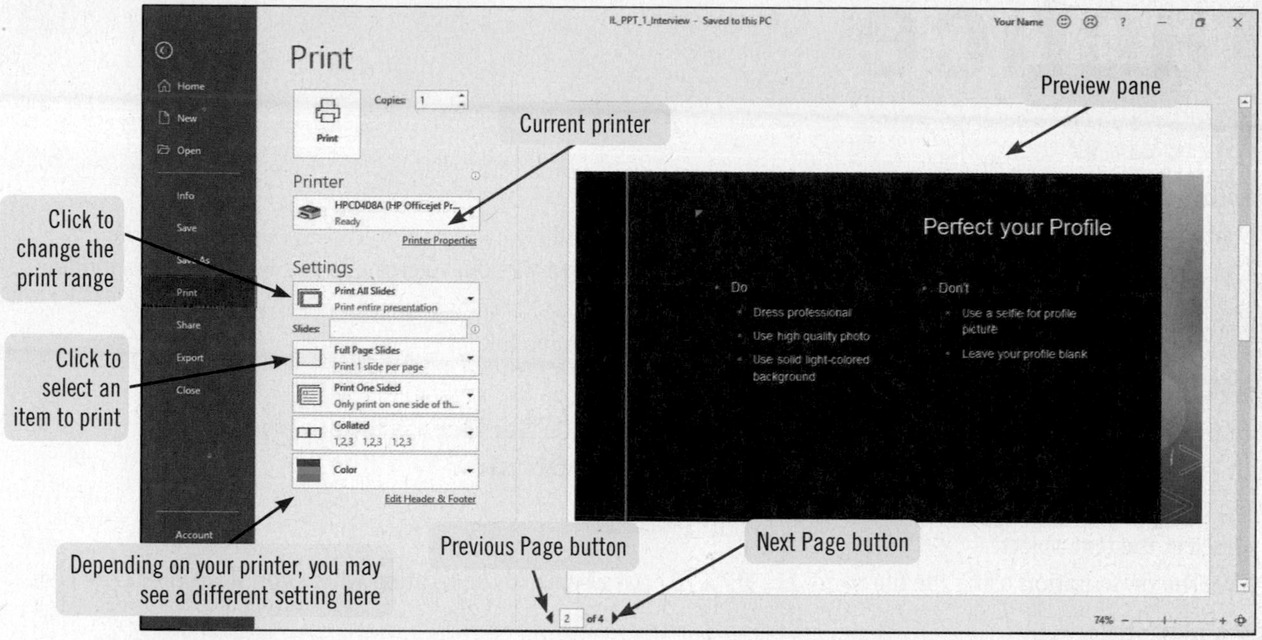

FIGURE 1-21: Print window with changed settings

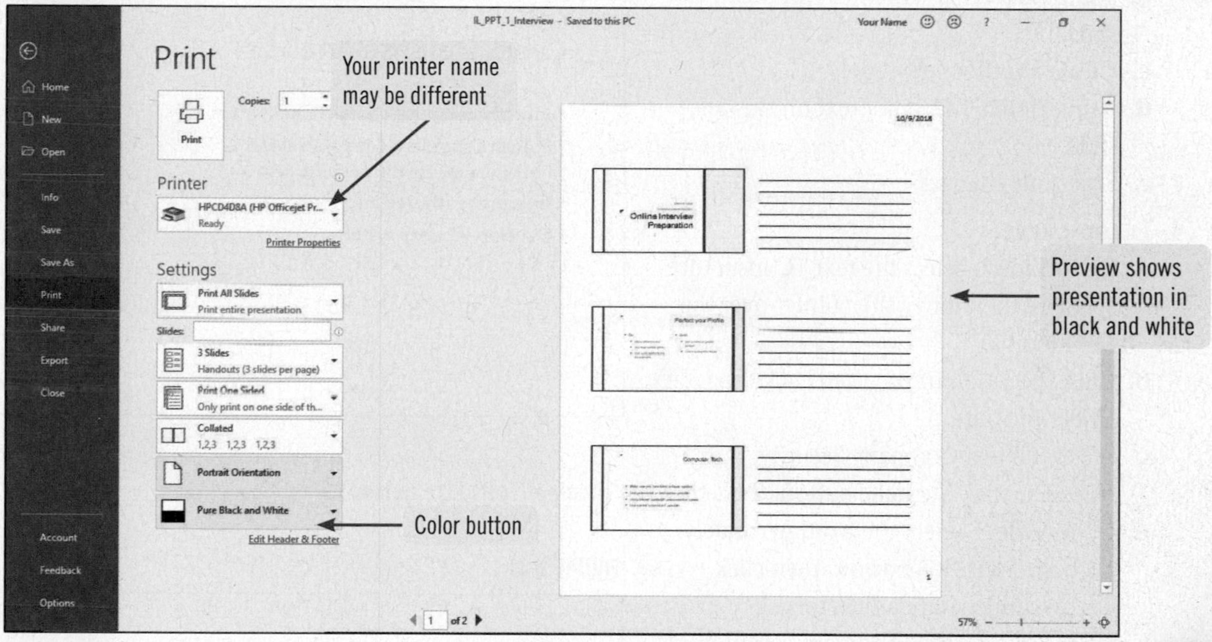

Office for the Web Apps

Some Office programs, PowerPoint for example, include the capability to incorporate feedback—called online collaboration—across the Internet or a company network. Using **cloud computing** (work done in a virtual environment), you can take advantage of web programs called Microsoft 365, which are simplified versions of the programs found in the Microsoft Office suite. Because these programs are online, they take up no computer disk space and are accessed using Microsoft OneDrive, a free service from Microsoft. Using Microsoft OneDrive, you and your colleagues can create and store documents in the "cloud" and make the documents available to whomever you grant access. To use Microsoft OneDrive, you need to create a free Microsoft account, which you obtain at the Microsoft website.

Practice

Skills Review

1. **Examine the PowerPoint window.**
   a. Start PowerPoint, if necessary then open a new blank presentation.
   b. Identify as many elements of the PowerPoint window as you can without referring to the lessons in this module.
   c. Be able to describe the purpose or function of each element.
   d. For any elements you cannot identify, refer to the lessons in this module.
2. **Enter slide text.**
   a. In the Slide pane in Normal view, enter the text **TC Insurance Services** in the title placeholder.
   b. In the subtitle text placeholder, enter **Company Security Division**.
   c. On the next line of the placeholder, enter your name.
   d. Deselect the text object.
   e. Save the presentation using the file name **IL_PPT_1_Analysis** to the location where you store your Data Files.
3. **Add a new slide.**
   a. Create a new slide using the Title and Content layout.
   b. Using **FIGURE 1-22**, enter text on the slide.
   c. Create another new slide.
   d. Using **FIGURE 1-23**, enter text on the slide.
   e. Save your changes.
4. **Format text.**
   a. Go to Slide 1, select the text TC Insurance Services, then move the pointer over the Mini toolbar.
   b. Click the Bold button, then click the Underline button.
   c. Select the text Company Security Division, click the Italic button, then click the Increase Font Size button.
   d. Go to Slide 2, select the word Accurately, click the Font Color arrow, then click Orange under Standard Colors.
   e. Go to Slide 3, select the word common in the third bullet point, click the Font Size arrow, then click 32.
   f. Click the Font button, click Algerian, then save your changes.

FIGURE 1-22

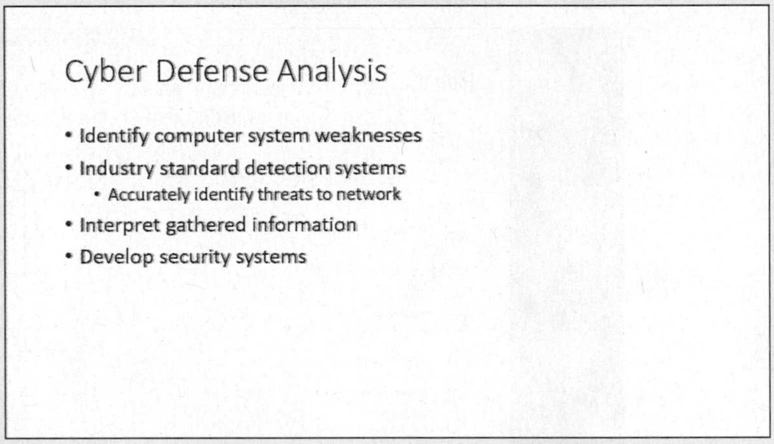

Cyber Defense Analysis
• Identify computer system weaknesses
• Industry standard detection systems
• Accurately identify threats to network
• Interpret gathered information
• Develop security systems

FIGURE 1-23

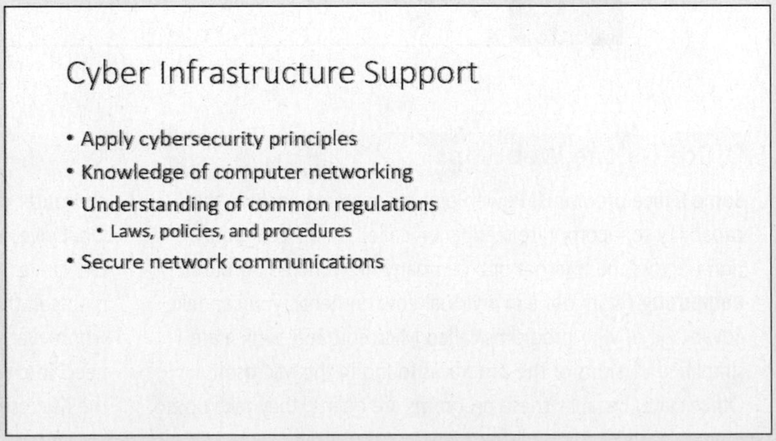

Cyber Infrastructure Support
• Apply cybersecurity principles
• Knowledge of computer networking
• Understanding of common regulations
• Laws, policies, and procedures
• Secure network communications

Skills Review (continued)

5. **Apply a design theme.**
   a. Click the Design tab.
   b. Click the Themes group More button, then point to all of the themes.
   c. Locate the Madison theme, then apply it to the selected slide.
   d. Go to Slide 1, click the Themes group More button, locate the Ion Boardroom theme, then apply it to Slide 1.
   e. Apply the Ion Boardroom theme to all of the slides in the presentation.
   f. Click the first design in the Design Ideas pane, then close the Design Ideas pane.
   g. Use the Next Slide button to move to Slide 2, then save your changes.
6. **Compare presentation views.**
   a. Click the View tab, then click the Slide Sorter button in the Presentation Views group.
   b. Click the Normal button in the Presentation Views group, then click the Notes button on the status bar.
   c. Click the Notes button on the status bar, then click the Next Slide button.
   d. Click the Slide Show button on the status bar.
   e. Click the More slide show options button, click Show Presenter View, then click the Pause button.
   f. Click the More slide show options button, then click Hide Presenter View.
   g. Advance the slides until a black screen appears, then click to end the presentation.
   h. Save your changes.
7. **Insert and resize a picture.**
   a. Select Slide 2 in the Slides tab, then click the Home tab.
   b. Click the Layout button, change the slide layout to Two Content, then insert the picture **Support_PPT_1_Group.jpg** from the location where you store your Data Files.
   c. Close the Design Ideas pane, then drag the left-middle sizing handle to the left.
   d. Click the Undo button, then drag the bottom-left corner sizing handle down to the left to increase the picture size.
   e. Drag the Zoom slider on the status bar to the right until 100% appears next to the Zoom slider.
   f. Click the Fit slide to current window button on the status bar, save your changes, then close the presentation.
8. **Check spelling.**
   a. Open the presentation IL_PPT_1-2.pptx from the location where you store your Data Files, then save it as **IL_PPT_ 1_Emergency**.
   b. Click the Next Slide button at the bottom of the vertical scroll bar.
   c. Click the Previous Slide button at the bottom of the vertical scroll bar until Slide 1 appears, then click the Review tab.
   d. Click the Spelling button in the Proofing group. The word incident is misspelled on Slide 2.
   e. Make sure the word incident is selected in the Spelling pane, then click the Change All button. The word Responsibilities is also misspelled.
   f. Click the Change button in the Spelling pane. A correctly spelled abbreviation appears in the Spelling pane.
   g. Click the Ignore All button.
   h. Click OK in the alert box, then save your changes.
9. **Print a PowerPoint presentation.**
   a. Print all the slides as handouts, 3 Slides, in color.
   b. Close the file, saving your changes.
   c. Exit PowerPoint.

Independent Challenge 1

You work for Riverwalk Medical Clinic (RMC), a large medical facility in Cambridge, Massachusetts. You have been asked to put together a presentation on the hospital's internship program. The presentation will be used to recruit interns from local colleges.

- **a.** Start PowerPoint, then open a new blank presentation.
- **b.** In the title placeholder on Slide 1, type **Riverwalk Medical Clinic**.
- **c.** In the subtitle placeholder, type **Medical Internship Program**, press ENTER, then type your name.
- **d.** Underline the text Medical Internship Program, then italicize your name.
- **e.** Save your presentation with the file name **IL_PPT_1_Intern** to the location where you store your Data Files.
- **f.** Use **FIGURE 1-24** and **FIGURE 1-25** to add two more slides to your presentation then select Slide 1.
- **g.** Apply the Wood Type design theme to the presentation, click the sixth design theme from the top in the Design Ideas pane, then close the Design Ideas pane.
- **h.** On Slide 3 format the color, font type, and font size of the words Oral interview to Red, 24 pt, Arial Black.
- **i.** Use the buttons on the View tab to switch between PowerPoint's views, then open and close Presenter View.
- **j.** Print the presentation using handouts, 3 Slides, in black and white.
- **k.** Save and close the file, then exit PowerPoint.

FIGURE 1-24

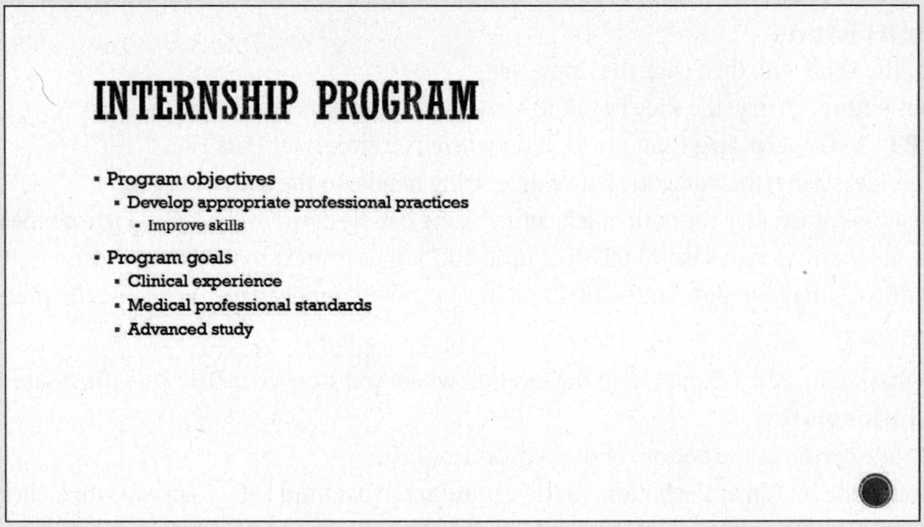

INTERNSHIP PROGRAM
Program objectives
Develop appropriate professional practices
Improve skills
Program goals
Clinical experience
Medical professional standards
Advanced study

FIGURE 1-25

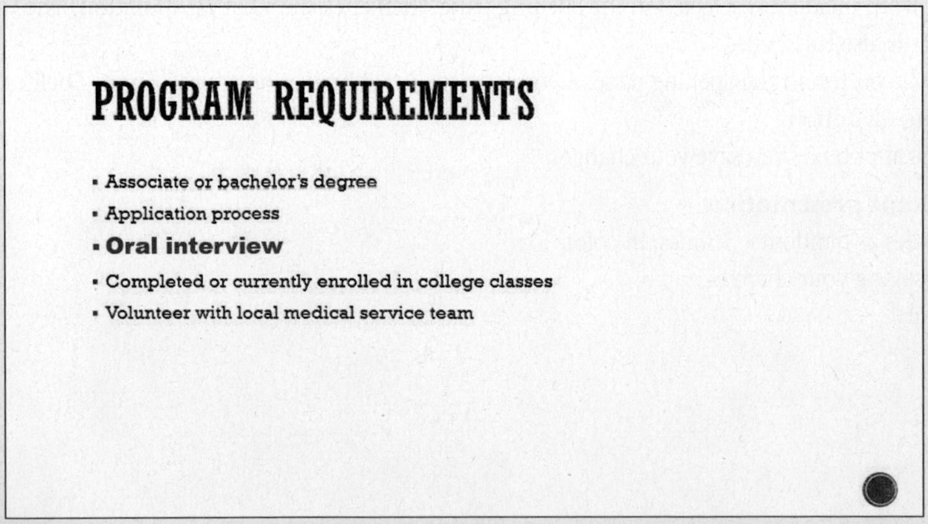

PROGRAM REQUIREMENTS
Associate or bachelor's degree
Application process

Completed or currently enrolled in college classes
Volunteer with local medical service team

Independent Challenge 2

You are an assistant in the Computer Science Department at City College and you have been asked to create a presentation on a new course being offered on artificial intelligence (AI). AI is a fast-growing industry and the Computer Science Dept. wants to have relevant classes for students to better prepare them for future jobs. You have already started working on the presentation and now you add and resize a picture, add a design theme, and run a spell check.

a. Start PowerPoint, open the presentation IL_PPT_1-3.pptx from the location where you store your Data Files, and save it as **IL_PPT_1_AI400**.
b. Apply the Circuit design theme to all the slides, apply a design theme from the Design Ideas pane similar to one shown in **FIGURE 1-26**, then close the Design Ideas pane.
c. Spell check the presentation. There is a misspelled word on Slide 3.
d. Drag Slide 3 above Slide 2 in the Slides tab, then change the slide layout to Two Content.
e. Insert the picture **Support_PPT_1_Group.jpg** from the location where you store your Data Files into the right content placeholder.
f. Resize the picture using a middle sizing handle, then undo the action by clicking the Undo button.
g. Resize the picture using a corner sizing handle, click the second design in the Design Ideas pane, then close the Design Ideas pane.
h. Switch views. Run through the slide show at least once.
i. Open and close Presenter view.
j. Close the presentation and exit PowerPoint.

FIGURE 1-26

PowerPoint

Visual Workshop

Create the presentation shown in **FIGURE 1-27** and **FIGURE 1-28**. Make sure you include your name on the title slide. Save the presentation as **IL_PPT_1_Allesco** to the location where you store your Data Files. Print the slides.

FIGURE 1-27

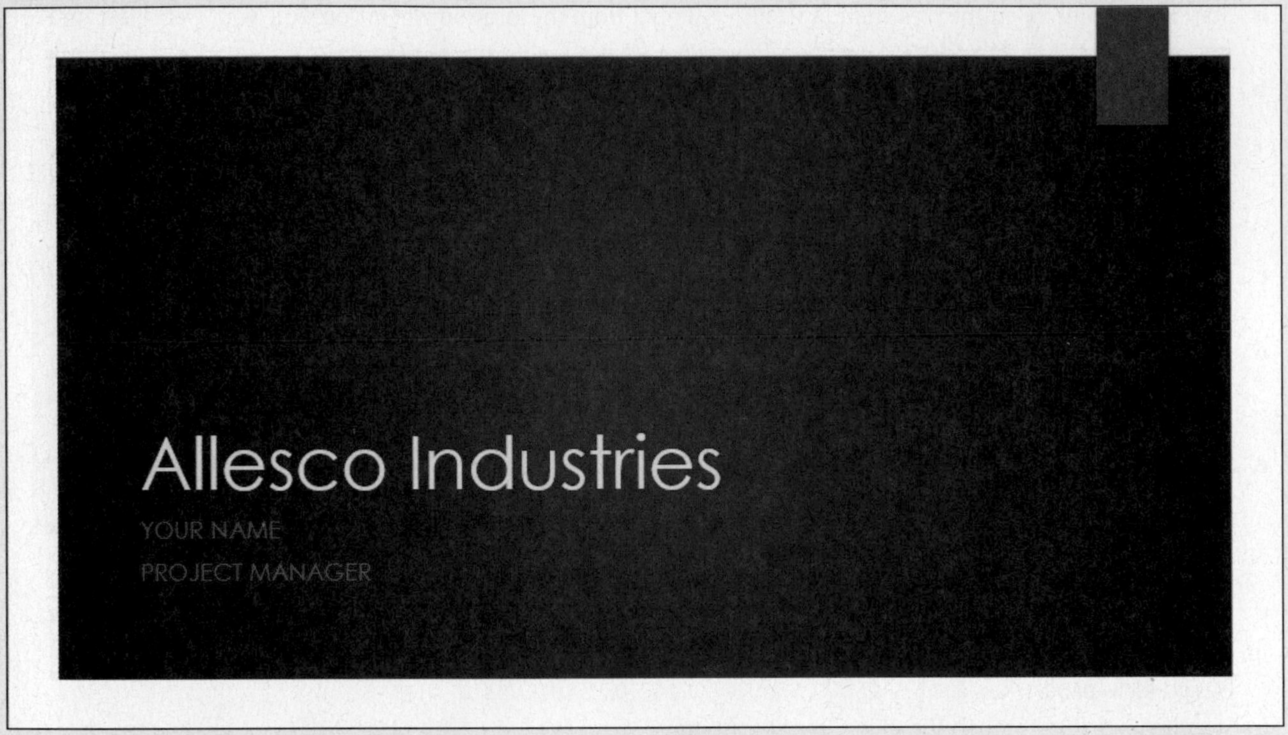

FIGURE 1-28

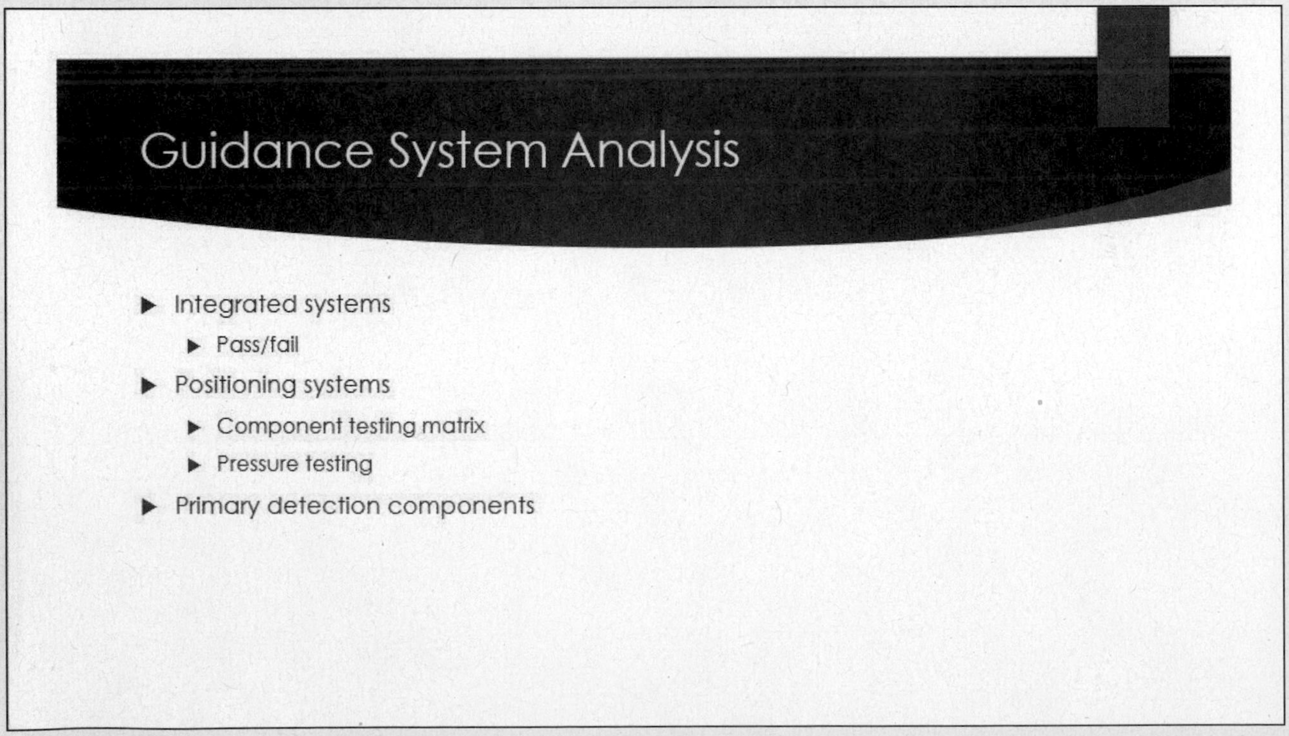

Modifying a Presentation

CASE You continue working on your global workforce presentation. In this module, you'll create a SmartArt graphic, draw and work with shapes, add slide footer information, and set slide transitions and timings in the presentation.

Module Objectives

After completing this module, you will be able to:

- Convert text to SmartArt
- Insert and style shapes
- Rotate and modify shapes
- Rearrange and merge shapes
- Edit and duplicate shapes
- Align and group objects
- Add slide footers
- Set slide transitions and timings

Files You Will Need

IL_PPT_2-1.pptx
IL_PPT_2-2.pptx
IL_PPT_2-3.pptx
IL_PPT_2-4.pptx
IL_PPT_2-5.pptx

PowerPoint
Module 2

Convert Text to SmartArt

Learning Outcomes
- Create a SmartArt graphic
- Modify the SmartArt design

Sometimes when you are working with text it just doesn't capture your attention. The ability to convert text to a SmartArt graphic provides a creative way to convey a message using text and graphics. A **SmartArt** graphic is a professional-quality diagram that graphically illustrates text. For example, you can show steps in a process or timeline, show proportional relationships, or show how parts relate to a whole. You can create a SmartArt graphic from scratch or create one by converting existing text you have entered on a slide. **CASE** *You want the presentation to appear visually dynamic, so you convert the text on Slide 4 to a SmartArt graphic.*

STEPS

1. **sam Start PowerPoint, open the presentation IL_PPT_2-1.PPTX from the location where you store your Data Files, then save it as IL_PPT_2_JCL**
   A presentation with the new filename appears in the PowerPoint window.
2. **Click the Slide 4 thumbnail in the Slides tab, click Service in the text object, then click the Convert to SmartArt Graphic button in the Paragraph group**
   A gallery of SmartArt graphic layouts opens. As with many features in PowerPoint, you can preview how your text will look prior to applying the SmartArt graphic layout by using PowerPoint's Live Preview feature. You can review each SmartArt graphic layout and see how it changes the appearance of the text.
3. **Move over the SmartArt graphic layouts in the gallery**
   Notice how the text becomes part of the graphic and changes each time you move the pointer over a different graphic layout. SmartArt graphic names appear in ScreenTips.

> **QUICK TIP**
> To enter text using the Text pane, click the Text pane control on the SmartArt graphic.

4. **Click the Vertical Block List layout in the SmartArt graphics gallery**
   A SmartArt graphic appears on the slide in place of the text object, and the SmartArt Design tab opens on the Ribbon, as shown in **FIGURE 2-1**. A SmartArt graphic consists of two parts: the SmartArt graphic and a Text pane where you type and edit text.

> **QUICK TIP**
> Text objects in the SmartArt graphic can be moved and edited like any other text object in PowerPoint.

5. **Click the SmartArt Design tab on the Ribbon, click the More button in the Layouts group, click More Layouts to open the Choose a SmartArt Graphic dialog box, click Pyramid, click the Pyramid List layout icon, then click OK**
   The SmartArt graphic changes to the new graphic layout. You can change how the SmartArt graphic looks by applying a SmartArt Style. A **SmartArt Style** is a preset combination of simple and 3-D formatting options that follows the presentation theme.
6. **Move slowly over the styles in the SmartArt Styles group, then click the More button in the SmartArt Styles group**
   A Live Preview of each style is displayed on the SmartArt graphic. The SmartArt styles are organized into sections; the top group offers suggestions for the best match for the document, and the bottom group shows you all the possible 3-D styles that are available.

> **QUICK TIP**
> Click the Convert button in the Reset group, then click Convert to Text to revert the SmartArt graphic to a standard text object.

7. **Move over the styles in the gallery, click Inset in the 3-D section, then click in a blank area of the slide outside the SmartArt graphic**
   Notice how the Inset style adds a shadow and an edge to achieve a 3-D effect. Compare your screen to **FIGURE 2-2**.
8. **Click the Slide 4 thumbnail in the Slides tab, then save your work**

FIGURE 2-1: Text converted to a Vertical Block List layout SmartArt graphic

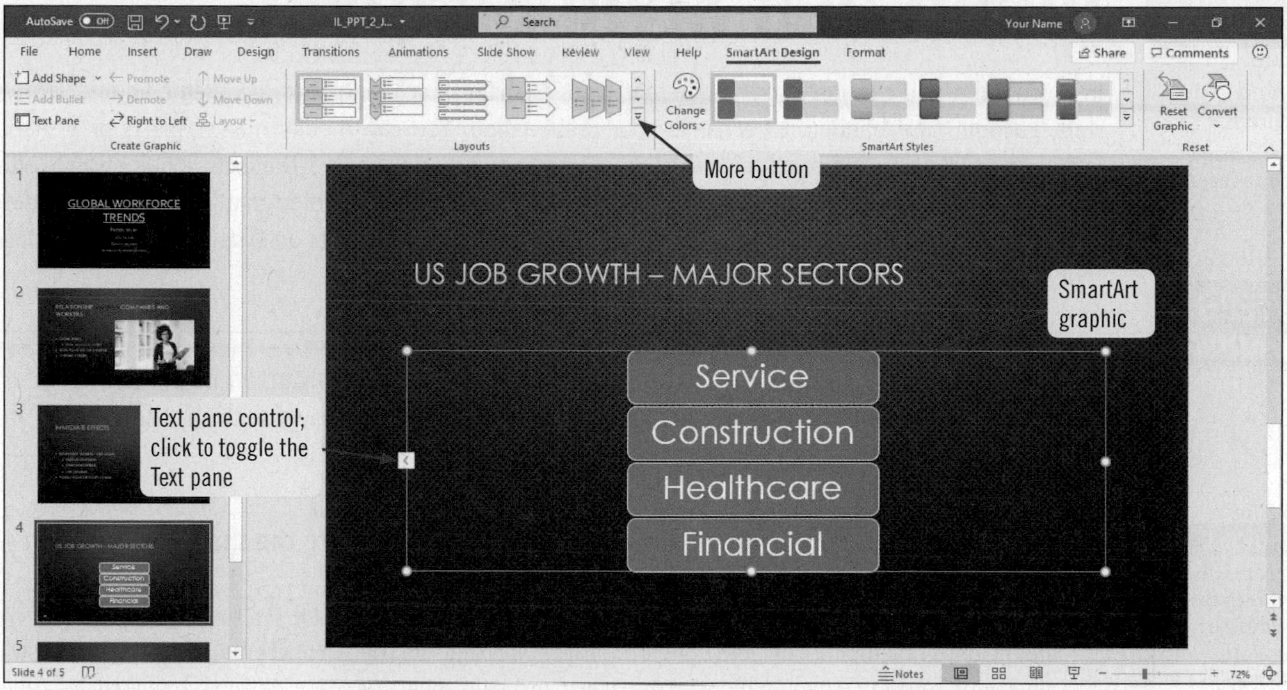

FIGURE 2-2: Final Pyramid List with Inset 3-D effect SmartArt graphic

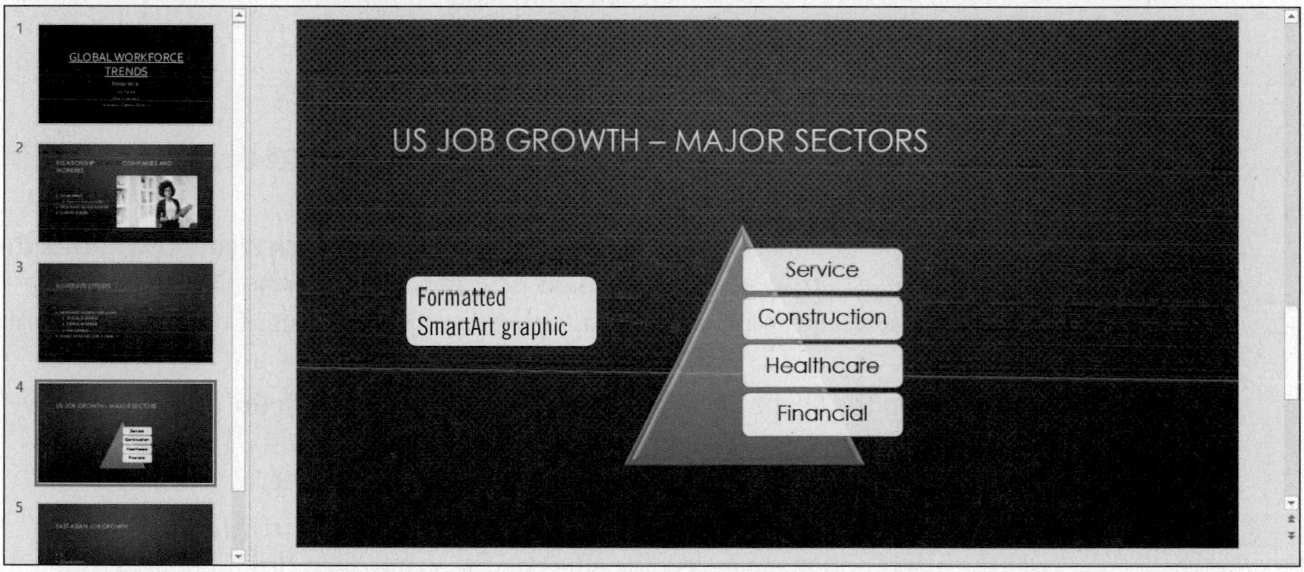

Entering and printing notes

You can add notes to your slides when there are certain facts you want to remember during a presentation or when there is additional information you want to hand out to your audience. Notes do not appear on the slides when you run a slide show. Use the Notes pane in Normal view or Notes Page view to enter notes for your slides. To open or close the Notes pane, click the Notes button on the status bar. To enter text notes on a slide, click in the Notes pane, then type the note. If you want to insert graphics as notes, you must use Notes Page view. To open Notes Page view, click the View tab on the Ribbon, then click the Notes Page button in the Presentation Views group. You can print your notes by clicking the File tab on the Ribbon to open Backstage view. Click Print, click the Full Page Slides list arrow in the Settings group (this button retains the last setting for what was printed previously so it might differ) to open the gallery, and then click Notes Pages. Once you verify your print settings, click the Print button. If you don't enter any notes in the Notes pane and print the notes pages, the slides print as large thumbnails with blank space below the thumbnails to handwrite notes.

Insert and Style Shapes

Learning Outcomes
- Create a shape
- Modify a shape's style

In PowerPoint you can insert many different types of shapes, including lines, geometric figures, arrows, stars, callouts, and banners to enhance your presentation. You can modify many aspects of a shape, including its fill color, line color, and line style, as well as add shadows and 3-D effects. A quick way to alter the appearance of a shape is to apply a Quick Style. A **Quick Style** is a set of formatting options, including line style, fill color, and effects. CASE *You decide to draw some shapes on Slide 3 of your presentation that complement the slide content.*

STEPS

1. **Click the Slide 3 thumbnail on the Slides tab, click the Shapes button in the Drawing group, click the Arrow: Pentagon button ▷ in the Block Arrows section, then position + in the blank area of Slide 3**
   ScreenTips help you identify the shapes.
2. **Press and hold SHIFT, drag + down and to the right to create the shape, as shown in FIGURE 2-3, release the mouse button, then release SHIFT**
   A block arrow shape appears on the slide, filled with the default theme color. Pressing SHIFT while you create the object maintains the object proportions as you change its size. A **rotate handle**—circular arrow—appears on top of the shape, which you can drag to manually rotate the shape. A yellow-orange circle—called an **adjustment handle**—appears in the upper-right portion of the shape. Some shapes have an adjustment handle that can be moved to change the most prominent feature of an object, in this case the shape of the arrow.
3. **Drag the adjustment handle left over the middle sizing handle**
   The tip of the arrow changes shape.
4. **Click the Shape Fill list arrow in the Shape Styles group, then click Orange, Accent 6**
   An orange fill color is applied to the shape.
5. **Click the Shape Outline list arrow in the Shape Styles group, click White, Text 1, click the Shape Outline list arrow again, point to Dashes, then click the Long Dash**
   The shape outline changes to a long white dash. You also have the option of using a Quick Style to format a shape.
6. **Click the ▾ in the Shape Styles group, move over the styles in the gallery to review the effects on the shape, then click Intense Effect—Gold, Accent 4**
   A gold Quick Style with coordinated gradient fill, line, and shadow color is applied to the shape.
7. **Click the Shape Effects button in the Shape Styles group, point to Reflection, move over the effect options to review the effect on the shape, then click Tight Reflection: Touching**
   A short faded reflection of the shape appears below the shape, as shown in FIGURE 2-4.
8. **Click a blank area of the slide, then save your work**
   Clicking a blank area of the slide deselects all selected objects.

TROUBLE
If your shape is not approximately the same size as the one shown in FIGURE 2-3, drag one of the corner sizing handles to resize the object.

QUICK TIP
To change the transparency of a shape or text object filled with a color, right-click the object, click Format Shape, click Fill, then move the Transparency slider.

FIGURE 2-3: Arrow shape added to slide

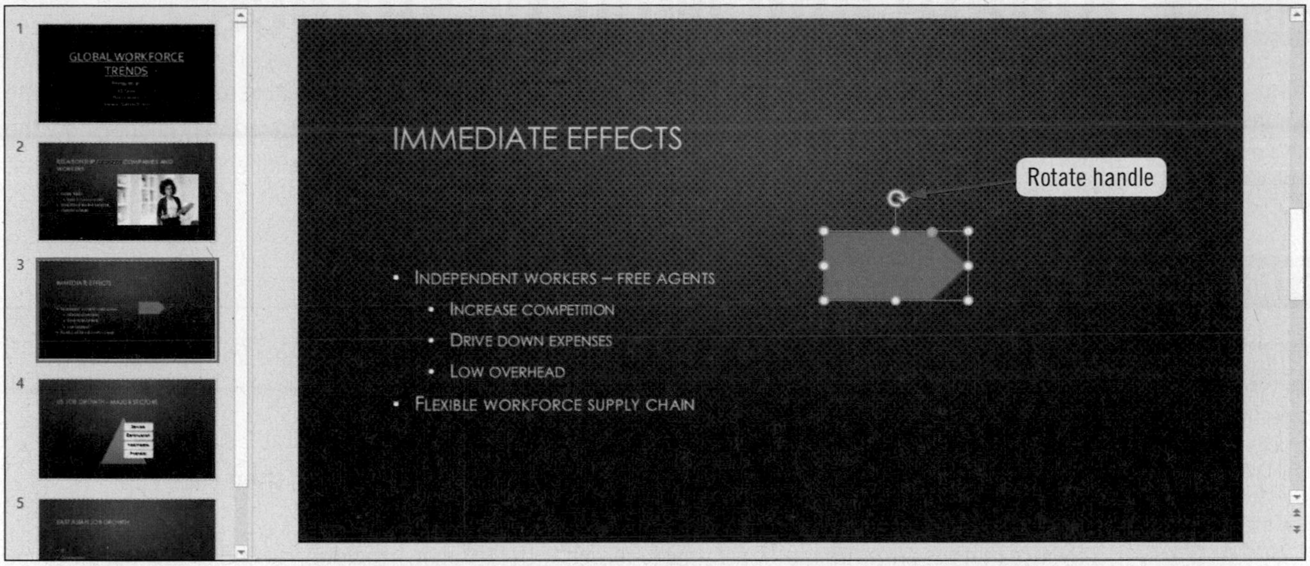

FIGURE 2-4: Styled arrow shape

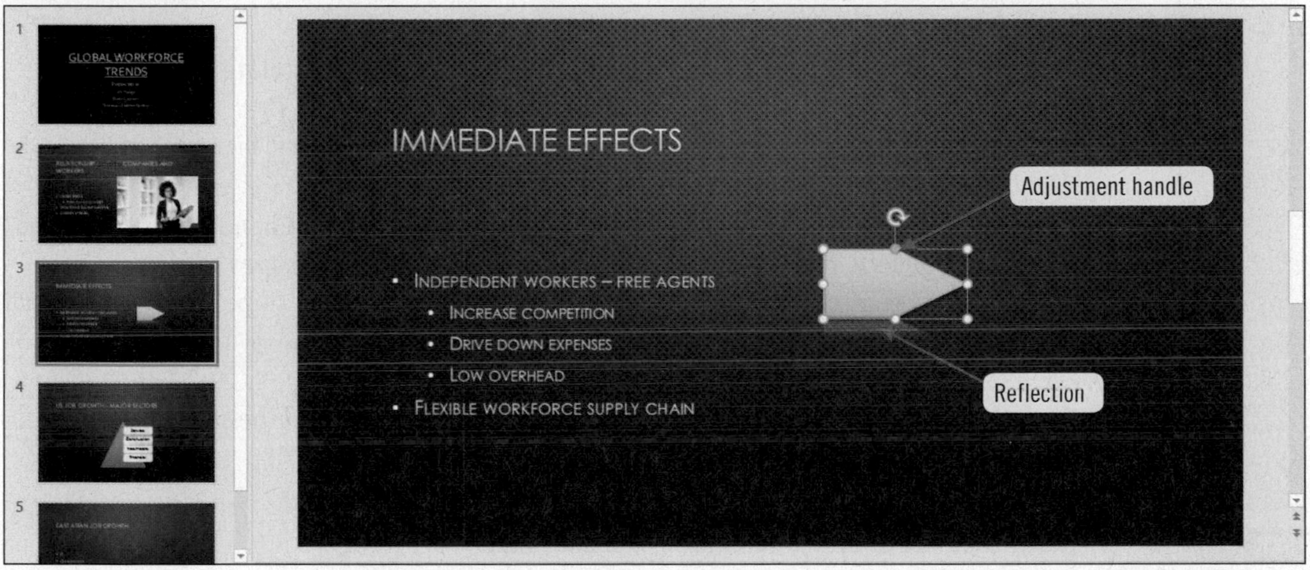

Using the Eyedropper to match colors

As you develop your presentation and work with different shapes and pictures, sometimes from other sources, there may be a certain color that is not in the theme colors of the presentation that you want to capture and apply to objects in your presentation. To capture a color on a specific slide, select any object on the slide, click any button arrow with a color feature, such as the Shape Fill button or the Shape Outline button in the Shape Styles group on the Shape Format tab, then click Eyedropper. Move the 🖉 over the color you want to capture and pause, or hover. As you hover over a color, a Live Preview of the color appears and the RGB (Red Green Blue) values, called coordinates, appear in a ScreenTip. Click when you see the color you want to capture. The new color now appears in any color gallery under Recent Colors. If you decide not to capture a new color, press ESC to close the Eyedropper without making any change.

Rotate and Modify Shapes

Learning Outcomes
- Rotate a shape
- Change a shape

Once you have created a shape, you have a number of formatting options available to you to enhance the shape. Some of these options include flipping and rotating the shape, which can radically change how the shape looks. Or, if a shape doesn't meet your needs, you can easily change to a different shape altogether.

CASE *You continue to work on the shape on Slide 3.*

STEPS

QUICK TIP
To apply a picture fill to a shape, select the shape, click the Shape Fill button in the Shape Styles group on the Shape Format tab, click Picture, then locate and insert a picture.

1. **Select the Block arrow shape on Slide 3, if necessary click the Shape Format tab on the Ribbon, then click the Rotate button in the Arrange group**
   The Rotate menu appears with two rotate options and two flip options.
2. **Move ↖ over all of the options to review the effect on the shape, then click Flip Horizontal**
   Notice that the arrow tip is now pointing to the left with the rotate handle on top, indicating that the shape has flipped horizontally, or rotated 180 degrees, as shown in **FIGURE 2-5**.
3. **Click the rotate handle on the shape, then drag to the right until the shape is approximately 45 degrees from where it started**
   The shape is now pointing toward the top of the slide and the reflection is under the shape. You decide to rotate the shape by a specific amount.
4. **Click the Undo button on the Quick Access Toolbar, click the Rotate button, then click Rotate Right 90°**
   The shape is now pointing up. It is 90 degrees from where it was just pointing and the rotate handle is to the right. It is easy to change the shape to any other shape in the shapes gallery.
5. **Click the Edit Shape button in the Insert Shapes group, point to Change Shape to open the shapes gallery, then click the Frame button in the Basic Shapes section**
   The block arrow shape changes to a frame shape. Notice that even though the shape has changed, it is still rotated 90 degrees from its original position and maintains the formatting changes you have already applied. You decide to rotate it back to its original position.
6. **Click the Rotate button, click Rotate Left 90°, click a blank area of the slide, then save your work**
   The shape is rotated back to its original position, as shown in **FIGURE 2-6**.

QUICK TIP
You can also use the Cut button in the Clipboard group on the Home tab to delete a slide.

7. **Right-click the Slide 5 thumbnail in the Slides tab**
   A shortcut menu appears with common slide commands. This slide is not needed, so you delete it from the presentation.
8. **Click Delete Slide, click the Slide 3 thumbnail in the Slides tab, then save your work**
   The fifth slide is deleted and Slide 3 appears in the Slide pane.

FIGURE 2-5: Flipped arrow shape

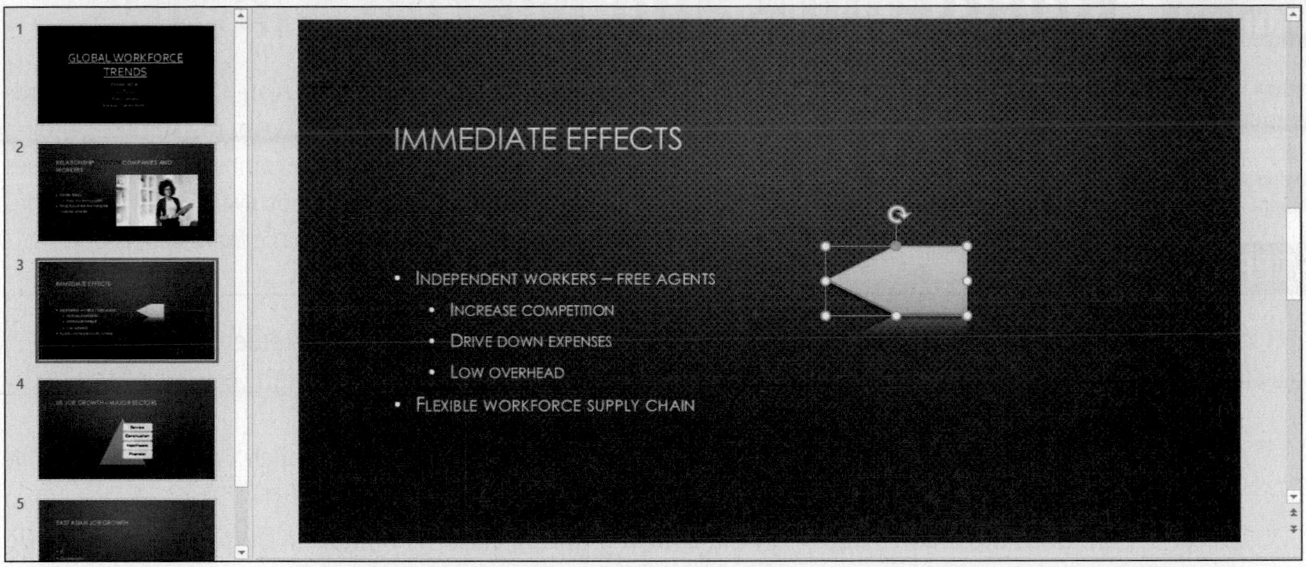

FIGURE 2-6: Frame shape

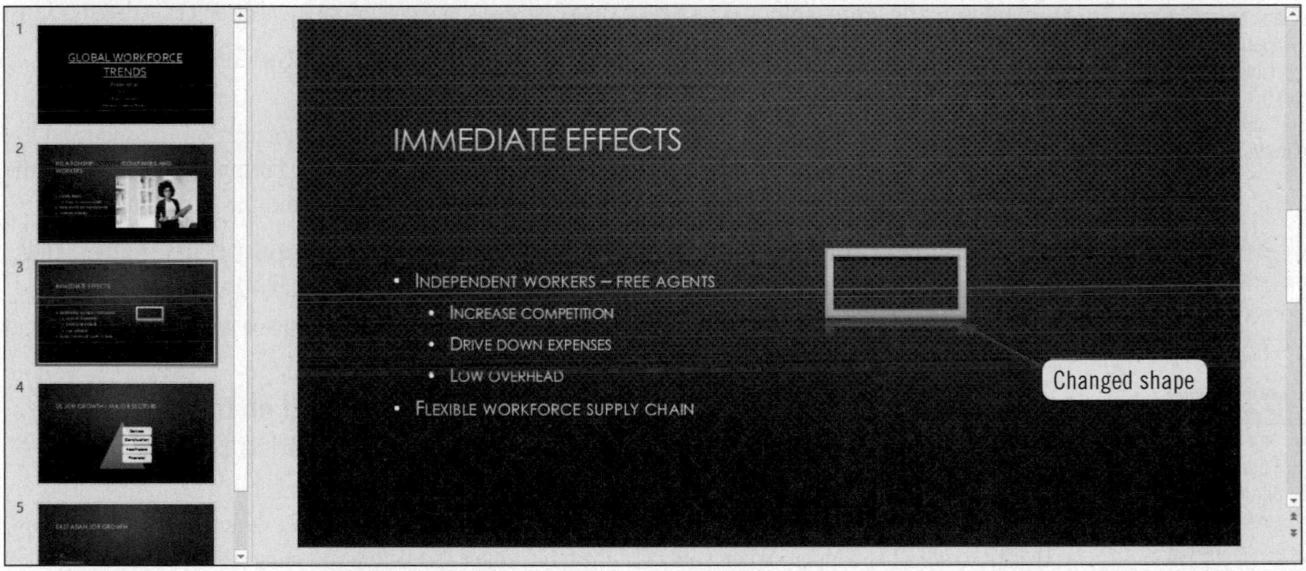

Aligning paragraph text

PowerPoint offers six ways to align paragraph text within a text object: Top, Middle, Bottom, Top Centered, Middle Centered, and Bottom Centered. To change paragraph text alignment, click the Home tab on the Ribbon, select the text you want to change, then click the Align Text button in the Paragraph group to open the Align Text menu. To see all the alignment options, click More Options in the Align Text menu, then click the Vertical alignment arrow.

Rearrange and Merge Shapes

Learning Outcomes
- Reorder shapes
- Combine shapes together

Every object on a slide is placed, or stacked, on the slide in the order it was created, like a deck of cards placed one on top of another. Each object on a slide can be moved up or down in the stack depending on how you want the objects to look on the slide. **Merging** shapes, which combines multiple shapes together, provides you the potential to create unique geometric shapes not available in the shapes gallery. **CASE** *You create a pentagon shape on Slide 3, then merge it with the frame shape.*

STEPS

1. **Click Independent in the text object, position ⇖ over the right-middle sizing handle, ⇖ changes to ⇔, then drag the sizing handle to the left until the right border of the text object is next to the word "AGENTS" in the text object**

   The width of the text object decreases. When you position ⇖ over a sizing handle, it changes to ⇔. This pointer points in different directions depending on which sizing handle it is over.

2. **Click the Shapes button in the Drawing group, click the Pentagon button ⬠ in the Basic Shapes section, press and hold SHIFT, drag down and to the right to create the shape, then release SHIFT**

   Compare your screen to FIGURE 2-7. A pentagon shape appears on the slide, filled with the default theme color. You can move shapes by dragging them on the slide.

> **TROUBLE**
> If Smart Guides do not appear, right-click a blank area of the slide, point to the Grid and Guides arrow on the shortcut menu, then click Smart Guides.

3. **Drag the pentagon shape over the frame shape, then use the Smart Guides that appear to position the pentagon shape in the center of the frame shape where the guides intersect**

   Smart Guides help you position objects relative to each other and determine equal distances between objects.

4. **Click the Selection Pane button in the Arrange group, then click the Send Backward button ▼ in the Selection pane once**

   The Selection pane opens on the right side of the window showing the four objects on the slide and the order they are stacked on the slide. The Send Backward and Bring Forward buttons let you change the stacking order. The pentagon shape moves back one position in the stack behind the frame shape.

5. **Press SHIFT, click the frame shape on the slide, release SHIFT to select both shapes, click the Merge Shapes button in the Insert Shapes group, then point to Union**

   The two shapes appear to merge, or combine, to form one shape. The merged shape assumes the theme and formatting style of the pentagon shape because it was selected first.

> **QUICK TIP**
> To move an object to the top of the stack, click the Bring Forward arrow in the Arrange group, then click Bring to Front. To move an object to the bottom of the stack, click the Send Backward arrow, then click Send to Back.

6. **Move ⇖ over the other merge shapes options to review the effect on the shape, click a blank area of the slide, click the pentagon shape, then click the Bring Forward button ▲ in the in the Selection pane once**

   Each merge option produces a different result. The pentagon shape moves back to the top of the stack. Now, you want to see what happens when you select the frame shape first before you merge the two shapes together.

7. **Click the frame shape, press SHIFT, click the pentagon shape, release SHIFT, click the Shape Format tab on the Ribbon, click the Merge Shapes button in the Insert Shapes group, then point to Union**

   The merged shape adopts the theme and formatting style of the frame shape.

8. **Point to each of the merge shapes options, then click Subtract**

   The two shapes merge into one shape. This merge option deletes the area of all shapes from the first shape you selected, so in this case the area of the pentagon shape is deleted from the frame shape. The merged shape is identified as a sequentially numbered Freeform in the Selection pane. See FIGURE 2-8.

9. **Click the Selection Pane button in the Arrange group, click a blank area of the slide, then save your work**

FIGURE 2-7: Pentagon shape added to slide

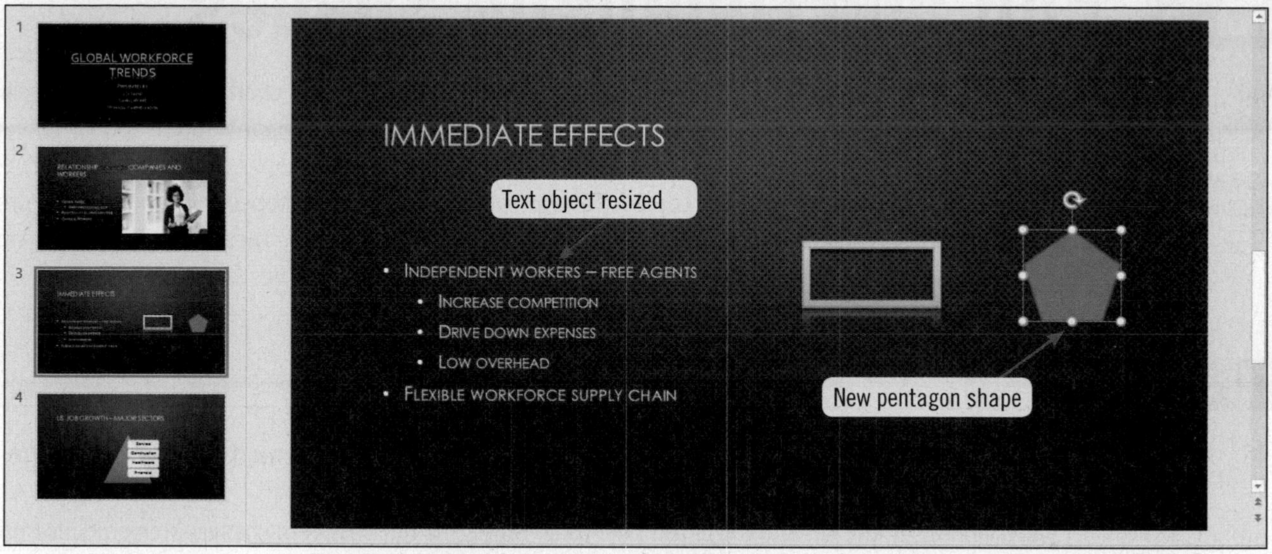

FIGURE 2-8: New Merged shape

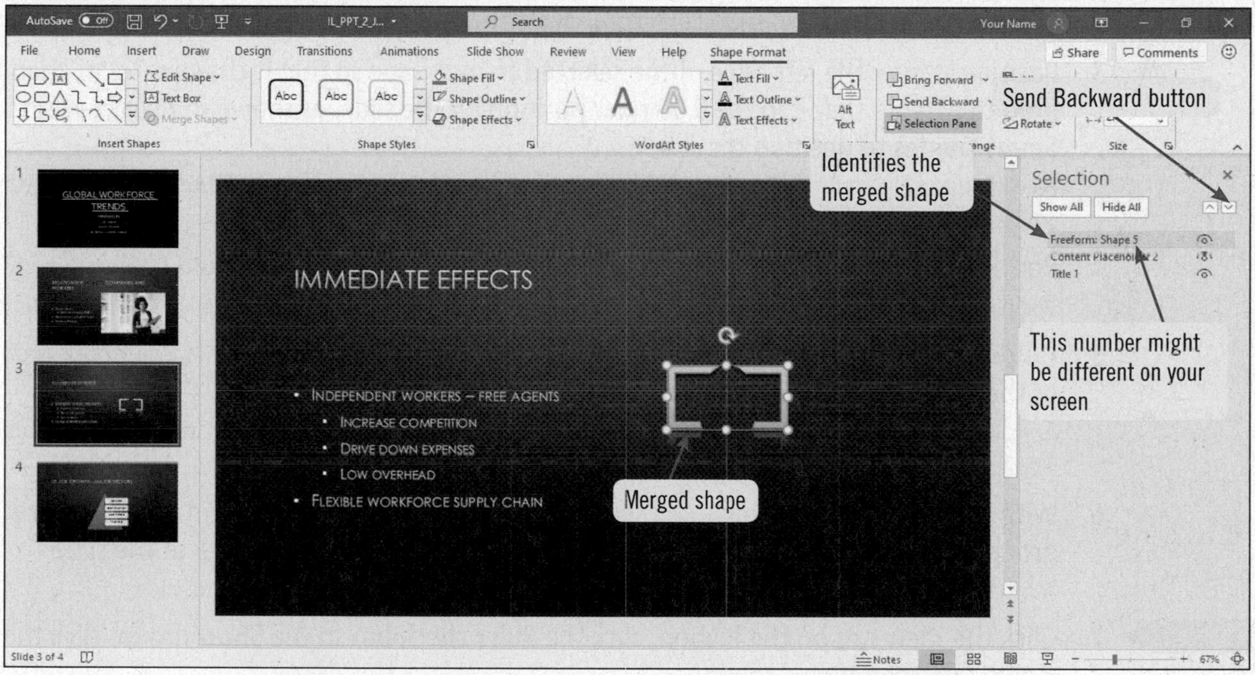

Changing the size and position of shapes

Usually when you resize a shape proportionally you can simply drag one of the corner sizing handles on the outside of the shape, but sometimes you may need to resize a shape more precisely. When you select a shape, the Shape Format tab appears on the Ribbon, offering you many different formatting options, including some sizing commands located in the Size group. The Width and Height commands in the Size group allow you to change the width and height of a shape. You also have the option to open the Format Shape pane, which allows you to change the size of a shape, as well as the rotation, scale, and position of a shape on the slide.

PowerPoint
Module 2

Edit and Duplicate Shapes

Learning Outcomes
- Modify shape, size, and design
- Duplicate shapes

Once you have created a shape, you still have the ability to refine its basic characteristics, which helps change the size and appearance of the shape. For example, if you create a shape and it is too large, you can reduce its size by dragging any of its sizing handles. Most PowerPoint shapes can have text attached to them. All shapes can be moved and copied. To help you resize and move shapes and other objects precisely, PowerPoint has rulers you can add to the Slide pane. Rulers display the measurement system your computer uses, either inches or metric measurements. **CASE** *You want three identical frame shapes on Slide 3. You first add the ruler to the slide to help you change the size of the frame shape you've already created, then you make copies of it.*

STEPS

1. **Right-click a blank area of Slide 3, click Ruler on the shortcut menu, then click the edge of the frame shape to select it**
   Rulers appear on the left and top of the Slide pane. Unless the ruler has been changed to metric measurements, it is divided into inches with ½" and ⅛" marks. Notice the current location of the pointer is identified on both rulers by a small dotted red line.
2. **Drag the middle-right sizing handle on the frame shape to the right approximately ½", then release the mouse button**
   The frame shape is now slightly wider.
3. **Position the pointer over the left edge of the selected frame shape so that it changes to the move pointer, then drag the frame shape to the 0.00 ruler position on the slide, as shown in FIGURE 2-9 using Smart Guides to position the shape**
   PowerPoint uses a series of evenly spaced horizontal and vertical lines—called **gridlines**—to align objects, which force objects to "snap" to the grid.
4. **Position the move pointer over the bottom part of the frame shape, then press and hold CTRL**
   The pointer changes to the copy pointer, indicating that PowerPoint makes a copy of the shape when you drag the mouse.
5. **Holding CTRL, drag the frame shape down until the frame shape copy is in a blank area of the slide, release the mouse button, then release CTRL**
   An identical duplicate copy of the frame shape appears on the slide and Smart Guides appear above and below the shape as you drag the new shape, which helps you align shapes.
6. **With the second frame shape still selected, click the Copy button in the Clipboard group, click the Paste button, then move the new shape to a blank area of the slide**
   You have duplicated the frame shape twice and now have three identical shapes on the slide.
7. **Click the View tab on the Ribbon, click the Ruler check box in the Show group, click the Home tab, then type Growth**
   The ruler closes, and the text you type appears in the selected frame shape and becomes a part of the shape. Now if you move or rotate the shape, the text moves with it. Compare your screen with **FIGURE 2-10**.
8. **Click the middle frame shape, type Supply, click the top frame shape, type Trends, click in a blank area of the slide, then save your work**
   All three frame shapes include text.

QUICK TIP
Press and hold ALT to temporarily turn the snap-to-grid feature off while dragging objects on the slide or dragging a sizing handle to make precise adjustments.

FIGURE 2-9: Merged shape moved on slide

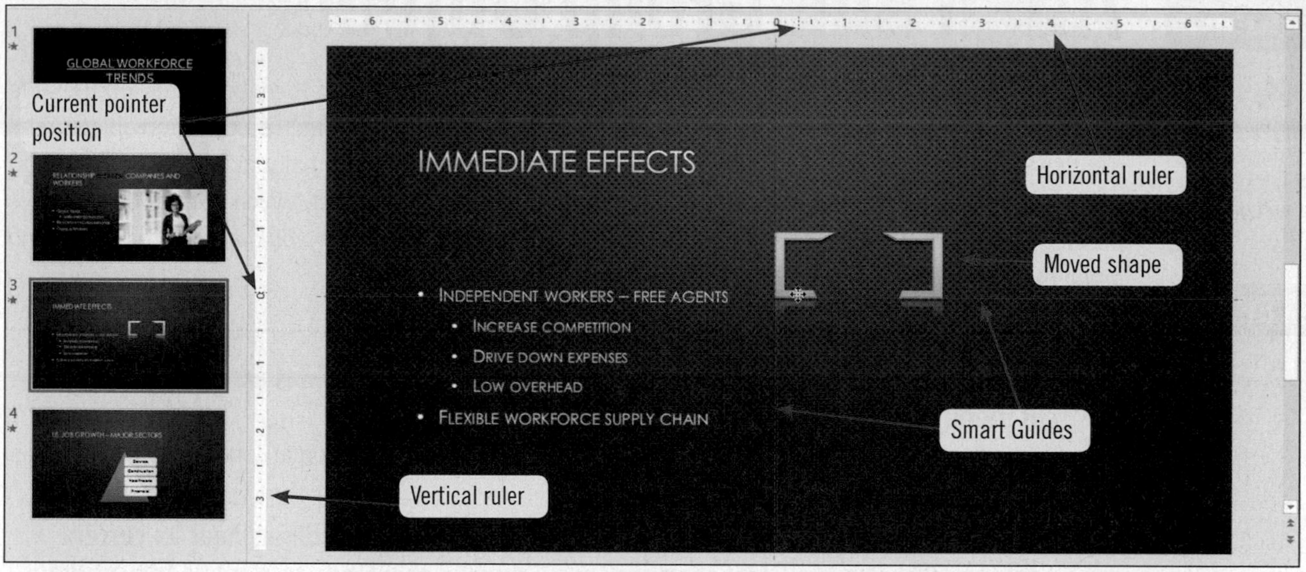

FIGURE 2-10: Duplicated shapes

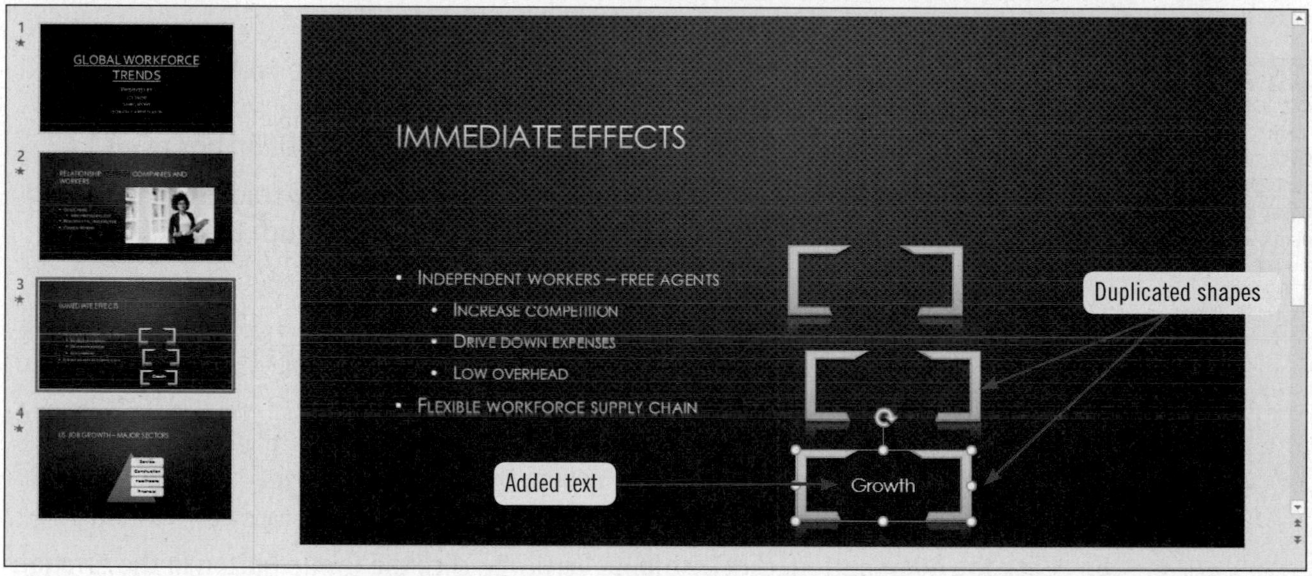

Editing points of a shape

If you want to customize the form (or outline) of any shape in the shapes gallery, you can modify its edit points. To display a shape's edit points, select the shape you want to modify, click the Shape Format tab on the Ribbon, click the Edit Shape button in the Insert Shapes group, then click Edit Points. Black edit points appear on the shape. To change the form of a shape, drag a black edit point. When you click a black edit point, white square edit points appear on either side of the black edit point, which allow you to change the curvature of a line between two black edit points. When you are finished with your custom shape, you can save it as a picture and reuse it in other presentations or other files. To save the shape as a picture, right-click the shape, then click Save as Picture.

PowerPoint **Module 2**

Align and Group Objects

Learning Outcomes
- Move shapes using guides
- Align and group shapes

After you are finished creating and modifying your objects, you can position them accurately on the slide to achieve the look you want. Using the Align commands in the Arrange group, you can align objects relative to each other by snapping them to the gridlines on a slide or to guides that you manually position on the slide. The Group command groups two or more objects into one object, which secures their relative position to each other and makes it easy to edit and move them. **CASE** *You are ready to position and group the frame shapes on Slide 3 to finish the slide.*

STEPS

1. **Right-click a blank area of the slide, point to the Grid and Guides arrow on the shortcut menu, then click Gridlines**
   Gridlines appear on the slide as a series of evenly spaced vertical and horizontal dotted lines. Gridlines can help you position objects on the slide.
2. **Drag the Trends shape until it snaps into place on a set of gridlines near its current position, click the View tab, then click the Gridlines check box to remove the gridlines**
   The shape snaps into place using gridlines.
3. **Right-click a blank area of the slide, point to Grid and Guides arrow on the shortcut menu, then click Guides**
   The guides appear as dotted lines on the slide and usually intersect at the center of the slide. Guides help you position objects precisely on the slide.
4. **Position ⇖ over the horizontal guide in a blank area of the slide, notice the pointer change to ÷, press and hold the mouse button until the pointer changes to a measurement guide box, then drag the guide up until the guide position box reads 1.83**
5. **Drag the vertical guide to the right until the guide position box reads 1.83, then drag the Trends shape so that the top and left edges of the shape touch the guides, as shown in FIGURE 2-11**
   The Trends shape attaches or "snaps" to the guides.
6. **Press and hold SHIFT, click the Supply shape, click the Growth shape, release SHIFT, then click the Shape Format tab on the Ribbon**
   All three frame shapes are now selected.
7. **Click the Align button in the Arrange group, then click Align Right**
   The two lower frame shapes move to the right and align with the top frame shape along their right edges.
8. **Click the Align button, click Distribute Vertically, click the Group button in the Arrange group, then click Group**
   The shapes are now distributed evenly among themselves and are grouped together to form one object without losing their individual attributes. Notice that the sizing handles and rotate handle now appear on the outer edge of the grouped object as shown in **FIGURE 2-12**, not around each individual object.
9. **Drag the horizontal guide to the middle of the slide until its guide position box reads 0.00, then drag the vertical guide to the middle of the slide until its guide position box reads 0.00**
10. **Click the View tab on the Ribbon, click the Guides check box in the Show group, click a blank area of the slide, then save your work**
    The guides are no longer displayed on the slide.

QUICK TIP
To quickly add a new guide to the slide, press CTRL, then drag an existing guide. The original guide remains in place. Drag a guide off the slide to delete it.

QUICK TIP
To duplicate a slide, right-click the slide thumbnail in the Slides tab, then click Duplicate Slide in the Shortcut menu.

FIGURE 2-11: Repositioned shape

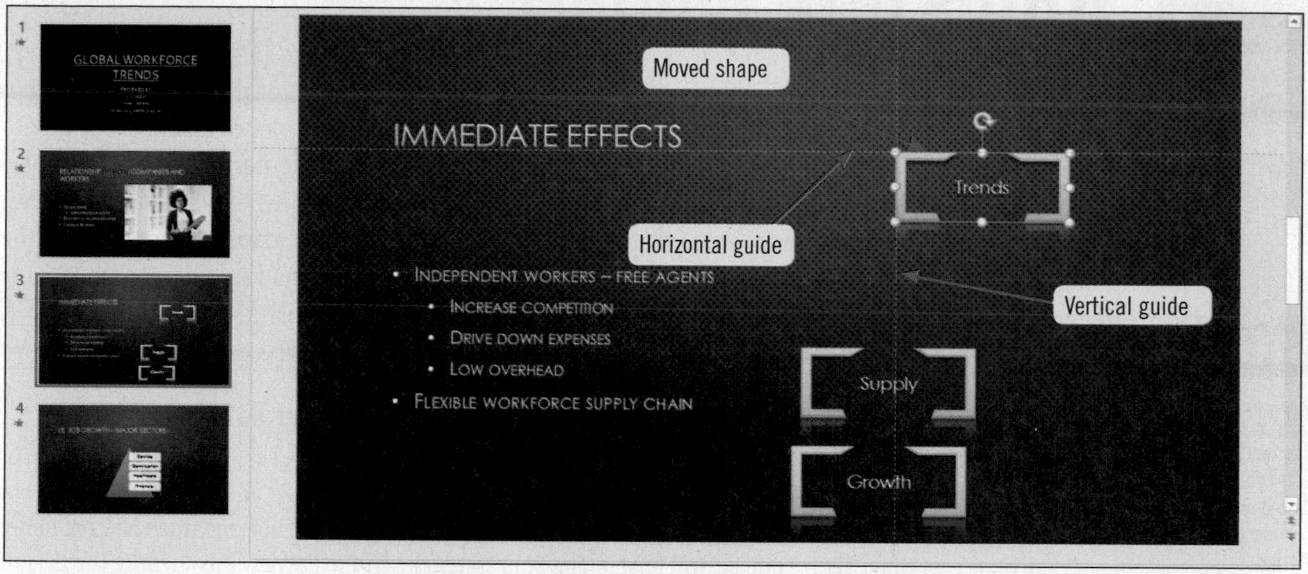

FIGURE 2-12: Grouped shapes

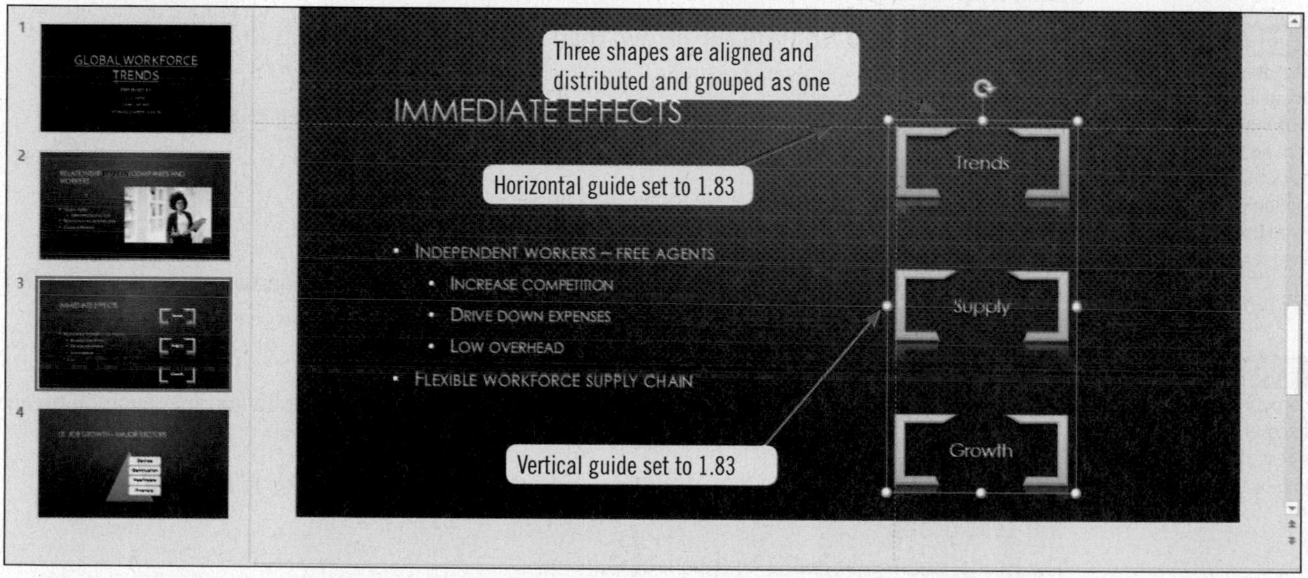

Distributing objects

There are two ways to distribute objects in PowerPoint: relative to each other and relative to the slide edge. If you choose to distribute objects relative to each other, PowerPoint evenly divides the empty space between all of the selected objects. When distributing objects in relation to the slide, PowerPoint evenly splits the empty space from slide edge to slide edge between the selected objects. To distribute objects relative to each other, click the Align button in the Arrange group on the Shape Format tab, then click Align Selected Objects. To distribute objects relative to the slide, click the Align button in the Arrange group on the Shape Format tab, then click Align to Slide.

Add Slide Footers

Learning Outcome
- Add footer text to slides

Footer text, such as a company, school, or product name, the slide number, or the date, can give your slides a professional look and make it easier for your audience to follow your presentation. Slides do not have headers. However, notes or handouts can include both header and footer text. You can review footer information that you apply to the slides in the PowerPoint views and when you print the slides. Notes and handouts header and footer text is visible when you print notes pages, handouts, and the outline. **CASE** *You add footer text that includes the date, slide number, and your name to the slides of the presentation to make it easier for the audience to follow.*

STEPS

QUICK TIP
The placement of the footer text objects on the slide is dependent on the presentation theme.

1. **Click the Insert tab on the Ribbon, then click the Header & Footer button in the Text group**
   The Header and Footer dialog box opens, as shown in **FIGURE 2-13**. The Header and Footer dialog box has two tabs: a Slide tab and a Notes and Handouts tab. The Slide tab is selected. There are three types of footer text: Date and time, Slide number, and Footer. The bold rectangles in the Preview box identify the default position of the three types of footer text placeholders on the slides.
2. **Click the Date and time check box to select it**
   The date and time options are now available to select. The Update automatically date and time option button is selected by default. This option updates the date and time to the date and time set by your computer every time you open or print the file.

QUICK TIP
If you want a specific date to appear every time you view or print the presentation, click the Fixed date option button, then type the date in the Fixed text box.

3. **Click the Update automatically arrow, then click the fourth option in the list**
   The month is spelled out in this option.
4. **Click the Slide number check box, click the Footer check box, click the Footer text box, then type your name**
   The Preview box now shows all three footer placeholders are selected.
5. **Click the Don't show on title slide check box**
   Selecting this check box prevents the footer information you entered in the Header and Footer dialog box from appearing on the title slide.

TROUBLE
If the grouped shapes cover the footer text, drag them up out of the way.

6. **Click Apply to All**
   The dialog box closes, and the footer information is applied to all of the slides in your presentation except the title slide. Compare your screen to **FIGURE 2-14**.
7. **Click the Slide 1 thumbnail in the Slides tab, then click the Header & Footer button in the Text group**
   The Header and Footer dialog box opens again.
8. **Click the Don't show on title slide check box to deselect it, click the Footer check box, then select the text in the Footer text box**

TROUBLE
If you click Apply to All in Step 9, click the Undo button on the Quick Access Toolbar and repeat Steps 7, 8, and 9.

9. **Type Always Looking Forward, click Apply, then save your work**
   The text in the Footer text box appears on the title slide. Clicking Apply applies this footer information to just the current slide.

FIGURE 2-13: Header and Footer dialog box

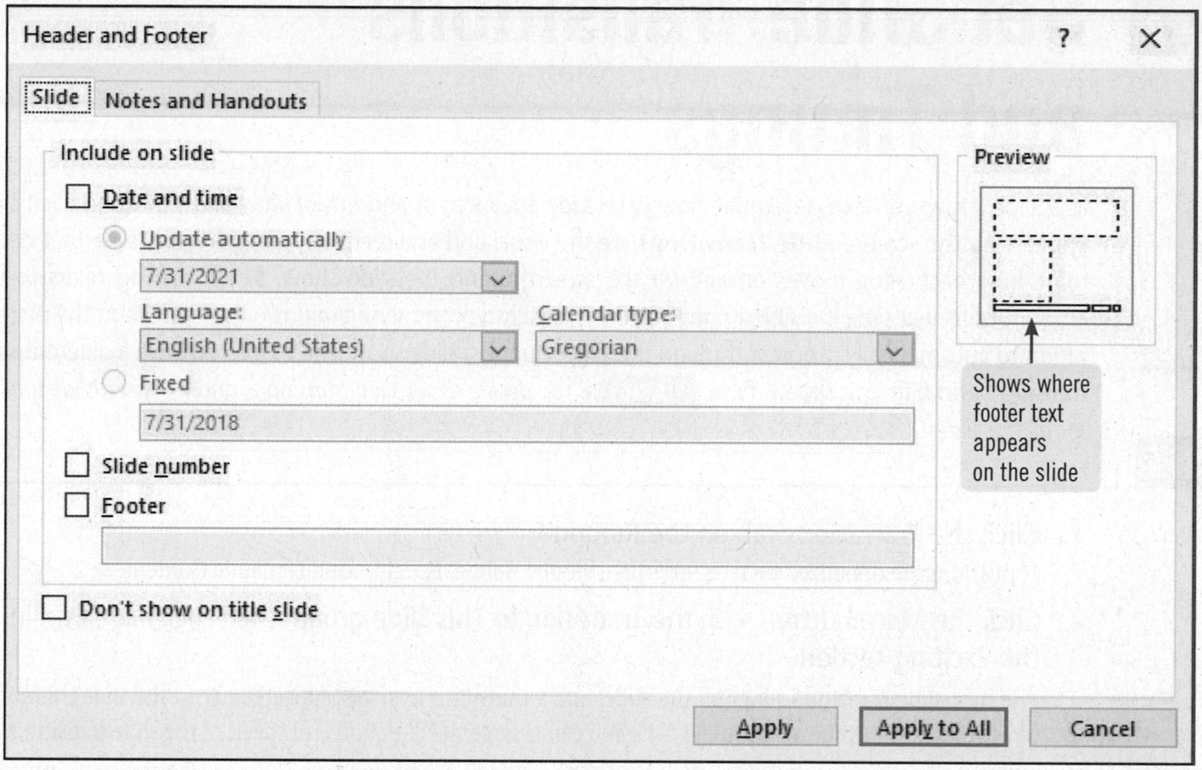

FIGURE 2-14: Footer information added to presentation

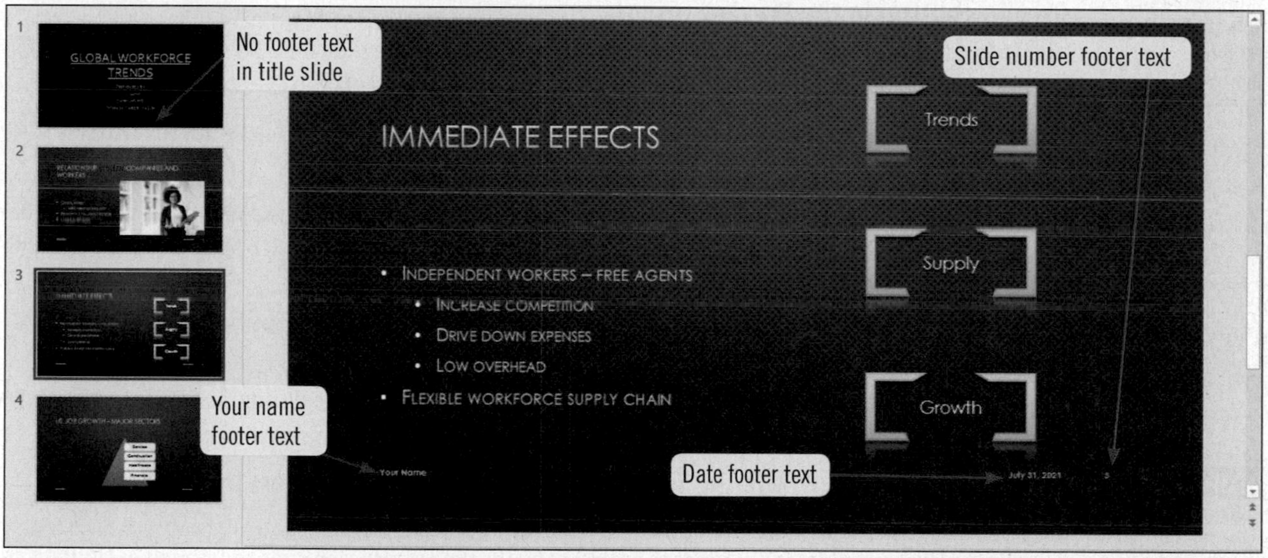

Creating superscript and subscript text

Superscript or subscript text is a number, figure, symbol, or letter that appears smaller than other text and is positioned above or below the normal line of text. A common superscript in the English language is the sign indicator next to a number, such as 1st or 2nd. Other examples of superscripts are the trademark symbol^{TM} and the copyright symbol$^{©}$. To create superscript text in PowerPoint, select the text, number, or symbol, then press CTRL SHIFT + at the same time. Probably the most familiar uses of subscript text are the numerals in chemical compounds and formulas, for example, H_2O and CO_2. To create subscript text, select the text, number, or symbol, then press CTRL = at the same time. To change superscript or subscript text back to normal text, select the text, then press CTRL SPACEBAR.

Set Slide Transitions and Timings

Learning Outcomes
- Apply and modify a transition
- Modify slide timings

In a slide show, you can determine how each slide advances in and out of view and how long each slide appears on the screen. **Slide transitions** are the visual and audio effects you apply to a slide that determine how each slide moves on and off the screen during the slide show. **Slide timing** refers to the amount of time a slide is visible on the screen. Typically, you set slide timings only if you want the presentation to automatically progress through the slides during a slide show. Each slide can have a different slide transition and different slide timing. CASE *You decide to set slide transitions and 7-second slide timings for all the slides.*

STEPS

1. **Click the Transitions tab on the Ribbon**
   Transitions are organized by type into three groups: Subtle, Exciting, and Dynamic Content.
2. **Click the More button in the Transition to This Slide group, then click Page Curl in the Exciting section**
   The new slide transition plays on the slide, and a transition icon appears next to the slide thumbnail in the Slides tab as shown in **FIGURE 2-15**. You can change the direction and speed of the slide transition.
3. **Click the Effect Options button in the Transition to This Slide group, click Double Right, click the Duration up arrow in the Timing group until 2.00 appears, then click the Preview button in the Preview group**
   The Page Curl slide transition now plays double from the left on the slide for 2.00 seconds. You can apply this transition with the custom settings to all of the slides in the presentation.

   > **QUICK TIP**
   > You can add a sound that plays with the transition from the Sound arrow in the Timing group.

4. **Click the Apply To All button in the Timing group, then click the Slide Sorter button on the status bar**
   All of the slides now have the customized Page Curl transition applied to them as identified by the transition icons located below each slide. You also have the ability to determine how slides progress during a slide show—either manually by mouse click or automatically by slide timing.
5. **Click the On Mouse Click check box under Advance Slide in the Timing group to clear the checkmark**
   When this option is selected, you have to click to manually advance slides during a slide show. Now, with this option disabled, you can set the slides to advance automatically after a specified amount of time.
6. **Click the After up arrow in the Timing group until 00:07.00 appears in the text box, then click the Apply To All button**
   The timing between slides is 7 seconds as indicated by the time under each slide thumbnail in **FIGURE 2-16**. When you run the slide show, each slide will remain on the screen for 7 seconds. You can override a slide's timing and speed up the slide show by using any of the manual advance slide commands.

   > **QUICK TIP**
   > Click the transition icon under any slide in Slide Sorter view to see its transition play.

7. **Click the Slide Show button on the status bar**
   The slide show advances automatically. A new slide appears every 7 seconds using the Page Curl transition.
8. **sam When you see the black slide, press SPACEBAR, save your changes, submit your presentation to your instructor, then exit PowerPoint**
   The slide show ends, and you return to Slide Sorter view with Slide 4 selected.

FIGURE 2-15: Applied slide transition

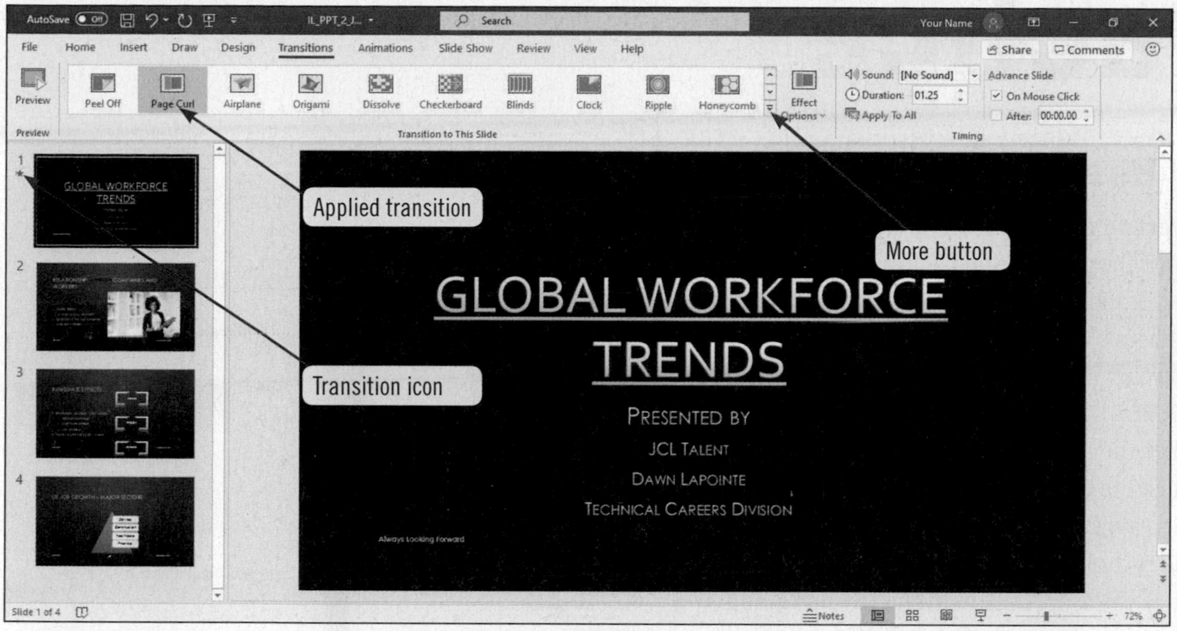

FIGURE 2-16: Slide Sorter view showing applied transition and timing

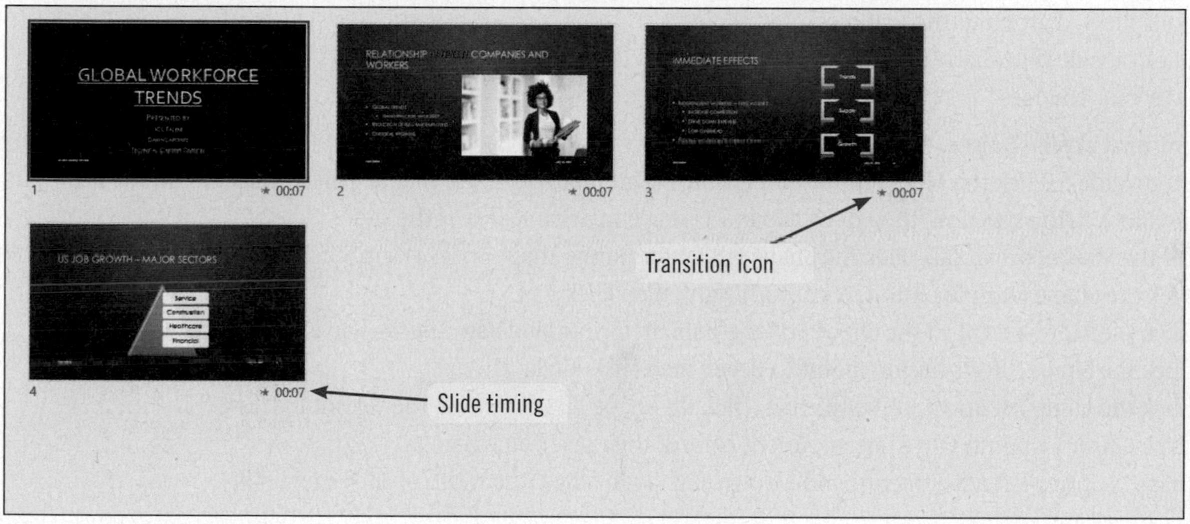

Asier Romero/Shutterstock.com

Inserting hyperlinks in a webpage

While creating a presentation there may be information on the Internet you want to reference or view during a slide show. Instead of re-creating the information in PowerPoint, you can insert a hyperlink on a slide that when clicked during a slide show will open the webpage directly from the Internet. To insert a hyperlink, select an object on the slide, such as a picture or text object, then click the Insert tab on the Ribbon. Click the Link button in the Links group to open the Insert Hyperlink dialog box. Click the Existing File or Web Page button in the link to section, then locate the webpage you want to link. Use the Address bar in the dialog box to insert the webpage address, then click OK. Now during a slide show, click the object with the hyperlink and you will view the linked webpage.

Practice

Skills Review

1. **Convert text to SmartArt.**
   a. Open the presentation IL_PPT_2-2.pptx from the location where you store your Data Files, then save it as **IL_PPT_2_Broker**. The completed presentation is shown in **FIGURE 2-17**.
   b. Click the text object on Slide 2.
   c. Click the Convert to SmartArt Graphic button, then apply the Basic Cycle graphic layout to the text object.
   d. Click the More button in the Layouts group, click More Layouts, click Process in the Choose a SmartArt Graphic dialog box, click Continuous Block Process, then click OK.
   e. Click the More button in the SmartArt Styles group, then apply the Metallic Scene style from the 3-D group to the graphic.
   f. Click outside the SmartArt graphic in a blank part of the slide.
   g. Save your changes.

FIGURE 2-17

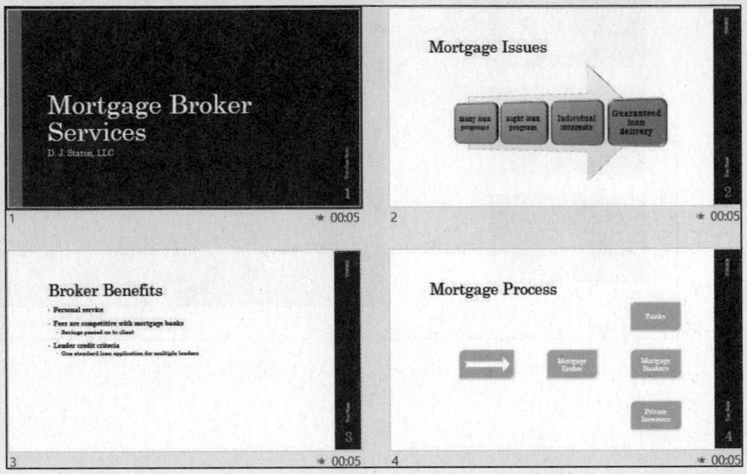

2. **Insert and style shapes.**
   a. Go to Slide 5, click the More button in the Drawing group to open the Shapes gallery, click the Arrow: Right button in the Block Arrows section, then draw about a 1" shape in a blank area of the slide.
   b. On the Shape Format tab, click the Shape Fill button in the Shape Styles group, click yellow under Standard Colors, click the Shape Outline button, point to Weight, then click 3 pt.
   c. Click the More button in the Shape Styles group, then click Moderate Effect—Olive Green, Accent 3.
   d. Click the Shape Effects button, point to Bevel, then click Angle.
   e. Click the Undo list arrow in the title bar, click the Shape Effects button, then point to Glow.
   f. Click Glow: 11 point; Olive Green, Accent color 3, then save your changes.
   g. Drag the lower-left adjustment handle down slightly to adjust the width of the arrow shaft.

3. **Rotate and modify shapes.**
   a. Click the arrow shape on the slide, click the Rotate button in the Arrange group, then click Flip Horizontal.
   b. Drag the Rotate handle to the left until the arrow is pointing to the bottom of the slide, click the Undo list arrow, then click Rotate Object.
   c. Click the Rotate button, then click Flip Horizontal.
   d. Click the Edit Shape button in the Insert Shapes group, point to Change Shape, then click Arrow: Notched Right in the Block Arrows section.
   e. Right-click the Slide 4 thumbnail in the Slides tab, click Delete Slide, then save your work.

4. **Rearrange and merge shapes.**
   a. Click the green arrow shape on Slide 4, then click the Shape Format tab.
   b. Drag the arrow shape over the top of the blank rectangle shape, center it on the rectangle shape using the SmartGuides, then adjust the shape if needed to make it fit in the space as shown in **FIGURE 2-18**.

Skills Review (continued)

c. Send the arrow shape back one level, press SHIFT, click the rectangle shape, then click the Merge Shapes button in the Insert Shapes group.

d. Point to each of the merge shapes options, click a blank area of the slide twice, then click the rectangle shape.

e. Send the rectangle shape back one level, then click a blank area of the slide.

f. Press SHIFT, click the arrow shape, click the rectangle shape, click the Merge Shapes button, click Combine, then save your work.

FIGURE 2-18

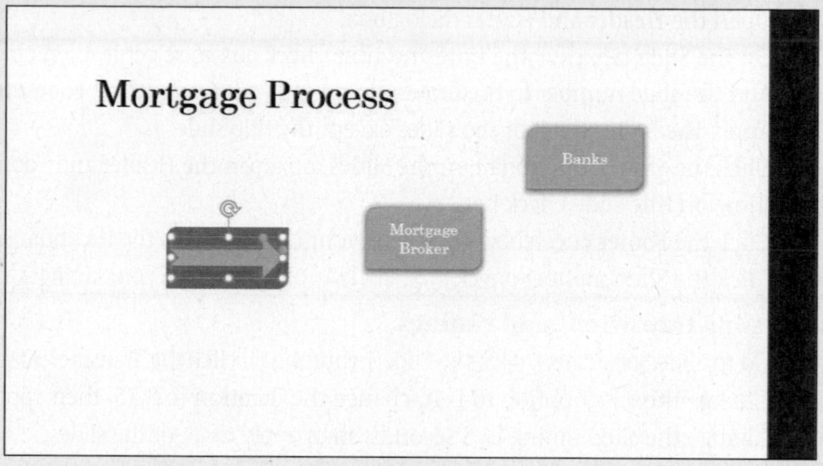

5. Edit and duplicate shapes.

a. Show Rulers, select the Banks shape, then using CTRL make one copy of the shape.

b. Using the ruler, move the new shape to approximately 3.5 (right of 0) on the horizontal ruler, then close the rulers.

c. Click the new shape, click the Copy button in the Clipboard group, then click the Paste button in the Clipboard group.

d. Move the new square shape to a blank area at the bottom of the slide, then select the text in the shape.

e. Type **Private Investors**, select the text in the other new rectangle shape, then type **Mortgage Bankers**.

f. Click the arrow shape, then drag the right-middle sizing handle to the right ¼".

g. Click a blank area of the slide, add the gridlines to the Slide pane, then save your changes.

6. Align and group objects.

a. Drag the Mortgage Broker rectangle shape down until its bottom edge snaps to a horizontal gridline, then click the Shape Format tab.

b. Press SHIFT, click the arrow shape, click the Mortgage Bankers shape, release SHIFT, then click the Align button in the Arrange group.

c. Click Align Middle, click the Align button, then click Distribute Horizontally.

d. Hide the gridlines, display the guides, then move the vertical guide to the right until 3.00 appears.

e. Move the Private Investors shape to the left until it is centered over the vertical guide, move the vertical guide back to 0.00, then hide the guides.

f. Select the three rectangle shapes on the right, click the Align button, then click Align Right.

g. Select all five square shapes, click the Group button in the Arrange group, click Group, then save your work. Your screen should look similar to **FIGURE 2-19**.

FIGURE 2-19

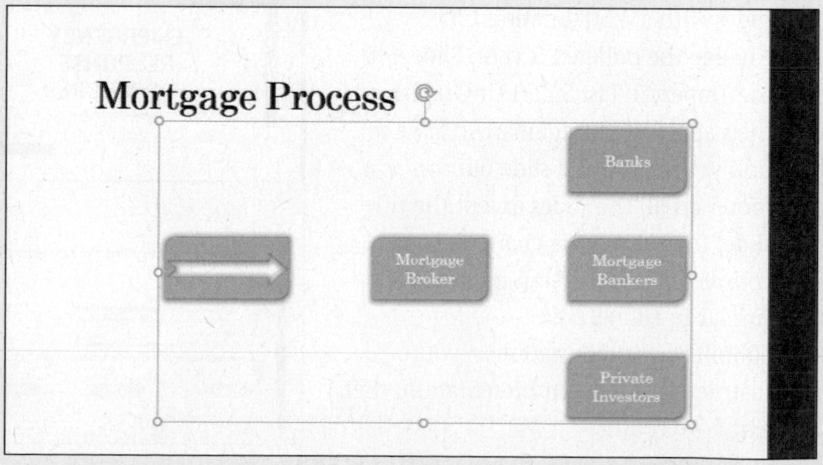

PowerPoint

Skills Review (continued)

7. Add slide footers.

a. Open the Header and Footer dialog box.

b. On the Slide tab, click the Date and time check box to select it, then click the Fixed option button.

c. Add the slide number to the footer, then type your name in the Footer text box.

d. Apply the footer to all of the slides except the title slide.

e. Click the Slide 1 thumbnail on the Slides tab, open the Header and Footer dialog box again, then click the Don't show on title slide check box.

f. Click the Footer check box, then type your class name in the text box.

g. Click the Slide number check box, click Apply, then save your changes.

8. Set slide transitions and timings.

a. Go to Slide Sorter view, click the Slide 1 thumbnail, click the Transitions tab, then apply the Wind transition to the slide.

b. Change the effect option to Left, change the duration to 2.75, then apply to all the slides.

c. Change the slide timing to 5 seconds, then apply to all of the slides.

d. Switch to Normal view, view the slide show, then save your work.

e. Submit your presentation to your instructor, close the presentation, then exit PowerPoint.

Independent Challenge 1

Riverwalk Medical Clinic (RMC) is a large medical facility in Cambridge, Massachusetts. You have been asked to create a presentation on the latest emergency response procedures for a staff training later in the week.

a. Start PowerPoint, open the presentation IL_PPT_2-3.pptx from the location where you store your Data Files, and save it as **IL_PPT_2_ERP**.

b. On Slide 3 display the guides in the Slide pane, move the horizontal guide down to 2.00, then move the vertical guide left to 5.00.

c. Drag the rectangle shape so its top and left edges snap into the guides, then move both guides back to 0.00 and hide the guides.

d. Move the left adjustment handle on the rectangle shape slightly to the right to change the shape of the rectangle.

e. Change the shape fill color to Rose, Accent 6, then change the shape outline to solid 1 ½-point black.

f. Duplicate the shape twice, align the shapes along their bottom edges across the slide, distribute the space horizontally between the shapes, then group the shapes.

g. Type **CPR** in the left shape, type **Airway kits** in the middle shape, then type **Crash cart** in the right shape.

h. Apply the Reveal transition to all the slides with a 4.50 duration time.

i Change the bulleted text on Slide 4 to the Trapezoid List SmartArt Graphic, then apply the Inset SmartArt style.

j. Add your name and slide number as a footer on all the slides except the title slide, then save your changes. Your completed presentation might look similar to **FIGURE 2-20**.

k. Submit your presentation to your instructor, close your presentation, then exit PowerPoint.

FIGURE 2-20

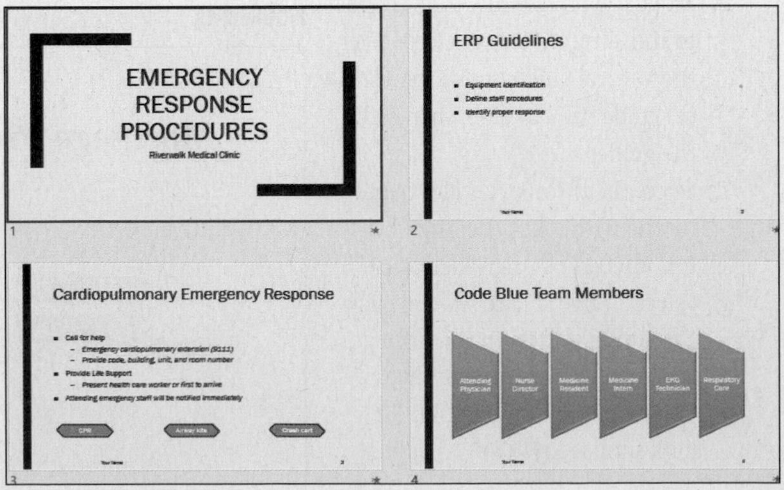

Independent Challenge 2

You are one of the assistants to the Career and Intern Program manager at Delvall Corp., a large engineering and manufacturing company. You have been asked by your manager to develop a new presentation outlining the details of the career and intern leadership program offered by Delvall. You continue working on the presentation you have already started.

a. Start PowerPoint, open the presentation IL_PPT_2-4.pptx from the location where you store your Data Files, and save it as **IL_PPT_2_Delvall**.
b. Go to Slide 4, show the rulers in the Slide pane, then drag the lower-right sizing handle on the shape down and to the right until the pointer reaches the 3 in the horizontal ruler.
c. Draw a 1" proportional chevron shape from the Block Arrows section of shapes. (*Hint*: to draw a specific size shape, position your pointer on the 0 of a ruler and drag until your pointer reaches the size you want on the ruler.)
d. Click the Shape Format tab, flip the shape horizontal, then drag the shape's rotate handle until the arrow is pointing up.
e. Select both shapes, then apply Intense Effect—Orange, Accent 2 from the Shape Styles group.
f. Apply the Preset 1 shape effect, then merge the two shapes together using the Union option, as shown in **FIGURE 2-21**.
g. Show gridlines in the Slide pane, drag the merged shape to the left until the shape's left and bottom edges are touching gridlines, then hide the gridlines.
h. Apply to all the slides the transition Random Bars with a duration of 2.00, then change the effect option to horizontal.
i. Delete Slide 2 from the presentation, add the slide number and your name as a footer on the slides, then save your changes.
j. Run a slide show, submit your presentation to your instructor, close your presentation, then exit PowerPoint.

FIGURE 2-21

PowerPoint

Visual Workshop

Open the presentation IL_PPT_2-5.pptx from the location where you store your Data Files, and save it as **IL_PPT_2_LaSalle**. Create the presentation shown in **FIGURE 2-22** and **FIGURE 2-23**. Add today's date as the date on the title slide. Create and duplicate the merged shape, which is made with an Arrow: Bent-Up shape and a Rectangle: Rounded Corners shape. The shapes are 1 ½" proportional shapes with the Subtle Effect—Dark Purple, Accent 2 applied to them. (*Hint*: The arrow shape is rotated 90 degrees before it's merged with the square shape.) Set the horizontal guide to 3 and the vertical guide to 1, as shown in **FIGURE 2-22**. The SmartArt graphic in **FIGURE 2-23** is created with the Basic Matrix layout and has the Moderate Effect style applied to it. Review your slides in Slide Show view, then add your name as a footer to the slides. Submit your presentation to your instructor, save your changes, close the presentation, then exit PowerPoint.

FIGURE 2-22

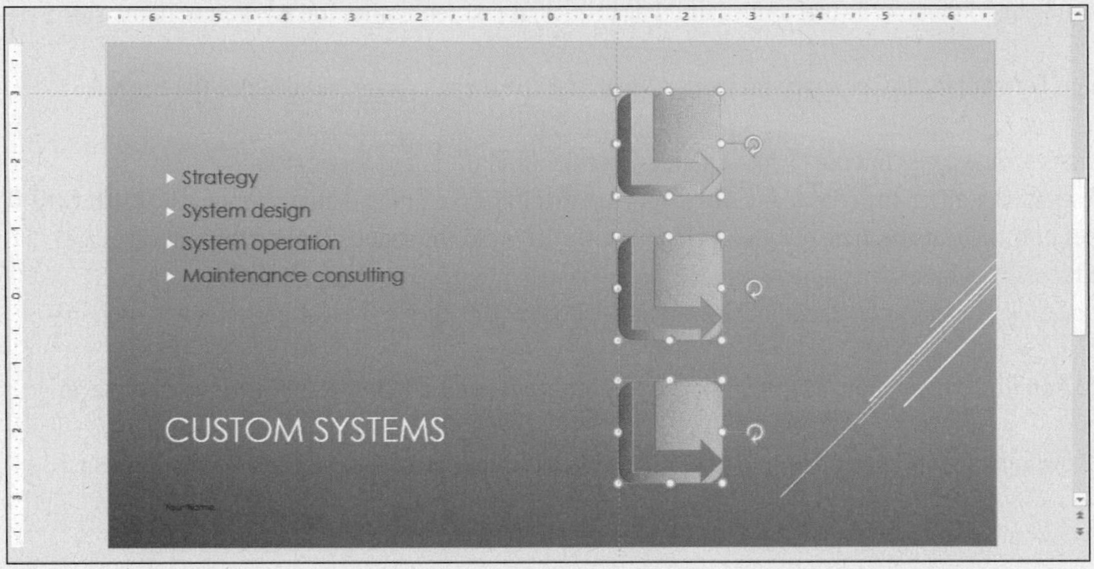

FIGURE 2-23

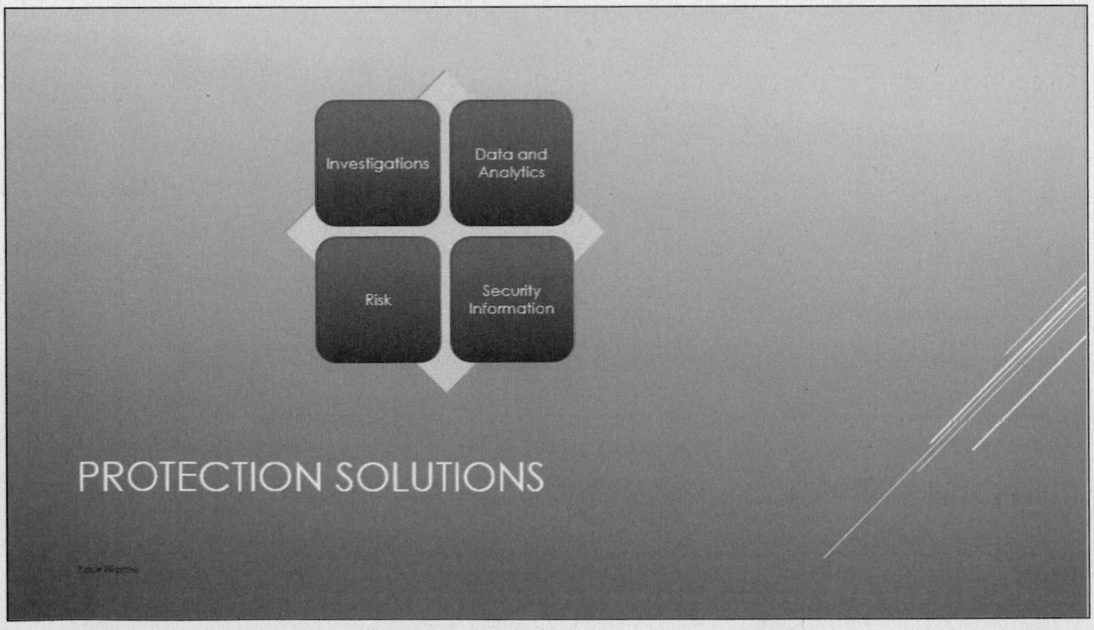

PowerPoint **Module 3**

Inserting Objects into a Presentation

CASE In this module, you continue working on the JCL Talent presentation by inserting and formatting a text box and then cropping and styling a picture. You also add visual elements into the presentation, including a chart, slides from another presentation, and a table. You format these objects using the powerful object-editing features in PowerPoint.

Module Objectives

After completing this module, you will be able to:

- Insert a text box
- Crop and style a picture
- Insert a chart
- Enter and edit chart data
- Insert slides from other presentations
- Insert a table
- Insert and format WordArt
- Animate objects
- Insert and edit digital video

Files You Will Need

IL_PPT_3-1.pptx
Support_PPT_3_Group.jpg
Support_PPT_3_Presentation.pptx
Support_PPT_3_Video.mp4
IL_PPT_3-2.pptx
Support_PPT_3_PMI.pptx
Support_PPT_3_Desk.mp4
IL_PPT_3-3.pptx
Support_PPT_3_ER.jpg
IL_PPT_3-4.pptx
Support_PPT_3_Invest.pptx
Support_PPT_3_Woman.jpg

PowerPoint
Module 3

Insert a Text Box

Learning Outcomes
- Insert a text box
- Format text in a text box
- Resize and move a text box

In most cases, you enter text on a slide using a title or content placeholder that is arranged on the slide based on a slide layout. Every so often you need additional text on a slide where the traditional placeholder does not place text. There are two types of text boxes: a text label, used for a small phrase where text doesn't automatically wrap inside the boundaries of a text box, and a word-processing box, used for a sentence or paragraph where the text wraps inside a text box. Either type of text box can be formatted and edited just like any other text object. **CASE** *You create a text box next to the SmartArt graphic on Slide 4, then edit and format the text.*

STEPS

1. **sam Start PowerPoint, open the presentation IL_PPT_3-1.pptx from the location where you store your Data Files, then save it as IL_PPT_3_JCL**
2. **Click the Slide 4 thumbnail on the Slides tab, click the Insert tab on the Ribbon, then click the Text Box button in the Text group**
   The pointer changes to ↓.
3. **Move ↓ to the blank area to the left of the SmartArt object on the slide, then drag the pointer + down and toward the right about 3" to create a text box**
   When you begin dragging, an outline of the text box appears, indicating the size of the text box you are drawing. After you release the mouse button, a blinking insertion point appears inside the text box, in this case a word-processing box, indicating that you can enter text.

QUICK TIP
To create a text label, click the Text Box button, position the pointer on the slide, click once, then enter your text.

4. **Type Last year's growth increased over 25% in all areas**
   Notice the text box increases in size as your text wraps to additional lines inside the text box. Your screen should look similar to **FIGURE 3-1**. After entering the text, you decide to edit the sentence.
5. **Drag I over the phrase in all areas to select it, position ↖ on top of the selected phrase, then press and hold the left mouse button**
   The pointer changes to ↖.
6. **Drag the selected words to the right of the word "growth", release the mouse button, then click to the left of the text box**
   A grey insertion line appears as you drag, indicating where PowerPoint places the text when you release the mouse button. The phrase "in all areas" moves after the word "growth". Notice there is no space between the words "growth" and "in" and the spelling error is identified by a red wavy underline.
7. **Right-click the red underlined words in the text box, then click "growth in" on the shortcut menu**
   Space is added between the two words in the text box.
8. **Move I to the edge of the text box, which changes to ✥, click the text box border (it changes to a solid line), then click the Shape Format tab on the Ribbon**
9. **Click the Shape Fill list arrow in the Shape Styles group, click the Gold, Accent 4 color box, click the Shape Outline list arrow in the Shape Styles group, point to Weight, then click 4½ pt**
   The text object is now filled with a gold color and has a thicker outline.
10. **Position ✥ over the text box edge, drag the text box to the Smart Guide on the slide as shown in FIGURE 3-2, then save your changes**

QUICK TIP
Click the Shape Effects list arrow in the Shape Styles group, then click one of the preset effects to change the style of a text object.

FIGURE 3-1: New text object

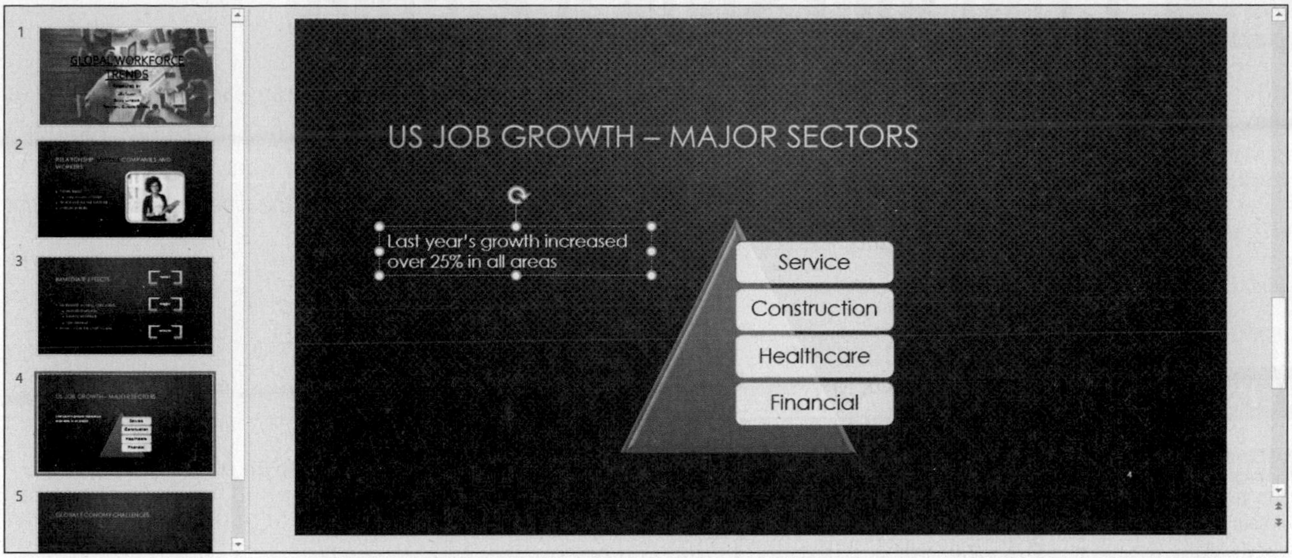

FIGURE 3-2: Formatted text object

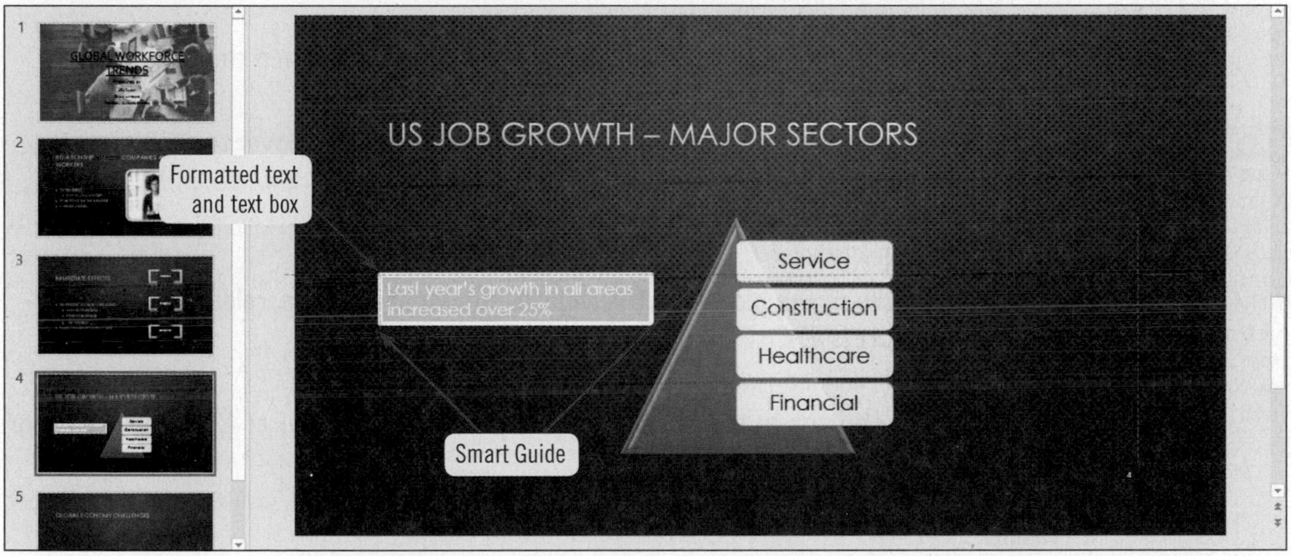

Changing text box defaults

You can change the default formatting characteristics of text boxes you create using the Text Box button on the Insert tab. To change the formatting defaults for text boxes, select an existing formatted text box, or create a new one and format it using any of the PowerPoint formatting commands. When you are ready to change the text box defaults of a text box that is not selected, press SHIFT, right-click the formatted text box, release SHIFT, then click Set as Default Text Box on the shortcut menu. Now, any text boxes you create will display the formatting characteristics of this formatted text box.

PowerPoint Module 3

Crop and Style a Picture

Learning Outcomes
- Crop a picture
- Apply a picture style
- Add effects to a picture
- Resize and move a picture

PowerPoint provides many editing tools that help you style a picture, such as transparency, sharpening or softening edges, color tone, and cropping. **Cropping** a picture hides a portion of the picture you don't want to see. The cropped portion of a picture is still available to you if you ever want to show that part of the picture again. **CASE** *In this lesson you crop and style a picture to best fit the slide, but first you format a picture you insert on the Slide Master.*

STEPS

QUICK TIP You can also insert a picture without a content placeholder by clicking the Pictures button in the Images group on the Insert tab.

1. **Click the Slide 1 thumbnail in the Slides tab, right-click a blank area of the slide, then click Format Background on the shortcut menu**
   The Format Background pane opens.
2. **Click Insert in the Format Background pane, click From a File in the Insert Pictures dialog box, navigate to the location where you store your Data Files, select the picture file Support_PPT_3_Group.jpg, then click Insert**
   The picture fills the slide.
3. **Drag the Transparency Slider to 50%, then close the Format Background pane**
   The slide background picture on Slide 1 is more transparent.
4. **Click the Slide 2 thumbnail in the Slides tab, click the picture, then click the Picture Format tab on the Ribbon**

QUICK TIP Click the Crop button list arrow to take advantage of other crop options, including cropping to a shape from the Shapes gallery and cropping to a common photo size or aspect ratio.

5. **Click the Crop button in the Size group, then place the pointer over the middle-left cropping handle on the picture**
   The pointer changes to ⊣. When the Crop button is active, cropping handles appear next to the sizing handles on the selected object.
6. **Drag the middle of the picture to the right as shown in FIGURE 3-3, release the mouse button, then press ESC**
   The picture would look better on the slide if it had a different color tone.
7. **Click the Color button in the Adjust group, then click Temperature: 4700 K in the Color Tone row**
   The options in the Color Tone row add more blue or orange to the picture, making it appear cooler or warmer.

QUICK TIP If you have multiple pictures on a slide, you can align them using guides or Smart Guides.

8. **Click the Corrections button in the Adjust group, then click Soften: 25% in the Sharpen/Soften section**
   The picture is slightly unclear.
9. **Click the More button ▾ in the Picture Styles group, then click Metal Rounded Rectangle (4th row)**
   The picture now has rounded corners with a metal-looking frame. Notice the picture has an adjustment handle that you can move.
10. **Drag the picture to the center of the blank area of the slide to the right of the text object, click a blank area on the slide, then save your changes**
    Compare your screen to FIGURE 3-4.

FIGURE 3-3: Using the cropping pointer to crop a picture

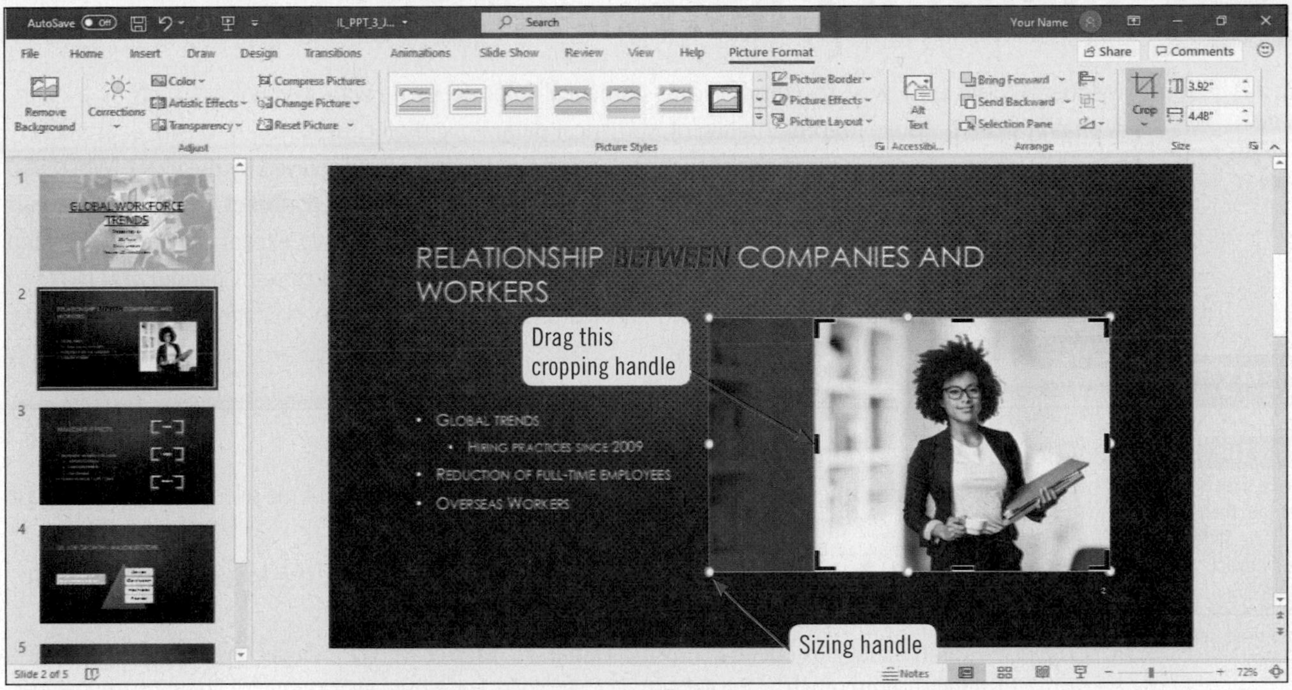

FIGURE 3-4: Cropped and styled picture

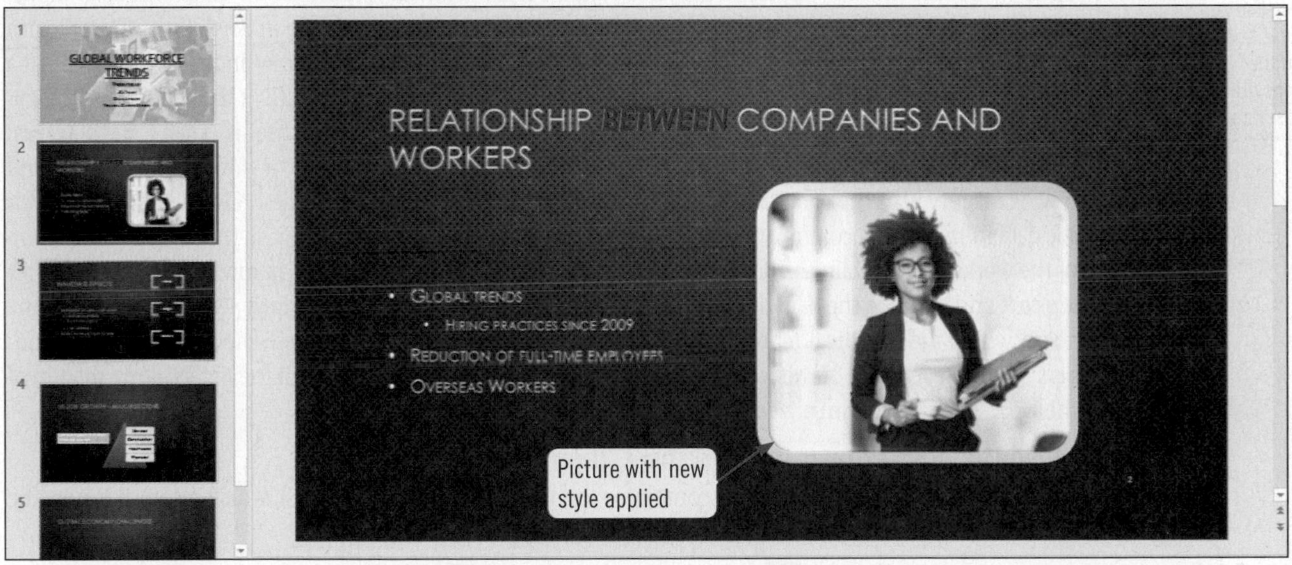

Inserting a screen recording

Using the Screen Recording button in the Media group on the Insert tab, you can record your computer screen with audio and insert the recording in a slide. For example, if you want to make a recording of an Internet video, locate and display the video on your computer screen. In PowerPoint on the slide where you want to insert the recording, click the Screen Recording button. On the toolbar, click the Select Area button, drag a selection box around the video, click the Audio button if necessary, then click the Record button on the toolbar. Click the video play button. When finished recording, click Windows Logo+SHIFT+Q to stop recording. PowerPoint opens and the recording appears on your slide. Click the Play button to review your recording.

Insert a Chart

Learning Outcome
- Insert a new chart on a slide

Frequently, the best way to communicate numerical information is with a visual aid such as a chart. A **chart** is the graphical representation of numerical data. PowerPoint uses Excel to create charts. Every chart has a corresponding **worksheet** that contains the numerical data displayed by the chart. When you insert a chart object into PowerPoint, you are embedding it. An **embedded object** is one that is a part of your presentation (just like any other object you insert into PowerPoint) except that an embedded object's data source can be opened, in this case using Excel, for editing purposes. Changes you make to an embedded object in PowerPoint using the features in PowerPoint do not affect the data source. **CASE** *You insert a chart on a new slide.*

STEPS

QUICK TIP
Right-click a slide in the Slides tab, then click Duplicate Slide to create an exact copy of the slide.

1. **Click the Slide 4 thumbnail in the Slides tab, then press ENTER**
   Pressing ENTER adds a new slide to your presentation with the slide layout of the selected slide, in this case the Title and Content slide layout.
2. **Click the Title placeholder, type Free Agency Trends, then click the Insert Chart icon in the Content placeholder**
   The Insert Chart dialog box opens as shown in **FIGURE 3-5**. Each chart type includes several 2D and 3D styles. The Clustered Column chart is the default 2D chart style. For a brief explanation of common chart types, refer to **TABLE 3-1**.

QUICK TIP
You can also add a chart to a slide by clicking the Chart button in the Illustrations group on the Insert tab.

3. **Click OK**
   The PowerPoint window displays a clustered column chart below a worksheet with sample data, as shown in **FIGURE 3-6**. The Chart Design tab on the Ribbon contains commands you use in PowerPoint to work with the chart. The worksheet consists of rows and columns. The intersection of a row and a column is called a **cell**. Cells are referred to by their row and column location; for example, the cell at the intersection of column A and row 1 is called cell A1. Each column and row of data in the worksheet is called a **data series**. Cells in column A and row 1 contain **data series labels** that identify the data or values in the column and row. "Category 1" is the data series label for the data in the second row, and "Series 1" is a data series label for the data in the second column. Cells below and to the right of the data series labels, in the shaded blue portion of the worksheet, contain the data values that are represented in the chart. Cells in row 1 appear in the chart **legend** and describe the data in the series. Each data series has corresponding **data series markers** in the chart, which are graphical representations such as bars, columns, or pie wedges. The boxes with the numbers along the left side of the worksheet are **row headings**, and the boxes with the letters along the top of the worksheet are **column headings**.
4. **Move the pointer over the worksheet, then click cell C4**
   The pointer changes to ✚. Cell C4, containing the value 1.8, is the selected cell, which means it is now the **active cell**. The active cell has a thick green border around it.
5. **Click the Close button on the worksheet title bar, then click the Quick Layout button in the Chart Layouts group**
   The worksheet window closes, and the Quick Layout gallery opens.
6. **Move over the layouts in the gallery, then click Layout 9**
   This new layout moves the legend to the right side of the chart and increases the size of the data series markers.
7. **Drag the chart straight up to center it on the slide**
8. **Click in a blank area of the slide to deselect the chart, then save your changes**
   The Chart Design tab is no longer active.

FIGURE 3-5: Insert Chart dialog box

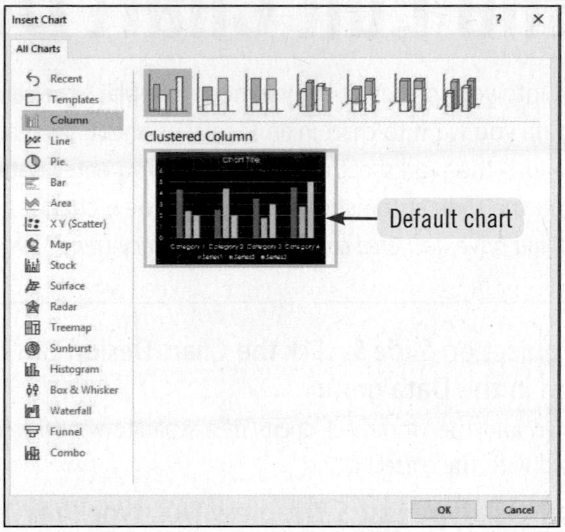

FIGURE 3-6: Worksheet open showing chart data

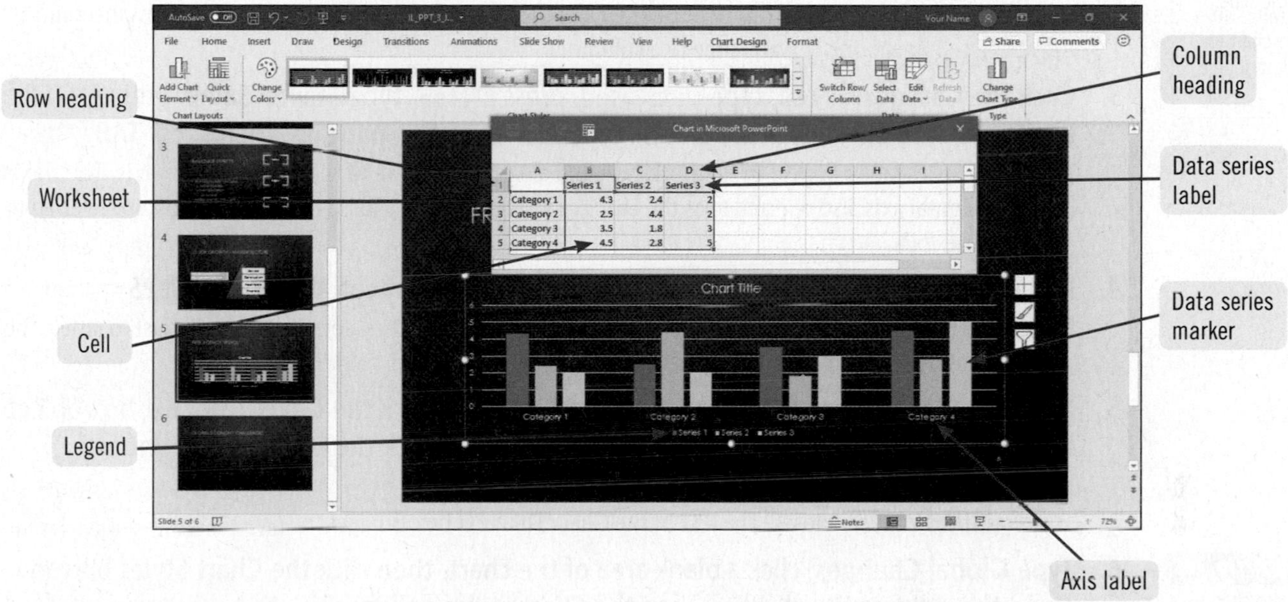

TABLE 3-1: Common chart types

chart type	icon looks like	use to
Column		Track values over time or across categories
Line		Track values over time
Pie		Compare individual values to the whole
Bar		Compare values in categories or over time
Area		Show contribution of each data series to the total over time
X Y (Scatter)		Compare pairs of values
Stock		Show stock market information or scientific data
Surface		Show value trends across two dimensions
Radar		Show changes in values in relation to a center point
Combo		Use multiple types of data markers to compare values

PowerPoint

Enter and Edit Chart Data

Learning Outcomes
- Change chart data values and labels
- Format a chart

After you insert a chart into your presentation, you need to replace the sample information with the correct data. If you have the data you want to chart in an Excel worksheet, you can import it from Excel; otherwise, you can type the data into the worksheet on the slide. As you enter data and make other changes in the worksheet, the chart on the slide automatically reflects the new changes. **CASE** *You enter and format internal company data you have gathered comparing free agency trends over the last five years.*

STEPS

1. **Click the chart object on Slide 5, click the Chart Design tab on the Ribbon, then click the Edit Data button in the Data group**

   The chart is selected and the worksheet opens in a separate window. The information in the worksheet needs to be replaced with the correct data.

2. **Click the Series 1 cell, type Last 5 Yrs, press TAB, type Prev 10 Yrs, press TAB, then type Next 5 Yrs**

   The data series labels you enter in the worksheet are displayed in the legend on the chart. Pressing TAB moves the active cell from left to right one cell at a time in a row. Pressing ENTER in the worksheet moves the active cell down one cell at a time in a column.

> **QUICK TIP**
> Click the chart in the PowerPoint window, then move your pointer over each bar in the chart to see the data source values.

3. **Click the Category 1 cell, type Decreased, press ENTER, type Stayed Same, press ENTER, type Increased Slightly, press ENTER, type Increased Dramatically, then press TAB**

   These data series labels appear in the worksheet and along the bottom of the chart on the *x*-axis. The *x*-axis is the horizontal axis also referred to as the **category axis**, and the *y*-axis is the vertical axis also referred to as the **value axis**.

4. **Enter the data shown in FIGURE 3-7 to complete the worksheet, then click cell E5**

   Notice that the height of each column in the chart, as well as the values along the *y*-axis, adjust to reflect the numbers you typed. You have finished entering the data in the Excel worksheet.

5. **Click the Close button on the worksheet title bar, click the Chart Title text box object in the chart, click the Home tab on the Ribbon, then click the Increase Font Size button in the Font group**

   The worksheet window closes. The text in the Chart Title text box is larger.

6. **Type Global Changes, click a blank area of the chart, then click the Chart Styles button to the right of the chart to open the Chart Styles gallery**

   The Chart Styles gallery opens on the left side of the chart with Style selected.

> **QUICK TIP**
> You can also change the chart style by clicking a style option in the Chart Styles group on the Chart Design tab.

7. **Scroll down the gallery, click Style 5, click Color at the top of the Chart Styles gallery, then click the Colorful Palette 2 in the Colorful section**

   The new chart style and color give the column data markers a professional look as shown in **FIGURE 3-8**.

8. **Click a blank area on the slide, then save the presentation**

   The Chart Styles gallery closes.

FIGURE 3-7: Worksheet data for the chart

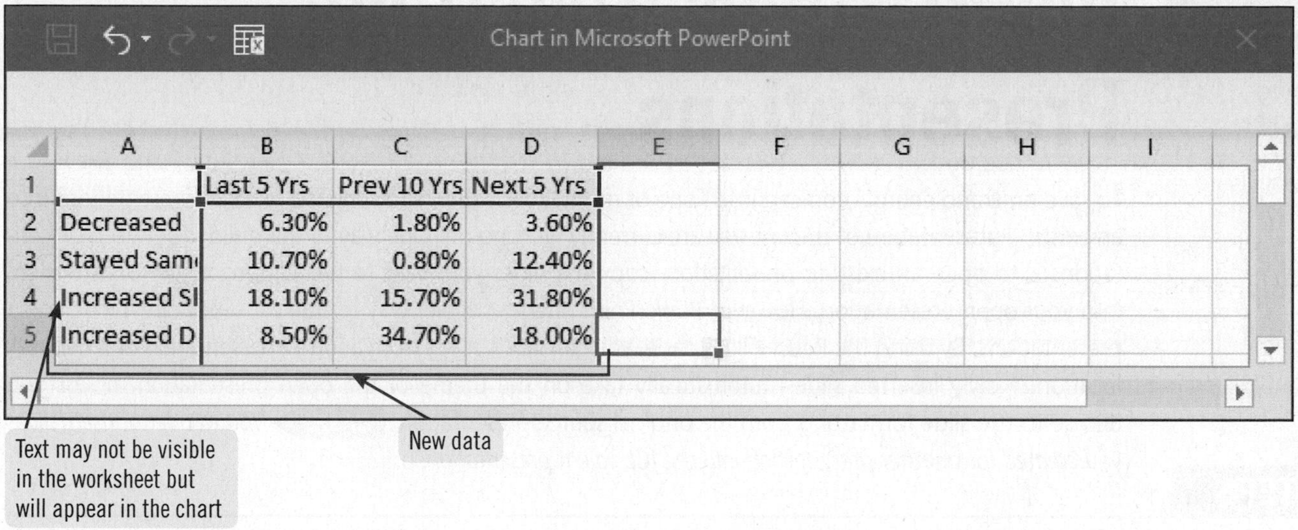

FIGURE 3-8: Formatted chart

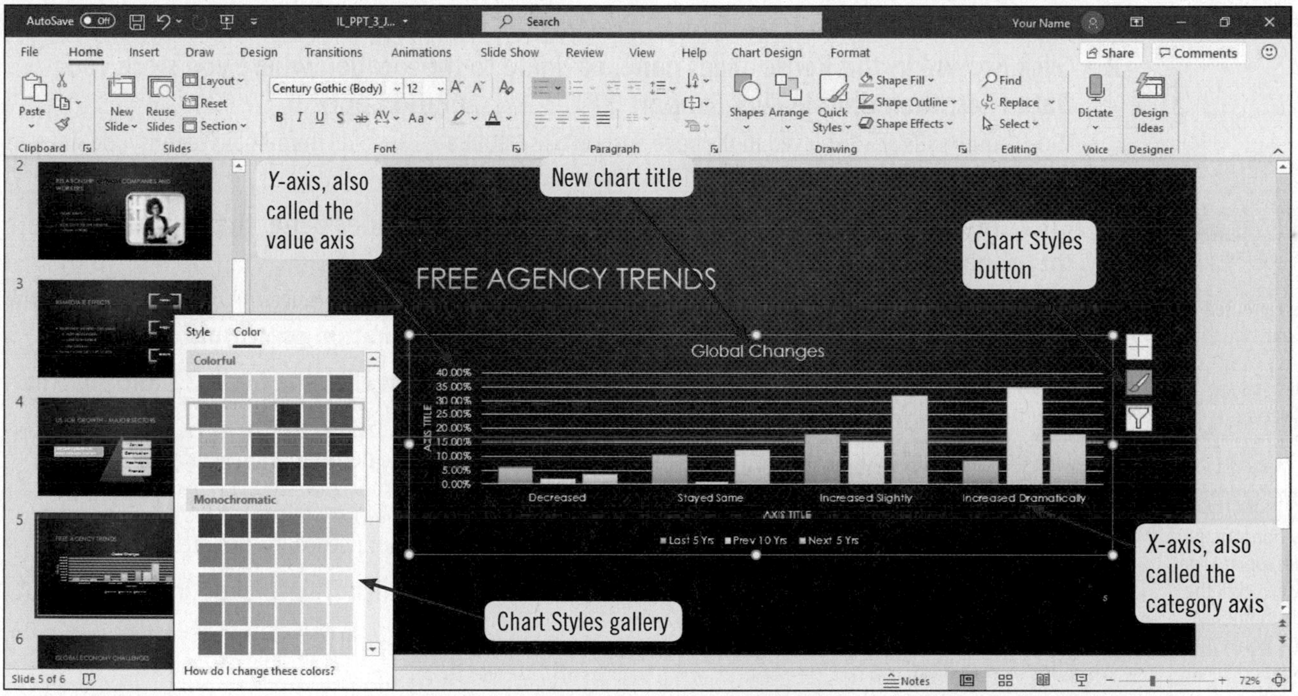

Adding a hyperlink to a chart

You can add a hyperlink to any object in PowerPoint, including a chart. Select that chart, click the Insert tab on the Ribbon, then click the Link button in the Links group. If you are linking to another file, click the Existing File or Web Page button, locate the file you want to link to the chart, then click OK. Or, if you want to link to another slide in the presentation, click the Place in This Document button, click the slide in the list, then click OK. Now, during a slide show you can click the chart to open the linked object. To remove the link, click the chart, click the Link button in the Links group, then click Remove Link.

Insert Slides from Other Presentations

Learning Outcome
- Insert slides from another presentation

To save time and energy, you can insert one or more slides you already created in other presentations into an existing presentation or the one you are currently working on. One way to share slides between presentations is to open an existing presentation, copy the slides you want to the Clipboard, then paste them into your open presentation. However, PowerPoint offers a simpler way to transfer slides directly between presentations. By using the Reuse Slides pane, you can insert slides from another presentation or a network location. Newly inserted slides automatically take on the theme of the open presentation, unless you decide to use slide formatting from the original source presentation. **CASE** *You decide to insert slides you created for another presentation into the JCL Talent presentation.*

STEPS

1. **Click the Slide 2 thumbnail in the Slides tab, then click the Reuse Slides button in the Slides group**
   The Reuse Slides pane opens on the right side of the presentation window and displays recently opened presentations.
2. **Click Browse in the Reuse Slides pane, navigate to the location where you store your Data Files, then double-click Support_PPT_3_Presentation.pptx**
   Slide thumbnails are displayed in the pane as shown in **FIGURE 3-9**. The slide thumbnails identify the slides in the **source presentation**, Support_PPT_3_Presentation.pptx.
3. **Click the Use source formatting check box in the Reuse Slides pane, then click the Slide 1 thumbnail in the Reuse Slides pane**
   The new slide appears in the Slides tab and Slide pane as the new Slide 3. Notice the new slide assumes the design style and formatting of your presentation, which is the **destination presentation**.
4. **Click the Slide 3 thumbnail in the Reuse Slides pane, then click the Slide 2 thumbnail in the Reuse Slides pane**
   The new Slides 4 and 5 assume the design style and formatting of the destination presentation.
5. **Click the Reuse Slides pane Close button**
   The Reuse Slides pane closes. You realize the last slide you inserted is not needed for this presentation.
6. **Right-click the Slide 5 thumbnail in the Slides tab, then click Delete Slide in the shortcut menu**
   Slide 5 is deleted.
7. **Click the Slide Sorter button in the status bar, then drag Slide 4 to the right of Slide 2**
8. **Click the Normal button in the status bar, then save the presentation**
   Slide 4 becomes Slide 3. Compare your screen to **FIGURE 3-10**.

QUICK TIP
To maintain the formatting and design of a reused slide, make sure the Use source formatting check box is selected.

QUICK TIP
To copy noncontiguous slides, open Slide Sorter view, click the first slide thumbnail, press and hold CTRL, click each additional slide thumbnail, release CTRL, then click the Copy button.

FIGURE 3-9: Presentation window with Reuse Slides pane open

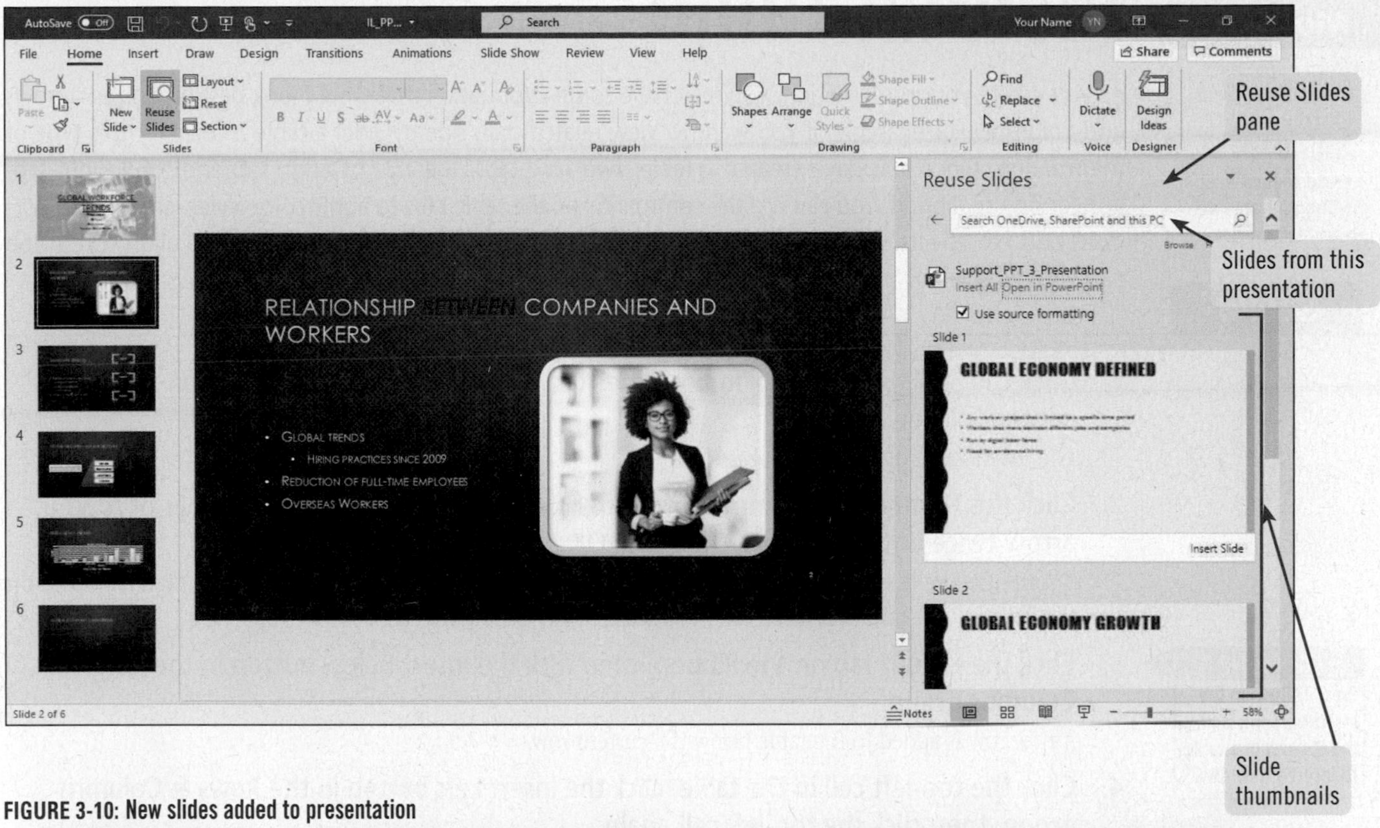

Asier Romero/Shutterstock.com

FIGURE 3-10: New slides added to presentation

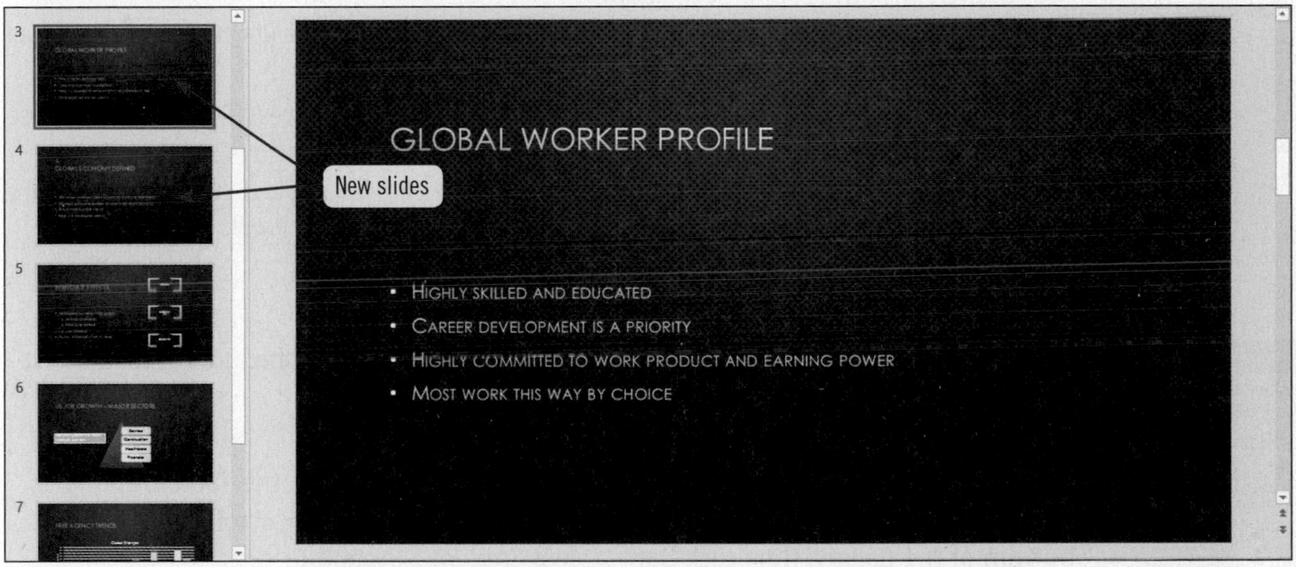

Working with multiple windows

Another way to work with information in multiple presentations is to arrange the presentation windows on your monitor so you see each window side by side. Open each presentation, click the View tab on the Ribbon in any presentation window, then click the Arrange All button in the Window group. Each presentation you have open is placed next to each other so you can easily drag, or transfer, information between the presentations. If you are working with more than two open presentations, you can overlap the presentation windows on top of one another. Open all the presentations you want, then click the Cascade button in the Window group. Now you can easily jump from one presentation to another by clicking the presentation title bar or any part of the presentation window.

PowerPoint

Insert a Table

Learning Outcomes
- Insert a table
- Add text to a table
- Change table size and layout

As you create your presentation, you may have some information that would look best organized in rows and columns. For example, if you want to view related data side by side, a table is ideal for this type of information. Once you have created a table, two new tabs, the Table Design tab and the Layout tab, appear on the Ribbon. You can use the commands on the table tabs to apply color styles, change cell borders, add cell effects, add rows and columns to your table, adjust the size of cells, and align text in the cells. **CASE** *You decide a table best illustrates the challenges of using free agency workers.*

STEPS

1. **Click the Slide 8 thumbnail in the Slides tab, then click the Insert Table icon in the content placeholder**
   The Insert Table dialog box appears.
2. **Click the Number of columns down arrow until 2 appears, click the Number of rows up arrow twice until 4 appears, then click OK**
   A formatted table with two columns and four rows appears on the slide, and the Table Design tab opens on the Ribbon. The table has 8 cells and you realize you need more cells.
3. **Click the Layout tab on the Ribbon, then click the Insert Below button in the Rows & Columns group**
   A new row is added to the table below the current row.
4. **Click the top-left cell in the table, click the Insert Left button in the Rows & Columns group, then click the top-left cell again**
   The table has a new column to the left of the current column and the insertion point is in the first cell of the table ready to accept text.
5. **Type Rank of Concerns, press TAB, type Free Agency Employer, press TAB, type Non-Free Agency Employer, then press TAB**
   The text you typed appears in the top three cells of the table. Pressing TAB moves the insertion point to the next cell; pressing ENTER moves the insertion point to the next line in the same cell.
6. **Enter the rest of the table information shown in FIGURE 3-11**
   The table would look better if it were formatted differently.
7. **Click the top-left cell in the table, click the Select button in the Table group, click Select Row, then click the Center button in the Alignment group**
   The text in the top row is centered horizontally in each cell.
8. **Click the Select button in the Table group, click Select Table, click the Table Design tab on the Ribbon, click the More button in the Table Styles group, scroll to the bottom of the gallery, then click Dark Style 2 - Accent 5/Accent 6**
   The table color changes to reflect the table style you applied.
9. **Click the Effects button in the Table Styles group, point to Cell Bevel, click Divot (3rd row), click a blank area of the slide, then save the presentation**
   The 3D effect makes the cells of the table stand out. Compare your screen with **FIGURE 3-12**.

QUICK TIP
Press TAB when the insertion point is in the last cell of a table to insert a new row.

QUICK TIP
Change the height or width of any table cell by dragging its borders.

QUICK TIP
To change the cell color behind text, click the Shading list arrow in the Table Styles group, then choose a color.

FIGURE 3-11: Inserted table with data

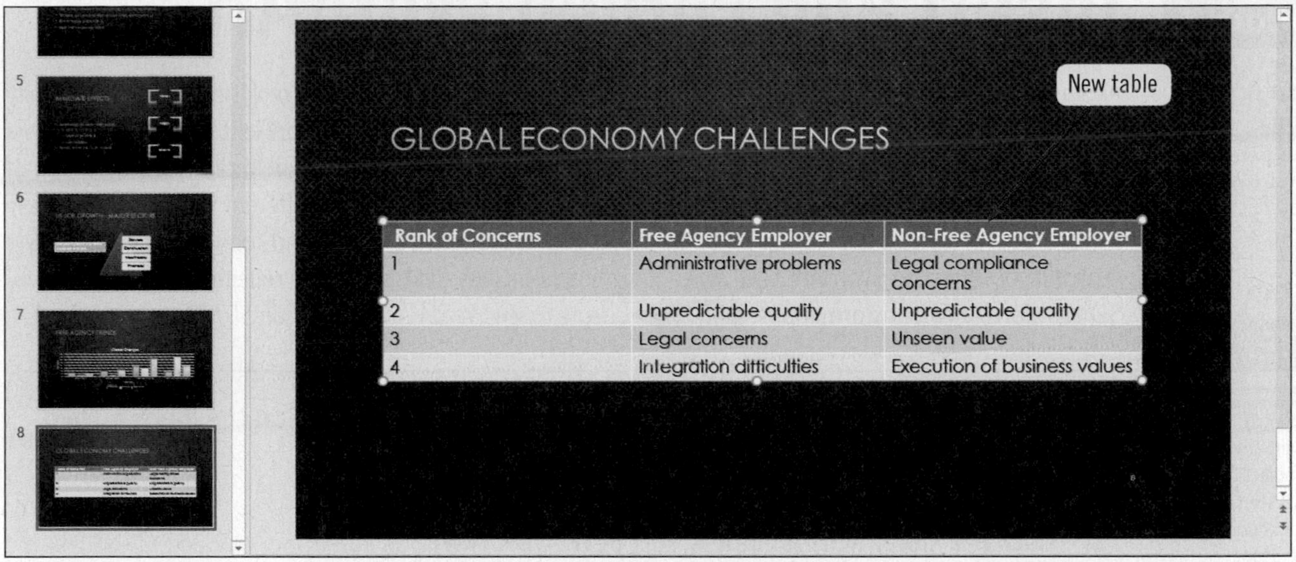

FIGURE 3-12: Formatted table

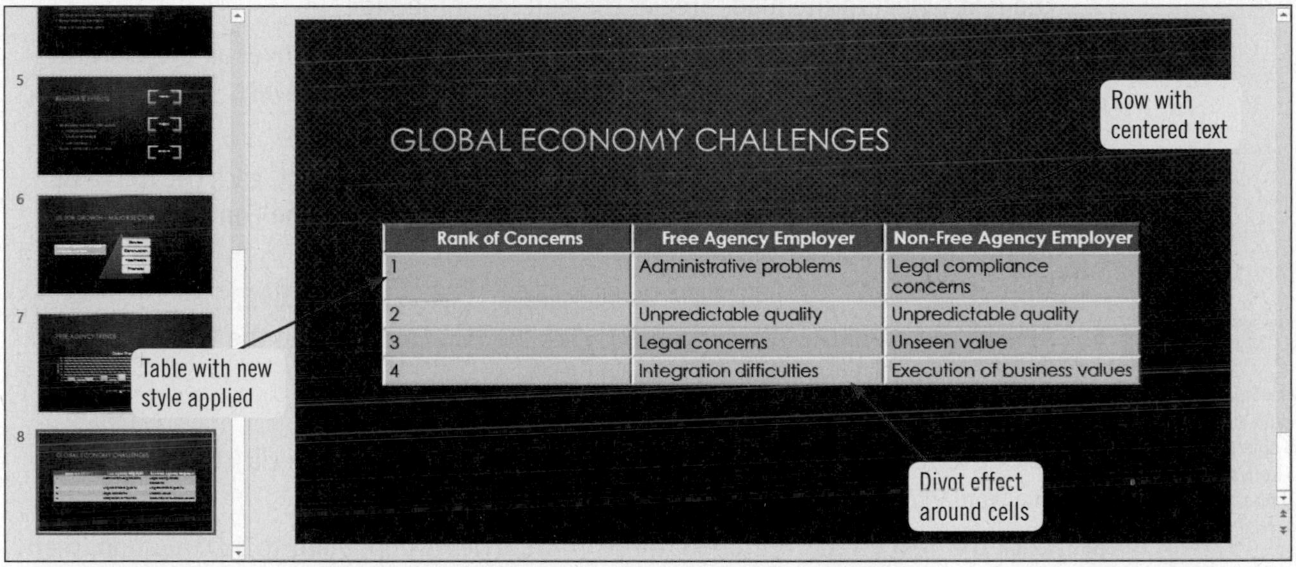

Setting permissions

In PowerPoint, you can set specific access permissions for people who review or edit your work so you have better control over your content. For example, you may want to give a user permission to edit or change your presentation but not allow them to print it. You can also restrict a user by permitting them to view the presentation without the ability to edit or print the presentation, or you can give the user full access or control of the presentation. To use this feature, you first access the information rights management services company. Then, to set user access permissions, click the File tab on the Ribbon, click Info, click the Protect Presentation button, point to Restrict Access, then click an appropriate option.

PowerPoint Module 3

Insert and Format WordArt

Learning Outcome
- Create, format, and resize WordArt

As you work to create an interesting presentation, your goal should include making your slides visually appealing. Sometimes plain text can come across as dull and unexciting in a presentation. **WordArt** is a set of decorative text styles, or text effects, you can apply to any text object to help direct the attention of your audience to a certain piece of information. You can use WordArt in two different ways: you can apply a WordArt text style to an existing text object that converts the text into WordArt, or you can create a new WordArt object. The WordArt text styles and effects include text shadows, reflections, glows, bevels, 3D rotations, and transformations. CASE *Create a new WordArt text object on Slide 3.*

STEPS

QUICK TIP
To convert any text or text object to WordArt, select the text or text object, click the Shape Format tab on the Ribbon, then click a WordArt style option in the WordArt Styles group.

1. **Click the Slide 3 thumbnail in the Slides tab, click the Insert tab on the Ribbon, then click the WordArt button in the Text group**
   The WordArt gallery appears displaying 20 WordArt text styles.
2. **Click Fill: Gold, Accent color 4; Soft Bevel (first row)**
   A text object appears in the middle of the slide displaying sample text with the WordArt style you just selected. The Shape Format tab is open on the Ribbon.
3. **Click the edge of the WordArt text object, then when the pointer changes to ✥, drag the text object to the blank area at the bottom of the slide**
4. **Click the More button ▾ in the WordArt Styles group, move ↖ over all the WordArt styles in the gallery, then click Fill: Tan, Accent color 3; Sharp Bevel**
   The sample text in the WordArt text object changes to the new WordArt style.
5. **Drag to select the text Your text here in the WordArt text object, click the Decrease Font Size button A˅ in the Mini toolbar so that 40 appears in the Font Size text box, then type Demand Drives Innovation**
   The text, "Demand Drives Innovation" is on the slide as WordArt. Compare your screen to **FIGURE 3-13**.

QUICK TIP
To convert a WordArt object to a SmartArt object, right-click the WordArt object, point to Convert to SmartArt on the shortcut menu, then click a SmartArt layout.

6. **Select the text in the WordArt object, click the Text Fill button in the WordArt Styles group, then click Tan, Accent 3, Darker 25%**
   The WordArt color is darker.
7. **Click the Text Outline button in the WordArt Styles group, then click White, Text 1**
   The WordArt outline is now white.
8. **Click the Text Effects button in the WordArt Styles group, point to 3-D Rotation, then click Perspective: Relaxed Moderately in the Perspective section (second row)**
   The off-axis effect is applied to the text object. You are unsure of this effect and apply another one.
9. **Click the Text Effects button, point to Transform, then click Triangle: Down in the Warp section (first row)**
   The effect is applied to the text object.
10. **Press SHIFT, drag the lower-right sizing handle down ½ inch, release SHIFT, click a blank area of the slide, then save your work**
    The text object is proportionally larger. Compare your screen to **FIGURE 3-14**.

FIGURE 3-13: WordArt inserted on slide

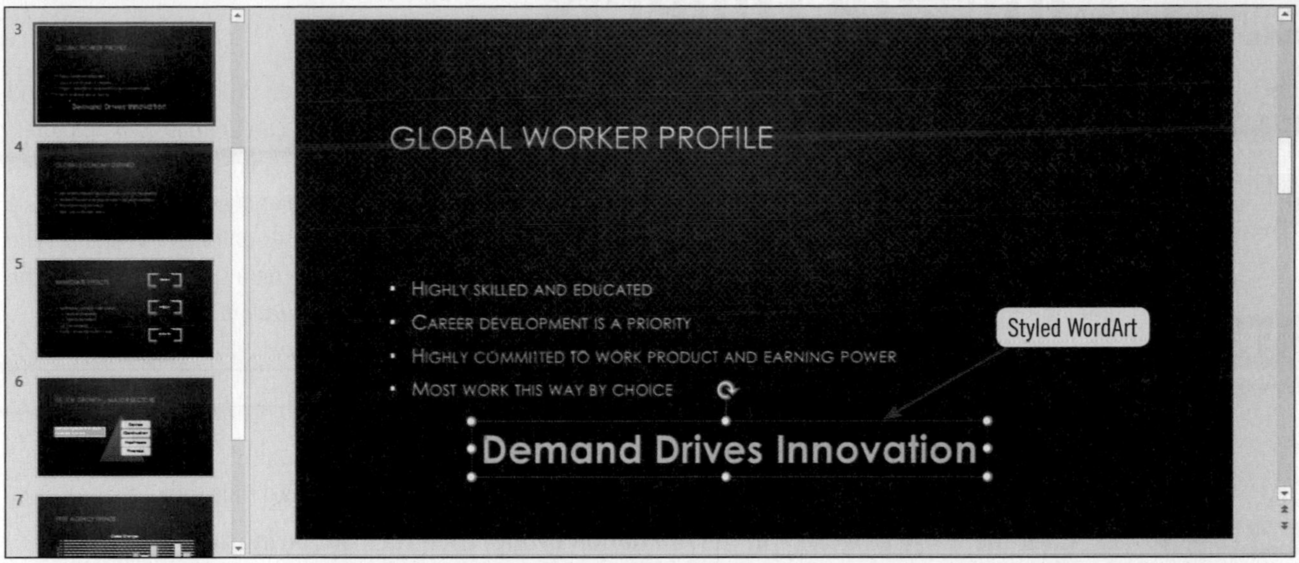

FIGURE 3-14: Formatted WordArt object

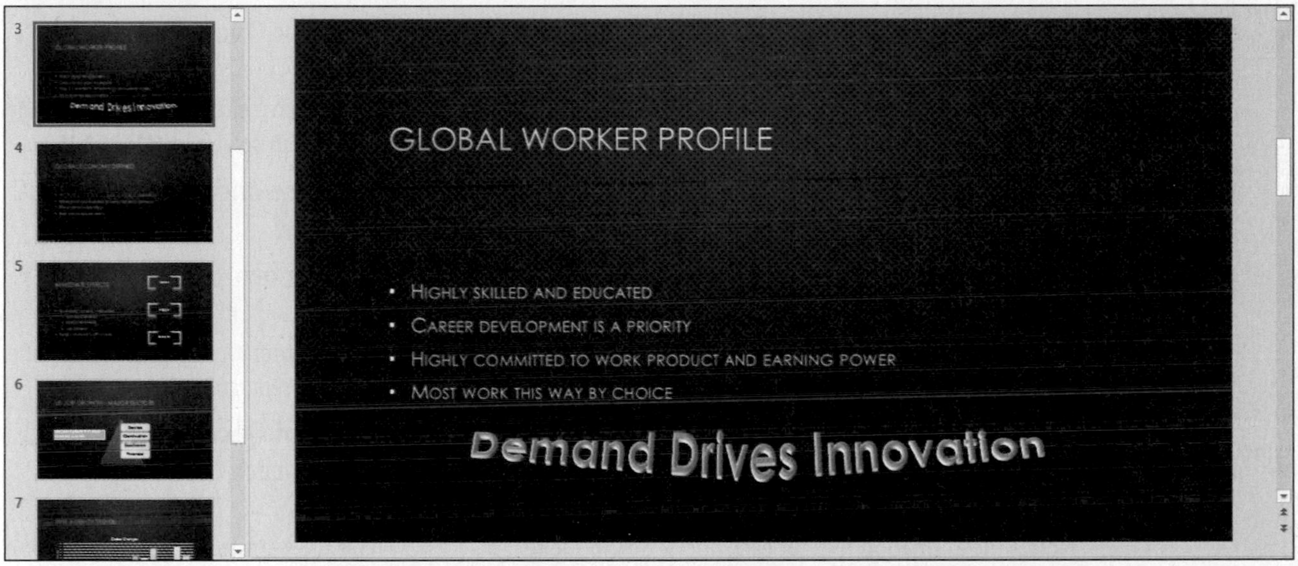

PowerPoint

Animate Objects

Learning Outcomes
- Animate objects
- Modify animation effects

Animations let you control how objects and text appear and move on the screen during a slide show and allow you to manage the flow of information and emphasize specific facts. You can animate text, pictures, sounds, hyperlinks, SmartArt diagrams, charts, and individual chart elements. Animations are organized into four categories: Entrance, Emphasis, Exit, and Motion Paths. The Entrance and Exit animations cause an object to enter or exit the slide with an effect. An Emphasis animation causes an object visible on the slide to have an effect, and a Motion Path animation causes an object to move on a specified path on the slide. **CASE** *You animate the text and graphics on several slides in the presentation.*

STEPS

1. **Click the Slide 6 thumbnail in the Slides tab, click the Animations tab on the Ribbon, then click the SmartArt object**

   Text as well as other objects, such as a shape or picture, can be animated during a slide show.

2. **Click the More button in the Animation group, then click Shape in the Entrance section**

   A small numeral 1, called an animation tag, appears on the slide. **Animation tags** identify the order in which objects are animated during a slide show.

3. **Click the Effect Options button in the Animation group, click All at Once, click the Effect Options button, then click Out**

   Effect options are different for every animation, and some animations don't have effect options. All of the objects in the SmartArt animate together in an outward direction. Compare your screen to **FIGURE 3-15**.

4. **Click the Slide Show button on the status bar, click your mouse once, then press ESC**

   The SmartArt object animates.

5. **Click the Slide 4 thumbnail in the Slides tab, click the bulleted list text object, then click Fade in the Animation group**

   The text object is animated with the Fade animation. Each line of text has an animation tag with each paragraph displaying a different number. Accordingly, each paragraph is animated separately.

6. **Click the Effect Options button in the Animation group, click All at Once, click the Duration up arrow in the Timing group until 01.50 appears, then click the Preview button in the Preview group**

   Notice the animation tags for each line of text in the text object now have the same numeral (1), indicating that each line of text animates at the same time.

7. **Click Economy in the title text object, click in the Animation group, scroll down, then click Arcs in the Motion Paths section**

   A motion path object appears over the shapes object and identifies the direction and shape, or path, of the animation. When needed, you can move, resize, and change the direction of the motion path. Notice the numeral 2 animation tag next to the title text object indicating that it is animated *after* the bulleted list text object. Compare your screen to **FIGURE 3-16**.

8. **Click the Move Earlier button in the Timing group, click the Slide Show tab on the Ribbon, then click the From Beginning button in the Start Slide Show group**

   Slide 1 appears in Slide Show view.

9. **Press SPACE to advance the slides, when you see the black slide, press ENTER, then save your changes**

QUICK TIP
There are additional animation options for each animation category located at the bottom of the animations gallery.

QUICK TIP
If you want to individually animate the parts of a grouped object, then you must ungroup the objects before you animate them.

FIGURE 3-15: Animation applied to SmartArt object

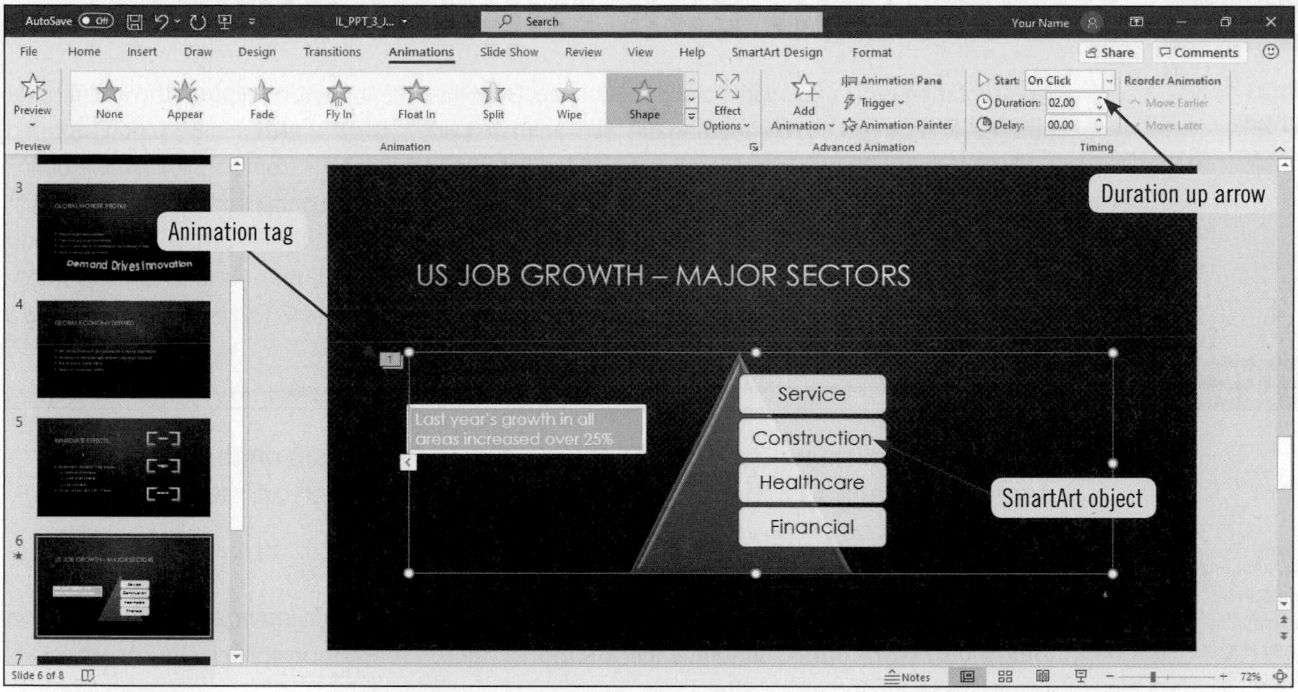

FIGURE 3-16: Motion path applied to title text object

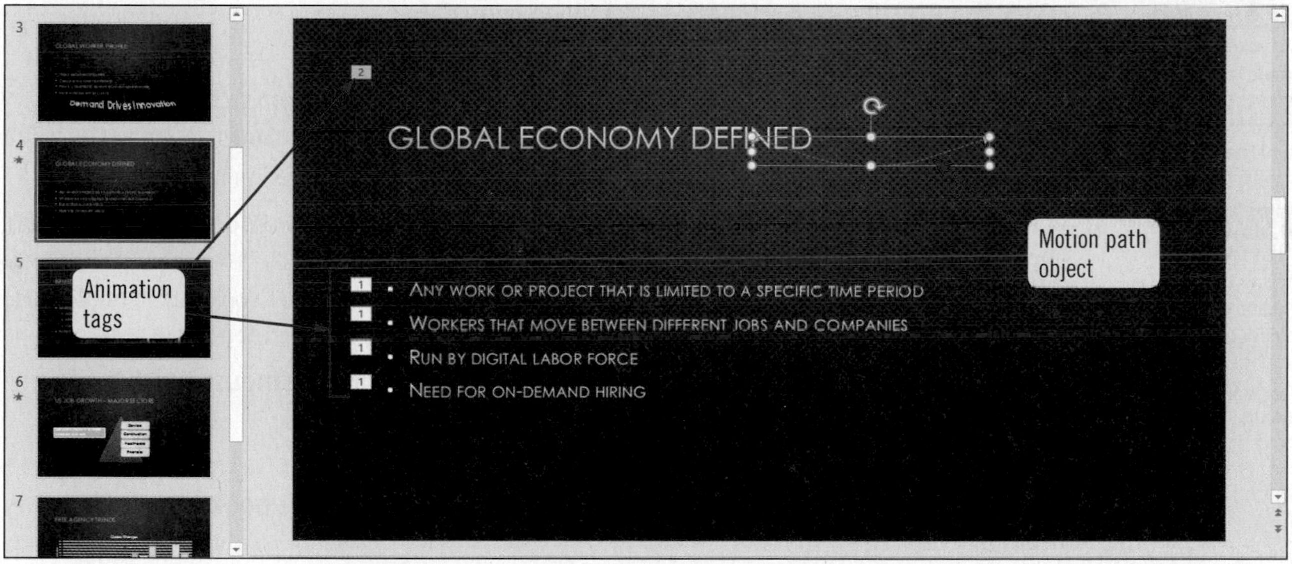

Attaching a sound to an animation

Text or objects that have animation applied can be customized further by attaching a sound for extra emphasis. First, select the animated object, then on the Animations tab, click the Animation Pane button in the Advanced Animation group. In the Animation Pane, click the animation you want to apply the sound to, click the Animation list arrow, then click Effect Options to open the animation effect's dialog box. In the Enhancements section, click the Sound list arrow, then choose a sound. Click OK when you are finished. Now, when you run the slide show, the sound you applied will play with the animation.

PowerPoint **Module 3**

Insert and Edit Digital Video

Learning Outcomes
- Link a video
- Add a bookmark

In your presentation, you may want to use special effects to illustrate a point or capture the attention of your audience. You can do this by inserting digital or animated video. **Digital video** is live action captured in digital format by a video camera. You can embed or link a digital video file from your hard drive or link a digital video file from a webpage on the Internet. **Animated video** contains multiple images that stream together or move to give the illusion of motion. If you need to edit the length of a video or add effects or background color to a video, you can use PowerPoint's video-editing tools to accomplish those and other basic editing tasks. CASE *You continue to develop your presentation by inserting and editing a video clip.*

STEPS

1. **Click the Slide 4 thumbnail in the Slides tab, click the Home tab on the Ribbon, right-click a blank area of the slide, point to Layout in the shortcut menu, then click Two Content**
   The slide layout changes and has two content placeholders.
2. **Click the Insert Video icon in the new Content placeholder, navigate to the location where you store your Data Files, click Support_PPT_3_Video.mp4, click the Insert list arrow, then click Link to File**
   The Support_PPT_3_Video.mp4 video clip displaying a black preview image is linked to the slide. By linking the digital video to the presentation, you do not increase the file size of the presentation, but remember, you need direct access to the location where the video file is stored in order to play it.
3. **Click the Play/Pause button in the video control bar**
   The short video plays through once but does not rewind to the beginning.
4. **Click the Playback tab on the Ribbon, click the Rewind after Playing check box in the Video Options group, then click the Play button in the Preview group**
   The video plays through once, and this time the video rewinds back to the beginning.
5. **Click the video control timeline at about 00:06.00, then click the Add Bookmark button in the Bookmarks group as shown in FIGURE 3-17**
   A yellow circle appears in the video control timeline, indicating the video has a bookmark. A **bookmark** can indicate a point of interest in a video; it can also be used to jump to a specific point in a video.
6. **Click the Slide Show button on the status bar, then click the mouse twice to view the animations on the slide**
   The text object animations play.
7. **Move over the video, the pointer changes to , then click the bookmark as shown in FIGURE 3-18**
   The video moves to the bookmarked frame.
8. **Click the Play/Pause button on the video**
   The video plays from the bookmarked frame to the end of the video and then rewinds to the beginning.
9. **Press ESC, click the Video Format tab on the Ribbon, click the More button in the Video Styles group, then click Reflected Bevel Black in the Intense section**
   A bevel effect is added to the video.
10. **sam Click a blank area of the slide, save your work, submit your presentation to your instructor, then exit PowerPoint**

QUICK TIP
Adjust the volume of the video using the Mute/Unmute control on the video control timeline.

QUICK TIP
You can also add fade effects to the beginning and end of a video using the Fade Duration commands in the Editing group.

QUICK TIP
Click the Reset Design button in the Adjust group to remove all formatting changes you made to the video.

FIGURE 3-17: Video clip inserted on the slide

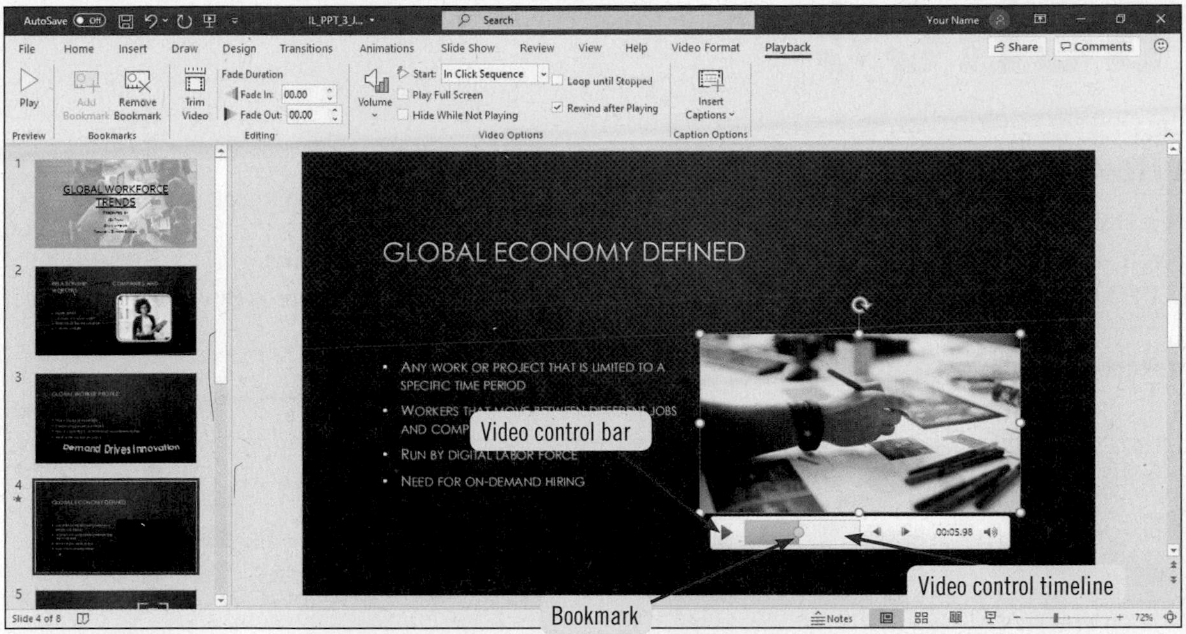

Nikita Sursin/Shutterstock.com

FIGURE 3-18: Video in Slide Show view with selected bookmark

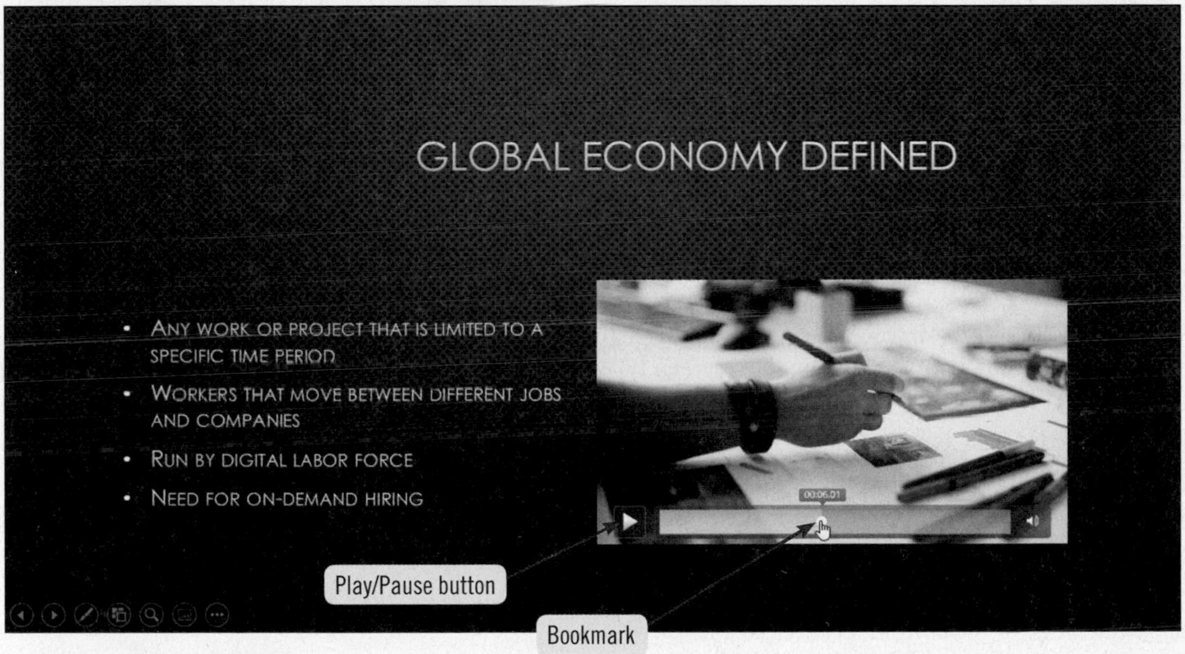

Nikita Sursin/Shutterstock.com

Saving a presentation as a video

You can save your PowerPoint presentation as a full-fidelity video, which incorporates all slide timings, transitions, animations, and narrations. The video can be distributed using a thumb drive, the Internet, or email. Depending on how you want to display your video, you have four resolution settings from which to choose: Ultra HD (4K), Full HD (1080p), HD (720p), and Standard (480p). The largest two settings, Ultra HD (3840 × 2160) and Full HD (1920 × 1080), are used for viewing on a computer monitor, projector, or other high-definition displays. The next setting, HD (1280 × 720), is used for uploading to the web or copying to a standard DVD. The smallest setting, Standard (852 × 480), is used on portable media players. To save your presentation as a video, click the File tab, click Export, click Create a Video, choose your settings, then click the Create Video button.

Practice

Skills Review

1. **Insert a text box.**
   a. Open IL_PPT_3-2.pptx from the location where you store your Data Files, then save it as **IL_PPT_3_Broker2**. You will work to create the completed presentation as shown in **FIGURE 3-19**.

FIGURE 3-19

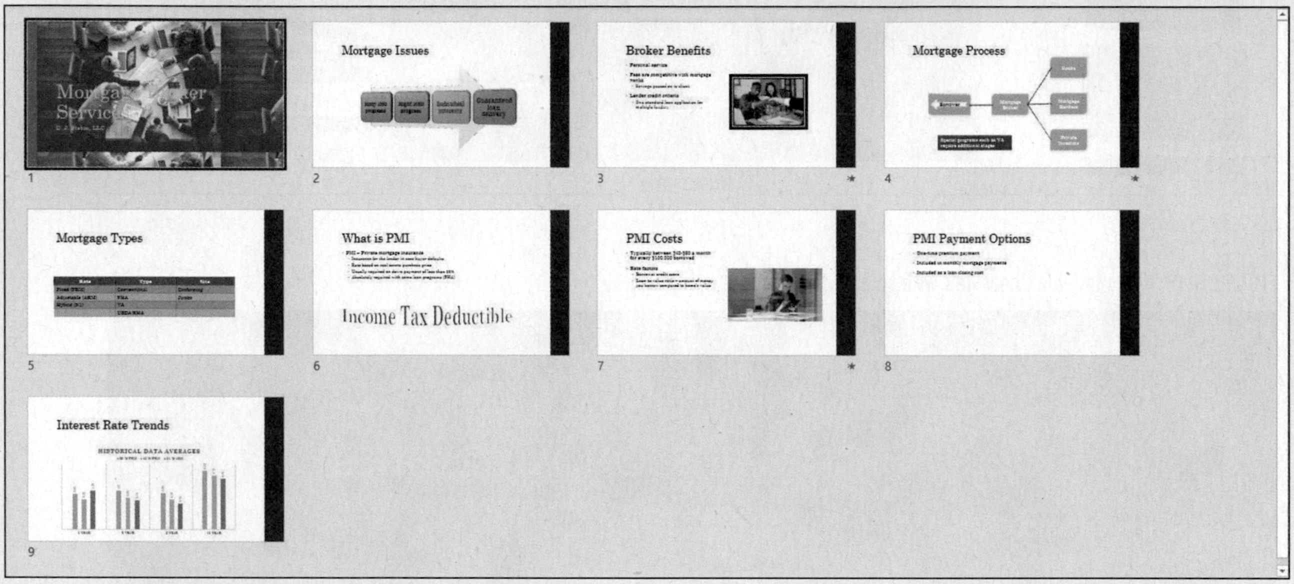

Rawpixel.com/Shutterstock.com; Gorodenkoff/Shutterstock.com; Jacob Lund/Shutterstock.com

   b. On Slide 4, insert a text box below the shapes, then type **Special programs require additional stages such as VA**
   c. Move the words "such as VA" after the word "programs", then add space between words, as necessary.
   d. Select the text object, then click the More button in the Shape Styles group on the Shape Format tab.
   e. Click Moderate Effect – Purple, Accent 5, then resize the text box to fit the text on two lines by dragging its sizing handles, if necessary. The second line of text begins with the word "require".
   f. Using Smart Guides, drag the text object so its right edge is centered on the slide and its bottom edge is aligned with the bottom edge of the bottom rectangle shape.

2. **Crop and style a picture.**
   a. Select Slide 3 in the Slides tab, then crop the left side of the picture up to the right cup on the table in the background.
   b. Drag the picture to the center of the blank area of the slide.
   c. Click the Color button, then change the color tone to Temperature: 8800 K.
   d. Click the Corrections button, then change the sharpness of the picture to Sharpen: 50%.
   e. Change the picture style to Double Frame, Black.
   f. Select Slide 1 in the Slides tab, open the Format Background task pane, then click the Picture or texture fill option button.

Skills Review (continued)

g. Click the Insert button in the task pane, click From a File, then insert the picture Support_PPT_3_Group.jpg from the location where you store your Data Files.

h. Click the Tile picture as texture check box in the task pane, close the Format Background pane, then save your changes.

3. Insert a chart.

a. Create a new slide after Slide 5 with a Title and Content layout and title it **Interest Rate Trends**.

b. Insert a Clustered Column chart, then close the worksheet.

c. Drag the chart down the slide away from the title, then apply the Layout 3 quick layout to the chart.

4. Enter and edit chart data.

a. Show the worksheet, enter the data shown in **TABLE 3-2** into the worksheet, then close the worksheet.

b. Type **Historical Data Averages** in the chart title text object then increase the font size of the chart title using the Increase Font Size button.

c. Click the Chart Styles button next to the chart, then change the chart style to Style 2.

TABLE 3-2

	30 Yr FRM	15 Yr FRM	5/1 Yr ARM
1 Year	3.82	3.19	4.19
3 Year	4.20	3.36	3.14
5 Year	3.89	3.19	2.75
10 Year	6.32	5.79	5.45

d. Click Color in the Charts Styles gallery, then change the color to Colorful Palette 3 in the Colorful section.

e. Close the Charts Styles gallery, then save your changes.

5. Insert slides from other presentations.

a. Go to Slide 5, then open the Reuse Slides pane.

b. Open Support_PPT_3_PMI.pptx from the location where you store your Data Files, then click the Use source formatting check box.

c. Insert the second slide thumbnail, insert the third slide thumbnail, then insert the first slide thumbnail.

d. Close the Reuse Slides pane, then open the Slide Sorter view.

e. Move Slide 8 between Slide 5 and Slide 6, switch to Normal view, then save your work.

6. Insert a table.

a. Go to Slide 5, then insert a table with two columns and four rows.

b. Add one more row and one more column to the table, then enter the information shown in **TABLE 3-3**.

c. On the Table Design tab, change the table style to Themed Style 1 – Accent 5.

d. On the Layout tab, select the top row, then center the text.

e. Select the whole table, open the Table Design tab, click the Effects button, point to Cell Bevel, then apply the Soft Round effect.

f. Move the table to the center of the blank area of the slide, then save your changes.

TABLE 3-3

Rate	Type	Size
Fixed (FRM)	Conventional	Conforming
Adjustable (ARM)	FHA	Jumbo
Hybrid (5/1)	VA	
	USDA/RHA	

7. Insert and format WordArt.

a. Go to Slide 6, then insert a WordArt text object using the style Gradient Fill, Gray.

b. Type **Income Tax Deductible**, apply the Transform text effect Inflate (sixth row in the Warp section) to the text object, then move the text object to the middle of the blank area of the slide.

c. Apply the 3-D Rotation text effect Perspective: Relaxed Moderately (second row in the Perspective section).

d. Change the text fill color to Dark Red, then change the text outline to Black, Text 1.

e. Apply the WordArt style Fill: Black, Text color 1; Outline: White, Background color 1; Hard Shadow: Purple, Accent color 5.

f. Increase the size of the WordArt object proportionally, view the slide in Slide Show view, then save your changes.

Skills Review (continued)

8. Animate objects.

a. Go to Slide 4, click the Animations tab, then select the four black arrow lines on the slide. (*Hint*: Use SHIFT to select the shapes.)

b. Apply the Wipe effect to the objects, click the Effect Options button, then apply the From Right effect.

c. Change the animation duration to 01.00, then preview the animations.

d. Click the Move Earlier button in the Timing group.

e. Go to Slide 3, click the title text object, then apply the animation Brush Color in the Emphasis section.

f. Click the Effect Options button, click Orange in Standard Colors, then open Slide Show view.

g. Click through the animations on Slides 3 and 4, press ESC when you see Slide 5, then save your work.

9. Insert and edit digital video.

a. Go to Slide 7, change the slide layout to Two Content, then click the Insert Video icon.

b. Locate the file Support_PPT_3_Desk.mp4 from the location where you store your Data Files, click the Insert list arrow, then click Link to File.

c. On the Playback tab, click the Rewind after Playing check box, then add a bookmark at about the 00:04.00 point on the video control timeline.

d. Apply the video style Center Shadow Rectangle, then preview the video clip in Slide Show view.

e. Switch to Normal view, then save your work.

f. Submit your presentation to your instructor, close your presentation, then exit PowerPoint.

Independent Challenge 1

Riverwalk Medical Clinic (RMC), is a large medical facility in Cambridge, Massachusetts. You continue to work on a presentation on the latest emergency response procedures for a staff training later in the week.

a. Start PowerPoint, open IL_PPT_3-3.pptx from the location where you store your Data Files, and save it as **IL_PPT_3_Riverwalk**. You will work to create the completed presentation as shown in **FIGURE 3-20**.

b. Add your name and today's date to Slide 1 in the Subtitle text box.

c. Go to Slide 4, change the slide layout to Two Content, click the Pictures icon in the content placeholder, then insert the file Support_PPT_3_ER.jpg from the location where you store your Data Files.

d. Crop the right side of the picture up to the red emergency sign next to the entrance, apply the Drop Shadow Rectangle picture style to the picture, click the Color button, then change the color tone to Temperature: 5300 K.

FIGURE 3-20

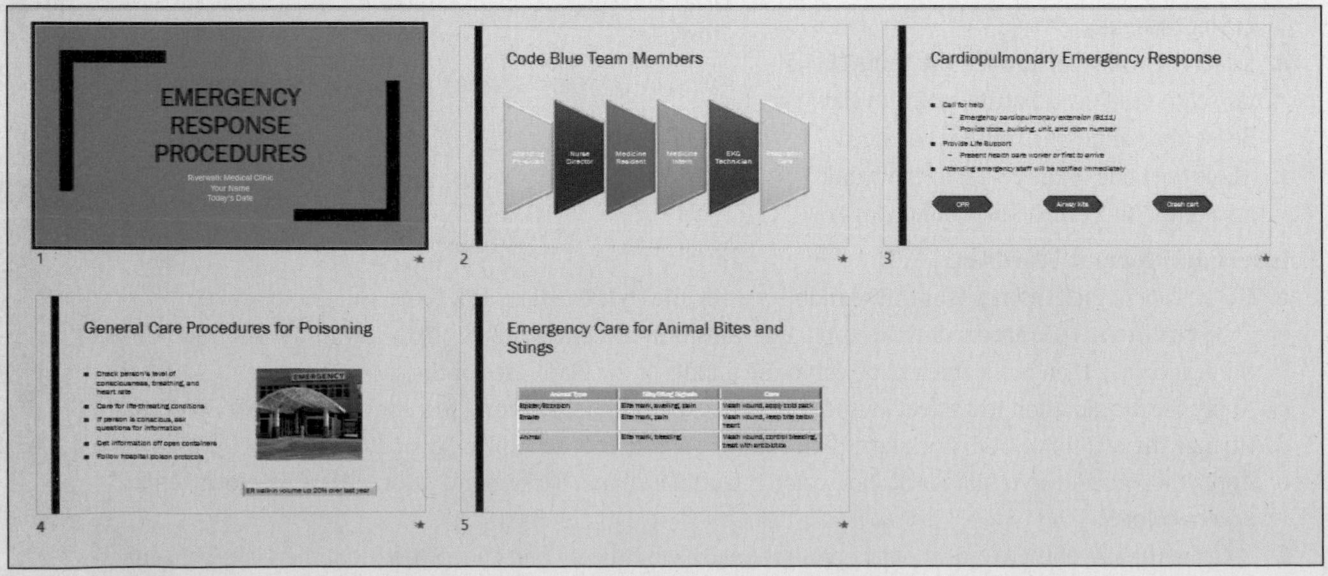

dcwcreations/Shutterstock.com

Independent Challenge 1 (continued)

e. Change the sharpness of the picture to Sharpen: 25%, then move the picture to the center of the blank area of the slide.
f. Insert a text box on the slide below the picture, type **ER walk-in volume up 20% over last year**, then change the text color to red.
g. Apply the shape style Colored Fill - Gold, Accent 2 to the text object, then apply the Preset 2 shape effect.
h. Go to Slide 5, create a new table, then enter the data in **TABLE 3-4**.
i. Apply the table style Medium Style 1 - Accent 2, apply the Round bevel effect, then center the text in the top row of the table.
j. Apply the Fly In animation to the SmartArt object on Slide 2, change the effect option to From Bottom-Right and the sequence to One by One, then change the duration to 01.00.
k. Add a Doors transition to all slides with a horizontal effect, and a duration time of 02.00.
l. View the final presentation in Slide Show view.
m. Save the presentation, submit the presentation to your instructor, close the file, then exit PowerPoint.

TABLE 3-4

Animal Type	Bite/Sting Signals	Care
Spider/Scorpion	Bite mark, swelling, pain	Wash wound, apply cold pack
Snake	Bite mark, pain	Wash wound, keep bite below heart
Animal	Bite mark, bleeding	Wash wound, control bleeding, treat with antibiotics

Independent Challenge 2

You are an associate at Myers Reed, a financial investment and management company, located in St. Louis, Missouri. One of your responsibilities is to create general presentations for use on the company website. As part of this presentation, you insert a chart, insert a video, add a WordArt object, and insert slides from another presentation. You finish the presentation by adding slide transitions and animations to the slides.

a. Open IL_PPT_3_4.pptx from the location where you store your Data Files, then save it as **IL_PPT_3_Reed**. You will work to create the completed presentation as shown in **FIGURE 3-21**.
b. Apply the Ion Design Theme, refer to Slide 1 in **FIGURE 3-21** and select the thumbnail in the Design Ideas task pane, then close the task pane.

FIGURE 3-21

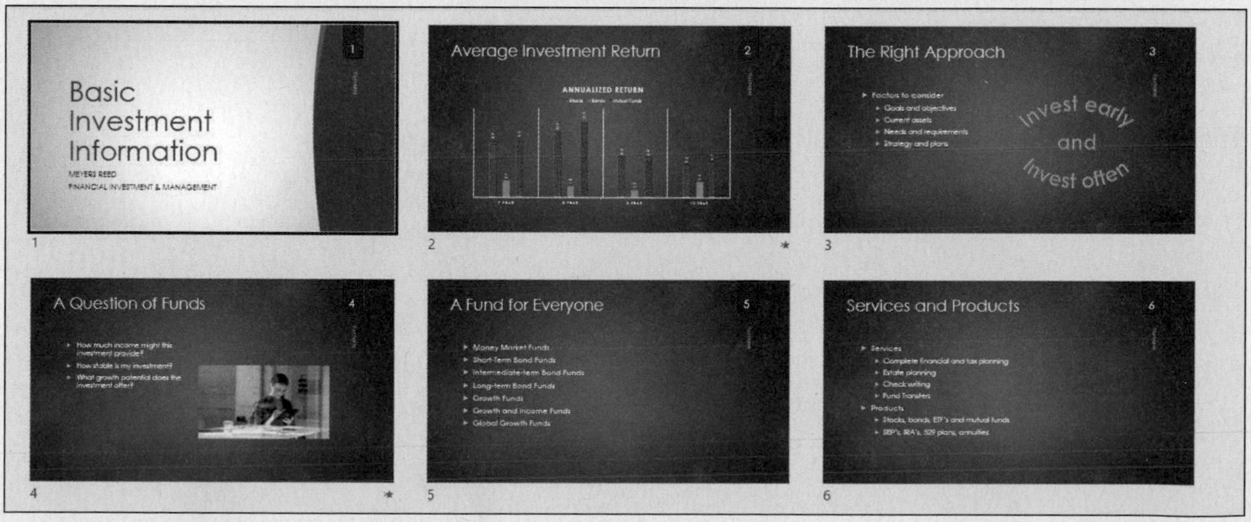

Gorodenkoff/Shutterstock.com

PowerPoint

Independent Challenge 2 (continued)

c. Insert a clustered column chart on Slide 2, then enter the data in **TABLE 3-5** into the worksheet.

d. Close the worksheet, format the chart using Style 2, change the color to Colorful Palette 3, then move the chart to the center of the blank area of the slide.

e. Type **Annualized Return** in the chart title text object, then decrease the font size to 20 point.

f. Open the Reuse Slides pane, open Support_PPT_3_Invest.pptx from the location where you store your Data Files, then insert Slides 2, 3, and 4.

g. Close the Reuse Slides pane, open Slide Sorter view, move Slide 5 between Slide 3 and Slide 4, then double-click Slide 3.

h. Insert a WordArt object using the Fill: Gold, Accent color 3; Sharp Bevel style, type **Invest early**, press ENTER, type **and**, press ENTER, then type **Invest often**.

i. Click the Text Effects button, point to Transform, apply the Button text effect from the Follow Path section, then move the WordArt object to a blank area of the slide.

j. Go to Slide 4, change the slide layout to Two Content, then link the video Support_PPT_3_Desk.mp4 from the location where you store your Data Files. (*Hint*: be sure to use the Link to File option when you link the video in this step.)

k. Insert a bookmark at about 00:03.00, rewind the video after playing, then apply the Center Shadow Rectangle video style.

l. Go to Slide 2, apply the animation Float In to the chart, apply the By Element in Category effect option, then set the duration to 01.50.

m. Apply the animation Random Bars to the slide title, then reorder the animation to first in the sequence.

n. Add your name and slide number as the footer on all of the slides, view the slide show, then save your work.

o. Submit the presentation to your instructor, close the presentation, then exit PowerPoint.

TABLE 3-5

	Stocks	Bonds	Mutual Funds
1 Year	8.9	2.7	9.3
3 Year	10.3	1.8	11.9
5 Year	6.6	1.3	6.4
10 Year	5.2	2.5	5.7

Visual Workshop

Create a one-slide presentation that looks like **FIGURE 3-22**. To complete this presentation, insert the picture file Support_PPT_3_Woman.jpg from the location where you store your Data Files to the slide background. Change the picture transparency to 30% and then format the text box with a 54-point, Orange, Accent 2 Calibri Light font and then apply a Tight Reflection: Touching text effect. Set the text object's top edge at 1.00 and its right edge on the slide center line. Add your name as footer text to the slide, save the presentation as **IL_PPT_3_Brookdale** to the location where you store your Data Files, then submit your presentation to your instructor.

FIGURE 3-22

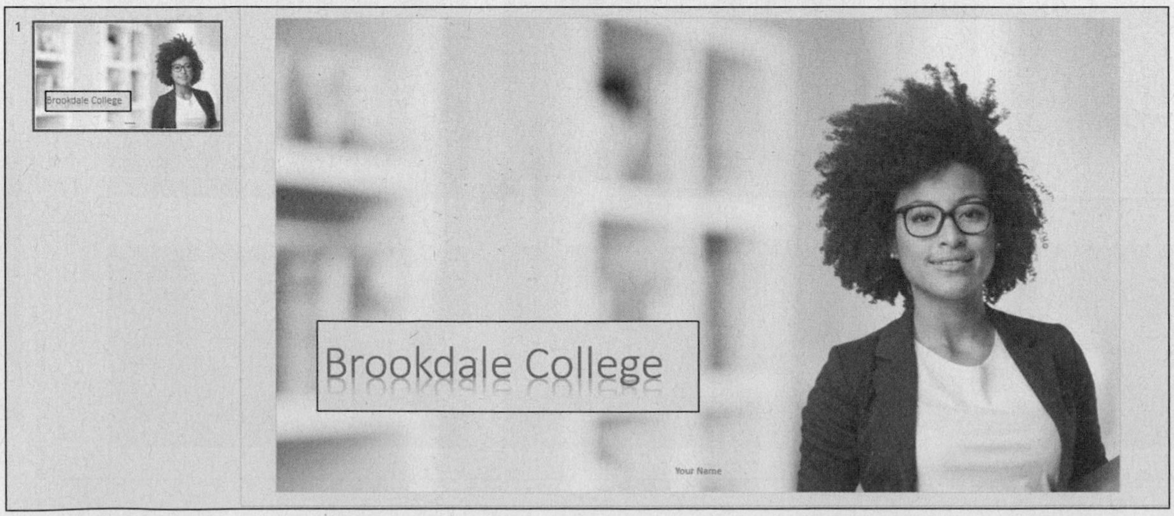

Asier Romero/Shutterstock.com

Integration **Module 3**

Integrating Word, Excel, Access, and PowerPoint

CASE Anthony Martinez, vice president of sales and marketing at the head office of JCL Talent, Inc., in Atlanta, GA, creates presentations for clients that often include objects from Word, Excel, and Access. He asks you to explore how to use linking and embedding in Office and then how to insert linked objects from Word, Excel, and Access into a PowerPoint presentation.

Module Objectives

After completing this module, you will be able to:

- Integrate data among Word, Excel, Access, and PowerPoint
- Import a Word outline into PowerPoint
- Embed an Excel worksheet in PowerPoint
- Link Access and Excel objects to PowerPoint
- Manage links

Files You Will Need

IL_INT_3-1.docx
IL_INT_3-2.accdb
IL_INT_3-3.docx
IL_INT_3-4.accdb
IL_INT_3-5.docx
IL_INT_3-6.accdb
IL_INT_3-7.docx
IL_INT_3-8.accdb
IL_INT_3-9.accdb

Integration
Module 3

Learning Outcome
- Identify integration options for Word, Excel, Access, and PowerPoint

Integrate Data among Word, Excel, Access, and PowerPoint

You can integrate information into a PowerPoint presentation using the linking and embedding techniques you learned with Word, Excel, and Access. As with those programs, you embed data created in other programs in PowerPoint when you want to be able to edit the data from within the destination file. You use linking when you want the linked data in the destination file to be updated when you change the data in the source file. In addition, you can import a Word outline into PowerPoint to automatically create slides without having to reenter information. The PowerPoint presentation in **FIGURE 3-1** includes information originally created in Word, Excel, and Access. **CASE** *Before you create the presentation, you review some of the ways you can integrate information among Word, Excel, Access, and PowerPoint.*

DETAILS

You can integrate Word, Excel, Access, and PowerPoint by:

- **Importing a Word outline into PowerPoint**

  In the course of your work, you may create Word documents that contain information that you also want to use in a PowerPoint presentation. Instead of retyping the information in PowerPoint, you can save time by importing it directly from Word into PowerPoint. **FIGURE 3-1** shows how a Word outline appears before and after it is imported into a PowerPoint presentation. Each Level 1 heading in the outline becomes a slide, and the Level 2 headings become bullets on the slides. Before you import a Word outline, you need to make sure all the headings and subheadings are formatted with heading styles. When you import an outline from Word to PowerPoint, you cannot create a link between the two files.

- **Embedding objects**

  Recall that when you embed an object, you do not create a link to the source file. However, you can use the source program tools to edit the embedded object within the destination file. An embedded object becomes a part of the PowerPoint file, which means that the file size of the PowerPoint presentation increases relative to the file size of the embedded object; a large embedded object, such as a graphic, will increase the size of the PowerPoint presentation considerably. To embed an object in a PowerPoint presentation, you use the Object command in the Text group on the Insert tab. In **FIGURE 3-1**, the table on Slide 3 is an embedded Excel worksheet object.

  To edit an embedded object, you double-click it. The source program starts, and the Ribbon and tabs of the source program appear inside the PowerPoint window.

- **Linking objects**

  When you link an object to a PowerPoint slide, a picture of the object is placed on the slide instead of the actual object. This representation of the object is connected, or linked, to the original file. The object is still stored in the source file in the source program, unlike an embedded object, which is stored directly on the PowerPoint slide. Any change you make to a linked object's source file is reflected in the linked object. The pie chart shown on Slide 4 of the presentation in **FIGURE 3-1** is linked to values entered in an Excel worksheet, which is, in turn, linked to data entered in an Access database. The differences between embedding and linking are summarized in **TABLE 3-1**.

  You can open the source file and make changes to the linked object as long as all files remain on your computer. When you move files among machines or transmit files to other people, the links will not be maintained. However, recipients can open and view the linked files. After opening the workbook in Excel, they need to click No, close the workbook without saving it, then reopen the workbook and click Don't Update. In Word, they click No to update links.

FIGURE 3-1: PowerPoint presentation with integrated objects

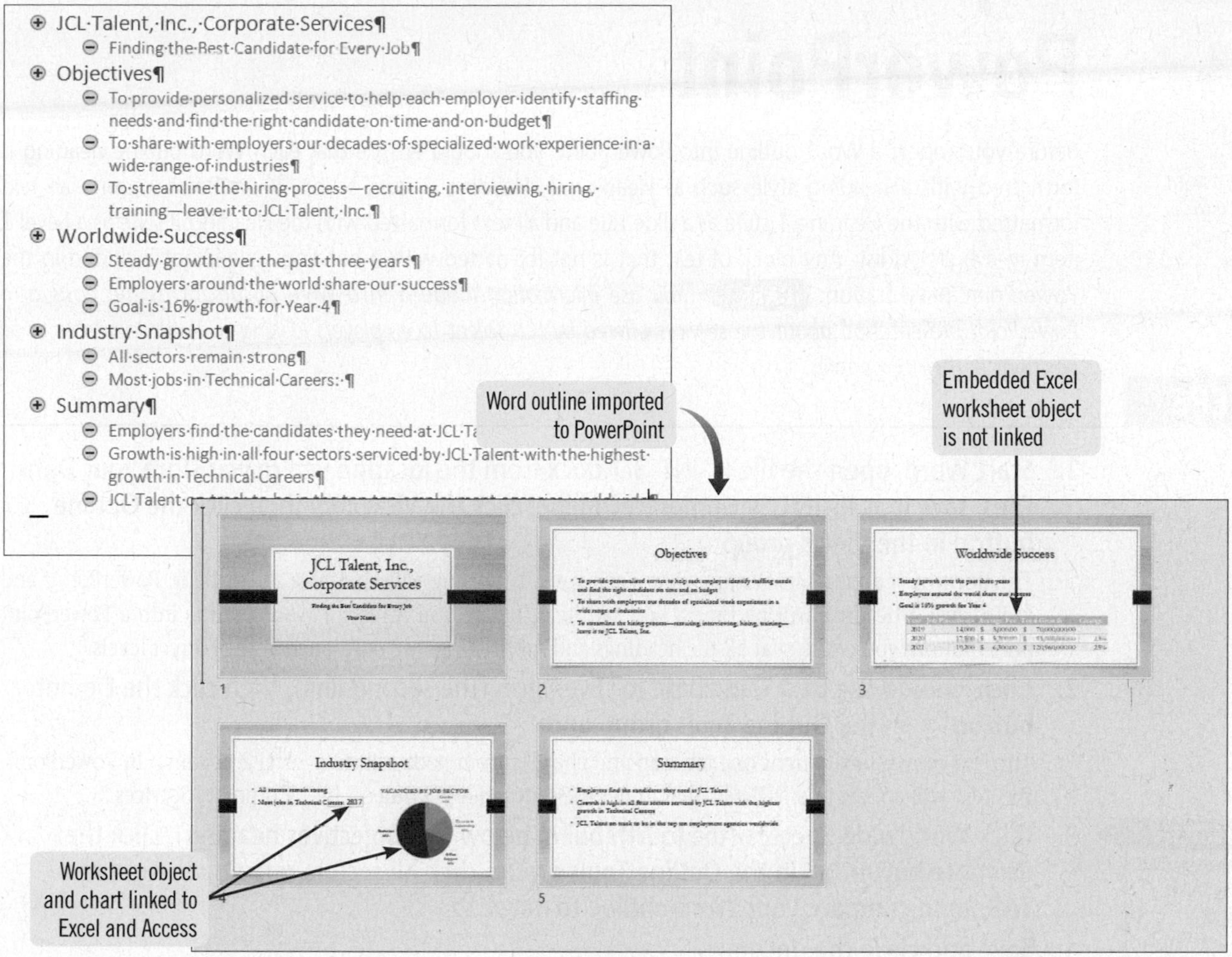

TABLE 3-1: Embedding vs. linking

	Embed	Link
User	You are the only user of an object and you want the object to be a part of your presentation	The object's source file is shared on a network or other users have access to the file and can change it
Availability	You want to open the object in its source program, even when the source file is not available	You are able to open the source file
Timeliness	Information does not change over time	You always want the object to include the latest information
Updating	You want to update the object manually while working in PowerPoint	You want the object to update automatically
File size	File size is not an issue	You want to keep the file size of the presentation small

Learning Outcomes
- Prepare a Word outline for PowerPoint
- Import a Word outline into PowerPoint

Import a Word Outline into PowerPoint

Before you import a Word outline into PowerPoint, you should ensure that each Word outline heading is formatted with a heading style such as Heading 1, Heading 2, and so on. PowerPoint imports all text formatted with the Heading 1 style as a slide title and all text formatted with the Heading 2 style as a Level 1 item in a bulleted list. Any block of text that is not formatted with a heading style is not included in the PowerPoint presentation. **CASE** *You use information included in a Word document as the basis of a PowerPoint presentation about the services offered by JCL Talent to employers looking to find candidates to fill positions in their companies.*

STEPS

1. **Start Word, open the file IL_INT_3-1.docx from the location where you store your Data Files, save it as IL_INT_3_CorporateOutline, click the View tab, then click the Outline button in the Views group**
   The document appears in Outline view. Each Level 1 heading will become a slide title in PowerPoint, and each Level 2 heading will become a bulleted item. Before you import a Word outline into a PowerPoint presentation, you check that all the headings and subheadings are positioned at the correct levels.
2. **Click Finding the Best Candidate for Every Job (the second line), then click the Demote button in the Outline Tools group once**
   The text moves to the right one tab stop and changes from body text to a Level 2 heading. In PowerPoint, this text will appear as a bulleted item under the slide title "JCL Talent, Inc., Corporate Services."
3. **Click Worldwide Success (the fourth bullet below the Objectives heading), click the Promote button in the Outline Tools group, click All sectors remain strong, press TAB, then compare your Word outline to FIGURE 3-2**
4. **Save and close the document**
5. **Start PowerPoint, create a blank presentation, then save it as IL_INT_3_CorporatePresentation in the location where you store your Data Files**
6. **Click the New Slide arrow in the Slides group, click Slides from Outline, navigate to the location where you stored IL_INT_3_CorporateOutline.docx, then double-click IL_INT_3_CorporateOutline.docx**
   The Thumbnails pane and the status bar indicate the presentation now contains six slides. Slide 1 is blank, and Slides 2 through 6 represent the Level 1 headings in the Word outline.
7. **Click Slide 1 in the Thumbnails pane, press DELETE, click the Layout button in the Slides group, click Title Slide, click the View tab, click the Outline View button in the Presentation Views group, click after Finding the Best Candidate for Every Job on Slide 1, press ENTER, then type your name**
   You change the slide layout for the first slide so the title and subtitle of the presentation and your name appear in the middle of the slide.
8. **Click the Design tab, click the More button in the Themes group, then click the Organic theme**
9. **Click the View tab, click the Slide Sorter button in the Presentation Views group, press CTRL+A to select all the slides, click the Home tab, click the Reset button in the Slides group, then save the presentation**
   The formatted presentation appears as shown in **FIGURE 3-3**.

QUICK TIP
You can also use TAB and SHIFT+TAB to demote and promote headings in Outline view.

QUICK TIP
When you import slides into PowerPoint, you need to reset the layout of the slides to conform to the PowerPoint slide design you have applied.

FIGURE 3-2: Edited outline in Word Outline view

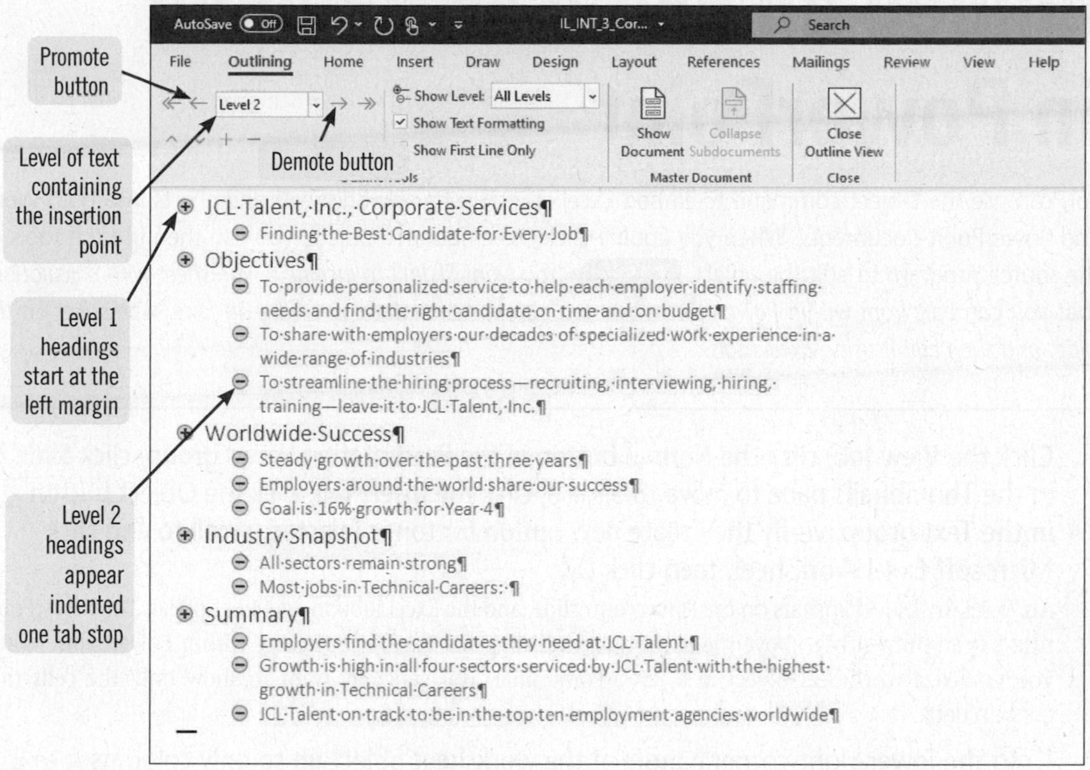

FIGURE 3-3: Formatted presentation in Slide Sorter view

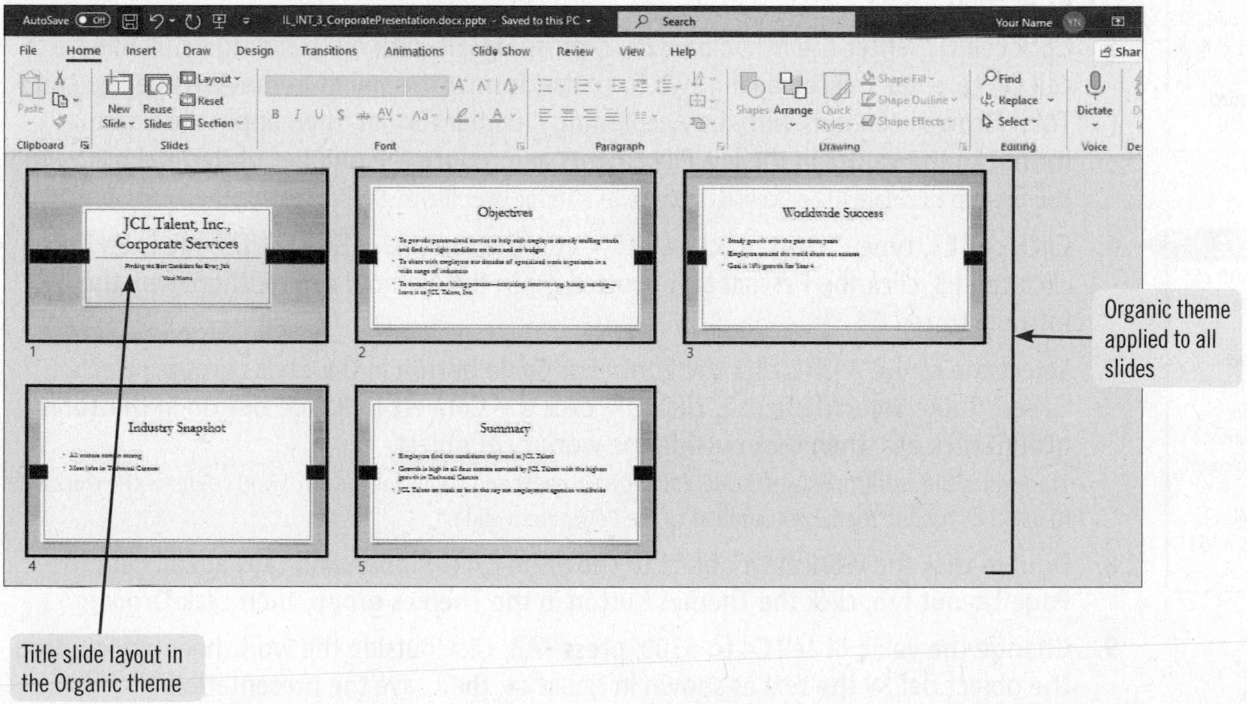

Embed an Excel Worksheet in PowerPoint

Learning Outcomes
- Embed a Worksheet object in PowerPoint
- Edit an embedded worksheet

You can use the Object command to embed Excel objects such as worksheets and charts into both Word and PowerPoint documents. When you double-click the embedded object, you can then use the tools of the source program to edit the object. **CASE** *You want Slide 3 to include a worksheet with calculations that you can edit from within PowerPoint when you obtain new data. You create an Excel worksheet on the slide, and then edit it using Excel tools.*

STEPS

1. **Click the View tab, click the Normal button in the Presentation Views group, click Slide 3 in the Thumbnails pane to move to Slide 3, click the Insert tab, click the Object button in the Text group, verify the Create new option button is selected, scroll to and click Microsoft Excel Worksheet, then click OK**

   An Excel worksheet appears on the PowerPoint slide, and the Excel Ribbon and tabs appear. The PowerPoint title bar and menu bar, above the Excel tools, indicate that Excel is operating within PowerPoint. When you embed a worksheet object in a PowerPoint slide, you generally want to show only the cells that contain data.

2. **Drag the lower-right corner handle of the worksheet object up so only columns A to E and rows 1 to 4 are visible, as shown in FIGURE 3-4**

   You want to clearly see the data you need to enter into the worksheet object.

3. **Click the Select All button in the upper-left corner of the embedded worksheet to select all the worksheet cells, change the font size to 24 point, then click cell A1**

4. **Enter the labels and values in the range A1:D4 as shown in FIGURE 3-5, widening columns as needed**

5. **Click cell D2, enter the formula =B2*C2, press ENTER, click cell D2, drag its fill handle to cell D4 to enter the remaining two formulas, format the values in the Average Fee and Total Growth columns with the Accounting Number format, then apply the Comma format to the values in the Job Placements and reduce the number of decimal places to 0**

   You need to calculate the percentage change in revenue over the past two years.

6. **Click cell E1, type Change, click cell E3, enter the formula =(D3-D2)/D3, press ENTER, click cell E3, click the Percent Style button in the Number group, then copy the formula to cell E4**

7. **Select the range A1:E4, click the Format as Table button in the Styles group, select Green, Table Style Medium 7, click OK, click the Convert to Range button in the Tools group, click Yes, then click outside the worksheet object**

   The embedded worksheet uses the default Office theme, and you want the fonts and colors of the worksheet to use the Organic theme you applied to the PowerPoint slide.

8. **Double-click the worksheet object to show the Excel Ribbon and tabs again, click the Page Layout tab, click the Themes button in the Themes group, then click Organic**

9. **Change the value in cell C4 to 6300, press TAB, click outside the worksheet object, drag the object below the text as shown in FIGURE 3-6, then save the presentation**

   The percentage growth for 2021 is now 25%.

TROUBLE
You move the mouse over the bottom-right corner of the embedded worksheet to show the resize pointer, then drag up and to the left until you see columns A to E and rows 1 to 4. You may need to adjust the view by dragging again.

TROUBLE
Press the arrow keys, use the scroll bars, or press CTRL+HOME to move to the top of the embedded worksheet.

TROUBLE
To set the width of column E, you will need to widen the worksheet object, double-click the column divider between columns E and F, then decrease the width of the workshop object so only columns A to E are visible.

FIGURE 3-4: Resizing the worksheet object

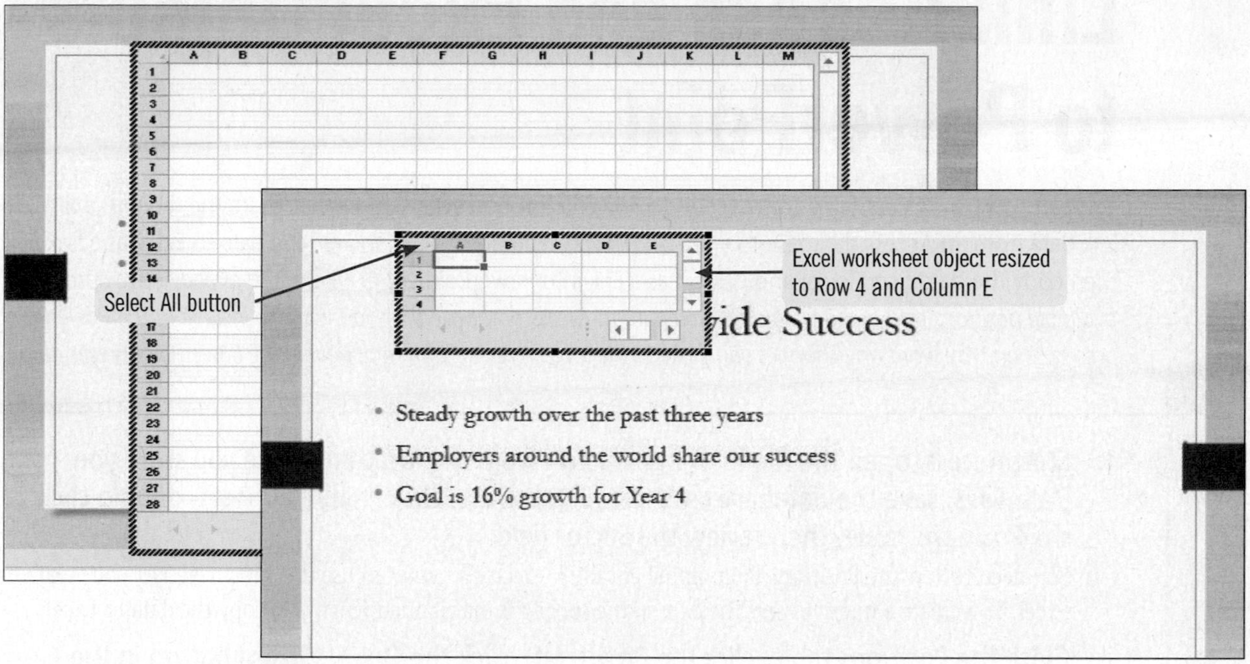

Steady growth over the past three years
Employers around the world share our success
Goal is 16% growth for Year 4

FIGURE 3-5: Labels and values entered in the Excel worksheet object

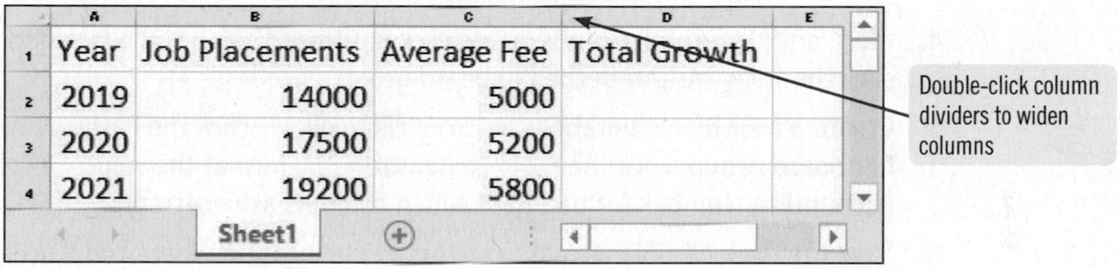

Year
Job Placements
Average Fee
Total Growth
2019 14000 5000
2020 17500 5200
2021 19200 5800
Sheet1
Double-click column dividers to widen columns

FIGURE 3-6: Completed Excel worksheet object

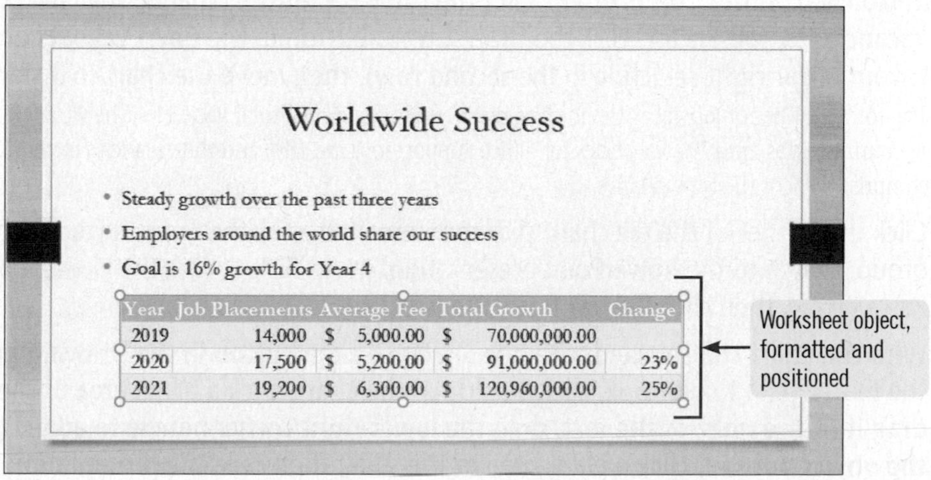

Steady growth over the past three years
Employers around the world share our success
Goal is 16% growth for Year 4

2021 19,200 $ 6,300.00 $ 120,960,000.00 25%

Integration
Module 3

Learning Outcomes
- Link an Access table to Excel
- Link an Excel chart to PowerPoint

Link Access and Excel Objects to PowerPoint

You can copy an Access table from Access to PowerPoint; however, you cannot paste the table as a link. To link data from an Access database to a PowerPoint presentation, you first copy the data to Excel as a link and then copy the data from Excel and paste it as a link into PowerPoint. **CASE** *You already have data about available positions and average salaries stored in an Access database that you want to include in the PowerPoint presentation. You want any changes you make to the table in Access also to appear in the PowerPoint presentation.*

STEPS

> **QUICK TIP**
> To save the database with a new name, click the File tab, click Save As, click the Save As button, navigate to the location where you store your Data Files, type the new filename, then click Save.

1. **Start Access, open the file IL_INT_3-2.accdb from the location where you store your Data Files, save the database as IL_INT_3_JobsData, click Enable Content, double-click the Positions table, then review the Sector field**
   You need to sort the Positions table alphabetically by Sector so you can use the data in a chart you create in Excel. You create a query to sort the data so the sorting is maintained when you copy the data to Excel.
2. **Close the Positions table, click the Create tab, click the Query Wizard button in the Queries group, click OK, click the Select All Fields button >> to add all the fields in the Positions table to the query, click Next, click Next, then click Finish**
3. **Click the Home tab, click the View button in the Views group to go to Design view, click the blank line below "Positions" in the [Sector] column, click the Sector Sort arrow, then select Ascending as shown in FIGURE 3-7**
4. **Close and save the Positions query, click Positions Query in the Navigation pane, then click the Copy button in the Clipboard group**
5. **Create a new blank workbook in Excel, click cell A1, click the Paste arrow in the Clipboard group, click the Paste Link button, format the values in column E with the Accounting Number format, then widen columns as necessary**
6. **Save the file as IL_INT_3_JobsbySectors in the location where you store your Data Files, click cell C23, then enter the labels and formulas as shown in FIGURE 3-8**
7. **Select the range C23:F24, click the Insert tab, click the Insert Pie or Doughnut Chart button in the Charts group, click the top-left pie style, change the chart title to Vacancies by Job Sector, click the Quick Layout button in the Chart Layouts group, select Layout 6 (far right selection in the second row), then move the chart so it starts in cell G1**
   The total number of job vacancies in the Creative sector is 16% of total vacancies, the vacancies for Finance & Accounting jobs are 17%, vacancies for Office Support jobs are 18% and the vacancies in the Technical Sector comprise 49% of the total salaries.

> **QUICK TIP**
> The chart you copied from Excel is linked by default to the source file but takes on the theme of the destination file.

8. **Click the border of the pie chart, click the Home tab, click the Copy button in the Clipboard group, switch to the PowerPoint presentation, show Slide 4, click the Home tab, click the Paste arrow, then click the Use Destination Theme & Link Data button**
9. **With the chart still selected, click the Shape Outline button in the Drawing group, click the Black, Text 1 color box, click outside of the chart, click a blank area of the chart, drag it to the right of the text, drag the lower-right corner handle to adjust the size as shown in FIGURE 3-9, click a blank area of the slide, then save the presentation**
   The chart is linked to the Excel worksheet and the Positions Query datasheet in Access. You will improve the chart's readability in the next lesson.

FIGURE 3-7: Sorting the Sector field in Query Design view

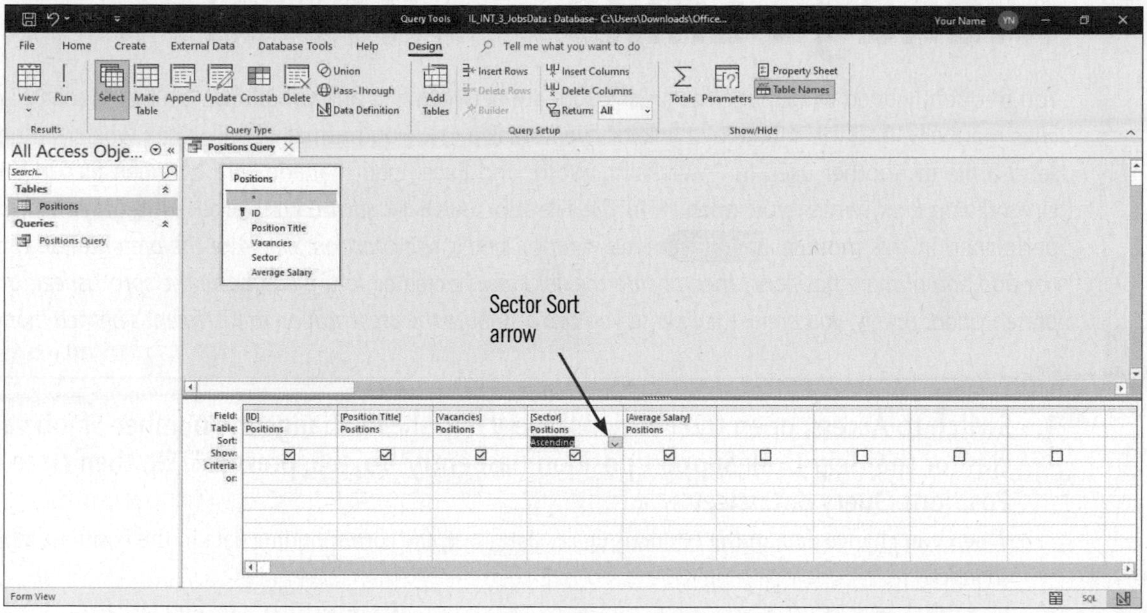

FIGURE 3-8: Formulas to calculate vacancies by sector

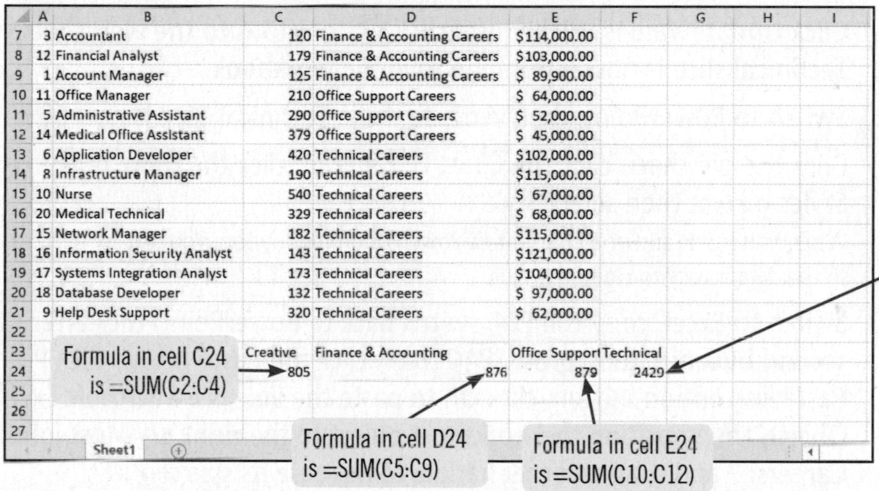

FIGURE 3-9: Linking a copied chart to PowerPoint

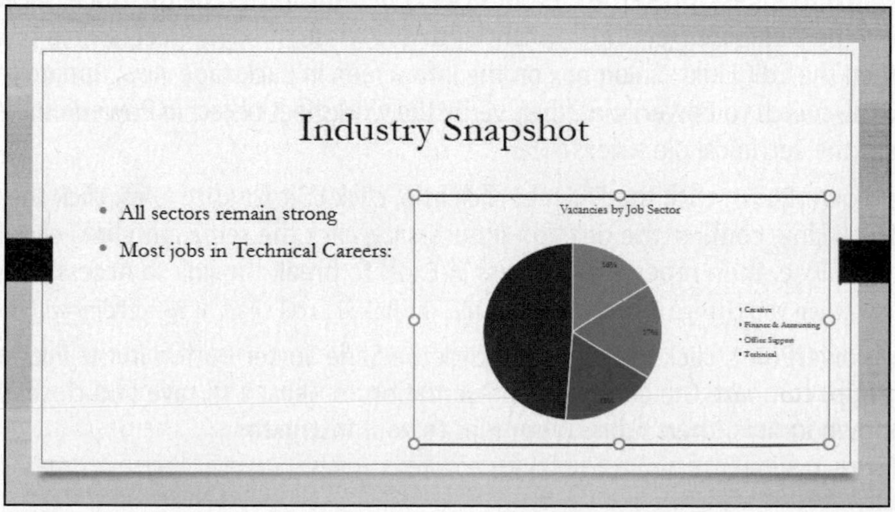

Manage Links

Learning Outcomes
- Manually update links
- Break links

You frequently need to manage the links you create between files and programs. You may need to update links manually, find the source of a link, or even break a link. You normally break a link when you need to send a file to another user. In PowerPoint, Word, and Excel, you manage links between files in the Edit Links dialog box, which you open from the File tab. **TABLE 3-2** summarizes all the integration tasks you performed in this module. **CASE** *You want to modify the chart on Slide 4 of the presentation to reflect the addition of more positions, then update the links you've created in the database, the spreadsheet, and the presentation. Finally, you break the links so you can distribute the presentation to JCL Talent's branch managers.*

STEPS

1. **Switch to Access, open the Positions Query datasheet, change the number of job vacancies for the Help Desk Support position (last entry) to 400, press ENTER, then close the Positions Query datasheet**

   When you change data in the Positions Query datasheet, the corresponding data in the Positions table also changes.

2. **Switch to Excel, click the File tab, click Info, then click Edit Links to Files in the lower-right corner of the screen, as shown in FIGURE 3-10**

   The Edit Links dialog box opens.

QUICK TIP
The linked values will automatically be updated in Excel if you wait a few minutes, but you can speed up the updating process by updating the values manually in the Edit Links dialog box.

3. **Click Update Values, click Close, click [back button] to return to the worksheet, verify that the Technical slice is now 50%, then save the workbook**
4. **Switch to PowerPoint, then verify that the Technical slice is now 50%**
5. **Click the pie chart, click the Chart Design tab, click the More button [More button] in the Chart Styles group, then select Style 9**

   When you insert an Excel chart into a PowerPoint presentation, you usually need to select a new chart style so the data is easy to read on a slide.

QUICK TIP
A value you copy from Excel and paste into PowerPoint as a link is formatted as an object that you can move and resize the same as you would any object.

6. **Switch to Excel, copy cell F24, switch back to PowerPoint, click after Careers: in the second bulleted item, press SPACEBAR, click the Paste arrow, click Paste Special, click the Paste link option button, click OK to paste the link as a Microsoft Excel Worksheet Object, then position the worksheet object to the right of "Most jobs in Technical Careers:," and drag a corner handle to increase its size slightly**

   The copied object appears as 2509.

7. **Switch to Access, open the Positions Query datasheet, change the Nurse vacancies to 700 and the Database Developer vacancies to 300, close the datasheet, switch to Excel and open the Edit Links dialog box on the Info screen in Backstage view, update the link in Excel, switch to PowerPoint, then verify the worksheet object in PowerPoint is now 2837 and the Technical pie slice is 53%**

TROUBLE
It is fine if a NULL link to the chart remains. This link is no longer active.

8. **In PowerPoint, click the File tab, click Info, click Edit Links to Files, click the top link, click Break Link, confirm the deletion if necessary, click the remaining link, click Break Link, click Close, then repeat the process in Excel to break the link to Access**

   Now when you change data in the Access file, the linked Excel chart in PowerPoint will not be updated.

9. **In PowerPoint, click the View tab, click the Slide Sorter button in the Presentation Views group, compare the completed presentation to FIGURE 3-11, save and close all open files and programs, then submit your files to your instructor**

FIGURE 3-10: Updating links using the File tab

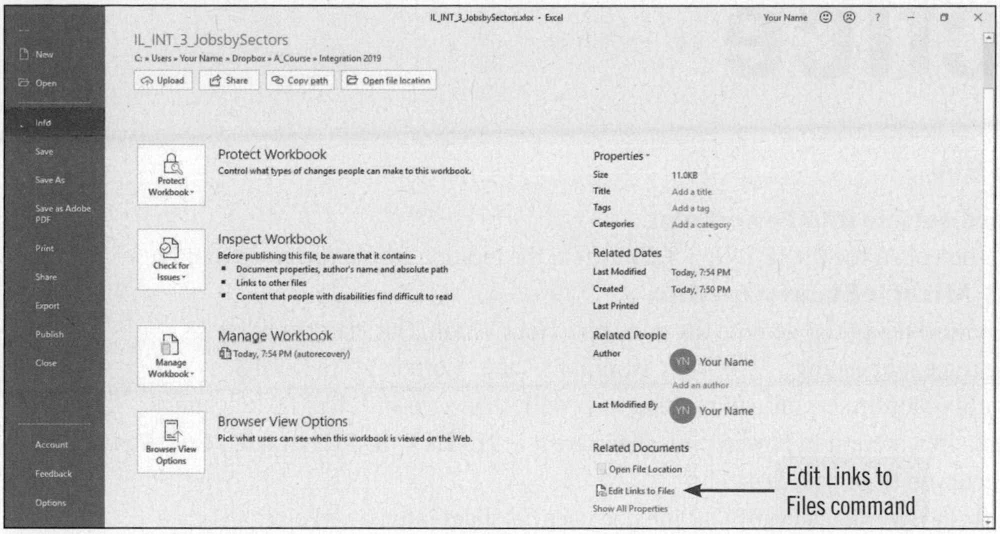

FIGURE 3-11: Completed presentation in Slide Sorter view

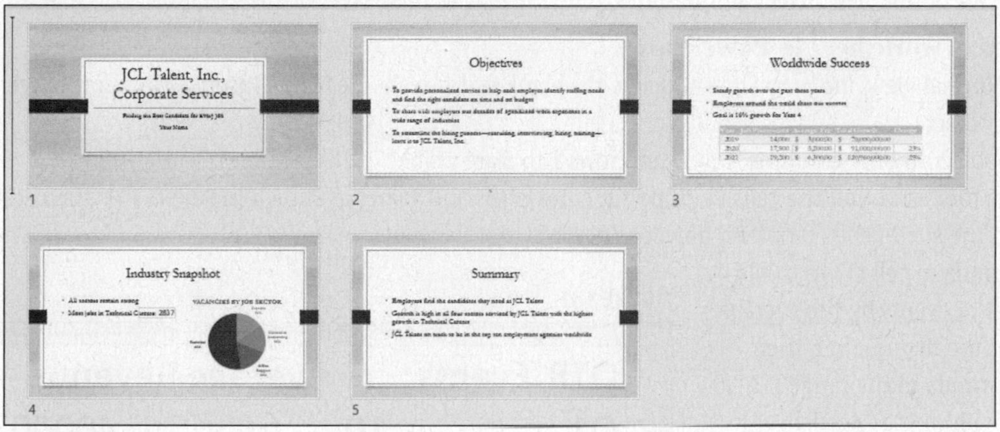

TABLE 3-2: Module 3 integration tasks

object	commands	source program(s)	destination program	result	connection	page no.
Word outline	In PowerPoint: New Slide/Slides from Outline	Word	PowerPoint	Word outline inserted into PowerPoint; Level 1 headings are slide titles, and Level 2 headings are text items	None	4
Excel worksheet	In PowerPoint: Insert/Object/ Create New	Excel	PowerPoint	Excel worksheet created in PowerPoint, then updated by double-clicking and using Excel tools	Embedded	6
Access query	Copy/Paste Link button	Access	Excel	Access query is pasted into Excel as a link; linked data can only be formatted in Excel	Linked	8
Excel chart	Copy/Paste Link using the Use Destination Themes and Link Data button	Access/Excel	PowerPoint	Chart created from linked Access query is pasted into PowerPoint as a link; when Access data changes, Excel and PowerPoint data is updated	Linked	8

Practice

Skills Review

1. **Import a Word outline into PowerPoint.**
   a. Start Word, then open the file IL_INT_3-3.docx from the location where you store your Data Files, then save it as **IL_INT_3_MiracleEventsOutline**.
   b. Switch to Outline view, then demote the body text "Your Vision, Our Plan" to Level 2.
   c. Demote the three subheadings: "Private," "Nonprofit," and "Corporate" to Level 3.
   d. Promote the Six-Month Revenue subheading to Level 1, then save and close the document.
   e. Open a blank presentation in PowerPoint, then save it as **IL_INT_3_MiracleEventsPresentation** in the location where you store your Data Files.
   f. Import the IL_INT_3_MiracleEventsOutline document as slides into PowerPoint.
   g. Delete the blank Slide 1, apply the Title Slide layout to the new Slide 1, then add your name below the subtitle on Slide 1.
   h. Apply the Vapor Trail theme with the pink variant (third variant from the left).
   i. Switch to Slide Sorter view, select all the slides, reset the layout, then save the presentation.

2. **Embed an Excel worksheet in PowerPoint.**
   a. Switch to Normal view, move to Slide 4, delete the blank text placeholder, then insert a Microsoft Excel Worksheet object.
   b. Resize the object so only columns A to D and rows 1 to 5 are visible.
   c. Change the font size of all the cells to 28 point, enter labels and values as shown in **FIGURE 3-12**, then adjust column widths and the size of the worksheet object as needed.
   d. Enter a formula in cell D2 to multiply the number of events by the average revenue for the first quarter, then copy the formula to the range D3:D5 and widen columns as needed.
   e. Apply the Vapor Trail theme to the embedded workbook, apply the Bright Green, Table Style Medium 13 convert the table to a range, format the dollar values in columns C and D with the Accounting Number format, then widen columns as needed. (*Hint*: To widen column D, resize the object to show column E, widen Column D, then reduce the object size again.)
   f. Right-align the worksheet object below the slide title.
   g. In the worksheet object, change the number of events in the third quarter to **15**, then save the presentation.

FIGURE 3-12

	A	B	C	D
1	QTR	Events	Average Revenue	Total
2	Q1	10	40000	
3	Q2	8	24000	
4	Q3	12	38000	
5	Q4	20	42000	

Sheet1

3. **Link Access and Excel objects to PowerPoint.**
   a. Start Access, open the file IL_INT_3-4.accdb from the location where you store your Data Files, save it as **IL_INT_3_MiracleEventsData**, then enable the content.
   b. Create a query called **Events Query** from the Events table, that contains all fields and that sorts the contents of the Category field in ascending order. (*Hint*: Remember to sort the Category field in Design view.)
   c. Close and save the query, copy it, create a new workbook in Excel, then paste the query datasheet as a link into cell A1.

Skills Review (continued)

d. Format the values in column F using the Accounting Number format, widen columns as necessary, enter **Total** in cell G1, enter the formula in cell G2 to multiply the Participants by the Per Person cost, then copy the formula to the range G3:G16 and widen the column as necessary.
e. In the range B18:D19, enter labels and formulas to calculate the total revenue from all the events in each of the three categories: Corporate, Nonprofit, and Private, widen columns as needed, then save the workbook as **IL_INT_3_MiracleEventsRevenue**.
f. Create a pie chart in the first 2D style from the range B18:D19, then apply Quick Layout 1 and move the chart to the right of the data.
g. Change the chart title to **Revenue by Event Category**, copy the chart, then paste it on Slide 5 in the PowerPoint presentation using the Use Destination Theme & Link Data option.
h. Move the worksheet object below the bullet point, add a black outline, then save the presentation.

4. Manage links.

a. In the Access query, change the per person cost for the Product Launch to **$150.00**, then close the query.
b. Switch to Excel, then if the value in cell F2 does not automatically update to $150.00, update the link in the Edit Links dialog box.
c. Switch to PowerPoint, then update the link, if necessary, and verify that the Corporate wedge is now 80%.
d. Size and position the pie chart so it fills the blank area on the slide attractively, then apply Chart Style 11.
e. In Excel, copy cell B19, then paste it as a linked worksheet object on Slide 5 in PowerPoint.
f. Position the Excel object after "is" and resize it so its font size is comparable to that of the bullet text.
g. In the Events Query datasheet in Access, change the number of participants in the Opening Gala to 2000, then close the datasheet.
h. Update the link in Excel, switch to PowerPoint, then, if necessary, update the links to the chart and the worksheet object. The worksheet object is now $1,880,200.00 and the Corporate slice is 77%.
i. Break the links to the Excel chart and worksheet, break the link from Excel to Access, view the presentation in Slide Sorter view, compare the presentation to **FIGURE 3-13**, save and close all open files and programs, then submit your files to your instructor.

FIGURE 3-13

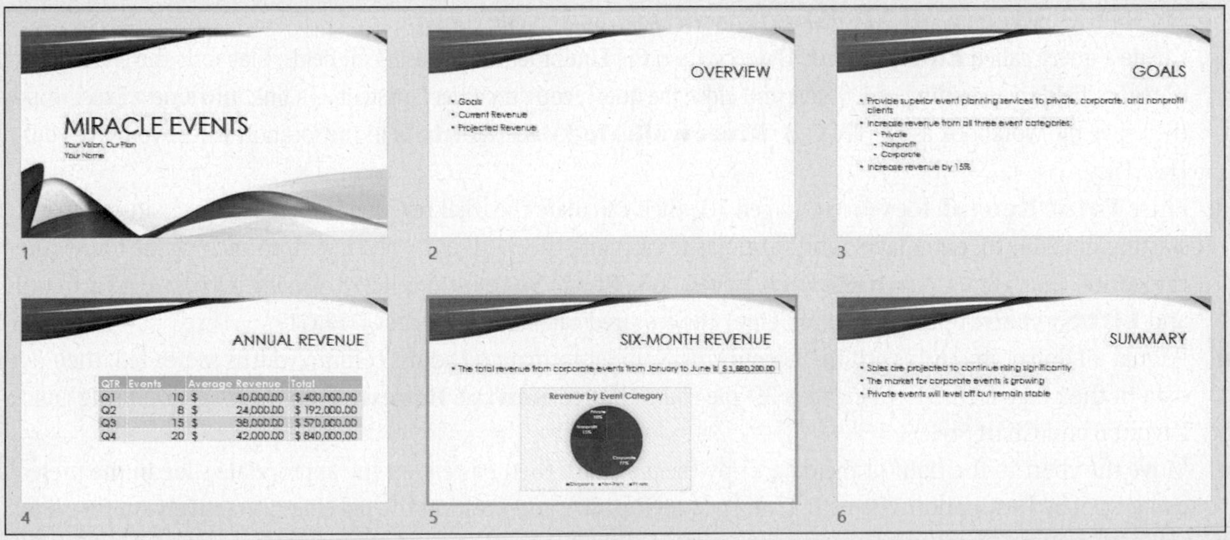

Independent Challenge 1

Riverwalk Medical Clinic in Cambridge, Massachusetts, operates a "Med Shed" that loans and rents medical equipment to patients. You have collected data about recent loans and rentals in an Access database, and now you need to create a presentation in PowerPoint that contains links to the loan and rental figures. You also need to import some of the slides needed for the presentation from a Word outline.

a. In Word, open the file IL_INT_3-5.docx from the location where you store your Data Files, then save it as **IL_INT_3_RiverwalkMedShedOutline**.

b. In Outline view, demote the subtitle text to Level 2, then demote the list of the four equipment categories (from "Ambulatory Equipment" to "Daily Living Aids") to Level 3.

c. Save and close the document.

d. Start a blank presentation in PowerPoint, then save it as **IL_INT_3_RiverwalkMedShedPresentation** in the location where you store your Data Files.

e. Insert the RiverwalkMedShed Outline document into PowerPoint, delete Slide 1, apply the Title Slide layout to the new Slide 1, then add your name below the subtitle on Slide 1.

f. In Slide Sorter view, reset the layout of all the slides, then apply the View theme with the variant that includes a red stripe along the right edge (third from the left in the selection of variants in the Variants group).

g. In Normal view on the new Slide 2 (Average Monthly Loans), embed an Excel Worksheet object resized to column B and row 5 with a 22 pt font size and containing the information and formatted as shown in **FIGURE 3-14**.

h. Enlarge the worksheet object to include row 6 and calculate the total number of monthly loans in cell B6.

i. Apply the View theme to the Excel worksheet, select the range A1:B6, apply the Brown, Table Style Medium 7, convert the table to a range, then left align the worksheet object with the title and bulleted item on the slide.

FIGURE 3-14

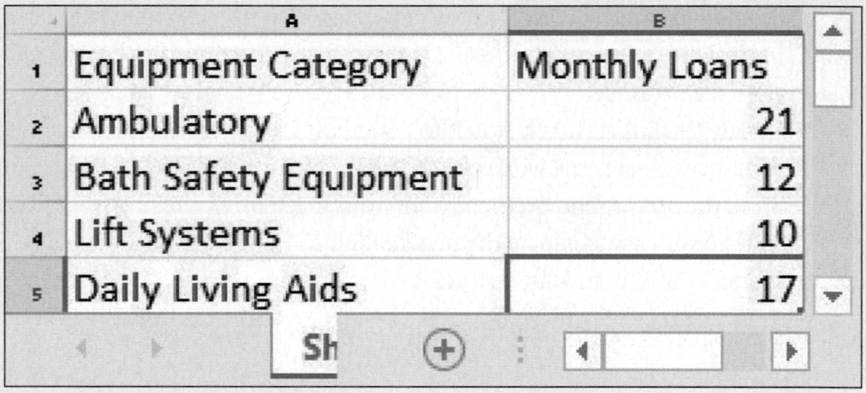

	A	B
1	Equipment Category	Monthly Loans
2	Ambulatory	21
3	Bath Safety Equipment	12
4	Lift Systems	10
5	Daily Living Aids	17

j. Start Access, open the file IL_INT_3-6.accdb the location where you store your Data Files, then save the database as **IL_INT_3_RiverwalkMedShedInventory** and enable content.

k. Create a query called **Equipment Query** from the Equipment table, using all fields, that sorts the contents of the Category field in ascending order. Save and close the query, copy the query, paste it as a link into a new Excel workbook, then save the workbook as **IL_INT_3_RiverwalkMedShedRentals** in the location where you save your Data Files.

l. Enter **Total Rental Revenue** in cell H1, then calculate the total revenue from rentals only in column H, then starting in cell D18, enter labels and formulas to calculate the total rental revenue from each of the four equipment categories. (*Hint*: Enter **Ambulatory** in cell D18, **Bath Safety** in cell E18, **Daily Living Aid** in cell F18, and **Lift System** in cell G18, then enter the required calculations in cells D19:G19.)

m. Format all dollar amounts with the Accounting Number format and adjust column widths as needed, then use the data in the range D18:G19 to create a 2D pie chart entitled **Rental Revenue by Category** using Quick Layout 6 and Chart Style 3.

n. Move the chart to the right of the data, copy the pie chart, then paste it on the appropriate slide in the presentation using the Use Destination Theme & Link Data option. Size and position the pie chart attractively on the slide.

o. In Excel, copy the total revenue from the rental of ambulatory equipment, then paste it as a linked worksheet object in the appropriate location on the slide containing the chart.

p. Size and position the worksheet object attractively, then enclose the chart in a black outline.

Independent Challenge 1 (continued)

q. In Access, change the rental rate for Forearm Crutches to **$20.00** and the quantity rented to **25**, then update the links in Excel and PowerPoint. The slice for Ambulatory equipment should be 53% as shown in **FIGURE 3-15**.

r. Break the links in Excel and PowerPoint, view the presentation in Slide Sorter view, compare it to **FIGURE 3-15** save and close all open files and programs, then submit your files to your instructor.

FIGURE 3-15

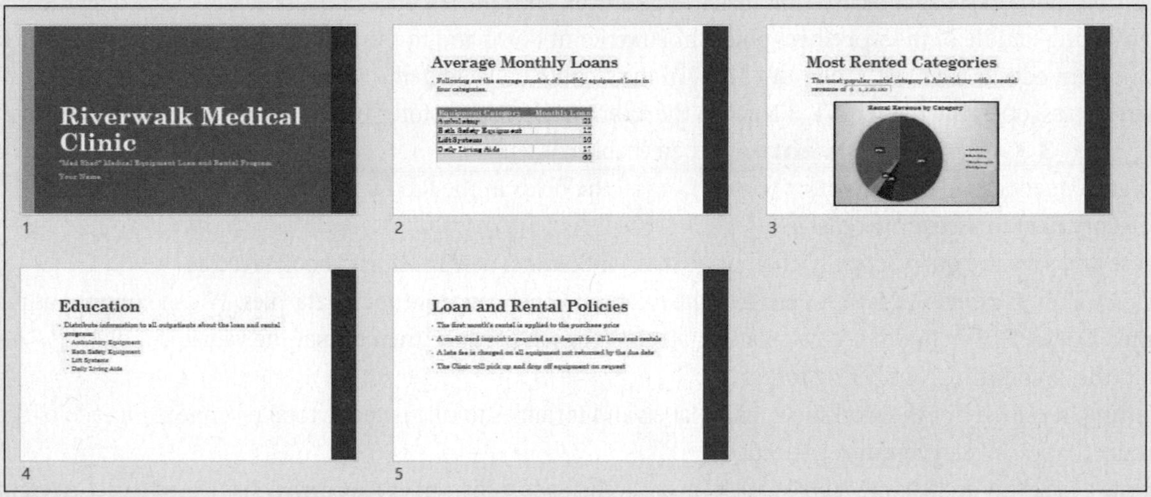

Independent Challenge 2

You are the Assistant Manager at Green Tech, a company that distributes eco-friendly products such as solar-powered battery chargers and energy-efficient appliances. To assist your customers, you have created a database of product information they can access online. You have also decided to create a short PowerPoint presentation from information you have stored in Word. The presentation will include data from the database, an embedded worksheet, and a linked chart.

a. Start Word, open the file IL_INT_3-7.docx from the location where you store your Data Files, switch to Outline view, then demote the subtitle to Level 2 and promote "Product Sales" to Level 1.

b. Save the document as **IL_INT_3_GreenTechOutline**, and close the document.

c. Start a new PowerPoint presentation, save it as **IL_INT_3_GreenTechPresentation**, then import the IL_INT_3_GreenTechOutline document into the presentation.

d. Delete the blank Slide 1, apply the Title Slide layout to the new Slide 1, add your name below the subtitle on Slide 1, then apply the Integral theme and apply the second variant from the left.

e. In Slide Sorter view, reset the layout of all the slides.

f. On Slide 2, embed an Excel Worksheet object displaying five columns and four rows, apply the 28-point font size so the cells are visible, then enter the information shown in **FIGURE 3-16** and adjust column widths.

g. Calculate the savings per product in cells D2 by subtracting the values in the Green Tech Cost column from the values in the Conventional Cost column.

h. In cell E2, enter the formula **=D2/B2** to calculate the percent savings on monthly power costs when using Green Tech products.

FIGURE 3-16

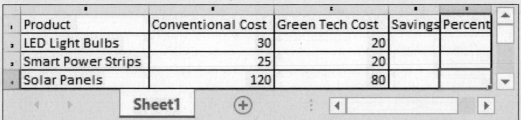

Product	Conventional Cost	Green Tech Cost	Savings	Percent
LED Light Bulbs	30	20		
Smart Power Strips	25	20		
Solar Panels	120	80		

Sheet1

Independent Challenge 2 (continued)

i. Copy the formulas for the other two product categories, format values with the Accounting Number (with zero decimal points) and Percent formats, then widen columns, as necessary.

j. Apply the Integral theme, select the range A1:E4, apply Dark Green, Table Style Medium 6, then convert the table to a range.

k. Make sure the completed table displays all five columns (you may need to readjust the width of the worksheet object).

l. Position the worksheet object so that its left edge is even with the left edge of the slide title, then drag the lower-right sizing handle of the worksheet object in PowerPoint down and to the right to increase the width of the object so its right edge is even with the word "top" in the second bulleted item.

m. Start Access, open the file IL_INT_3-8.accdb the location where you store your Data Files, save the database as **IL_INT_3_GreenTechInventory**, then enable content.

n. Create a query called **Products Query** from all the fields in the Products table that sorts the contents of the Category field in ascending order.

o. Close and save the query, copy it, then paste it as a link into a new Excel workbook saved as **IL_INT_3_GreenTechRevenue** in the location where you store your Data Files. Widen columns as needed. Enter **Total Sales** in cell G1, calculate total sales for each product, then format the values in Columns F and G with the Accounting Numbering format.

p. Starting in cell C15 of the worksheet, enter labels and formulas to calculate the total revenue from each of the four product types. Widen columns as needed.

q. Create a pie chart of the totals, apply Quick Layout 1, then add a chart title: **Revenue by Product Category**. Move the chart to the right of the data.

r. Copy the chart, then paste it using the Use Destination Theme & Link Data paste option on the appropriate slide in the presentation. Add a black border, then resize and reposition the pie chart to fit the space attractively.

s. Apply Chart Style 12 to the chart and remove the legend. (*Hint*: Click the Add Chart Element button in the Chart Layouts group on the Chart Design tab, point to Legend, then click None.)

t. Copy cell F16 in the source workbook, then paste it as a linked worksheet object in the appropriate place following the colon in the bulleted item and enlarge as needed.

u. In the Access query, change the Price of the Air Purifier to **1200**, the price of Low Power Air Conditioner to **2000** and the price of the solar panels to **5000**, then close the query.

v. Update links in Excel and PowerPoint. Verify that the value of the worksheet object is now $1,668,600.00 as shown in **FIGURE 3-17**.

w. In Excel and PowerPoint, break the links, view the presentation, save and close all open files and programs, then submit your files to your instructor.

FIGURE 3-17

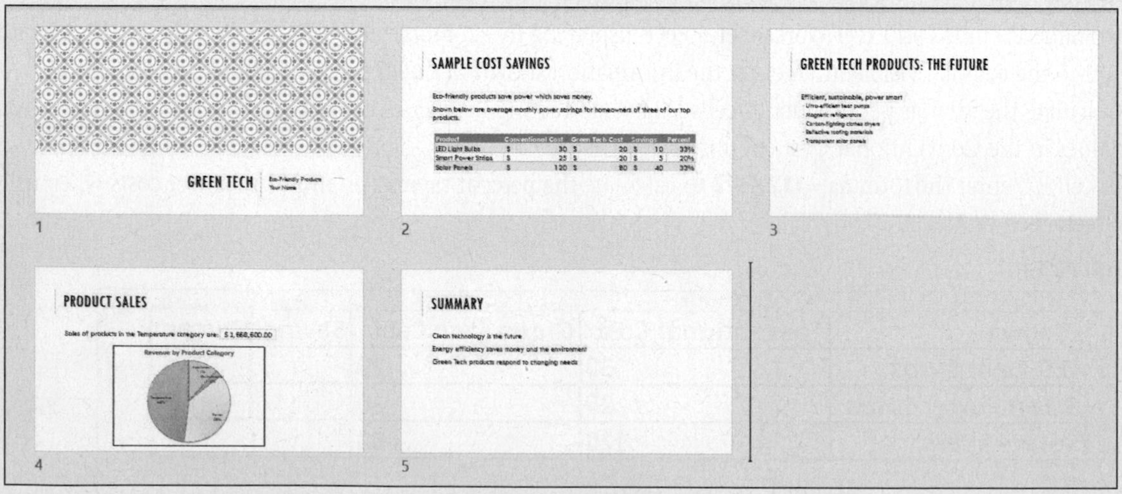

Visual Workshop

For a college course on tourism in New Zealand at Memorial University in Arizona, you have decided to create a presentation that focuses on popular hotels in various locations. The presentation will contain one slide displaying a pie chart showing the breakdown of hotel guests by location. In Access, open the file IL_INT_3-9.accdb from the location where you store your Data Files, then save the database as **IL_INT_3_NewZealandHotels**. Create a query called **Hotels Query** that includes all fields and that sorts the Hotels table in ascending order by Location. Copy the query, paste it as a link into Excel, then create the 2D pie chart similar to the one shown in **FIGURE 3-18**, and save the Excel workbook as **IL_INT_3_NewZealandHotelsData**. As shown in the figure, create a one-slide PowerPoint presentation called **IL_INT_3_NewZealandHotelsPresentation**, apply the Title Only slide layout, then copy the pie chart from Excel and paste it onto the slide using the Use Destination Theme & Link Data option. Format the slide as shown: add the slide title, apply the Dividend slide design with the Green variant (third from the left), apply a black border of the chart, format the chart with Quick Layout 6 and Style 9, then remove the chart title from the chart. Switch to Access, open the Hotels query, change the number of guests who stayed at the Lakeview Resort in Queenstown to **150**, close the query, update the links in Excel and PowerPoint, then enter your name in the slide footer. Break the link to the Excel workbook and PowerPoint presentation, save and close all open files and programs, then submit your files to your instructor.

FIGURE 3-18

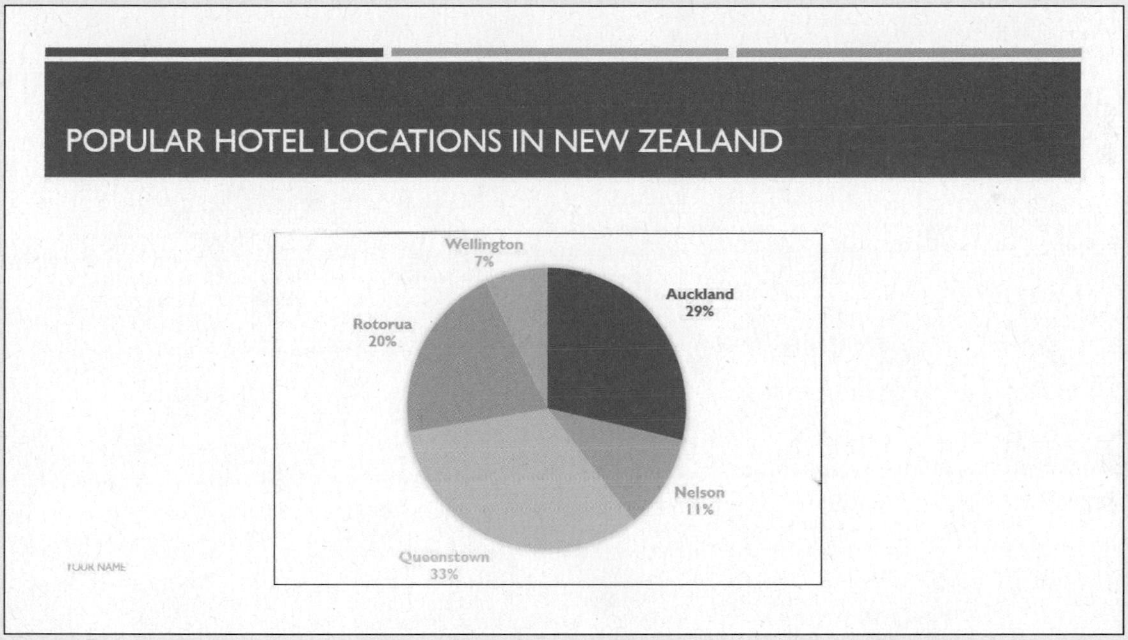

Index

D

E

F

G

H

I

J

K

L

M

Q

R

S

T

U

V

W

X

Y

Z